OXFORD MONOGRAPHS IN INTERNATIONAL HUMANITARIAN AND CRIMINAL LAW

Series Editors

SUZANNAH LINTON
Member of the Expert Committee, International Academy of the Red Cross & Red Crescent at Suzhou University and Adjunct Professor at the School of International Law, China University of Political Science and Law (CUPL)

PHILIPPA WEBB
Professor of Public International Law, The Dickson Poon School of Law, King's College London

SALVATORE ZAPPALÀ
Professor of International Law at the University of Catania

International Criminal Tribunals and Domestic Accountability

OXFORD MONOGRAPHS IN INTERNATIONAL HUMANITARIAN AND CRIMINAL LAW

This series emerged through the vision of the late Antonio Cassese. Since then the series has published original and innovative works on challenging issues in international humanitarian law and international criminal justice, primarily by emerging authors. Given the ever-growing intersection of these areas with other fields of international law such as the jus ad bellum, and disciplines such as criminology, sociology, and history, the scope of the series also incorporates these perspectives. Fresh approaches and new ideas for improving conceptual and practical challenges are welcomed. The series editors encourage submissions from around the world, and will consider edited collections, although the primary focus is on authored works.

ALSO PUBLISHED IN THIS SERIES

Accountability for Mass Starvation
Testing the Limits of the Law
Edited by Bridget Conley, Alex de Waal, Catriona Murdoch, and Wayne Jordash KC

The Defence of Mistake of Law in International Criminal Law
A Study on Ignorance and Blame
Antonio Coco

The Use of Force against Individuals in War under International Law
A Social Ontological Approach
Ka Lok Yip

Non-Binding Norms in International Humanitarian Law
Efficacy, Legitimacy, and Legality
Emily Crawford

Doing Justice to History
Confronting the Past in International Criminal Courts
Barrie Sander

International Criminal Tribunals and Domestic Accountability

In the Court's Shadow

PATRYK I. LABUDA

OXFORD
UNIVERSITY PRESS

OXFORD
UNIVERSITY PRESS

Great Clarendon Street, Oxford, OX2 6DP,
United Kingdom

Oxford University Press is a department of the University of Oxford.
It furthers the University's objective of excellence in research, scholarship,
and education by publishing worldwide. Oxford is a registered trade mark of
Oxford University Press in the UK and in certain other countries

First Edition published in 2023

Published in the United States of America by Oxford University Press
198 Madison Avenue, New York, NY 10016, United States of America

British Library Cataloguing in Publication Data

Data available

Library of Congress Control Number: 2023936282

ISBN 978–0–19–886884–2

DOI: 10.1093/oso/9780198868842.001.0001

Printed and bound in the UK by
TJ Books Limited

Advance Praise

Domestic prosecution of international crimes has become the mantra of international criminal law since the establishment of the International Criminal Court (ICC) in 2002. In *International Criminal Tribunals and Domestic Accountability: In the Court's Shadow*, Patryk Labuda expertly unpacks the assumption that international criminal tribunals such as the ICC catalyse domestic prosecutions. He deftly exposes the paradox of the increasing turn to domestic prosecutions of international crimes, which he argues may empower authoritarian elites, instead of providing meaningful accountability. Labuda's thoughtful book is a must read for anyone interested in the future of international criminal law.

Charles C Jalloh
Distinguished University Professor, Florida International University

In offering both broad historical context and fine-grained case study illustration, Labuda expands our understanding of complementarity in both theory and practice. Whatever one's opinion about the appropriate relationship between the International Criminal Court and national judiciaries, this book is an eye-opening and essential read.

Kim Thuy Seelinger
Research Associate Professor, Brown School, Washington University
Special Adviser on Sexual Violence in Conflict to the
Prosecutor of the International Criminal Court

Patryk Labuda's book is about light and shadows. Labuda encourages international legal institutions to step out of shadows of their own making; to stop overshadowing victims and domestic contexts; and to shade in colour rather than shroud things in their own image. Labuda's work is to law what Caravaggio's *chiaroscuro* is to the canvas—Labuda illuminates, places candles in the darkness, and reveals what is obscured. This excellent book offers wise counsel about how international criminal law enforcement can combat the increasingly illiberal swagger of our political times.

Mark A Drumbl
Class of 1975 Alumni Professor of Law and Director,
Transnational Law Institute, Washington and Lee University

This is a timely book that effectively analyses the turn to positive complementarity underpinned by a shift towards domestic accountability, as a response to the problematic interventions of international criminal tribunals. It assesses the relocation of the anti-impunity agenda closer to the locus of the crimes at the state level, and interrogates the important role that societal actors have to play in engaging national institutions in pursuing redress and accountability for atrocities. This is a superlative study that needs to be engaged with by analysts, policymakers, and practitioners of international criminal justice.

Tim Murithi
Head of Programme at Institute for
Justice and Reconciliation, Cape Town
Professor of African Studies, University of the
Free State and Stellenbosch University in South Africa
Author of Judicial Imperialism: The Politicisation of
International Criminal Justice in Africa

This thoughtful and perceptive examination of international criminal justice has been greatly enriched by Patryk Labuda's research on site, in the living laboratories of Africa. He examines the inexorable tension between national justice systems and the international mechanisms that is sometimes understood, at least as far as the International Criminal Court is concerned, applying the enigmatic notion of complementarity. This book will be of great value to practitioners as well as academics.

William A Schabas
Professor of International Law, Middlesex University

Series Editors' Preface

We are very pleased to publish Dr Patryk I. Labuda's important book, *International Criminal Tribunals and Domestic Accountability* in the Oxford Monographs in International Humanitarian and Criminal Law series. Both the topic and the author perfectly fit the series and its spirit: cross-cutting studies on topical issues by brilliant (young) scholars possibly with relevant practical experience in the field. The study tackles a lynchpin of international criminal law and does so with depth and competence.

The debate on the primacy or complementarity of international criminal tribunals vis-à-vis domestic jurisdiction is one of the core areas of institutional difference between the foundational era of the United Nations ad hoc tribunals (and before them the Nuremberg and Tokyo experience) and the 'new world' of international criminal justice dominated by the establishment of the International Criminal Court (ICC) and the premise that justice is better delivered at the domestic level. There are several reasons for this shift, among them the idea that communities directly affected by the crimes are better served by accountability being established with greater proximity. The centrality of domestic jurisdiction in the ICC framework might have been a strategic diplomatic tool, indispensable to secure sufficient support by states and eventually gather consensus in a treaty-based system of international criminal justice. However, in international criminal justice more broadly, the centrality of domestic jurisdiction has been seen as a mechanism to render accountability more effective. In this respect, it must be recognized that already in the years immediately following the establishment of the Yugoslavia and Rwanda tribunals it had become clear that international tribunals located in countries away from the crime scenes were not ideal for establishing accountability for international crimes, as these tribunals could be perceived as distant entities which would never really understand the situation on the ground, let alone do justice for such serious crimes. The experiences of the Special Court for Sierra Leone, the Extraordinary Chambers in the Courts of Cambodia, and other hybrid tribunals signalled shifting in this direction. Whether this shift was artificially motivated by political bias against the ad hoc tribunals or the genuine expression of a vision of justice as a process closer to directly affected communities is actually beside the point, since with the establishment of the ICC, the affirmation of a sort of primary duty of domestic jurisdictions became the rule.

In this regard, the author appropriately refrains from a merely theoretical approach and has chosen to base his analysis on three case studies. This is wise, for in so doing the book avoids merely restating obvious theoretical principles which are the basis of the competing views (primacy vs complementarity) and actually contributes fresh ideas based on a more empirical approach. The three case studies—Rwanda, Sierra Leone, and the Democratic Republic of the Congo—eventually show different aspects of the interplay between international courts and domestic processes and how they can lead to different outcomes.

Dr Labuda highlights some trends that are underpinning developments in international criminal law which are evidence of the paradigm shift which has placed domestic jurisdiction at the centre of the system. According to Dr Labuda this has led to (a) the need for increasingly cooperative approaches; (b) positive complementarity in the form of strengthened capacity building; and (c) the importance of domesticating international norms.

There is no doubt, as Dr Labuda lucidly highlights, that in the past thirty years there has been a radical paradigm shift which has placed domestic jurisdiction at the centre of the justice enterprise. It would be too easy to say that no one size fits all; although eventually this seems the conclusion that one must draw from the case studies. More broadly, Dr Labuda's work also helpfully considers other forms of participation of the international community in accountability processes, such as hybrid tribunals and other entities created or supported by the United Nations or other international entities (e.g. Kosovo, the Central African Republic, South Sudan).

In any event, irrespective of the theoretical stance and 'ideological' approach that can be taken on the issue, there is no doubt that today (nearly thirty years after the establishment of the ICTY) there is a panoply of mechanisms at the disposal of the international community to promote accountability through a diversified mix of international and domestic measures and institutions.

This book by Dr Labuda is not only a contribution to the academic debate but will be a useful tool for a better informed and fact-based analysis leading to well-crafted options in future situations.

The Editors

Acknowledgements

This book has been quite a journey. It began as a doctorate in international criminal law at the Geneva Graduate Institute but morphed into a reckoning with the rationales of peacebuilding and transitional justice, originating in my work in the Democratic Republic of Congo (DRC) over a decade earlier. A series of black swan events in the last two years delayed this manuscript, and I thank Oxford University Press for their patience.

I have incurred many debts along the way. I would like to begin by thanking everyone who was interviewed for this project, most of them in Rwanda, Sierra Leone, and the DRC. This book would not have been possible without visits to the three countries and the countless hours that my interlocutors gave me. Over the years, interviews also took place in locations as disparate as Cape Town, Bangui, Tunis, Dakar, New York, and The Hague. The names of my interlocutors do not always appear in the text, but the final product is partly theirs—thank you all.

The help and support of colleagues and friends was essential over the years. Heartfelt thanks to Paola Gaeta, my doctoral supervisor, for her patience, steadfast support, and for introducing me to the magical world of the Geneva Academy. Je souhaite adresser mes remerciements chaleureux à Robert Roth pour son soutien indéfectible, ses conseils et son amitié. I would also like to express my gratitude to Bill Schabas and Giovanni Distefano for their intellectual inspiration in Geneva (and to Bill for facilitating contacts in the country studies). My thanks to Gerhard Kemp, Sarah Nouwen, Ryan Goodman, Ibrahim Tommy, Alain Werner, Célestin Tukala, Eugène Bakama, Ian Johnstone, Kevin Heller, and Ingo Venzke for welcoming me to their institutions or facilitating visits to, and research in, Stellenbosch, Cambridge, Kinshasa, Freetown, Goma, New York, Medford, and Amsterdam over the years. A special thank you to Jenny and Gerard for being such wonderful hosts in Kin. I am eternally indebted to the Swiss National Science Foundation for their generous fellowships, the ZEIT Foundation for its travel grant, and the Wayamo Foundation for involving me in several enriching international justice projects.

Many people contributed to this text over the years. In addition to those mentioned above, I would like to thank Roland Adjovi, Eugène Bakama, Mohamed Bangura, Antonio Coco, Thierry Cruvellier, Geoff Dancy, Christian De Vos, Emile Dhekana, Kate Gibson, Mark Kersten, Nico Krisch, Ryan Liss, Tim Longman, Sarah Nouwen, Beth van Schaack, Priya Urs, Karolina Wierczyńska, Marcel Wetsh'okonda, Sergey Vasiliev, and Ingo Venzke for sharing insights and reviewing drafts along the way. This book benefited from conversations at conferences on the International Criminal Court in Accra, on African courts in Niamey, the European

Society of International Law annual meeting in Naples, the Stanford Junior Faculty Forum, the American Society of International Law's Research Forum in Los Angeles and its Transitional Justice Working Group in New York, the Amsterdam Center for International Law, and finally the Asser Institute in The Hague.

Na zakończenie, wielkie podziękowania należą się mojej rodzinie, która się przyczyniła do tej podróży intelektualnej na różne sposoby: mama nauczyła mnie marzyć, siostra walczyć, a ojciec (za dużo) myśleć. Je remercie affectueusement Pusia et Benoit, ma famille genevoise, qui ont alimenté ce projet avec des festins intellectuels et culinaires à Montchoisy. Ma plus grande dette va à Elvincia pour m'avoir soutenu tout au long de ce projet.

Dakar
20 July 2022

Contents

Table of Cases, Laws, and Resolutions

INTERNATIONAL CRIMINAL TRIBUNAL FOR RWANDA

SPECIAL COURT FOR SIERRA LEONE

INTERNATIONAL CRIMINAL COURT

UN DOCUMENTS

RWANDA

SIERRA LEONE

DEMOCRATIC REPUBLIC OF CONGO

UNITED KINGDOM

NETHERLANDS

EUROPEAN COURT OF HUMAN RIGHTS

List of Abbreviations

AC	Appeals Chamber
ACC	Anti-Corruption Commission [Sierra Leone]
ACHPR	African Court of Human and People's Rights
ACJHR	African Court of Justice and Human Rights
AFRC	Armed Forces Revolutionary Council [Sierra Leone]
ASP	Assembly of States Parties [International Criminal Court]
AU	African Union
BCUNDH	UN Joint Human Rights Office [DR Congo]
CAPS	Prosecution Support Cells [DR Congo]
CAR	Central African Republic
CICC	Coalition for the International Criminal Court
DFID	Department for International Development
DOMAC	Impact of International Courts on Domestic Criminal Procedures in Mass Atrocity Cases [Project]
DRC	Democratic Republic of the Congo
ECCC	Extraordinary Chambers in the Courts of Cambodia
EU	European Union
FARC	Revolutionary Armed Forces of Colombia
FIDH	Fédération Internationale pour les droits humains
GNU	Government of National Unity [Rwanda]
HRFOR	UN Human Rights Field Operation in Rwanda
HRW	Human Rights Watch
ICC	International Criminal Court
ICT	international criminal tribunal
ICTJ	International Center for Transitional Justice
ICTR	International Criminal Tribunal for Rwanda
ICTY	International Criminal Tribunal for the former Yugoslavia
ICU	International Crimes Unit [Rwanda]
ILC	International Law Commission
JCCD	Jurisdiction, Complementarity and Cooperation Division [ICC]
MCC	Military Criminal Code [DRC]
MICT	Mechanism for International Criminal Tribunals
MONUC	UN Organization Mission in the DRC
MONUSCO	UN Organization Stabilization Mission in the DRC
MoU	memorandum of understanding
NGO	non-governmental organization
NPPA	National Public Prosecution Authority (Rwanda)
OHCHR	Office of the High Commissioner for Human Rights
OSJI	Open Society Justice Initiative

OTP	Office of the Prosecutor
PTC	Pre-Trial Chamber
RPE	Rules of Procedure and Evidence
RPF	Rwandan Patriotic Front
RSCSL	Residual Special Court for Sierra Leone
RUF	Revolutionary United Front
SCSL	Special Court for Sierra Leone
SLCMP	Sierra Leone Court Monitoring Programme
TC	Trial Chamber
TRC	Truth and Reconciliation Commission
UK	United Kingdom
UN	United Nations
UNAMIR	UN Mission in Rwanda
UNAMSIL	UN Mission in Sierra Leone
UNDP	United National Development Programme
UNGA	United Nations General Assembly
UNHCR	UN High Commissioner for Refugees
UNSC	United Nations Security Council
UNSG	United Nations Secretary General
US[A]	United States [of America]
WSB	West Side Boys
WVS	Witness and Victim Section [Sierra Leone]

1
Introduction

> When an international tribunal ... is created, it must be endowed with primacy over national courts. Otherwise, human nature being what it is, there would be a perennial danger of international crimes being characterized as 'ordinary crimes' ... or proceedings being 'designed to shield the accused' ... or cases not being diligently prosecuted ... If not effectively countered by the principle of primacy, any one of those stratagems might be used to defeat the very purpose of the creation of an international criminal jurisdiction, to the benefit of the very people whom it has been designed to prosecute.
>
> *Prosecutor* v. *Tadić*, Appeals Chamber ICTY, 1995[1]

> The Rome Statute was never intended to replace national courts, and the system it created will only succeed if there is genuine national action. The ICC through the principle of complementarity was engineered to incentivize accountability efforts [at] the national level.
>
> Fatou Bensouda, ICC Prosecutor, 2014[2]

> Our Court will deal with only a few cases over the years but the impact of its cases and rulings extends to at least 110 States which are Parties to the Rome Statute and even beyond to reach non States Parties. [This is] the shadow of the Court.
>
> Luis Moreno Ocampo, ICC Prosecutor, 2010[3]

International criminal justice has experienced a paradigm shift. For decades, it was associated with the promise of new international criminal tribunals (ICTs). Established in 1993, the International Criminal Tribunal for the former Yugoslavia

[1] AC, *Prosecutor v Tadić* (Decision on the Defence Motion for Interlocutory Appeal on Jurisdiction) ICTY IT-94-1 (2 October 1995) para 58.

[2] Fatou Bensouda, 'Local Prosecution of International Crimes: Challenges and Prospects', speech delivered at 7th Annual Prosecutors Colloquium, Arusha, Tanzania, November 2014 <icc-cpi.int/iccdocs/otp/otp-statement-141105.pdf>.

[3] Luis M Ocampo, 'Keynote Address', Council of Foreign Relations, Washington, DC, 4 February 2010 <icc-cpi.int/sites/default/files/NR/rdonlyres/A80CDDDD-8A9A-432E-97CE-F6EAD700B5AE/281527/100204ProsecutorsspeechforCFR.pdf>.

International Criminal Tribunals and Domestic Accountability. Patryk I. Labuda,
Oxford University Press. © Patryk I. Labuda 2023. DOI: 10.1093/oso/9780198868842.003.0001

(ICTY) received jurisdictional primacy over national courts. A year later, the statute of the International Criminal Tribunal for Rwanda (ICTR) enshrined its priority vis-à-vis Rwandan institutions. Expressing a then dominant assumption, the landmark *Tadić* judgment explained matter of factly that states could not be trusted with prosecutions of international crimes. At the time, this claim was uncontroversial; even self-explanatory. Given the dearth of domestic trials of genocide, crimes against humanity and war crimes during the Cold War, the revival of international criminal justice in the 1990s revolved around Security Council-mandated ad hoc tribunals and, in due course, efforts to create a permanent institution.

Adopted in 1998, the Rome Statute marked the culmination of an idealistic project dating back to the nineteenth century.[4] As noted by the UN Secretary General, '[u]ndoubtedly, the most significant recent development in the international community's long struggle to advance the cause of justice and rule of law was the establishment of the International Criminal Court [ICC]'.[5] Yet, while it embodies the dreams of generations of international lawyers, the ICC also recognizes the primacy of states—not the Court itself—to prosecute 'the most serious crimes of concern to the international community as a whole'.[6]

As the years have gone by and the ICC has struggled to hold international trials, attention has increasingly shifted away from The Hague towards accountability processes at the national level. Complementarity, a norm born in the interstices of the Rome Statute, is usually credited with this development. In line with its founding treaty, the ICC exercises mere 'complementary' jurisdiction while states have priority to prosecute serious crimes.[7] Where the ICTY and ICTR took for granted that international prosecutors and judges must 'counter' state 'stratagems' to avoid accountability, complementarity proceeds on the opposite assumption: states can and should be trusted to carry out credible trials, and national and international actors should work together to eradicate the 'impunity gap'. Nearly three decades after *Tadić*, it has become an article of faith that domestic trials of genocide, crimes against humanity, and war crimes are a key ingredient in the fight against impunity. Many even argue that the future of international criminal justice is domestic.[8]

The shift in emphasis could not be starker. Upending expectations about how the 'fight against impunity' should function, states have emerged as the primary sites for the enforcement of international criminal law. In less than a generation,

[4] Rome Statute of the International Criminal Court, 2187 UNTS 90, entered into force 1 July 2002 (Rome Statute), preamble.

[5] *Report of the Secretary-General on the Rule of Law and Transitional Justice in Conflict and Post-Conflict Societies* (23 August 2004) S/2004/616, para 49.

[6] Rome Statute, preamble. See also Marlies Glasius, *The International Criminal Court: A Global Civil Society Achievement* (Routledge 2006) 5–14.

[7] Rome Statute, preamble, arts 1 and 17.

[8] International Nuremberg Principles Academy, 'Is the Future of International Criminal Justice Domestic?', annual conference, 12–14 May 2022 <nurembergacademy.org>; Max Du Plessis, 'The Future of International Criminal Justice Is Domestic' (*iLawyer*, 17 September 2014) <ilawyerblog.com/future-international-criminal-justice-domestic/>.

complementarity has evolved into a multifaceted norm defining not only the ICC's institutional design but also a vocabulary of global governance that extends beyond the Rome Statute. Marshalling the rhetoric of complementarity, successive ICC prosecutors have argued that the key to the ICC's success are states who take up the burden of prosecution domestically. Echoing the call for positive complementarity, activists and scholars celebrate the consolidation of a 'Rome System of Justice', wherein the ICC, prodding states into action, intervenes only as a 'court of last resort' while the bulk of anti-impunity work happens at the national level.[9] Instead of sporadic trials in The Hague, it is now the 'shadow' of international intervention that epitomizes the promise of crime prevention, conflict resolution, and a transnational rule of law.

Against the backdrop of the (positive) complementarity turn, defined as a shift towards the domestic enforcement of international criminal law, this book analyses whether and how the shadow of ICTs mobilizes states to fight impunity at the national level. Do international tribunals encourage states to carry out domestic prosecutions of international crimes? How does the ICC's track record compare to other tribunals, including those that had primacy? Based on three case studies, this book examines the complex relationship between international intervention and domestic accountability, illuminates longer-term trends in international criminal law enforcement, and interrogates the consequences of a shift to domestic accountability *qua ultima ratio* of the global anti-impunity project.

1. Domestic Accountability in the Shadow of ICTs

Data from around the world suggest that prosecutions of international crimes and serious human rights violations have increased in the past few decades. Employing the metaphor of the 'justice cascade', Kathryn Sikkink has called this a 'dramatic new trend in world politics toward holding individual state officials, including heads of state, criminally accountable'.[10] Others describe these developments as the 'age of accountability' and the 'anti-impunity turn'.[11]

It now seems settled that a combination of litigation and prosecution in international, regional, and domestic forums has contributed to increased attention

[9] For details on 'shadow of the ICC', 'Rome system of justice', 'court of last resort', and anti-impunity, see Chapters 2 and 3 in this volume.

[10] Kathryn Sikkink, *The Justice Cascade: How Human Rights Prosecutions Are Changing World Politics* (Norton 2011) 5; Kathryn Sikkink and Hun Joon Kim, 'The Justice Cascade: The Origins and Effectiveness of Prosecutions of Human Rights Violations' (2013) 9 Annual Review of Law and Social Science 269 (situating the 'justice cascade' within the scholarly literature).

[11] Ban-Ki Moon, 'The Age of Accountability' <un.org/sg/en/content/sg/articles/2010-05-27/age-accountability>; Kathryn Sikkink, 'The Age of Accountability. The Global Rise of Individual Criminal Accountability' in Francesca Lessa and Leigh A Payne (eds), *Amnesty in the Age of Human Rights Accountability. Comparative and International Perspectives* (CUP 2012). On the turn to anti-impunity (critically), see Karen Engle, Zinaida Miller and Dennis Davis (eds), *Anti-Impunity and the Human Rights Agenda* (CUP 2016).

to accountability for serious crimes than in the past. But less understood are the mechanisms that enable the domestic enforcement of international criminal law. Why do states prosecute international crimes if they did not do so before? To what extent does international intervention influence government action and vice versa?

Based on three case studies, this book analyses whether and how the shadow of ICTs incentivizes state action and the conditions under which states exercise jurisdiction over serious violations that may amount to international crimes. As noted by Yuval Shany, 'the ability of international courts to attain their institutional goals depends not only on those cases they actually adjudicate, but also on the court's "shadow" ... the mere threat of adjudication'.[12] By focusing on how ICT institutional design conditions relations with states, this book interrogates an assumption among international criminal lawyers that the ICC's complementarity norm encourages domestic accountability, and in doing so, it explores how the field's trajectory may have evolved differently had the ICC received primacy, as many 'friends of the Court' hoped in the mid-1990s.

This question may have seemed academic in the 2000s. As a permanent institution, the complementarity-based ICC was widely expected to displace primacy-based ad hoc tribunals. However, this assumption no longer holds. Mired in a semi-permanent crisis for well over a decade, the ICC's high-profile acquittals and threats of individual and collective withdrawal have prompted calls for reform.[13] With investigations underway in well over a dozen countries and additional interventions on the horizon, the ICC is said to be overstretched. As noted by Beth van Schaack, '[o]riginally envisioned as a standing institution that would obviate the need for new ad hoc courts, it is now clear that the ICC cannot handle all the atrocity situations ravaging our planet'.[14]

Confirming this trend, the last decade has seen a revival and proliferation of proposals for ad hoc (Syria and Ukraine), hybrid (Central African Republic (CAR)), South Sudan, Kosovo, Sri Lanka), and regional criminal courts, including the African Court of Human and People's Rights (ACHPR).[15] As the first hybrid tribunal to operate in parallel with an ICC investigation, the Special Criminal Court in CAR has primacy over national courts while purporting to 'reverse' the Rome Statute's complementarity norm vis-à-vis the ICC.[16] Envisaged by the 2014 Malabo

[12] Yuval Shany, *Assessing the Effectiveness of International Courts* (OUP 2014) 76–77.

[13] Douglas Guilfoyle, 'This Is Not Fine. The International Criminal Court in Trouble' (*EJIL:Talk!*, 21 March 2019) <ejiltalk.org/part-i-this-is-not-fine-the-international-criminal-court-in-trouble/>.

[14] Beth van Schaack, 'The Building Blocks of Hybrid Justice' (2016) 44 Denver Journal of International Law and Policy 169.

[15] Mark Kersten, 'As the Pendulum Swings—The Revival of the Hybrid Tribunal' in Mikkel Jarle Christensen and Levi Ron (eds), *International Practices of Criminal Justice: Social and Legal Perspectives* (Routledge 2017). In this book, ad hoc tribunals refer to the ICTY and ICTR, though strictly speaking hybrid tribunals (including the SCSL) are also ad hoc tribunals.

[16] Patryk I Labuda, 'The Special Criminal Court in the Central African Republic: Failure or Vindication of Complementarity?' (2017) 15 Journal of International Criminal Justice 175; Patryk I Labuda, 'Institutional Design and (Non-)Complementarity: Regulating Relations between

Protocol (but still not operational), the ACHPR is expected to function with a form of complementary jurisdiction modelled on the Rome Statute, though the African Union (AU) has left open how regional prosecutions should relate to ICC cases.[17] Other investigative mechanisms, some of whose mandates overlap with the ICC and other tribunals, have also proliferated.[18]

This book examines how the ICC and new tribunals should regulate relations with states to maximize benefits to affected populations. While lawyers have spilt much ink on the theory of concurrent jurisdiction, how ICT institutional design relates to the aims of international criminal justice remains understudied.[19] The dearth of comparative country studies epitomizes a paradox. The design of tribunals like the ICC was grounded on assumptions about their effects—unverifiable at the time of their creation. Although terms like complementarity, primacy, hybridity, and 'those bearing greatest responsibility' were debated to different degrees, the architects of the ICTs created in the late 1990s and 2000s made educated guesses about how these institutions would operate and their short- and longer-term effects.

Yet these assumptions are still rarely interrogated. This is best illustrated by the evolving debate around complementarity, which Karim Khan—sworn in as the third ICC prosecutor in June 2021—has made a centrepiece of his outreach to states.[20] A neologism subject to an endless plurality of interpretations, the term is usually assimilated with a few core beliefs: (1) that states have priority to prosecute international crimes; (2) as a 'court of last resort', the ICC intervenes when states fail to prosecute and, in doing so, prods states into action; and (3) transnational stakeholders should support the ICC and states in this endeavour. Although largely unintended, the ICC's ability to support states' accountability efforts is now seen as consistent with the Rome Statute's original design. Advocacy groups and academics promote expansive readings of 'positive complementarity' that frame the ICC as a catalyst for domestic reforms, including claims about (quasi-)legal obligations to domesticate ICC crimes and prohibitions of amnesties.[21] As argued by Rod

Hybrid Tribunals and Other Judicial Institutions' in Kirsten Ainley and Mark Kersten (eds), *Hybrid Justice: Innovation and Impact in the Prosecution of Atrocity Crimes* (OUP forthcoming).

[17] Charles C Jalloh, Kamari Maxine Clarke and Vincent O Nmehielle (eds), *The African Court of Justice and Human and Peoples' Rights in Context: Development and Challenges* (CUP 2019); Miles Jackson, 'Regional Complementarity. The Rome Statute and Public International Law' (2016) 14 Journal of International Criminal Justice 1061.

[18] Zachary D Kaufman, 'The Prospects, Problems and Proliferation of Recent UN Investigations of International Law Violations' (2018) 16 Journal of International Criminal Justice 93.

[19] See Yuval Shany, *Questions of Jurisdiction and Admissibility before International Courts* (CUP 2016). This research distinguishes between primacy and a restrictive mandate, though both are based on ICT jurisdictional priority. See further Chapter 3 in this volume.

[20] Kai Ambos, 'The Return of "Positive Complementarity"' (*EJIL:Talk!*, 3 November 2021) <ejiltalk.org/the-return-of-positive-complementarity/>.

[21] Philippa Webb and Morten Bergsmo, 'International Criminal Courts and Tribunals, Complementarity and Jurisdiction' [2010] *Max Planck Encyclopedia of Public International Law* <opil.ouplaw.com/display/10.1093/law:epil/9780199231690/law-9780199231690-e1381>. On the 'duty' to

Rastan, 'the Rome Statute is about more than the establishment of a new court: it creates a global compliance system for the enforcement of international criminal law'.[22]

Complementarity's surprising evolution from weakness (a principle of jurisdictional limitation) to strength (the ICC as global enforcer of norms) will be explored in Chapter 2. However, an unintended consequence of complementarity's rhetorical rise is the assumption that the ICC's institutional design is a blueprint for international criminal law enforcement. For instance, in their appropriately entitled *The ICC in an Effective Global Justice System*, Linda Carter, Mark Ellis, and Charles Jalloh suggest that 'because states have the first option to investigate and prosecute [at the ICC], it is far more likely that there will be national prosecutions than was ever the case with the ICTY, ICTR or SCSL [Special Court for Sierra Leone]'.[23] While asking an important question—how to design an effective global justice system?—a premise is conflated with a desired outcome by assuming that the ICC, by virtue of complementarity, enables domestic accountability. Along these lines, Cedric Ryngaert argues that impact 'in conflict-ridden' states 'will be stronger if national courts, rather than international tribunals, assume their investigative and prosecutorial responsibilities [which] is why the international community has embraced the complementarity principle'.[24] This, in turn, takes for granted not only that domestic courts are better at adjudicating international crimes, but also that domestic institutions operate more effectively under complementarity than other forms of concurrent jurisdiction.

Complementarity's potential to cast a shadow over states is a familiar trope in advocacy and scholarship. But other ICTs are burdened with their own self-fulfilling prophecies. It is often suggested that hybrid courts have a greater impact on states than purely international tribunals because they comprise a mix of international and national elements, have a 'demonstration effect',[25] are 'more

prosecute, 'prohibition' of amnesty, and 'duty' to domesticate the Rome Statute, see Sarah MH Nouwen, *Complementarity in the Line of Fire. The Catalysing Effect of the International Criminal Court in Uganda and Sudan* (CUP 2013) 40–43.

[22] Rod Rastan, 'Complementarity: Contest or Collaboration' in Morten Bergmo (ed), *Complementarity and the Exercise of Universal Jurisdiction for Core International Crimes* (Torkel Opsahl 2010) 131.

[23] Linda Carter, Mark Ellis and Charles Jalloh, *The International Criminal Court in an Effective Global Justice System* (Edward Elgar 2016) 25.

[24] Cedric Ryngaert, 'The Principle of Complementarity: A Means of Ensuring Effective International Criminal Justice' in Cedric Ryngaert (ed), *The Effectiveness of International Criminal Justice* (Intersentia/COST Office 2009) 170. For further examples, see eg Mark A Drumbl, 'Impunities' in Kevin Jon Heller and others (eds), *The Oxford Handbook of International Criminal Law* (OUP 2020) 240; Florian Jessberger and Julia Geneuss, 'The Many Faces of the International Criminal Court' (2012) 10 Journal of International Criminal Justice 1081, 1088.

[25] Thierry Cruvellier, 'From the Taylor Trial to a Lasting Legacy: Putting the Special Court Model to the Test' (ICTJ 2009).

legitimate',[26] or that their 'spill-over effect' promotes 'the democratic legal training of local members of the prosecution and judiciary'.[27] Meanwhile, despite mainly negative evaluations of primacy, the ICTY and ICTR's experience of referring cases to states under rule 11*bis* is often offered uncritically as a model for the ICC's relations with states.[28]

In short, while there is a rich academic literature on doctrines and case law, the relationship between ICT institutional design and the goals of international criminal justice requires further study. As argued by Carsten Stahn, '[t]he choice of institutional models and investment in justice remains dictated by "faith-based", rather than "fact-based" considerations'.[29] To take this conversation forward, this book studies how three tribunals—the ICTR, ICC, and SCSL—regulated relations with national jurisdictions and what their experiences tell us about the capacity of ICTs to influence domestic accountability processes.

2. The (Positive) Complementarity Turn in International Criminal Justice

A quick look at the landscape of ICTs reveals that international trials of international crimes are on the decline. While the ICTY prosecuted 161 accused in twenty years, the ICC has shepherded just a handful of trials to completion in the same amount of time. Combined with its disproportionate rate of acquittals, the ICC has struggled to demonstrate its value.[30]

In the shadow of the ICC's (rare) proceedings in The Hague, a realignment of expectations has taken place. Domestic trials are the new promise of international criminal law. In fact, as this book argues, a (positive) complementarity turn—a turn to the domestic enforcement of the law of genocide, crimes against humanity, and war crimes—has occurred. This turn captures a shift grounded on an increasingly consensual *modus vivendi* between ICTs and states. It comprises three elements: states functioning as primary enforcement actors in the fight against

[26] Padraig McAuliffe, 'Hybrid Tribunals at Ten: How International Criminal Justice's Golden Child Became an Orphan' (2011) 7 Journal of International Law and International Relations 1.

[27] Antonio Cassese, 'Role of Internationalized Courts and Tribunals in the Fight Against International Criminality' in Cesare Romano, André Nollkaemper and Jann Kleffner (eds), *Internationalized Criminal Courts. Sierra Leone, East Timor, Kosovo, and Cambodia* (OUP 2004) 6.

[28] But see Padraig McAuliffe, 'Bad Analogy. Why the Divergent Institutional Imperatives of the Ad Hoc Tribunals and the ICC Make the Lessons of Rule 11 bis Inapplicable to the ICC's Complementarity Regime' (2015) 11 International Organizations Law Review 345.

[29] Carsten Stahn, 'Input, Output and "Local" Acceptance: Analyzing Impact and Effects of the International Criminal Court' (*Post-Conflict Justice*, 10 December 2014) <postconflictjustice.com/input-output-and-local-acceptance-analyzing-impact-and-effects-of-the-international-criminal-court/>.

[30] For ICTY and ICC case figures, see <icty.org and icc-cpi.int>. On acquittals in international criminal law, see Richard J Goldstone, 'Acquittals by the International Criminal Court' (*EJIL:Talk!*, 18 January 2019) <ejiltalk.org/acquittals-by-the-international-criminal-court/>.

impunity; ICTs prioritizing cooperation with state actors to foster domestic accountability; and resultant ontological shifts in international criminal justice as a field of practice geared to building state capacity.[31] In short, the turn to domestic accountability constitutes a paradigm shift in how international criminal law is institutionalized, enforced, and rationalized.[32]

Nearly three decades after *Tadić*, states are increasingly understood as the frontline in the global fight against impunity. Although complementarity, the Rome Statute's regulation of concurrent jurisdiction, is the semantic source of this shift, this trend is not limited to the ICC. As will be seen in subsequent chapters, the rise of domestic accountability manifests in different ways and in different places. At the ICTR and ICTY, completion strategies prioritized domestic trials in Rwanda and former Yugoslav states. In Sierra Leone, some features of the Special Court's mandate foregrounded its link to the domestic sphere, while a new concept—legacy—reinforced the domestic dimension of international intervention. A similar emphasis on the longer-term national 'appropriation' of international criminal law guides the hybrid court in CAR, as well as initiatives in South Sudan, Liberia, and Ukraine. After a brief hiatus in the 2000s, prosecutions under universal jurisdiction are again on the rise.[33]

Yet, while there is a distinct turn to the enforcement of international criminal law domestically, ICTs' contribution to this process is more complex than is often assumed. To explain how the shadow of ICTs shapes domestic accountability and vice versa, this book develops a three-tiered typology of ICT–state relations based on accommodation, iteration, and isolation.[34] While any of these three relationships may transpire at different ICTs at different points in time, some elements of institutional design seem more conducive to positive, iterative relationships. Specifically, while some ICT mandates are likely to generate conditionality-based relations, which may in turn influence states' accountability preferences over time, other institutional design features are likely to foster accommodative divisions of labour.

[31] It is important to dissociate two aspects of (positive) complementarity: an element of institutional design (at the ICC) as opposed to an idea underlying international criminal law enforcement premised on cooperation (at all ICTs). This book argues that the vocabulary of '(positive) complementarity' matters in that it captures two core elements of an ideational turn in international criminal justice: an emphasis on *domestic* accountability and *consensual* ICT–state relations geared towards (state) capacity building. On conceptualizations of complementarity, positive complementarity, and cooperation, see Chapter 2 in this volume. For other uses of this phrase, see Mark Kersten, 'The Complementarity Turn in International Criminal Justice' (*Justice in Conflict*, 30 September 2014) <justiceinconflict.org/2014/09/30/the-complementarity-turn-in-international-criminal-justice/>; Christopher Gevers, 'Back to the Future? Civil Society, the "Turn to Complementarity" in Africa and Some Critical Concerns' in Sarah Williams and Hannah Woolaver (eds), *Civil Society and International Criminal Justice in Africa: Challenges and Opportunities* (Juta 2016).

[32] For the term 'paradigm', see Thomas S Kuhn, *The Structure of Scientific Revolutions* (University of Chicago Press 1962).

[33] Máximo Langer and Mackenzie Eason, 'The Quiet Expansion of Universal Jurisdiction' (2019) 30 European Journal of International Law 779.

[34] These terms will be explained in Chapter 2 in this volume.

Yet others may result in isolation. Although the ICC's complementarity norm is, in theory, conducive to iteration, its prosecutor and judges have interpreted the Rome Statute to foster mainly accommodation with states, reducing the scope for cross-pollination of international and domestic best practices and the emergence of a more polycentric system of international criminal law enforcement.[35]

Although there is now more scepticism about the ICC's 'shadow effects' on domestic accountability, ideas associated with complementarity have nevertheless revolutionized how international criminal law stakeholders rationalize the global fight against impunity. In particular, certain rhetorical elements flowing from complementarity seem to have engendered ideational and behavioural changes in how ICTs, donors, and non-governmental organizations (NGOs) interact with states. Advocated initially by the first ICC Prosecutor, Luis Ocampo, and later embraced by civil society and academics, a rhetorical conflation of complementarity with partnership means that the ICC increasingly understands its *raison d'être* as cooperation (accommodation) with—instead of a more relational and at times confrontational (iterative) posture vis-à-vis—states. Nearly three decades after the post-Cold War revival of ICTs, there is a widespread belief that partnership with states can overcome impunity and, accordingly, international intervention is increasingly rationalized in such terms.

As this book argues, this aspect of the complementarity turn—a shift from iterative, push–pull bargaining over domestic accountability to accommodative-cum-cooperative relations with government counterparts—may transform the ontology of international criminal justice. For one, it seems that the crimes of non-state actors increasingly displace state-sponsored criminality as a justification for international criminal law enforcement. For another, states are increasingly cast as a solution to—rather than the root cause of—impunity that ICTs were originally established to overcome. Amounting to an unexpected rehabilitation of state power in international relations, this reorientation of assumptions in international criminal justice—where the coercive tool of criminal law is subordinated to state consent—has consequences for domestic accountability processes that this study begins to disentangle based on the experiences of Rwanda, Sierra Leone, and the Democratic Republic of the Congo (DRC).

While the ICC's poor track record of prosecuting incumbent government officials and, conversely, its focus on non-state actors are familiar tropes,[36] this book unpacks these phenomena by shifting the frame to how government and civil society actors respond to, absorb, and deflect international intervention. It suggests that international criminal justice may be drifting towards an increasingly consensual system of enforcement. Going forward, a growing number of

[35] With few exceptions to date, the ICC has struggled to engender iterative relations with government counterparts. On Colombia, see Chapters 4 and 7 in this volume.

[36] For the existing literature, see Chapters 2, 4, and 7 in this volume.

domestic prosecutions targeting non-state actors, inconvenient political opponents, or cross-border fugitives are likely to be supplemented by token international trials if and when states agree to outsource suspects for prosecution in The Hague. However, the ICC and other ICTs will function less as a tool to challenge unaccountable states and more as an item on the international community's statebuilding agenda. Enabled by a cottage industry of NGOs and donors, governments will make strategic use of ICT interventions to monopolize criminal jurisdiction in their territories, while international partners, marshalling the battle cry of (positive) complementarity, provide resources to support uneven domestic trials of some crimes (but not others) and some perpetrators (but not others).

By isolating the phenomenon of 'unintended diversionary complementarity'—national prosecutions of lower-level, politically unconnected perpetrators for unsystematic crimes—while eliding more complex questions around the quality and aims of such proceedings, this book argues that ICT intervention may entrench national political elites and promote authoritarian power at the expense of affected populations' aspirations for emancipatory justice, which in turn raises questions about the desirability of criminal law as a transitional justice tool. Accordingly, it is argued in the following chapters that the turn to (positive) complementarity may have prompted more fundamental distortions in international criminal justice, not only at the international level (trials limited to non-state actors) but especially at the national level, where state-initiated prosecutions of serious crimes serve to consolidate the authority of elites and exacerbate transitional regimes' authoritarian tendencies. Driven by the incentives and rhetoric of complementarity, international actors strengthen prosecution services and courts, but are unable to challenge the executive branch which condones impunity for some people and some crimes. While advocates strive to promote domestic accountability as part of a human rights-based transitional justice agenda, complementarity's 'authoritarian shadow' may ultimately serve to mainstream a well-known pathology of ICTs—victors' justice—into the domestic sphere.

3. Research Method, Limitations, and Terminology

This book contributes to a growing body of interdisciplinary scholarship that studies how international law and institutions influence the behaviour of state and non-state actors.[37] While there is a considerable literature on international

[37] Tom Ginsburg and Gregory Shaffer, 'How Does International Law Work?' in Peter Cane and Herbert Kritzer (eds), *The Oxford Handbook of Empirical Research* (OUP 2012) 755; Jeffrey L Dunoff and Mark A Pollack (eds), *Interdisciplinary Perspectives on International Law and International Relations: The State of the Art* (CUP 2013). For the rich human rights literature, see Courtney Hillebrecht, *Domestic Politics and International Human Rights Tribunals: The Problem of Compliance* (CUP 2014), Thomas Risse-Kappen, Stephen C Ropp and Kathryn Sikkink (eds), *The Persistent Power of Human Rights: From*

criminal law doctrines and the ICTs' institutional architectures, their effects on societies in, and emerging from, conflict are less well understood. Echoing an 'empirical turn' in the legal sciences, where interdisciplinary tools are used to study 'the conditions under which international law is formed and has effects',[38] this book combines deductive legal methods and an inductive, interpretivist social science approach to generate sociolegal insights into how international norms shape and are, in turn, shaped by interactions between international civil servants (especially prosecutors and their staff) and different state-based actors (government and civil society).[39] While drawing on critical approaches, this book seeks also to develop evidence-based recommendations to move beyond the status quo. As Dustin Sharp observes recently, pushing transitional justice debates forward 'over a decade into the critical turn will require a higher degree of engagement with "the how" of implementing the critical vision', since 'many critical theory ideals—such as participation and local ownership—have become ritualized mantras devoid of substance' and 'pitched at a level of generality bordering on sloganeering'.[40]

Accordingly, it is useful to clarify what this book is not about. It is not an analysis of whether the ICC, ICTR, or SCSL were more effective, induced more compliance, or had a greater impact (cast a longer shadow) at the national level.[41] This is also not a study of whether domestic or international proceedings are 'better' or 'fairer'.[42] Such questions would require different evaluative frameworks and, as this book argues, framing accountability debates in terms of a stark 'international' versus 'national' binary may be part of the problem rather than a solution.

Against the backdrop of institutional design norms conditioning ICT–state relations,[43] this book draws on three qualitative case studies and 'grounded theory'

Commitment to Compliance (CUP 2013); Beth A Simmons, *Mobilizing for Human Rights: International Law in Domestic Politics* (CUP 2009).

[38] Tom Ginsburg and Gregory Shaffer, 'The Empirical Turn in International Legal Scholarship' (2012) 106 American Journal of International Law 1. In international criminal law, see Sergey Vasiliev, 'On Trajectories and Destinations of International Criminal Law Scholarship' (2015) 28 Leiden Journal of International Law 701.

[39] On interpretivism, see Rachel Ormston and others, 'The Foundations of Qualitative Research' in Jane Ritchie and others (eds), *Qualitative Research Practice: A Guide for Social Science Students and Researchers* (2nd edn, Sage 2013) 11–12.

[40] Dustin N Sharp, 'What Would Satisfy Us? Taking Stock of Critical Approaches to Transitional Justice' (2019) 13 International Journal of Transitional Justice 570, 589; see also Kazuo Ohgushi, 'A Critical Note on "Hypercritical" Studies of Transitional Justice' (2015) 79 Journal of Social Science 83. On human rights, see Kathryn Sikkink, *Evidence for Hope: Making Human Rights Work in the 21st Century* (Princeton UP 2017); Gráinne de Búrca, *Reframing Human Rights in a Turbulent Era* (OUP 2021).

[41] On effectiveness, see Shany (n 12). On compliance and its limits, see Robert Howse and Ruti Teitel, 'Beyond Compliance: Rethinking Why International Law Really Matters' (2010) 1 Global Policy 127.

[42] On the merits of domestic and international trials, see Beatrice I Bonafé, 'Coordinating Concurrent Legal Orders in the Prosecution of International Crimes' (2013) 2 Global Constitutionalism 316.

[43] On institutional design and its relationship to social science research in international criminal law, see Jens Meierhenrich, 'The Practice of International Law: A Theoretical Analysis' (2013) 76 Duke Journal of Comparative & International Law 1.

to assess when, why, and how tribunals influence domestic accountability processes and, in turn, how states influence the actions of tribunals.[44] As defined by Alexander George and Andrew Bennett, the case study approach consists of a 'detailed examination of an aspect of a historical episode to develop or test historical explanations that may be generalizable to other events'.[45] Process tracing 'involves looking at evidence within an individual case ... to derive and/or test alternative explanations of that case, [which] ... may or may not provide a theoretical explanation relevant to the wider phenomenon of which the case is an instance'.[46] While the book engages with emerging quantitative scholarship on ICTs, it does so only to contextualize its qualitative case-based analysis.

Qualitative research and comparative case studies raise questions about the replicability of their data and findings.[47] This research does not generate data points according to rigid, predefined categories—in line with the precepts of quantitative research—but analyses patterns of behaviour extrapolated from phenomena observed across the cases, without formulating strict hypotheses about how ICTs operate in other contexts.[48] Qualitative case studies necessarily give a partial picture of the whole, and shed light on micro processes but without establishing general principles. By comparing different ICT–state relations, this study acknowledges the context-specific nature of each state's accountability process while starting a discussion about the effects of institutional design choices that will have to be assessed by other scholars in other contexts.

The book uses various primary and secondary sources to trace and 'unpack' connections between the actions of ICT and government actors. In addition to publications about the ICTR, ICC, and SCSL, including legal texts, civil society reports, memoirs of decision makers and other scholars' work, information on Rwanda, Sierra Leone, and the DRC is based on legislation, court transcripts, monitoring reports, government statements. Complementing the author's work experience, research visits to the DRC, Rwanda, Sierra Leone, Arusha, and The Hague allowed interviews with judges, prosecutors, attorneys, police officers, government officials, civil society representatives, and diplomats.[49] In total, over 220 semi-structured

[44] On qualitative research generally, see Ormston and others (n 39) 2. On grounded theory, see Kathy Charmaz, *Constructing Grounded Theory* (Sage 2006).

[45] Alexander L George and Andrew Bennett, *Case Studies and Theory Development in the Social Sciences* (MIT Press 2005) 5; Bent Flyvbjerg, 'Five Misunderstandings about Case-Study Research' (2006) 12 Qualitative Inquiry 219.

[46] Andrew Bennett, 'Process Tracing: A Bayesian Perspective' in Janet M Box-Steffensmeier, Henry E Brady and David Collier (eds), *The Oxford Handbook of Political Methodology*, vol 1 (OUP 2008) 704.

[47] Jane Lewis and Jane Ritchie, 'Generalising from Qualitative Research' in Ritchie and others (n 39).

[48] George and Bennett (n 45) 5–6.

[49] Some information about the DRC is based on the author's work there in 2010–11, but the usual research process was used to generate data. Research visits took place as follows: Kigali (August–September 2015), Arusha (September 2015; October 2016), Freetown (March 2016), Goma, Bukavu, and Kinshasa (September 2015; April 2016, August 2016; July–August 2019), in addition to visits to The Hague in 2015, 2016, 2018, 2019, 2020, and 2021.

interviews with domestic actors and officials from the ICC, ICTR, and SCSL were carried out between 2015 and 2021.[50] In addition, professional and research visits to three other ICC situations—Sudan, CAR, and Libya—between 2012 and 2019 allowed engagement with justice actors (while this book's main ICC case study is the DRC, insights from other situations inform the analysis).

Following a 'snowball' approach, the interview process in Rwanda, Sierra Leone, and the DRC led to interviewees with more targeted knowledge.[51] As data on the three case studies accumulated, people with direct knowledge of specific events or processes were contacted. No financial incentives were offered to interviewees and most interviews were transcribed by hand. Identifying information has been withheld for most interviewees, except where consent for attribution was received.

Several considerations dictated the choice of Rwanda, Sierra Leone, and the DRC as case studies. When this research began, just over a dozen countries had 'hosted' ICTs. As the ICC had to be compared to tribunals that regulated their relationships to states differently, the SCSL was chosen as an example of a hybrid tribunal focused on a narrow group of perpetrators (the Extraordinary Chambers in the Courts of Cambodia's (ECCC's) mandate is similar, but it acted as a substitute for domestic courts and dealt with crimes from a more distant past). The ICTY could have served as a case of primacy, but there were fewer similarities between African (the ICC was only active in Africa at the time) and former Yugoslav justice systems, introducing a different baseline against which to assess ICT effects. This issue is addressed further in Chapter 7.[52]

Although, in 2013, seven ICC situations were eligible, the DRC was chosen to allow meaningful comparisons with Rwanda and Sierra Leone, where the ICTR and SCSL had operated for a decade or more. Investigations in Kenya, Côte d'Ivoire, Libya, and Mali began between 2010 and 2013, reducing the scope for process tracing. By contrast, the ICC prosecutor had opened his first investigation in the DRC in June 2004 (Uganda followed a month later) and, having previously worked in this francophone country which had been studied less than Uganda, the author opted for it as an active case of complementarity. Where possible, connections to the experience of other ICTs or other ICC countries are made throughout this book.

The choice of case studies shapes the empirical foundations and theoretical implications of this research. The ICTR's impact on accountability in Rwanda is different from the ICTY's role in Bosnia or Serbia, much like the ICC's effects in DRC differ from the Mali or Sudan investigations, or preliminary examinations, such as Colombia or Guinea. Although the ICC's status as a permanent tribunal sets it

[50] Brian C Rathbun, 'Interviewing and Qualitative Field Methods: Pragmatism and Practicalities' in Box-Steffensmeier, Brady and Collier (n 46).

[51] Rathbun (n 50) 696.

[52] See World Justice Project, Rule of Law Index. According to the 2019 Index, this book's three case studies were ranked 40 (Rwanda), 98 (Sierra Leone), and 124 (DRC), respectively.

apart from ad hoc tribunals with jurisdiction over single conflicts, this difference in institutional design, rather than obviating the need for comparison, feeds into the analysis. Acknowledging such differences, this book formulates hypotheses about ICT–state relations that will have to be assessed in other contexts.

A few words about terminology. The term 'domestic accountability' describes government action relating to criminal law intended to fight 'impunity' for serious crimes. In principle, it does not cover civil, administrative, or disciplinary proceedings at the national level.[53] As will be explained in Chapter 3, serious crimes may be prosecuted by states as either ordinary crimes or international crimes, provided contextual elements are met. Chapters 4 to 6 introduce the three variables—domestic prosecutions, capacity building, and norm internalization—that serve to establish the parameters of ICT influence on domestic accountability and vice versa. Complementarity refers to the ICC's institutional design, whereas the 'complementarity turn' refers to a shift to domestic accountability at all ICTs, which—as this book argues—privileges cooperation as a means of incentivizing states to fight impunity.

4. The Case Studies: Rwanda, Sierra Leone, and the DR Congo

By way of background, the book's three case studies are introduced below. Chapters 4 to 6 will expand on these themes.

4.1 Rwanda: zero-impunity, prosecutions, and traditional justice

The genocide against the Tutsi was the culmination of a four-year conflict between the Rwandan Patriotic Front (RPF), a Tutsi-led armed group led by Paul Kagame, and the pro-Hutu government of President Juvénal Habyarimana.[54] The 1993 Arusha Accords ushered in a tense power-sharing agreement between the belligerents, but the downing of Habyarimana's plane on 6 April 1994 unleashed a wave of violence over the next three months, with an estimated 500,000 to one million victims.[55] After capturing Kigali in July 1994, the RPF established a government

[53] 'Updated Set of Principles for the Protection and Promotion of Human Rights through Action to Combat Impunity, E/CN.4/2005/102/Add.1' (2005). The French term 'lutte contre l'impunité' is more common in the francophone world as a phrase equivalent to international criminal justice.

[54] On the genocide, its antecedents, and aftermath, see Gérard Prunier, *The Rwanda Crisis: History of A Genocide* (1st edn, Columbia UP 1995); André Guichaoua, *De la guerre au génocide: Les politiques criminelles au Rwanda 1990–1994* (Karthala 2005). For the official designation 'genocide against the Tutsi', which consolidated in the 2000s, and its exclusion of violence against moderate Hutu and Twa, see Scott Straus, 'The Limits of a Genocide Lens: Violence against Rwandans in the 1990s' (2019) 21 Journal of Genocide Research 504. Hereafter, the shorter term 'Rwandan genocide' is used.

[55] On the numbers of victims, see Jens Meierhenrich, 'How Many Victims Were There in the Rwandan Genocide? A Statistical Debate' (2020) 22 Journal of Genocide Research 72.

of national unity (GNU), based formally on a power-sharing deal with moderate Hutus. However, fighting against Hutu extremists continued in parts of Rwanda, eventually spilling into the neighbouring DRC, where military operations continued until 2002 and occasionally thereafter, leading to accusations of serious crimes.[56]

As will be explained in the next chapters, the Rwandan justice system was in ruins in the aftermath of the genocide and many suspects had fled the country. The UN Security Council established the ICTR in late 1994 but placed the Tribunal in Arusha, Tanzania. Although the ICTR's jurisdiction ran concurrently with that of Rwandan courts, primacy allowed the Tribunal to 'override' domestic proceedings subject to specific conditions. Meanwhile, Rwanda's multilayered domestic response to the genocide unfolded in the ICTR's shadow. The GNU initially considered various transitional justice options, but a 'maximum' accountability policy was deemed most appropriate for mass crimes.[57] In addition to some 10,000 people tried in Rwandan ordinary courts, over one million people were held accountable before customary *gacaca* courts. After operating concurrently with national institutions for twenty years, the ICTR closed its doors in 2015. Based in The Hague and Arusha, the Mechanism for International Criminal Tribunals (MICT) performs certain essential 'residual' functions in the wake of the ICTR's closure.[58]

4.2 Sierra Leone: amnesty, truth and reconciliation, and prosecutions

Triggered by the Revolutionary United Front (RUF)'s invasion from Liberia in 1991, Sierra Leone's civil war lasted for over a decade. In addition to the RUF, the main belligerents included the Sierra Leone Army (SLA), the Armed Forces Revolutionary Council (AFRC), and the Civil Defence Force (CDF). In 1998, troops from West African countries deployed to stem the violence, followed by the UN's—at the time—largest peacekeeping mission in 1999. In May 2000, after the kidnapping of some 500 peacekeepers, British troops intervened in their former colony, gradually bringing about a cessation of hostilities by early 2002. It is estimated that between 50,000 and 75,000 people died in the war.[59]

[56] On Rwanda's involvement in the Congo Wars, see Gérard Prunier, *Africa's World War: Congo, the Rwandan Genocide, and the Making of a Continental Catastrophe* (OUP 2010).

[57] For 'maximum accountability', see Nicholas A Jones, *The Courts of Genocide: Politics and the Rule of Law in Rwanda and Arusha* (Routledge 2010) 52.

[58] Statute of the International Residual Mechanism for Criminal Tribunals, annex to UNSC Res 1966 (22 December 2010) S/RES/1966.

[59] William A Schabas, 'Conjoined Twins of Transitional Justice? The Sierra Leone Truth and Reconciliation Commission and the Special Court' (2004) 2 Journal of International Criminal Justice 1082.

Sierra Leone has struggled with conflict since independence in 1961. After the 1996 Abidjan peace agreement provided a blanket amnesty to the RUF and the SLA, amnesty was again on the table when ceasefire negotiations resumed. Although a peace agreement signed in Lomé in 1999 again foresaw a blanket amnesty for the warring parties, the UN representative reportedly appended a note refusing to recognize its applicability to international crimes. The UN later argued it was not bound by this aspect of the Lomé amnesty, laying the groundwork for the SCSL.[60]

Established in 2002 to prosecute suspects bearing greatest responsibility, the Special Court operated alongside a truth-seeking process. Mandated to create a historical record and promote healing, the Sierra Leonean Truth and Reconciliation Commission (TRC) investigated violations but lacked the power to recommend individuals for prosecution.[61] While the government continued to adhere to the Lomé amnesty for pre-1999 crimes, in the shadow of the SCSL's high-profile trials in Freetown and amid capacity-building projects for the national justice system, Sierra Leonean courts prosecuted over fifty people for post-1999 war-related crimes. Recurrent civil society demands to repeal the Lomé amnesty have been ignored to this day, preventing national trials for pre-1999 events.

4.3 DR Congo: partial amnesty, failed truth-seeking, and prosecutions

Ranging from 1996 to 2003, the First and Second Congo Wars involved several foreign armies, and various armed domestic proxies and local militias. Estimates of casualties vary from several hundred thousand to millions killed.[62] Published in 2010, a UN report identified over 600 incidents of potential war crimes and crimes against humanity committed between 1993 and 2003.[63] In 1999, the UN deployed what became one of its largest ever peacekeeping missions, but conflict in eastern Congo continues to this day, with as many as 100 armed groups still active.[64]

Following the Inter-Congolese Dialogue and a power-sharing agreement with the main belligerents, the Transitional Constitution, adopted in 2003, embraced the language of reconciliation and human rights. Despite mandating a national

[60] On the Lomé agreement, see Priscilla Hayner, 'Negotiating Peace in Sierra Leone: Confronting the Justice Challenge' (ICTJ and Centre for Humanitarian Dialogue 2007).

[61] Sierra Leone Truth and Reconciliation Commission Report <sierraleonetrc.org>.

[62] Prunier (n 56) 181–284; Human Security Report, *The Causes of Peace and the Shrinking Costs of War* (2011) 123–31.

[63] OHCHR, 'Rapport du Projet Mapping concernant les violations les plus graves des droits de l'homme et du droit international humanitaire commises entre mars 1993 et juin 2003 sur le territoire de la République démocratique du Congo' (2010).

[64] Jason K Stearns, *The War That Doesn't Say Its Name. The Unending Conflict in the Congo* (Princeton UP 2021).

amnesty, it excluded war crimes, crimes against humanity, and genocide from its ambit.[65] A truth commission operated from 2003 to 2006 but it is considered a failure. Following his ratification of the Rome Statute in 2002,[66] President Joseph Kabila requested the ICC to open an investigation in March 2004. The ICC prosecutor's investigation—opened in June 2004 and still active at the time of writing—has run in parallel with domestic trials. As of 2022, Congolese authorities have prosecuted dozens of international crimes and hundreds of serious ordinary crimes in the ICC's shadow.

5. Book Outline

The next six chapters examine how ICTs influence domestic accountability processes and specifically how choices of institutional design shape prosecutions, capacity building, and norm internalization at the national level. Chapter 2 explains the origins and rationales of today's emphasis on domestic accountability in international criminal law and its rhetorical association with complementarity. Although the relationship of the ICC to national jurisdictions was a key issue during the drafting of the Rome Statute, the now common emphasis on supporting the domestic fight against impunity, known as 'positive complementarity', emerged as a post hoc rationalization after the ICC's establishment and ties in with analogous developments at the ICTR and SCSL. After tracing the ascendancy of (positive) complementarity as a multipurpose accountability and global governance vocabulary, Chapter 2 introduces the book's practice-based tripartite analytical framework for analysing ICT–state relations and considers the implications of a state-driven accountability system for the traditional justifications of international criminal law enforcement.

Against the backdrop of the (positive) complementarity turn, Chapter 3 examines how ICTs regulate(d) their relationship to states. By analysing the mandates and jurisprudence of the ICTR, SCSL, and ICC, the chapter illuminates similarities and differences between their institutional design, explains the relationship of each tribunal to national jurisdictions, and assesses the potential of each arrangement to incentivize states' responses to serious crimes. Based on the law of primacy, a hybrid/restrictive mandate, and complementarity, this chapter argues that, rather than fixed bodies of norms that generate specific procedural or substantive outcomes, these three arrangements also express general values or a

[65] Martien Schotsmans, 'La justice transitionnelle pendant la période de la transition en RDC' in Stefaan Marysse, Filip Reyntjens and Stef Vandeginste (eds), *Annuaire des Grands Lacs 2006–2007* (Harmattan 2007) 204–06.

[66] In fact, the DRC, a signatory since 8 September 2000, ratified the Rome Statute on 30 March 2002, helping to bring the ICC into existence on 1 July 2002 <treaties.un.org>; William A Schabas, *An Introduction to the International Criminal Court* (4th edn, CUP 2011) 24.

dominant institutional preference for international, domestic, or mixed enforcement of international criminal law. While no ICT mandate was designed as such to encourage domestic trials of serious crimes, the case law explains how ideas about the fight against impunity have changed over time and why some institutional arrangements are better able to adjust to these changes than others.

The next three chapters examine how the shadow of ICTs influences domestic accountability processes, with domestic trials (Chapter 4), capacity building (Chapter 5), and norm internalization (Chapter 6) serving as variables to assess whether international intervention had generally positive (iteration), neutral (accommodation), or negative (isolation) effects on the willingness and ability of governments to pursue accountability for serious crimes. Chapter 4 examines to what extent the ICTR, SCSL, and ICC encouraged authorities in Rwanda, Sierra Leone, and the DRC to initiate national proceedings and, in turn, how government officials and civil society in these countries shaped international prosecutorial strategy. It argues that, despite ICTs' divergent institutional designs, international investigative practices are generally similar and divisions of labour depend less on mandates than on governments' willingness to cooperate with international prosecutors, although primacy may provide stronger incentives than complementarity for international civil servants to challenge states over state crimes.

Chapter 5 examines how the ICTR, SCSL, and ICC shaped capacity building for the national justice sectors in Rwanda, Sierra Leone, and the DRC, in particular by revitalizing criminal justice institutions and magistrates' expertise. It reveals that, while ICTs rarely intervene directly to support national institutions, development partners regularly draw on their 'symbolic shadow', with concepts like 'positive complementarity' and 'legacy' serving as rhetorical slogans to rationalize international–national capacity building. Chapter 5 argues that, while the term positive complementarity is now a shorthand for financial and technical assistance to national justice systems and there is much advocacy around how 'positive complementarity' partners can collaboratively build the capacity of courts and prosecution services, a reluctance to critically evaluate such statebuilding projects—lest host governments withdraw their consent—may end up strengthening authoritarian tendencies and romanticize domestic accountability to the exclusion of international alternatives.

Chapter 6 examines how the ICTR, SCSL, and ICC influenced domestic actors in Rwanda, Sierra Leone, and the DRC to enact normative reforms and to what extent international norms are respected in national trials of serious crimes. It argues that, while the Rome Statute increasingly functions as a global code for international crimes, it inadvertently privileges a sovereignty-friendly, outcomes-oriented vision of accountability. Rather than mainstream process-oriented fair trial rights, states under the shadow of ICC intervention may prioritize the holding of trials as such, to repel external scrutiny without addressing the underlying conditions that enable impunity. Based on the DRC case study, this chapter also explains the phenomenon of 'unintended diversionary complementarity', whereby state actors use domestic trials selectively to target certain perpetrators and certain crimes, eliding complex questions around the quality and aims of domestic and international trials in fostering emancipatory justice.

Extrapolating from the three case studies, Chapter 7 examines three trends in the field of international criminal justice: a turn from 'coercive' intervention to 'cooperative' rule-of-law strategies, the phenomenon of 'unintended diversionary complementarity', and the turn from investigations to preliminary examinations as sites of iterative strategies at the ICC. After identifying three intervening factors that define the conditions of possibility for iterative practices in ICT–state relations—temporal constraints, prosecutorial leadership, and intrastate politics—the chapter turns to reforms that can be implemented at the ICC to enhance the enforcement of international criminal law in an increasingly illiberal political climate. It shows that, notwithstanding complementarity's rhetorical salience, the determinants of the ICC's 'success' are still associated with The Hague, rather than the states in which it intervenes. In challenging binary distinctions between national and international responses to serious crimes, this chapter suggests how the ICC can cast as long a shadow as possible by engendering iterative relations vis-à-vis states through what it calls 'relational complementarity'.

Situating the turn to domestic accountability in a longer-term chronological perspective, the Epilogue examines the ideational changes prompted by the vocabulary of (positive) complementarity. It argues that, by revolutionizing how civil society, scholars, and tribunals talk and act in regard to serious crimes, complementarity has altered the imaginary of international criminal law stakeholders and may become an ideology that transforms the ontology of international criminal law from a counter-hegemonic project to a consent-based statebuilding enterprise.

2
The (Positive) Complementarity Turn in International Criminal Justice

The promise of domestic accountability is rhetorically associated with the word complementarity, a term that refers to states' priority to prosecute serious crimes and the ICC's subsidiary enforcement powers. Complementarity's design of checks and balances is said to provide a positive mix of incentives to states, the ICC, and other accountability stakeholders to collectively administer the fight against impunity in a decentralized system of international criminal law enforcement. In fact, as this book argues, some aspects of primacy, a different mechanism to regulate international–state interactions may, over time, generate more positive incentives for the domestic enforcement of international criminal law.

Yet, even if complementarity, as the term is currently interpreted, does not always incentivize domestic accountability, its rhetorical features and the cooperation incentives embedded in the ICC's institutional design have transformed the debate over the enforcement of international criminal law. In particular, the vocabulary of 'positive complementarity' has had profound implications for how tribunals, states, civil society, and academics rationalize the global fight against impunity. Not only are states now rhetorically understood as the primary enforcers of international criminal law, but international actors are also expected to support domestic anti-impunity initiatives, regardless of whether states address the root causes of impunity. Complementarity may incarnate deeper transformations in the ontology of international criminal law which has evolved from a counter-hegemonic project to a managerial, statebuilding enterprise geared towards the crimes of non-state actors and consolidating the authority of incumbent governments.

The chapter begins by explaining the origins of today's emphasis on domestic accountability in international criminal law and its rhetorical association with complementarity. It then traces the ascendancy of (positive) complementarity as a vocabulary of global governance before introducing the book's analytical framework for analysing ICT–state relations. The chapter ends with the ideational implications of prioritizing state-driven accountability and embracing the language of 'positive complementarity' for the evolving justifications of international criminal law.

International Criminal Tribunals and Domestic Accountability. Patryk I. Labuda,
Oxford University Press. © Patryk I. Labuda 2023. DOI: 10.1093/oso/9780198868842.003.0002

1. The Rise and Fall of Domestic Accountability in Time and Space

International criminal law is a relatively young subfield of international law. By most accounts, the idea of holding individuals criminally accountable for serious crimes under international law can be traced to the post-First World War efforts to prosecute the German Kaiser and the post-Second World War Nuremberg and Tokyo trials. While recent scholarship nuances this linear genealogy,[1] a common theme running through the history of international criminal justice is its *ideational* preference for international tribunals.[2] As noted by Carsten Stahn, '[t]hroughout much of the nineteenth and twentieth centuries, international criminal law has been driven by the ideal of international criminal jurisdiction'.[3]

Created in 1993 and 1994 respectively, the ICTY and ICTR epitomized the international community's belief in the superiority of international enforcement. Endowed with primacy, both tribunals received expansive powers to take cases away from states, which—as explained forcefully in the 1995 *Tadić* judgment—were considered inherently ill-suited to adjudicating international crimes. As José Alvarez observes:[4]

> 'primacy' over national courts ... reflects the prevailing wisdom that trials organized within the regions affected by mass atrocities should either be discouraged, as within the Balkans where they are likely to be political show trials that would undermine public support for the rule of law, or kept at a distance, as within Rwanda, where such second-best alternatives would prove selective in applying the law and less competent in applying the requirements of the treaty and customary law developments that have emerged in the fifty years since Nuremberg.

As will be seen in Chapter 3, although the architects of the ad hoc tribunals endorsed concurrent jurisdiction, they viewed domestic trials as an unavoidable

[1] Mark Lewis, *The Birth of the New Justice: The Internationalization of Crime and Punishment, 1919–1950* (OUP 2014). Immi Tallgren and Thomas Skouteris (eds), *The New Histories of International Criminal Law: Retrials* (OUP 2019). Frédéric Mégret and Immi Tallgren (eds), *The Dawn of a Discipline: International Criminal Justice and Its Early Exponents* (CUP 2020).

[2] See eg Benjamin B Ferencz, *An International Criminal Court, a Step toward World Peace: A Documentary History and Analysis* (Oceana 1980). It is important to dissociate the *ideational* preference for ICTs from the fact of (sporadic) national trials of serious crimes occurring after the First and Second World Wars. For the converse idea of states qua primary enforcement sites in the post-First World War era, see Kirsten Sellars, 'The First World War, Wilhelm II, and Article 227: The Origin of the Idea of "Aggression" in International Criminal Law' in Claus Kress and Stefan Barriga (eds), *The Crime of Aggression. A Commentary* (CUP 2017) 30–31.

[3] Carsten Stahn, *A Critical Introduction to International Criminal Law* (2019) 6; Florian Jessberger, 'International v. National Prosecutions of International Crimes' in Antonio Cassese (ed), *Oxford Companion to International Criminal Justice* (OUP 2009) 208.

[4] José E Alvarez, 'Crimes of States/Crimes of Hate: Lessons from Rwanda' (1999) 24 Yale Journal of International Law 365, 376.

compromise, at best, or a necessary evil, at worst. For instance, when Radovan Karadžić, the President of Republika Srpska, proposed in 1997 that his case be tried 'by the courts of his homeland' rather than before the ICTY, '[t]he international community immediately dismissed this suggestion as a transparent attempt to circumvent justice'.[5] As Yuval Shany observes, 'the international community did not in the past view national courts as meaningful partners in the international response to mass atrocity situations'.[6]

The Rome Statute would transform these assumptions about the superiority of international trials. Endowed with 'complementary jurisdiction', the ICC is required to respect states' priority to prosecute genocides, crimes against humanity, and war crimes (and aggression as of 2018).[7] This marked a break with past assumptions. Despite its potentially global remit, the ICC would act as a subsidiary enforcement body. Well known in global governance theory, the principle of subsidiarity would be applied to international crimes, albeit under a different name.[8] Known colloquially as complementarity, the ICC's institutional design would in due course spawn a revolution in international criminal law enforcement, with states gradually emerging as the frontline in the global fight against impunity.

Yet, while it is often associated with the ICC, the ascendancy of domestic accountability for international crimes is a product of several trends that coalesced at around the same time in the late 1990s and early 2000s. Amid criticisms of 'costly' international trials and the 'remoteness' of justice delivered in The Hague and Arusha, the 'national' dimension of international criminal law grew exponentially in the former Yugoslavia and Rwanda.[9] When called upon to sanction crimes in East Timor, Cambodia, and Sierra Leone, the UN opted for 'hybrid' tribunals, restricted to a narrow group of perpetrators, located in-country, closer to affected populations, and, in some cases, designed to maximize impact at the national level.[10] As the ICTY and ICTR prepared to shut down in the mid-2000s, international prosecutors began arguing that '[n]ational legal systems have a vital

[5] Cited in Bartram S Brown, 'Primacy or Complementarity: Reconciling the Jurisdiction of National Courts and International Criminal Tribunals' (1998) 23 Yale Law Journal 383, 384.

[6] Yuval Shany, 'The Role of National Courts in Advancing the Goals of International Criminal Tribunals' (2009) 103 Proceedings of the Annual Meeting of the American Society of International Law 210, 211.

[7] Rome Statute, preamble and art 5. On the ICC's jurisdiction over aggression, activated in July 2018, and its modified jurisdictional regime as well as doubts over the applicability of complementarity, see Pål Wrange, 'The Crime of Aggression: Domestic Prosecutions and Complementarity' in Kress and Barriga (n 2).

[8] On subsidiarity, see Markus Jachtenfuchs and Nico Krisch, 'Subsidiarity in Global Governance' (2016) 79 Law and Contemporary Problems 1.

[9] Also labelled 'tribunal fatigue', see 'State Department Views on the Future for War Crimes Tribunals' (2002) 96 American Journal of International Law 482; David Scheffer, 'Challenges Confronting International Justice Issues' (1998) 4 New England International and Comparative Law Annual 1.

[10] Daphna Shraga, 'The Second Generation UN-Based Tribunals: A Diversity of Mixed Jurisdictions' in Cesare Romano, André Nollkaemper and Jann Kleffner (eds), *Internationalized Criminal Courts: Sierra Leone, East Timor, Kosovo, and Cambodia* (OUP 2004).

role in the prosecution of these grave crimes. International institutions need step in only when national systems lack the strength or impartiality to hold the most serious offenders to account.'[11] As early as 2002, William Burke-White argued that 'the future of international criminal law enforcement will largely be at the domestic level'.[12]

The turn to the domestic enforcement of international criminal law is a multi-causal phenomenon that has seeped into the practice of the ad hoc tribunals, hybrid courts, and the ICC in a variety of ways. By and large, however, it is the term complementarity that conveys the emphasis on, and implicitly the superiority of, domestic accountability. Exemplifying this trend, the ICTY and ICTR mobilized the language of complementarity to describe their completion strategies and rule 11*bis* transfers while their jurisdiction remained grounded on primacy.[13] As explained by the ICTR in its final report, '[b]y referring these indictments to national jurisdictions for trial, the Tribunal also gave practical effect to the principle of complementarity', whereby '[n]ational authorities, and not the Tribunal, became primarily responsible for conducting and completing proceedings against the accused'.[14] A similar emphasis on complementarity *qua* domestic dimension of international intervention can be observed recently in CAR, where donors and human rights groups work to maximize the Special Criminal Court's legacy for the ordinary justice system.[15]

In these and other instances, complementarity functions as a cognitive shortcut for the ideal of sanctioning international crimes domestically. Put differently, aside from the Rome Statute's institutional design vis-à-vis states, complementarity epitomizes a broader set of assumptions, ideas, and expectations that resonate beyond the ICC. The next sections trace key inflection points in complementarity's rise as a global governance vocabulary before turning to its ideational implications within the field of international criminal justice.

[11] Joint Statement of the Prosecutors, Prosecutors Colloquium 'Challenges of International Criminal Justice' (25–27 November 2004, Arusha, Tanzania); Luis M Ocampo, Hassan Jallow, Carla Del Ponte, David Crane <unictr.org/sites/unictr.org/files/news/newsletters/November2004.pdf>.

[12] William Burke-White, 'A Community of Courts: Toward a System of International Criminal Law Enforcement' (2002) 24 Michigan Journal of International Law 1, 3.

[13] On case transfers under r 11*bis*, see Chapter 3 in this volume.

[14] Report on the Completion of the Mandate of the ICTR as at 15 November 2015, S/2015/884, 17 November 2015, para 61; see also ICTR–OTP, 'Complementarity in Action: Lessons Learned from the ICTR Prosecutor's Referral of International Criminal Cases to National Jurisdictions for Trial' (2015). In scholarship, see eg William A Schabas, 'Anti-Complementarity: Referral to National Jurisdictions by the UN International Criminal Tribunal for Rwanda' (2009) 13 Max Planck Yearbook of United Nations Law 29.

[15] Amnesty International, '"On Trial, These Warlords Lowered Their Eyes": The Central African Republic's Challenging Pursuit of Justice' (2020) AFR 19/3185/2020. On legacy and complementarity, see Elizabeth M Evenson and Alison Smith, 'Completion, Legacy, and Complementarity at the ICC' in Carsten Stahn (ed), *The Law and Practice of the International Criminal Court* (OUP 2015). See also Chapter 5 in this volume.

2. From Subsidiarity to Shadow: Tracing Complementarity's Ascendance

Adopted in July 1998, the Rome Statute was greeted with both optimism and anxiety. On the one hand, international justice advocates celebrated the prospect of a permanent tribunal catering to victims of international crimes around the world. William Pace, the leader of the Coalition for the ICC, argued 'the ICC will deter; the ICC will prevent .... the ICC will save millions of humans from suffering unspeakably horrible and inhumane death in the coming decades'.[16] On the other hand, with some powerful states voting against the Statute, many worried that the ICC might never come into existence. Philippe Kirsch, a key actor in Rome and subsequently the ICC's first president, notes that '[w]hen we finished the conference in Rome, the pessimists were saying twenty years and the optimists were saying ten years'.[17]

The ICC's institutional design was controversial. Of particular concern were the prosecutor's independence and the Security Council's powers vis-à-vis the ICC. Underpinning these questions, however, was the quasi-ontological issue of the ICC's future relationship to states. Over time, the neologism complementarity (though it would never be incorporated into the Rome Statute) coalesced among diplomats.[18] Reconciling the incongruity of a criminal court with *coercive* enforcement powers in an international legal system predicated on state *consent*, complementarity allowed the ICC to depart from the institutional design of earlier tribunals which operated on the basis of primacy vis-à-vis domestic actors.[19]

At the time, few anticipated the meteoric rise of complementarity—a term that is, after all, absent from the Rome Statute—which has come to define a global project of international criminal law enforcement. Fewer yet could have predicted the term's rehabilitation. An admissibility mechanism designed to protect states and limit the ICC's powers, complementarity was initially viewed as a defeat. As noted by Silvia Fernandez de Gurmendi, a participant in the Rome conference who later occupied many ICC leadership positions, 'many left Rome with the feeling that the complementarity provisions, which failed to recognize primacy ... were a necessary but regrettable concession ... that could weaken the future institution'.[20]

De Gurmendi was hardly alone. A range of commentators worried that the ICC's lack of primacy vis-à-vis states made it weaker than the ad hoc tribunals.

[16] Quoted in David L Bosco, *Rough Justice: The International Criminal Court in a World of Power Politics* (OUP 2014) 3.

[17] Quoted ibid 56; see further ibid 2–5.

[18] Immi Tallgren, 'Completing the "International Criminal Order": The Rhetoric of International Repression and the Notion of Complementarity in the Draft Statute for an International Criminal Court' (1998) 67 Nordic Journal of International Law 107.

[19] Alvarez (n 4) 385.

[20] Silvia Fernandez de Gurmendi, 'Foreword' in Carsten Stahn and Mohamed M El Zeidy (eds), *The International Criminal Court and Complementarity* (CUP 2011) xxvi.

Speaking just before Rome, Louise Arbour, then ICTY/R Prosecutor, aptly conveyed the sense of alarm:[21]

> I would like to discuss the complementarity and primacy of international tribunals and possibly a permanent court over domestic institutions. I have been told in many circles that this is not a negotiable issue before the Rome conference. If that is correct, then I am very disappointed. But, since I am not in the business of taking no for an answer quickly, I think it is important that we forcefully examine the question of whether we should concede that the lack of primacy of a permanent international court is acceptable.

The same negative sentiment abounded after Rome. Antonio Cassese warned that '[c]omplementarity might lend itself to abuse . . . [and] amount to a shield used by states to thwart international justice'.[22] Arbour continued to argue that the absence of primacy allowed states to withhold cooperation and shield suspects from prosecution, and predicted that jurisdictional conflicts would take years to resolve.[23] Others noted that '[t]he ICC starts the game at a terrible disadvantage' and that 'a very real risk' exists that it 'will be forced to confine its proceedings . . . to confirming the charges before trial and then suspending proceedings because the accused is absent'.[24]

At the time, it was generally acknowledged that complementarity, which gave the ICC 'subsidiary' or 'residual' jurisdiction, was mainly a concession to states and arguably the price to be paid if a global court was to be established at all.[25] Over the years, however, this passive and reactive reading of complementarity changed.

[21] Louise Arbour and Aryeh Neier, 'History and Future of the International Criminal Tribunals for the Former Yugoslavia and Rwanda' (1998) 13 American University International Law Review 1495, 1500. Before Rome, see also Lawyers Committee for Human Rights, 'Establishing an International Criminal Court: Major Unresolved Issues in the Draft Statute'.

[22] Antonio Cassese, 'The Statute of the International Criminal Court: Some Preliminary Reflections' (1999) 10 European Journal of International Law 144, 159.

[23] Louise Arbour and Morten Bergsmo, 'Conspicuous Absence of Jurisdictional Overreach' (1999) 1 International Law FORUM du droit international 13, 14; Jennifer Llewellyn and Sandra Raponi, 'The Protection of Human Rights through International Criminal Law: A Conversation with Madame Justice Louise Arbour, Chief Prosecutor for the International Criminal Tribunals for the Former Yugoslavia and Rwanda' (1999) 57 University of Toronto Faculty Law Review 83, 96–97.

[24] Paolo Benvenuti, 'The Complementarity of the International Criminal Court to National Criminal Jurisdictions' in Flavia Lattanzi and William Schabas (eds), *Essays on the Rome Statute of the International Criminal Court*, vol 1 (Il Sirente 1999) 50; See also Leila N Sadat, *The International Criminal Court and the Transformation of International Law: Justice for the New Millennium* (Transnational 2002) 122; André Klip, 'Complementarity and Concurrent Jurisdiction' (2004) 21 Nouvelles Etudes Pénales 187; Padraig McAuliffe, 'Bad Analogy: Why the Divergent Institutional Imperatives of the Ad Hoc Tribunals and the ICC Make the Lessons of Rule 11 Bis Inapplicable to the ICC's Complementarity Regime' (2015) 11 International Organizations Law Review 345, 369–73. But see Morten Bergsmo, 'The Jurisdictional Régime of the International Criminal Court (Part II, Articles 11–19)' (1998) 6 European Journal of Crime, Criminal Law and Criminal Justice 29, 43–47.

[25] Carsten Stahn, 'Complementarity: A Tale of Two Notions' (2008) 19 Criminal Law Forum 87, 90; Douglas Guilfoyle, *International Criminal Law* (OUP 2016) 109–10.

For one, the ad hoc tribunals struggled to accomplish their goals, raising questions about the wisdom of primacy.[26] For another, activists and academics advocated 'progressive' and 'teleological' readings of the Rome Statute that privileged the 'cosmopolitan' goals of international criminal justice.[27] Over time, international civil servants in chambers and the Office of the Prosecutor (OTP) selectively championed reinterpretations of complementarity that nominally strengthened the ICC vis-à-vis states.

In fact, before the ICC had even launched operations in mid-2003, a group of court officials, activists, and state representatives kick-started the process of reimagining complementarity. Morten Bergsmo, legal adviser to the ICTY prosecutor who later became the ICC prosecutor's first legal adviser, launched a consultation process to assess 'the main risks' and 'threat[s]' awaiting his future boss (Ocampo would be sworn in on 16 June 2003).[28] Among several initiatives, Bergsmo picked a group of twelve experts to assess 'the potential legal, policy and management challenges which are likely to confront the OTP as a consequence of the complementarity regime of the Statute'.[29]

Drafted by prominent international lawyers, including Cassese and Elizabeth Wilmshurst, the 'informal' paper on 'the principle of complementarity in practice' put forward practical recommendations for the OTP.[30] However, the paper's most lasting contribution lay elsewhere. By adopting a shared vision of the Rome Statute's admissibility norms, the experts redefined the ICC's ontology in a state-centric system of international criminal law enforcement. Emphasizing states' pre-existing duties to prosecute international crimes, the experts argued that '[t]he complementarity regime serves as a mechanism to encourage and facilitate the compliance of States with their primary responsibility to investigate and prosecute core crimes'.[31] By foregrounding state responsibilities and the ICC's oversight function, the debate over national primacy and international subsidiarity was turned upside down. Rather than a victory for states, complementarity could become a tool for the ICC to promote change. In Ocampo's words, complementarity went from a 'restriction' to a 'benefit'.[32]

[26] For an early critique of primacy, see Alvarez (n 4).

[27] Padraig McAuliffe, 'From Watchdog to Workhorse: Explaining the Emergence of the ICC's Burden-Sharing Policy as an Example of Creeping Cosmopolitanism' (2014) 13 Chinese Journal of International Law 259.

[28] Morten Bergsmo, 'Institutional History, Behaviour and Development' in Morten Bergsmo, Klaus Rackwitz and Tianying Song (eds), *Historical Origins of International Criminal Law*, vol 5 (Torkel Opsahl 2017) 6–7 and 17–19.

[29] ICC-OTP, 'Informal Expert Paper: The Principle of Complementarity in Practice' (2003) 2; Morten Bergsmo and Tianying Song, 'The Principle of Complementarity in Practice' in Bergsmo, Rackwitz, and Song (n 28).

[30] ICC-OTP (n 29).

[31] ibid 3.

[32] Remarks by Luis Moreno Ocampo. ICTR Newsletter, 'Prosecutors Colloquium, Challenges of International Criminal Justice, Arusha, Tanzania, 25–27 November 2004' (2004) 16; Fernandez de Gurmendi (n 20) xxvi ('barrier' vs 'opportunity').

Building on this reading, the OTP's early policies realigned the goals and determinants of the ICC's success. Prefiguring Ocampo's June 2003 inaugural speech as prosecutor, where he suggested that 'the absence of trials before [the ICC], as a consequence of the regular functioning of national institutions, would be a major success', the experts noted that 'complementarity can magnify the effectiveness of the ICC beyond what it could achieve through its own prosecutions [by] prompt[ing] a network of ... States Parties and other States to carry out consistent and rigorous national proceedings'.[33] Similarly, the OTP's first official policy paper emphasized that states were the 'most effective and efficient means of bringing offenders to justice' and that, given its limited resources, 'a major part of the external relations and outreach strategy of [the OTP] will be to encourage and facilitate States to carry out their primary responsibility of investigating and prosecuting crimes'.[34] In a reversal of past assumptions, states went from unreliable partners to the first line of defence in the fight against impunity, and the ICC's potential to spur domestic accountability became the benchmark of its success.[35]

Mainstreamed by a Jurisdiction, Complementarity and Cooperation Division (JCCD) within the OTP, complementarity thus redefined became a central element of prosecutorial discretion.[36] Although it did not yet feature in its earliest strategies, the word 'positive complementarity' emerged to describe the OTP's relationship to states. Citing 'a positive approach' to complementarity, a 2006 strategy affirmed that the prosecutor 'encourages genuine national proceedings where possible; relies on national and international networks; and participates in a system of international cooperation'.[37] All subsequent OTP strategies have affirmed the importance of positive complementarity.[38]

Against the backdrop of (positive) complementarity, the prosecutor also began to situate the ICC within a global governance paradigm. 'A Court based on the principle of complementarity', argued the OTP, 'ensures the international rule of law by creating an interdependent, mutually reinforcing international system of justice' known as the 'Rome System of Justice'.[39] Amplifying a vision of the ICC as a tool for change within the global order, the prosecutor marshalled the 'shadow' metaphor. '[T]he issue is not what the court is doing', explained Ocampo in 2009, 'the shadow ... is the most important part ... because the system is based on the

[33] ICC-OTP (n 29) 3–4.

[34] ICC-OTP, 'Paper on Some Policy Issues before the Office of the Prosecutor' (2003) 2 and 5.

[35] Rod Rastan, 'Complementarity: Contest or Collaboration' in Morten Bergsmo (ed), *Complementarity and the Exercise of Universal Jurisdiction for Core International Crimes* (Torkel Opsahl 2010) 131.

[36] ICC-OTP, 'Regulations of the Office of the Prosecutor, ICC-BD/05-01-09' (2009) reg 7. On the origins of the JCCD, see also Bergsmo (n 28).

[37] ICC-OTP, 'Report on Prosecutorial Strategy' (14 September 2006) 5.

[38] On the origins of positive complementarity, see Bergsmo (n 28) 14–15.

[39] ICC-OTP (n 37) 5 and 10. For the 'Rome system of justice', see William Burke-White, 'Proactive Complementarity: The International Criminal Court and National Courts in the Rome System of Justice' (2008) 49 Harvard International Law Journal 53.

idea the national court will do it'.[40] He would later clarify that '[a] court isolated in The Hague could never end impunity' and that 'its impact depends on the size of its "shadow" '.[41]

In similar terms, Fatou Bensouda, the second prosecutor, would later argue that 'the shadow of the court ... has given substance to the now widely accepted notion that impunity for atrocity crimes and the blanket amnesties ... are no longer an option'.[42] Echoing this vocabulary, the UN Secretary General, Ban Ki-moon, noted at the 2010 Kampala Review Conference:[43]

> The old era of impunity is over. In its place, slowly but surely, we are witnessing the birth of a new 'age of accountability' ... Those who thought the court would be little more than a 'paper tiger' have been proved wrong. To the contrary, the ICC casts an increasingly long shadow.

Yet, while the OTP initially served as the engine for creative reimaginations of complementarity, other actors have used the word for their own ends. Adopting teleological readings of complementarity, civil society groups encourage states not only to organize domestic trials but also to enact rule-of-law reforms, support victims, outlaw amnesties, and delegitimize alternative justice mechanisms. A key element of transnational advocacy is legislative reform, with NGOs leveraging complementarity to urge domestication of international norms, in particular through Rome Statute implementing legislation, or risk 'being considered unable and unwilling genuinely to investigate and prosecute crimes within the [ICC]'s jurisdiction'.[44] Although scholars question the normative basis of such claims, complementarity has, in Frédéric Mégret's words, become 'a sort of global package of norms that have to be adopted by states that become part of the ICC club'.[45] As Mégret emphasizes, '[i]mplementation ... is the long shadow of complementarity'.[46]

[40] 'Pursuing International Justice: A Conversation with Luis Moreno Ocampo' (4 February 2010) <cfr.org/event/pursuing-international-justice-conversation-luis-moreno-ocampo-0>.

[41] Luis M Ocampo, 'Prologue. The Prosecutor's Use of Legal Policies' in Martha Minow, Cora C True-Frost and Alex Whiting, *The First Global Prosecutor* (University of Michigan Press 2015) 10; Luis M Ocampo, 'A Positive Approach to Complementarity: The Impact of the Office of the Prosecutor' in Stahn and El Zeidy (n 20).

[42] '2017 Oxford Global Justice Lecture by Fatou Bensouda, Prosecutor of the International Criminal Court' (24 October 2017) <law.ox.ac.uk/news/2017-10-24-2017-oxford-global-justice-lecture-fatou-bensouda-prosecutor-international-criminal> (at 23:46).

[43] Ban Ki-moon, 'The Age of Accountability' (27 May 2010) <un.org/sg/en/content/sg/articles/2010-05-27/age-accountability>.

[44] Amnesty International, 'The International Criminal Court: Checklist for Effective Implementation' (2000) IOR 40/011/2000 2. On NGOs and complementarity, see Christian M De Vos, *Complementarity, Catalysts, Compliance. The International Criminal Court in Uganda, Kenya, and the Democratic Republic of Congo* (CUP 2020) 58–67.

[45] Frédéric Mégret, 'Too Much of a Good Thing?: Implementation and the Uses of Complementarity' in Stahn and El Zeidy (n 20) 362.

[46] ibid 363. On the diffusion of international crimes, see Mark S Berlin, *Criminalizing Atrocity. The Global Spread of Criminal Laws against International Crimes* (OUP 2020).

Over time, implementation has become part of a broad donor-driven capacity-building agenda known simply as positive complementarity. At the Kampala Review Conference, the Assembly of States Parties (ASP) argued that positive complementarity—defined as 'actions whereby national jurisdictions are strengthened and enabled to conduct genuine national investigations and trials'—may 'contribute to closing the impunity gap, enhancing the prevention of crimes and promoting the rule of law, with potential positive effects for international peace and security'.[47] In addition to legislative reform, the ASP singled out technical assistance, capacity building, and physical infrastructure as elements of positive complementarity.[48] In a similar vein, the EU has embraced ICC action plans to implement complementarity, including through legislative and technical assistance, capacity building, training for judges, prosecutors, registrars, police, civil society, and the construction and rehabilitation of infrastructure.[49] According to the ASP, '[e]xperience shows the importance of a holistic approach to enhancing national capacity, taking into account the entire judicial cycle from initiating investigations to enforcing sentences'.[50]

Positive complementarity's ascendancy as a multipurpose rule-of-law vocabulary is not confined to the ICC. Under the proposed Malabo Protocol, the African Court of Justice and Human Rights (ACJHR) is to be based on complementary jurisdiction vis-à-vis African states parties and—without defining the term—'complementarity' between the African Court and other AU treaty bodies, including the African Commission on Human and Peoples' Rights and the African Committee of Experts on the Rights and Welfare of the Child.[51] Scholars 'generalize' complementarity to regional human rights bodies and even international investment tribunals.[52] While not citing complementarity directly, the UN has endorsed an expansive vision of the ICC's role in rule-of-law promotion, where it is part of 'a multilateral system that aims to end impunity and establish the rule of law'.[53]

[47] ICC–ASP, 'Report of the Bureau on Stocktaking: Complementarity, Taking Stock of the Principle of Complementarity: Bridging the Impunity Gap' (18 March 2010) ICC–ASP/8/51 paras 16 and 53. More recently, see ICC–ASP, 'Report of the Bureau on Complementarity' (6 December 2021) ICC–ASP/20/22.

[48] ICC–ASP, 'Report of the Bureau on Stocktaking' (n 47) para 17.

[49] Council of the European Union, 'Joint Staff Working Document on Advancing the Principle of Complementarity: Toolkit for Bridging the Gap between International and National Justice (22 February 2013); Council of the European Union, 'Decision on the ICC, 2011/168/CFSP (21 March 2011); Council of the European Union, 'EU Action Plan on ICC, 12080/11 (12 July 2011) 15–16.

[50] ICC–ASP, 'Report of the Bureau on Stocktaking' (n 47) para 18.

[51] Protocol on the Statute of the African Court of Justice and Human Rights (as Amended by the Malabo Protocol), reproduced in Amnesty International, 'Malabo Protocol; Legal and Institutional Implications of the Merged and Expanded African Court', AFR 01/3063/2016 (2016) arts 27, 38, and 46 (H). See Solomon T Ebobrah, 'Towards a Positive Application of Complementarity in the African Human Rights System: Issues of Functions and Relations' (2011) 22 European Journal of International Law 663.

[52] Simon Hentrei, 'Generalising the Principle of Complementarity: Framing International Judicial Authority' (2013) 4 Transnational Legal Theory 419.

[53] Declaration of the High-Level Meeting of the General Assembly on the Rule of Law at the National and International Levels, UNGA, A/RES/67/1 (30 November 2012) para 23.

Taken together, the ICC, the ASP, and civil society have revolutionized the meaning and purpose of complementarity. Instead of a weakness, complementarity is now viewed as a 'positive' instrument that can be leveraged to advance domestic prosecutions, capacity building, and norm implementation. With the ICC sitting at the apex of a global system of international criminal justice, in which different stakeholders work together to promote accountability for the most serious crimes, the imagery of the ICC casting as long a shadow as possible over states has arguably eclipsed its original function as a subsidiary court.

3. The Mechanics of Complementarity as Global Governance

Embraced by the negotiators of the Rome Statute because the term was new and devoid of normative substance, complementarity's plasticity has proved well suited to evolutionary interpretation.[54] In fact, so accepted are various 'big ideas' about the term that scholars routinely mistake them for the ICC's original design rather than innovation.[55] However, aside from rehabilitating complementarity, the practical, rather than theoretical, challenge of regulating relations with states awaited the ICC and especially its first prosecutor.

As noted, the ICC's institutional design elicited concern initially. Bereft of primacy, the prosecutor was expected to face—and, observers feared, likely to lose—admissibility challenges from states. In particular, justifying ICC involvement by labelling a state 'unwilling or unable' could trigger backlash. As noted by Robert Cryer, 'for the ICC to take a case it must have determined that the relevant State(s) are unwilling or unable genuinely to prosecute themselves', which 'hardly bodes well for the willingness of the national authorities concerned to provide suspects or evidence'.[56] Crucially, unlike the ICTR/Y, underpinned by Chapter VII powers, cooperation with the ICC hinges on states' voluntary consent. William Schabas observes that the 'relationship between international justice and national justice ... is far from "complementary" ... the two systems function in opposition and to some extent with hostility vis-à-vis each other'.[57]

Concerns about hostility did not come to pass, however. Although it was to be guided by two principles—where 'partnership' highlights that 'the relationship with States ... can and should be a positive, constructive one' and '[v]igilance mark[ing]

[54] Tallgren (n 18) 110. But see Mohamed M El Zeidy, *The Principle of Complementarity in International Criminal Law: Origin, Development, and Practice* (Martinus Nijhoff 2008) (tracing ideas about types of 'complementarity' to the early twentieth century).

[55] On 'big ideas' of complementarity, see Sarah MH Nouwen, *Complementarity in the Line of Fire: The Catalysing Effect of the International Criminal Court in Uganda and Sudan* (CUP 2013) (albeit critically of 'big ideas', based on a dichotomy between 'pure' law vs ideas and policy).

[56] Robert Cryer, *Prosecuting International Crimes: Selectivity and the International Criminal Law Regime* (CUP 2005) 157.

[57] William A Schabas, *An Introduction to the International Criminal Court* (4th edn, CUP 2011) 191.

the converse principle' that '[t]he Prosecutor must . . . verify that national procedures are carried out genuinely'—the OTP pivoted to conflict avoidance and stimulating cooperation with states.[58] Complementarity became an unlikely vehicle for this, with the 2003 expert paper again breaking ground by endorsing consensual approaches to concurrent jurisdiction and de-emphasizing the Rome Statute's textual injunctions. 'Although it is common to emphasize the "unwilling or unable" test in Article 17', stressed the experts, in 'appropriate circumstances' there is 'no need to label the State as "unwilling" or "unable" before it can co-operate with the Court'.[59] '[T]he Prosecutor's objective is not to "compete" with States for jurisdiction' the experts noted, before adding that there may be 'situations where the [OTP] and the State concerned agree that a consensual division of labour is in the best interests of justice'.[60]

Drawing on this interpretation of complementarity, Ocampo developed an alternative vision of the ICC's relationship to states. Instead of vigilance or hostility vis-à-vis governments, the OTP stressed three alternatives: (1) the Statute did not forbid governments to request investigations in their territories (self-referrals);[61] (2) 'divisions of labour' were permissible and potentially desirable; and (3) states need not oppose international trials of crimes arising from their territory. 'There may be cases where inaction by States is the appropriate course of action', noted the OTP and gave the example of '[g]roups bitterly divided by conflict [who] may oppose prosecutions at each other's hands and yet agree to a prosecution by a Court perceived as neutral and impartial'.[62] Although it lacks a basis in the Statute, burden sharing based on perpetrator status was proposed by the OTP—'a two-tiered approach to combat[ting] impunity'—where the ICC 'will initiate prosecutions of the leaders who bear most responsibility' and 'encourage national prosecutions, where possible, for the lower-ranking perpetrators'.[63]

As will be seen in Chapter 3, concepts such as self-referrals and uncontested admissibility consolidated to justify these policy innovations. Not impermissible per se yet 'quite extraordinary' when they happened, self-referrals from Uganda and the DRC—the ICC's first investigations that went on to define the implementation of complementarity—came under sharp criticism.[64] As early as 2004, Paola Gaeta stressed that 'self-referral is not necessarily the most straightforward option' and warned of 'possible pitfalls', including ICC politicization.[65] Florian Jessberger and Julia Geneuss observe that 'the practice of self-referrals ultimately turns the very

[58] ICC-OTP (n 29) 3–4.
[59] ibid 7 and 19.
[60] ibid 4.
[61] On the law applicable to self-referrals, see Chapter 3 in this volume.
[62] ICC-OTP (n 34) 5; ICC-OTP (n 29) 19.
[63] ICC-OTP (n 34) 3.
[64] Cryer (n 56) 162.
[65] Paola Gaeta, 'Is the Practice of "Self-Referrals" a Sound Start for the ICC?' (2004) 2 Journal of International Criminal Justice 949, 952.

idea of complementarity inside out', concluding more cautiously '[w]hether self-referrals are to be regarded as blessing or curse for the ICC is still up for debate'.[66] More scathingly, Padraig McAuliffe notes that a 'division of labour based on State referrals finds no support in the *travaux préparatoires* or academic commentary before 2003' and 'contrary to the presentation of burden-sharing by its advocates, there was nothing inevitable about its emergence as a policy option, and nor is it something explicitly required by the Rome Statute'.[67]

Over time, while still nominally guided by partnership and vigilance vis-à-vis states, the OTP increasingly emphasized cooperation over supervision. Calculating that cooperation allowed the ICC to fight impunity more effectively than confronting states over their failures to prosecute, Ocampo worked to strengthen partnerships with governments to 'encourage States to initiate their own proceedings' by 'develop[ing] formal and informal networks of contacts' and 'providing [states] with the information gathered by the [OTP]'.[68] The 2009–12 strategy advocated 'a proactive policy of cooperation aimed at promoting national proceedings' in particular by 'providing information … to national authorities', 'sharing databases of non-confidential materials or crime patterns' and 'acting as a catalyst with development organizations' to promote 'relevant accountability efforts'.[69] However, in response to the ASP's admonition that the ICC should not be involved in capacity building,[70] the second prosecutor's strategies from 2012 to 2015, 2016 to 2018, and 2019 to 2021 de-emphasized the OTP's direct support for domestic proceedings and focused on partnerships with third-party law enforcement and civil society.[71]

Prosecutorial strategy under Fatou Bensouda evolved in other ways as well. The importance of self-referrals as a method of initiating investigations decreased relative to her *proprio motu* power, while positive complementarity rose to prominence in preliminary examinations (the pre-investigation phase used to assess whether to open investigations).[72] As emphasized in a 2013 policy paper on preliminary examinations, '[w]here potential cases falling within the jurisdiction of the [ICC] have been identified, the [OTP] will seek to encourage, where feasible, genuine national investigations and prosecutions by the States concerned'.[73] As will be seen

[66] Florian Jessberger and Julia Geneuss, 'The Many Faces of the International Criminal Court' (2012) 10 Journal of International Criminal Justice 1081, 1089.

[67] McAuliffe (n 27) 277 and 294; see also Ahmed S Hassanein, 'Self-Referral of Situations to the International Criminal Court: Complementarity in Practice—Complementarity in Crisis' (2017) 17 International Criminal Law Review 107, 111 and 114. For a defence of self-referrals, see Darryl Robinson, 'The Controversy over Territorial State Referrals and Reflections on ICL Discourse' (2011) 9 Journal of International Criminal Justice 355.

[68] ICC-OTP (n 34) 5.

[69] ICC-OTP, 'Prosecutorial Strategy 2009–2012' (2010) paras 16–17.

[70] ICC-ASP, 'Report of the Bureau on Stocktaking' (n 47) paras 4 and 16.

[71] ICC-OTP, 'Strategic Plan June 2012–2015' (2013) paras 64–67; ICC-OTP, 'Strategic Plan 2016–2018' (2015) paras 92–98; ICC-OTP, 'Strategic Plan 2019–2021' (2019) paras 49–52.

[72] On jurisdictional triggers, see Schabas (n 57) 157–82.

[73] ICC-OTP, 'Policy Paper on Preliminary Examinations' (2013) para 101; Sara Wharton and Rosemary Grey, 'The Full Picture: Preliminary Examinations at the International Criminal Court' (2019) 56 Canadian Yearbook of International Law 1.

in Chapters 4 and 7, Bensouda experimented with a mix of carrots and sticks to galvanize domestic responses in some countries, but the OTP's practices in preliminary examinations came under sharp criticism towards the end of her term. After Karim Khan's ascension to office in 2021, another shift in the OTP's approach to positive complementarity seemed afoot, with an end to prolonged preliminary examinations and a new species of 'cooperation agreements' in some countries.[74]

Yet, despite differences in emphasis under Ocampo, Bensouda, and now Khan, an overarching trend is the OTP's privileging of partnership over vigilance vis-à-vis states. As noted by Kai Ambos, 'cooperation is (now) seen as the essential tool to support (positive) complementarity'.[75] Indeed, in the ICC's official lexicon, cooperation, complementarity, and positive complementarity are almost always used interchangeably.[76] Nevertheless, because the case law on article 17 (as will be seen in Chapter 3) sits uneasily with OTP strategies and ICC discourse on positive complementarity, scholars have developed a wide range of theories about different types of complementarity. One especially prominent view is that the Rome Statute's admissibility rules in articles 17–20 are distinct from positive complementarity *qua* prosecutorial strategy. As the OTP itself has explained, 'complementarity has two dimensions: (i) the admissibility test ... which is a judicial issue; and (ii) the positive complementarity concept, *i.e* a proactive policy of cooperation aimed at promoting national proceedings'.[77]

Although viewing admissibility as distinct from (positive) complementarity—a view premised on a stark binary between (judge-made) law and (prosecutorial) policy—has been embraced at various times by chambers, the ASP, and academics, Chapter 3 will argue that admissibility norms are inextricably intertwined with policy and hence (positive) complementarity—in both its judicial and prosecutorial manifestations—is better understood as a tool of global governance.[78] Such

[74] ICC, 'ICC Prosecutor, Mr Karim A.A. Khan QC, Concludes the Preliminary Examination of the Situation in Colombia with a Cooperation Agreement with the Government Charting the next Stage in Support of Domestic Efforts to Advance Transitional Justice' (28 October 2021) <icc-cpi.int/news/icc-prosecutor-mr-karim-khan-qc-concludes-preliminary-examination-situation-colombia>; ICC, 'ICC Prosecutor, Mr Karim A.A. Khan QC, Opens an Investigation into the Situation in Venezuela and Concludes Memorandum of Understanding with the Government' (5 November 2021) <icc-cpi.int/news/icc-prosecutor-mr-karim-aa-khan-qc-opens-investigation-situation-venezuela-and-concludes>. See further Chapter 7, section 4.3 in this volume.

[75] Kai Ambos, *Treatise on International Criminal Law. Volume III: International Criminal Procedure* (1st edn, OUP 2016) 329.

[76] ICC–ASP, 'Report of the Bureau on Complementarity' (n 47) para 53; ICC Press Release, 'ICC Holds High-Level Regional Symposium on Cooperation and Complementarity in Niger' (27 October 2017) ICC-CPI-20171027-PR1340; ICC Press Release, 'ICC Holds High-Level Regional Symposium on Cooperation and Complementarity in Senegal' (25 May 2022) ICC-CPI-20220525-PR1656 <icc-cpi.int/news/icc-holds-high-level-regional-conference-cooperation-and-complementarity-senegal>.

[77] ICC–OTP (n 69) para 16.

[78] For chambers, see Chapter 3 in this volume. ICC–ASP, 'Report of the Court on Complementarity, ICC-ASP/11/39' (16 October 2012) para 2; Ambos (n 75) 332 (the so-called policy of positive complementarity is indeed a mere prosecutorial policy, largely operating without an explicit or implicit legal basis in the Statute); Nouwen (n 55) 97–98 (not inherent to complementarity); Rastan (n 35) 83. But see Carsten Stahn, 'Taking Complementarity Seriously. On the Sense and Sensibility of "Classical",

a multifaceted reading of (positive) complementarity can be traced to William Burke-White's vision of the ICC's role in world affairs based on 'a tiered system of prosecutorial authority' within a 'Rome System of Justice'.[79] Noting that 'international and domestic governance structures (such as courts) are engaged in … governance efforts whereby each level of authority continuously cross-influences, reshapes, and, ideally, reinforces activities at other levels of governance', Burke-White believed the ICC and states would engage in 'political and legal interactions', including 'everything from the political posturing of national officials and the reform of domestic courts to the application of the complementary criteria by international officials', whereby 'each level is continuously responding to and impacting actions at the other level'.[80]

Other scholars have analysed the ICC's relations with states through similar 'managerial' and 'systemic' approaches to (positive) complementarity. Jann Kleffner argues that complementarity may generate 'a pull effect' towards compliance by 'legitimising' state behaviour, serve as a 'coercive mechanism' to reprimand non-compliant states, enable 'managerial' compliance through cooperation, and promote 'norm internalisation' within national legal systems.[81] Stahn embraces a two-tiered 'systemic vision' of complementarity that comprises a classical 'vertical' dimension based on the [ICC]'s role as a 'watchdog' extracting 'compliance through threat' versus an 'amicable' dimension aiming to foster national proceedings 'through burden sharing and mutual interaction'.[82] More recently, Christian De Vos stresses complementarity's 'cooperative' and 'coercive' dimensions, with the ICC oscillating between 'stimulat[ing] national prosecutorial activity through threatened intervention' and a 'managerial function, wherein it supports … national jurisdictions'.[83] Put differently, while scholars diverge on the mechanics, these global governance models focus on how the (positive) complementarity norm structures ICC–state interactions and how the international and national levels mutually shape accountability for serious crimes.[84]

As a multifaceted term that defies categorization, (positive) complementarity designates both the ICC's admissibility framework and a diverse set of ideas about

"Positive" and "Negative" Complementarity' in Stahn and El Zeidy (n 20) 233 (challenging 'the assumption that "positive" complementarity is merely a policy principle').

[79] Burke-White (n 39) 56.

[80] William Burke-White, 'Complementarity in Practice: The International Criminal Court as Part of a System of Multi-Level Global Governance in the Democratic Republic of Congo' (2005) 18 Leiden Journal of International Law 557, 558–59.

[81] Jann K Kleffner, *Complementarity in the Rome Statute and National Criminal Jurisdictions* (OUP 2008) 311–12.

[82] Stahn (n 78) 251. For an updated systemic vision with four functions, see Carsten Stahn, 'Revitalizing Complementarity a Decade after the Stocktaking Exercise', Policy Brief Series No 115 (Torkel Opsahl 2020).

[83] De Vos (n 44) 8.

[84] For further examples, see Christoph Burchard, 'Complementarity as Global Governance' in Stahn and El Zeidy (n 20); Cryer (n 56) 143–44.

how the shadow of international intervention mobilizes states to fight impunity. Accordingly, this book uses the terms complementarity and positive complementarity interchangeably to analyse the ICC and other ICTs' actions *qua* global governance actors.[85] To avoid possible confusion, however, the next section moves beyond the multiple meanings of (positive) complementarity and proposes an alternative vocabulary to analyse how ICTs and states interact with one another.

4. Beyond Complementarity: Reimagining Relations with States

While its surprising evolution from weakness to strength is familiar scholarly terrain by now, complementarity's discursive rehabilitation and multiplicity of meanings carries the risk of terminological and disciplinary confusion. Whereas the legal literature emphasizes interpretation of norms but downplays how norms relate to outcomes on the ground, social scientists analyse the effects of ICT interventions but pay insufficient attention to how the law circumscribes the actions of international civil servants and state actors.

To bridge this gap, this book develops an original analytical framework to analyse how ICT and states interact with one another. It argues that the interplay of domestic and international jurisdiction reflects a more complex set of institutional design features than complementarity and primacy, two terms that fail to capture the complexity of how ICTs interact with state-based actors. While ICT mandates structure and circumscribe how international civil servants interact with governments, concurrent jurisdiction must be analysed alongside other mandated features such as personal jurisdiction, cooperation obligations, trigger mechanisms, operational time frames, and hybrid institutional design features. Viewed in isolation, a complementarity-type framework embedded in an ICT mandate is no more or less likely to incentivize domestic accountability than primacy; however, different elements of ICT mandates, viewed holistically, may create divergent incentives for international civil servants and government actors to engage with one another.

Drawing on findings from its case studies, this book proposes a typology of ICT–state relations, which it categorizes according to three 'ideal-type' relationships: iteration, accommodation, and isolation (see Figure 2.1). As with all ideal types, this typology does not map precisely onto reality.[86] These three relationships depend on whether international civil servants and government actors cooperate with,

[85] By contrast, the word 'admissibility', when used, means the Rome Statute's arts 17–20, though admissibility rulings are just another way of (not) enacting (positive) complementarity (see Chapter 3 in this volume).

[86] Kim Sung Ho, 'Max Weber' in Edward N Zalta (ed), *Stanford Encyclopedia of Philosophy* (2021) <plato.stanford.edu/archives/sum2021/entries/weber/>.

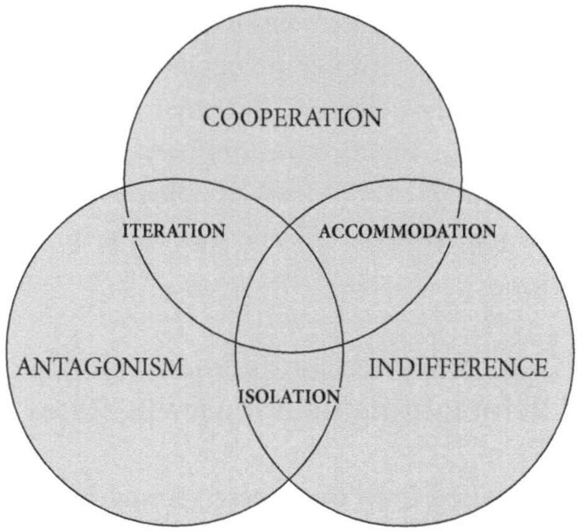

Figure 2.1 Typology of state–international criminal tribunal relations

ignore, or are in conflict with one another. While iteration captures international–domestic interactions that produce shifts in domestic accountability preferences, accommodation is neutral in terms of how ICTs influence states while isolation has dissuasive effects.

As defined in this study, iteration refers to dialectical and dynamic processes of negotiation, contestation, and consensus building involving governments and ICTs. This term seeks to capture the process of ICTs engaging domestic actors, and vice versa, in debates over prosecutorial strategy, strengthening institutions to overcome 'capacity' shortfalls, exercising oversight of domestic reforms and trials, and adjusting international prosecutorial strategy in response to domestic feedback. This term has parallels with experimentalist forms of governance, which respond to the 'failures of "command-and-control" regulation in a turbulent, fast-moving world', and emphasize 'a recursive process of provisional goal-setting and revision based on learning from the comparison of alternative approaches to advancing them in different contexts'.[87] Critically, iteration requires push–pull relationships that go beyond agreements to divide labour and not interfere with one another's work.

In contrast to iteration, accommodation encapsulates a range of primarily hands-off and consensual relationships, whereby international civil servants and government officials agree, formally or informally, to divide their work but also to refrain from challenging the other's *modus operandi*. Scholarship uses a range

[87] Charles F Sabel and Jonathan Zeitlin, 'Experimentalism in Transnational Governance: Emergent Pathways and Diffusion Mechanisms' [2011] Green Working Paper: Global Re-ordering: Evolution through European Networks 4, Gráinne de Búrca, 'Human Rights Experimentalism' (2017) 111 American Journal of International Law 277.

of labels, such as 'burden sharing', 'opportunism', and 'substitution', to capture this non-interventionist dynamic. Significantly, ICTs and governments often posit accommodation as a desirable relationship based on managerialism, in particular geared towards capacity building,[88] even though it means that ICTs and states are unlikely to adjust their behaviour in response to the actions of the other.

Lastly, isolation refers to relationships that oscillate between indifference and hostility, where international civil servants and government officials ignore each other, refuse to enter negotiations on accountability, or withdraw from any formal relationship altogether (as in Rome Statute withdrawals). A key challenge for international civil servants is how to steer antagonistic relations towards iteration rather than isolation.

As ideal types, these three relationships are not to be treated as airtight categories. Minor changes, for instance in domestic or international prosecutorial strategy, may shift one type of relationship to the other. However, this typology downplays merely consensual relations for the realization of international criminal justice aims. Drawing on Monica Hakimi's work on the 'value' of 'legal conflict' in international law, this book emphasizes that the architects and interpreters of ICT mandates should prioritize iterative dynamics based on push–pull relationships between tribunals and states. While much international law is predicated on the 'cooperation thesis', namely that 'conflict impedes cooperation and is a problem for international law to overcome', Hakimi argues that cooperative and conflictual relations between different stakeholders in international law are in fact 'interdependent' and 'symbiotic'.[89] As she notes, '[i]nternational law is cooperative, even when it is contentious, in that it establishes ground rules that the participants all accept and use to structure their interactions and that '[a]rguing through international law is itself a kind of cooperation'.[90]

As will be seen in Chapter 3, ICT mandates define the parameters within which tribunals and states negotiate the exercise of jurisdiction over serious crimes. Although mandates conventionally allocate powers in three ways—primacy,

[88] On managerialism qua 'cooperative, problem-solving approach' to compliance with international law (as opposed to coercion), see Abram Chayes and Antonia H Chayes, *The New Sovereignty: Compliance with International Regulatory Agreements* (Harvard UP 1995) 1–28. On human rights compliance and the importance of capacity building in areas of limited statehood, see Thomas Risse and Tanja A Börzel, 'Human Rights: The New Agenda' (The Transatlantic Relationship and the Future Global Governance 2012) Working Paper 07. On managerialism in international law and beyond, see Richard Clements, 'Governing International Criminal Justice: Managerial Practices and the International Criminal Court' (PhD dissertation, University of Cambridge 2019) 35–36.

[89] Monica Hakimi, 'The Work of International Law' (2017) 58 Harvard International Law Journal 1, 5–6; see also Monica Hakimi, 'Constructing an International Community' (2017) 111 American Journal of International Law 317, 319–20.

[90] Hakimi, 'Work of International Law' (n 89) 6. On law as an argumentative practice, see also Ian Johnstone, *The Power of Deliberation: International Law, Politics and Organizations* (OUP 2011); Martti Koskenniemi, *From Apology to Utopia the Structure of International Legal Argument* (CUP 2005). This book draws on Hakimi but other theories of international law may lend themselves to a similar argument.

hybridity, and complementarity—norms embedded in such mandates can usually, despite their different underpinnings, be interpreted as either a rationalization for accommodation or as conditionality-based tools geared to iteration. To date, international civil servants at ICTs have almost always interpreted their mandates to mean the former by eliding issues of sovereign duties to prosecute, evaluative assessments of domestic justice, and state duties towards victims and defendants. Questioning the emphasis on mere cooperation with states—an idea that is increasingly seen as synonymous with complementarity—Chapter 7 will suggest that ICT mandates should be designed to ensure a degree of *strategic conflict* that must be overcome through *tactical* bargaining between international civil servants and their government counterparts. If mandates can be too easily reinterpreted to entrench *strategic* accommodation, this will decrease pressure on both international civil servants and government actors to engage one another in iterative processes of dialogue and consensus building.

5. International Criminal Tribunals, Complementarity, and Statebuilding

International criminal law's relationship to sovereignty is complex. For instance, by disregarding immunities of state officials, including heads of state and government, international trials can be said to deprive states of their privileged position within the global legal order. Schabas observes that until the mid-1990s, 'international criminal justice had concerned itself with leaders—politicians, generals, bankers, judges—who belonged to or were associated with the highest levels of the state apparatus' and 'the crimes with which they were charged had a link to state policy'.[91] Accordingly, international criminal law enforcement against such state actors is sometimes seen as counter-hegemonic in nature.

Emblematic of this counter-hegemonic ethos, the Nuremberg and Tokyo tribunals prosecuted state-sponsored crimes of the Nazi regime and Imperial Japan. Drawing on the post-Second World War precedent, the ICTY and ICTR also targeted crimes committed primarily by military and political actors from former Yugoslav states and the Rwandan Hutu government. In total, the two ad hoc tribunals prosecuted over 200 government officials at different levels of command, including former heads of state and ministers. While there are many criticisms

[91] William A Schabas, *Unimaginable Atrocities: Justice, Politics, and Rights at the War Crimes Tribunals* (OUP 2012) 128–29; Alvarez (n 4); David Luban, 'State Criminality and the Ambition of International Criminal Law' in Tracy Isaacs and Richard Vernon (eds), *Accountability for Collective Wrongdoing* (CUP 2011). But see Ryan Liss, 'Crimes Against the Sovereign Order: Rethinking International Criminal Justice' (2019) 113 American Journal of International Law 727. On the duality of sovereignty, see Frédéric Mégret, 'The Politics of International Criminal Justice' (2002) 13 European Journal of International Law 1261.

of Nuremberg and the ad hoc tribunals, in particular that of victors' justice, there can be little doubt that the state and its crimes were the target of international intervention.[92]

Although the ICC's treaty-based design was different from previous ICTs, its 'anti-statist' ontology was initially not in doubt. As Payam Akhavan notes, '[b]ased on the experience of the ad hoc Yugoslav and Rwanda Tribunals, the assumption was that the ICC would be acting against states'.[93] Like its predecessors, the Rome Statute disregards immunities of government officials and the defence of superior orders. Moreover, the ICC's prospective and potentially global mandate allows it, in principle at least, to avoid the ad hoc tribunals' many limitations. David Bosco suggests that the ICC 'represents a remarkable transfer of authority from sovereign states to an international institution' and that '[o]n paper at least, the [ICC] is a striking advance for the legalist worldview against the traditional concept of sovereignty'.[94]

Nevertheless, other features of the ICC's institutional design challenge this perspective. For one, the ICC's authority extends only as far as states consent to its jurisdiction. To be sure, the Security Council can refer situations to the prosecutor for investigation, but the hegemonic nature of the permanent five members' decision-making runs counter to the ICC's universalist aspirations. For another, the ICC depends on the availability of resources from 'friendly' states parties.[95] This and other factors lead scholars like Robert Cryer to ask 'whether the ICC is really that threatening to sovereignty in the first place'.[96]

Nearly twenty years after it began investigations, the ICC's relationship to sovereignty remains a key preoccupation. Although a handful of trials have featured deposed government officials, cases have been brought to completion against non-state actors from just three countries: the DRC, Mali, and Uganda.[97] Significantly, despite investigations in fifteen additional countries, the OTP has yet to secure the arrest of a single sitting government official, with the voluntary appearance of the Kenyan president underscoring the enforcement limits of the ICC.

[92] Payam Akhavan, 'International Criminal Justice in the Era of Failed States: The ICC and the Self-Referral Debate' in Stahn and El Zeidy (n 20) 286.

[93] Akhavan (n 92).

[94] Bosco (n 16) 2 and 4.

[95] As seen in the response to post-2022 Ukraine, in the context of interstate aggression, states may be willing to steer ICC investigations towards certain crimes. See Reed Brody, 'The ICC at 20: Elusive Success, Double Standards and the "Ukraine Moment"' (*JusticeInfo*, 30 June 2022) <justiceinfo.net/en/102866-icc-20-elusive-success-double-standards-ukraine-moment.html>.

[96] Robert Cryer, 'International Criminal Law vs State Sovereignty: Another Round?' (2005) 16 European Journal of International Law 979, 983.

[97] See Paola Gaeta and Patryk I Labuda, 'Bilan des quinze premières années de la Cour pénale internationale' in Julian Fernandez and Xavier Pacreau (eds), *Commentaire du Statut de Rome. Commentaire article par article* (Pédone 2019). On the *Ongwen* trial (from Uganda), see Tonny Kirabira, 'Ongwen at the International Criminal Court' (2021) 25(7) American Society of International Law: Insights.

The literature recognizes the ICC's struggles to prosecute incumbent state officials and criticizes states' 'manipulation' and 'instrumentalization' of the Court to prosecute rivals in The Hague.[98] But an equally important trend may be how national political elites harness intervention to implement rule-of-law reforms and launch selective proceedings while international partners fail to monitor or evaluate such trials, lest their capacity-building projects be undermined. By shifting the frame to domestic struggles over the enforcement of international criminal law, including in nominally cooperative states, this book draws attention to the effects and paradoxes of prioritizing domestic accountability as an *ultima ratio* of international criminal justice. It will suggest that, whereas the state used to be viewed as the root cause of impunity, growing support for national trials of serious crimes may inadvertently rehabilitate the state as a *locus* of anti-impunity promise. With states seen increasingly not as *a cause* but as *a solution* to impunity, the domestic enforcement of international criminal law may serve not only to fight impunity but also to consolidate the authority of (unaccountable) political elites. In doing so, the (positive) complementarity norm may be doing unacknowledged damage at the national level.

[98] See Oumar Ba, *States of Justice: The Politics of the International Criminal Court* (CUP 2020); Phil Clark, *Distant Justice: The Impact of the International Criminal Court on African Politics* (CUP 2018). On non-state actors, see Frédéric Mégret, 'Is the ICC Focusing Too Much on Non-State Actors?' in Margaret M deGuzman and Diane M Amann (eds), *Arcs of Global Justice: Essays in Honour of William A. Schabas* (OUP 2018). Conversely, for a defence of self-referrals and the ICC's focus on non-state actors, see Akhavan (n 92).

3

Institutional Design

Regulating Relations between States and ICTs

1. Institutional Design, Concurrent Jurisdiction, and Shadow Effects

Relations between states and international institutions depend on various factors, one of which is their institutional design.[1] Although scholars agree that design choices shape the subsequent performance of international institutions, research is limited on how such choices impact the efficacy of ICTs. Carsten Stahn's observation that '[t]he search for appropriate institutional designs to deal with mass atrocities is still very much "a work in progress" ' remains as apposite today as it was over fifteen years ago.[2]

The constitutive instruments of international tribunals determine how mandated goals are to be accomplished, with various norms facilitating cooperation, preventing a duplication of tasks, and avoiding unnecessary conflict vis-à-vis other institutions and states.[3] Mandated norms on jurisdiction and admissibility are crucial, as they delineate a tribunal's judicial activity while answering baseline questions such as who can access a tribunal? What issues can be litigated? However, equally important are their 'shadow effects'.[4] As Yuval Shany explains, international courts' ability 'to attain the goals prescribed by their mandate providers is decisively influenced by their jurisdictional powers and the rules on admissibility'. However, goal attainment 'depends not only on those cases they actually adjudicate, but also on the court's "shadow"—that is, on the court's impact on actors and issues that *could be brought* before the court'.[5]

While international tribunals can use a variety of arrangements to regulate relations with states, the institutional design of ICTs vis-à-vis states traditionally focuses on concurrent jurisdiction and admissibility. In Antonio Cassese's words,

[1] Erik Voeten, 'Making Sense of the Design of International Institutions' (2019) 22 Annual Review of Political Science 147.

[2] Carsten Stahn, 'The Geometry of Transitional Justice: Choices of Institutional Design' (2005) 18 Leiden Journal of International Law 425, 425.

[3] Yuval Shany, *Regulating Jurisdictional Relations between National and International Courts* (OUP 2007) 15–20 and 34–36; Yuval Shany, *The Competing Jurisdictions of International Courts and Tribunals* (OUP 2003) 117–26.

[4] Yuval Shany, *Assessing the Effectiveness of International Courts* (OUP 2014) 67–68.

[5] ibid 67 and 76 (emphasis added).

International Criminal Tribunals and Domestic Accountability. Patryk I. Labuda,
Oxford University Press. © Patryk I. Labuda 2023. DOI: 10.1093/oso/9780198868842.003.0003

concurrent jurisdiction arises when 'one or more States may assert their criminal jurisdiction over a specific crime ... and at the same time, an international tribunal is empowered to adjudicate the same crime by virtue of its Statute'.[6] While it is accepted that states and ICTs have, in principle, coequal claims to prosecute genocide, crimes against humanity, and war crimes, jurisdictional overlap can be more contentious than in other areas of international law, especially if states that should nominally hold perpetrators accountable, encourage, or condone such crimes. Indeed, situations of state-sponsored criminality are when the fight against impunity clashes with sovereignty, necessitating creative dispute resolution to overcome state non-cooperation.[7]

Accordingly, ICT statutes create webs of relationships with states, including by regulating admissibility. For instance, the exercise of international jurisdiction can be subject to state consent, or conversely international judges or prosecutors can be empowered to compel states to defer cases to international adjudication, refer cases to states for domestic adjudication, monitor the exercise of domestic jurisdiction, or sanction the exercise of domestic jurisdiction.[8] Other norms in ICT statutes, for instance on mixed jurisdiction, the seniority of suspects or the gravity of crimes, also structure interactions between states and tribunals. Likewise, non-normative elements of institutional design, for instance an ICT's ability to hire national staff, may indirectly influence the exercise of jurisdiction at the national and international levels.[9]

While these and other institutional design elements influence ICT–state relations, no theory of concurrent authority or distributive principle regulates the prosecutions of international crimes at the international and national levels. As Leila Sadat observes, 'jurisdictional boundaries are fluid and, particularly at their interface, controversy remains as to the appropriate allocation of jurisdiction between national and international courts'.[10] Nevertheless, over time, two arrangements have come to define a division of labour in international criminal law. Under primacy, ICTs enjoy priority to exercise jurisdiction over international crimes while states have concurrent but secondary powers to punish perpetrators. Under

[6] Antonio Cassese, *International Criminal Law* (1st edn, OUP 2003) 348. Another option is exclusive jurisdiction, eg the Special Tribunal for Lebanon had *quasi*-exclusive jurisdiction vis-à-vis Lebanese tribunals.

[7] Harmen van der Wilt and others (eds), *System Criminality in International Law* (CUP 2009); Jann K Kleffner, *Complementarity in the Rome Statute and National Criminal Jurisdictions* (OUP 2008) 56.

[8] Sarah MH Nouwen and Dustin M Lewis, 'Jurisdictional Arrangements and International Criminal Procedure' in Göran Sluiter and others (eds), *International Criminal Procedure. Rules and Principles* (OUP 2013) 116–17.

[9] On hybrid tribunals' constitutive elements, see Sarah Williams, *Hybrid and Internationalised Criminal Tribunals: Selected Jurisdictional Issues* (Hart 2012) 201–51.

[10] Leila N Sadat, 'Understanding the Complexities of International Criminal Tribunal Jurisdiction' in William A Schabas and Nadia Bernaz (eds), *Routledge Handbook of International Criminal Law* (Routledge 2010) 197.

complementarity, states have priority to exercise jurisdiction while an ICT exercises concurrent and secondary authority.[11]

As will be seen in this chapter, this binary can be misleading. In fact, primacy and complementarity both give rise to varied ICT–state interactions. For one, while both arrangements are based on concurrent jurisdiction, international judges and prosecutors have the power to decide the key question of *when* or *why* domestic and international courts may proceed. For another, practice rarely conforms to these archetypes and terms such as absolute or strict primacy, international or domestic primacy, subsidiarity, negative and positive complementarity, radical and reverse complementarity have all been used to make sense of developments that deviate from classical formulations of concurrent jurisdiction.[12] As Sarah Nouwen and Dustin Lewis observe, because 'there is no … "concurrent" jurisdiction, or "primacy" or "complementarity" of jurisdiction in the abstract', such 'labels have been put on specific arrangements in specific statutes that provide for the specific circumstances in which an [ICT] may or may not exercise jurisdiction'.[13] Moreover, as will be seen, rather than fixed bodies of norms that generate specific procedural interactions or substantive outcomes, these arrangements also embody values or preferences for international, domestic or mixed trials, which change over time and affect interpretation in practice.

2. (International) Primacy

Primacy is the term that designates an ICT arrangement premised on concurrent jurisdiction, where the international tribunal has priority to investigate, prosecute and adjudicate international crimes. Although it seems like a simple method of regulating concurrent jurisdiction, the scope and mechanics of primacy may vary, as will be seen by comparing the practice of the ICTR and the SCSL.

2.1. The original aims

The ICTR was established in November 1994. A UN commission of experts had initially recommended expanding the ICTY's mandate to Rwanda, but the Security Council created a standalone ad hoc tribunal. Appended to a Chapter VII

[11] For other classifications, see Antonio Cassese and others, *Cassese's International Criminal Law* (3rd edn, OUP 2013) 291–93; Gerhard Werle and Florian Jessberger, *Principles of International Criminal Law* (3rd edn, OUP 2014) 90–95.

[12] See Mohamed M El Zeidy, 'From Primacy to Complementarity and Backwards: (Re)-Visiting Rule11*bis* of the Ad Hoc Tribunals' (2008) 57 International and Comparative Law Quarterly 403; Carsten Stahn, 'Introduction: Bridge over Troubled Waters?' in Carsten Stahn and Mohamed M El Zeidy (eds), *The International Criminal Court and Complementarity* (CUP 2011) 7.

[13] Nouwen and Lewis (n 8) 117.

resolution, the ICTR's mandate mentioned goals such as national reconciliation, restoration, and maintenance of peace, and putting an end to atrocities.[14]

Regulating relations with Rwanda was one of the main challenges facing the ICTR's architects. Led by the victorious RPF, Rwanda's post-genocide government had initially requested an international tribunal to 'avoid any suspicion of [Rwanda] wanting to organize speedy, vengeful justice' and to 'enhance the exemplary nature of a justice that would be seen to be completely neutral and fair'.[15] Although foreign powers, in particular the United States, pressured the new Rwandan leadership to request a tribunal,[16] Rwanda ended up voting against the ICTR (by coincidence, it held one of the Security Council's revolving seats), foreshadowing a complex relationship with international actors.[17]

Rwanda opposed several elements of the ICTR's design, including an overly restrictive temporal mandate, its 'inappropriate and ineffective' structure, and placing the Tribunal outside of Rwandan territory (arguing this would undermine national reconciliation and weaken the 'harmonization of international and national jurisprudence').[18] As will be seen in Chapter 5, the post-genocide government was especially critical of the drafters' decision to exclude the death penalty from the ICTR Statute. In addition, Rwanda's negative vote can probably be explained by the RPF realizing belatedly it would not be able to control the Tribunal.[19]

The ICTR's regulation of concurrent jurisdiction was less controversial than one might expect. Echoing debates from the ICTY's establishment, the ICTR was expected to work alongside Rwandan courts.[20] Neither the ICTR's architects nor Rwanda expected international trials to supplant domestic accountability. The statute also foresaw 'international cooperation to strengthen the Courts and Judicial System of Rwanda, having regard in particular to the necessity for those Courts to deal with large numbers of suspects'.[21] However, concurrent jurisdiction

[14] The International Criminal Tribunal for the Prosecution of Persons Responsible for Genocide and Other Serious Violations of International Humanitarian Law Committed in the Territory of Rwanda and Rwandan Citizens responsible for genocide and other such violations committed in the territory of neighbouring States, between 1 January 1994 and 31 December 1994. Annexed to UNSC Res 955 (8 November 1994) S/RES/955 (ICTR Statute) preamble and paras 6–8.

[15] UNSC, S/PV.3453 (8 November 1994) 14.

[16] Gerald Gahima, *Transitional Justice in Rwanda: Accountability for Atrocity* (Routledge 2013) 83–88; David Scheffer, *All the Missing Souls. A Personal History of the War Crimes Tribunals* (Princeton UP 2012) 74–86.

[17] See Daphna Shraga and Ralph Zacklin, 'The International Criminal Tribunal for Rwanda' (1996) 7 European Journal of International Law 501, 504.

[18] UNSC (n 15) 13–16.

[19] Payam Akhavan, 'The International Criminal Tribunal for Rwanda: The Politics and Pragmatics of Punishment' (1996) 90 American Journal of International Law 501, 505; Olivier Dubois, 'Les juridictions pénales nationales du Rwanda et le Tribunal international' (1997) 79 Revue Internationale de la Croix-Rouge 763.

[20] *Report of the Secretary General on the Establishment of the ICTY* (3 May 1993) S/25704, para 64; William A Schabas, *The UN International Criminal Tribunals: The Former Yugoslavia, Rwanda, and Sierra Leone* (CUP 2006) 125–26. But see Virginia Morris and Michael P Scharf, *The International Criminal Tribunal for Rwanda* (Transnational 1998) 308–12.

[21] ICTR Statute, preamble (recital 9). There was no analogous clause in the ICTY Statute.

in the Statute did not resolve the more contentious question of who should have priority to prosecute. As Roy Lee notes, '[i]n contrast to the case of the former Yugoslavia ... Rwanda seemed anxious that its national courts should proceed before the [ICTR]'.[22]

Nevertheless, in 1994, the primacy of Rwandan courts vis-à-vis the ICTR was never seriously considered. With most Rwandan magistrates killed or displaced, and the country's infrastructure in ruins, the domestic justice system seemed to be in no position to hold trials. Moreover, international actors feared that cooperation with Rwandan actors, for instance by consensually apportioning cases, might undermine the Tribunal's independence and impartiality.[23] In the end, like the ICTY, the ICTR's primacy was viewed as an inherent attribute of an international tribunal established under Chapter VII of the UN Charter.[24]

Rwanda conceded primacy relatively early on, but other aspects of the Tribunal's jurisdiction elicited more debate. In particular, the ICTR Statute failed to predetermine the gravity of crimes to be adjudicated, meaning that, in theory, the ICTR could choose to focus on 'lesser crimes' while 'relegating to a secondary level the genocide'.[25] Anticipating the dangers of an independent prosecutor, Rwanda objected that 'instead of devoting its meagre human resources, and probably equally meagre financial ones, to trying the crime of crimes, genocide, [the ICTR] intends to disperse its energy by prosecuting crimes that come under the jurisdiction of internal tribunals'.[26] Put differently, as early as 1994, the post-genocide authorities argued for a division of labour, whereby the ICTR would focus on genocide crimes while the RPF self-scrutinized allegations against its own troops.[27]

Ultimately, the ICTR's primacy covered all state (including Rwandan) courts and it had unlimited personal jurisdiction, allowing it to prosecute any perpetrator regardless of their affiliation or rank.[28] However, this jurisdictional set-up still offered little guidance on the mechanics of primacy. Following the ICTY's example, the UN decided that 'the details of how the primacy [would] be asserted shall be set out in the rules of procedure and evidence'.[29] In practice, the Tribunal's relationship to domestic accountability efforts was to depend on judicial rule-making, statutory interpretation, and prosecutorial discretion.

22 Roy S Lee, 'The Rwanda Tribunal' (1996) 9 Leiden Journal of International Law 37, 55.

23 Madeline Morris, 'The Trials of Concurrent Jurisdiction: The Case of Rwanda' (1997) 7 Duke Journal of Comparative & International Law 349, 353, 357–58, and 362; Cassese (n 6) 339 and 349.

24 TC, *Prosecutor v Kanyabashi* (Decision on the Defence Motion on Jurisdiction) ICTR-96-15-T (18 June 1997) (*Kanyabashi* Jurisdiction Decision) para 32; El Zeidy (n 12) 403.

25 UNSC (n 15) 15–16.

26 ibid.

27 Scheffer (n 16) 82–84; Shraga and Zacklin (n 17) 504.

28 ICTR Statute, arts 1 and 8; Cécile Aptel, 'A propos du Tribunal pénal international pour le Rwanda' [1997] International Review of the Red Cross 721.

29 *Report of the Secretary General* (n 20) para 65; Antonio Cassese, International Criminal Law (2nd edn, OUP 2008) 324–28.

Overall, the ICTR's institutional design attempted to reconcile Rwandan and international interests. However, given the Rome Statute's recognition of state priority just four years later, it may come as a surprise that Rwanda never objected to primacy in the Security Council.[30] The most persuasive explanation is that (international) primacy was considered self-explanatory at the time. Symbolizing a mid-1990s consensus, the revival of international criminal law revolved around Nuremberg-type courts with priority vis-à-vis 'unreliable' state counterparts. To be sure, the international community accepted that states *also* had a role in combating impunity, but the primary response was at the international level.

2.2. Nipped in the bud: the false promise of 'open-ended' and 'conditional' primacy

In line with the ICTR Statute, concurrent jurisdiction, including primacy, meant that '[a]t any stage of the procedure, the Tribunal may formally request national courts to defer to its competence'.[31] The details of primacy were regulated by judge-made Rules of Procedure and Evidence (RPE). Adopted in 1995, rule 9 specified that:[32]

> Where it appears to the Prosecutor that in any such investigations or criminal proceedings instituted in the courts of any State:
> (i) the act being investigated or which is the subject of those proceedings is characterised as an ordinary crime;
> (ii) there is a lack of impartiality or independence, or the investigations or proceedings are designed to shield the accused from international criminal responsibility, or the case is not diligently prosecuted; or
> (iii) what is in issue is closely related to, or otherwise involves, significant factual or legal questions which may have implications for investigations or prosecutions before the Tribunal, the Prosecutor may propose to the Trial Chamber designated by the President that a formal request be made that such court defer to the competence of the Tribunal.

Taken together, the ICTR Statute and RPE established what can be described as a system of 'open-ended' and 'conditional' primacy.[33] First, the Tribunal had jurisdiction to prosecute all suspects of specified international crimes (open-ended

[30] Scheffer (n 16) 82; Kingsley C Moghalu, *Rwanda's Genocide: The Politics of Global Justice* (Palgrave Macmillan 2005) 33–36.
[31] ICTR Statute, art 8.
[32] Rules of Procedure and Evidence ICTR, ITR/3/REV.1 (1995), r 9, entered into force 29 June 1995, as amended (ICTR RPE). Rule 9(i) and (ii) draw on ICTR Statute, art 9(2).
[33] For 'conditional primacy', including at the ICTY, see Nouwen and Lewis (n 8) 126–27.

personal jurisdiction). Second, while this jurisdiction ran concurrently with that of Rwandan authorities (and other states), the ICTR could assert priority subject to specific conditions, in particular if national institutions tried to subvert justice by charging ordinary crimes or conducting 'sham' proceedings, or if significant issues arose during international proceedings (conditional primacy).

Procedurally, only the prosecutor could initiate deferrals with the judges assessing the merits of such requests. By contrast, states, including Rwanda, could not try to reclaim cases once international proceedings had begun (although states could argue against primacy by way of *amicus curiae* if a crime was already being handled domestically and the prosecutor requested deferral).[34] The ICTR's primacy provisions mirrored the ICTY, though differences emerged over time.[35]

Although some scholars emphasize the ICTR's broad discretion to override state jurisdiction, it did not have 'absolute primacy' or an unconditional power to override and divest national courts of cases.[36] On the contrary, the conditions embedded in primacy speak to the prevailing assumptions about the interplay of international and domestic accountability in the mid-1990s. At its heart was the ICTR's power to monitor domestic proceedings and intervene if Rwanda or other states shielded suspects from justice.[37] In *Tadić*, the judges explained that primacy was necessary to prevent domestic 'stratagems' that could subvert 'the very purpose of the creation of an international criminal jurisdiction'.[38] In its first annual report, Cassese observed that the ICTY was 'not meant to deprive national courts of their criminal jurisdiction ... However ... [it] has been endowed with the power to intervene at any stage of national proceedings and take over from them, whenever this proves to be in the interests of justice'.[39] In short, implicit in primacy was the idea that international institutions should qualitatively assess domestic justice to challenge states' unreliable exercise of jurisdiction.

In practice, the ICTY and ICTR never took this confrontational path. Instead, pioneering a strategy that the ICC revitalized years later, international judges developed formalistic Tribunal-centric statutory readings to justify the assertion of

[34] Robert Cryer, *Prosecuting International Crimes: Selectivity and the International Criminal Law Regime* (CUP 2005) 130–31.

[35] On the ICTY, see Nouwen and Lewis (n 8) 118–22.

[36] See Cryer (n 34) 130–31; Cassese and others (n 11) 294.

[37] Daphna Shraga and Ralph Zacklin, 'The International Criminal Tribunal for the Former Yugoslavia' (1994) 5 European Journal of International Law 360, 371; Cryer (n 34) 130; José E Alvarez, 'Crimes of States/Crimes of Hate: Lessons from Rwanda' (1999) 24 Yale Journal of International Law 365.

[38] AC, *Prosecutor v Tadić* (Decision on the Defence Motion for Interlocutory Appeal on Jurisdiction) ICTY IT-94-1 (2 October 1995) para 58. See also Separate Opinion of Judge Sidhwa (2 October 1995) paras 84 and 90 (TC, *Prosecutor v Tadić* (Decision on the Defence Motion on Jurisdiction) IT-94-1-T (10 August 1995) para 41)).

[39] Antonio Cassese (as ICTY president), *First Annual Report of the ICTY* (29 August 1994) A/49/342, S/1994/1007, para 20 (also 87–89); *Kanyabashi* Jurisdiction Decision, paras 7 and 31; Cassese (n 6) 349 ('[national] proceedings would have been highly biased').

international jurisdiction at the expense of domestic proceedings. In *Musema*, Switzerland was ordered to defer to the ICTR's competence because the Tribunal is 'the appropriate jurisdiction to examine the case ... taking into account the seriousness of the factual charges and of the legal questions'.[40] Following an almost identical line of reasoning, in *Bagosora*, Belgium was ordered to defer to the ICTR's competence because 'the continuation of parallel investigations by the [B]elgian courts ... might be detrimental to the [international] investigations, including the testimonies [of witnesses]'.[41]

In reality, policy considerations weighed on the ad hoc tribunals' deferral decisions. In *Tadić*, the ICTY divested Germany of the case mainly to generate work for the Tribunal.[42] Belgium and Switzerland were ordered to suspend national proceedings and surrender suspects to Arusha because, inter alia, their national legislation failed to criminalize genocide or crimes against humanity, which meant that, under the ICTR's *ne bis in idem* rules, a risk existed that domestic proceedings would preclude a subsequent trial at the ICTR. However, rather than ground their deferral order on rule 9(i), which explicitly recognized the 'ordinary crime' exception and carried a 'shaming' element by emphasizing deficient national norms, chambers granted all four deferral requests against 'friendly' states like Belgium and Switzerland because the cases purportedly involved 'significant factual or legal questions'.[43] Similarly, at the ICTY, even when the prosecutor applied for a deferral alleging sham domestic proceedings, the judges still opted for rule 9(iii)'s less controversial 'significant factual or legal questions' standard to justify their priority of jurisdiction'.[44]

In other words, rule 9(iii) emerged as an escape valve, a conflict-avoidance tool, that allowed international judges to mask their incentives for deferrals and avoid shaming states over the deficiencies of concurrent domestic accountability efforts.[45] Yet, while rule 9(iii) detached primacy from evaluative assessments, it also deprived states of incentives to enhance domestic standards or challenge international jurisdiction. Even if a national trial was conducted in good faith,

[40] TC, *Prosecutor v Musema* (Decision on the Application by the Prosecutor for a Formal Request for Deferral) ICTR-96-5-D (12 March 1996) para 11.

[41] TC, *Prosecutor v Bagorosa* (Decision on the Application by the Prosecutor for a Formal Request for Deferral) ICTR-96-7-D (17 May 1996) para 12; Morris and Scharf (n 20) 322–25.

[42] TC, *Prosecutor v Tadić* (Decision on the Application by the Prosecutor for a Formal Request for Deferral to the Competence of the [ICTY] in the Matter of Duško Tadić) IT-94-1-D (8 November 1994); Mohamed M El Zeidy, *The Principle of Complementarity in International Criminal Law: Origin, Development, and Practice* (Martinus Nijhoff 2008) 141–42; Cryer (n 34) 130–31.

[43] On the ICTR's (confused) reasoning with respect to *ne bis in idem*, see Tom Vander Beken, Gert Vermeulen and Tom Ongena, 'Belgium, Concurrent National and International Criminal Jurisdiction and the Principle "ne Bis in Idem"' (2002) 73 Revue internationale de droit pénal 811, 837.

[44] TC, *Prosecutor v Mrskić, Sljivancanin & Radić* (Decision on the Proposal of the Prosecutor for a Request to the Federal Republic of Yugoslavia to Defer the Pending Investigations and Criminal Proceedings to the Tribunal) IT-95-13-R61 (10 December 1998) paras 4–5.

[45] Morris and Scharf (n 20) 322–25; Kai Ambos, *Treatise on International Criminal Law. Volume III: International Criminal Procedure* (1st edn, OUP 2016) 267.

international judges could ignore such efforts and override domestic efforts on the thinnest of pretences: 'significant factual and legal issues'. As Robert Cryer observes, by allowing the ad hoc tribunals to demand transfers of suspects at will, this provision made the limits to international jurisdiction 'more illusory than real'.[46]

In light of this, it is not surprising that the ICTR never formally invoked primacy after 1996. States had understood the message. Despite the ad hoc tribunals' conditionality-based primacy framework, judicial interpretation enshrined a Tribunal-centric reading of concurrent jurisdiction. Over the next decade, Zambia, Cameroon, Kenya, Tanzania, South Africa, Benin, Togo, Angola, Mali, and the DRC all transferred suspects to Arusha without any effort to launch domestic proceedings or litigation over primacy. France and the UK eventually also transferred several suspects.[47]

While, at first glance, it may seem surprising that the ICTR never invoked primacy against Rwanda, this does not mean that they agreed on concurrent jurisdiction. As will be seen in Chapter 4, relations were more complex than this absence of litigation over primacy might suggest. Against the backdrop of a nascent case law on concurrent jurisdiction that ignored domestic accountability standards, international prosecutors invoked primacy over senior perpetrators, even though the Statute lacked a norm to this effect, while contestation over primacy moved outside the courtroom.

2.3. 'Targeted' (quasi-absolute) primacy over high-level suspects

In June 1997, the ICTR's plenary of judges amended rule 9 to allow deferrals in light of, inter alia, the seriousness of the offences, the status of the accused at the time of the alleged offences, and the general importance of the legal questions involved in the case.[48] The shift in emphasis is clear. Although the prosecutor retained the power to request, and the judges the power to approve, deferrals, the conditionality attached to primacy was different. Rather than evaluate domestic proceedings, ICTR officials would henceforth consider the gravity of crimes and the status of suspects, in addition to the previous clause on 'important legal questions'.

In theory, the RPE continued to impose conditions for international trials to pre-empt domestic proceedings. In practice, primacy no longer depended on the

[46] Cryer (n 34) 1303. On the ICTY's different experience with primacy vis-à-vis former Yugoslav states under the Rules of the Road programme, see Chapter 4 in this volume; see also Aleksandar Kontic and David Tolbert, 'The International Criminal Tribunal for the Former Yugoslavia: Transitional Justice, the Transfer of Cases to National Courts, and Lessons for the ICC' in Göran Sluiter and Carsten Stahn (eds), *The Emerging Practice of the International Criminal Court* (Brill 2008).

[47] For details, see Kate Gibson, 'Reliance upon and Complications with State Cooperation' (2014) <unictr.irmct.org/sites/unictr.org/files/publications/compendium-documents/ii-reliance-complications-state-cooperation-gibson.pdf>.

[48] ICTR RPE, r 9, as amended 6 June 1997. On the ICTY, see Nouwen and Lewis (n 8) 120.

ICTR's relationship to domestic accountability processes. In its amended form, rule 9 became a formalistic assessment of cases that the international prosecutor had preselected. By creating an almost irrebuttable presumption, the RPE transformed the ICTR's jurisdictional relations vis-à-vis Rwanda (and other states), validating a normative shift in favour of uncontested international jurisdiction. As noted by Alexander Zahar and Göran Sluiter, amended rule 9 'is exclusively oriented to the wishes of the Tribunal and offers practically unfettered discretion as regards referral'.[49]

While these far-reaching changes in institutional design occurred by judicial fiat and with minimal external consultation, their practical significance was limited. This iteration of rule 9 was never invoked against any state. In fact, by the time the rule was adopted, facts on the ground foreshadowed a new phase of ICT–state relations. As the Arusha detention centre filled up with genocide suspects and the first trials began in mid-1997, concerns about sham domestic justice and a lack of international cases yielded to a pragmatic realization that states could alleviate the ICTR's swelling case docket. In 1999, Switzerland prosecuted its first Rwandan genocide case, followed by Belgium two years later.[50]

The ICTR's case against Bernard Ntuyahaga brought into focus evolving attitudes to concurrent jurisdiction. Ntuyahaga was under investigation by both Rwanda and Belgium (he was suspected of murdering ten Belgian peacekeepers). However, when an ICTR judge declined to confirm several charges against Ntuyahaga in 1998, Prosecutor Arbour attempted to transfer his case to a domestic court on the basis that a revised indictment was no longer 'within the framework of a global policy aimed at shedding light on the events that occurred in Rwanda in 1994'.[51] In other words, Ntuyahaga's case, after the judge had rejected certain charges, was no longer important enough to justify an international trial. But Arbour faced a curious legal problem. Although Rwanda and Belgium wanted to prosecute Ntuyahaga, the ICTR Statute did not allow referrals to states.

At the time, primacy operated in only one direction. The ICTR's architects had not even considered that domestic justice might be an alternative, let alone a superior one, to international trials. Unable to request Ntuyahaga's transfer to Belgium, Arbour petitioned to withdraw the original indictment and simultaneously order his transfer to the custody of the Tanzanian authorities who would, in turn, extradite him to Belgium. The Trial Chamber agreed to withdraw the

[49] Alexander Zahar and Göran Sluiter, *International Criminal Law: A Critical Introduction* (OUP 2008) 450–51. But see TC, *Decision on the Prosecutor's Request for Deferral and Motion for Order to the Former Yugoslav Republic of Macedonia*, IT-02-55-MISC.6 (4 October 2002).

[50] Luc Reydams, 'Niyonteze v. Public Prosecutor' (2002) 96 American Journal of International Law 231; Luc Reydams, 'Belgium's First Application of Universal Jurisdiction: The Butare Four Case' (2003) 1 Journal of International Criminal Justice 428.

[51] TC, *Prosecutor v Ntuyahaga* (Decision on Prosecutor's Motion to Withdraw Indictment) ICTR-98-40-T (18 March 1999) (*Ntuyahaga* Withdrawal Decision); ICTR, *Fourth Annual Report* (7 September 1999) A/54/315, S/1999/943, paras 34–39.

indictment but decided it had no legal authority to order his transfer to any state for purposes of detention.[52] As a result, the judges ordered Ntuyahaga's unconditional release.

The *Ntuyahaga* decision provides a snapshot of extant assumptions about concurrent jurisdiction. In its ruling, the judges described ICTR proceedings as 'complementary to those of national jurisdictions' and acknowledged Belgium's amicus brief on the ICTY's rule 11*bis* which allowed case referrals to national courts.[53] Yet, cognizant of normative developments at both the ICTY and ICC (the ruling summons complementarity without quoting from the Rome Statute, adopted just months earlier), the chamber concluded that:[54]

> the primacy recognized by the [ICTR] Statute is clear inasmuch as the Tribunal may request any national jurisdiction to defer investigations or ongoing proceedings, whereas the reverse, namely the deferral of investigations and proceedings by the Tribunal to any national jurisdiction, is not provided for.

Notwithstanding the judges' formalism, Ntuyahaga was eventually arrested by Tanzanian authorities, extradited to, and convicted by Belgium.[55] However, the ICTR would have to wait several more years before rule 11*bis* allowed referrals to national courts. In 1999, international criminal law's turn to domestic enforcement had yet to reach Arusha.

2.4. The completion strategy and rule 11*bis*: conditionality in action

Although expectations for the ICTR and ICTY were initially high, optimism yielded to concerns about soaring costs and the slow pace of international prosecutions. Amid a series of critical reports in the late 1990s, the Security Council requested a review of the ICTY's performance followed by similar stocktaking for the ICTR. Ultimately, this led to the adoption of completion strategies for both tribunals.[56]

[52] *Ntuyahaga* Withdrawal Decision.

[53] See Michael Bohlander, 'Referring an Indictment from the ICTY and ICTR to Another Court—Rule 11 Bis and the Consequences for the Law of Extradition' (2006) 55 International and Comparative Law Quarterly 219.

[54] *Ntuyahaga* Withdrawal Decision.

[55] Moghalu (n 30) 102–04. Another prominent case was the ICTR's order to release Jean-Bosco Barayagwiza in 1999. Rwanda again requested a transfer, but Barayagwiza's Arusha trial ultimately went ahead. See Thierry Cruvellier, *Le Tribunal des Vaincus: Un Nuremberg pour le Rwanda?* (Calmann-Lévy 2006) 169.

[56] On the origins of the Completion Strategy, see Daryl A Mundis, 'The Judicial Effects of the "Completion Strategies" on the Ad Hoc International Criminal Tribunals' (2005) 99 American Journal of International Law 142.

Adopted in 2003–4, the ICTR Completion Strategy mandated the completion of investigations by 2004, trials by 2008, and appeals by 2010.[57] Additional judges would be recruited to reduce the backlog of pending cases. On concurrent jurisdiction, the Security Council urged the ICTR to 'formalize a detailed strategy . . . to transfer cases involving intermediate- and lower-rank accused to competent national jurisdictions, as appropriate, including Rwanda, in order to allow the ICTR to achieve its objective'.[58] It also called on 'the international community to assist national jurisdictions . . . in improving their capacity to prosecute cases transferred'.[59] The Council also appointed a separate prosecutor for the ICTR (the two ad hoc tribunals had previously shared a single prosecutor).[60]

By revamping the ICTR's relations with states, the Completion Strategy required the prosecutor to focus on 'the most senior leaders suspected of being most responsible', within a strict time frame. This had four consequences: pursuing 'the most senior' and 'most responsible' went from an internal prosecutorial and RPE-sanctioned goal to an operational imperative and arguably a legal obligation;[61] the possibility of new indictments against high-ranking suspects was limited to one year, crippling the OTP's ability to pursue new cases; issuing new indictments for other classes of offenders was eliminated altogether; and cases before the ICTR involving mid- and low-level suspects had to be offloaded to national jurisdictions. In short, despite primacy, the exercise of jurisdiction was severely constrained.

Glimpses of the ICTR's complex relationship with Rwanda can be seen in the Completion Strategy. Although the Security Council required cases to be sent back to national jurisdictions, including Rwanda, it was more cautious about the prospect of trials before Rwandan courts than the ICTY's strategy regarding proceedings in the former Yugoslavia. Whereas, at the ICTY, a 'war crimes chamber' within the state court of Bosnia and Herzegovina was to be established and donors were encouraged to provide financial support 'to ensure the success of domestic prosecutions', the Security Council made no analogous appeal for Rwanda.[62]

To enable referrals, the ICTR adjusted its RPE and specifically rule 11*bis* (the rule itself pre-dated the Completion Strategy).[63] Its core features are as follows: (1)

[57] UNSC Res 1523 (28 August 2003) S/RES/1503, para 7.

[58] ibid preamble, line 8.

[59] ibid para 1.

[60] ibid para 8 and annex; see further Chapter 4 in this volume.

[61] Questioning the legality of the Completion strategies, as the ICTR/Y statutes were never formally amended, see Gregory P Lombardi, 'Legitimacy and the Expanding Power of the ICTY' (2003) 37 New England Law Review 887, 895–97.

[62] UNSC Res 1523, preamble, line 11 and para 5; UNSC Res 1534 (26 March 2004) S/RES/1534, paras 9–10. As will be discussed below and in Chapters 4–6, cooperation with Rwanda repeatedly broke down, and it took much longer for Rwanda to emerge as a destination for case referrals. For the ICTR, the Security Council only issued a general call to the DRC, Congo-Brazzaville, Kenya, and Rwanda to cooperate with the ICTR in bringing indictees before the Tribunal. UNSC Res 1523, para 3; UNSC Res 1534, para 2.

[63] For the rule's history, see Bohlander (n 53). ICTR RPE, r 11*bis*, adopted 6 July 2002 (Suspension of Indictment in Case of Proceedings before National Courts), amended 23/24 April 2004 (Referral of the Indictment to Another Court), amended 21 May 2005 (death penalty excluded), amended 1 April

ICTR judges could refer cases back to Rwanda and other national jurisdictions, as long as (2) states guaranteed defendants a fair trial, which—after 2005—included (3) a guarantee not to impose the death penalty;[64] (4) ICTR organs would continue to monitor the exercise of jurisdiction by states, and if necessary (5) ICTR judges could revoke the referral—at any point before a state's final determination of guilt or innocence—if a state failed to meet these requirements. Procedurally, only the prosecutor and judges had the power to initiate referrals (states could not initiate referrals) and any final decision on whether or not to refer cases or revoke referrals required judicial approval.[65]

Although rule 11*bis* remained grounded on primacy in that the ICTR had the power to divest any state of a case before a final conviction or acquittal, it turned the practice of concurrent jurisdiction upside down. By 2004, domestic prosecutions of genocide suspects had been underway in Rwanda and abroad, but the Completion Strategy forced the ICTR, for the first time, to grapple with the merits of domestic accountability. The Tribunal was ill-prepared for the task. In due course, the rule 11*bis* case law revealed a number of challenges.

While referrals to any state were possible, the ICTR initially focused on states who had custody of alleged genocidaires and whose justice systems were considered independent and impartial. In 2007, two genocide suspects under indictment by the ICTR but still physically present in France were referred for trial to French courts (in practice, this meant that the ICTR simply agreed not to pursue the transfer of said suspects to Arusha).[66] However, further referrals to European

2011 (r 11*bis* then incorporated into the MICT Statute with further changes, see below). The relevant fragments of the 2011 version are reproduced: '(A) If an indictment has been confirmed, whether or not the accused is in the custody of the Tribunal, the President may designate a [TC] which shall determine whether the case should be referred to the authorities of a State: (i) in whose territory the crime was committed; or (ii) in which the accused was arrested; or (iii) having jurisdiction and being willing and adequately prepared to accept such a case, so that those authorities should forthwith refer the case to the appropriate court for trial within that State.... (C) In determining whether to refer the case in accordance with paragraph (A), the [TC] shall satisfy itself that the accused will receive a fair trial in the courts of the State concerned and that the death penalty will not be imposed or carried out. (D) Where an order is issued pursuant to this Rule ... (iii) the Prosecutor shall provide to the authorities of the State concerned all of the information relating to the case which the Prosecutor considers appropriate and, in particular, the material supporting the indictment; (iv) the Prosecutor may, and if the [TC] so orders, the Registrar shall, send observers to monitor the proceedings in the courts of the State concerned. The observers shall report, respectively, to the Prosecutor, or through the Registrar to the President ... (F) At any time after an order has been issued pursuant to this Rule and before the accused is found guilty or acquitted by a court in the State concerned, the [TC] may *proprio motu* or at the request of the Prosecutor and upon having given to the authorities of the State concerned the opportunity to be heard, revoke the order and make a formal request for deferral within the terms of Rule 10. (G) Where an order issued pursuant to this Rule is revoked by the Trial Chamber, it may make a formal request to the State concerned to transfer the accused to the seat of the Tribunal, and the State shall accede to such a request without delay in keeping with Article 28 of the Statute.'

64 RPE, r 11*bis* as amended 21 May 2005.

65 ICTR trial chambers could order referrals *proprio motu* or upon request from the Prosecutor (r 11*bis*, para (B) [not reproduced above]).

66 TC, *Prosecutor v Wenceslas Munyeshyaka* (Decision on the Prosecutor's Request for the Referral of Munyeshyaka's Indictment to France) ICTR-2005-87-1 (20 November 2007); TC, *Prosecutor v Laurent*

states ran into legal obstacles. In *Bagaragaza*, chambers decided that, despite its willingness to prosecute a suspect, Norway lacked subject-matter jurisdiction over genocide, complicity in, and conspiracy to commit, genocide.[67] In rejecting Norway's motion to bring a charge of homicide (an ordinary crime), the Appeals Chamber clarified that states willing to receive referrals must be able to charge the same crimes as in the ICTR Statute, although it was not strictly necessary to prosecute the same crime or conduct that the Tribunal had charged in its original indictment.[68] Similar jurisdictional hurdles foreclosed Bagaragaza's transfer to the Netherlands.[69]

In light of these obstacles to prosecutions in third states, Rwanda emerged as the forum of first and last resort for rule 11*bis*. Rwanda's jurisdictional claim was obvious and the RPF's willingness to prosecute genocidaires not in doubt. However, other rule 11*bis* conditions, that of 'adequate preparation', including 'fair trial guarantees', created problems.[70] After time-consuming litigation, different trial and appeals chambers rejected five separate rule 11*bis* applications during the course of 2008. Based in Arusha, the judges concluded that Rwanda's justice system failed to provide adequate fair trial guarantees for two interrelated reasons: first, its penalty structures, specifically the possibility of life imprisonment in isolation, did not meet international standards, and, second, an effective defence could not be guaranteed, compromising the suspect's right to a fair trial.[71]

Bucyibaruta (Decision on the Prosecutor's Request for the Referral of Laurent Bucyibaruta's Indictment to France) ICTR-2005-85-1 (20 November 2007).

[67] TC, *Prosecutor v Michael Bagaragaza* (Decision on the Prosecution Motion for Referral to the Kingdom of Norway) ICTR-2005-86-R11*bis* (19 May 2006) para 16.

[68] AC, *Prosecutor v Michael Bagaragaza* (Decision on Rule 11*bis* Appeal) ICTR-05-86-AR11bis (30 August 2006) paras 16–18; Roland Adjovi, 'Regards sur la justice et les droits de l'homme en Afrique. L'affaire Baragaraza' in Paul Tavernier (ed), *Regards sur les droits de l'homme en Afrique* (Harmattan 2008).

[69] TC, *Prosecutor v Michael Bagaragaza* (Decision on Prosecutor's Request for Referral of the Indictment to the Kingdom of Netherlands) ICTR-2005-86-R11*bis* (13 April 2007); TC, *Prosecutor v Michael Bagaragaza* (Decision on Prosecutor's Extremely Urgent Motion for Revocation of the Referral to the Kingdom of Netherlands pursuant to Rule 11*bis*(F) and Rule 11*bis*(G)) ICTR-2005-86-11*bis* (17 August 2007) paras 11–12.

[70] ICTR RPE, r 11*bis*(C).

[71] TC, *Prosecutor v Yussuf Munyakazi* (Decision on Prosecutor's Request for Deferral to the Republic of Rwanda) ICTR-97-36-R11*bis* (28 May 2008); TC, *Prosecutor v Kanyarukiga* (Decision on Prosecutor's Request for Deferral to the Republic of Rwanda) ICTR-2002-78-R11*bis* (6 June 2008) (TC *Kanyarukiga*); TC, *Prosecutor v* Ildephonse Hategekimana (Decision on Prosecutor's Request for Deferral to the Republic of Rwanda) ICTR-00-55B-R11*bis* (19 June 2008) (TC *Hategekimana*); TC, *Prosecutor v Jean-Baptiste Gatete* (Decision on Prosecutor's Request for Deferral to the Republic of Rwanda) ICTR-2000-61-Rule11*bis* (17 November 2008) (TC *Gatete*); TC, *Prosecutor v Fulgence Kayishema* (Decision on Prosecutor's Request for Deferral to the Republic of Rwanda) ICTR-01-67-Rule11*bis* (16 December 2008); AC, *Prosecutor* v *Yussuf Munyakazi* (Decision on the Prosecution's Appeal against Decision on Referral under Rule 11*bis*) ICTR-97-36-R11*bis* (8 October 2008); AC, *Prosecutor u Kanyarukiga* (Decision on the Prosecutor's Appeal against Decision on Referral under Rule 11*bis*) ICTR-02-78-R11*bis* (30 October 2008); AC, *Prosecutor v Ildephonse Hategekimana* (Decision on Prosecutor's Appeal for Request under Rule 11*bis*) ICTR-00-553-R11bis (4 December 2008). For a detailed analysis, see Alhagi BM Marong and Charles C Jalloh, 'Transfer of Cases under the Jurisprudence of the ICTR and Lessons Learnt for the ICC' in Alhagi BM Marong and Charles C Jalloh (eds), *Promoting Accountability*

This first round of rule 11*bis* decisions generated controversy. At the ICTY, chambers had interpreted rule 11*bis* as a formalistic legal assessment of the right to a fair trial, concentrating narrowly on national legislation in force at the time of the referral. By contrast, the ICTR's judges adopted a mixed legal-cum-factual test, examining not just legal frameworks but also the 'objective' realities of a fair trial in Rwanda, and how domestic institutions applied the country's laws.[72] Adding fuel to the controversy, ICTR referrals to France had applied the pure 'legal' test to assess French standards, prompting accusations of double standards.[73]

Chapter 5 will examine how rule 11*bis* impacted the Rwandan justice system, but the case law marks the first time that international judges assessed a domestic accountability process from a qualitative sociolegal perspective. By reviewing submissions from various parties, including amicus curiae briefs from civil society and external experts, the ICTR forged a holistic vision of Rwanda's judiciary, prosecution, police and penitentiary services, and the bar association. Chambers reached many positive findings about justice standards in Rwanda, albeit with conflicting views at the trial and appellate levels. For instance, the judges agreed that domestic laws and conditions of detention prior to and during trial were, by and large, in line with international standards,[74] and that the judiciary was sufficiently impartial and independent from the executive.[75]

However, the ICTR refused to allow referrals for a few interrelated reasons. First, despite abolishing the death penalty in 2007, inconsistencies in national law left open the possibility that a suspect transferred from Arusha would receive a sentence of life imprisonment in isolation. According to the ICTR, this form of punishment violated the prohibition of torture.[76] Second, the judges found that the accused would not be able to call witnesses residing inside and outside Rwanda on the same conditions as the prosecution, undermining the principle of equality

under International Law for Gross Human Rights Violations in Africa: Essays in Honour of Prosecutor Hassan Bubacar Jallow (Martinus Nijhoff 2015).

[72] TC *Kanyarukiga*, para 33; TC *Hategekimana*, para 35.

[73] Jesse Melman, 'The Possibility of Transfer(?): A Comprehensive Approach to the International Criminal Tribunal for Rwanda's Rule 11bis To Permit Transfer to Rwandan Domestic Courts' (2010) 79 Fordham Law Review 1271, 1298–1305; Amelia S Canter, '"For These Reasons, the Chamber Denies the Prosecutor's Request for Referral": The False Hope of Rule 11 Bis' (2009) 32 Fordham International Law Journal 1614, 1651; Andrew Wallis, 'International Courts: Justice vs. Politics' Open Democracy (27 February 2013) <opendemocracy.net/en/andrew-wallis/international-courts-justice-vs-politics>; Martin Ngoga, 'The ICTR Completion Process and Resultant Consequences on Rwanda's Justice System' New Times Rwanda (24 October 2008) <newtimes.co.rw/section/read/5493>.

[74] TC *Gatete*, para 31; TC *Kanyarukiga*, para 33; TC *Hategekimana*, para 35. The only exception were the conflicting provisions on the death penalty, see below. See also TC *Kanyarukiga*, paras 27–29.

[75] AC *Munyakazi*, paras 28–29 reversing TC *Munyakazi*, paras 36–48.

[76] AC *Munyakazi*, paras 16–20; AC *Kanyarukiga*, paras 12–17; TC *Kanyarukiga*, paras 95–96. For more on the death penalty, see Chapter 5 in this volume. See also Alex Obote-Odora, 'Transfer of Cases from the International Criminal Tribunal for Rwanda to Domestic Jurisdictions' (2012) 5 African Journal of Legal Studies 147, 162.

of arms.[77] Third, despite formal guarantees in Rwandan law, defence counsel for genocide suspects encountered serious practical impediments to their work, in particular threats, intimidation, and the possibility of arrest,[78] difficulties in getting documents from the authorities,[79] and obstacles to meeting witnesses.[80] Lastly, chambers acknowledged that the ICTR's monitoring system, reliant in part on OTP monitors, did not adequately ensure that such failures would be noticed.[81]

Despite backlash, Rwanda ended up cooperating with the ICTR on a second round of referrals.[82] In June 2011, the Tribunal approved its first referral to Rwanda in the seminal *Uwinkindi* case:[83]

> Rwanda has made material changes in its laws and has indicated its capacity and willingness to prosecute cases referred by this Tribunal. This gives the Referral Chamber confidence that the case of the Accused ... will be prosecuted consistent with internationally recognised fair trial standards enshrined in the Statute of this Tribunal and other human rights instruments.

Following *Uwinkindi*, chambers approved eight other cases for transfer in 2012 and 2013.[84] The most striking feature of the post-*Uwinkindi* case law is that ICTR judges had reverted, without openly acknowledging it, to a formalistic legal analysis of domestic justice standards. In other words, while the approvals reaffirmed the rule 11*bis* case law's substantive requirements, the judges focused on abstract norms rather than attempting to evaluate the practical sociolegal realities of a fair trial. For instance, in *Uwinkindi*, post-2008 legislative reforms—life imprisonment in isolation had been abolished in the meantime—were cited to dismiss concerns about applicable penalties.[85] Less convincingly, chambers again focused on legislative tweaks to revise their assessment of the unavailability of defence witnesses,[86]

[77] TC *Munyakazi*, para 66; TC *Kanyarukiga*, paras 73 and 81; TC *Hategekimana*, para 71. Specifically, a new national witness protection programme did not provide sufficient guarantees of independence, witnesses testifying on behalf of suspects could be prosecuted for genocide denial, and reliance on video-link technology for remote testimony from witnesses living abroad could give the prosecution service an unfair advantage over defence counsel. On the Rwandan justice minister's statement that witnesses from abroad would be arrested if they testified in Rwanda, see Obote-Odora (n 76) 167.

[78] TC *Gatete*, para 52; TC *Kanyarukiga*, paras 61–62.

[79] TC *Kanyarukiga*, para 62.

[80] ibid; AC *Kanyarukiga*, para 21.

[81] AC *Kanyarukiga*, para 38.

[82] On Rwanda's criticisms, see further Chapter 5 in this volume.

[83] Referral Chamber, *Prosecutor v Jean-Bosco Uwinkindi* (Decision on the Prosecutor's Request for Referral to the Republic of Rwanda, ICTR-2001-75-R11*bis*) 28 June 2011 (TC *Uwinkindi*), para 223; AC, *Prosecutor v Jean Uwinkindi* (Decision on Uwinkindi's Appeal against the Referral of His Case to Rwanda and Related Motions) ICTR-01-75-AR11*bis* (16 December 2011).

[84] At the time of the ICTR's closure, in December 2015, nine cases had been successfully referred to Rwanda and two to France <www.unmict.org/en/cases>.

[85] TC *Uwinkindi*, para 51; Referral Chamber, *Prosecutor v Bernard Munyagishari* (Decision on the Prosecutor's Request for Referral to the Republic of Rwanda) ICTR-2005-89-R11*bis* (6 June 2012) (TC *Munyagishari*), para 85.

[86] TC *Uwinkindi*, para 90; TC *Munyagashari*, paras 107–08 and 117.

or the working conditions of defence counsel,[87] despite evidence that the practicalities of defending genocide suspects had become less fair after 2008.[88] In effect, by ignoring the practical realities of a (un)fair trial, chambers conceded that Rwanda had to be given an opportunity to prove itself.[89]

Given this dissonance in the case law, Cedric Ryngaert criticizes the referrals 'as a foregone conclusion for which *ex post* some legal arguments had to be found'.[90] Critical of the case law, albeit on different grounds, Nicola Palmer suggests that 'the rulings highlight the severe disconnect' between the Tribunal and the domestic justice system because the ICTR was measuring Rwanda's progress against the wrong standards, by 'not tak[ing] sufficient account of the domestic practice of genocide trials in Rwanda' and 'underpinned by an assumption that the domestic courts should have been pursuing the same objectives as the [ICTR]'.[91] A likely explanation for the ICTR's lenient approach in the second round of referrals may have been its improved monitoring programme, which allowed—following the judges' amendment of rule 11*bis* just two months before *Uwinkindi*—the registrar to monitor transferred cases separately from OTP monitors. In theory, this two-track monitoring scheme gave genocide suspects an extra level of protection, though it remains debatable—as will be seen in Chapter 6—to what extent the ICTR was willing to challenge Rwandan authorities over their domestic trials.

At the time of the ICTR's closure in December 2015, only three fugitives—Félicien Kabuga, Protais Mpiranya, and Augustin Bizimana—remained on the docket, due to their perceived seniority. Under the MICT Statute, the Mechanism retained 'the power to prosecute ... the persons indicted by the ICTY or the ICTR who are among the most senior leaders suspected of being most responsible' whereas other less important indictees may only be tried in Arusha after the MICT has 'exhausted all reasonable efforts to refer the case[s]' to national jurisdictions.[92] Following Kabuga's surprise arrest in mid-2020, the MICT's decision to exercise

[87] TC *Uwinkindi*, paras 154–59.

[88] On post-2008 conditions, see Marong and Jalloh (n 71).

[89] TC *Uwinkindi*, paras 90, 103; AC *Uwinkindi*, para 83; Obote-Odora (n 76) 177.

[90] Cedric Ryngaert, 'State Cooperation with the International Criminal Tribunal for Rwanda' in James D Meernik, Thordis Ingadóttir and Dawn L Rothe (eds), *The Realities of International Criminal Justice* (Brill 2013) 141.

[91] Nicola Palmer, 'Transfer or Transformation? A Review of the Rule 11*bis* Decisions of the International Criminal Tribunal for Rwanda' (2012) 20 African Journal of International and Comparative Law 1, 2. Commentary on r 11*bis* is generally less critical after *Uwinkindi*. See Alhagi Marong, Charles C Jalloh and David Kinnecome, 'Concurrent Jurisdiction at the ICTR: Should the Tribunal Refer Cases to Rwanda?' in Emmanuel Decaux, Adama Dieng and Malick Sow (eds), *Des droits de l'homme au droit international pénal. Etudes en l'honneur d'un juriste africain, feu le juge Laïty Kama* (Martinus Nijhoff 2007); Obote-Odora (n 76). Critically, see Jennifer Wren Morris, 'The Trouble with Transfers: An Analysis of the Referral of Uwinkindi to the Republic of Rwanda for Trial' (2012) 90 Washington University Law Review 505.

[92] The primacy provisions are no longer in the RPE, but directly in the MICT Statute. Statute of the International Residual Mechanism for Criminal Tribunals, annex to UNSC Res 1966 (22 December 2010) S/RES/1966, art 6. MICT Statute, art 6 diverges somewhat from the ICTR's r 11*bis* by incorporating requirements from the ICTY's r 11*bis*.

primacy and prosecute him in Arusha appeared to be driven—notwithstanding his prominent role as an alleged genocide mastermind—mainly by institutional inertia rather than any principled jurisdictional rationale. Palmer, for instance, emphasizes that it is unclear why Kabuga's case needs to be tried in Arusha in light of the ICTR's previous rule 11*bis* rulings.[93]

Although the overall trend has been to encourage trials in Rwanda, Kabuga's international trial epitomizes how ICTs struggle to justify asserting jurisdiction over high-level perpetrators at the expense of states. While the MICT also retains primacy, and may revoke cases sent back to Rwandan and French courts, it has declined to reassert jurisdiction over a single referral and this eventuality seems increasingly unlikely as time goes by, primarily due to the UN's financial constraints.

2.5. Rehabilitating the domestic: from 'conditional' to 'absolute' primacy and back

In a system of concurrent national–international jurisdiction, the primacy norm allows an ICT to exercise jurisdiction over international crimes, including by obliging states to recognize its priority. The ICTR initially required deferrals from states under three conditions: the ordinary crimes exception, 'sham' national proceedings; or the importance of an international case. Primacy in this iteration was the mirror image of admissibility at the ICC—not 'absolute' priority, but a conditionality tool to pre-empt deficient domestic trials or affirm the superiority of international trials on specific issues.

Although these deferral criteria later shifted, the pre-Completion iteration of primacy consecrated the privileged place of ICTs atop the international criminal justice architecture as the forum of choice, especially for high-level suspects. With the ICTY and ICTR prosecuting senior perpetrators, the original primacy norm captures a mid-1990s consensus wherein states are a secondary forum in the fight against impunity. As Serge Brammertz and Kevin Hughes observe, '[*Tadić*'s] articulation of the meaning of primacy stands as a high-water mark of belief in the transformative power of international criminal courts'.[94]

[93] Nicola Palmer, 'Who Should Try Félicien Kabuga?' (*Opinio Juris*, 20 May 2020) <opiniojuris.org/2020/05/20/who-should-try-felicien-kabuga/>. Unlike the ICTY, where 'the level of the responsibility of the accused' was part of the r 11*bis* conditionality scheme and produced (conflicting) case law, the ICTR referral process eschewed this issue—only for it to re-emerge in *Kabuga*. On the ICTY case law, see David Tolbert and Aleksandar Kontić, 'The International Criminal Tribunal for the Former Yugoslavia ("ICTY") and the Transfer of Cases and Materials to National Judicial Authorities: Lessons in Complementarity' in Stahn and El Zeidy (n 12) 906–08; Alex Odora-Obote, 'Investigations and Case Selection' in Anne-Marie de Brouwer and Alette Smeulers (eds), *Elgar Companion to the International Criminal Tribunal for Rwanda* (Edward Elgar 2017) 258–64.

[94] Serge Brammertz and Kevin C Hughes, 'From Primacy to Complementarity: The International Criminal Tribunal for the Former Yugoslavia, 1993–2015' in Morten Bergsmo and others (eds), *Historical Origins of International Criminal Law. Volume 4* (Torkel Opsahl 2015) 188.

This belief proved incomplete. As early as 1998, *Ntuyahaga* illustrated the shortcomings of an institutional approach that ignored the benefits of national trials. As negative attitudes towards domestic accountability evolved, including under the impulse of the Rome Statute, the Security Council forced a reckoning with the assumptions underpinning primacy. Despite concerns about the Rwandan judiciary, rule 11*bis* required cases to be transferred to states subject to minimal international standards. By 2015, with eleven cases sent back to Rwanda, the ICTR's legacy report carried the seemingly self-explanatory title 'complementarity in action', symbolizing an ideational shift in how ICTs and states work together to fight impunity.[95] At both the ICTR and ICTY, the rule 11*bis* transfer process epitomized a shift to domestic accountability, even if the MICT retains primacy to this day.

3. A Hybrid and Restrictive Mandate

The SCSL shared many elements of institutional design with the ICTR, including primacy. However, there were important differences. Its defining jurisdictional feature was a mandate restricted ab initio to perpetrators who 'bear the greatest responsibility'. While ICTs often target variously defined high-level perpetrators—'most responsible' or 'greatest responsibility'[96]—mandates that expressly impose this restriction affect the exercise of concurrent jurisdiction in ways that are not fully explored in the literature.

In addition, the Special Court's relations with Sierra Leone were affected by its location (based in Freetown) and a mix of other jurisdictional (mixed crimes) and institutional (mixed staffing) elements, earning the SCSL the moniker of a 'hybrid' tribunal.[97] Although subject-matter jurisdiction, staff nationality, and location are not a function of ICT–state relations in the same way as complementarity or primacy, these elements of institutional design shaped the SCSL's interactions with Sierra Leone, making them integral to an analysis of its 'shadow effects' on domestic accountability.[98]

[95] ICTR–OTP, 'Complementarity in Action: Lessons Learned from the ICTR Prosecutor's Referral of International Criminal Cases to National Jurisdictions for Trial' (2015).

[96] For the Nuremberg, Tokyo, and Cambodia tribunals, see Luc Reydams and Jed Odermatt, 'Mandates' in Luc Reydams, Jan Wouters and Cedric Ryngaert (eds), *International Prosecutors* (OUP 2012).

[97] For the term 'hybrid', see n 9; OHCHR, 'Rule-of-Law Tools for Post-Conflict States. Maximizing the Legacy of Hybrid Courts' (2008). Against hybridity as a legal category, see Roger O'Keefe, *International Criminal Law* (OUP 2015) 86–87.

[98] Accordingly, this study adopts the shorthand 'hybrid' and 'restrictive' mandate to capture how the SCSL's institutional design impacted Sierra Leone. On the relationship between hybrid tribunals and restrictive mandates, see Cesare Romano, 'Mixed Criminal Tribunals (Sierra Leone, East Timor, Kosovo, Cambodia)' *Max Planck Encyclopedia of Public International Law* (2006) paras 29–31.

3.1. The original aims

The SCSL was established in January 2002 at the end of Sierra Leone's decade-long civil war. The impetus for its creation came from Sierra Leone's political leaders, who had become disillusioned with failed peacemaking efforts, though foreign persuasion—in particular US and UK interests—likely played a significant role.[99] In June 2000, then Sierra Leonean President, Ahmad Tejan Kabbah, requested the UN Secretary General to set up a 'special court' that would 'try and bring to credible justice ... members of the [RUF] and their accomplices'.[100] Kabbah initially requested a Security Council-mandated ad hoc court modelled on the ICTY/R, but—after several rounds of negotiations—the UN and his government signed a bilateral treaty creating a special court (demands to grant Chapter VII powers resurfaced after 2002—mainly to enable Charles Taylor's arrest outside the territory of Sierra Leone—but the SCSL never obtained such powers).[101]

The Tribunal's legal framework remained open in Kabbah's initial invitation letter but was already 'designed to be narrow' and focused on 'the most responsible violators and the leadership of the [RUF]'.[102] Its jurisdiction eventually grew to encompass all parties to the civil war, but it seems UN negotiators consistently argued for a restrictive mandate. As a result, the SCSL's temporal jurisdiction was restricted to crimes committed after 1996 (rather than 1991) and its territorial jurisdiction encompassed only Sierra Leone (and not Liberia, from where Taylor fomented the civil war).[103] Most importantly, the Special Court's personal jurisdiction was limited to those bearing 'greatest responsibility'.

The SCSL's institutional design embodied a mixed approach to international and domestic justice. Whereas the Sierra Leonean government, the judiciary, and civil society groups had expressed 'a clear preference ... for a national court with a strong international component',[104] the Security Council requested the Secretary

[99] Luc Reydams, Jan Wouters and Cedric Ryngaert, 'The Politics of Establishing International Criminal Tribunals' in Luc Reydams, Jan Wouters and Cedric Ryngaert (eds), *International Prosecutors* (OUP 2012) 68–69; International Crisis Group, 'The Special Court for Sierra Leone: Promises and Pitfalls of a "New Model"' (2003).

[100] Alhaji A Tejan Kabbah, 'Letter Dated 12 June 2000, with an Enclosure, from the President of the Republic of Sierra Leone, to the President of the [UNSC] on the Proposed Special Court for Sierra Leone [Letter Annexed to Letter Dated 9 August 2000 from the Permanent Representative of Sierra Leone]' S/2000/786.

[101] Agreement between the United Nations and the Government of Sierra Leone on the Establishment of a Special Court for Sierra Leone, 14 January 2002 [SCSL Statute]. On chapter VII, see International Crisis Group (n 99).

[102] Kabbah (n 100) enclosure to letter, para 2; Alison Smith, 'The Expectations and Role of International and National Civil Society and the SCSL' in Charles C Jalloh (ed), *The Special Court for Sierra Leone and Its Legacy* (CUP 2013).

[103] Report of the Secretary General on the establishment of a [SCSL] (4 October 2000) S/2000/915 (UNSG SCSL Report), para 32; Letter from the Secretary General to the President of the UN Security Council (28 December 2001) S/2001/1320; Chandra Lekha Sriram, 'Wrong-Sizing International Justice? The Hybrid Tribunal in Sierra Leone' (2005) 29 Fordham International Law Journal 472, 483–84.

[104] *Fifth Report of the Secretary General on UNAMSIL* (31 July 2000) S/2000/751, para 9.

General to 'negotiate an agreement ... to create an independent special court'.[105] Echoing concerns from the ICTR, questions surfaced about justice standards in Sierra Leone, including use of the death penalty.[106] Ultimately, the UN opted for a 'strong and independent' international court with national elements, rather than a domestic institution with international support.[107]

Accordingly, SCSL organs comprised both international and Sierra Leonean officials, but the drafters ensured that foreigners had decision-making power. Its focus was on international crimes, but the SCSL mandate also included domestic crimes to foster local ownership. Unlike the ICTR and ICTY, the Special Court would be located in Freetown, Sierra Leone's capital, closer to the people who had experienced the crimes to be adjudicated.[108]

By contrast, the SCSL's architects ignored other institutional design features with ramifications for domestic accountability, in particular concurrent jurisdiction. Although the UN noted a 'pressing need for international cooperation to assist in strengthening the judicial system of Sierra Leone' and 'arrangements regarding cooperation, assistance and sharing of information', the SCSL Statute failed to mention capacity building.[109] Equally important, as will be seen in Chapter 4, while the SCSL statute clarified that amnesty 'shall not be a bar to prosecution' at the international level, it left open the domestic validity of the 1999 Lomé amnesty that 'ensure[d] that no official or judicial action is taken against [combatants] in respect of anything done by them in pursuit of their objectives'.[110]

3.2. Primacy and rule 11*bis*: law without practice

Modelled on the ICTR's primacy framework, the SCSL Statute allowed the Special Court to 'request a national court to defer to its competence'.[111] Under the SCSL's RPE, copied initially from the ICTR RPE, chambers approved requests initiated by the prosecutor if domestic proceedings were or should be the subject of an SCSL investigation in light of, inter alia, the seriousness of the offences, the status of the accused, or the general importance of the legal questions involved.[112] Like at the ICTR, no procedural rule allowed Sierra Leonean authorities to contest primacy.

105 UNSC Res 1315 (14 August 2000) S/RES/1315, para 1.

106 *Fifth Report of the Secretary General on UNAMSIL* (n 104) para 10.

107 UNSG SCSL Report, para 10; Special Court Agreement, 2002, Ratification Act, 29 March 2002, Supplement to the Sierra Leone Gazette Vol CXXXIII, No 22, 25 April 2002, art 11(2).

108 SCSL Statute, art 1(1).

109 UNSC Res 1315, preamble and para 11; UNSG SCSL Report, paras 8 and 28; Smith (n 102) 55–56.

110 Lomé Peace Agreement, art IX. On the UN special representative's reservation to the amnesty, see Schabas (n 20) 34.

111 SCSL Statute, art 8. For an early analysis, see Abdul Tejan-Cole, 'The Special Court for Sierra Leone: Conceptual Concerns and Alternatives' (2001) 1 African Human Rights Law Journal 107, 113–14.

112 The ICTR RPE, incorporated *mutatis mutandis* on 16 January 2002, were amended in March 2003, and thereafter several times until 2012 (SCSL RPE). SCSL RPE, rr 9–11 and 11*bis*.

While primacy at the SCSL tracked the ICTR's framework, there were three differences. First, unlike the ICTR's original primacy rules geared to countering 'ordinary crimes' and 'sham trials', the SCSL RPE conditioned ab initio the Special Court's deferral power on factors such as gravity and perpetrator seniority, which echoes the SCSL's jurisdictional focus on greatest responsibility.[113]

Second, the SCSL also adopted elements of the ICC's institutional design. It recognized states' primacy to prosecute peacekeepers subject to the condition that if 'the sending State is unwilling or unable genuinely to carry out an investigation or prosecution, the [SCSL] may, if authorized by the Security Council ... exercise jurisdiction over such persons'.[114] While 'unable or unwilling genuinely' echoes the Rome Statute, the trigger—Security Council authorization—conditioned the exercise of jurisdiction over peacekeepers on both legal and political factors.[115] In practice, neither the SCSL prosecutor nor any state attempted to activate the Special Court's subsidiary jurisdiction over peacekeepers.

Third, the Special Court's primacy over (non-peacekeeping) perpetrators extended only to Sierra Leonean national courts—but not the courts of other states. Accordingly, the SCSL lacked the authority to obligate other states—for example, if Liberia began to prosecute Taylor—to defer to its competence (similarly, the SCSL could issue requests for cooperation to foreign state institutions, but they were not bound to comply).[116]

It appeared initially that, much like in Rwanda, the scope of primacy vis-à-vis Sierra Leonean institutions might give rise to litigation. As a dualist country, Sierra Leone had to adopt legislation to give legal effect to Kabbah's agreement with the UN establishing the SCSL. However, the Special Court Ratification Act purported to grant the Sierra Leonean Attorney General discretionary power over primacy-based deferral requests. Accordingly, '[w]here, pursuant to Article 8 of the [SCSL] Statute, the Attorney General receives any request for deferral or discontinuance of proceedings, he shall grant the request, *if in his opinion* there are sufficient grounds for him to do so'.[117] In other words, by granting the Attorney General coequal power to assess the validity of SCSL primacy requests, the Act conflicted with the SCSL's exclusive authority to take binding decisions on concurrent jurisdiction.

As will be explained in Chapter 4, no Attorney General was forced to approve a deferral request because the SCSL never formally invoked primacy—despite instances of jurisdictional overlap—against Sierra Leone. Yet, unexpectedly, disputes

[113] SCSL RPE, r 9(ii)(b).

[114] SCSL Statute, art 1(2) and (3); Ousman Njikam, *The Contribution of the Special Court for Sierra Leone to the Development of International Humanitarian Law* (Duncker Humblot 2013) 62–70.

[115] Scheffer (n 16) 323–29.

[116] SCSL RPE, r 9(C) and (E); Cassese (n 29) 341–42; UNSG SCSL Report, para 10.

[117] Special Court Agreement Ratification Act, 19 March 2002, art 14 (emphasis added). But see arts 20 (orders of the Court) and 23 (arrest and delivery of persons), suggesting that SCSL orders and arrest warrants were legally binding for Sierra Leonean authorities. See also Headquarters Agreement between the Republic of Sierra Leone and the Special Court for Sierra Leone, 22 October 2003, art 20.

over primacy emerged in the context of the SCSL's relationship with Sierra Leone's TRC. As a *sui generis* domestic institution with investigative powers over the same crimes as the SCSL, the TRC's relationship to the Special Court raised novel legal questions that neither the Special Court nor the TRC statutes resolved.[118]

Disagreements emerged over, inter alia, the authority of one institution to compel the other to share information and witness testimony. SCSL chambers invoked their primacy to reject a request for testimony from the TRC on one occasion, but litigation over primacy had little long-term significance.[119] Similarly, despite adopting rule 11*bis* for the referral of a single outstanding indictment, this rule never triggered debates over concurrent jurisdiction in Sierra Leone. Unlike the ICTR, which spent a decade referring indictments, neither the SCSL nor its successor, the Residual Special Court for Sierra Leone (RSCSL) have activated rule 11*bis*.[120]

3.3. 'Targeted' primacy: litigating 'greatest responsibility'

In international criminal law, concurrent jurisdiction is usually analysed through the lens of primacy and complementarity, i.e. rules of jurisdictional priority. But other jurisdictional norms embedded in ICT mandates also influence the distribution of cases between ICTs and states. From the perspective of Sierra Leone, where civil society and victim groups advocated accountability in domestic courts, the SCSL Statute's rules on concurrent jurisdiction (primacy) proved less important than its regulation of personal jurisdiction (greatest responsibility).

Unlike the ICTR, which initially had primacy over all national courts and personal jurisdiction over perpetrators of any seniority (open-ended primacy), the

[118] For details, see Tom Perriello and Marieke Wierda, 'The Special Court for Sierra Leone under Scrutiny' (ICTJ 2006) 40–43; Charles C Jalloh, 'Toward Greater Synergy between Courts and Truth Commissions in Post-Conflict Contexts' in William A Schabas, Margaret M deGuzman and Diane M Amann (eds), *Arcs of Global Justice: Essays in Honour of William A. Schabas* (OUP 2018); Abdul Tejan-Cole, 'The Complementary and Conflicting Relationship between the Special Court for Sierra Leone and the Truth and Reconciliation Commission' (2003) 6 Yale Human Rights and Development Journal 139, 151–53; Witness to Truth, Report of the Sierra Leone TRC, vol 3B (2004) ch 6.

[119] AC, *Prosecutor v Norman* (Decision on Appeal by the [TRC] for Sierra Leone and Chief Samuel Hinga Norman JP against the Decision of His Lordship, Mr Justice Bankole Thompson to Deny the TRC's Request to Hold a Public Hearing) SCSL-2003-08-PT (28 November 2003) para 4. The SCSL prosecutor's decision to not use TRC-generated information avoided potential conflict. On conflict and dispute resolution, see Elizabeth M Evenson, 'Truth and Justice in Sierra Leone: Coordination between Commission and Court' (2004) 104 Columbia Law Review 730, 744–47, 755–59.

[120] SCSL RPE, r 11*bis*, adopted by the plenary of judges, 27 May 2008. It incorporated the ICTR and elements of the ICTY's r 11*bis* but omitted the power to revoke cases. See Sigall Horovitz, 'How International Courts Shape Domestic Justice: Lessons from Rwanda and Sierra Leone' (2013) 46 Israel Law Review 339, 361; Statute of the Residual Special Court for Sierra Leone, annexed to the Agreement between the United Nations and the Government of Sierra Leone on the Establishment of a Residual Special Court for Sierra Leone, 11 August 2010 (RSCSL Statute), art 1, RSCSL Statute and RSCSL RPE, r 11*bis*; Tiyanjana Mphepo, 'The Residual Special Court for Sierra Leone. Rationale and Challenges' (2014) 14 International Criminal Law Review 177.

SCSL's primacy of jurisdiction was limited from the outset to one group of perpetrators, namely those bearing 'greatest responsibility' ('targeted primacy'). According to article 1(1) of the SCSL Statute:[121]

> The Special Court shall … have the power to prosecute persons who *bear the greatest responsibility* for serious violations of international humanitarian law and Sierra Leonean law committed in the territory of Sierra Leone since 30 November 1996, including those leaders who, in committing such crimes, have threatened the establishment of and implementation of the peace process in Sierra Leone.

This clause is usually analysed from the SCSL's vantage point, but from the perspective of Sierra Leonean courts the Statute's regulation of concurrent and personal jurisdiction had two consequences. First, Sierra Leone had concurrent but subsidiary jurisdiction over suspects with greatest responsibility. Second, national courts enjoyed de facto exclusive jurisdiction to prosecute anyone outside the scope of greatest responsibility. As noted by Michaela Frulli, the SCSL Statute established 'a possible limitation in favour of national jurisdictions dealing with cases of a lesser scale' through its 'norms relating to the *rationae personae* jurisdiction'.[122]

The centrality of the 'greatest responsibility' clause was not lost on the UN and Sierra Leoneans. During negotiations on the SCSL Statute, the UN Secretary General and Security Council clashed, with the former advocating broader and more inclusive language (most responsible) while the latter pushed for narrowly tailored authority (greatest responsibility). Although it ultimately incorporated the Security Council's language, the SCSL Statute failed to define 'greatest responsibility'. Adding to the uncertainty, two different versions of the phrase appeared in the Statute. Under article 1(1), the Special Court had the power 'to prosecute persons who bear the greatest responsibility … including those leaders',[123] whereas the OTP's powers in article 15 extended to persons 'who bear the greatest responsibility' without any qualification.[124]

As will be seen in Chapter 4, interpretation of 'greatest responsibility' generated debate in Sierra Leone. Given the government's refusal to overturn the Lomé amnesty, which barred civil-war-related domestic prosecutions, 'greatest responsibility' emerged as an admissibility filter for accountability *tout court*. By the same token, defendants tried repeatedly to leverage 'greatest responsibility' to have their cases dismissed due to a perceived lack of seniority. Litigation revolved around two issues: first, did the category of perpetrators bearing 'greatest responsibility' cover only political and military leaders, or did it also include notorious individuals of

[121] SCSL Statute, art 1(1) (emphasis added).

[122] Michaela Frulli, 'The Special Court for Sierra Leone: Some Preliminary Comments' (2000) 11 European Journal of International Law 857, 863.

[123] SCSL Statute, art 1 (Competence of the Special Court).

[124] ibid art 15 (the Prosecutor).

lower rank? Second, was the clause a jurisdictional requirement *stricto sensu* or, alternatively, non-binding guidance for prosecutorial discretion?

The historical record suggests that the Security Council wanted to restrict the mandate to a narrow group of military and political leaders directly responsible for the conflict.[125] By contrast, the Secretary General argued for a wider concept of 'most responsible', reasoning that, '[w]hile those "most responsible" obviously include the political or military leadership, others ... down the chain of command may also be regarded "most responsible" judging by the severity of the crime or its massive scale'.[126] Although the Security Council rejected the Secretary General's attempts to replace 'greatest responsibility' in the Statute with 'most responsible', SCSL trial chambers concluded that greatest responsibility extended to lower-ranking perpetrators accused of especially gruesome crimes.[127]

The nature of the 'greatest responsibility' clause turned on the (ir)relevance of the word 'including' in article 1(1). One trial chamber concluded that it was both a jurisdictional requirement and statutory guidance for the SCSL prosecutor,[128] while another trial chamber suggested that 'greatest responsibility' only related to prosecutorial discretion but did not restrict SCSL personal jurisdiction.[129] Endorsing the latter view, the Appeals Chamber concluded that 'it is the Prosecutor who has the responsibility and competence to determine who are to be prosecuted' whereas chambers had the responsibility of 'try[ing] such persons who the prosecutor has consequently brought before it as persons who bear the greatest responsibility'.[130]

The Appeals Chamber's ruling is difficult to square with the SCSL Statute's language, purpose, and historical record. However, it makes sense in its procedural context. To argue that 'greatest responsibility' was a jurisdictional requirement

[125] *Fifth Report of the Secretary General on UNAMSIL* (n 104) para 10 ('those most responsible'); UNSC Res 1315, para 3 ('persons who bear the greatest responsibility ... including those leaders'); UNSG SCSL Report, para 29 ('I propose, however, that the more general term "persons most responsible" should be used'); *Report of the Security Council Mission to Sierra Leone* (16 October 2000) S/2000/992, para 50 ('the purpose was to indict only those persons who bore the greatest responsibility'); Letter from the Security Council to the Secretary General (22 December 2000) S/2000/1234, para 1 ('continue to hold the view that ... should have personal jurisdiction over persons who bear the greatest responsibility').

[126] UNSG SCSL Report, para 30; Draft Statute annexed to Report, art 1.

[127] TC, *Prosecutor v Norman, Fofana, Kondewa* (Decision on the Preliminary Defence Motion on the Lack of Personal Jurisdiction filed on behalf of Moimina Fofana) SCSL-04-14-PT (3 March 2004) (CDF decision), para 40; TC, *Prosecutor v Brima, Kamara, Kanu* (Decision on Defence Motions for Judgment of Acquittal pursuant to Rule 98) SCSL-04-16-T (31 March 2006) (AFRC no-motion decision), paras 35–36; TC, *Prosecutor v Brima* (Judgment, SCSL-04-16-T) 20 June 2007 (AFRC Judgment), paras 655–59 obiter. For a detailed analysis of the 'greatest responsibility' case law, see Charles C Jalloh, 'Prosecuting Those Bearing "Greatest Responsibility": The Contributions of the Special for Sierra Leone' in Charles C Jalloh (ed), *The Sierra Leone Special Court and its Legacy: The Impact for Africa and International Criminal Law* (CUP 2013).

[128] CDF decision, para 27; TC, *Prosecutor v Fofana* (Judgment) SCSL-04-14-T (2 August 2007) paras 91–92.

[129] AFRC Judgment, paras 652–53.

[130] AC, *Prosecutor v Brima, Kamara, Kanu* (Judgment) SCSL-2004-16-A (22 February 2008) (AFRC Appeals Decision) para 281.

meant an accused's status had to be proved beyond a reasonable doubt, like all jurisdictional requirements. While it is uncontroversial that ICTs should dismiss charges due to an absence of temporal jurisdiction (e.g. if an alleged crime did not take place within the temporal mandate) or subject-matter jurisdiction (e.g. if it is not proven that an armed conflict existed for the purpose of war crime charges), dismissal due to insufficient seniority creates difficulties, especially on appeal. For instance, the Appeals Chamber argued it was 'inconceivable that after a long and expensive trial the [judges] could conclude that although the commission of serious crimes has been established beyond reasonable doubt against the accused', a case should be thrown out 'on the ground that it has not been proved that the accused was not one of those who bore the greatest responsibility'.[131]

Accordingly, no defendant was ultimately found 'insufficiently' senior or responsible. However, the SCSL's experience suggests that litigation over perpetrator seniority should be resolved akin to admissibility questions in the pretrial phase, before time and resources are spent on prosecuting a case to completion. Architects of ICTs must also consider what to do with suspects who are found insufficiently senior, as the drafters of the SCSL Statute, relying on the ICTR Statute as a model, arguably failed to appreciate the significance that 'greatest responsibility' would acquire in Sierra Leone, where the Lomé amnesty ensured that the stakes of whether a defendant bore greatest responsibility became exceptionally high.[132]

Critical of the Special Court's 'greatest responsibility' case law, Charles Jalloh argues that, while 'greatest responsibility' served to 'establish a relatively cheap and time limited ad hoc court that would prosecute only a small group of people', it is not desirable to include 'general statements of personal jurisdiction' in 'a criminal tribunal instrument'.[133] Similarly, Margaret deGuzman argues that ICT architects 'should avoid including jurisdictional requirements limiting personal jurisdiction based on degree of responsibility'.[134] Yet the fact remains that ICTs focus on variously defined senior perpetrators.[135] Not only does the SCSL's jurisprudence shed light on a term that is often used but rarely theorized, Chapter 4 explains how the mere fact of litigation—and uncertainty as to the outcome of such challenges—influenced interactions with Sierra Leonean authorities.

[131] ibid para 283.

[132] On the link between suspect status and admissibility before the ad hoc tribunals, see Ambos (n 45) 268.

[133] Jalloh, 'Prosecuting Those Bearing "Greatest Responsibility"' (n 127) 621.

[134] Margaret M deGuzman, 'SCSL Symposium: Who Bears the Greatest Responsibility for International Crimes?' (*Opinio Juris*, 18 March 2021) <opiniojuris.org/2021/03/18/scsl-symposium-who-bears-the-greatest-responsibility-for-international-crimes/>.

[135] On the ECCC, see Stuart Ford, 'Senior Leaders and Those Most Responsible at the Extraordinary Chambers in the Courts of Cambodia' (2021) 15 Florida International University Law Review 31.

3.4. Hybrid crimes: insulating the international from domestic scrutiny

In addition to its regulation of jurisdictional matters, the SCSL Statute contained hybrid features that structured relations with Sierra Leonean institutions. First, the prosecutor could charge not only war crimes and crimes against humanity but also two ordinary domestic crimes, namely offences relating to the abuse of girls under the 1926 Prevention of Cruelty to Children Act and offences relating to the wanton destruction of property under the 1861 Malicious Damage Act.[136] Second, the SCSL Statute empowered the Sierra Leonean government to appoint Sierra Leonean judges and a deputy prosecutor.[137] As will be seen in Chapter 5, although the appointment prerogative was initially meant to empower the national justice system, the government distanced later itself from these aims, foreshadowing a more isolationist relationship than advocates of hybridity envisioned.[138]

3.5. Searching for domestic impact: reconciling hybridity with a restrictive mandate

At the time of its establishment, the SCSL was considered a novel experiment in international criminal justice. Given their blending of international and national elements, the 'promise' of 'third-generation' hybrid courts lie in their ability to 'combine the best of two worlds, the purely domestic and the purely international prosecution of international crimes, and to transcend the shortcomings of each world taken separately'.[139] As noted by Cassese, the Special Court 'was designed to improve on the [ICTs] for the former Yugoslavia and Rwanda', which were 'marred by four essential flaws': their 'costly nature', the 'excessive length' of proceedings, their 'remoteness from the territory where crimes had been committed', and 'the unfocussed character of the prosecutorial targets resulting in trials of a number of low-ranking accused'.[140]

Based in Freetown, the SCSL's hybrid institutional features were expected to have a 'demonstration effect' on domestic institutions, inter alia, by promoting ownership and legitimacy, building institutional capacity, and enhancing norm internalization.[141] While the SCSL Statute did not mandate capacity building

[136] SCSL Statute, art 5.

[137] ibid arts 12 and 15(4).

[138] The Special Court Agreement, 2002 Ratification Amendment Act, 24 October 2002.

[139] Laura A Dickinson, 'The Promise of Hybrid Courts' (2003) 97 American Journal of International Law 295; Sarah MH Nouwen, '"Hybrid Courts": The Hybrid Category of a New Type of International Crimes Courts' (2006) 2 Utrecht Law Review 190, 190–91.

[140] Antonio Cassese, 'Report on the Special Court for Sierra Leone' (2006) 8.

[141] On demonstration effect, see Thierry Cruvellier, 'From the Taylor Trial to A Lasting Legacy: Putting the Special Court Model to the Test' (ICTJ 2009) and Chapter 6. For early optimism about the SCSL's transformative potential, see Charles C Jalloh, 'Special Court for Sierra Leone: Achieving Justice?'

as a standalone goal, so-called legacy advocacy emerged—as will be seen in Chapter 5—shortly after operations began. As noted later by Daphna Shraga, an SCSL architect, 'the success of any mixed tribunal ... will be measured also by its legacy of enhanced international standards of justice and a generation of skilled judges and prosecutors trained in the principles and procedures of international criminal justice'.[142]

While it is known for its hybridity, an equally important feature of the SCSL's design was its restrictive mandate. As Jalloh observes, '[t]here is no aspect of the [Special] Court's jurisdiction that was more controversial than the notion that it should prosecute only those persons bearing "the greatest responsibility"'.[143] Combined with the SCSL's brief (three-year) projected lifespan, this clause loomed large in Sierra Leone and symbolized assumptions about international criminal justice in the early 2000s. With the ad hoc tribunals experiencing setbacks and the ICC emerging as a permanent option for future crimes, the SCSL focused on just a handful of perpetrators, and steered a middle course between unreliable national courts and ineffective international tribunals.

4. Complementarity (Domestic Primacy or Subsidiarity)

Complementarity is a multifaceted term that has acquired an independent meaning in international criminal law. Strictly speaking, it refers to an arrangement based on concurrent jurisdiction, where states have priority to investigate, prosecute, and adjudicate international crimes while an ICT intervenes as a backstop subject to specific conditions. Yet, while it has generated copious commentary, the nature and scope of the complementarity norm before the ICC are deeply contested, partly because the term itself does not appear in the Rome Statute.[144] This section focuses on the Rome Statute's admissibility norms that regulate the

(2011) 32 Michigan Journal of International Law 395, 396; Marieke Wierda, 'Comparison of the Legacy of the Special Court for Sierra Leone and the ICC Intervention in Uganda from a Practical Perspective' (2009) 103 Proceedings of the Annual Meeting of the American Society of International Law 218, 219.

[142] Daphna Shraga, 'The Second Generation UN-Based Tribunals: A Diversity of Mixed Jurisdictions' in Cesare Romano, André Nollkaemper and Jann Kleffner (eds), *Internationalized Criminal Courts. Sierra Leone, East Timor, Kosovo, and Cambodia* (OUP 2004) 15.

[143] Jalloh, 'Prosecuting Those Bearing "Greatest Responsibility"' (n 127) 590. In this sense, see also David M Crane, 'The Bright Red Thread. The Politics of International Criminal Law—Do We Want Peace or Justice? The West African Experience' in Leila N Sadat (ed), *Forging a Convention for Crimes Against Humanity* (CUP 2010) 65.

[144] The term may also be a misnomer. See Andrew Clapham, 'Issues of Complexity, Complicity and Complementarity: From the Nuremberg Trials to the Dawn of the New International Criminal Court' in Philippe Sands, *From Nuremberg to The Hague: The Future of International Criminal Justice* (CUP 2003) 64; Cryer (n 34) 145; Padraig McAuliffe, *Transitional Justice and Rule of Law Reconstruction* (Routledge 2013) 203.

question of when the ICC may proceed with a case to complement states' primary jurisdiction. While noting how the case law alters the balance of power in the ICC's favour, it also highlights tensions between the case law and the global governance goals of (positive) complementarity examined in Chapter 2.

4.1. The original aims

Although ideas of a permanent tribunal for international crimes date back to the nineteenth century, negotiations on the future ICC began in earnest after the Cold War.[145] In 1998, after several years of diplomatic negotiations, 148 delegations assembled in Rome finalized the legal framework of the ICC. The Rome Statute came into force in July 2002.

Given its potentially global jurisdiction, the ICC's relationship to states was one of the most important negotiation items. Unlike the ad hoc tribunals imposed by way of Chapter VII resolutions, a permanent tribunal based on a multilateral treaty required buy-in from consenting states. Already in 1990, one member of the International Law Commission (ILC) observed that 'the extent to which national sovereignty was affected by the establishment of a court would very much depend on whether the court was intended to replace, compete with or *complement* national jurisdiction'.[146] In language almost identical to the Rome Statute, the ILC's Second Draft Statute from 1994 stated that 'the court is intended to be complementary to national criminal justice systems'.[147] The seeds of a normative principle had been planted.

As negotiations on the Statute proceeded from 1994 to 1998, the 'ambiguous notion' of complementarity emerged as a rhetorical device for states with different ideas about the ICC.[148] As Kristina Miskowiak notes, complementarity functioned as 'an empty box in which one could put whatever one liked without having to reveal the intentions behind it'.[149] Over time, as delegations presented their views, the Statute's admissibility procedure became increasingly complex. While there is

[145] Christopher K Hall, 'The First Proposal for a Permanent International Criminal Court' (1998) 322 International Review of the Red Cross 57; Jo Stigen, *The Relationship between the International Criminal Court and National Jurisdictions: The Principle of Complementarity* (Martinus Nijhoff 2008) 35–39.

[146] Yearbook of the International Law Commission, Summary Records of the Meetings of the Forty Second Session (1990) vol 1, pt 1, A/CN.4/SER.A/1990/Add.1, para 36 (emphasis added).

[147] ILC Draft Statute 1994, preamble, see *Yearbook of International Law Commission* (1994) vol 2, pt 2, ACN.4/SER.A/1994/Add.1, 26–27.

[148] Kristina Miskowiak, *The International Criminal Court: Consent, Complementarity and Cooperation* (DJOF 2000) 45.

[149] ibid; see also Immi Tallgren, 'Completing the "International Criminal Order": The Rhetoric of International Repression and the Notion of Complementarity in the Draft Statute for an International Criminal Court' (1998) 67 Nordic Journal of International Law 107. But see Ryan Liss, 'The Coherence of Complementarity and the Structure of International Criminal Law' [2023 forthcoming].

no single original intent behind complementarity, several themes defined negotiations leading up to Rome.[150]

First, the ICC's regulation of *ne bis in idem* presaged a different approach to concurrent jurisdiction than at the ad hoc tribunals. Whereas early drafts mirrored the ICTY/R's rules, including the 'ordinary crimes' exception, some delegations worried that this solution, derived from primacy, created a hierarchy of crimes and gave the ICC too much leeway to assert jurisdiction at the expense of states. Ultimately, states may prosecute ordinary—as opposed to international—crimes, and this is not a reason for the ICC to assert jurisdiction at the expense of domestic courts.[151]

Second, while it was fairly uncontroversial that the ICC should defer to states parties prosecuting on the basis of territorial jurisdiction, it was less clear whether states parties with other jurisdictional titles (for instance, nationality or universal jurisdiction), or non-member states should be able to pre-empt the ICC's exercise of jurisdiction. Ultimately, delegations advocating an expansive vision of state priority prevailed and the ICC must defer to any state that wishes to prosecute.[152]

Third, despite its more deferential approach to domestic jurisdiction, the Rome Statute contained a major concession to the ICC: it was the Court's judges, not states, that had decision-making authority on admissibility. As noted by Miskowiak, 'it is a victory of great significance that the Rome Conference was able to adopt a provision to the effect that the [ICC] itself will be competent to determine when it has priority'.[153] Radical pro-sovereignty options failed, for instance ad hoc conferrals of jurisdiction or states deciding for themselves whether they were willing or able to genuinely prosecute.[154]

Fourth, despite late efforts impose primacy at the ICC,[155] a sensitive question was how the ICC would justify exercising jurisdiction at the expense of states. Early

[150] On the debates, see Fanny Benedetti, *Negotiating the International Criminal Court: New York to Rome, 1994–1998* (Martinus Nijhoff 2014) 166. Kleffner (n 7) 70–97; Stigen (n 145) 44–86.

[151] *Report of the Ad Hoc Committee on the Establishment of the ICC*, GAOR 50, supp 22, A/50/22, 1995 (Ad Hoc Report) para 43; *Report of the Preparatory Committee on the Establishment of the ICC, Proceedings of the Preparatory Committee during March–April and August 1996*, GAOR 51, supp 22, vol 1, A/51/22, 1996, para 171; John T Holmes, 'The Principle of Complementarity' in Roy S Lee (ed), *The International Criminal Court: The Making of the Rome Statute. Issues, Negotiations, Results* (Kluwer 1999) 57–58.

[152] Ad Hoc Report, paras 39–51. See Holmes (n 151) 61–62; Kleffner (n 7) 91. But see Britta Lisa Krings, 'The Principles of "Complementarity" and Universal Jurisdiction in International Criminal Law: Antagonists or Perfect Match?' (2012) 4 Goettingen Journal of International Law 737.

[153] See Miskowiak (n 148) 49.

[154] Line Engbo Gissel, 'Nomos and Narrative in International Criminal Justice' (2022) 20 Journal of International Criminal Justice 117; William A Schabas, *The International Criminal Court: A Commentary on the Rome Statute* (2nd edn, OUP 2016) 448; Kleffner (n 7) 84; John T Holmes, 'Complementarity: National Courts versus the ICC' in Antonio Cassese, Paola Gaeta, and John RWD Jones (eds), *The Rome Statute of the International Criminal Court: A Commentary* (OUP 2002) 672.

[155] See Chapter 2, section 2 in this volume. Sharon A Williams, 'Article 17: Issues of Admissibility' in Otto Triffterer (ed), *Commentary on the Rome Statute of the International Criminal Court: Observers' Notes, Article by Article* (1st edn, Nomos-Verl-Ges 1999) 385–93.

drafts allowed the ICC to intervene if national trial procedures were 'less preferable', 'ineffective', or 'not available'.[156] Over time, the words 'unwilling', 'unable', and 'genuine' emerged as compromise language that gave the admissibility assessment an objective flavour, protecting states from an interventionist court.[157]

Although many issues were not regulated expressly, for instance the ICC's relationship to transitional justice mechanisms, complementarity was a compromise between pro-sovereignty and internationalist visions of international criminal law. Its principal rationale, however, seems to have been limiting the ICC's powers vis-à-vis states. ICC intervention was understood as the exception, not the norm. As Markus Benzing observes, '[t]he most apparent underlying interest that the complementarity regime … is designed to protect and serve is the *sovereignty* both of State parties and third states'.[158] Yet, while the ICC's rules on concurrent jurisdiction appeared to foreshadow tense relations with states, the practice has been uneven.

4.2. An admissibility framework open to challenge

To operationalize the preamble, according to which it 'shall be complementary to national criminal jurisdictions',[159] article 17 provides that 'the Court shall determine that a case is inadmissible' under the following conditions:

> (a) The case is being investigated or prosecuted by a State which has jurisdiction over it, unless the State is unwilling or unable genuinely to carry out the investigation or prosecution;
>
> (b) The case has been investigated by a State which has jurisdiction over it and the State has decided not to prosecute the person concerned, unless the decision resulted from the unwillingness or inability of the State genuinely to prosecute;

[156] Report of the International Law Commission on the Work of Its Forty-Fifth Session (3 May–23 July 1993) A/48/10, 101; 1994 ILC Draft Statute, preamble, recital 3; Holmes (n 154) 670–71.

[157] On 'unable or unwilling genuinely', see Holmes (n 151) 48–51; Kleffner (n 7) 85–86; Holmes (n 154) 674–79.

[158] Markus Benzing, 'The Complementarity Regime of the International Criminal Court: International Criminal Justice between State Sovereignty and the Fight against Impunity' (2003) 7 Max Planck Yearbook of United Nations Law 591, 595 (emphasis in original); Holmes (n 151) 70–73; Lijun Yang, 'On the Principle of Complementarity in the Rome Statute of the International Criminal Court' (2005) 4 Chinese Journal of International Law 121, 122; Cassese (n 29) 343; Holmes (n 154) 668; Karolina Wierczyńska, *Przesłanki Dopuszczalności Wykonywania Jurysdykcji Przez Międzynarodowy Trybunał Karny* (Wydawnictwo Naukowe Scholar 2016) 265; Michael A Newton, 'The Complementarity Conundrum: Are We Watching Evolution or Evisceration?' (2010) 8 Santa Clara Journal of International Law 115, 115.

[159] Rome Statute, preamble, arts 1 and 17.

(c) The person concerned has already been tried for conduct which is the subject of the complaint, and a trial by the Court is not permitted under article 20, paragraph 3;

(d) The case is not of sufficient gravity to justify further action by the Court.

2. In order to determine unwillingness in a particular case, the Court shall consider, having regard to the principles of due process recognized by international law, whether one or more of the following exist, as applicable:

(a) The proceedings were or are being undertaken or the national decision was made for the purpose of shielding the person concerned from criminal responsibility for crimes within the jurisdiction of the Court referred to in article 5;

(b) There has been an unjustified delay in the proceedings which in the circumstances is inconsistent with an intent to bring the person concerned to justice;

(c) The proceedings were not or are not being conducted independently or impartially, and they were or are being conducted in a manner which, in the circumstances, is inconsistent with an intent to bring the person concerned to justice.

3. In order to determine inability in a particular case, the Court shall consider whether, due to a total or substantial collapse or unavailability of its national judicial system, the State is unable to obtain the accused or the necessary evidence and testimony or otherwise unable to carry out its proceedings.

Article 17 regulates case (in)admissibility (may the ICC exercise jurisdiction over a case?). However, the Statute also requires complementarity assessments of 'situations', comprising 'potential cases', before the OTP may launch an investigation and prosecute specific cases.[160] As will be seen in Chapters 4 and 7, situational complementarity became an important aspect of preliminary examinations, where the OTP assessed potential investigations and the prosecution of potential cases.

The Rome Statute's allocation of jurisdictional authority between states and the ICC can be summarized as follows: (1) states have jurisdictional priority over all suspects and all crimes, but (2) the ICC may assert jurisdiction if (3) a case is not insufficiently grave and (4) a state fails to exercise jurisdiction genuinely, due to either (5) its inability or (6) unwillingness. From the state's perspective, these rules acknowledge states' jurisdictional primacy and the ICC's subsidiarity (also known as a 'court of last resort'). From the ICC's perspective, the Statute recognizes its authority to complement states when they fail to exercise jurisdiction.[161] Contrary to

[160] ibid art 53(1); Ambos (n 45) 272–73 and 279; Rod Rastan, 'Situation and Case: Defining the Parameters' in Stahn and El Zeidy (n 12) 422–36. A doctrinal analysis of the Statute and the case law is beyond the scope of this book.

[161] Ambos (n 45) 268. The ICC has acknowledged states' primacy: AC, *Prosecutor v Germain Katanga & Matthieu Ngudjolo* (Judgment on the Appeal of Mr Germain Katanga against the Oral Decision of Trial Chamber II of 12 June 2009 on the Admissibility of the Case) ICC-01/04-01/07 OA 8 (25 September 2009) (*Katanga* Appeals Judgment) para 85. On 'court of last resort', see ASP, 'Report of the Bureau on Stocktaking: Complementarity. Taking Stock of the Principle of Complementarity: Bridging the Impunity Gap' (18 March 2010) ICC-ASP/8/51, para 2.

the ad hoc tribunals, where the prosecutor invoked primacy against states, complementarity can be invoked by states, defendants, or ICC judges, with articles 18 and 19 regulating the procedural aspects of such challenges.[162]

Although article 17 seems to revolve around the definitions of 'unable or unwilling' (U/U) that establish a conditionality scheme to justify the exercise of ICC jurisdiction, the first ten years have altered its normative content. Three issues deserve emphasis. First, instead of contesting ICC jurisdiction, states have invited the prosecutor to intervene through 'self-referrals', inverting the assumptions that guided the pre-Rome negotiations. Second, complementarity is seen increasingly as an element of prosecutorial discretion, whereas judicial review of admissibility is considered optional unless states affirmatively lodge challenges. Third, ICC organs have put forward purposive and strict constructions of article 17 to augment their discretion, with U/U becoming something of a dead letter.

4.3. Avoiding conflict: self-referrals and uncontested admissibility

As an admissibility rule, complementarity regulates the narrow legal question of whether the ICC may proceed to investigate and prosecute a specific case. However, as noted in Chapter 2, complementarity qua global governance relies on the ICC's 'shadow effect', where the mere threat of international intervention influences state behaviour. As Rob Cryer observes:[163]

> The outcome of complementarity is that if the Prosecutor becomes interested in a situation subject to the jurisdiction of the ICC, then although he cannot force the parties to prosecute any offenders, steps can be taken to prompt the relevant States into taking action. This is because States, particularly in relation to offences by their nationals, are more likely to prefer to investigate at the national level, rather than have an investigation proceeded with in public by an independent international investigator ... Important in this regard are the powers of the ICC not only to *embarrass States severely by determining them to be unwilling or unable to prosecute, but also to prosecute offences committed by their nationals ... in a very public forum.*

[162] Rome Statute, arts 18–19; ICC RPE, rr 51–62.

[163] Cryer (n 34) 164 (emphasis added); William Burke-White, 'The Domestic Influence of International Criminal Tribunals: The International Criminal Tribunal for the Former Yugoslavia and the Creation of the State Court of Bosnia & Herzegovina' (2008) 46 Columbia Journal of Transnational Law 279, 308. But see Sarah MH Nouwen, *Complementarity in the Line of Fire: The Catalysing Effect of the International Criminal Court in Uganda and Sudan* (CUP 2013) 104–09.

Greenawalt notes further that 'applying the complementarity standard ... means that, in many cases, it is a state's justice system that is on trial and not just the individual accused'.[164]

However, when states began self-referring situations in their own territories to the ICC, the core assumption underpinning complementarity's shadow effect, namely that states would contest international jurisdiction to prevent being labelled 'unwilling or unable' to provide 'genuine' accountability, was called into question.[165] From 2004 to 2006, governments in Uganda, the DRC, and CAR invited ICC intervention, and the pace of self-referrals has remained high ever since, with Mali, Côte d'Ivoire, Gabon, Palestine, and Venezuela all proactively triggering the ICC's jurisdiction.

Self-referrals had a major impact not only on the ICC's first two decades of trials, most of which stem from self-referring countries, but also on the article 17 case law. Where governments actively invite the ICC to exercise jurisdiction, and thereby implicitly concede unwillingness or inability to genuinely prosecute, it may seem superfluous to assess complementarity. Accordingly, some argue that self-referrals amount to complementarity 'waivers', or that states should be 'estopped' from withdrawing a referral and contesting ICC jurisdiction.[166] Although ICC judges have rejected the suggestion that self-referrals obviate the need to litigate case admissibility, the case law is shaped by interpretations based on consensual exercises of jurisdiction that are not easily transferrable to instances of contested jurisdiction.[167] An enduring side effect of this case law is that article 17, a provision originally premised on *contesting* rather than *conceding* international jurisdiction, is now filtered through the doctrine of 'inactivity' and associated concepts.

4.4. From conditionality (unable or unwilling) to consensuality (inactivity)

Although observers believed that the ICC's future hinged on its relationship to states as epitomized by complementarity's U/U standard,[168] ICC organs have

[164] Alexander Greenawalt, 'Admissibility as a Theory of International Criminal Law' in Margaret deGuzman and Valerie Oosterveld (eds), *Elgar Companion to the International Criminal Court* (Edward Elgar 2020) 63.

[165] On trigger mechanisms and the controversies surrounding self-referrals, see Chapter 2, section 3 in this volume.

[166] El Zeidy (n 42) 211–22; William Burke-White and Scott Kaplan, 'Shaping the Contours of Domestic Justice: The International Criminal Court and an Admissibility Challenge in the Uganda Situation' (2009) 7 Journal of International Criminal Justice 257, 261–62, and 276; Claus Kress, '"Self-Referrals" and "Waivers of Complementarity": Some Considerations in Law and Policy' (2004) 2 Journal of International Criminal Justice 944.

[167] *Katanga* Appeals Judgment, para 85.

[168] Holmes (n 154) 672–78; Dan Sarooshi, 'Prosecutorial Policy and the ICC: Prosecutor's Proprio Motu Action or Self-Denial?' (2004) 2 Journal of International Criminal Justice 940, 912; Paolo Benvenuti, 'The Complementarity of the International Criminal Court to National Criminal

recalibrated concurrent jurisdiction in favour of uncontested international discretion.[169] As noted in Chapter 2, reinventing complementarity began at the OTP, which argued in 2003 that 'there is no need to examine ... unwillingness or inability' if a state remains inactive.[170] Few appreciated the significance of this argument at the time, but it revolutionized the exercise of concurrent jurisdiction.

The logic behind 'inaction' lies in the language of article 17, which conditions admissibility on cases '*being* investigated or prosecuted' or cases that '*have been* investigated or prosecuted'.[171] This formulation seems to leave a gap: what happens before a state begins an investigation and there is (still) no case? Based on a formalistic reading of this provision, the OTP suggested and chambers validated the argument that, in the absence of a state investigation, article 17's U/U test is inapplicable in its entirety and all ICC cases are *ipso facto* admissible, without any further inquiry into why a state has failed to exercise its jurisdiction.

It is no coincidence that this interpretation of complementarity emerged in the context of self-referrals, where states like the DRC and Uganda invited the ICC into their territories and the OTP selected cases over which states were eager not to exercise jurisdiction. This nominally positivist reading of article 17 had immense policy ramifications. In such cases, it was convenient for both the inviting state and the OTP not to dwell on article 17's U/U scheme focused on the reasons for states' failure to prosecute. Inaction allowed the ICC to proceed without labelling 'cooperative' states 'unwilling or unable' or challenging domestic proceedings for a lack of 'genuineness'. Not only did state 'inaction' accelerate the OTP's work by incentivizing agreements with states on the prosecution of specific perpetrators, it also facilitated the work of chambers, who could ignore state motives for failing to prosecute without carrying out qualitative sociolegal assessments of domestic justice.

To date, inactivity has served as the admissibility rationale for every single case prosecuted before the ICC, beginning with its first case against Thomas Lubanga. At the time of his transfer to The Hague, Lubanga was in detention on domestic

Jurisdictions' in Flavia Lattanzi and William Schabas (eds), *Essays on the Rome Statute of the International Criminal Court*, vol 1 (Il Sirente 1999) 43; Zahar and Sluiter (n 49) 489. While the shorthand 'U/U' is used in this chapter, it encompasses 'genuineness'. The point is that under 'unable or unwilling genuinely' the ICC must perform a *qualitative* assessment of domestic justice. The majority view is that the condition for the exercise of ICC jurisdiction is the 'genuineness' of a state's exercise of jurisdiction, rather than 'unwillingness or inability' as such (O'Keefe (n 97) 555–60); Rod Jensen, 'Complementarity, "Genuinely" and Article 17: Assessing the Boundaries of an Effective ICC' in Jann K Kleffner and Gerben Kor (eds), *Complementary Views on Complementarity* (TMC Asser Press 2006). But see Diane Bernard, 'Beyond Hierarchy: Standard of Review and the Complementarity of the International Criminal Court' in Lukasz Gruszczynski and Wouter Werner (eds), *Deference in International Courts and Tribunals: Standards of Review and Margin of Appreciation* (OUP 2014) 375.

169 Yuval Shany, 'Jurisdiction and Admissibility' in Cesare Romano, Karen Alter, and Yuval Shany (eds), *The Oxford Handbook of International Adjudication* (OUP 2014) 799–800.

170 ICC–OTP, 'Informal Expert Paper. The Principle of Complementarity in Practice' (2003) 7.

171 Article 17(1)(a)–(b) (emphasis added).

charges of international crimes.[172] Yet, despite its domestic case, the Congolese government consented to Lubanga's prosecution in The Hague pursuant to a request from the first ICC prosecutor. When called upon to assess the (in)admissibility of Lubanga's case before the ICC, chambers struggled with article 17. Acknowledging doubts about the DRC's 'inability' to prosecute Lubanga, the judges pointed out that that there were ongoing national proceedings and that the court system in Ituri had undergone reform.[173] Nevertheless, the judges decided that the DRC's 'inability', as defined in article 17, was immaterial because domestic charges of genocide and crimes against humanity did not include the OTP's war crime charge of enlisting and using child soldiers and, therefore, the 'DRC cannot be considered to be acting in relation to the specific case before the [ICC]'.[174] Put differently, as the DRC was 'inactive' in relation to the ICC's child soldier case, it no longer mattered whether the DRC was 'unable' or 'unwilling' to 'genuinely' prosecute Lubanga on other charges.

In complementarity jurisprudence, state 'inaction' emerged as an ingenious sleight of hand to ignore the U/U scheme. While the judges in *Lubanga* still expressed hesitation, noting that the separation between inaction and U/U was an '[i]nterpretation *a contrario* of Article 17',[175] the ICC has since doubled down on the two prongs of admissibility. According to the Appeals Chamber in *Katanga*:[176]

> [I]n considering whether a case is inadmissible under article 17 … the initial questions to ask are (1) whether there are ongoing investigations or prosecutions, or (2) whether there have been investigations in the past, and the State having jurisdiction has decided not to prosecute the person concerned. It is only when the answers to these questions are in the affirmative that one has to look to the second halves of sub-paragraphs (a) and (b) and to examine the question of unwillingness and inability. To do otherwise would be to put the cart before the horse. It follows that in case of inaction, the question of unwillingness or inability does not arise; inaction on the part of a State having jurisdiction (that is, the fact that a State is not investigating or prosecuting, or has not done so) renders a case admissible.

As a two-step admissibility test, complementarity asks first whether a state is active. If not, an ICC case is automatically admissible. Only if a state has initiated or concluded proceedings can one examine 'unwillingness' or 'inability' to 'genuinely' investigate or prosecute.

[172] PTC, *Prosecutor v Lubanga* (Decision on the Prosecutor's Application for a Warrant of Arrest) ICC-01/04-01/06-08 (10 February 2006) (*Lubanga* Warrant) para 33–34.

[173] ibid para 36.

[174] ibid para 39.

[175] ibid para 29, fn 19.

[176] *Katanga* Appeals Judgment, para 78. For a detailed analysis, see Ben Batros, 'The Evolution of the ICC Jurisprudence on Admissibility' in Stahn and El Zeidy (n 12).

Reaffirmed repeatedly since then, the two-step complementarity test is now considered 'the correct',[177] 'black and white text',[178] 'unambiguous'[179] reading of article 17. Yet alternative interpretations were and remain possible. In *Katanga*, the Trial Chamber explored a teleological reading of 'unwillingness' under article 17(2), including a state declining to exercise its domestic jurisdiction and complying with its duty to prosecute by facilitating an international trial.[180] The OTP has conspicuously ignored the 'inaction' test in preliminary examinations and applied complementarity 'prospectively', sometimes for years, to give states time to develop their ability or willingness and launch genuine domestic proceedings.[181] An alternative contextual reading is that not only a state's decision to drop,[182] but also its failure to begin, an investigation or prosecution could be treated as prima facie evidence of obstructing justice or inability, which chambers may ask states to rebut through consultations.[183]

Jurisprudential debates notwithstanding, the upshot of the 'inactivity' doctrine is that, while volumes of ink have been spilled parsing the terms 'unwilling', 'unable', and 'genuine', these and other terms that require a qualitative sociolegal appreciation of national proceedings have played little role in the case law. ICC judges have only found cases admissible for reasons other than the U/U scheme.

Even in cases like *Gaddafi*, where Libya's 'inability' to arrest was an important feature of admissibility litigation, the case was ultimately declared admissible due to Libya's 'inactivity' in regard to the ICC's case.[184] Similarly, ICC judges are reluctant to interpret the term 'unwilling genuinely' expansively to challenge states' primacy to prosecute serious crimes. As confirmed in *Al-Senussi*, the ICC is unlikely to exercise jurisdiction in lieu of a state that fails to provide a fair trial because 'unwilling genuinely' only comes into play if national proceedings 'lead to a suspect evading justice ... in the equivalent of sham proceedings that are concerned

[177] Darryl Robinson, 'Comments on Chapter 4' in Kleffner and Kor (n 168) 141 (in relation to Claudia C Aravena, 'The Admissibility Test before the International Criminal Court under Special Consideration of Amnesties and Truth Commission' in Kleffner and Kor (n 168)).

[178] Darryl Robinson, 'The Mysterious Mysteriousness of Complementarity' (2010) 21 Criminal Law Forum 67, 68.

[179] ibid. Critically, see William A Schabas, 'The Rise and Fall of Complementarity' in Stahn and El Zeidy (n 12) 158–61.

[180] TC, *Prosecutor v Germain Katanga and Mathieu Ngudjolo* (Reasons for the Oral Decision on the Motion Challenging the Admissibility of the Case) ICC-01/04-01/07-1213-tENG (16 June 2009) (Katanga oral Decision) paras 74–81.

[181] Independent Expert Review of the ICC and the Rome Statute System, 'Final Report' (2020), para 724.

[182] Article 17(1)(b). But see *Katanga* Appeals Judgment, paras 80, 82–83.

[183] Patryk I Labuda, 'Relational Complementarity (Working Paper)'. For textual counter-arguments, see Robinson (n 178).

[184] AC, *Prosecutor v Saif Al-Islam Gaddafi and Abdullah Al-Senussi* (Judgment on the Appeal of Libya against the Decision of Pre-Trial Chamber I of 31 May 2013 entitled 'Decision on the Admissibility of the Case against Saif Al-Islam Gaddafi') ICC-01/11-01/11-547-Red (21 May 2014) (AC *Gaddafi*) paras 212–14. Inability similarly featured in *dicta* in Jean Pierre-Bemba's admissibility proceedings.

with that person's protection'.[185] By contrast, domestic convictions, including after an unfair trial, are—absent exceptional circumstances—unlikely to ever be 'inconsistent with an intent to bring the person concerned to justice'.[186] As argued by the Appeals Chamber, '[the ICC] was not established to be an international court of human rights, sitting in judgment over domestic legal systems to ensure that they are compliant with international standards of human rights'.[187]

Put differently, on the rare occasions the ICC had an opportunity to weigh in on the scope of 'unwilling genuinely' by interrogating the quality of domestic proceedings, the judges severed ICC oversight of national trials from fair trial considerations. In doing so, the judges also reduced the OTP's ability to challenge states over, and thereby influence, the fairness of domestic prosecutions. As a result, somewhat extraordinarily, while state obstructionism remains a primary obstacle to accountability, no case has ever been found admissible due to a state's unwillingness or inability to genuinely prosecute twenty years after the Rome Statute's entry into force.

Equally important, while 'inaction' is presented as a logical consequence of statutory interpretation, this approach to case admissibility has the policy benefit of allowing ICC organs to eschew conflict over politically sensitive domestic standards and validate the OTP's case selection on the basis of facially neutral constructions not codified in the Rome Statute, in particular the progeny of the 'inaction' doctrine: the 'same person, same conduct' standard.

4.5. Consolidating international supremacy: 'same case, same conduct'

Despite article 17's discursive emphasis on U/U, complementarity jurisprudence turns on a different—'same person, same conduct'—test for determining 'whether the case that the State is investigating sufficiently mirrors the one that the Prosecutor is investigating'.[188] The main consequence is to reverse the object

[185] AC, *Prosecutor v Saif Al-Islam Gaddafi and Abdullah Al-Senussi* (Judgment on the Appeal of Mr Abdullah Al-Senussi against the Decision of Pre-Trial Chamber I of 11 October 2013 entitled 'Decision on the Admissibility of the Case against Abdullah Al-Senussi') ICC-01/11-01/11-565 (24 July 2014) (AC *Senussi*) para 230.

[186] ibid; see also PTC, *Prosecutor v Saif Al-Islam Gaddafi and Abdullah Al-Senussi* (Decision on the Admissibility of the Case against Abdullah Al-Senussi, ICC-01/11-01/11-466-Red (11 October 2013) (PTC *Senussi*). On complementarity and fair trial, see Kevin J Heller, 'The Shadow Side of Complementarity: The Effect of Article 17 of the Rome Statute on National Due Process' (2007) 17 Criminal Law Forum 255; Elinor Fry, 'Between Show Trials and Sham Prosecutions: The Rome Statute's Potential Effect on Domestic Due Process Protections' (2012) 23 Criminal Law Forum 35; F Mégret and M Giles Samson, 'Holding the Line on Complementarity in Libya: The Case for Tolerating Flawed Domestic Trials' (2013) 11 Journal of International Criminal Justice 571; Hugo J van der Merwe, 'The Show Must Not Go On: Complementarity, the Due Process Thesis and Overzealous Domestic Prosecutions' (2015) 15 International Criminal Law Review 40.

[187] AC *Senussi*, para 219. Critically on this, see Chapter 7, section 4.3 in this volume.

[188] AC *Gaddafi*, paras 2 and 73.

of complementarity assessments from state behaviour to ICC charging preferences: instead of focusing on whether states are capable and willing to genuinely hold perpetrators accountable, admissibility litigation begins and usually ends with an examination of the parameters of the prosecutor's case.

How did OTP charging policy come to displace state behaviour as the core complementarity question? Although it lacks support in the Rome Statute's drafting history, the 'same case' test is again derived from a textual reading of article 17.[189] Beginning with *Lubanga*, most ICC suspects have been subject to some form of domestic criminal process, which precludes findings of state inactivity as such. However, it remains to be decided what the scope of the 'case' is, and as long as the domestic and international cases do not overlap, the state may still be found inactive with respect to part of the case. As argued by chambers in *Lubanga*, 'it is a condition *sine qua non* for a case ... to be inadmissible that national proceedings encompass both the person and the conduct which is the subject of the case before the [ICC]'.[190]

While the same-person prong is less controversial—it is generally accepted that states should prosecute the same perpetrators as the ICC to prevent ICC cases from being admissible[191]—the specific conduct that the same perpetrator must be charged with raises more questions. To make an ICC case inadmissible, must a state prosecute the same suspect as the ICC for all—or, crucially, only some—of the crimes that the OTP wants to charge them with? The stakes are high because if a state is required but fails to prosecute the exact same case, the inactivity doctrine implies that the state is inactive in relation to part of the ICC's case, and no analysis of whether a state is willing or able genuinely to prosecute its case is necessary. In other words, 'inactivity' combined with the 'same case' test reverses the balance of power between states and the ICC by making the parameters of international case selection—rather than state behaviour—the decisive factor in whether cases are admissible or not.

The degree of 'sameness' between ICC and national proceedings has driven most litigation to date, with Kenya and Libya arguing that '[t]here simply must be a leaway [*sic*] in the exercise of discretion in the application of the principle of complementarity',[192] and that a state should be allowed 'a margin of appreciation in determining the parameters of its domestic investigation thereby encouraging

[189] In this sense, see Gideon Boas and others, *International Criminal Procedure* (CUP 2011), 74–75.

[190] *Lubanga* Warrant, paras 31 (and 37).

[191] But see Kevin J Heller, 'Radical Complementarity' (2016) 14 Journal of International Criminal Justice 637, 640–44; PTC, *Prosecutor v William Ruto, Henry Kosgei & Joshua Sang* (Application on Behalf of the Government of the Republic of Kenya Pursuant to Article 19 of the ICC Statute) ICC-01/09-01/11 and ICC-01/09-02/11 (31 March 2011) para 32.

[192] *Prosecutor v Francis Muthaura, Uhuru Kenyatta and Mohammed Ali*, Corrigendum to the 'Document in Support of the "Appeal of the Government of Kenya against the Decision on the Application by the Government of Kenya Challenging the Admissibility of the Case Pursuant to Article 19(2)(b) of the Statute'" ICC-01/09-02/11 (21 June 2011) para 43.

national accountability and local ownership of the judicial process'.[193] Yet, as even critics acknowledge, a textual reading of the Statute seems to require that ICC and domestic cases be the same.[194]

Illustrating the policy-driven logic of case admissibility, after the early case law adopted a requirement of near absolute sameness, ICC judges began showing some understanding for state prosecution preferences in the Libya cases. In *Gaddafi*, chambers clarified that 'a domestic investigation or prosecution for "ordinary crimes", to the extent that the case covers the same conduct, shall be considered sufficient' and hence 'Libya's current lack of legislation criminalising crimes against humanity does not per se render the case admissible'.[195] Accordingly, a state may, for example, charge murder—as opposed to the crime against humanity of murder—to forestall an ICC case against the same suspect. While this put to rest the most expansive pro-ICC interpretations, requiring *identical* domestic charges (and imposing an implicit duty to domesticate international crimes), as defined in the Rome Statute, it still left open what specific conduct a state must address to avoid breaching the 'same case' test, and, consequently, a finding of 'inactivity' in relation to the OTP's case. After *narrowing* the 'same conduct' test to 'same incidents' in *Katanga* and other cases,[196] different judicial panels in cases from Kenya, Libya, and Côte d'Ivoire broadened the 'same conduct' standard to '*substantially* the same conduct'.[197] The qualifier 'substantially' nominally increased states' margin of appreciation in tailoring their domestic cases, but disagreement persists in jurisprudence and scholarship as to the degree to which national proceedings should 'mirror' an ICC case, with 'soft' and 'hard' mirror theses echoing three theories—charge, sentence, and process—to assess domestic proceedings.[198]

Although scholarly critique focuses on the 'same conduct' prong of the same-case test, other aspects of the case law privilege OTP discretion over domestic

[193] Application on Behalf of the Government of Libya relating to Abdullah Al-Senussi pursuant to Article 19 of the ICC Statute, ICC-01/11-01/11 (2 April 2013) para 43.

[194] Heller (n 191); Rod Rastan, 'What Is "Substantially the Same Conduct"?' (2017) 15 Journal of International Criminal Justice 1.

[195] PTC, *Prosecutor v Saif Al-Islam Gaddafi and Abdullah Al-Senussi* (Public Redacted Decision on the Admissibility of the Case against Saif Al-Islam Gaddafi) ICC-01/11-01/11-344-Red (31 May 2013) (PTC *Gaddafi*) para 88.

[196] *Katanga* Appeals Judgment; PTC, *Prosecutor v Laurent Gbagbo* (Decision on the Prosecutor's Application Pursuant to Article 58 for a Warrant of Arrest against Laurent Koudou Gbagbo) ICC-02/11-01/11 (30 November 2011) para 10.

[197] AC, *Prosecutor v William Ruto, Henry Kosgei & Joshua Sang* (Judgment on the Appeal of the Republic on Kenya Against the Decision of Pre-Trial Chamber II of 30 May 2011 entitled 'Decision on the Application by the Government of Kenya Challenging the Admissibility of the Case Pursuant to Article 19(2)(b) of the Statute') ICC-01/09-02/11-274 (30 August 2011) paras 40 and 47; PTC, *Prosecutor v Simone Gbagbo* (Public Redacted Version of Decision on Côte d'Ivoire's Challenge to the Admissibility of the Case against Simone Gbagbo) ICC-02/11-01/12-47-Red (11 December 2014) (PTC *S. Gbagbo* Decision) para 32; AC *Gaddafi*, paras 63–84; PTC *Al-Senussi*, para 79.

[198] Darryl Robinson, 'Three Theories of Complementarity: Charge, Sentence, or Process?' (2012) 53 Harvard International Law Journal Online 65; Kevin J Heller, 'A Sentence-Based Theory of Complementarity' (2012) 53 Harvard International Law Journal 202, 241.

charging policy as the benchmark for case admissibility. Notably, ICC judges have maintained that complementarity hinges on the conduct being investigated 'at the time' of the admissibility decision, which strongly implies that ICC organs need not wait for domestic investigations to unfold.[199] Equally important, ICC judges have stopped assessing admissibility *proprio motu,* implying that complementarity is an optional feature that states must actively contest for it to be a justiciable matter (in turn, raising questions as to the relevance of defence challenges under article 19).[200] Most significantly, not only must states actively challenge admissibility, they also bear 'the burden of proof to show that the case is inadmissible',[201] and to 'discharge that burden', states must show 'specific investigative steps', such as 'interviewing witnesses or suspects, collecting documentary evidence, or carrying out forensic analyses'.[202]

The last argument is particularly problematic and illustrates the stakes of the case law. By requiring states to show progress in investigating and prosecuting cases, the judges essentially reintroduce the U/U scheme through the backdoor and cloak qualitative appraisals of domestic prosecutorial efforts in the technical language of 'inactivity'. In reality, the rigid formalities of 'inactivity' and 'same case' allow both chambers and the OTP to enact their policy preferences with regard to surrendering (*Senussi*) or maintaining (all other cases) suspects on the ICC case docket, while avoiding article 17 conditionality and evaluating the quality of parallel domestic accountability efforts.

By the same token, chambers and the OTP have shown no interest in state and defence requests to share evidence or information to facilitate domestic trials in accordance with positive complementarity. Under article 93(10), 'the [ICC] may, upon request, cooperate with and provide assistance to a State Party conducting an investigation into or trial in respect of conduct which constitutes a [Rome Statute] crime'.[203] Yet judges have rejected such requests in several proceedings, arguing that support for domestic accountability is a policy and aspirational goal not required by the Rome Statute.[204]

[199] *Katanga* Appeals Judgment, para 56; AC, *Prosecutor v Francis Muthaura, Uhuru Kenyatta and Mohammed Ali* (Judgment on the Appeal of the Republic of Kenya against the Decision of Pre-Trial Chamber II of 30 May 2011 entitled 'Decision on the Application by the Government of Kenya Challenging the Admissibility of the Case Pursuant to Article 19(2)(b) of the Statute') ICC-01/09-02/11 OA (30 August 2011) (*Kenyatta* Appeals Judgment).

[200] *Lubanga* Warrant; PTC, *Prosecutor v Germain Katanga* (Decision on the Evidence and Information Provided by the Prosecution for the Issuance of a Warrant of Arrest for German Katanga) ICC-01/04-01/07-4 (6 July 2007); PTC, *The Prosecutor v Ahmad Harun and Ali Abd-Al-Rahman* (Decision on the Prosecution Application under Article 58(7) of the Statute) ICC-02/05-01/07-I-Corr (27 April 2007).

[201] *Kenyatta* Appeals Judgment, para 61.

[202] ibid paras 61 and 40; PTC S. *Gbagbo*, para 35.

[203] Rome Statute, art 93(10).

[204] TC, *Prosecutor v Germain Katanga and Mathieu Ngudjolo Chui* (Public Redacted Version of 19 March 2009, Prosecution Response to Motion Challenging the Admissibility of the Case by the Defence of Germain Katanga, pursuant to Article 19(2)(a)) ICC-01/04-01/07 (30 March 2009) paras 100–01; TC, *Prosecutor v Francis Muthaura, Uhuru Kenyatta and Mohammed Ali* (Decision on the Application

4.6. Importing a restrictive mandate through gravity

Admissibility at the ICC is sometimes equated with complementarity. In fact, under article 17, cases 'not of sufficient gravity' are also inadmissible.[205] Put differently, while states may prosecute less grave crimes, the ICC must focus on grave crimes.

The general idea behind gravity, that the ICC should not handle 'insignificant' situations and cases, is unimpeachable. However, agreement on what is 'grave enough' to merit the ICC's attention is contentious. Chambers have proposed different criteria to assess gravity, including 'quantitative and qualitative' elements related to the scale, nature, manner of commission of crimes; the impact on victims, and aggravating circumstances.[206] Similarly, the OTP has adopted policies to reduce criticism that gravity appraisals are too subjective—with limited success. As noted by deGuzman, 'although ... [international] prosecutors and judges, have sought to explain gravity in qualitative as well as quantitative terms, their efforts have failed to yield an understanding of the term sufficient to bolster the legitimacy of their decisions'.[207]

ICC organs sometimes suggest that the ICC's mandate is to prosecute those 'most responsible'. In fact, defendants' degree of seniority or responsibility is not—unlike the SCSL's 'greatest responsibility' clause—expressly mentioned in the Rome Statute.[208] While not a function of personal jurisdiction as such, perpetrators' degree of responsibility has featured in gravity assessments. In its policies, the OTP has suggested that charges target those bearing 'greatest responsibility' or those 'most responsible' (the wording has fluctuated), while keeping open the possibility of cases against mid- and low-level perpetrators.[209] For instance, according to the OTP's 2016 Case Selection policy, 'most responsible does not necessarily equate with the *de jure* hierarchical status of an individual within a structure, but will be

by the Government of Kenya Challenging the Admissibility of the Case pursuant to Article 19(2)(b) of the Statute) ICC-01/09-02/11-96 (30 May 2011) paras 28–31.

[205] Rome Statute, art 17(1)(d). For the drafting history, see William A Schabas, *An Introduction to the International Criminal Court* (4th edn, CUP 2011) 200. As with complementarity, article 17 nominally requires gravity assessments of cases only, but in fact the gravity of situations must also be evaluated (Ambos (n 45) 284–85).

[206] PTC, *Decision Pursuant to Article 15 of the Rome Statute on the Authorization of an Investigation into the Situation in the Republic of Kenya*, ICC-01/09-19 (31 March 2010) para 62; ICC–OTP, 'Policy Paper on Preliminary Examinations' (2013) paras 59–66; ICC–OTP, 'Policy Paper on Case Selection and Prioritisation' (2016) para 32; ICC–OTP, 'Regulations of the Office of the Prosecutor, ICC-BD/05-01-09' (2009), reg 29(2).

[207] Margaret M deGuzman, *Shocking the Conscience of Humanity: Gravity and the Legitimacy of International Criminal Law* (OUP 2020) 2.

[208] See Reydams and Odermatt (n 96) 110.

[209] ICC–OTP, 'Report on Prosecutorial Strategy' (14 September 2006) 5; ICC–OTP, 'Prosecutorial Strategy 2009–2012' (2010) para 19; ICC–OTP, 'Strategic Plan June 2012–2015' (2013) para 4a; ICC–OTP, 'Strategic Plan 2016–2018' (2015) 5 and 9; ICC–OTP, 'Strategic Plan 2019–2021' (2019) paras 5 and 24.

assessed on a case-by-case basis ... on the basis of, *inter alia*, the nature of the unlawful behaviour; the degree of their participation and intent; the existence of any motive involving discrimination; and any abuse of power or official capacity'.[210]

However, as with perpetrator status at the SCSL, the value of importing this criterion into the ICC's admissibility framework remains uncertain. To date, no case has ever been dismissed because of insufficient gravity, including a perpetrator's insufficient degree of responsibility. In *Ntaganda* the Appeals Chamber rejected the argument that 'any perpetrators other than those at the very top are automatically excluded from the exercise of the jurisdiction of the [ICC]'.[211] A similar challenge failed in *Al Hassan*.[212] In other words, international trials of low- and mid-level defendants do not make cases 'insufficiently grave' and, hence, inadmissible before the ICC.[213]

The effects of the OTP's policy on perpetrator status for state prosecutorial choices are rarely considered. For instance, Kai Ambos and Ignaz Stegmiller argue that 'the ICC Prosecutor mainly selects the persons from the top of the (state) hierarchy for his cases' while '[o]thers are left to national criminal justice systems, encouraging territorial and third states to take measures against those offenders and to close the impunity gap'.[214] But, as will be seen in Chapter 4, there is little evidence of coordination between the ICC and states based on perpetrator seniority. In fact, the 2020 Independent Expert Review confirmed suspicions that ICC case selection—despite prosecutorial claims to the contrary—is guided mainly by opportunism rather than any division of labour with states.[215]

4.7. Plausible deniability: from conditional admissibility to consensual and targeted quasi-primacy

The ICC's regulation of concurrent jurisdiction broke with the institutional design of earlier ICTs. Under the Rome Statute, states have priority over international crimes while international trials perform a backstop function. Circumscribed by

[210] ICC–OTP, 'Case Selection and Prioritisation' (n 206) para 43.

[211] AC, *Judgment on the Prosecutor's Appeal against the Decision of Pre-Trial Chamber I entitled 'Decision on the Prosecutor's Application for Warrants of Arrest, Article 58'* ICC-01/04-169 (18 July 2006) para 75.

[212] AC, *Prosecutor v Al Hassan* (Judgment on the Appeal of Mr Al Hassan against the Decision of Pre-Trial Chamber entitled 'Décision relative à l'exception d'irrecevabilité pour insuffisance de gravité de l'affaire soulevée par la défense) ICC-01/12-01/18-601-Red (19 February 2020).

[213] Given the ICC's problems, support seems to be growing for trials of lower-level suspects. See Ward Ferdinandusse and Alex Whiting, 'Prosecute Little Fish at the ICC' (2022) 19 Journal of International Criminal Justice 759.

[214] Kai Ambos and Ignaz Stegmiller, 'Prosecuting International Crimes at the International Criminal Court: Is There a Coherent and Comprehensive Prosecution Strategy?' (2013) 59 Crime, Law and Social Change 415, 418.

[215] See Chapter 7 in this volume.

an admissibility procedure, the exercise of ICC jurisdiction was to be reserved for narrow circumstances. As noted by William Schabas, complementarity was 'very much the contrary of the scheme established for the *ad hoc* tribunals'.[216]

The practice of complementarity has upended assumptions about the ICC's relationship to states. First, self-referrals have incentivized accommodationist practices, whereby the OTP and states agree to consensually distribute cases. ICC trials have all resulted from uncontested admissibility (even when, as in *Katanga*, defendants launch challenges), premised on the 'inactivity' doctrine, rather than arrests against the wishes of territorial states or contested admissibility based on states' inability or willingness to genuinely prosecute. As will be seen in Chapter 4, while this *modus operandi* enhances state cooperation and allows international trials to proceed with fewer obstacles, it has produced a short-term opportunistic case selection and an imbalanced case docket, with international cases limited to deposed state or non-state actors.

Second, in developing a jurisprudence that all but ignores article 17's carefully drafted conditions, ICC judges have unilaterally recalibrated the Rome Statute's jurisdictional equilibrium in their favour. It is the decision-making power to draw lines around cases ('same case') that defines complementarity rather than the parameters of state behaviour ('inability', 'unwillingness', and 'genuineness'). Yet this ICC-centric case law is in tension with the global governance ideals of positive complementarity. On one hand, ICC judges argue that there is very little space for domestic accountability considerations in deciding case admissibility; on the other, as will be seen in Chapter 4, the OTP applies complementarity prospectively in preliminary examinations to enable states to develop 'capacity' and 'willingness' before deciding whether to open investigations, thereby contradicting the 'inactivity' and 'same case' tests and generating backlash from some ICC stakeholders.

Third, similar to the ICTR, ICC judges have embraced conflict-avoidance interpretive techniques to eschew politically sensitive issues of domestic capacity (inability), political will (unwillingness), and fair trial standards (genuineness). Instead of analysing why states fail to ensure justice in specific cases, admissibility is subordinated to the parameters of prosecutorial charging (same case). Criticism has focused on how the 'same conduct' standard may be too narrow and intrude on state sovereignty but equally problematic is that international trials proceed at the expense of holistic sociolegal analyses of the respective merits of international and domestic accountability processes. By focusing on technical distinctions between domestic and international proceedings, ICC judges refrain from evaluating states' good faith but, in doing so, they unwittingly sanitize domestic accountability processes while denying legitimacy to international trials.

[216] Schabas (n 205) 191.

In the end, despite the Rome Statute's apparent emphasis on state-driven accountability, the ICC has yet to witness a jurisprudential shift towards prioritizing and evaluating domestic trials, akin to the ICTR/Y's rule 11*bis* case law. ICC officials publicly claim that states are the first line of defence while the ICC serves as a 'court of last resort' and a 'catalyst for compliance', but the dissonance between the article 17 case law, which privileges international trials based on technical line-drawing and the ICC's limited attention to domestic accountability processes has generated a range of critiques.[217] Most significantly, the ICC-centric jurisprudence, which focuses on the parameters of international case selection while implying that the conditions of domestic accountability are an aspirational but non-binding goal in the Rome Statute, seems based on an artificial dichotomy between the judge-made law of admissibility (complementarity) and prosecutorial policy on positive complementarity.

This dichotomy is unpersuasive insofar as admissibility decisions are ultimately always policy-driven. As Shany observes, 'rules on admissibility provide international courts with important policy tools that mediate between their legal powers, their institutional goals, and the prevailing environmental conditions that surround them'.[218] Unlike jurisdictional norms, which leave international civil servants with little discretion to exercise mandated powers, complementarity is a policy tool that allows judges 'to engage in some degree of case selection according to their internal policy preferences and in response to external expectations'.[219] In other words, strict or flexible readings of article 17—as seen in the evolution and relaxation of the 'same conduct' test—are a form of policymaking relating to case allocation, no matter judges' insistence they merely 'interpret' or 'apply' the law.

Despite various ideas on how to reconcile positive complementarity with article 17, judges have avoided defining the relationship between international and domestic accountability. International trials proceed without analysing why such trials are needed in the first place, including states' failures to prosecute genuinely, and instead unchecked prosecutorial discretion defines the limits of the ICC's shadow effects on domestic accountability. The results have been mixed, with Libya and Côte d'Ivoire's refusals to surrender Gaddafi and Simone Gbagbo showing the limits of conflict-avoidance techniques. Notably, after an Ivorian court convicted and sentenced Gbagbo to twenty years' imprisonment, the ICC still insisted on her transfer to The Hague because the domestic trial did not concern the same

[217] Nouwen (n 163) 11 (arguing complementarity lives a 'double life') and 51–58; Carsten Stahn, 'Admissibility Challenges before the ICC: From Quasi-Primacy to Qualified Deference?' in Carsten Stahn (ed), *Law and Practice of the International Criminal Court* (OUP 2015) 246 (describing the pre-*Senussi* case law as 'quasi-primacy'); Christian M De Vos, *Complementarity, Catalysts, Compliance. The International Criminal Court in Uganda, Kenya, and the Democratic Republic of Congo* (CUP 2020) 103 (and the literature cited therein).

[218] Shany (n 4) 68.

[219] ibid.

case (rather than possible flaws in domestic proceedings).[220] As noted by Kevin Heller, 'that Côte d'Ivoire can be considered "inactive" ... [is] only because the ICC's judges have imposed structural limits on national proceedings that are inconsistent with the [Rome] Statute and counterproductive in practice'.[221] As will be discussed in Chapter 7, whether justifying trials in The Hague based on states' unwillingness or inability to genuinely prosecute, including in cases of unfair trials, would incentivize iteration (and extend the ICC's shadow) or merely exacerbate isolation has yet to be tested.

5. Unpacking the Nexus of ICT Institutional Design, International Trials, and Domestic Accountability

While it is customary to associate the promise of domestic accountability with the ICC and (positive) complementarity, this chapter explains that ICT–state relations are influenced not only by the distribution of jurisdictional authority but also other elements of institutional design, as well as evolving institutional policy preferences and ideas about the superiority of international, domestic, or mixed trials. Several trends can be discerned across the ICTR, SCSL, and ICC.

First, while most ICTs operate on the basis of concurrent jurisdiction, which increases the scope for interaction between ICTs and states, mandates address the conditionalities of concurrent jurisdiction differently. Complementarity, the original primacy framework[222] and rule 11*bis* generated a web of interdependencies, allowing international civil servants and domestic institutions to mutually shape accountability for serious crimes. But differences exist between these frameworks. Under rule 11*bis*, states' ability to influence the exercise of concurrent jurisdiction hinged on ICTs' incentives to 'relinquish' primacy. By contrast, under article 17, the ICC's incentives are, in theory, irrelevant, so long as states wish to carry out genuine prosecutions. In theory, therefore, the Rome Statute increases states' leverage vis-à-vis international actors and enhances the scope for push–pull relations over case allocation; however, the 'same case' jurisprudence effectively insulates prosecutorial and judicial preferences from state challenges to ICC jurisdiction, reducing—rather than stimulating—dialogue over the exercise of concurrent jurisdiction.

Second, while complementarity and rule 11*bis* condition the exercise of concurrent jurisdiction on the domestic justice system's performance, the standards

[220] AC, *Prosecutor v Simone Gbagbo* (Judgment on the Appeal of Côte d'Ivoire against the Decision of Pre-Trial Chamber I of 11 December 2014 entitled 'Decision on Côte d'Ivoire's Challenge to the Admissibility of the Case against Simone Gbagbo') ICC-02/11-01/12 OA (27 May 2015).

[221] Heller (n 191) 639–40.

[222] While the original r 9 created a degree of interdependence between the ICTR and Rwanda, the analysis will focus on r 11*bis* (see n 33).

of evaluation are different. Under rule 11*bis*, the exercise of domestic jurisdiction depended on a state's observance of fair trial standards, enabling the ICTR to assert primacy whenever a national court failed to provide defendants with due process, irrespective of whether a fair trial made it easier or harder to secure convictions or acquittals. By contrast, according to the article 17 case law, the ICC may only assert jurisdiction if a state shields a defendant from accountability. Crucially, the opposite is not true: barring exceptional circumstances, unfair domestic trials aimed at securing convictions are likely to be deemed compatible with ending impunity. Accordingly, the ICC's ability to challenge states is restricted to the hardest cases of bad faith obstructionism, while it lacks any normative incentive to encourage better performance in cooperative states that may nonetheless use trials for political ends.

Third, regardless of statutory injunctions, international civil servants are reluctant to evaluate the performance of domestic justice systems. Even when rules embedded in ICT mandates require qualitative appraisals ('unwilling', 'genuinely', 'lack of impartiality and independence', 'designed to shield the accused', 'not diligently prosecuted'), judges search for neutral ways ('significant legal and factual issues', 'inactive', 'same conduct') to assert international jurisdiction. Conflict-avoidance techniques create a gap between mandates that condition ICT intervention on states' failure to live up to their legal obligations on the one hand, and jurisprudential standards that avoid passing judgement on states' performance or explaining why international intervention is needed on the other. With the exception of the ICTR's rule 11*bis* practice, this approach has been geared to preserving cooperation with incumbent governments, but it inadvertently sanitizes domestic flaws while delegitimizing international trials that proceed on ICT-centric rationales rather than an evaluation of the relative merits of both.

Fourth, the decision-making power to adopt rules or binding interpretations matters more than detailed legal frameworks regulating when ICTs and states may exercise jurisdiction.[223] Under primacy, evolving judge-made rules gave the ICTR great latitude to require states to desist from or, alternatively, to enable states to exercise jurisdiction under rule 11*bis*. By the same token, notwithstanding the Rome Statute's codification aimed at reducing prosecutorial and judicial activism, narrow ICC-centric readings of article 17 have allowed ICC organs to accomplish policy aims—mainly, the admissibility of cases when the OTP secures custody of suspects—as easily as the ad hoc tribunals switched from 'absolute' and 'targeted' primacy to 'promoting' domestic trials under rule 11*bis*.

Fifth, international prosecutors and judges proceed on the assumption that their mandate is to prosecute high-level suspects. A 'burden-sharing' logic based on perpetrator status can be found in some mandates (the SCSL or the completion

[223] See Jack Goldsmith and Stephen D Krasner, 'The Limits of Idealism' (2003) 132 Daedalus 47, 54.

phase ICTR), but it rarely translates into intelligible prosecutorial strategy or case law. Left unregulated by mandates is the assumption that states will fill the gap and handle other perpetrators. But ICT mandates, prosecutorial strategy, and case law often fail to explain why states should not prosecute senior suspects themselves, engendering disagreements when states and ICTs both wish to exercise jurisdiction. Aside from time-consuming litigation, international civil servants' power to draw jurisdictional and admissibility boundaries relating to perpetrator status seem to accomplish little if states' jurisdictional counterclaims are not evaluated.

Sixth, the flexibility of institutional design matters for ICT–state relations. Despite its name, primacy proved an adaptable framework, allowing international actors to adjust norms to take cognizance of changing circumstances in Rwanda. Starting from a position of strength, the ICTR recalibrated concurrent jurisdiction to accommodate domestic accountability. By contrast, while its jurisdiction is activated in different ways—state (self)-referrals, Security Council authorization, and *proprio motu*—the ICC's admissibility rules seem to assume that relationships with states are relatively homogeneous. By failing to analyse different types of state cooperation, non-cooperation, and obstructionism, the complementarity case law reflects a disconnect between judge-made norms originating in self-referrals that ignore most of article 17 and positive complementarity that aims to reconcile the benefits of international trials with domestic accountability.

Lastly, it is often said that ICTs regulate their relations with states in different ways, with primacy and complementarity serving as a paradigmatic binary. Ambos notes, for instance, that 'either the international tribunal enjoys primacy, or it is subsidiary (complementary) to the respective national jurisdiction'.[224] Similarly, hybrid tribunals are said to constitute 'a third approach to deal with international crimes ... offer[ing] a midway between international and domestic justice'.[225] In reality, while demarcations between primacy and complementarity, or between hybrid and international courts, correspond to certain baseline institutional design features, the ICTR, SCSL, and ICC case law underscores that ICT mandates are more than just fixed bodies of norms that generate specific procedural interactions or substantive outcomes. They can also be understood as expressions of general values or dominant—but subject to change—institutional preferences in favour of domestic or international trials, or something in between that 'deal[s] with the artificial distinction between the domestic and the international by simply collapsing it'.[226]

Viewed in these terms, despite an ideational turn to domestic accountability, international prosecutors and judges struggle to reconcile their operational

[224] Ambos (n 45) 266.

[225] Carsten Stahn, *A Critical Introduction to International Criminal Law* (CUP 2019) 197.

[226] Frédéric Mégret, 'In Defence of Hybridity: Towards a Representational Theory of International Criminal Justice' (2005) 38 Cornell Journal of International Law 725, 747.

mandates with global governance visions of international criminal law enforcement. While ICT mandates usually make the exercise of international and domestic jurisdiction interdependent and mutually co-constitutive, international civil servants usually deploy conflict-avoidance interpretive techniques to shield international case selection from challenge, rather than treat concurrent jurisdiction as a matter of policy geared to, for instance, the promotion of domestic trials or charging hybrid forms of criminality. In doing so, not only is a judicial and prosecutorial dialogue about the benefits and shortcomings of international, mixed, or domestic accountability vis-à-vis certain types of criminality or certain categories of perpetrators foreclosed; in fact, ICTs may also lose opportunities—as will be seen in the next three chapters—to cast a longer shadow over accountability processes by negotiating the terms of case selection, capacity building, and norm internalization with their state counterparts.

4
International Intervention and Domestic Prosecutions

1. Introduction

The next three chapters assess how the shadow of ICTs influences state-driven accountability processes and to what extent inferences can be made between incentive structures embedded in ICT mandates, actions taken by international tribunal officials, and government responses to atrocity crimes. To understand the conditions under which the ICTR, SCSL, and ICC shaped state accountability policies and vice versa, this book uses three variables—domestic prosecutions (Chapter 4), capacity building (Chapter 5), and norm internalization (Chapter 6)—to assess if international intervention had generally positive (iteration), neutral (accommodation), or negative (isolation) effects on the willingness and ability of governments to pursue accountability for international crimes.

Against this backdrop, Chapter 4 examines to what extent the ICTR, SCSL, and ICC's institutional design encouraged domestic prosecutions of serious crimes in Rwanda, Sierra Leone, and the DRC. As seen in Chapter 2, the ICC's ability to cast a shadow and encourage domestic prosecutions through complementarity is considered one of the Rome Statute's greatest virtues. In this regard, the ICC is often contrasted with the ad hoc tribunals, where primacy was said to dissuade states from prosecuting suspects. As seen in Chapter 3, although the SCSL is one of the few to explicitly mandate a division of labour based on perpetrator status, the ICTR's rule 11*bis* established an analogous, conditionality-based procedure for referrals of intermediate and low-ranking perpetrators to states, including Rwanda.

Focusing on areas of synergy, antagonism, and indifference, this chapter assesses how international civil servants influence domestic prosecutorial policy and, in turn, how state-based actors shape international prosecutors' case selection. It argues that, despite ICTs' divergent elements of institutional design, international investigative practices are generally similar and divisions of labour depend less on mandates than on governments' (un)willingness to cooperate with international prosecutors. While evidence of ICTs positively influencing domestic prosecutorial policy is uncommon and there is a risk of states free-riding on international trials, primacy may provide stronger incentives than complementarity for international civil servants to challenge the impunity of state-affiliated suspects.

International Criminal Tribunals and Domestic Accountability. Patryk I. Labuda,
Oxford University Press. © Patryk I. Labuda 2023. DOI: 10.1093/oso/9780198868842.003.0004

2. The International Criminal Tribunal for Rwanda

2.1. Early prosecutorial strategy: investigations 'all over the place'

The ICTR's original mandate and prosecutorial strategy are often mischaracterized. As explained in Chapter 3, primacy does not mean absolute priority vis-à-vis states. Nor did the Tribunal have personal jurisdiction over 'most responsible' suspects when it was established. In reality, the ICTR's conditional primacy and open-ended personal jurisdiction allowed it to prosecute any perpetrator, including when national proceedings failed to meet specified qualitative criteria.

The ICTR's 'open-ended' and 'conditional' primacy shaped the prosecutors' early prosecutorial decisions and interactions with Rwandan officials. According to initial estimates, the Tribunal was expected to prosecute as many as 400 individuals, though 'diplomats in Kigali predict[ed] that less than a dozen [would] actually come to trial ... in the first year'.[1] The first prosecutor, Richard Goldstone,[2] hinted early on that he would focus on top-level suspects, but neither he nor his successor, Louise Arbour, implemented a clear strategy to limit the number of suspects or to prioritize investigations in Rwanda.[3] Focused primarily on the ICTY, Goldstone and Arbour spent most of their time in The Hague, and left the coordination of Rwandan issues to others.[4]

In the meantime, deputy prosecutor Honoré Rakotomana, based full-time in the Kigali field office, developed his own strategy focused on mid-level suspects and geographically delineated parts of the country. Rakotomana was dismissed in early 1997 after an internal UN inquiry 'uncovered serious operational deficiencies and mismanagement in the [ICTR]'s administration'.[5] Questioning his leadership, the investigation found that Rakotomana 'did not redirect the limited resources of the [OTP] to pursue key figures in the genocide, nor did [Goldstone] take affirmative steps to ensure this new focus'.[6]

[1] 'Report of the Secretary General on the United Nations Assistance Mission for Rwanda [UNAMIR]' (4 June 1995) S/1995/457, para 30; Donatella Lorch, 'As Rwanda Trials Open, a Nation Struggles' *New York Times* (7 April 1995) <nytimes.com/1995/04/07/world/as-rwanda-trials-open-a-nation-struggles.html>.

[2] Goldstone was preceded, briefly, by Ramon Escovar Salom (John Hagan, *Justice in the Balkans: Prosecuting War Crimes in the Hague Tribunal* (University of Chicago Press 2003) 55–56).

[3] The general idea of targeting senior suspects existed from the beginning but it was not acted upon, see Madeline Morris, 'The Trials of Concurrent Jurisdiction: The Case of Rwanda' (1997) 7 Duke Journal of Comparative & International Law 349, 363. See also Frederick de Vlaming, 'Selection of Defendants' in Luc Reydams, Jan Wouters and Cedric Ryngaert (eds), *International Prosecutors* (OUP 2012) 549–57 (concluding, more generously, Arbour had developed a strategy for the ICTR by the end of her term).

[4] Louise Arbour, 'The Crucial Years' (2004) 2 Journal of International Criminal Justice 396. But see Richard J Goldstone, *For Humanity: Reflections of a War Crimes Investigator* (Yale UP 2000) 113.

[5] 'ICTR Second Annual Report' (13 November 1997) A/52/582 S/1997/868, 2 (Summary).

[6] UNGA, 'Report of the Secretary-General on the Activities of the Office of Internal Oversight Services: Financing of the ICTR' (1997) A/51/789, para 56. On Rakotomana, see Véronique Parqué, 'Le Tribunal pénal international pour le Rwanda' in Stefaan Marysse and Filip Reyntjens (eds), *Annuaire des Grands Lacs 1996–1997* (Harmattan 1997) 151–56.

Reflecting on these years, Luc Côté, an ICTR investigator from 1995 to 1999, noted that 'there was little strategy. We identified a number of targets to get the ball rolling and it grew from there.'[7] Stephen Rapp, former chief of prosecutions, recalled that 'when [he] joined the ICTR in May 2001 … [he] immediately confronted the reality that our investigative force over in Kigali had been directed to begin thirty new cases every year'.[8] Former ICTR staff explained that, while ICTR investigations were mainly target-driven, an uncoordinated approach to evidence collection meant that investigators roamed Rwanda searching for leads, without any overarching strategy and that the list of suspects remained open-ended for years.[9] A senior OTP official criticized a 'non-existent' prosecutorial strategy, with investigations 'all over the place' and investigators going 'as far as possible for as long as possible' to collect 'the biggest possible *per diems*'.[10]

Under Carla Del Ponte, appointed prosecutor in 1999, an internal strategy based on levels of responsibility, geographical case distribution, institutional complicity (military, media, etc.), and thematic (e.g. sexual) crimes consolidated.[11] However, Laurent Walpen, a former Geneva police chief hired as head of investigations by Del Ponte, conceded that, as late as 2001, investigators were still pursuing leads against 2,000 suspects.[12] Only later, as discussions began on a completion strategy, was this number reduced to a list of 200, then to 110, and ultimately 90 suspects.[13] Writing in 2004, Walpen argued that 'had we worked on this limited number of suspects from the beginning, there is little doubt the ICTR would have finished its work by now'.[14]

[7] ICTR Newsletter, 'Prosecutors Colloquium, Challenges of International Criminal Justice, Arusha, Tanzania, 25–27 November 2004' (2004) 5.

[8] Stephen J Rapp, 'The Challenge of Choice in the Investigation and Prosecution of International Crimes in Post-Conflict Sierra Leone' in Charles C Jalloh (ed), *The Sierra Leone Special Court and Its Legacy* (CUP 2013) 24.

[9] Interviews with former ICTR officials, The Hague, Netherlands, Geneva, Switzerland and phone interviews, 23 November 2015, 20 June 2016, and 8 December 2016. See also International Crisis Group, 'Tribunal pénal international pour le Rwanda: le compte à rebours' (International Crisis Group 2002) 6–9; Alison Des Forges and Timothy Longman, 'Legal Responses to Genocide in Rwanda' in Eric Stover and Harvey Weinstein (eds), *My Neighbor, My Enemy. Justice and Community in the Aftermath of Mass Atrocity* (CUP 2004) 53.

[10] Interview with former ICTR official, Geneva, Switzerland, 20 June 2016. On investigations, see Alain Ribaux, 'Folie meurtrière au pays des milles collines: carnet de notes d'un enquêteur suisse au Rwanda' [1996] Receuil de jurisprudence neuchâteloise 12, 26–30. On early ICTR investigations and overlapping mandates with UN human rights inquiries, see Martin Seutcheu, 'Working Together to Prosecute Human Rights Criminals: An Insider Account of the Relationship between Human Rights Organizations and the International Criminal Tribunal for Rwanda' (unpublished manuscript).

[11] Internal ICTR prosecutorial document (on file with author). This strategy systematized choices arrived at by Goldstone and Arbour.

[12] Laurent Walpen, 'La conduite des enquêtes, un défi majeur pour la justice pénale internationale' (2004) 12 Centre international de formation à l'enseignement des droits de l'homme et de la paix: Thématique 35, 39; Kingsley C Moghalu, *Rwanda's Genocide: The Politics of Global Justice* (Palgrave Macmillan 2005) 133–34.

[13] Walpen (n 12) 39. For figures, including the 'gamma list', see also Rapp (n 8) 25; Alex Odora-Obote, 'Investigations and Case Selection' in Anne-Marie de Brouwer and Alette Smeulers (eds), *Elgar Companion to the International Criminal Tribunal for Rwanda* (Edward Elgar 2017) 253.

[14] Walpen (n 12) 39 (author translation).

These figures provide the context for the ICTR prosecutor's relations with Rwanda. Contrary to retrospective claims about a 'limited mandate' and 'targeted prosecutions', open-ended, primacy-based investigations initially extended to a very large number of perpetrators, including mid- and even low-level suspects. As a result, not only did the ICTR and Rwanda formally have concurrent jurisdiction; a real possibility existed that international and domestic prosecutions would overlap.

2.2. Open-ended primacy in action: dissuasive or iterative competition?

In hindsight, Rwanda and the ICTR could have conducted concurrent but separate prosecutions, with the former focusing on genocide suspects who remained in the country after July 1994 and the latter targeting fugitives who had fled abroad. In fact, during Security Council debates on the ICTR's establishment, Rwanda seemed to acknowledge the Tribunal's advantage in pursuing genocidaires scattered around the world.[15] Nevertheless, accommodation based on a consensual division of labour did not come to pass immediately. On the contrary, a race to locate high-value suspects triggered tension over the contours of primacy.

The ICTR initially had a robust and expansive understanding of primacy, extending to both genocidaires abroad and potential targets inside Rwanda. In line with the ICTR's original regulation of primacy, Goldstone contemplated 'divesting' Rwandan courts of jurisdiction over suspects arrested in Rwanda. As noted by Martin Seutcheu, a former OTP official, the ICTR 'sought out NGOs to monitor national prosecutions of Rwandan genocide, in order to establish whether the Tribunal should exercise its primacy over domestic courts', with civil society 'act[ing] as trial observers within the Rwandan judicial system in order to ensure . . . the openness of the trials and the fairness of the proceedings'.[16] Ultimately, neither Goldstone nor his successors divested Rwanda of ongoing cases, owing largely to the ICTR's increasing workload. A former OTP official explained that, after an initial period of uncertainty, an 'informal arrangement' emerged whereby the ICTR focused on suspects abroad while leaving those inside Rwanda to national authorities.[17]

[15] See Payam Akhavan, 'The International Criminal Tribunal for Rwanda: The Politics and Pragmatics of Punishment' (1996) 90 American Journal of International Law 501, 505.

[16] Seutcheu (n 10) 9. Interviews with former ICTR and UN officials, Geneva, Switzerland, 25 January 2016 and 19 January 2018. See also Ian Martin, 'After Genocide: The UN Human Rights Field Operation in Rwanda' in Alice H Henkin (ed), *Honoring Human Rights: From Peace to Justice. Recommendations to the International Community* (Aspen Institute 1998) 106–08.

[17] Interview with former ICTR official, Geneva, Switzerland, 12 June 2015.

Nevertheless, disagreement remained over primacy in regard to fugitives abroad. Unforeseen during negotiations of the ICTR Statute, it was the prestige of 'candidates for prosecution' that triggered a race to locate suspects. It turned out that Rwanda's new RPF political elite would not be satisfied with trials of low-level genocidaires. In his memoir, David Scheffer, then US ambassador at large for war crimes, explains how during a visit to Kigali, Gerald Gahima, then deputy minister of justice (and later prosecutor general), lost his temper, arguing that Rwanda 'need[ed] some big fish to put on trial here!'.[18]

Few in 1994 expected Rwanda to track down fugitives dispersed around the world. It was assumed also that no state would send suspects back for trial before Rwanda's courts. But these assumptions proved incomplete. As noted by Côté, 'it should be recognized that ... the ICTR Prosecutor, slower to organize himself, arrived belatedly, after Rwandan authorities had requested extraditions of certain suspects'.[19] Notably, in March 1996, Cameroon arrested more than a dozen suspects pursuant to concurrent extradition requests from Belgium and Rwanda, including former government officials considered among those most responsible for the genocide, Théoneste Bagosora, Ferdinand Nahimana, and Anatole Nsengiyumya.[20]

The stakes could not be higher. At the time, neither Rwanda nor the ICTR had initiated a single trial. Faced with Rwanda's extradition requests, Goldstone proved unwilling to concede primacy. Goldstone later claimed he 'preferred to suggest closing down the tribunal than to defer a major criminal involved in the genocide'.[21] Negotiations between the OTP and Rwandan authorities ultimately produced a compromise.[22] According to Madeline Morris, an American lawyer advising the Rwandan government, Goldstone insisted on the ICTR exercising primacy over several senior genocidaires, whereas Rwanda would be allowed to proceed with its extradition requests for the remaining suspects.[23] However, after Bagosora's transfer to Arusha in January 1997, Cameroon unexpectedly rejected Rwanda's other extradition requests, which paved the way for more transfers to

[18] David Scheffer, *All the Missing Souls: A Personal History of the War Crimes Tribunals* (Princeton UP 2012) 113.

[19] Luc Côté, 'Le Tribunal pénal International pour le Rwanda: Un tribunal dans la tourmente' in Filip Reyntjens and Stefaan Marysse, *L'Afrique des Grands Lacs, Annuaire 2005–2006* (Harmattan 2006) 425 (author translation).

[20] Thierry Cruvellier, *Le tribunal des vaincus: un Nuremberg pour le Rwanda?* (Calmann-Lévy 2006) 28.

[21] Quoted in Peskin, *International Justice in Rwanda and the Balkans: Virtual Trials and the Struggle for State Cooperation* (CUP 2008) 173.

[22] Interviews with Richard Goldstone and Rwandan officials, Cape Town, South Africa and other locations, 23 March and 16 September 2016, 21 October 2017. Participants in these negotiations agree that a compromise was reached, but there are two understandings of what the compromise entailed. Some believe the ICTR agreed to exchange Bagosora for Karamira. Others argue the deal was to exchange the high-level perpetrators caught in Cameroon for other 'less prominent' suspects.

[23] Morris (n 3) 365; Goldstone (n 4) 112–13.

the ICTR.[24] According to Scheffer, diplomatic pressure from the US government helped persuade Cameroon to cooperate with the ICTR.[25]

As this nine-month 'tug of war' over Bagosora and his confederates unfolded, Goldstone clashed with Rwanda over Froduald Karamira, a prominent politician and genocide supporter.[26] Rwanda—not the ICTR—had found Karamira in Bombay and convinced India to deport him. However, during his flight back to Kigali, in June 1996, Karamira left the transit area in Addis Ababa and refused to continue his journey. Though unaware of Karamira's whereabouts prior to his 'escape' from the airport, Goldstone asked Ethiopia to halt Karamira's deportation.[27] Under pressure from Rwanda, however, Goldstone withdrew his request. He later argued that, despite the ICTR's primacy, he had exercised discretion to prevent relations with Rwanda from deteriorating further in light of the Bagosora standoff, though others suggest that the RPF-led authorities threatened to break off cooperation.[28] Goldstone's decision, criticized by human rights groups, paved the way for Karamira's trial, death sentence, and subsequent execution in Rwanda.[29]

After these two high-profile clashes over Bagosora and Karamira, the race for high-ranking genocidaires abroad moved behind the scenes. Agnes Ntamabyariro, a pre-genocide justice minister, was tracked down in Zambia and likely kidnapped by Rwandan intelligence operatives. Her domestic trial in Rwanda finished nearly a decade after she 'resurfaced' in Kigali in 1997.[30] A senior OTP official explained that the ICTR had hoped Valérie Bemeriki, a prominent genocide instigator whom the Rwandan army had apprehended during operations in the DRC, would be transferred to Arusha to stand trial in the *Media* case.[31] However, the Tribunal chose not to litigate primacy when Rwanda refused to hand her over. Bemeriki was eventually tried and sentenced to life imprisonment in a gacaca court.[32]

In the end, the ICTR never formally invoked primacy to request the Rwandan government to relinquish custody of a single suspect. Nevertheless, primacy contributed to tensions between the ICTR and Rwanda. In its official position on the

[24] On Bagosora's (complex) transfer to Arusha, see TC, *Prosecutor v Bagosora* (Judgement and Sentence) ICTR-98-41-T (18 December 2008) Annex A, paras 2285–93; Parqué (n 6) 144. On Belgium's extradition request (dropped upon the ICTR's request), see Vandermeersch, 'La loi du 22 mars 1996 relative à la reconnaissance du Tribunal pour l'ex-Yougoslavie et du Tribunal international pour le Rwanda et à la coopération avec ces tribunaux' [1996] *Revue de droit pénal et de criminologie* 855.

[25] Scheffer (n 18) 111–12.

[26] For the term 'tug of war', see Morris (n 3).

[27] On Karamira, see Peskin (n 21) 172–77; Cruvellier (n 20) 29–33.

[28] Peskin (n 21) 175.

[29] Amnesty International, 'International Criminal Tribunal for Rwanda. Trials and Tribulations' (1998) IOR 40/003/1998; ICTR Press Release (29 April 1998) ICTR/INFO/9-2-117.

[30] Cruvellier (n 20) 27–28; TRIAL profile, Agnes Ntamabyariro <trialinternational.org/latest-post/agnes-ntamabyariro/>.

[31] Interview with former ICTR officials, Geneva, Switzerland and The Hague, Netherlands, 12 June 2015 and 23 November 2015.

[32] VOA, 'Rwanda: la prison à perpétuité pour la journaliste Valérie Bemeriki' (14 December 2009) <voaafrique.com/a/a-46-2009-12-14-voa5-91979374/1377631.html>.

ICTR from 1997, the Rwandan government criticized that '[t]he prosecutors have never determined policy as to whom the tribunal should pursue [and] have never indicated the kind of cases they wish to prosecute before the tribunal and those they expect to be tried by national courts'.[33] Writing in 1997, Frederik Harhoff, then an ICTR legal adviser, acknowledged Rwandans' 'perfectly understandable' fear 'that the Tribunal would always intervene and effectively bar the Rwandan prosecution from ever bringing any of the former leaders of the genocide campaign to trial in Rwanda'.[34] Referring to the general idea of primacy qua supremacy, Scheffer explains that Rwandan officials complained '[they] were shown no respect by tribunal authorities', and that 'primacy of jurisdiction did not mean primacy of character or political wisdom'.[35]

Yet, although negative perceptions of primacy persist among many Rwandan officials to this day, it had other effects as well. While Rwanda initially opted for a 'go-slow policy'[36] on genocide accountability—as Human Rights Watch (HRW) notes, the authorities 'appeared unwilling to prosecute [genocide] perpetrators, either because they lacked confidence in judges named by the previous government or because they saw some political interest in detaining large numbers of persons indefinitely'[37]—tensions over primacy accelerated reforms. To be sure, the RPF's shift to an anti-impunity policy over other transitional justice options after 1995 (when, for instance, amnesty was rejected), arose from various homegrown factors, including a desire to exercise 'political and social control' over the majority Hutu population and thereby consolidate its authority.[38] However, activists explained that the ICTR's shadow, in particular the race to locate fugitives and the threat of divesting Rwandan courts of cases, pressured the RPF to launch domestic trials and ensure basic fair trial rights.[39] As will be seen below, the threat of prosecutions of RPF crimes also meant the government's behaviour remained in the spotlight.[40]

[33] 'The Position of the Government of the Republic of Rwanda on the International Criminal Tribunal for Rwanda' (1997) (on file with author).

[34] Frederik Harhoff, 'Consonance or Rivalry? Calibrating the Efforts to Prosecute War Crimes in National and International Tribunals' (1997) 7 Duke Journal of Comparative & International Law 571, 584.

[35] Scheffer (n 18) 113–14. Scheffer notes that Gahima complained that ICTR officials 'argue[d] their points under the shield of Security Council authority rather than the mutual relationship we must have'. See also Des Forges and Longman (n 9) 54.

[36] Gérard Prunier, *The Rwanda Crisis: History of a Genocide* (2nd edn, Hurst 2002) 366; Stef Vandeginste, 'L'approche "vérité et réconciliation" du génocide et des crimes contre l'humanité au Rwanda' in Filip Reyntjens and Stefaan Marysse, *Annuaire des Grands Lacs 1997–1998* (Harmattan 1998) 99–102.

[37] HRW, 'World Report 1996' (1997) <hrw.org/reports/1996/WR96/Africa-08.htm>.

[38] Prunier (n 36) 365–72; Des Forges and Longman (n 9) 59–60.

[39] Interviews with former NGO officials, Brussels, Belgium and Boston, USA, 17 November 2016 and 25 April 2017.

[40] Interview with former UN official, Geneva, Switzerland, 19 January 2018.

A range of international actors assisted the judicial authorities in preparing prosecutions. One initiative involved support for the Rwandan prosecution service to conduct a 'triage' of cases by opening case files against prisoners, bringing charges against suspects for whom there was evidence, and releasing those against whom evidence was insufficient. In addition to these reforms, the prosecution service drew up a list of around 2,000 priority, category 1 genocidaires.[41] Despite delays, national trials started in the last days of December 1996. Not coincidentally, Karamira, a category 1 defendant, one of the first to be put on trial, was sentenced to death by February 1997.[42] As explained by one analyst, the rush to prosecute people like Karamira was driven in part by the RPF's desire to be seen by Rwandans as delivering justice more effectively than the ICTR, whose first trial against Jean-Paul Akayesu began in late 1996 (and eventually concluded in 1998).[43]

As will be seen in Chapter 6, ordinary courts in Rwanda eventually tried several thousand people for genocide-related crimes (a term that is broader than the international definition of genocide, including, for instance, property offences).[44] Yet, while opinions diverge on their merits, national trials advanced in parallel with cases in Arusha with little interaction. An uneasy relationship solidified between the ICTR and Rwandan authorities, punctuated by recurring cooperation challenges, for instance in the infamous controversy over Barayagwiza's release.[45]

However, public clashes over the distribution of suspects ended after Goldstone's tussles over prominent fugitives. Based in Kigali, ICTR investigators depended on the RPF for access to crime sites but rarely asked for assistance otherwise, while national magistrates conducted separate investigations into suspects apprehended in Rwanda.[46] Jean de Dieu Mucyo, a justice minister from 1999 to 2003, explained later that, while he could not be sure who was on the ICTR's list of targets, national

[41] Cruvellier (n 20) 85. On the prioritization scheme, see Daniel De Beer, *Loi rwandaise du 30 août 1996 sur l'organisation des poursuites des infractions constitutives du crime de génocide ou de crimes contre l'humanité. Commentaire et jurisprudence* (2nd edn, Alter Egaux 1999).

[42] Tribunal de 1ère instance de Kigali, *Ministère public v Karamira* (Judgment) RP 006/KIG/CS, RMP433/SI2/CT/KP (14 February 1997); Vandeginste (n 36); William A Schabas, 'Genocide, Impunity and Accountability in Rwanda: Is It Reasonable to Expect a Devastated Legal System to Deal Justly with Those Who Destroyed It?' *Inroads: A Journal of Opinion* (1 January 1997).

[43] Interview with NGO official, undisclosed location, 25 April 2017. E-mail exchange with foreign expert, 28 March 2019.

[44] Scholars and NGOs seem to rely on data from LIPRODHOR, a Rwandan human rights group. LIPRODHOR, *Rescapés et droits humains. Problèmes actuels des rescapés huit ans après le génocide* (2002) 44; Sigall Horovitz, *Rwanda: International and National Responses to the Mass Atrocities and Their Interaction* (DOMAC 2010) 33–34. But see Barbora Hola and Hollie Nyseth Brehm, 'Punishing Genocide: A Comparative Empirical Analysis of Sentencing Laws and Practices at the International Criminal Tribunal for Rwanda, Rwandan Domestic Courts, and Gacaca Courts' (2016) 10 Genocide Studies and Prevention 59 (suggesting a lower number of people held accountable).

[45] On cooperation challenges and *Barayagwiza*, well covered in the literature, see Peskin (n 21) 170–85; Gerald Gahima, *Transitional Justice in Rwanda: Accountability for Atrocity* (Routledge 2013) 106–08; Morris (n 3) 363–64.

[46] Interviews with former ICTR and Rwandan officials, undisclosed locations, 20 June and 16 September 2016; Gregory Townsend, 'Structure and Management' in Reydams, Wouters and Ryngaert (n 3) 245–55.

magistrates were aware of primacy and felt it 'unnecessary' to duplicate investigations if they had reason to believe the ICTR was already handling a case.[47]

All in all, OTP officials did not interfere in domestic cases, which concerned different suspects and, by the same token, Rwandan authorities mostly ignored the ICTR. An agreement on case distribution never materialized, but concerns over primacy dissipated as the Tribunal and Rwanda acquired custody of suspects and each launched its own trials.[48] A consensual modus vivendi on genocide cases would, however, be put to the test in relation to the crimes of the incumbent government.

2.3. ICTR versus Kagame: probing the coercive limits of primacy

The RPF's role in the armed conflict that culminated in the 1994 genocide is steeped in controversy. Allegations of widespread killings emerged as early as June 1994 when a UN report suggested that between 25,000 and 45,000 civilians may have been killed by RPF troops.[49] HRW argues that up to 30,000 perished in widespread and premeditated attacks.[50] Equally controversial, it remains unclear who shot down President Habyarimana's plane on 6 April, the event that triggered the genocide (albeit responsibility for this attack should not be conflated with responsibility for the genocide).[51]

Although the ICTR's mandate covered allegations against the RPF, the first two prosecutors decided not to confront Rwanda's new political leaders. Goldstone never opened an investigation into alleged RPF crimes, suggesting alternatively that he received no evidence to implicate the RPF or that genocide crimes outweighed the RPF's 'revenge killings'.[52] In fact, Goldstone's disclaimers notwithstanding, ICTR officials present in Rwanda in the mid-1990s concede that the issue of alleged RPF crimes was controversial and openly discussed from the beginning, with the ICTR's primacy placing the RPF in a 'defensive posture' vis-à-vis Arusha.[53]

[47] Interview with Jean de Dieu Mucyo, Kigali, Rwanda, 26 August 2015.

[48] A memorandum of understanding was signed in 1999, but it did not address the distribution of cases. Preamble of Memorandum of Understanding, 3 June 1999 (on file). On consensual distribution of suspects, see further Morris (n 3) 364; Harhoff (n 34) 584.

[49] Luc Reydams, Jan Wouters and Cedric Ryngaert, 'The Politics of Establishing International Criminal Tribunals' in Reydams, Wouters and Ryngaert (n 3) 34–35.

[50] Alison Des Forges, *'Leave None to Tell the Story'. Genocide in Rwanda* (2020 reissue, HRW; International Federation of Human Rights 1999) 500.

[51] Luc Reydams, 'Politics or Pragmatism? The International Criminal Tribunal for Rwanda and the Burying of the Investigation into the Assassination of President Juvénal Habyarimana' (2018) 40 Human Rights Quarterly 989. On responsibility for the 6 April attack, as opposed to responsibility for the genocide, see Alex De Waal, 'Writing Human Rights and Getting It Wrong' [2016] *Boston Review*.

[52] Interview with Richard Goldstone, Cape Town, South Africa, 23 March 2016. Goldstone (n 4); Morris (n 3) 362; Peskin (n 21) 189–91; Filip Reyntjens, *Political Governance in Post-Genocide Rwanda* (CUP 2013) 243–44. But see Reydams (n 51) 995.

[53] Interview with former UN officials, Geneva, Switzerland and by phone, 19 January 2018 and 9 May 2019.

In addition to allegations from 1994, NGO and UN investigations uncovered continuing, post-1994 crimes attributable to the RPF, especially in the eastern part of Rwanda, near the border with Zaire (present-day DRC). In April 1995, RPF troops killed as many as 4,000 civilians in the Kibeho refugee camp, in the presence of UN monitors.[54] When the RPF invaded Zaire in 1997, allegations of widespread crimes again triggered international condemnation and various inquiries.[55]

Although these post-1994 events were beyond its temporal mandate, they increased pressure on the ICTR to look into allegations from 1994. Arbour launched a brief inquiry into the 6 April attack, but decided that an isolated incident was outside her mandate.[56] Her decision remains controversial.[57] An investigation in France into the downing of Habyarimana's plane was followed later by Spain's inquiry into the killings of Spanish nationals in 1994.[58] Neither translated into trials, though both inquiries brought to light disturbing allegations of RPF crimes.

In response to these allegations, the RPF maintains its military justice system has fully addressed allegations against its own troops. According to HRW, military courts in Rwanda prosecuted thirty-two RPF soldiers, of whom fourteen were convicted, with suspects, usually of a low-military rank, receiving sentences of no more than six years' imprisonment.[59] In one well-documented case from 1994, Sam Bigabiro's life sentence was eventually commuted.[60] Fred Ibingira, the commander who oversaw the Kibeho massacre, was sentenced to eighteen months' imprisonment for 'failing to give assistance to a person in danger', and he continued

[54] 'Report of the Secretary General on UNAMIR' (n 1) paras 10–16; Ian Martin, 'Hard Choices After Genocide. Human Rights and Political Failures in Rwanda' in Jonathan Moore (ed), *Hard Choices: Moral Dilemmas in Humanitarian Intervention* (Rowman & Littlefield 1998).

[55] OHCHR, *Rapport du Projet Mapping concernant les violations les plus graves des droits de l'homme et du droit international humanitaire commises entre mars 1993 et juin 2003 sur le territoire de la République démocratique du Congo* (2010).

[56] Documents revealed later suggest that a preliminary case file had been opened. 'Michael Hourigan Affidavit on Investigation into 6 April 1994 Attack' <rwandadelaguerreaugenocide.univ-paris1.fr/wp-content/uploads/2010/01/Annexe_49.pdf>; Carla Del Ponte, *Madame Prosecutor: Confrontations with Humanity's Worst Criminals and the Culture of Impunity: A Memoir* (Other Press 2009) 180; Peskin (n 21) 190; Moghalu (n 12) 137.

[57] André Guichaoua, *De la guerre au génocide. Les politiques criminelles au Rwanda 1990–1994* (Karthala 2005); Reydams (n 51); Peskin (n 21) 190. But see Peter Robinson and Golriz Ghahraman, 'Can Rwandan President Kagame Be Held Responsible at the ICTR for the Killing of President Habyarimana?' (2008) 6 Journal of International Criminal Justice 981.

[58] On French investigations, see Vanessa Thalmann, 'French Justice's Endeavours to Substitute for the ICTR' (2008) 6 Journal of International Criminal Justice 995. On Spain, see anonymous, 'The Spanish Indictment of High-Ranking Rwandan Officials' (2008) 6 Journal of International Criminal Justice 1003. See also Del Ponte (n 56) 222–41. Lars Waldorf, '"A Mere Pretense of Justice": Complementarity, Sham Trials, and Victor's Justice at the Rwanda Tribunal' (2011) 33 Fordham International Law Journal 1221, 1241–45.

[59] HRW, 'Law and Reality. Progress in Judicial Reform in Rwanda' (2008) 89–95. Some internal investigations and commissions of inquiry appear also to have resulted in disciplinary action against individual RPF soldiers. HRW (n 37); Reuters, 'Rwanda Army Opens the Trial of 14 Soldiers' (3 May 1995) <nytimes.com/1995/05/03/world/rwanda-army-opens-the-trial-of-14-soldiers.html>.

[60] Des Forges (n 50) 483 and 499; HRW (n 59) 107.

his military service upon release, eventually rising to the rank of general.[61] Prior to the *Kabgayi* trial (discussed later in this section), the last military trial for allegations dating from 1994 occurred in 1998.[62]

However, upon closer inspection, data on Rwanda's domestic accountability processes for RPF crimes are fragmentary and self-referential. Not only does HRW's evidence contradict that of the Fédération International pour les droits humains (FIDH) and the ICTR,[63] this internally inconsistent information is all based on self-reporting from the Rwandan government. NGOs were not allowed to observe military court proceedings against members of the RPF. The UN had limited access based on personal connections rather than an official monitoring agreement, and the ICTR never monitored such trials.[64]

Doubts remain not only as to how many trials actually took place, but more importantly whether military proceedings should be considered credible.[65] For most activists, UN officials and Rwandan dissidents, these were sham trials. As noted by one activist, 'it was a bit of a smokescreen ... a response to criticisms that nothing was being done'.[66] A UN official who leveraged personal relationships with the RPF top brass to attend some sessions explained that the trials were 'only for the international community to show that we follow international norms'.[67] Acknowledging that 'justice was being done to show to [the] international community', a former government official emphasized that the RPF had no internal policy to hold its own decision makers accountable beyond sporadic crimes by low-level foot soldiers.[68] Even Martin Ngoga, then Rwandan deputy prosecutor general, seemed to admit at an ICTR-sponsored event in 2004, that only some RPF crimes had been prosecuted and conceded that '[c]ompromises are made to stabilize the society'.[69]

All in all, while Rwanda prosecuted few RPF crimes, especially if they implicated high-ranking officers, the diplomatic community, beset by its own 'guilt over

[61] Waldorf (n 58) 1228; Timothy Longman, *Memory and Justice in Post-Genocide Rwanda* (CUP 2017) 124.

[62] Waldorf (n 58) 1227.

[63] For data on RPF trials, see HRW (n 59) 103–09; FIDH, 'Victims in the Balance. Challenges Ahead for the International Criminal Tribunal for Rwanda' (2002) Report No 329/2, 15–18 and 64–70. The same figures are quoted by Del Ponte (n 56) 179. In 2008 and 2009, Rwanda and Prosecutor Jallow cited prosecutions of 42 RPF soldiers, with 19 held accountable for 1994 events, including 12 convictions and sentences, 5 acquittals, and 2 unresolved cases. See 'Hassan Jallow Response to Kenneth Roth' <hrw.org/sites/default/files/related_material/2009_06_Rwanda_Jallow_Response.pdf>; UNSC (4 June 2009) S/PV.6134, 33.

[64] Phone interview with Rwandan activist, 2 May 2017. On monitoring generally, see Martin (n 16) 123.

[65] Phone interviews with former NGO officials, 2 and 11 May 2017. Interview with former UN official, New York, 14 May 2019. Attempts by the author to contact the Rwandan military prosecution service in Kigali in 2015 were unsuccessful. On the risks of research into the Rwandan military, see also Patryk I Labuda, 'Review Essay: The International Criminal Tribunal for Rwanda and Post-Genocide Justice 25Years on' (2020) 30 European Journal of International Law 1113, 1130.

[66] Phone interview with Rwandan human rights activist, 2 May 2017.

[67] Phone interview with former UN official, 3 March 2021.

[68] Phone interview with former Rwandan government official, 25 May 2017.

[69] ICTR Newsletter (n 7) 17.

letting the genocide happen', applied minimal pressure on the RPF over such allegations. Acknowledging 'guilt syndrome', international activists noted that the UN would not always cooperate with them on investigations implicating the RPF in crimes.[70]

While the ICTR had authority to prosecute allegations against the RPF from 1994, it was only Carla Del Ponte, the third prosecutor, who finally turned to this issue. In theory, as no domestic military trials (by the Rwandan government's own admission) involved charges of war crimes or crimes against humanity, this alone allowed the Tribunal to assert primacy under the 'ordinary crimes' exception. However, rather than challenge the credibility of military proceedings, the OTP pivoted to serious allegations that the Rwandan military had not investigated at all.

In late 2000, acting against the recommendations of her staff, Del Ponte called a meeting with Paul Kagame to inform him of a 'special investigation'.[71] Invoking the ICTR's primacy and Chapter VII authority, she hoped to extract cooperation to investigate three of the thirteen sites that her office had identified.[72] Elected president in 2000 (albeit de facto leader since July 1994), Kagame appeared to acquiesce. However, the authorities failed to respond to subsequent cooperation requests. In particular, the military prosecutor, Andrew Rwigamba, rebuffed the OTP's repeated attempts to establish channels of communication with the military.[73] Meanwhile, Rwanda's nominally civilian authorities started blocking witnesses from travelling to and testifying in Arusha, forcing the suspension of ongoing genocide trials. As explained later by a senior ICTR attorney, the Rwandan government had 'signaled to the ICTR that if we continued it would cause the abortion of cases against genocidaires'.[74] Acting at the behest of the military, the RPF was using blackmail to extract concessions from the Tribunal.[75]

Over time, the Rwandan government formulated four main objections to the special investigation: that it would facilitate attempts to draw an equivalence of blame between Hutu genocidaires and Tutsi liberators; that RPF cases would slow down the ICTR's already 'ineffective' investigations; that the special investigation constituted foreign interference, violated Rwanda's sovereignty, and jeopardized peace and security in the region; and that the domestic military justice system had dealt or would deal with crimes that were, in any event, mere 'revenge killings', acts

[70] On genocide guilt, see Susan M Thomson, *Whispering Truth to Power: Everyday Resistance to Reconciliation in Postgenocide Rwanda* (University of Wisconsin Press 2013) 83–84; Moghalu (n 12) 49; Zinaida Miller, 'Anti-Impunity Politics in Post Genocide Rwanda' in Karen Engle, Zinaida Miller and Dennis Davis (eds), *Anti-Impunity and the Human Rights Agenda* (CUP 2016) 167.

[71] ICTR Press Release, 'Prosecutor Outlines Future Plans' (13 December 2000) ICTR/INFO-9-2-254-ENG <ictr-archive09.library.cornell.edu/ENGLISH/PRESSREL/2000/254.html>; Del Ponte (n 56) 184.

[72] Del Ponte (n 56) 183–85; International Crisis Group (n 9) 14–15.

[73] Interviews with former senior OTP official and senior Rwandan official, undisclosed location, 20 June and 16 September 2016. On the shift to non-cooperation in mid-2002, see Del Ponte (n 56) 224–26.

[74] Interview with former ICTR official, undisclosed location, 23 November 2015.

[75] Gahima (n 45) 109; Del Ponte (n 56) 226.

of individual insubordination, or mistakes.[76] Kagame articulated iterations of these objections to the Security Council and domestic audiences on various occasions.[77]

Facing obstructionism, Del Ponte's special investigation had stalled by mid-2002.[78] Although she referred Rwanda's non-cooperation to the Security Council, the political climate surrounding the ICTR's mandate was evolving. In addition to the UN's emerging completion strategy, a new US administration under George W. Bush was more sceptical of international criminal justice. According to Del Ponte, the United States supported Kagame's efforts to quash the special investigation in exchange for Rwanda's help in undermining the then newly established ICC.[79]

The ICTR's primacy emerged as a bone of contention. In line with US support for states' primacy (what became known as complementarity in the Rome Statute), the US ambassador for war crimes and a former ICTR trial attorney, Pierre Prosper, suggested that Del Ponte transfer the RPF case files to Rwandan prosecutors. According to Del Ponte, a draft agreement, brokered by Prosper, required her to 'share with the government of Rwanda a list of sites where massacres may have been committed' and 'any evidence related to these alleged massacres'.[80] Although she would be able to review the ensuing investigations and trials, Del Ponte would 'not seek an indictment or otherwise bring a case before the [Tribunal] until it is determined that [the government of Rwanda] investigation or prosecution was *not genuine*'.[81] Prosper later defended the compromise as a way to implement complementarity.[82]

There is disagreement as to the details. Some argue she accepted the deal only to later backtrack, but Del Ponte ultimately refused the offer, invoking what she believed to be the Tribunal's absolute primacy.[83] Under the agreement, Rwandan courts would have had the first opportunity to prosecute but, unlike primacy's

[76] FIDH (n 63) 16–17; Peskin (n 21) 208–09.

[77] Letter to the UN Secretary General from the Permanent Representative of Rwanda to the UN (26 July 2002) S/2002/842. President Paul Kagame, press conference broadcast on *Radio Rwanda*, 2 July 2002, quoted in Longman (n 61) 107; Paul Kagame, 'Preface' in Phil Clark and Zachary D Kaufman (eds), *After Genocide: Transitional Justice, Post-Conflict Reconstruction and Reconciliation in Rwanda and Beyond* (Hurst 2008) xxiii; Mohamed C Othman, *Accountability for International Humanitarian Law Violations: The Case of Rwanda and East Timor* (Springer 2005) 78–79.

[78] International Crisis Group, 'Tribunal pénal international pour le Rwanda: pragmatisme de rigeur' (2003) 7–8; Cruvellier (n 20) 242. But see Del Ponte (n 56) 229.

[79] On the US approach, see William A Schabas, *An Introduction to the International Criminal Court* (4th ed, CUP 2011) 25–34; Del Ponte (n 56) 230–41; Gahima (n 45) 109–12. On the US delegation to Rome, see Scheffer (n 18) 163–97.

[80] Del Ponte (n 56) 233.

[81] ibid 234. Emphasis added.

[82] Pierre Richard Prosper, Remarks at ICTR Conference, 'Model or Counter-Model for International Criminal Justice? The Perspectives of the Stakeholders', Session 2: The Prosecutions, Geneva, Switzerland, 9 July 2009 <genevaconference-tpir.univ-paris1.fr>.

[83] Del Ponte (n 56) 231–33. There is disagreement as to what happened at a high-level meeting in Washington in May 2003. Most scholars imply that Del Ponte agreed to Rwanda prosecuting the RPF domestically, but Del Ponte has argued in her memoirs that no agreement was reached (Gahima (n 45) 111; Moghalu (n 12) 144–45).

original rule 9 or the Rome Statute's admissibility rules, there was no mechanism to determine under what conditions the ICTR could reassert primacy. Arguing it was 'unskilfully vague', Del Ponte interpreted the agreement as a manoeuvre to kill the special investigation.[84]

Del Ponte's determination to investigate RPF crimes likely contributed to her removal as ICTR prosecutor in 2003 (the Security Council extended only her ICTY appointment).[85] Her replacement, Hassan Jallow, based full-time in Arusha, became the first standalone ICTR prosecutor. Although in splitting the ICTY/R prosecutorial functions, the UN instructed Jallow to investigate 'allegations of violations by the members of the [RPF]', his handling of the special investigation was 'marked by ambiguity'.[86] Jallow later announced his criteria for prosecutorial discretion under the Completion Strategy, but sidestepped the Security Council's mention of RPF investigations.[87] He also emphasized the importance of 'national reconciliation' in exercising discretion and that the ICTR was primarily a genocide court.[88]

Jallow later decided to pursue a back channel with Rwandan authorities modelled on the 2003 agreement that Del Ponte had rejected.[89] Reviving the original conception of primacy that aligns with complementarity's emphasis on the quality of domestic proceedings, Jallow announced in 2008 that Rwanda would be given an opportunity to prosecute one case on a 'clear understanding that any such prosecutions in and by Rwanda should be effective, expeditious, fair and open to the public'.[90] The OTP would also monitor the proceedings which 'will of course be without prejudice to the primacy of the ICTR's jurisdiction over these crimes'.[91] As explained by Jallow:[92]

> We did not give our OTP file to the Rwandans ... so we requested that they investigate it separately from our own investigation in order to protect our witnesses, but I saw the dossier and I approved the indictment against the four military officers ... they had to submit their investigations and indictment for my approval,

[84] Del Ponte (n 56) 234. Expressly as complementarity, see International Crisis Group (n 78) 8.

[85] Agence Hirondelle, 'Carla Del Ponte, si j'avais eu le choix, je serai restée procureur au TPIR' (14 September 2003). On the rationales behind a single prosecutor, see Moghalu (n 12) 127–37.

[86] UNSC Res 1503 (27 August 2003) S/RES/1503, para 3; Peskin (n 21) 227.

[87] Hassan B Jallow, 'Prosecutorial Discretion and International Criminal Justice' (2005) 3 Journal of International Criminal Justice 145, 151 (arguing the UNSC's mention of RPF investigations was not directed at him). See also Hassan Jallow, Remarks at ICTR Conference, Model or Counter Model for International Criminal Justice? The Perspectives of the Stakeholders: Session 5: Prosecutors Debate, 11 July 2009.

[88] Interview with Hassan Jallow, Arusha, Tanzania, 10 September 2015. See also Vlaming (n 3) 560–62. On the ICTR having 'primary responsibility' for genocide, see Rapp (n 8) 28; Peskin (n 21) 187–90.

[89] On the impulse for Jallow's outreach, see Waldorf (n 58) 1238 (noting Rwanda's interest in r 11*bis* referrals, and the French and Spanish indictments of the RPF).

[90] UNSC, S/PV.5904 (4 June 2008) 11.

[91] ibid.

[92] Interview with Hassan Jallow, Arusha, Tanzania, 10 September 2015.

> in order for us to make sure that the right charges were being brought and against the right people ... I wanted to see the Rwandan state itself prosecuting its own people, very senior people, and the effect that that could have perhaps on reconciliation ... and so we insisted that they do it publicly, and with monitoring from the Office.

Of the potential cases, the slaying of several prominent Catholic clergymen, including the Archbishop of Kigali, in June 1994 had always stood out. The RPF had essentially acknowledged responsibility for this massacre.[93] Following negotiations with the OTP, Rwandan military prosecutors charged two low-level and two high-ranking RPF soldiers. Monitored intermittently by OTP officials, a Rwandan military tribunal found the two captains guilty of the war crime of murder but acquitted Gen. Wilson Gumisiriza and Maj. Wilson Ukwishaka of command responsibility.[94] The verdict was confirmed on appeal in February 2009.[95]

The *Kabgayi* trial elicited much attention. As Gumisiriza also featured in the Spanish case against the RPF, a genuine trial would have strengthened the Rwandan government's argument that a foreign prosecution was not necessary.[96] However, *Kabgayi* had the opposite effect, with human rights groups condemning the lack of adversarial proceedings, questionable procedures, and inadequate ICTR monitoring. Acquittals of the two high-ranking officers, whose command responsibility was not seriously examined at trial, was considered particularly damning.[97] Labelling the trial a 'political whitewash' and 'a miscarriage of justice', HRW urged Jallow 'to recall the case' to Arusha.[98]

Jallow refused to assert primacy, explaining later to the Security Council that the *Kabgayi* trial 'was an open and public trial, and ... [t]he report of my monitors indicates that the standards of fair trial were observed'.[99] Elsewhere, Jallow noted that 'a fair trial clearly has the potential for acquittals and for convictions ... it's not really the outcome which is the critical factor. It's the process.'[100] By the same token, the Rwandan justice minister argued that a 'five year sentence [was] not a small punishment for a person who admitted to hav[ing] committed the crime'.[101]

93 Waldorf (n 58) 1246–48.

94 Le tribunal militaire (Kigali) [Military Tribunal] (24 October 2008) RP 0151/08/TM (on file).

95 Haute cour militaire (25 February 2009) RPA 0062/08/HCM (on file). For details, see Leslie Haskell and Lars Waldorf, 'The Impunity Gap of the International Criminal Tribunal for Rwanda: Causes and Consequences' (2011) 34 Hastings International and Comparative Law Review 49, 59–68.

96 On the link to the Spanish indictment, see Waldorf (n 58) 1243–45.

97 Kenneth Roth, 'Human Rights Watch: Letter to the Prosecutor of the ICTR Regarding the Prosecution of RPF Crimes' <hrw.org/news/2009/05/26/letter-prosecutor-international-criminal-tribunal-rwanda-regarding-prosecution-rpf>; Letter from Academics to UN, 'Ensuring ICTR Prosecutions for RPF War Crimes' <uk-africa.blogspot.ch/2009/06/ensuring-ictr-prosecutions-for-rpf-war.html>.

98 Roth (n 97). On monitoring, see Waldorf (n 58) 1254.

99 UNSC, S/PV.6134 (4 June 2009) 33.

100 Jallow (n 87).

101 Quoted in Sigall Horovitz, 'How International Courts Shape Domestic Justice: Lessons from Rwanda and Sierra Leone' (2013) 46 Israel Law Review 339, 348.

Jallow's assessment was controversial within the ICTR. One official conceded that Jallow had, in fact, overridden the advice of his OTP team, which had concluded *Kabgayi* failed to meet the required standards and advocated asserting primacy over the case.[102] Others noted that some ICTR officials were upset by the perception that Jallow had 'bowed to the Rwandan government'.[103] Striking also is the incongruence of ICTR judges rejecting Rwanda's transfer petitions under rule 11*bis* on fair trial grounds in 2008, while the prosecutor found the military justice system's handling (and acquittals) of far more controversial prosecutions of incumbent government-affiliated officials up to standard.[104]

As a rather unique trial of incumbent government actors occurring in the shadow of an ICT, *Kabgayi* illustrates the limitations and politicization of domestic accountability for international crimes. While it is clear the Rwandan military justice system never would have prosecuted the two RPF commanders in the absence of international pressure, their acquittals may have strengthened the political elite rather than promoting any sense of intrastate accountability or justice for Hutu victims.[105] As Horovitz observes, Kabgayi's potential 'recognition of Hutu victimhood and Tutsi accountability and its message that all conflict-related victims have an equal right to justice . . . was not met'.[106] Noting that ICTs may be 'unable or reluctant to recognize sham national proceedings designed to shield the accused', Waldorf warned also that *Kabgayi* might be a harbinger for the ICC's complementarity practice.[107]

2.4. Rule 11*bis*: foregrounding the iterative potential of primacy

With Del Ponte struggling and Jallow later refusing to prosecute RPF crimes, the ICTR's institutional priorities shifted. Under the Completion Strategy, the prosecutor was required to focus on 'senior leaders' and 'most responsible', while sending other cases to national jurisdictions subject to a fair trial.[108] The Tribunal's

[102] Interview with former OTP official, undisclosed location, 16 November 2016. Kenneth Roth, 'Human Rights Watch: Letter to the ICTR Chief Prosecutor Hassan Jallow in Response to His Letter on the Prosecution of RPF Crimes' <hrw.org/news/2009/08/14/letter-ictr-chief-prosecutor-hassan-jallow-response-his-letter-prosecution-rpf>.

[103] Phone interview with former ICTR official, 9 May 2019.

[104] In this sense, see Roth (n 97).

[105] For evaluations of the trial, see also Haskell and Waldorf (n 95) 75–78; Roland Adjovi, 'L'affaire Gumisiriza devant la justice militaire rwandaise' (2010) 18 African Yearbook of International Law/Annuaire africain de droit international 451, 458–60. For Rwandan perspectives on the trial and its contribution to reconciliation, see Sigall Horovitz, 'Rwanda's Kabgayi Trial between International Justice and National Reconciliation' in Mikkel Jarle Christensen and Ron Levi (eds), *International Practices of Criminal Justice Social and Legal Perspectives* (Routledge 2017) 241–50.

[106] Horovitz (n 105) 232.

[107] Waldorf (n 58) 1223–24. In this sense, presciently, see also Makau Mutua, 'From Nuremberg to the Rwanda Tribunal: Justice or Retribution?' (2000) 6 Buffalo Human Rights Law Review 77.

[108] See Chapter 3 in this volume.

jurisdiction remained primacy-based and the prosecutor retained authority to interpret the mandate, but cost-cutting incentives required the OTP to develop partnerships with states to decrease a bloated case docket. As Jallow acknowledged, 'it was not until the passing of . . . the completion strategy that there was a more determined focus on this process of identifying and concentrating on what is regarded as [the] "serious" cases'.[109]

In fact, the prospect of referrals existed prior to the Completion Strategy, albeit in a non-systematic manner. As explained in Chapter 3, in *Ntuyahaga* and *Barayagwiza*, Rwandan authorities had encouraged the ICTR to withdraw indictments and hand over suspects for domestic prosecution. Around this time, informal discussions also began between Rwandan prosecutors and senior OTP officials about referring cases.[110] According to former ICTR officials, no official agreement was possible primarily because of concerns over the death penalty and the domestic judiciary's lack of independence.[111] However, the OTP did from time to time use informal channels of communication to support domestic proceedings, which also built trust with Rwandan actors along the way.[112] The OTP occasionally relied on information from Rwandan officials to support its Arusha trials.[113]

As explained in Chapter 3, to implement the Completion Strategy, the OTP initially sought to transfer low- and mid-level suspects to states with a stronger rule of law. It was only when these rule 11*bis* referrals ran into obstacles that the OTP engaged Rwandan authorities on case transfers systematically. Jallow's full-time posting to Arusha allowed him to devote more time to his Rwandan counterparts. A series of meetings in 2005 and 2006, including in Kigali, led to the transmission of up to fifty-five case files to the National Public Prosecution Authority (NPPA).[114] Marking a break with past assumptions, the OTP shared, officially for the first time, files with Rwandan counterparts, subject to witness confidentiality requirements. Jallow later observed that the transmissions were an important confidence-building measure.[115]

[109] Jallow (n 87) 151.

[110] Interviews with former ICTR officials, Geneva, Switzerland, 25 January and 13 July 2016; International Crisis Group (n 9) 7–8.

[111] Interviews with former ICTR officials, Geneva, Switzerland, 12 June 2015, 25 January, 20 June and 13 July 2016.

[112] Horovitz (n 44) 62–64. But see Cruvellier (n 20) 187.

[113] Interview with former ICTR official, The Hague, 24 November 2015.

[114] ICTR-OTP, 'Complementarity in Action: Lessons Learned from the ICTR Prosecutor's Referral of International Criminal Cases to National Jurisdictions for Trial' (2015) 7. On transmissions of case files as opposed to r 11*bis* cases under indictment, see Alex Obote-Odora, 'Transfer of Cases from the International Criminal Tribunal for Rwanda to Domestic Jurisdictions' (2012) 5 African Journal of Legal Studies 147, 150. On the prosecutor's freedom (or not) to transmit case files, see Alhagi Marong, Charles C Jalloh and David Kinnecome, 'Concurrent Jurisdiction at the ICTR: Should the Tribunal Refer Cases to Rwanda?' in Emmanuel Decaux, Adama Dieng and Malick Sow (eds), *Des droits de l'homme au droit international pénal. Etudes en l'honneur d'un juriste africain, feu le juge Laïty Kama* (Martinus Nijhoff 2007) 170–72.

[115] Interview with Hassan Jallow, Arusha, Tanzania, 10 September 2015; Richard Karegyesa, 'Empowering Domestic Jurisdictions: Lessons from the ICTR Referral of Cases'. International Symposium on the Legacy of the ICTR, Arusha, Tanzania, 6 November 2014 (on file).

The process of sending ICTR indictments—as opposed to case files—to Rwanda was more complex. As will be explained in Chapter 5, to ensure that the Rwandan justice system met the conditions of rule 11*bis*, the entire Tribunal—Registry, chambers, and OTP—provided capacity building. After the first round of referrals was rejected over fair trial concerns, Rwanda continued to cooperate with the Tribunal, leading to a second round of capacity-building efforts and, ultimately, several referrals. In addition to these rule 11*bis* referrals, Rwanda continues to track suspects and request extraditions and deportations to this day, with an estimated 1,000 fugitives still unaccounted for.[116] As will be seen in subsequent chapters, the ICTR's diffusion of normative standards and positive evaluations of Rwandan justice standards likely facilitated outreach to states where such suspects reside.

2.5. Unpacking primacy's effects on domestic prosecutions

The literature on the ICTR's impact on prosecutions in Rwanda is thin. Most scholars, however, view the OTP's strategy as epiphenomenal at best, or dissuasive at worst, for Rwanda's home-grown accountability process. Writing in 2009 (before rule 11*bis* referrals had been approved), Horovitz argued that the ICTR 'did not play a role in encouraging national prosecutions of genocide perpetrators'.[117] Focusing on government crimes, Lars Waldorf suggests that the prosecutor '[b]y failing to prosecute *any* RPF crimes ... has rendered "victor's justice"', choosing 'to acquiesce in a pretense of justice rather than recognize an absence of justice'.[118]

Similar sentiments abound in scholarship on the ICTY and the 'Rules of the Road' programme. As William Burke-White observes:[119]

> [under] the Rules of the Road Agreement, which stipulated that the ICTY had to review case files from Bosnia & Herzegovina, Croatia, and Serbia before domestic indictments could be issued ... [l]ocal judicial authorities were required to forward case files to the ICTY [OTP] for review and approval. Without such

[116] For recent data, see TRIAL International, 'Universal Jurisdiction Annual Review 2020' (2020); Ivan Mugisha, 'Rwanda Issues New Indictments for Genocide Suspects' *East African* (12 December 2020) <theeastafrican.co.ke/tea/news/east-africa/rwanda-issues-new-indictments-for-genocide-suspects-3226516>.

[117] Horovitz (n 44) 69.

[118] Waldorf (n 58) 1272 and 1277.

[119] William Burke-White, 'The Domestic Influence of International Criminal Tribunals: The International Criminal Tribunal for the Former Yugoslavia and the Creation of the State Court of Bosnia & Herzegovina' (2008) 46 Columbia Journal of Transnational Law 279, 312–13 (emphasis added); Alejandro Chehtman, 'Developing Local Capacity for War Crimes Trials: Insights from BiH, Sierra Leone, and Colombia' (2013) 49 Stanford Journal of International Law 297, 320–21. For a more balanced and positive assessment, in line with this book's findings, see Diane Orentlicher, *Some Kind of Justice: The ICTY's Impact in Bosnia and Serbia* (OUP 2018) 328–34.

> approval, domestic prosecutors would be unable to proceed with the case. Though the intent of the Rules of the Road program—to prevent politically motivated domestic prosecutions by one ethnic group against another—may have been benign, the result was a further barrier to domestic prosecutions ... [it] sanctioned the exercise of domestic jurisdiction sufficiently to *deter national action*.

One-dimensionally negative assessments of the ad hoc tribunals' impact on domestic prosecutorial policy, in particular of primacy's dissuasive effects, misapprehend how international case selection shaped the domestic accountability landscape in Rwanda. For one, the prosecutor's initially robust reading of primacy allowed the ICTR to set the terms of the post-genocide accountability debate. Backed by a Chapter VII mandate, the OTP established a permanent office in Kigali while launching a worldwide effort to track high-level fugitives, virtually all of whom had departed Rwanda after 1994. Despite Rwanda's tracking efforts, the reality was that most states would have refused to extradite people to a justice system that was only beginning to rebuild.[120]

International trials in Arusha also shaped the process of rebuilding domestic justice institutions. By challenging the new political elite's authority to criminally sanction the previous regime, the race for high-ranking suspects, coupled with the threat of deferrals, likely accelerated the convening of domestic trials. Although primacy-based deferrals never eventuated on Rwandan soil (primacy only helped to gain custody of suspects abroad), the possibility that Goldstone would challenge Rwanda's exercise of jurisdiction, coupled with pressure from development partners to ensure defence rights, triggered debates—as will be seen in Chapters 5 and 6—over justice standards before national courts. Therefore, while top-down, coercive pressure from the ICTR was not a primary cause of domestic prosecutions in Rwanda, the shadow of international intervention, including the ICTR's non-consensual approach to primacy, provided an important point of international leverage vis-à-vis the country's emerging political elite.

Yet, while the ICTR's robust mandate put pressure on the post-genocide authorities in the early phase, primacy's iterative potential was short-lived. Goldstone's tough line on jurisdictional disputes dissipated as soon as the ICTR had enough suspects to keep itself busy and, over time, a tacit division of labour replaced the race for defendants. Faced with the task of running complex trials in Arusha, Arbour avoided clashes with Rwanda. As international trials of genocidaires began, the RPF's support became crucial not only for OTP investigators (who continued to search for evidence in Rwanda) but also for the logistics of trials, which could only take place if the RPF allowed Rwandan witnesses to fly to Arusha to testify in

[120] In this sense, see Moghalu (n 12) 198.

court. Against this backdrop, the Rwandan government increasingly dictated the terms of its relationship with the ICTR.

As the terms of this uneven relationship came into focus, so did the coercive limits of Chapter VII-based primacy. Although, given the vagaries of its temporal mandate, the ICTR only had jurisdiction over crimes committed until 31 December 1994, the OTP was haunted by allegations of continuing RPF crimes. Adopting an unconditional reading of primacy, Del Ponte discounted domestic trials of RPF soldiers, fearing—not without reason—that the military would not hold its own to account. Yet, despite primacy and the nominal threat of Security Council action, the ICTR could not force Rwanda's military to cooperate with her special investigation. In the end, unlike the ICTY's experience in former Yugoslav states, the threat of indictments against RPF leaders was insufficient to overcome obstructionism.[121]

By realigning ICTR priorities, the Completion Strategy imposed a revised conditionality-based relationship with Rwanda. As will be seen further in Chapters 5 and 6, instead of competition, rule 11*bis* foregrounded international–domestic synergies based on a consensual distribution of suspects, with the mutual benefits of rule 11*bis*—transfers allowed the ICTR to decrease its caseload while the RPF delivered on its anti-impunity policy—driving iterative negotiations. However, in the background of rule 11*bis* loomed the unresolved issue of RPF crimes. Unlike his predecessor, Jallow embraced a conciliatory approach, reinterpreting primacy as a conditionality tool to outsource an emblematic case while retaining the authority to evaluate the ensuing domestic trial. Although *Kabgayi* is a unique example of international civil servants fostering a controversial domestic prosecution of high-level incumbent state officials, its outcome raises questions about the standards by which to evaluate national proceedings and prosecutorial negotiation tactics. Rather than a tool to contest state impunity, Jallow's push for a domestic trial may have reinforced RPF control rather than promote accountability for crimes against Hutus.

The ICTR's failure to prosecute RPF crimes and influence Rwanda's one-sided accountability landscape remains its greatest shortcoming.[122] But this outcome was not foreordained; the OTP arguably had opportunities to act differently. For one, investigations could have started earlier, ideally under Goldstone, when the RPF had yet to consolidate control.[123] For another, Jallow could have used the carrot of

[121] On the ICTY vis-à-vis Serbia, see Orentlicher (n 119) 383–87 and 406–25.

[122] Scott Straus, 'The Limits of a Genocide Lens: Violence against Rwandans in the 1990s' (2019) 21 Journal of Genocide Research 504; Peskin (n 21) 186–234. But see Charles C Jalloh and Andrew Morgan, 'International Criminal Justice Processes in Rwanda and Sierra Leone: Lessons for Liberia' in Charles C Jalloh and Olufemi Elias, *Shielding Humanity: Essays in International Law in Honour of Judge Abdul G. Koroma* (Brill 2015) 470–73; William A Schabas, 'Selecting Cases at the International Criminal Tribunal for Rwanda' in Charles C Jalloh and Alhagi BM Marong, *Promoting Accountability under International Law for Gross Human Rights Violations in Africa. Essays in Honour of Prosecutor Hassan Bubacar Jallow* (Brill 2015).

[123] International Crisis Group (n 78) 9.

rule 11*bis* referrals to demand Rwandan concessions on the RPF file (to be sure, this strategy could have backfired, leaving the OTP with un-transferred rule 11*bis* cases). It may also be that international prosecutors never pushed hard enough. According to Gahima, the Rwandan prosecutor general who later went into exile, the ICTR 'never seriously pressured the Rwandan government to cooperate with or support investigations of abuses attributable to its military'.[124]

Ultimately, while the Completion Strategy promoted iterative practices by forcing the ICTR to engage Rwanda over genocide prosecutions, it decreased the OTP's leverage over RPF crimes. After the Completion Strategy, the threat of new investigations was not plausible and Rwanda knew it could wait out the Tribunal. Moreover, unlike the ICTY, which received international backing to effect arrests, the United States supported, sometimes overtly, the RPF in its struggle against the ICTR.

3. The Special Court for Sierra Leone

3.1. Prosecutorial strategy: targeted or target-driven?

After the Special Court's establishment in January 2002, the UN Secretary General appointed David Crane, a US government attorney, to be the first prosecutor.[125] Crane and a few members of the future SCSL–OTP arrived in Freetown to begin investigations in the summer of 2002. Although violence had by then decreased and a peace agreement ending the civil war had been signed, Sierra Leone remained a volatile environment where a relapse into conflict remained a possibility.[126]

The SCSL is known primarily for its hybridity, but prosecutorial discretion was shaped by its restrictive mandate. Crane's freedom to select cases for prosecution was constrained in three ways. First, perpetrators had to bear 'greatest responsibility'. Second, only crimes committed after the Abidjan peace agreement were prosecutable, meaning almost half the civil war was outside the SCSL's temporal jurisdiction. Third, given the SCSL's projected three-year operational timeframe and funding constraints, it was clear from the outset that the list of suspects could not be long. Put differently, to a greater extent than at other ICTs, investigations, prosecutions and trials before the SCSL had to materialise quickly.[127]

[124] Gahima (n 45) 112; Peskin (n 21) 222–25.

[125] President SCSL, 'First Annual Report SCSL' 5; International Crisis Group, 'The Special Court for Sierra Leone: Promises and Pitfalls of a "New Model"' (2003).

[126] David M Crane, 'The Bright Red Thread. The Politics of International Criminal Law: Do We Want Peace or Justice? The West African Experience' in Leila N Sadat (ed), *Forging a Convention for Crimes against Humanity* (CUP 2010).

[127] Rapp (n 8) 24–26 and 34–35. Interview with former OTP official, Cape Town, South Africa, 23 March 2016.

Against this backdrop, it is not surprising that Crane's prosecutorial strategy formed over the course of just several months in late 2002 and early 2003. There has long been speculation that the selection of cases may have been influenced by external considerations, including US and British foreign policy.[128] In particular, some have argued that Keith Biddle, a senior British police officer seconded by the UK government to lead the Sierra Leonean police force, provided Crane with a list of suspects before investigations started in mid-2002.[129] Interviews reveal scepticism as to the existence or relevance of such a list, especially since the ringleaders of the main warring factions were generally known.[130] Crane maintains that those bearing 'greatest responsibility' for atrocities in the Sierra Leonean civil war were selected free of political pressure, based on a 'four corners' strategy involving travel and consultations with Sierra Leoneans around the country.[131]

Irrespective of whether prosecutions at the SCSL were (merely) targeted or target-driven (based on a list), the Special Court's restrictive mandate forced the OTP to reduce, in a short amount of time, the number of potential indictees from 30,000 to 20.[132] Moreover, within just months of beginning investigations, the Special Court had custody of its first suspects. On 10 March 2003, three days after indictments had been approved by the SCSL's judges, seven individuals were arrested in 'Operation Justice' in different parts of Freetown. Despite concerns about collusion between the Sierra Leonean government and indictees, Crane and his staff succeeded in keeping the operation secret not only from government officials but also the UN peacekeeping mission.[133] All but one of the initial seven targets ended up in the SCSL's custody by nightfall on March 10.[134]

Uniquely among ICTs, the SCSL brought charges against the main belligerents in the civil war. From the beginning, Crane argued that the SCSL's mandate should be interpreted to mean those bearing greatest responsibility within each faction.[135]

[128] Chris Mahony, 'A Political Tool? The Politics of Case Selection at the Special Court for Sierra Leone' in Kirsten Ainley, Rebekka Friedman and Chris Mahony (eds), *Evaluating Transitional Justice. Accountability and Peacebuilding in Post-Conflict Sierra Leone* (Palgrave Macmillan 2015) 77; International Crisis Group (n 125) 13.

[129] Tom Perriello and Marieke Wierda, 'The Special Court for Sierra Leone under Scrutiny' (ICTJ 2006) 27; Vlaming (n 3) 564. But see Crane (n 126) 67–68.

[130] Phone interview with international experts, 9 January 2017 and 6 April 2017. Interviews with former SCSL officials, The Hague, Netherlands and Geneva, Switzerland, 19 November 2016 and 7 July 2016.

[131] Mahony (n 128) 90–91; Crane (n 126) 70 ('Frankly, it was understood . . . who the "local favorites" were')

[132] Crane (n 126) 75; International Crisis Group (n 125) 3. Critically, see Charles C Jalloh, 'Special Court for Sierra Leone: Achieving Justice?' (2011) 32 Michigan Journal of International Law 395, 420.

[133] Crane (n 126) 70–77; David M Crane, 'The Take Down: Case Studies Regarding "Lawfare" in International Criminal Justice: The West African Experience' (2010) 43 Case Western Reserve Journal of International Law 201, 206–11.

[134] Phone interviews with former SCSL officials and international experts, 9 January, 17 March, and 4 July 2017. President SCSL (n 125) 14–15.

[135] On pursuing leaders within each group as a prosecutorial strategy, see Rapp (n 8) 29–30; Crane (n 126); Jalloh (n 132) 421–28.

Few were surprised by the indictments against Foday Sankoh of the RUF or Alex Tamba Brima of the AFRC, but many Sierra Leoneans considered the CDF—a militia with close ties to the incumbent government of President Kabbah—as liberators. In fact, Sam Hinga Norman had become deputy minister of interior by the time of his arrest. Given his position, it was his own police officers, albeit on secondment to the SCSL, who carried out the physical act of arrest in his office.[136] Illustrative of how controversial his trial would be, Peter Penfold, a British High Commissioner to Sierra Leone during the civil war, went on to testify in Norman's defence at trial.[137]

Although the CDF cases generated much criticism, this was hardly the only case selection controversy. Many Sierra Leoneans felt that 'greatest responsibility' should mean direct perpetrators who committed gruesome atrocities, rather than commanders who gave orders far from the battlefield.[138] Another critique was that, while Crane claimed to prosecute within each faction, neither ECOMOG peacekeepers nor the Sierra Leonean Army were charged.[139] Some have also noted the absence of charges against the financiers of the war.[140] Most importantly, many disagreed that those charged from the three main belligerent factions were, in fact, the most senior. In particular, it was suggested that President Kabbah should have, as Norman's superior, also been charged on grounds of command responsibility or, conversely, that Augustine Gbao was prosecuted mainly because he had committed crimes against peacekeepers (which mattered for the UN but less so for Sierra Leoneans).[141]

Despite these and other controversies, Crane's prosecutorial strategy stands out for the fact that he succeeded in bringing charges and effecting arrests against a sitting senior government official. As Kenneth Rodman observes, 'in a normal sovereign state', Norman 'would have control over the arresting units'.[142] No other ICT has managed to use coercive power against the territorial state to such effect, which in turn raises questions about the incumbent administration's relationship with the

[136] William A Schabas, 'Conjoined Twins of Transitional Justice? The Sierra Leone Truth and Reconciliation Commission and the Special Court' (2004) 2 Journal of International Criminal Justice 1082, 1092; International Crisis Group (n 125) 6–7 and 10.

[137] Lansana Gberie, 'The Civil Defense Forces Trial: Limit to International Justice?' in Charles C Jalloh (ed), *The Sierra Leone Special Court and Its Legacy: The Impact for Africa and International Criminal Law* (CUP 2013) 636.

[138] Thierry Cruvellier, 'From the Taylor Trial to a Lasting Legacy: Putting the Special Court Model to the Test' (ICTJ 2009) 19–20; Priscilla Hayner, *'Negotiating Peace in Sierra Leone: Confronting the Justice Challenge'* (ICTJ and Centre for Humanitarian Dialogue 2007) 26; Perriello and Wierda (n 129) 28.

[139] Kenneth Rodman, 'Justice Is Interventionist: The Political Sources of the Judicial Reach of the Special Court for Sierra Leone' (2013) 13 International Criminal Law Review 63, 84. Interviews with former SCSL officials, Cape Town, South Africa and by phone 23 March 2016 and 6 April 2017.

[140] Interviews with former SCSL officials, Geneva, Switzerland, 7 July 2016. Kirsten Ainley, 'Evaluating the Success of Transitional Justice in Sierra Leone and Beyond' in Kirsten Ainley, Rebekka Friedman and Chris Mahony (eds), *Evaluating Transitional Justice: Accountability and Peacebuilding in Post-Conflict Sierra Leone* (Palgrave Macmillan 2015) 247.

[141] Phone interview with former SCSL official, 2 August 2016. See also Rodman (n 139) 74–77.

[142] Rodman (n 139) 78.

SCSL. Although some argue that Kabbah sacrificed Norman, an inconvenient political rival, interviews with former OTP officials and Sierra Leoneans suggest that Crane's targeting of the CDF was not a strategy that he 'negotiated' with the government.[143] In particular, interviewees confirmed that the SCSL–OTP opened a file on Kabbah, though there was ultimately not enough evidence to substantiate an actual case file against him.[144]

Interpretations diverge, but it is likely that Crane's case selection, including an indictment against a senior government official, was enabled mainly by the Sierra Leonean state's fragility and the presence of the British army and UN peacekeepers, reducing the sovereignty constraints that traditionally prevent ICTs from enforcing mandates over state opposition. Unusually for ICTs, the Sierra Leonean police force—which played a role in investigations, as will be discussed in Chapter 5—was headed by a foreign national rather than someone from the domestic political establishment. It helped also that Crane brought indictments soon after the cessation of hostilities. As Rodman observes:[145]

> [the SCSL's] willingness to try both winners and losers has ... been praised as an important precedent in countering victor's justice. Yet the ability of the SCSL to pursue exemplary prosecutions regardless of peace negotiations or political alignment was a function of political conditions absent in other cases. First, Sierra Leone was a failed state inordinately dependent on the international actors supportive of trials for security and economic reconstruction ... Second, the strong international military presence on the ground minimized the risk that prosecution would destabilize the peace process. That was primarily because the UK and UN-supported enforcement missions effectively defeated the RUF ...

In total, the SCSL charged thirteen individuals, ten of whom stood trial between 2004 and 2013. But it is important not to project backward from these numbers in interpreting the court's impact on Sierra Leone. Even after the first indictments were enforced in 2003, no one on the Sierra Leonean side knew for sure how far 'greatest responsibility' would extend.[146] For instance, in 2004, HRW observed that 'the existing indictments reflect[ed] an inappropriately narrow interpretation of the court's mandate' and encouraged the OTP to 'include other perpetrators who, while not at the top of the chain of command, were regional or mid-level

[143] On Norman and his relationship with Kabbah, see Gberie (n 137) 630; Mahony (n 128) 90 and 94. But see George K Kieh, 'State-Building in Post-Civil War Sierra Leone' (2005) 4 African and Asian Studies 163, 178; Jalloh and Morgan (n 122) 486; Solomon E Berewa, *A New Perspective on Governance, Leadership, Conflict and Nation Building in Sierra Leone* (AuthorHouse 2011) 179–81.

[144] Interviews with former OTP and Sierra Leonean officials, Cape Town, South Africa and by phone, 23 March 2016 and 17 March 2017.

[145] Rodman (n 139) 77.

[146] President SCSL (n 125) 14–15.

commanders'.[147] Charles Taylor's arrest in 2006 fuelled speculation about additional cases, including sealed indictments against Muamar Gaddafi, then president of Libya and Blaise Compaoré, then president of Burkina Faso.[148]

In other words, in the public eye, the SCSL's case docket remained open after 2003. Although 'greatest responsibility' left only so much room for manoeuvre—HRW acknowledged that there could be no more 'than a couple of additional indictments'—the uncertainty around the prospect of future indictments shaped interactions with government and civil society actors in Sierra Leone.[149]

3.2. The SCSL and domestic prosecutions: neutral or dissuasive?

Accountability for Sierra Leone's civil war is usually equated with the SCSL and the TRC. However, two multi-defendant 'ordinary crimes' trials and several treason trials for war-related events took place in the shadow of the Special Court's intervention. In March 2002, before Crane had been appointed prosecutor, Sierra Leonean prosecutors charged Foday Sankoh and some forty-nine codefendants from the RUF on charges of murder, conspiracy to murder and shooting with intent to commit murder, relating to multiple deaths after a demonstration in front of Sankoh's house in May 2000 (*RUFP* case). Two months later, thirty-one members of the West Side Boys (WSB), a splinter group of the Sierra Leonean Army, were indicted on charges of murder and aggravated robbery for incidents that took place after the 1999 Lomé amnesty (*WSB* case).[150]

The *RUFP* and *WSB* trials, which took place at the High Court in Freetown—a few kilometres from the SCSL's three trials—did not formally involve charges of war crimes or crimes against humanity (as will be discussed in Chapter 6, international crimes had not, for the most part, been domesticated in Sierra Leone). Importantly also, the *RUFP* and *WSB* cases concerned post-Lomé events, which made them ineligible for amnesty under Sierra Leonean law. Yet these two trials implicated several of the SCSL's future defendants, which meant that—as in Rwanda—the distribution of cases between national and international prosecutors created jurisdictional overlap.

However, the similarities end there. Unlike Rwanda's tug of war with the ICTR over genocidaires, Sierra Leone conceded international jurisdiction. For instance, Sankoh, the RUF leader and most senior accused in the *RUFP* trial, was transferred

[147] HRW, 'Bringing Justice: The Special Court for Sierra Leone. Accomplishments, Shortcomings, and Needed Support' (2004) 5.

[148] For other potential indictees, see Cruvellier (n 138) 20.

[149] HRW (n 147) 5.

[150] For the facts of both cases, this chapter draws on Sigall Horovitz, *Sierra Leone: Interaction between International and National Responses to the Mass Atrocities* (DOMAC 2009) 26–27; Horovitz (n 101) 358.

to the Special Court in March 2003.[151] Although he died just a few months later, before his international trial had begun, Crane never formally invoked primacy against Sierra Leone. Instead, it appears then Attorney General, Eke Holloway, suspended domestic proceedings against Sankoh.[152] Similarly, Santigie Kanu, another suspect in Pademba prison on domestic charges, was transferred 'consensually' to the SCSL in September 2003.[153]

With the allocation of defendants happening behind the scenes, not only was primacy never litigated; equally important, the number of suspects prosecuted domestically depended on the SCSL's interpretation of 'greatest responsibility'. As noted previously, Crane's case selection raised many questions, but less researched is the extent to which deals with 'insider witnesses' prevented Sierra Leonean prosecutors from bringing charges domestically, in particular in the *RUFP* and *WSB* cases.[154] For instance, while it is generally accepted that some perpetrators had to receive some form of immunity from international prosecution in exchange for their cooperation with the OTP, some observers question whether insider witnesses bore 'greater' responsibility than the defendants who eventually appeared before the Special Court.[155] Equally problematic, some suspects-cum-insiders were released from domestic custody in exchange for their cooperation, thereby preventing Sierra Leonean prosecutors from bringing charges. As noted by one official, 'awed by the authority of the UN … nobody within the domestic system was prepared to take a tough line … with those who had been prosecution witnesses at the Special Court and then prosecute them domestically'.[156]

The SCSL's inward-looking approach to case selection augured a relationship with Sierra Leonean authorities marked by isolation, rather than interdependence and mutual learning. Contrary to expectations, the OTP did not sign a cooperation agreement to facilitate the sharing of information and evidence with Sierra Leonean prosecutors.[157] As will be seen in Chapters 5 and 6, except for Sierra Leonean police officers seconded to the OTP, international investigations

[151] *Prosecutor v Foday Sankoh* (Warrant of Arrest and Order for Transfer and Detention) SCSL-2003–2-I (7 March 2003); ICTJ, 'The Special Court for Sierra Leone: The First Eighteen Months' 5.

[152] Interviews with international experts, Nuremberg, Germany and by phone, 9 January 2017 and 20 October 2017. See also Chapter 3, section 3.1 in this volume.

[153] President SCSL (n 125) 9.

[154] But see Jennifer Easterday, 'The Consequences of Witness Payments at the Special Court for Sierra Leone' in Charles C Jalloh (ed), *The Sierra Leone Special Court and Its Legacy* (CUP 2013); Sara Kendall and Michelle Staggs, *From Mandate to Legacy: The Special Court for Sierra Leone as a Model for 'Hybrid Justice'* (War Crimes Studies Center Berkeley 2005) 21.

[155] Interviews with former SCSL officials, Geneva, Switzerland, 7 July 2016 and London, UK, 25 March 2017 and Nuremberg, Germany, 19 October 2016.

[156] Phone interview with former SCSL official, 16 December 2016. See also Thierry Cruvellier, 'The Massaquoi Affair: Special Report on the Judas of Sierra Leone' (*JusticeInfo*, 7 April 2020) <justiceinfo.net/en/tribunals/mixed-tribunals/44085-the-massaquoi-affair-special-report-on-the-judas-of-sierra-leone-part-1.html>.

[157] Horovitz (n 150) 48. Phone interviews with former SCSL staff and international experts, 9 January and 17 March 2017.

advanced with no input from state actors, and Crane's failure to charge ordinary crimes under national law may have discouraged analogous charging by domestic prosecutors.

Meanwhile, against the backdrop of the SCSL's high-profile trials in Freetown, the two domestic trials lingered in obscurity. Amid reports of 'gross judicial abuses, detention without charges, a lack of defence counsel, the taking of statements under severe duress, and physical abuse [resulting] in a number of deaths', the *RUFP* and *WSB* proceedings took years to weave their way to trial.[158] In 2006, the High Court finally announced verdicts and lengthy sentences against over a dozen suspects.[159] Among those sentenced were mid-level rebel commanders that were cited as potential SCSL targets (but who failed to make the cut), notably Mohamed Savage who received a sentence of sixty years' imprisonment.[160] Although these domestic proceedings advanced alongside the SCSL's trials, there is little evidence that the Special Court's presence enhanced respect for international standards.[161]

Aside from the *RUFP* and *WSB* trials, which involved charges of serious crimes, accountability for wartime events in Sierra Leone has traditionally been limited to treason. For instance, in 1998, at the height of the Sierra Leonean civil war, courts prosecuted hundreds of suspects for treason, with twenty-four AFRC defendants ultimately executed.[162] In a similar fashion, Sierra Leonean authorities occasionally used treason charges in the post-civil war era, notably against former AFRC and RUF commanders, including Jonny Paul Koroma for a failed coup attempt in 2003,[163] and in 2006 against a former RUF spokesperson, Omrie Golly, for an attempted coup plot.[164] However, these post-civil war treason proceedings suffered from serious politicization and shifting power constellations.[165]

In fact, any semblance of domestic criminal accountability for the civil war proved ephemeral. Shortly before the 2007 elections, outgoing president Kabbah

[158] Clare Da Silva, 'Will Justice Prevail?' *The Guardian* (4 June 2007) <theguardian.com/commentisfree/2007/jun/04/willjusticeprevail>; Open Society Justice Initiative, 'Legacy: Completing the Work of the Special Court for Sierra Leone' (2011) 15.

[159] High Court of Sierra Leone, *The State v Foday Kallay & ors* (Judgment by the Honourable Mr Justice PO Hamilton) (5 April 2006) (*WSB*) (on file); High Court of Sierra Leone, *The State v Foday Sankoh & ors* (Judgment by the Honourable Mr Justice PO Hamilton) (11 April 2006) (on file).

[160] *WSB* trial transcript, 29.

[161] The verdicts ignore SCSL norms and international jurisprudence (Horovitz (n 101) 359). In line with Sierra Leone's practice of 'trial by ambush', prosecutors conducted no preliminary investigations and suspects were neither informed of the charges nor had access to defence counsel before trial. Chehtman (n 119) 301; Horovitz (n 150) 27. On 'trial by ambush', see Chapter 6, section 3.4 in this volume.

[162] For details, see Chapter 6, section 3.3 in this volume; Berewa (n 143) 123.

[163] Horovitz (n 150) 53; Da Silva (n 158).

[164] High Court of Sierra Leone, *The State v Omrie Golly and ors* (6 July 2007) (on file); Horovitz (n 150) 54; Institute for Security Studies, 'Sierra Leone. A Country Review of Crime and Criminal Justice, 2008' (2009) 66.

[165] Mohamed Suma, 'Politics of Death Penalty in Post-Conflict Sierra Leone: An Opportunity for Reform or a Missed Opportunity?' in Madoka Futamura and Nadia Bernaz, *The Politics of the Death Penalty in Countries in Transition* (Routledge 2014) 169.

released everyone who had been convicted in the *RUFP* trial, pre-empting an appeal in their cases.[166] After the opposition came to power in 2007, charges were dropped against Golly and, in 2008, several warlords previously sentenced to death for a coup attempt in 2003 were acquitted.[167] The *WSB* trial ended equally ignominiously—before the Court of Appeal could examine the defendants' appeal, all ten were released for unknown reasons in 2008.[168]

Sierra Leone's post-civil war domestic trials have received scant attention. Although almost eighty people were tried by the High Court, international NGOs focused their advocacy on the Special Court.[169] One NGO official acknowledged that the SCSL may have created a perception among government officials and activists that enough was being done to advance accountability in Sierra Leone—'not that we don't think it's important, [but] we didn't have time to follow [the post-Lomé prosecutions], or advocate for them'.[170] Echoing this sentiment, Sierra Leonean activists acknowledged that the Special Court was the main priority for them.[171]

The SCSL's high-profile trials seem also to have engendered a false sense of accommodation between the Tribunal and Sierra Leonean actors. An international expert noted that the Special Court's 'greatest responsibility' mandate 'decreased pressure' on the Sierra Leonean judiciary.[172] By the same token, SCSL officials did not consider encouraging or supporting domestic trials to be within their mandate. For instance, Desmond de Silva, the first deputy prosecutor who later succeeded Crane as chief prosecutor, dismissed the idea of supporting domestic cases, arguing that 'our job was to deal with the people who bore the greatest responsibility ... we had enough on our plate'.[173] Another senior OTP official argued that, while it would have been desirable to encourage fair trials at the national level, 'my impression was they didn't want the SCSL involved in this, [there were] sensitivities around prosecuting people from all sides, so it was politically tricky'.[174] Yet another OTP staff noted 'a strong hesitancy' to do domestic prosecutions given the political elite's complicity in war-related crimes.[175] In short, aside from its physical presence in Freetown and proximity to domestic trials, the Special Court's mandate seems to have provided no incentive to, and may have had a dissuasive effect on, OTP officials and human rights groups to challenge practices before national courts.

166 Horovitz (n 150) 27–28.
167 Mohamed Fofanah, 'Death Penalty—Sierra Leone: Successful Appeal Strengthens Case for Abolition' *IPS News Agency* (12 December 2008) <ipsnews.net/2008/12/death-penalty-sierra-leone-successful-appeal-strengthens-case-for-abolition/>.
168 Horovitz (n 101) 358.
169 Phone interviews with NGO staff, 6 April and 9 August 2017.
170 Phone interviews with NGO representatives, 7 April and 13 August 2017.
171 Interviews with civil society activists, Freetown, Sierra Leone, 11, 13 and 16 March 2016.
172 Interview with international expert, Nuremberg, Germany, 20 October 2017.
173 Phone interview with Desmond de Silva, 3 July 2017.
174 Interview with former senior SCSL official, London, UK, 9 February 2017.
175 Phone interview with former OTP official, 17 March 2017.

3.3. Failed iteration: amnesty repeal, rule 11*bis*, and drawdown

Although the Special Court's architects had initially hoped for a brief, three-year operational timeframe, it soon turned out that complex international trials did not lend themselves to quick resolution. With first instance proceedings still ongoing in the three main trials in 2006, Antonio Cassese suggested that 'realistically' the SCSL should 'complete its judicial activity by the end of 2009'.[176] These estimates changed again after Taylor's arrest necessitated additional trial and appellate proceedings.[177] In the end, the SCSL operated in Sierra Leone for over a decade, with the RSCSL taking over in 2013 and carrying out limited operations in Freetown to this day.

During this period, the SCSL contributed to domestic accountability debates, some of which still continue in a more limited fashion.[178] In particular, against the backdrop of the 1999 Lomé peace agreement, which provided for truth-seeking and a blanket amnesty, the SCSL raised questions about the (il)legality of amnesties under both international and domestic law. Uniquely among ICTs (for complex reasons originating in Lomé), the SCSL Statute declared that '[a]n amnesty granted to any person falling within the jurisdiction of the Special Court ... shall not be a bar to prosecution'.[179] Building on this, in March 2004, the Appeals Chamber rejected a defence challenge that the Lomé amnesty prevented their prosecution, arguing inter alia that amnesty was 'not only incompatible with, but is in breach of an obligation of a state towards the international community as a whole'.[180]

While the Appeals Chamber decision is usually hailed as a landmark on the illegality of amnesties in international law, it also stimulated civil society efforts to overturn the Lomé amnesty at the national level.[181] Shortly after the decision, a magistrate court in Freetown dismissed a test case brought by a Sierra Leonean attorney. Although this meant the Lomé amnesty had been implicitly upheld, Sierra Leonean activists acknowledged that the SCSL's jurisprudence provided an initial stimulus for their repeal effort.[182] One human rights activist explained that attorneys sought also to challenge the amnesty's legality before the Sierra Leonean

[176] Antonio Cassese, 'Report on the Special Court for Sierra Leone' (2006) 1.

[177] For the Taylor trial, see Luc Côté, 'Independence and Impartiality' in Reydams, Wouters and Ryngaert (n 3) 386–88; Cruvellier (n 138) 12–14.

[178] On Fambul Tok, see Shankar Vedantam and Maggie Penman, 'Fambul Tok: Forgiveness and "Family Talk" in Sierra Leone' *National Public Radio* <npr.org/2016/01/26/463861864/fambul-tok-forgiveness-and-family-talk-in-sierra-leone?t=1655385235966>.

[179] SCSL Statute, art 10. On the SCSL and amnesty, see William A Schabas, *Unimaginable Atrocities: Justice, Politics, and Rights at the War Crimes Tribunals* (OUP 2012) 173–76.

[180] AC, *Prosecutor v Kallon and Kamara* (Decision on Challenge to Jurisdiction. Lomé Accord Amnesty) SCSL-2004-15/16-AR72(E) (13 March 2004) para 73; Leila N Sadat, 'The Lomé Amnesty Decision of the Special Court for Sierra Leone' in Charles C Jalloh (ed), *The Sierra Leone Special Court and Its Legacy* (CUP 2013).

[181] But see critically n 211 (and accompanying test) in this section on the Appeals Chamber decision.

[182] Interview with activist and foreign expert, Freetown, Sierra Leone, and Nuremberg, Germany, 15 March 2016 and 20 October 2017. Phone interview with former SCSL judge, 4 August 2016.

Supreme Court, but he averred that 'it was made clear to me in informal discussions' that judges of the Supreme Court 'would not touch this issue'.[183]

Despite resistance from Sierra Leone's political establishment, including in this case the judiciary, civil society continued to search for ways to prosecute pre-Lomé crimes. To potentially influence the government, the truth commission and other organizations named several high-ranking suspects worthy of prosecution (one of whom, Gibril Massaquoi, would later stand trial in Finland).[184] Some NGOs, for instance the Centre for Accountability and the Rule of Law, pushed for an executive or legislative repeal of the Lomé amnesty.[185] Some even argued that a repeal was not legally necessary, with Cassese encouraging the SCSL to 'hand over to the Sierra Leonean Director of Public Prosecution copies of all the evidence [they] may have collected against middle-level defendants or against the so-called notorious criminals'.[186]

Evidence sharing as a means of encouraging domestic prosecutions was contemplated. Having amassed considerable evidence in the course of their investigations, including against perpetrators who met the 'greatest responsibility' threshold but could not be charged due to budgetary constraints, SCSL officials suggested as early as 2004 that evidence would be transferred to Sierra Leonean prosecutors to facilitate domestic proceedings. For instance, Al White, then chief of investigations, noted that 'he intend[ed] to provide local justice officials with investigative reports about individuals who the Special Court decided not to pursue, as they were found to be just under the threshold for prosecution within the mandate of the court'.[187]

However, this transfer of evidence appears never to have happened. While it is not clear why—some argue the applicability of the death penalty constituted an obstacle to sharing files[188]—the Sierra Leonean government's increasingly negative stance on the possibility of domestic prosecutions may have limited prospects for cooperation.[189] For instance, a senior official in the Attorney General's office conceded that previous administrations had purposely avoided any discussion of domestic prosecutions.[190] At the same time, civil society groups seemed wary of distracting from international trials, with HRW warning that '[t]he Special Court

[183] Interview with Sierra Leonean activist, Cape Town, 23 March 2016.

[184] HRW (n 147) 6.

[185] HRW, 'Justice in Motion. The Trial Phase of the Special Court for Sierra Leone' (2005) 38; Ibrahim Tommy, 'Lessons from the SCSL in the Fight against Impunity' (2012) <asf.be/wp-content/uploads/2012/10/Lessons-from-the-Special-Court-for-Sierra-Leone.pdf>.

[186] Cassese (n 176) para 285.

[187] HRW (n 147) 38. Interview with human rights activist, Freetown, Sierra Leone, 10 March 2016.

[188] Phone interview with former OTP official, 4 July 2017. See also ICTJ and UNDP, 'The "Legacy" of the Special Court. Draft for Discussion' (2003) 9 (on file).

[189] Interview with civil society activist, Freetown, Sierra Leone, 10 March 2016. Interviews with former SCSL officials, undisclosed location, 18 November 2016, by phone, 4 July 2017; Cape Town, South Africa, 23 March 2016 and by phone 17 March 2017.

[190] Interview with senior prosecutor, Freetown, Sierra Leone 15 March 2016.

does not have the mandate or the resources to become extensively involved in possible prosecutions in the local courts'.[191]

Nevertheless, contestation over possible prosecutions in Sierra Leone re-emerged after Stephen Rapp became chief prosecutor in late 2006. Arriving from the ICTR, where he had served as head of prosecutions, Rapp had witnessed first-hand the rule 11*bis* process vis-à-vis Rwanda. After discovering that the OTP had unused evidence, including against high-level suspects, he considered bringing a new case. As Rapp later recalled:[192]

> [w]hen I came to the SCSL ... for all practical purposes the issue [of case selection] was settled. However, I did have investigators who then recommended to me that we prosecute at least one additional person. I weighed that question for some time, but declined to proceed on practical grounds because of the difficulties and time necessary to make an arrest, and the limitation of the Court's resources that made it impossible to ensure, if we pursued that case, that we would complete it.

While considering an additional international trial, Rapp also reached out to Kabbah's outgoing administration about repealing the Lomé amnesty and bringing prosecutions in the Sierra Leone justice system. After the 2007 elections catapulted the opposition into power, Rapp again engaged the new administration on these issues. However, his efforts encountered cross-party resistance from the political establishment. Rapp later explained that '[he] dealt with three ministers of justice ... but [they were] not interested'.[193] Ultimately, he failed also to convince international donors to finance a new trial before the SCSL.[194]

The political establishment's unwillingness to prosecute serious crimes from the civil war solidified towards the end of the SCSL's mandate. In mid-2008, with the three main trials completed and the Taylor trial underway, the Special Court adopted rule 11*bis* to allow a referral of Jonny Paul Koroma's unenforced indictment to a national jurisdiction.[195] Although Rapp exhorted Sierra Leone to acquire the will and capacity to prosecute Koroma if he were found alive, the government never showed interest in his case.[196] According to UN officials, despite Sierra Leone being the territorial state and thus a natural destination for Koroma's trial,

[191] HRW (n 147) 38.
[192] Rapp (n 8) 25.
[193] Author interview with Stephen Rapp, undisclosed location.
[194] Rapp (n 8) 25.
[195] Cruvellier (n 138) 43. In 2017, it was reported that Koroma had, contrary to previous news, lived in hiding in Sierra Leone before passing away. See 'Johnny Paul Koroma Dead and Laid to Rest' *Sierra Express Media* (20 August 2017) <sierraexpressmedia.com/?p=82074>. This has never been confirmed by the SCSL and the veracity of this report is in doubt.
[196] Cruvellier (n 138) 43.

the RSCSL was forced to conclude an agreement with a Nordic country because of Sierra Leone's refusal to reconsider their position on domestic prosecutions.[197]

The government's policy of non-prosecution again took centre stage in 2013, when it emerged that Ibrahim Bah—one of Taylor's arms traffickers, long rumoured to be among the SCSL's targets who failed to make the 'greatest responsibility' cut—was living in Freetown.[198] After news of Bah's whereabouts broke, prompting his arrest and detention in Freetown, NGOs tried to press charges in Sierra Leonean courts. However, rather than wait for a domestic trial, the government deported Bah to Senegal with no advance warning or a legal rationale. Then Attorney General, Frank Kargbo, argued that '[i]t was out of consideration for the best interests of the country that the government decided to expel [Bah] from its territory'.[199] In a later interview, he confirmed that 'our position was we would not prosecute, [that] it would open up old wounds, so we thought it would be best to offer him up to our international partners, but no one showed up in three months so we deported him'.[200]

Although accountability for civil war crimes remains a pressing issue not only in Sierra Leone but also in neighbouring Liberia (where efforts to set up a hybrid court continue), civil society advocacy has shifted to universal jurisdiction cases prosecuted outside of West Africa, for instance in Finland, Switzerland, and the United States.[201] Following the SCSL's closure in 2013, the Residual Special Court has played an increasingly limited role in Sierra Leone while sharing information with prosecutorial authorities from third states. RSCSL officials confirmed that there were no ongoing communications with their Sierra Leonean counterparts about future domestic prosecutions in Sierra Leone, acknowledging for instance that they had not intervened to encourage Bah's prosecution.[202]

Ultimately, the Special Court's poor track record of encouraging domestic prosecutions reflects a mix of international and domestic policy considerations. On one hand, while some limited advocacy to repeal the Lomé amnesty continues in Sierra Leone, successive administrations—from opposing political factions—have maintained that amnesty was necessary for reconciliation. As explained by Kargbo,

[197] Interview with former SCSL officials, The Hague, Netherlands, 23 November 2015 and undisclosed location, 18 November 2016.

[198] Phone interview with former SCSL official, 6 April 2017.

[199] Cited in *BBC*, 'Sierra Leone "Deports" Taylor Ally Ibrahim Bah' (7 August 2013) <bbc.com/news/23599725>. See also Corey Boulet, 'Trusted Ally of Charles Taylor Located in Sierra Leone' *Voice of America* (20 June 2013) <voanews.com/a/trusted-ally-of-charles-taylor-located-in-sierra-leone/1685770.html>.

[200] Interview with former justice minister Franklyn Kargbo, Freetown, Sierra Leone, 14 March 2016.

[201] On Liberia, see Emmanuelle Marchand and Lisa-Marie Rudi, 'Extraterritorial Cases and National Accountability: The Liberian Quest for Justice' (*Armed Groups and International Law*, 15 June 2020) <armedgroups-internationallaw.org/2020/06/15/extraterritorial-cases-and-national-accountability-the-liberian-quest-for-justice/>.

[202] Interviews with former SCSL official and RSCSL officials, undisclosed location and by phone, 23 November 2015, 18 November 2016, and 10 May 2017. Sierra Leonean authorities have reportedly cooperated with requests for prosecutions abroad under universal jurisdiction.

political will 'was directed elsewhere ... the national thinking was that we do a few in SCSL, largely due to international pressure I may add, and the rest through the TRC'.[203] Echoing this sentiment, the deputy attorney general explained that 'we wanted to get on with our lives'.[204] Similarly, Joseph Kamara, then Attorney General and a former deputy SCSL prosecutor, confirmed publicly in 2016 there were no plans to repeal the amnesty.[205]

On the other hand, the SCSL's restrictive mandate gave it little leverage to threaten new international indictments, which in turn likely had a chilling effect on its ability to extract cooperation from government actors. A senior Sierra Leonean prosecutor argued that 'there was never a policy to ask for prosecutions, you can't impose this on government ... we could always withhold cooperation and [the SCSL] knew it ... instead we gave them cooperation and facilitated for the trials [of] the RUF, CDF, AFRC'.[206] UN officials explained that pressuring or encouraging domestic prosecutions was never within the SCSL's mandate. Brenda Hollis, the fourth and final SCSL prosecutor (who later also became RSCSL prosecutor), noted that, while she may have interpreted the mandate more broadly than her predecessors, it was too late to bring new cases by the time she was appointed in 2010.[207] Ultimately, while crystallizing attention on a handful of trials, a restrictive mandate may have decreased interaction between domestic and international actors over the ensuing impunity gap.

3.4. Unpacking a restrictive mandate's effects on domestic prosecutions

It was assumed initially that the Special Court might encourage prosecutions of lower-level defendants in national courts.[208] Yet, while international and domestic prosecutorial policy turned out to be intertwined at the margins, such a division of labour based on perpetrator status never materialized. As noted by Yuval Shany, Sierra Leone epitomizes 'the *prosecutorial-depressing* potential of international judicial intervention ... the existence of the [SCSL] was invoked by local politicians and lawyers as one reason why the amnesty provisions of the Lomé agreement ... should not be reopened'.[209]

203 Interview with former justice minister Franklyn Kargbo, Freetown, Sierra Leone, 14 March 2016.

204 Interview with deputy attorney general, Arrow Bockarie, Freetown, Sierra Leone, 15 March 2016.

205 Author conversation with Joseph Kamara, Nuremberg, Germany, 30 September 2016. See also Horovitz (n 150) 20; Chehtman (n 119) 324.

206 Interview with senior Sierra Leonean prosecutor, Freetown, Sierra Leone, 15 March 2016.

207 Interview with Brenda Hollis, 15 March 2016, Freetown, Sierra Leone.

208 Michaela Frulli, 'The Special Court for Sierra Leone: Some Preliminary Comments' (2000) 11 European Journal of International Law 857 863.

209 Yuval Shany, 'How Can International Criminal Courts Have a Greater Impact on National Criminal Proceedings? Lessons from the First Two Decades of International Criminal Justice in Operation' (2013) 46 Israel Law Review 431, 439; Horovitz (n 150) 57.

Drawing parallels with other hybrid tribunals, Shany notes 'a similar lack of interest in local follow-up to internationalized prosecutions' in Timor-Leste and Cambodia.[210] While future research should address whether restrictive mandates have the effect of decreasing interest in domestic prosecutions, it should not be assumed retrospectively that the SCSL was bound to be a dissuasive force in Sierra Leone's accountability landscape. Much like at the ICTR, where Rwanda's attitude to high-level targets was not factored into its original institutional design, the SCSL's influence on domestic prosecutions emerged through some degree of happenstance.

While a restrictive mandate may decrease pressure on government actors to prosecute domestically, the behaviour of SCSL officials amplified these isolationist dynamics. For one, a cooperation agreement was never signed, reducing points of interaction with the Sierra Leonean government. For another, although it confirmed the inapplicability of amnesties in international proceedings, the SCSL declined to weigh in on the amnesty's validity under Sierra Leonean law, reducing pressure on similarly situated Sierra Leonean judges to address the issue. As Horovitz observes, '[h]ad the judges considered it within their interest or authority to encourage national atrocity-related trials in Sierra Leone, they might have addressed the amnesty's applicability in cases before Sierra Leonean national courts'.[211] To be sure, the SCSL's pronouncements had no legally binding effect national courts, but they would have constituted a persuasive authority for domestic litigants.

At the same time, the Special Court's successful track record of targeted prosecutions raises important questions about the proper interplay of international and domestic trials. On the one hand, because of the SCSL's 'greatest responsibility' mandate, the OTP felt that a perpetrator's relative seniority not only gave it absolute priority but also that international trials justified interference with national proceedings. Although disputes over concurrent jurisdiction never formally occurred and the SCSL's four trials are usually hailed as successful prosecutions, the distribution of defendants through backdoor diplomacy sits uneasily with the SCSL's goal of promoting national ownership. This narrative also obscures how the OTP's cases depended on cooperation from insider witnesses, some of whom escaped accountability altogether by compelling Sierra Leone to drop domestic charges.

On the other hand, while defendants like Sankoh (had he lived long enough) and Kanu may well have been tried domestically in the absence of the SCSL, the politicized nature of Sierra Leone's post-civil war trials suggest that international prosecutions are sometimes preferable to flawed domestic accountability.

[210] Shany (n 209) 439.
[211] Horovitz (n 101) 360.

Similarly, while Crane's prosecution of Norman remains an exceptional case of a high-ranking government official arrested in office (literally), its symbolic importance remains contested. For instance, Michael Vagias notes approvingly that 'it is a rare instance of a court that brought proceedings to bear upon suspects of the incumbent government'.[212] But Sierra Leoneans often view this case differently. For instance, Charles Jalloh criticizes 'a legally correct but politically blind insistence on carrying out equal prosecutions against all the parties to the conflict without regard to their consequences in healing, or worsening, the raw wounds of an ethnically, emotionally, and politically divided nation'.[213]

As will be seen in Chapter 6, the political and societal dynamics behind Norman's prosecution remain open to (re)interpretation. However, it remains a fact that, over time, the SCSL's restrictive mandate became a convenient excuse for both international and domestic audiences to halt further accountability measures. International partners used budgetary constraints to thwart further indictments, while Sierra Leonean government actors cited 'greatest responsibility' as proof that the state had provided its fair share of criminal accountability—for the most senior perpetrators, no less. To a large extent, this policy reflected the political elite's conscious prioritization of reconciliation over punishment. Somewhat unexpectedly, therefore, the SCSL may have enabled successive administrations to free-ride on its high-profile trials while falling back on the truth process and Lomé amnesty to avoid revisiting the civil war.

It is unclear whether the SCSL's architects should have done anything to change these isolationist dynamics. The UN could have, in line with Kabbah's initial proposal, created a joint prosecution team with the Sierra Leonean attorney general to secure greater involvement from national authorities. But such an arrangement opened the door to domestic politics and, at any rate, Rapp's failed efforts to refer cases illustrate the limits of institutional tweaks in the absence of political will.[214] Ultimately, the Sierra Leonean political elite could have refused to revisit the Lomé amnesty no matter the SCSL's institutional design or external pressure, even if this retrospective rationalization obscures how fluid the accountability landscape was throughout the 2000s. In hindsight, the SCSL's handful of trials may have been most dissuasive for advocacy efforts, with bottom-up accountability initiatives, including efforts to repeal the Lomé amnesty, receiving less attention. In total, almost eighty people were tried by the High Court, but the two major civil war trials in the domestic judiciary are largely forgotten in Sierra Leone.

212 Michail Vagias, 'Hybrid Court Resilience and the Selection of Cases' (2020) 33 Leiden Journal of International Law 1029, 1035.

213 Jalloh (n 132) 459; Gberie (n 137). See also n 143.

214 Horovitz (n 150) 66.

4. The International Criminal Court

4.1. Prosecutorial strategy: imbuing complementarity with (extralegal) meaning

The ICC's beginnings and its DRC investigation are closely intertwined. In July 2003, just one month after his inauguration as the first prosecutor, Luis Moreno Ocampo indicated that his office was monitoring the crisis in Ituri, a province in north-eastern DRC.[215] Two months later, at the second annual meeting of the ASP, Ocampo signalled he was 'ready to seek authorization from a Pre-Trial Chamber to start an investigation under [his] proprio motu powers' but clarified that '[the ICC's] role could be facilitated by a referral or active support from the DRC'.[216] According to ICC officials and Congolese activists, the prosecutor remained in contact with then Congolese president, Joseph Kabila, during late 2003 and early 2004. Kabila was open to an international investigation, but he worried it could backfire if the prosecutor targeted his allies.[217]

By opening a preliminary examination in January 2004, Ocampo signalled that a *proprio motu* investigation was forthcoming but continued to encourage the Congolese authorities to proactively request the ICC's intervention.[218] Kabila obliged in March 2004. In a 'self-referral' letter, he explained that 'because of the exceptional situation in my country, the competent authorities are unfortunately not capable of investigating [international] crimes, nor are they able to conduct the necessary prosecutions without the participation of the [ICC]'.[219] In reality, OTP officials in The Hague had drafted the letter for Kabila to rubber-stamp. Not coincidentally, the letter contains a reference to complementarity, specifically article 17's 'inability' condition.[220] It remains unclear to what extent Kabila's self-referral—a frank avowal of the state's lack of capacity to perform a core attribute

[215] Press Release, 'Communications Received by the Office of the Prosecutor of the ICC' (16 July 2003) pids-009.2003-EN; Schabas (n 79) 38.

[216] 'Report of Luis Moreno Ocampo, Second Annual ASP Meeting' (8 September 2003) <www.icc-cpi.int/NR/rdonlyres/C073586C-7D46-4CBE-B901-0672908E8639/143656/LMO_20030908_En.pdf>.

[217] Interview with civil society activists and military prosecutor, Kinshasa, DRC and Dakar, Senegal, 16 and 17 August 2016, 7 July 2017. See also Pascal K Kambale, 'A Story of Missed Opportunities? The Role of the International Criminal Court in the Democratic Republic of Congo' in Christian M De Vos, Sara Kendall and Christian Stahn (eds), *Contested Justice: The Politics and Practice of International Criminal Court Interventions* (CUP 2015) 175–76.

[218] Godfrey M Musila, *Between Rhetoric and Action: The Politics, Processes and Practice of the ICC's Work in the DRC* (Institute for Security Studies 2009) viii.

[219] Reproduced in Musila (n 218) annex I.

[220] Interview with ICC official, The Hague, Netherlands, 18 November 2016. Similarly, see Sarah MH Nouwen, *Complementarity in the Line of Fire: The Catalysing Effect of the International Criminal Court in Uganda and Sudan* (CUP 2013) 113.

of sovereignty—reflected a domestic power struggle, international pressure, or a combination of both.[221]

As seen in Chapter 2, this self-referral was, at the time, part of an emerging trend at the OTP. Although ICC jurisdiction over crimes is activated in three ways, self-referrals had procedural (obviating judicial scrutiny of the permissibility of an investigation) and logistical (promising greater cooperation from the state than the other, non-consensual triggers) benefits for the OTP. Three months prior to the DRC self-referral, Yoveri Museveni had similarly 'invited' the ICC to intervene against the Lord's Resistance Army in northern Uganda, including in areas abutting Ituri.[222] By opening investigations in the DRC and Uganda two self-referrals from central Africa became, in the space of just a few months, testing grounds for the ICC's emerging prosecutorial strategy, including its approach to complementarity.

These two investigations put to the test various assumptions espoused in the OTP's early policy papers. For one, with Ocampo invoking the gravity of Uganda and the DRC relative to other situations (notably Iraq), the highly discretionary notion of gravity displaced states' willingness or ability to fight impunity as the primary justification for international intervention.[223] For another, an extralegal reading of complementarity qua burden sharing sidestepped certain legal questions relating to states' primacy under the Rome Statute.[224] In his 2003 ASP speech, Ocampo signalled this novel understanding:[225]

> The Court and the territorial State may agree that a consensual division of labour could be an effective approach. Groups bitterly divided by conflict may oppose prosecutions at each other's hands and yet agree to a prosecution by a Court perceived as neutral and impartial. The Office could cooperate with the national authorities by prosecuting the leaders who bear most responsibility for the crimes. National authorities with the assistance of the international

[221] Interviews with ICC officials, Congolese politicians and civil society actors, The Hague, Netherlands, Kinshasa, DRC, 18 November 2016, 21 April and 16, 17, 18, 19 August 2016, and 7 July 2017. See further Valérie Arnould, 'Transitional Justice in Peacebuilding: Dynamics of Contestation in the DRC' (2016) 10 Journal of Intervention and Statebuilding 321 (arguing that the invitation was domestically driven, not externally imposed). But see Phil Clark, 'Chasing Cases: The ICC and the Politics of State Referral in the Democratic Republic of Congo and Uganda' in Carsten Stahn and Mohamed El Zeidy (eds), *The International Criminal Court and Complementarity: From Theory to Practice*, vol 2 (CUP 2011); Kambale (n 217) 176.

[222] On the politics of the Uganda referral, including tensions within the OTP, see Sarah MH Nouwen and Wouter G Werner, 'Doing Justice to the Political: The International Criminal Court in Uganda and Sudan' (2010) 21 European Journal of International Law 941.

[223] Interview with Luis M Ocampo and former OTP official, Cambridge, MA and Tunis, Tunisia, 8 March 2017 and 5 October 2018. On Iraq, see David L Bosco, *Rough Justice: The International Criminal Court in a World of Power Politics* (OUP 2014) 89–91; see generally Matthew R Brubacher, 'Prosecutorial Discretion within the International Criminal Court' (2004) 2 Journal of International Criminal Justice 71, 178–84.

[224] ICC-OTP, 'Paper on Some Policy Issues before the Office of the Prosecutor' (2003) 5.

[225] 'Report of Luis Moreno Ocampo' (n 216).

community could implement appropriate mechanisms to deal with other individuals responsible.

Managerial in nature, the OTP's strategy in the DRC was premised on two conditions. First, the ICC and Congolese authorities would consensually apportion cases based on a distinction between high- and low-level perpetrators. In doing so, Ocampo arrogated to himself a power that the Rome Statute, contrary to the SCSL and ICTR mandates, withheld from the ICC—states had jurisdictional primacy over *all* suspects. Second, in exchange for its support to international trials, the Congolese government could count on foreign aid to support domestic proceedings against lower-level suspects. Implicit was also that the OTP would support parallel domestic justice efforts rather than monitor and evaluate their 'genuineness' with a view to asserting jurisdiction. In a confidential letter to Kabila, Ocampo echoed this theme, emphasizing the potential benefits of partnership with the ICC and suggesting, inter alia, that '[i]n return, the international community may take a more resolved stance in the reconstruction of the national judiciary and in the re-establishment of the rule of law in the [DRC]'.[226]

The JCCD became Ocampo's 'engine room' for outreach to states, managing relations with governments along this burden-sharing model.[227] As explained by a former official, 'Ocampo didn't see the OTP as a purely operational structure, he saw the Court as having diplomatic relevance' where 'JCCD became the central element ... [and] the Investigations and Prosecutions Divisions were expected to respond to whatever [Ocampo] had worked out with JCCD'.[228] Signed in 2004, a cooperation agreement 'establish[ed] practical mechanisms of cooperation and assistance necessary for the effective and swift conduct of investigations and prosecutions'.[229] Implying a degree of international supervision, it required the DRC to inform the OTP 'as soon as possible of any investigation or prosecution ... by the national authorities concerning [ICC] crimes', but—as will be seen next—it came to epitomize a deferential, hands-off logic to the fight against impunity, where consensual relations between ICC and the Kabila government mutually shaped interactions.[230]

[226] Letter from Luis Ocampo to President Joseph Kabila (25 September 2003) (on file). For a different division of labour, see William Burke-White, 'Complementarity in Practice: The International Criminal Court as Part of a System of Multi-Level Global Governance in the Democratic Republic of Congo' (2005) 18 Leiden Journal of International Law 557, 570–72; see also Justine Tillier, 'The ICC Prosecutor and Positive Complementarity: Strengthening the Rule of Law?' (2013) 13 International Criminal Law Review 507, 525–26.

[227] On the JCCD, see Chapter 2 in this volume.

[228] Phone interview with former ICC official, 8 December 2016.

[229] DRC and OTP, Judicial Cooperation Agreement (6 October 2004) reproduced in Musila (n 218) annex 2, art 1 (and art 7).

[230] ibid art 35; see also art 37 ('[OTP] may ... provide assistance to [DRC] for those investigations, prosecutions, and any eventual trials for crimes that fall within [ICC jurisdiction]').

4.2. Complementarity in action: trading iteration for accommodation

The ICC's intervention in the DRC was an important event at both the national and international levels. In 2004, many hoped that the ICC would be able to challenge, if not fully eradicate, the lack of accountability for serious crimes.[231] Yet, while the Congolese government has nominally supported the ICC's investigation over the intervening years, burden sharing has played out differently in practice. Despite OTP assurances, its prosecutorial policy has been driven by short-term opportunism rather than a long-term anti-impunity strategy.

The shift from burden sharing to ICC-centric opportunism occurred swiftly. Some of Ocampo's statements, including on positive complementarity and the need to support domestic prosecutions, generated opposition in The Hague. By 2005, ICC judges had spent over two years with little work. One former ICC judge conceded that Ocampo's policies, in particular his claim that an absence of cases would be evidence of success, created concern.[232] Acknowledging impatience among its Hague-based staff, ICC officials noted that Ocampo's policies seemed to ignore the practical reality that states parties would not support a multimillion-dollar budget with no international trials.[233]

An ICC with few cases provoked disquiet not only among Hague-based international civil servants but also human rights NGOs which had no illusions about the obstacles to domestic accountability. In the DRC, groups like HRW were among the most active proponents of ICC intervention. Similarly, Congolese civil society groups advocated international trials, cognizant of the local justice system's capacity shortfalls.

The OTP's prosecutorial strategy evolved soon after investigations started in the DRC. According to a senior ICC official, 'at that time, complementarity was not really the main focus; it was about getting the first cases off the ground'.[234] Asked about a division of labour with Congolese authorities, he responded 'I've never heard of that, I am quite sure that nothing of this nature existed, [and] I was in Kinshasa many times'.[235] Rather than engage its national counterparts on case distribution, the OTP focused on gathering evidence and apprehending suspects—any suspect—as soon as possible.[236] Much like *Tadić* at the ICTY, the ICC's first arrest in the DRC bore the marks of opportunism rather than principled

[231] For an early take, see Aryeh Neier, 'Accountability for State Crimes: The Past Twenty Years and the Next Twenty Years' (2003) 35 Case Western Reserve Journal of International Law 351, 357–58.

[232] Interview with former ICC judge, Geneva, Switzerland, 21 October 2016.

[233] Interview with ICC official, The Hague, Netherlands, 18 November 2016. Phone interview with former ICC officials, 15 November and 8 December 2016. See also William A Schabas, '"Complementarity in Practice": Some Uncomplimentary Thoughts' (2008) 19 Criminal Law Forum 5.

[234] Interview with former senior ICC official, Nuremberg, Germany, 1 October 2016.

[235] ibid.

[236] Phone interviews with former ICC officials, 7 and 8 December 2016. Schabas (n 233) 32–33.

case selection. In early 2006, Thomas Lubanga, a mid-level warlord, in detention awaiting trial on war crimes and genocide charges, and facing the death penalty, was transferred to The Hague pursuant to an ICC arrest warrant.[237]

As seen in Chapter 3, *Lubanga* produced litigation over complementarity, with chambers finding his case admissible. Irrespective of the contrived 'inactivity' rationale that justified Lubanga's international trial, the OTP had factual reasons to insist on his transfer to The Hague when it did. According to OTP officials, Congolese prosecutors had made so little progress building their domestic case that military judges could have ordered Lubanga's release from pretrial detention due to detention time limits under domestic criminal procedure.[238] Ocampo's rushed opportunism turned out to be risky—at the time of his surrender, OTP investigators had collected weak evidence of child soldiering—which later almost thwarted the case at trial. However, while his trial exposed questionable investigative practices (covered in the literature),[239] the case also portended an accommodationist reading of complementarity, where the ICC refused to call out the Congolese authorities for their inability or unwillingness to genuinely prosecute Lubanga but relied instead on 'the same case' doctrine to justify the exercise of international jurisdiction.[240]

Accommodation came back with a vengeance a few years later, when the cases of Katanga and Ngudjolo, two mid-level militiamen integrated into the Congolese military, were outsourced for trial in The Hague.[241] Forced to address complementarity because Katanga unexpectedly challenged admissibility, chambers again ignored why the Congolese state, despite its jurisdictional primacy and duty to prosecute serious crimes, refused to progress its domestic case. To elide the inconvenient fact that Katanga was being prosecuted domestically and hence the DRC was not 'inactive', the Pre-Trial Chamber accepted at face value assurances from the Congolese judicial authorities, who 'expressly reject[ed] the idea that the DRC could henceforth try Katanga'.[242] When counsel for Katanga pointed out that

[237] PTC, *Prosecutor v Lubanga* (Decision concerning Pre-Trial Chamber I's Decision of 10 February 2006 and the Incorporation of Documents into the Record) ICC-01/04-01/06-08-US Corr (24 February 2006) para 33; Adam Hochschild, 'The Trial of Thomas Lubanga' [2009] The Atlantic <theatlantic.com/magazine/archive/2009/12/the-trial-of-thomas-lubanga/307762/>.

[238] Interview with OTP official, The Hague, Netherlands, 23 November 2015. See also Paul Seils, 'The Selection and Prioritization of Cases by the Office of the Prosecutor of the International Criminal Court' in Morten Bergsmo (ed), *Criteria for Prioritizing and Selecting Core International Crimes Cases* (2nd edn, Forum for International Criminal and Humanitarian Law 2010) 74.

[239] Christian M De Vos, 'Investigating from Afar: The ICC's Evidence Problem' (2013) 26 Leiden Journal of International Law 1009; M Miraglia, 'Admissibility of Evidence, Standard of Proof, and Nature of the Decision in the ICC Confirmation of Charges in Lubanga' (2008) 6 Journal of International Criminal Justice 489. For a history of the DRC investigation, see TC, *Prosecutor v Thomas Lubanga* (Judgment pursuant to Article 74) ICC-01/04-01/06 (14 March 2012) paras 124–77.

[240] See discussion in Chapter 3 in this volume; *Lubanga* Warrant.

[241] On seniority, see Kambale (n 217) 178–79.

[242] TC, *Prosecutor v Germain Katanga and Mathieu Ngudjolo* (Transcript of Oral Hearing) ICC-01/04-01/07 (12 June 2009) (author translation); see also *Observations of the DRC on the Challenge to the Admissibility made by the Defence for Katanga*, ICC-01/04-01/07-1189-Anx (1 June 2009) 4.

Congolese authorities had previously requested evidence from the ICC to facilitate domestic proceedings, the OTP responded that '[t]he ICC was not created to be an international investigative bureau with resources to support national authorities' and there is no 'obligation on the ICC to render assistance to States'.[243]

Put differently, by 2009, not only was the ICC not asking whether Congolese authorities were able or willing to genuinely prosecute Katanga, the OTP was also openly disavowing its burden-sharing prosecutorial policy. Rather than interrogate a reading of the Rome Statute that allowed the OTP to encourage states to *not* prosecute—after all, complementarity supposedly channels the opposite assumption—the Appeals Chamber doubled down and rationalized states' outsourcing of suspects for trial in The Hague on the basis that the ICC 'does not have the power to order States to open investigations or prosecutions domestically' and that 'there may be merit in the argument that the sovereign decision of a State to relinquish its jurisdiction in favor of the Court may well be seen as complying with the "duty to exercise [its] criminal jurisdiction"'.[244] As Susanna Sácouto and Katherine Clearly observe, while legally 'defensible', the decision 'effectively authorizes the [OTP] to engage in practices that may be inconsistent with one of the fundamental principles underlying the founding of the ICC'.[245]

It was in the DRC that complementarity came to be redefined as a form of accommodation with host governments, rather than an iterative concept where the ICC supports but also monitors governments' capacity or willingness to prosecute genuinely. As noted in Chapter 3, *Katanga* reversed the Rome Statute's assumptions by allowing the ICC to ignore qualitative appraisals of domestic proceedings, or why an international trial was necessary or preferable to domestic accountability.

Although it was intended as a quick fix for a nascent institution in need of trials, *Lubanga* and *Katanga* became a model for prosecutorial strategy in the DRC and beyond. Instead of advocating a potentially iterative division of labour with national prosecutors, in which hard cases—involving senior suspects whom, for instance, the army shielded—would be prioritized by the ICC, the OTP continued to prioritize cases that the Kabila administration did not oppose. The arrest of Jean-Pierre Bemba, a former warlord turned vice president who lost the disputed 2006 presidential election, eliminated Kabila's main political rival. This was followed by uncontroversial cases—from Kabila's perspective—against two foreign nationals, Callixte Mbarushimana and Sylvestre Mudacumura, affiliated with militias operating in eastern DRC (who could have, if arrested, been prosecuted by Rwanda or France).[246]

[243] *Prosecutor v Katanga* (Prosecution Response to Motion Challenging the Admissibility of the Case) ICC-01/04-01/07 (30 March 2009) paras 100–01 (see Chapter 3 in this volume).

[244] *Katanga* Appeals Judgment, paras 85–86 (see Chapter 3 in this volume).

[245] Susana Sácouto and Katherine Cleary, 'The *Katanga* Complementarity Decisions: Sound Law But Flawed Policy' (2010) 23 Leiden Journal of International Law 363, 369; Schabas (n 233) 6–7.

[246] On these cases, see <icc-cpi.int/drc>.

As a result, the ICC's prosecutions in the DRC have targeted only non-state actors and Kabila rivals in particular.[247] Congolese government officials acknowledge that they succeeded in pushing the prosecutor to focus on certain suspects, with one senior Kabila adviser conceding later that 'Lubanga was a question of political opportunity; he didn't have as much support as Bemba, so his transfer posed no risk of disorder and that was convenient for us'.[248] Nevertheless, both Ocampo and his successor, Fatou Bensouda, continued to deploy the language of complementarity. In 2009, Olivia Swaak-Goldmann, an external relations adviser, explained the OTP's strategy for the DRC as follows:[249]

> An example of how the [OTP] has put its policy of positive complementarity into practice is our investigation into the Kivus case ... As with all our cases, we will only prosecute a small number of potential perpetrators ... the [OTP] is trying to develop a proactive complementarity approach with other judicial institutions that are ready to prosecute some perpetrators from the various groups involved in the area ... including the DRC and Rwandan authorities, and beyond, including national authorities outside of the region ... The aim is to ensure full coverage of the victimization patterns as well as to make sure that those responsible at the different levels of the relevant groups will be prosecuted by the most relevant authorities, whether it is by the Court or national authorities genuinely willing and able to do so.

Accordingly, to foster a 'coordinated approach', the OTP reportedly considered 'sharing information on ongoing cases' and 'transfer of cases or evidence'.[250]

Triannual OTP strategies have all embraced similar 'cooperative' readings of positive complementarity.[251] However, implementation has proved difficult. On the one hand, ICC officials acknowledge that Congolese authorities share information and provide access to crime sites, victims, and witnesses. On the other hand, the OTP has struggled to share evidence, in particular due to the absence of witness protection guarantees at the national level.[252] At times, insufficient cooperation has

[247] Phil Clark, *Distant Justice: The Impact of the International Criminal Court on African Politics* (CUP 2018) 79–80.

[248] Interview with senior adviser, Kinshasa, DRC, 19 August 2016. Stemming officially from the CAR I situation, Bemba's case was driven by military rivalries and electoral politics in the DRC. Interviews with Congolese activists and former minister, Kinshasa, DRC and Dakar, Senegal, 19 April and 19 August 2016 and 7 July 2017.

[249] Olivia Swaak-Goldman, 'Relations between National and International Criminal Courts in the Aftermath of Atrocity Situations' in *Proceedings of the Annual Meeting*, vol 103 (American Society of International Law 2009) 216.

[250] ibid, 217.

[251] ICC–OTP, 'Strategic Plan 2019–2021' (2019); ICC–OTP, 'Strategic Plan 2016–2018' (2015) objective 9.

[252] Interview with OTP officials, The Hague, Netherlands, 23 and 24 November 2015. Interviews with Congolese military magistrates, Goma and Kinshasa, DRC, 4 September 2015, 23 April and 17 August 2016. See also Eric Witte, *Putting Complementarity into Practice: Domestic Justice for International Crimes in DRC, Uganda and Kenya* (Open Society Foundations 2011) 26.

created tensions. In 2016, Toussaint Muntazini, then Congolese military advocate general, took the unusual step of publicly expressing 'frustration at having so little benefit from the ICC's consideration, when it could reasonably expect a better fate'.[253] A senior Congolese military magistrate noted that the ICC usually declined requests because of 'witness protection concerns' but argued that 'different ICC organs' were 'passing the buck for non-cooperation'.[254] An OTP official responded that the office had, in fact, received few concrete requests relating to cases that the ICC had investigated.[255]

The truth lies somewhere in the middle. Despite criticisms of cooperation as a 'one-way street', it seems the OTP has occasionally supported domestic efforts, for instance by assisting in exhumations and helping military magistrates investigate a case of mass rape.[256] Yet, while such instances of cooperation are insufficient for the Congolese and UN officials, they obscure a more fundamental transformation in the ICC's division of labour with the DRC. While it exercises de facto primacy over a handful of cases that national authorities want prosecuted internationally, the OTP refuses to challenge the military over outstanding cases. Epitomizing this mentality, a senior OTP official explained the ICC's division of labour with the DRC as 'they do what we do not do'.[257]

4.3. In the ICC's shadow: NGO justice and the rise of human rights prosecutions

Although Congolese law dating from the 1970s criminalized genocide, war crimes, and crimes against humanity, no trials in furtherance of these norms appear to have taken place prior to the 2000s. It was only in late 2004 that a military tribunal convicted Congolese army troops for a mass crime, including the murder of sixty people and destroying and pillaging hundreds of homes.[258] While the trial in *Ankoro* did not yet feature charges of international crimes, a flurry of trials in 2005 and 2006 produced convictions for war crimes, crimes against humanity, and other

[253] Toussaint Muntazini Mukimapa, 'The Congolese Experience with the Complementary Role of the ICC' (*Justice Info*, 4 August 2016) <justiceinfo.net/en/justice-reconciliation/28669-the-congolese-experience-with-the-complementary-role-of-the-icc.html>.

[254] Interview with senior Congolese military magistrate, 23 April 2016.

[255] Interview with senior Congolese military magistrate, 26 July 2019. Interview with OTP official, The Hague, Netherlands, 23 November 2015.

[256] Interview with UN official, Brussels, Belgium, 16 November 2016. Interview with unnamed source, The Hague, Netherlands, 23 November 2015 and phone interview with MONUSCO official, 2 August 2016. See also ICC, 'Overall Response to the "Independent Expert Review". Preliminary Analysis of the Recommendations' (2021) para 503.

[257] Interview with ICC official, The Hague, Netherlands, 23 November 2015.

[258] Cour militaire du Katanga, Affaire *Ankoro*, RP 01/2003 & RP 02/2004 (20 décembre 2004). See Avocats Sans Frontières, 'Etude de jurisprudence: L'application du Statut de Rome de la Cour pénale internationale par les juridictions de la République démocratique du Congo' (2009) 112.

military offences in three provinces. In June 2006, a conviction for crimes against humanity was confirmed on appeal in a case of mass rape in *Songo Mboyo*.[259]

While the OTP and Congolese authorities failed to enact a 'division of labour', the temporal proximity of these domestic military trials and ICC intervention raises questions about the impetus for prosecutorial initiatives. A combination of support and pressure from international actors appear to have been instrumental. Around 2003, the UN peacekeeping mission—known initially as MONUC, later rebranded as MONUSCO—became more involved in human rights and transitional justice.[260] In many areas of the country, where state institutions had all but collapsed after decades of mismanagement, compounded by the Second Congo War, the UN was the only actor with capacity to conduct investigations. Lacking both resources and experience with mass crimes, Congolese magistrates relied on international actors for transportation to crime sites, forensic expertise, and witness interviewing.[261]

Congolese magistrates and activists acknowledge the severe shortcomings in domestic capacity and expertise in these years, but, while international support was crucial for fact-finding and investigations, it is only state institutions that conduct criminal proceedings. Pointing to this nuance, one senior UN official observed 'we led them by the hand for investigations but not the trials themselves'.[262] To support the rollout of military trials, around 2005, a few NGOs began trainings on international criminal law, with courses on topics such as sexual violence crimes and investigation techniques. A Congolese attorney explained that 'it was no coincidence' that the same military magistrates who received training went on to launch prosecutions of international crimes.[263] Reflecting the extent of their influence over state-run criminal proceedings, an activist explained that judges and prosecutors sought and obtained advice throughout the early trials, even though these 'informal consultations' on international criminal norms likely breached the confidentiality of criminal proceedings under domestic law.[264]

There is no public repository of domestic cases, but estimates indicate that military tribunals have prosecuted over fifty cases of war crimes and crimes against humanity since 2005.[265] Equally important, hundreds of perpetrators have been

[259] Cour Militaire de l'Equateur, *Songo Mboyo* (7 June 2006) RPA 014/06.

[260] UNSC Res 1493, S/RES/1483 (28 July 2003) para 11. On MONUC's early support, see Roberto Ricci, 'Human Rights Challenges in the DRC: A View from MONUC's Human Rights Section' in Mark Malan and Joao Gomes Porto (eds), *Challenges of Peace Implementation: The UN Mission in the DRC* (Institute for Security Studies 2004); Federico Borello, *A First Few Steps: The Long Road to a Just Peace in the Democratic Republic of the Congo* (ICTJ 2004) 18–20.

[261] Interviews with former MONUC officials, by phone and Geneva, Switzerland, 14 January 2016 and 12 June 2017.

[262] Phone interview with former MONUC staff, 14 January 2016.

[263] Interviews with human rights activist and attorney, Kinshasa, DRC, 20 April and 18 August 2016.

[264] ibid.

[265] For pre-2010 trials, see OHCHR (n 55) 410–21. For 2009–2014 investigations in Ituri, North and South Kivu, see Sofia Candeias and others, 'The Accountability Landscape in Eastern DRC: Analysis of the National Legislative and Judicial Response to International Crimes (2009–2014)' (ICTJ 2015) 17

tried for serious but ordinary domestic crimes in so-called mobile courts which operate, as will be discussed in Chapter 5, with support from the UN, donors and NGOs.[266] In 2016, in cooperation with the UN and the International Center for Transitional Justice, the Congolese prosecution service finalized a prioritization strategy for 'emblematic cases' based on criteria such as the gravity of crimes, numbers of victims, perpetrator characteristics and operational challenges, with 65 case files shortlisted for follow-up in five provinces.[267] Landmark cases from the last five years include a 2016 trial of a regional parliamentarian in a notorious case of child rape, the conviction of a high-ranking army officer, Colonel 106, for crimes against humanity in 2017, the long-delayed trial and conviction of 'Cheka', a warlord wanted for mass rape in Walikale, and the first trials of Kamuina Nsapu insurgents in Kasai province.[268]

As will be seen in Chapter 5 and 6, the UN, donors, and NGOs continue to play a support role to this day. But the links between international intervention and domestic accountability are complex. On the one hand, military trials extend only so far, with magistrates still facing challenges in prosecuting politically sensitive cases and no strategy for crimes committed before 2002. While they are cited as evidence of the ICC's shadow or complementarity in action, domestic trials may reinforce rather than challenge existing power structures, producing the phenomenon of 'unintended diversionary complementarity'. On the other hand, contrary to early speculation, the DRC has never initiated trials to prevent the ICC from exercising jurisdiction and, in fact, as noted previously, on three occasions—Lubanga, Katanga, and Ngudjolo—the military suspended proceedings to facilitate prosecutions in The Hague. While this has spawned scholarly arguments that relations between the ICC and Congolese judicial actors are 'competitive', the DRC is primarily a case of accommodation.[269] The prosaic reality is that the political elites willingly 'surrendered' jurisdiction over suspects like Lubanga, and Congolese courts would have struggled to launch any prosecutions without international help.

and 20–23 and 41–67. For recent trials, see UNDP and EU, 'Projet d'appui à la Justice Militaire en République démocratique du Congo à travers le renforcement du programme des cellules d'appui aux poursuites (février 2015–décembre 2018)' (2019).

[266] Open Society Foundations, 'Justice in DRC: Mobile Courts Combat Rape and Impunity in Eastern Congo' (2013) 7 <opensocietyfoundations.org/sites/default/files/justice-drc-20130114.pdf>; HRW, 'Soldiers Who Rape, Commanders Who Condone: Sexual Violence and Military Reform in the Democratic Republic of Congo' (2009).

[267] UNDP and EU (n 265) 15–25.

[268] Daniele Perissi and Karen Naimer, 'Achieving Justice for Child Survivors of Conflict-Related Sexual Violence in the Democratic Republic of the Congo' (2020) 18 Journal of International Criminal Justice 293; Lauren Wolfe, 'What It Takes to Get an Alleged Mass Rapist and 67 Militiamen Arrested in Congo' [2016] *Foreign Policy* <foreignpolicy.com/2016/06/23/how-i-got-an-alleged-mass-rapist-and-67-militiamen-arrested-in-congo/>; Ephrem Rugiririza, 'First Trial in Kasai for Crimes of the Kamuina Nsapu Rebellion' (*JusticeInfo*, 8 November 2021) <justiceinfo.net/en/84096-first-trial-kasai-crimes-kamuina-nsapu-rebellion.html>.

[269] See Chapter 5, section 4.5 in this volume. For 'competitive', see Clark (n 247) 150.

Significantly, while trials of serious crimes have proliferated independently from The Hague, the ICC has cast a symbolic shadow over domestic accountability efforts, with UN officials explaining, for instance, that, in liaising with their Congolese counterparts, MONUC leveraged the DRC's 'duty' under the Rome Statute to encourage military magistrates to launch prosecutions of international crimes.[270] As will be explained in Chapter 6, the Statute has also served as an interpretive tool in domestic proceedings, with magistrates applying international standards to overcome inconsistencies in domestic law. In other words, even when it is not formally involved, strategic use is made of the ICC's presence and the language of complementarity to support accountability initiatives.

4.4. Inadmissibility in reverse: complementarity as pretext for ICC inaction

Despite many domestic military trials, the political establishment has placed limits on international criminal law when its interests are at stake. For instance, when, in 2013, the Sudanese President, Omar Al-Bashir, attended a regional summit in Kinshasa, the government refused to enforce the ICC's request for his arrest.[271] An ICC official noted that government officials had been informed in advance of their obligation to enforce the warrant,[272] but a senior adviser to Kabila explained bluntly: 'we weren't going to arrest a sitting head of state … the DRC is a strong supporter of the ICC but … [its] policies in Africa raise certain problems'.[273]

While Al-Bashir's arrest saga is emblematic of the limits to the ICC's coercive power on the African continent and beyond,[274] another case illustrates even more starkly the Congolese government's ambivalence towards the ICC. Although the DRC is often lauded as the most cooperative ICC state party, for several years the Kabila administration refused to arrest Bosco Ntaganda, a Rwandan commander of an Ituri armed group later reintegrated into the national army under a peace agreement.[275] Despite international pressure, Emmanuel-Janvier Luzolo Bambi

[270] Interviews with human rights activists and UN officials, Kinshasa, DRC, 25 April and 18 August 2016. Phone interview with former MONUC official, 14 January 2016. Interview with former MONUC official, Geneva, Switzerland, 12 June 2017.

[271] For details, see Patryk I Labuda, 'The ICC in the DRC: A Decade of Partnership and Antagonism' in Kamari Clarke, Abel Knottnerus, and Eefje de Volder (eds), *Africa and the ICC: Perceptions of Justice* (CUP 2016) 282–83.

[272] Interview with ICC official, Kinshasa, DRC, 18 April 2016.

[273] Interview with senior Kabila adviser, Kinshasa, DRC, 19 August 2016. On the AU's position on immunities, see Paola Gaeta and Patryk I Labuda, 'Trying Sitting Heads of State: The African Union versus the ICC in the Al Bashir and Kenyatta Cases' in Ilias Bantekas and Charles C Jalloh (eds), *The International Criminal Court and Africa* (OUP 2018).

[274] Franziska Boehme, '"We Chose Africa": South Africa and the Regional Politics of Cooperation with the International Criminal Court' (2016) 11 International Journal of Transitional Justice 50.

[275] Interview with state representative, The Hague, Netherlands, 23 November 2015. See also *Africa News*, 'Dans le cadre de la cooperation entre la RD Congo et la CPI: Fatou Bensouda chez le

Lessa, justice minister from 2008 to 2012 and the ICC's interlocutor for the trials of Lubanga, Katanga, and Ngudjolo, openly militated against Ntaganda's arrest as the price of peace.[276] Acknowledging the impasse, several senior Congolese stakeholders explained that Ntaganda was 'a political decision', meaning the government at the highest levels had decided not to cooperate with the ICC.[277] In a surprising turn of events, Ntaganda ended up turning himself in to the US embassy in Rwanda, from where he was transferred to The Hague, but this happened only after he had taken up arms against the Congolese army and his M23 rebellion was defeated in open combat.[278]

Although Luzolo later rationalized his position—'we had always said and knew that it would happen, but one had to wait for the right moment ... for political reasons it had to wait'—the Ntaganda arrest saga epitomizes the obstacles to prosecuting government-affiliated commanders in the DRC.[279] For years, the UN, civil society, and foreign governments have urged the ICC to take a harder line against Kabila's top brass (some of whom, it should be noted, are implicated in pre-2002 crimes, over which the ICC lacks temporal jurisdiction).[280] One human rights activist observed in 2016, 'we know the big boys are "off the hook" ... the financiers of the war have not been gone after', but expressed cautious optimism that 'with Bensouda things are changing a little'.[281]

These hopes proved premature. Not only did Bensouda not bring a single case against Kabila loyalists; the OTP declined also to monitor the few domestic trials that implicated high-ranking government officials. This abdication of oversight responsibility on the ICC's part is significant. As seen in Chapter 3, under the Rome Statute, sham trials allow the ICC to assert jurisdiction at the expense of national courts under the 'unwilling genuinely' prong of complementarity (even after trials are completed, the ICC has powers to reassert jurisdiction under *ne bis in idem*).[282] Although ICC intervention against sham trials is sensitive, these are the hardest cases of state-sanctioned impunity, where government institutions organize judicial proceedings that whitewash allegations of criminal activity. It is in these cases that the ICC's shadow can expose structural deficiencies in domestic justice efforts.

PGR Kabange Numbi' (14 March 2014) <mediacongo.net/article-actualite-1391_dans_le_cadre_-de_la_cooperation_entre_la_rdc_et_la_cpi_fatou_bensouda_chez_le_pgr_kabange_numbi.html>.

276 Interview with NGO representative, Goma, DRC, 2 September 2015. See also Arnould (n 221) 329 (noting the government's attempts to 'sound out' the ICC about a suspension of the Ntaganda warrant under Rome Statute, art 16).

277 Interview with DRC Prosecutor General and senior Kabila adviser, Kinshasa, DRC, 26 April and 19 August 2016.

278 Pete Jones and David Smith, 'Notorious Warlord Gives Himself up to International Criminal Court' *The Guardian* (19 March 2013) <theguardian.com/world/2013/mar/19/africa-congo>.

279 Interview with Emmanuel-Janvier Luzolo Bambi Lessa, Kinshasa, DRC, 21 April 2016.

280 See eg UNSC Res 2463 (2019) preamble.

281 Interview with human rights activist, Kinshasa, DRC, 22 April 2016.

282 See Chapter 3 in this volume; Rome Statute, art 20.

Yet, in line with its deferential approach, the OTP has not monitored proceedings in the DRC, even in the high-profile 2014 *Minova* trial which implicated thirty-nine Congolese troops in a notorious mass rape. The military organized this trial after intense lobbying from donors, the UN, and NGOs. In 2014, after two months of proceedings, a military tribunal convicted two rank-and-file soldiers of one rape each and several soldiers for the war crime of pillage. Low-ranking officers were acquitted while senior commanders bearing overall responsibility were never charged.[283] Noting shortcomings at various stages of the proceedings, HRW concluded that '[n]ational trials such as the one held to prosecute the Minova crimes ... discourag[e] victims and [entrench] the perception that justice is arbitrary and that high-level commanders are protected no matter what happens'.[284] Despite unprecedented media attention, the OTP declined to exercise jurisdiction, reinforcing the perception it would not jeopardize its relationship over the crimes of Kabila allies. Organized with international support, *Minova* exposed the limitations of NGO-supported trials.[285]

The prosecutor's strategy came under renewed scrutiny when Kabila refused to step down as president after the end of his second (and last) term in 2016. As violence and abuses surged in several cities and in Kasaï province, the EU and United States imposed sanctions on high-level civilian, military, and police officials.[286] In the meantime, Bensouda limited herself to periodic press releases assuring that she continued to 'carefully monitor' the DRC situation.[287] Although security forces loyal to Kabila are accused of killing hundreds of protesters, the OTP has failed to bring any prosecutions for the crimes committed during the 2015–18 electoral crisis.

While Kabila eventually left office in 2019, two years after the end of his constitutional mandate and after a controversial deal with an opposition leader, a notable feature of the OTP's public relations strategy during the electoral crisis was Bensouda's use of complementarity as a rationale for *not* exercising jurisdiction. In

[283] HRW, 'Justice on Trial. Lessons from the Minova Rape Case in the Democratic Republic of Congo' (2015).

[284] ibid 4.

[285] Interviews with activist and UN official, Goma, DRC, 3 September 2015. Phone interview with UN official, 2 August 2016.

[286] UN Joint Human Rights Office, 'Unlawful, Unjustified and Disproportionate Use of Force in the Context of the Management of Public Demonstrations in the DRC from January 2017 to January 2018' (March 2018); BCUNDH, 'Preliminary Investigation Report on Human Rights Violations and Violence Perpetrated during Demonstrations in Kinshasa between 19 and 21 September 2016' (2016); Steve Wembi, 'Senior Congo Officials Linked to Kabila Face Sanctions for Rights Abuses' *New York Times* (2 June 2017) <nytimes.com/2017/06/02/world/africa/congo-officials-sanctioned.html>.

[287] ICC, 'Statement by the Prosecutor of the International Criminal Court, Fatou Bensouda, on Her Office's Mission to the Democratic Republic of the Congo from 16 to 20 October 2016' (2016) <icc-cpi.int/Pages/item.aspx?name=161020-otp-statement-congo>; ICC, 'Statement of the Prosecutor of the International Criminal Court, Fatou Bensouda, Regarding the Situation in the Kasaï Provinces, Democratic Republic of the Congo' (2017) <icc-cpi.int/Pages/item.aspx?name=170331-otp-stat>.

March 2017, the OTP 'urge[d] the competent DRC authorities, in accordance with the principle of complementarity, which lies at the heart of the Rome Statute . . . and which confers on States Parties the primary responsibility to investigate and prosecute, to take all measures required to conduct genuine investigations'.[288] By this time, thirteen years into the OTP's investigation, reminding the government of its duty to prosecute ignored that the justice system had failed to discharge its 'primary responsibility' against a single high-ranking Kabila ally. In an ironic gloss on the ICC's case law, complementarity served not to challenge the Congolese judiciary's 'inaction', but as a shield to excuse the OTP's own inaction.[289]

To be sure, how much pressure the ICC prosecutor can apply against state actors, without provoking backlash or a breakdown in cooperation, is contested. Prompted about the OTP's reluctance to challenge Kabila, some OTP officials cited legal obstacles, for instance the ICC's lack of jurisdiction over pre-2002 crimes or a lack of evidence against Kabila allies. Others acknowledged the political context. One OTP official, drawing a sharp distinction between the ICC and politics, argued 'we will not be drawn into the election process . . . we are not there to topple the government'.[290] Echoing a more conciliatory approach to state power, Bensouda disavowed in 2014—during one of two visits to Kinshasa during her mandate—that the ICC functioned as a 'sword of Damocles' hanging over African countries.[291] Her confession was certainly curious as Bensouda had previously explained positive complementarity as a 'proactive policy of cooperation and consultation, aimed at promoting national proceedings and at positioning itself as a sword of Damocles, ready to intervene in the event of unwillingness or inability by national authorities'.[292]

The ICC's growing unwillingness to confront the Kabila administration did not go unnoticed in the DRC, where several senior magistrates acknowledged that the OTP never tried to apply pressure over cases implicating government actors. But reactions to the prosecutor's risk-averseness vary. One senior military magistrate affirmed 'we are not accountable to the ICC . . . [it] can come and observe but it is not here to teach us lessons'.[293] At the same time, he argued that the threat of ICC intervention could, despite the risk of backlash, prove beneficial in unblocking investigations stalled due to political obstruction. Yet reconciling cooperation with the need for principled pressure has proved a daunting task. At one point, Kabila

[288] ICC, 'Situation in the Kasaï Provinces' (n 287).

[289] This argument was developed initially in Patryk I Labuda, 'Taking Complementarity Seriously: Why Is the International Criminal Court Not Investigating Government Crimes in Congo?' (*Opinio Juris*, 28 April 2017) <opiniojuris.org/2017/04/28/33093/>.

[290] Interview with OTP official, The Hague, Netherlands, 6 July 2018.

[291] *Africa News* (n 275).

[292] Fatou Bensouda, 'Reflections from the International Criminal Court Prosecutor' (2012) 45 Case Western Reserve Journal of International Law 505, 507.

[293] Interview with senior Congolese military magistrate, Kinshasa, DRC, 26 July 2019.

allies reportedly brandished the threat of Rome Statute withdrawal in the run up to the 2018 elections.[294]

Although the OTP still employs the rhetoric of burden sharing and positive complementarity in the DRC, its place in the Congolese accountability landscape is ill defined. Formally, the ICC retains jurisdiction over, and disclaims any intention of closing, the DRC investigation. But, beyond general exhortations to investigate domestically, for instance in a 2020 press release on violence in Ituri, there is no evidence of a country-wide strategy to address impunity.[295] Acknowledging the absence of a strategy, one senior OTP official noted that complementarity refers to the ICC's presence and collaboration with NGOs, but that encouraging domestic prosecutions, which he considered merely 'aspirational', reveals 'a mismatch between aspirations and reality'.[296] In practice, therefore, the fight against impunity is led by the UN and NGOs, while many serious crimes remain beyond the justice system's reach. A senior OTP official conceded that the prosecutor needs to 're-assess the situation' and 'develop a strategy' or 'simply leave'.[297]

4.5. Unpacking complementarity's effects on domestic prosecutions

As early as 2005, William Burke-White, a champion of positive complementarity qua 'system of multi-level global governance', pointed to the DRC as evidence that the ICC was 'altering incentives at the national level and catalyzing reform efforts'.[298] Following his lead, commentators have used the DRC's military trials as a prime case study of 'complementarity in action', where the ICC serves as a 'global catalyst' for domestic prosecutions.[299] Some even claim, optimistically, that 'most of these [domestic] cases were against senior members of the Congolese army', which could in turn raise questions about the relevance of trials in The Hague.[300]

294 TRIAL International, 'ICC Withdrawal: Kinshasa Issues Alarming Statement' (17 September 2018) <trialinternational.org/latest-post/icc-withdrawal-kinshasa-issues-alarming-statement/>.

295 ICC, 'Statement by the Prosecutor of the ICC, Fatou Bensouda, Regarding the Situation in Ituri, DRC' (4 June 2020) <icc-cpi.int/Pages/item.aspx?name=200604-icc-prosecutor-statement-ituri-drc>.

296 Interview with OTP official, The Hague, Netherlands, 24 November 2015.

297 Phone interview with OTP official, 27 August 2019. The UN High Commissioner for Human Rights has criticized the persistence of impunity for government crimes: Sonia Rolley, 'RDC: d'après Michelle Bachelet, "Les crimes contre l'humanité sont confirmés"' *Radio France Internationale* (28 January 2020) <rfi.fr/fr/podcasts/20200128-rdc-apr%C3%A8s-michelle-bachelet crimes-contre-humanit%C3%A9-sont-confirm%C3%A9s>.

298 Burke-White (n 226) 574.

299 Geraldine Mattioli and Anneke Woudenberg, 'Global Catalyst for National Prosecutions? The ICC in the Democratic Republic of Congo' in Nicholas Waddell and Phil Clark, *Courting Conflict? Justice, Peace and the ICC in Africa* (Royal African Society 2008).

300 Richard Goldstone, Phil Clark and Dan Plesch, 'Justice for War Criminals and Human Rights Abusers: Beyond the Nuremberg—ICC Model' (*9BR International*, 31 July 2019) <9bri.com/justice-for-war-criminals-and-human-rights-abusers-beyond-the-nuremberg-icc-model/>. The citation refers to a sample of 382 cases from Maniema and South Kivu provinces tried between 2009 and 2012—not the DRC as a whole.

With the OTP's investigation still underway, conclusions about the ICC's impact on domestic prosecutions are necessarily tentative. However, overly positive appraisals of positive complementarity can be put into perspective. Since 2005, Congolese magistrates have indeed tried over fifty cases of international crimes as well as hundreds of ordinary crimes that could have potentially met the threshold of war crimes and crimes against humanity. To date, no other ICC investigation has seen as much domestic prosecutorial activity (Colombia and a few other preliminary examinations raise different questions, as will be seen below). Yet, as impressive as these figures are, Bosnia and Herzegovina had, by 2005—when the ICTY Completion Strategy kicked in—already prosecuted over fifty international crimes cases under its 'rules of the road' programme that apparently discouraged prosecutions.[301] Rwanda had also tried thousands in the ICTR's shadow before rule 11*bis* was put in place.

To be sure, unlike in Sierra Leone and Rwanda, where most crimes stopped either shortly (SCSL) or a few years (ICTR) after the tribunals intervened, recurring cycles of violence in eastern Congo have formed the backdrop to the ICC's in-country presence. Yet, despite these contextual differences, the Congolese case study remains relevant as it sheds light on the OTP's modus operandi in the first twenty years. Epitomizing a general shift from iteration to accommodation at the ICC, the DRC investigation has not fulfilled the most optimistic predictions of the ICC's shadow pushing states to do justice domestically, including by encouraging the national authorities to launch admissibility challenges to obviate the need for international trials. But this is hardly surprising. In a country as vast as the DRC, no justice system could address thousands of crimes, at least not immediately.

By the same token, there was always going to be a role for ICC prosecutions in the DRC. It is the types of cases and rationales underpinning transfers to The Hague, rather than the fact that international trials have taken place, that raise questions about the OTP's strategy in Congo. As noted in Chapter 3, by conditioning intervention on states' 'unwillingness' or 'inability' to 'genuinely' prosecute, the Rome Statute seems to anticipate conditionality-based iterative relations between the ICC and states. By contrast, self-referrals and the 'inaction' doctrine have produced a diametrically opposite set of accommodative interactions by allowing the ICC to ignore domestic shortcomings in the pursuit of triable cases. The DRC illustrates as well as any situation why the 'inaction' and 'same case' jurisprudence is counterproductive. There is no doubt that many cases from the DRC were admissible and hence prosecutable by the ICC, yet the case law substituted a conditionality-based dialogue with Congolese authorities over the domestic judiciary's flaws, for OTP-led backdoor diplomacy with the political elite in Kinshasa. As a result, rather than Ocampo and Bensouda emphasizing the hard

[301] Burke-White (n 119) 287.

cases of shielding, the Kabila administration agreed to halt imperfect but ongoing investigations against a handful of suspects—Lubanga, Katanga, Ngudjolo—who would be prosecuted internationally based on the purportedly unique gravity of their crimes.

What is unconvincing about the ensuing trials is not their taking place in The Hague—as will be seen in Chapter 6, the Congolese justice system never would have prosecuted people like Katanga fairly—but the misleading rationale underpinning these transfers. Instead of using Hague-based trials as an opportunity to rationalize and legitimize the exercise of international jurisdiction by acknowledging the Congolese judiciary's struggle to prosecute domestically, the OTP based its case selection on the promises of government actors to not interfere with international prosecutions. In so doing, the case law missed an opportunity to set benchmarks for domestic reform that would enable successful admissibility challenges in the future and spur civil society advocacy around national trials. In other words, rather than cast a shadow over domestic prosecutorial strategy, complementarity—reinterpreted as partnership—sanitized accommodation with government actors while delegitimizing international trials in The Hague that proceeded on spurious grounds of national 'inaction'.

The shift from iteration to accommodation amplifies a rhetorical chasm between complementarity as a public relations slogan and the realities of ICC prosecutorial strategy. Although, colloquially, complementarity came to encapsulate the idea that the ICC and state authorities work together to 'complement each other', by shifting the focus from conditionality-based relations with Congolese state actors to rhetorical promises of partnership, the ICC unwittingly created false expectations that it could never meet. Despite OTP strategies emphasizing cooperation under the banner of positive complementarity, its leadership separated itself from sensitive debates on domestic prosecutorial strategy, with the first two prosecutors visiting the DRC a handful of times and a limited field presence hampered by budgetary constraints. With the ICC's cases amounting to little more than opportunistic prosecutions but little in the way of burden sharing, Congolese military magistrates complained that the OTP declined to support them, for instance by sharing evidence.

In other words, from a burden-sharing strategy, complementarity morphed into a marriage of convenience that absolved both ICC and Congolese actors from confronting the most serious crimes. As early as 2009, Laura Davis and Priscilla Hayner observed that '[d]espite the intention spelled out in [the Rome Statute] to complement and give precedence to investigations and prosecutions in national courts, the national justice sector seems to use the ICC as an excuse for not pursuing such cases'.[302] The same dynamic can be seen in reverse, with

[302] Laura Davis and Priscilla Hayner, *Difficult Peace, Limited Justice: Ten Years of Peacemaking in the DRC* (ICTJ 2009) 30. On complementarity as a marriage of convenience, see also Nouwen (n 220).

complementarity becoming an excuse for ICC inaction. Despite well-documented crimes by Kabila allies, complementarity served as a rhetorical shield for an OTP wary of jeopardizing a partnership that allowed it—by receiving cooperation for its Hague trials of Kabila rivals—to maintain a semblance of action in the DRC. In sum, rather than devise a holistic strategy to close the impunity gap, both the ICC and Congolese authorities pointed to complementarity as an excuse for their inaction on difficult cases.

Meanwhile, in the ICC's shadow, the impetus for domestic trials has come mainly from proactive Congolese magistrates and development partners. While some observers suggest that ICC intervention harmed domestic prosecutorial efforts, it must also be recognized that civil society and state actors have harnessed the ICC's shadow to advocate a large number of prosecutions. Nevertheless, while invoking complementarity tactically to rationalize national trials, NGO and donors face constraints and are often unable to surmount the political impediments to accountability. As will be seen in Chapter 6, 'NGO justice' concentrates on less contentious violations while ignoring the structural impunity that enables mass crimes to continue, with too many trials implicating former rebels or low-level suspects. In short, in the absence of credible threats of ICC prosecution, the political elite retains control over the domestic accountability process.

5. Interim Conclusion: Domestic Prosecutions in the Court's Shadow

Popularized by its first prosecutor, the idea that the ICC could, through complementarity, encourage domestic prosecutions was expected to set it apart from the primacy-based ad hoc tribunals. As seen in Sierra Leone, a primacy-based restrictive mandate may have even depressed domestic prosecutorial activity. Yet the ICC's 'shadow effects' have confounded expectations for several interrelated reasons.

First, delegations to Rome may have hoped to reverse the ad hoc tribunals' primacy by giving the ICC 'complementary' jurisdiction, but international prosecutors—like judges, as seen in Chapter 3—have interpreted their mandated powers similarly. Aside from the ICTR/Y's initial phase of open-ended investigations with dozens of indictments, prosecutors increasingly replicate the SCSL's strategy of numerically limited cases. Like their counterparts, ICC prosecutors also interpret their mandate to prioritize 'high-level' or 'most responsible' suspects.

While they have not adhered to this rule *à la lettre*—mid- and low-level suspects were targeted in the ad hoc tribunals' early phases as well as in the DRC, CAR, and Mali situations—the ICC now follows a 'targeted primacy' model, whereby charges are sought against a small number of suspects. Complementarity plays little role—other than as a rhetoric of partnership—in how ICTs and national prosecutors conduct investigations. Acknowledging continuity, a senior magistrate explained that investigations at the ICTY and ICC were conducted 'exactly the same way', adding that 'from an operational perspective there cannot be any difference ... there has to be a cut-off point where the case is ours'.[303] Yet, while narrow case selection arguably reduces costs, it also fosters—as Paul Seils argues—an inward, 'looking-for-business' mentality to international prosecution, reducing points of interaction and incentives to start an iterative dialogue with states over case distribution.[304]

Second, although the Rome Statute was expected—by giving states an opportunity to pre-empt international trials—to coax or even shame states into action, the shadow of international intervention has generally proved insufficient to overcome the obstacles to domestic prosecutions. Drawing on her study of ICC investigations in Sudan and Uganda, where 'patronage networks' fuel cycles of impunity, Sarah Nouwen concludes that 'the sovereignty and reputational costs incurred by ICC interference' are not comparatively greater than 'the practical and political costs' of launching national proceedings against people who benefit from the state's protection.[305] The same pattern can be seen in the DRC and beyond. Although ICT intervention raises awareness of international criminal law, and empowers NGOs and other stakeholders to advocate domestic prosecutions, international prosecutors are reluctant to intrude on national prosecutorial strategy, for instance by sharing evidence or, more controversially, by monitoring trials with a view to galvanizing action. By the same token, ICTs often serve as an excuse for domestic inaction, with national authorities 'free-riding' on international trials. Despite a commitment to independence, international prosecutors struggle to resist the opportunity for triable cases, especially when faced with obstructionism in relation to other cases.[306]

That being said, despite the limitations of their coercive power vis-à-vis obstructionist states, the ICTY, SCSL, and ICTR experiences suggest that prosecutors at primacy-based tribunals may find it harder to ignore government wrongdoing altogether. While the challenges to overcoming the interests of political and military elites are the same under primacy (and the ICTR managed to directly spur just one high-level prosecution against the wishes of the RPF), the ICC's institutional design, in particular the Rome Statute's consent-based nature coupled with the (now real) threat of withdrawals, undermines the ICC's ability to advocate prosecutions of government-affiliated actors. In addition to the threat of non-cooperation,

[303] Interview with former ICTY and ICC official, undisclosed location, 5 April 2017.

[304] Paul F Seils, 'Making Complementarity Work: Maximizing the Limited Role of the Prosecutor' in Carsten Stahn and Mohamed M El Zeidy (eds), *The International Criminal Court and Complementarity* (CUP 2011) 989.

[305] Nouwen (n 220) 398; on domestic 'patronage networks' and cycles of impunity, see further 367–406.

[306] Shany (n 209) 437–38.

present at the ad hoc tribunals, the ICC prosecutor must consider the possibility that governments—as in the case of Burundi and the Philippines—will simply withdraw from the Rome Statute rather than face the threat of indictments against their officials.[307]

Third, the intrastate political obstacles to domestic prosecutions combined with the operational imperative that cases remain 'ours' means that cooperation with government actors, especially from the executive branch with foreign relations decision-making power, often trumps other institutional design features such as primacy or complementarity.[308] Although, in theory, governments have a non-negotiable obligation to cooperate, state non-cooperation (the mere threat thereof is usually enough) has occurred at all ICTs. In response, prosecutorial and judicial interpretation of primacy and complementarity adjust to accommodate state concerns. While article 17 seemed to anticipate iterative, conditionality-based relations with states, ICC judges validated Hague-centric theories of uncontested admissibility that made international case selection dependent on states' willingness to cooperate rather than their shortcomings in prosecuting domestically. Accordingly, Ocampo focused initially on crimes of purportedly unique gravity committed by—from the state's perspective—politically uncontroversial suspects, usually mid-level and easier to apprehend. While such targets did not jeopardize cooperation and resulted in accommodation with leaders in Uganda and the DRC, opportunistic prosecutions also decreased pressure on the ICC to engage governments on iterative anti-impunity strategies, as will be seen in the next two chapters.

Initially, most of the ICC's activities and 'shadow effects' revolved around accommodationist self-referrals. However, an early outlier was Kenya,[309] where the OTP embraced a positive complementarity strategy consisting of a mix of 'carrots and sticks' to influence the post-2007 election accountability process. After the Kenyan government failed to meet pre-agreed upon benchmarks and reneged on promises to self-refer (arguing inter alia that self-referrals were 'an option reserved for failed states'), the OTP opened a *proprio motu* investigation and pivoted to a three-tiered accountability strategy involving trials in The Hague against senior suspects, a domestic tribunal for lower-level perpetrators, and a truth commission.[310] Against the backdrop of charges against six senior officials, including

[307] On the broken taboo of withdrawals, see Patryk I Labuda, 'Africa and the ICC: Shattered Taboos, and the Status Quo' (*EJIL: Talk!*, 23 November 2016) <ejiltalk.org/africa-and-the-icc-shattered-taboos-and-the-status-quo/>.

[308] On complementarity and cooperation, including the ICC's embeddedness in patronage networks, see Nouwen (n 220) 392 and 402.

[309] In 2011, Burke-White still argued that '[n]oticeably absent from the Prosecutor's current framing of positive complementarity are more proactive visions of the concept, particularly using the threat of investigation and prosecution ... to encourage national governments to prosecute crimes domestically or engaging in any direct capacity-building efforts'. See William Burke-White, 'Reframing Positive Complementarity' in Stahn and Zeidy (n 304) 346.

[310] Lionel Nichols, *The International Criminal Court and the End of Impunity in Kenya* (Springer 2014) 74–81.

Uhuru Kenyatta and William Ruto who leveraged their Hague cases to become president and vice president respectively, the investigation collapsed, with 'little evidence that the OTP's strategy of positive complementarity made any significant contribution to its stated objective of ending impunity'.[311] Christian De Vos calls Kenya 'a cautionary tale' about the prosecutor's 'hubris', the OTP's 'poor quality' preparations, and 'the ability of governments to obstruct and hobble a Court that relies on State co-operation'.[312]

While Kenya remains a prominent case of iterative, push–pull dynamics vis-à-vis government actors at the ICC, its shortcomings prompted a re-evaluation of prosecutorial strategy. Positive complementarity remained a rhetorical priority during Bensouda's term, but the OTP focused on cultivating state cooperation in investigations while the iterative ideals of positive complementarity shifted entirely to preliminary examinations, which became—in Stahn's words—'a new species of proceedings, somewhere between internal analysis, atrocity alert, and monitoring of situations', including 'ambitious rationales' such as 'early warning, deterrence and complementarity'.[313] On Bensouda's watch, the OTP applied the Rome Statute's 'unwilling', 'unable', and 'genuinely' criteria prospectively to entire situations (outside of case admissibility challenges) to influence state accountability policies.

Several inquiries became experimental laboratories for the OTP's tactics in the pre-investigation phase. Originating in 2004, the Colombia examination spanned nearly two decades, with the government putting in place a new legal framework and specialist institutions to address allegations of serious crimes from a fifty-year conflict. However, as elsewhere, the core question remained the state's ability and willingness to translate rule-of-law reforms into genuine prosecutions—and thereby avoid an ICC investigation. Despite a track record of cases against armed groups and lower-level state agents, allegations against senior government officials, especially the command responsibility of army officers for so-called false positives killings, remain a challenge to this day, as the government implements a peace agreement with the FARC rebels.[314] Although scholars disagree about the OTP's shadow effects, including its role in the peace negotiations with the FARC,

[311] ibid 249; Sosteness F Materu, *The Post-Election Violence in Kenya: Domestic and International Legal Responses* (Asser 2015) 106–15.

[312] Christian M De Vos, '"Magical Legalism" and the International Criminal Court: A Case Study of the Kenyan Preliminary Examination' in Morten Bergsmo and Carsten Stahn (eds), *Quality Control in Preliminary Examination*, vol 2 (Torkel Opsahl 2018) 283.

[313] Carsten Stahn, 'Damned If You Do, Damned If You Don't' (2017) 15 Journal of International Criminal Justice 413.

[314] The acronym 'FARC' stands for Revolutionary Armed Forces of Colombia. In addition to receiving communications from local civil society and monitoring the Colombian situation from The Hague, the OTP dispatched delegations on several occasions to engage with authorities on obstacles to domestic proceedings. In 2012, the OTP published a report assessing Colombia's progress and signalled what needed to be done to stave off an ICC investigation. See ICC–OTP, 'Situation in Colombia. Interim Report' (2012); ICC, 'The Office of the Prosecutor Concludes Mission to Colombia' (2 March 2015) ICC-OTP-20150302-PR1090 <icc-cpi.int/Pages/item.aspx?name=pr1090>.

Colombia is considered an emblematic preliminary examination, illustrating how iterative dynamics can work in practice.[315]

For much of Bensouda's term, preliminary examinations seemed to offer great promise. After all, in the pre-investigation phase, the OTP and states share the goal of preventing an ICC investigation by mobilizing domestic responses. However, despite extensive outreach to state authorities, including in Georgia, Guinea, the UK, Nigeria, and Ukraine, evidence of the OTP galvanizing national prosecutorial activity remained mixed. Since 2010, the OTP has attempted to persuade the Guinean authorities to carry out a single trial of a prominent massacre.[316] In Nigeria, ten years of outreach failed in 2020 when Bensouda announced she would seek authorization for an investigation.[317] Although the UK became the first country to stave off an ICC investigation, at least temporarily, after the OTP found national proceedings sufficient to address allegations from Iraq,[318] the length and lack of results in preliminary examinations came under sharp criticism towards the end of Bensouda's term.

As will be seen in Chapter 7, the third prosecutor, Karim Khan, has signalled a novel prosecutorial strategy, with investigations re-emerging as the main sites for (positive) complementarity. Whether Khan is able to overcome his predecessors' track record and incentivize national trials, including against incumbent government actors, remains an open question, however.

[315] See Courtney Hillebrecht, Alexandra Huneeus and Sandra Borda, 'The Judicialization of Peace' (2018) 59 Harvard International Law Journal 279; René Urueña, 'Prosecutorial Politics: The ICC's Influence in Colombian Peace Processes, 2003–2017' (2017) 111 American Journal of International Law 104; Marina Aksenova, 'The ICC Involvement in Colombia: Walking the Fine Line Between Peace and Justice' in Bergsmo and Stahn (n 312) vol 1; Kai Ambos, *The Colombian Peace Process and the Principle of Complementarity of the International Criminal Court: An Inductive, Situation-Based Approach* (Springer 2010). In October 2021, the prosecutor closed the preliminary examination and signed a new cooperation agreement, which—at the time of writing—cannot be assessed. See further Chapter 7 in this volume.

[316] HRW, 'Guinea: Coup Further Complicates Massacre Justice. Efficient, Fair Trial Should Hold 2009 Stadium Abusers Accountable' (26 September 2021) <hrw.org/news/2021/09/26/guinea-coup-further-complicates-massacre-justice>. After this manuscript was submitted, the trial began in September 2022. See V*oice of Africa News*, 'Guinea Trial for 2009 Massacre Begins on Anniversary' (29 September 2022) <voanews.com/a/guinea-trial-for-2009-massacre-begins-on-anniversary-/6768886.html> (last accessed 1 December 2022).

[317] ICC, 'Statement of the Prosecutor, Fatou Bensouda, on the Conclusion of the Preliminary Examination of the Situation in Nigeria' (11 December 2020) <icc-cpi.int/Pages/item.aspx?name=201211-prosecutor-statement>. However, as of mid-2022, Khan had yet to open an investigation, see 'ICC Prosecutor, Mr Karim A.A. Khan QC, Concludes First Official Visit to Nigeria' (22 April 2022) <icc-cpi.int/news/icc-prosecutor-mr-karim-aa-khan-qc-concludes-first-official-visit-nigeria>.

[318] ICC–OTP, 'Situation in Iraq/UK. Final Report' (2020).

5
International Intervention and Capacity Building

1. Introduction

To assess how the shadow of ICTs influences state-driven accountability processes and whether international intervention has generally positive (iteration), neutral (accommodation), or negative (isolation) effects on governments' willingness and ability to pursue accountability for international crimes, this chapter examines to what extent elements of the ICTR, SCSL, and ICC's institutional design encouraged capacity building for the national justice sectors in Rwanda, Sierra Leone, and the DRC, in particular by revitalizing criminal justice institutions and local expertise.

For states to be able to launch investigations and prosecutions of serious crimes, functioning national institutions are a prerequisite. Accordingly, the ICTR Statute anticipated 'the need for international cooperation to strengthen the Courts and Judicial System of Rwanda' and its Completion Strategy later emphasized that 'strengthening of competent national judicial systems is crucially important to the rule of law'.[1] Although the SCSL Statute contained no analogous clauses, the concept of legacy, which emerged in the interstices of its hybrid and restrictive mandate, came to define this aspect of its mission. It was assumed also that 'national location' boosts 'the national capacity-building contribution' of tribunals, 'allowing them to bequeath their physical infrastructure ... to national justice systems, and to build the skills of national justice personnel'.[2]

Echoing the ICTR preamble, the Rome Statute affirms that the 'effective prosecution' of the most serious crimes 'must be ensured by taking measures at the national level and by enhancing international cooperation'.[3] Additionally, in line with complementarity, the ICC may exercise jurisdiction over a case 'due to a total or substantial collapse or unavailability of [a state's] national judicial system', which implies that a state's (lack of) capacity to prosecute may matter for admissibility assessments.[4] Initially, no jurisdictional provisions at the ICTR or SCSL spoke to

[1] UNSC Res 955 (8 November 1994) S/RES/955, preamble; UNSC Res 1534 (26 March 2004), S/RES/1534 para 9.

[2] Report of the Secretary General, 'The Rule of Law and Transitional Justice in Conflict and Post-Conflict Societies' (2004) S/2004/616 para 44.

[3] Rome Statute, preamble.

[4] ibid art 17(3); see also art 93(10). On the importance of state capacity, see Morten Bergsmo, Olympia Bekou and Annika Jones, 'Complementarity and the Construction of National Ability' in

International Criminal Tribunals and Domestic Accountability. Patryk I. Labuda,
Oxford University Press. © Patryk I. Labuda 2023. DOI: 10.1093/oso/9780198868842.003.0005

domestic capacity as directly, but the rule 11*bis* conditionality scheme—echoing the ICC's complementarity norm—later made case referrals contingent on, inter alia, national institutions' ability to adhere to fair trial standards.

As seen in Chapter 2, the term positive complementarity, which now extends beyond the ICC, has become a shorthand for international financial and technical assistance to national justice systems. Focusing on areas of synergy, antagonism, and indifference, this chapter assesses to what extent the shadow of ICTs incentivizes the building of state institutions' capacity and, in turn, how state actors influence international capacity-building priorities. It argues that, while there is increased attention to how ICTs, foreign partners, and state-based actors can work together to improve infrastructure or develop practitioner expertise, the turn to (positive) complementarity may also legitimize authoritarian practices while romanticizing domestic accountability to the exclusion of international responses.

2. The International Criminal Tribunal for Rwanda

2.1. Specialist genocide courts and the waning shadow of international influence

The Rwandan genocide had catastrophic effects on society at large.[5] Like most of its state institutions, Rwanda's domestic justice system had imploded. Courthouses, prisons, and other infrastructure lay in ruins. Only 270 out of 800 magistrates who survived the carnage remained inside the country.[6] Given the fragile nature of its pre-genocide institutions, William Schabas argues that post-1994 capacity building was more about building than rebuilding the justice sector, which had 'never been more than a corrupt caricature of justice'.[7]

Justice reform faced unique political, logistical, and financial challenges. On the one hand, the RPF, an invading army, aimed to assert control over state institutions to impose its accountability preferences on legal professionals drawn primarily from the Hutu majority.[8] On the other, (re)building state institutions capable of

Carsten Stahn and Mohamed M El Zeidy (eds), *The International Criminal Court and Complementarity* (CUP 2011) 1055–56 and 1059–63.

[5] Gérard Prunier, *Africa's World War: Congo, the Rwandan Genocide, and the Making of a Continental Catastrophe* (OUP 2010) 11.

[6] François-Xavier Nsanzuwera, *La magistrature rwandaise dans l'étau du pouvoir exécutif* (Collectif des Ligues et Associations des Droits de l'Homme au Rwanda 1993) 63–79 ; Sigall Horovitz, 'Rwanda: International and National Responses to the Mass Atrocities and Their Interaction' (DOMAC 2010) 21–22.

[7] William A Schabas, 'Justice, Democracy, and Impunity in Post-Genocide Rwanda: Searching for Solutions to Impossible Problems' (1996) 7 Criminal Law Forum 523, 531.

[8] Prunier (n 5) 10–15; Filip Reyntjens, *Political Governance in Post-Genocide Rwanda* (CUP 2013) 213–22.

processing large numbers of cases depended on foreign aid. After a brief honeymoon in late 1994 up until mid-1995, rule-of-law reform transformed into a delicate balancing act between the RPF's sovereignty demands and the human rights concerns of foreign actors.

Post-genocide Rwanda was an epicentre of international intervention. UNAMIR, the peacekeeping mission that was on the ground during the genocide, was joined in September 1994 by one of the UN's first fully fledged human rights field missions, run by the then newly established Office of the High Commissioner for Human Rights (OHCHR).[9] Known as HRFOR, the mission received a mandate to, inter alia, 'implement programs of technical cooperation, particularly in the area of the administration of justice'.[10] The UN worked alongside several UN rapporteurs, and an eclectic mix of francophone and anglophone NGOs, led by RCN-Justice et Démocratie, Avocats Sans Frontières, African Rights, and Penal Reform International. A number of nascent domestic human rights groups, in particular LIPRODHOR, worked together with these and other international actors, including the ICTR.

It took some time for the new Rwandan authorities—a brittle coalition of RPF-led Tutsis and moderate Hutu that formed the Government of National Unity (GNU)—to develop an institutional policy on post-genocide accountability. Initially, both a truth and reconciliation commission, modelled on the South African truth-seeking process, and traditional justice mechanisms were considered. However, after the RPF gained the upper hand around mid-1995, the authorities gradually prioritized a criminal justice response, including large-scale genocide trials.[11]

At first, it appeared that Rwanda might experiment with a hybrid judicial mechanism, comprising both national and international magistrates. However, this project fell apart under pressure from RPF hardliners. Arguing that even a temporary secondment of international judges would be 'unconstitutional' and 'a breach of the sovereignty' of Rwanda, the RPF-led authorities blocked a hybrid court.[12] Alluding to the internal struggle between moderate Hutus and RPF-aligned Tutsis, Schabas

[9] Ian Martin, 'After Genocide: The UN Human Rights Field Operation in Rwanda' in Alice H Henkin (ed), *Honoring Human Rights: From Peace to Justice. Recommendations to the International Community* (Aspen Institute 1998).

[10] Martin (n 9) 101; Todd A Howland, 'Mirage, Magic, or Mixed Bag? The UN High Commissioner for Human Rights' Field Operation in Rwanda' (1999) 21 Human Rights Quarterly 1, 16–17.

[11] Projet d'appui à la reconstruction du système judiciaire rwandais du Ministère de la justice (7 November 1994) TCB/BT2/8/Add.9. Rwanda, Office of the President, Recommendations of the Conference Held in Kigali from 1 to 5 November 1995, on 'Genocide, Impunity, and Accountability': Dialogue for a National and International Response, Kigali, 1995.

[12] Prunier (n 5) 12; Stef Vandeginste, 'Poursuite des présumés responsables du génocide et des massacres politiques devant les juridictions rwandaises' in Stefaan Marysse and Filip Reyntjens (eds), *Annuaire des Grands Lacs 1996–1997*, vol 1 (Harmattan 1997) 93; William A Schabas, 'Genocide, Impunity and Accountability in Rwanda: Is It Reasonable to Expect a Devastated Legal System to Deal Justly with Those Who Destroyed It?' *Inroads: A Journal of Opinion* (1 January 1997).

explains that when the first post-genocide justice minister, Alphonse Nkubito was killed and replaced in September 1995 by his chief of staff, Martha Mukamurenzi, the new Rwandan administration 'made it clear that large numbers of foreign jurists were not what was required, and that justice in Rwanda would be done by Rwandans, with assistance from abroad playing only a secondary role'.[13] A former UN official explained that the 'hybrid' option was supported by moderate Hutus, but the RPF feared it might be held accountable for its own actions if international experts were integrated into the Rwandan justice system.[14]

After her appointment, Mukamurenzi emphasized domestic solutions to the genocide. Rejecting foreign influence, specialized genocide chambers became the preferred institutional response.[15] Chambers were to be placed in each of the twelve first instance (civilian) tribunals. The War Council, sitting atop the military justice system, had an additional chamber. As noted in Chapter 1, several thousand trials of genocidaires took place before the chambers, which briefly became the focal point for post-genocide justice in Rwanda, though the community justice system of *gacaca*—as will be seen later—emerged as the primary accountability forum in the 2000s.

International actors contributed to the institutionalization of the chambers in different ways. The UN and NGOs provided extensive training for magistrates, many of whom had to be recruited into the legal profession for the first time. For instance, the Belgian group, RCN Justice et Démocratie, liaised with Nkubito to develop a training curriculum for new magistrates, many of whom lacked any formal legal training and would go on to prosecute and judge genocidaires before the specialized chambers. International aid helped to refurbish courts and international experts provided technical assistance.[16]

An important albeit controversial initiative involved foreign attorneys, who would provide pro bono representation to genocide suspects before the specialized chambers. Although this initiative was supported by the Rwanda Bar Association and the Rwandan judiciary, it created a perception that foreigners, already heavily criticized for their inaction during the genocide, were again supporting genocidaires. For instance, Robert Van Lierop, on behalf of the American Bar Association, 'strongly advise[d] against... being involved in this effort' because

[13] William A Schabas, 'Genocide Trials and Gacaca Courts' (2005) 3 Journal of International Criminal Justice 879, 883; see also Gerald Gahima, *Transitional Justice in Rwanda: Accountability for Atrocity* (Routledge 2013) 64–65.

[14] Interview with former HRFOR official, Geneva, Switzerland, 19 January 2018.

[15] Organic Law 08/1996 of 1996 on the Organization of Prosecutions for Offenses constituting the Crime of Genocide or Crimes Against Humanity committed since 1 October 1990, Official Gazette, Year 35, 17, 1 September 1996, art 19. On civilian and military courts, see Daniel De Beer, *Loi rwandaise du 30 août 1996 sur l'organisation des poursuites des infractions constitutives du crime de génocide ou de crimes contre l'humanité. Commentaire et jurisprudence* (2nd edn, Alter Egaux 1999) 78–82.

[16] Interview with former NGO officials, Brussels, Belgium, 17 November 2016. See also Martin (n 9); Peter H Sennett and Gregory P Noone, 'Working with Rwanda toward the Domestic Prosecution of Genocide Crimes' (1997) 12 St John's Journal of Legal Commentary 425.

'we would not wish to be perceived by citizens of Rwanda, and other Africans, as experienced and "high powered" lawyers from a developed country ... defending those against whom accusations of participating in genocide have been made'.[17] Ultimately, legislation was amended and foreign attorneys did intervene in domestic genocide cases.[18]

The ICTR, which was based in Arusha, several hundred kilometres away, played a limited role in domestic accountability initiatives. On occasion, Tribunal officials participated in trainings, and there were regular communications with Rwandan justice actors.[19] But cooperation focused squarely on facilitating Arusha-based trials. As noted by an expert embedded in the Rwandan justice sector, 'the ICTR let its distrust be known ... [it] refused any collaboration ... it had disdain [for us], what is this justice of yours?'.[20] In many ways, ICTR officials made a calculated decision to avoid domestic justice as much as possible. In Thierry Cruvellier's phrase, 'the principle of ignorance', or 'minimal exposure to Rwanda's political and historical torments' of international civil servants, 'took firm root at the Arusha-based tribunal', with some judges even thinking 'it was inappropriate for them to visit Rwanda or meet with its authorities'.[21]

Many Rwandans as well as some international observers criticized the ICTR's separation from the domestic realm. Arguing, in 1997, that '[t]he Tribunal does not appear to be fulfilling an important part of its mandate', Lierop observed that '[i]f there is any assistance to Rwanda's judicial system by the Tribunal, it is almost imperceptible'.[22] In the same vein, the Rwandan government bemoaned the lack of support from Arusha, noting that 'as an international judicial body', the ICTR 'should be at the fore front in spearheading efforts to rehabilitate and reconstruct the judicial system of Rwanda'.[23]

The truth probably lies somewhere in the middle. With the RPF excluding international actors from strategic decision-making on post-genocide accountability, the ICTR had little ability to influence government policy and had legitimate reasons to remain detached from domestic politics. Notably, the UN appears to have supported a hybrid court with the participation of foreign magistrates, yet the RPF—as seen above—opted for a purely domestic institution that maximized their ability to control the judicial process.

[17] Robert F Van Lierop, 'Rwanda Evaluation: Report and Recommendations' (1997) 31 International Lawyer 887, 905.

[18] For details, see Mark A Drumbl, 'Rule of Law Amid Lawlessness: Counseling the Accused in Rwanda's Domestic Genocide Trials' (1998) 29 Columbia Human Rights Law Review 545.

[19] See eg ICTR Fourth Annual Report (7 September 1999) A/54/315 S/1999/943, para 63. Interviews with former ICTR officials, New York, NY and by phone, 9 May and 8 August 2019.

[20] Interview with foreign expert, Brussels, Belgium, 17 November 2016.

[21] Thierry Cruvellier, *Le Tribunal des vaincus: un Nuremberg pour le Rwanda?* (Calmann-Lévy 2006) 133.

[22] Van Lierop (n 17) 902.

[23] 'The Position of the Government of the Republic of Rwanda on the International Criminal Tribunal for Rwanda' (1997) (on file with author).

Tension only increased as time went by. International actors were initially reluctant to criticize the RPF for its policies, largely because of guilt over their failure to stop the 1994 genocide. However, reports of the RPF's human rights abuses received more and more international attention. Whereas the UN and some foreign donors felt that, in exchange for aid, they should have a say in charting Rwanda's post-accountability landscape, the RPF's aversion to foreign oversight grew with NGO- and UN-backed denunciations of government-sponsored abuses. In response to these criticisms, the RPF initially emphasized HRFOR's capacity-building mandate, to the exclusion of its monitoring powers. However, in 1998, after a series of critical human rights reports, the government ejected HRFOR from Rwanda.[24]

From 1994 to 1999, government policy on accountability was increasingly driven by internal power struggles within a narrow English-speaking RPF elite. Centred around Paul Kagame, who became president in 2000 and has remained in office ever since, the RPF came to exercise absolute control over a marginalized political opposition. Against the backdrop of these centralizing tendencies, the UN, donors, and NGOs had less influence on justice reform strategies. While the rejection of a hybrid tribunal was an early harbinger of resistance to foreign involvement, the *gacaca* courts came to epitomize a homegrown accountability alternative. As Kagame would explain later, it was an 'African solution to an African problem'.[25]

2.2. *Gacaca*: challenging international oversight

'A bed of soft green grass' or 'small grass', the word *gacaca* in Kinyarwanda refers to a system of community dispute resolution in Rwanda.[26] With tens of thousands of genocide suspects lingering in prisons in the 1990s, it became apparent that neither the specialized chambers nor the Arusha-based ICTR would be able to prosecute more than a fraction of those involved in the genocide.

As noted previously, some form of 'traditional justice' had been contemplated in the immediate aftermath of the genocide, but the idea of adapting *gacaca* to genocide justice grew organically, independently from the ICTR and, to some extent, in opposition to international intervention. As Nicola Palmer observes, 'just as the establishment of the domestic courts was in part a reaction to the criticisms

[24] *Report of UN High Commissioner for Human Rights on the Human Rights Field Operation in Rwanda* (11 September 1998) A/53/367, para 14. Interviews with former HRFOR officials, New York, NY and by phone, 14 May 2019 and 3 March 2021.

[25] HRW, *Justice Compromised: The Legacy of Rwanda's Community-Based Gacaca Courts* (2011) 1. But see Barbara Oomen, 'Donor-Driven Justice and Its Discontents: The Case of Rwanda' (2005) 36 Development and Change 887 (arguing that, while billed as 'local' justice, gacaca were framed by Western donors and consultants); Howland (n 10) 28.

[26] See <www.gacaca.rw/about>; Timothy Longman, *Memory and Justice in Post-Genocide Rwanda* (CUP 2017) 111.

that the Rwandan government raised against the ICTR, so *gacaca* was in part a response to the international criticisms and domestic challenges raised against the national courts' prosecutions'.[27] As one Rwandan government official noted, *gacaca* emerged at the confluence of the ICTR's primacy—which he assimilated with the Tribunal's raw power to appropriate cases—and national courts' capacity shortfalls.[28]

Gacaca is now reflexively associated with 'mass justice for mass atrocity', but the RPF was initially divided on whether traditional dispute resolution could be adapted to mass killing.[29] As noted by Phil Clark, '[*g*]*acaca* was not an automatic institutional choice to deal with genocide crimes ... [t]he eventual decision to adopt *gacaca* ... was highly controversial'.[30] While a government commission eventually endorsed this accountability mechanism in 1999,[31] *gacaca* courts should also be seen as part of wider reforms in the justice sector in the late 1990s and early 2000s. This included drafting a new constitution, reforming the judicial police, mandatory legal training for justice sector officials, and decoupling the Minister of Justice and Attorney General offices, to enhance, in principle, the judiciary's independence from the executive.[32]

Rolled out in phases over the next few years, *gacaca*'s aims included truth-seeking, establishing a list of victims and perpetrators, accelerating and enhancing the publicity of trials, absolute criminal accountability, punishment coupled with reconciliation and unity of Rwandans, and a traditional Rwandan solution to Rwandan problems, based on arbitration.[33] Much like the specialized chambers, the *gacaca* process was nominally intended to promote reconciliation by eliciting confessions, based on a differentiated hierarchy of guilt. Over time, however, as Bert Ingelaere and others have shown, it shifted from reconciliation to more retributive forms of accusatory justice.[34]

The decentralized *gacaca* court system reached much deeper into Rwandan society than the specialized chambers. After a pilot programme launched in 2001,

[27] Nicola Palmer, *Courts in Conflict: Interpreting the Layers of Justice in Post-Genocide Rwanda* (OUP 2015) 46.

[28] Interview with Rwandan official, Kigali, Rwanda, 12 August 2015.

[29] Lars Waldorf, 'Mass Justice for Mass Atrocity: Rethinking Local Justice as Transitional Justice' (2006) 79 Temple Law Review 1.

[30] Phil Clark, 'Hybridity, Holism, and "Traditional" Justice: The Case of the Gacaca Courts in Post-Genocide Rwanda' (2007) 39 George Washington International Law Review 765, 775; see also Phil Clark, *The Gacaca Courts, Post-Genocide Justice and Reconciliation in Rwanda. Justice without Lawyers* (CUP 2010) 22–23.

[31] On the origins and politics of establishing gacaca, see Longman (n 26) 112; Bert Ingelaere, 'From Model to Practice: Researching and Representing Rwanda's "Modernized" Gacaca Courts' (2012) 32 Critique of Anthropology 388, 391–92; Reyntjens (n 8) 222–23; Gahima (n 13) 159–60.

[32] See Alfred Ndahiro, Joseph Rwagatare and Alphonse Nkusi (eds), *Rwanda: Rebuilding of a Nation* (Fountain 2015) 135–44.

[33] On the goals of gacaca, see Schabas (n 13) 891–892.

[34] Bert Ingelaere, *Inside Rwanda's Gacaca Courts: Seeking Justice after Genocide* (University of Wisconsin Press 2016).

the new court system spread around the country and operated until 2012.[35] By the mid-2000s, *gacaca's* jurisdiction covered most of the then still unresolved genocide crimes. In total, Rwanda's community court system handled some two million cases, involving almost one million suspects, including over a million property cases. Most cases—up to 67 per cent—concerned property, not physical integrity, crimes.[36] As Cruvellier and Ephrem Rugiriza argue, 'the vast majority' of suspects were found guilty though '[g]uilty of what is not always clear'.[37] Despite early suggestions to the contrary, RPF crimes did not fall under the jurisdiction of *gacaca*, meaning that only genocide crimes were adjudicated, reinforcing a narrative of Tutsi-only victimhood and Hutu-only guilt for the events of 1994.[38]

From the outset, *gacaca's* unique blend of retributive and restorative justice elicited intense curiosity. Some argued that the Rwandan government should be given a chance to fashion a sui generis accountability response. However, *gacaca* also came under severe criticism, especially from human rights groups. Focusing on the judges' lack of professional training and insufficient due process guarantees for defendants, especially a lack of legal representation or the ability to challenge evidence, NGOs questioned the legitimacy of a justice mechanism that ignored individual rights.[39] The RPF ignored these critiques for the most part, although a short-lived attempt to give *gacaca* jurisdiction over category 1 offenders—which would make the death penalty applicable in non-traditional legal proceedings—may have been dropped after donors threatened to withhold funding.[40]

In principle, *gacaca* did not handle the most serious cases or the most high-profile suspects, most of whom remained within the jurisdiction of the ICTR or the ordinary criminal courts.[41] As such, international proceedings rarely overlapped with *gacaca*. However, some suspects, for instance Emmanuel Bagambiki, acquitted by the ICTR, were reprosecuted *in absentia* by *gacaca* courts.[42] ICTR decisions also discussed evidence gathered by *gacaca*, with some OTP officials noting that *gacaca* findings influenced their investigations.[43]

[35] Organic Law 40/2000 of 26/01/2001 Setting up Gacaca Jurisdictions and Organizing Prosecutions for Offences Constituting the Crime of Genocide or Crimes against Humanity Committed between 1 October 1990 and 31 December 1994; Schabas (n 13) 892–94; Clark (n 30) 777.

[36] Ingelaere (n 34) 56; see also Phil Clark, 'How Rwanda Judged Its Genocide' (Africa Research Institute 2012) 3.

[37] Thierry Cruvellier and Ephrem Rugiririza, 'Rwanda: The Most Judged Genocide in History' (*JusticeInfo*, 4 April 2019) <justiceinfo.net/en/40846-rwanda-the-most-judged-genocide-in-history.html>.

[38] Reyntjens (n 8) 225; Longman (n 26) 124.

[39] For a brief overview of the literature and generations of gacaca scholarship, see Ingelaere (n 31).

[40] Interview with former NGO official, Brussels, Belgium, 17 November 2016. See also Paul C Bornkamm, *Rwanda's Gacaca Courts: Between Retribution and Reparation* (OUP 2012) 42–43.

[41] Clark, *Gacaca Courts* (n 30) 72–75.

[42] But Bagambiki was prosecuted domestically on different charges (Horovitz (n 6) 60–61).

[43] Interview with former ICTR official, Geneva, Switzerland, 13 July 2016. Palmer (n 27) 83–84; Clark, *Gacaca Courts* (n 30) 204–05. See also ICTR r 11*bis* decisions examined in Chapter 3 in this volume, where *gacaca* convictions and *ne bis in idem* are discussed.

Although *gacaca* and the ICTR influenced each other's operations only at the margins, Rwanda's homegrown accountability system received much scrutiny, with opinions divided on the merits. At one end of the spectrum, proponents defend the Rwandan government's experiment. Notably, Clark argues that *gacaca,* judged on its own terms, is a 'remarkable success' in its 'holistic response to the legacies of the genocide, pursuing via popular participation both pragmatic and profound objectives'.[44] But most assessments are more measured and, on the whole, critical. Charity Wibabara concludes that '[g]acaca was the necessary evil of resolving the problem of the case backlog that was in the country after the genocide, where ordinary justice could not be applied ... [and] justifies why it was better to do justice, albeit unsatisfactorily, than not to do justice at all'.[45] According to Lars Waldorf, '[f]ar from being a model for future transitional justice efforts, gacaca offers some profound cautionary lessons about how local justice should be adapted after mass atrocity'.[46] Drawing attention to its wider political consequences, Anuradha Chakravarty argues *gacaca* consolidated 'authoritarian rule', enabling 'the RPF regime's entrenchment and survival'.[47]

Gacaca courts had by the mid-2000s displaced ordinary courts as the main accountability forum. However, after their phasing out in 2012, the ordinary justice system re-emerged as the primary venue for trials, especially extraditions and deportations from third states and rule 11*bis* referrals.[48]

2.3. In the ICTR's shadow: rule 11*bis*, iteration, and two-tier justice

As noted previously, Rwanda's decimated justice sector received a significant injection of international aid in the aftermath of the genocide. Over the years, a range of international organizations and donors, chiefly the EU, UN, the UK, USA, Belgium, the Netherlands, and Germany, provided financing, training, and technical expertise to revive the legal profession and stand up the court system. Support initially focused on operational necessities, but as Rwandan justice actors consolidated their authority, capacity building turned to more granular issues, such as improving judgment drafting or forensic investigation techniques.[49]

[44] Clark, *Gacaca Courts* (n 30) 27–28.

[45] Charity Wibabara, *Gacaca Courts versus the International Criminal Tribunal for Rwanda and National Courts: Lessons to Learn from the Rwandan Justice Approaches to Genocide* (Nomos 2014) 214–15; similarly, HRW (n 25) 1; Longman (n 26) 280–81.

[46] Waldorf (n 29) 86; see also Gahima (n 13); Pietro Sullo, *Beyond Genocide: Transitional Justice and 'Gacaca' Courts in Rwanda: The Search for Truth, Justice and Reconciliation* (TMC Asser Press 2018).

[47] Anuradha Chakravarty, *Investing in Authoritarian Rule. Punishment and Patronage in Rwanda's Gacaca Courts for Genocide Crimes* (CUP 2016) 5.

[48] Organic Law 04/2012/OL of 15/06/2012 terminating Gacaca Courts and determining mechanisms for solving issues which were under their jurisdiction.

[49] For an overview, see Alejandro Chehtman and Ruth Mackenzie, 'Annex. Section B. International Criminal Law Capacity Development Projects—Rwanda' in Alejandro Chehtman and Ruth Mackenzie

Contrary to the ICTR's limited support for capacity building in the 1990s, the Completion Strategy catalysed a new approach. United by the goal of ensuring case referrals to Rwanda, the ICTR's different organs—the OTP, judges, and Registry—engaged different Rwandan judicial institutions, in particular the NPPA, judges, and judicial service, to ensure compliance with the conditionality scheme in rule 11*bis*. As noted in Chapter 4, negotiations between Rwandan authorities and the ICTR on referrals began as early as 2004, initially on case files rather than rule 11*bis* indictments.[50] To ensure that the rule 11*bis* cases were successfully transferred back to Kigali, Rwanda created a special task force to coordinate negotiations with the ICTR.[51] On various occasions, delegations from the NPPA and the Kigali Bar Association travelled to Arusha to engage on technical, legal, and logistical matters.[52] After ICTR chambers rejected a first round of referrals, cooperation strengthened, leading to intense, and even more intrusive negotiations on rule-of-law reforms. In particular, the OTP provided hands-on mentoring and technical advice to the NPPA. One OTP adviser was eventually embedded full-time within the NPPA in Kigali.[53]

Throughout the rule 11*bis* process, ICTR organs provided extensive training for their Rwandan counterparts. Operating (frequently) with financial support from donors (rather than from the UN budget), ICTR officials gave courses on topics such as investigations, crime analysis, case and evidence management, trial advocacy, indictment drafting, and witness and victim protection.[54] The ICTR also played a more hands-on role in creating a witness and victim protection mechanism within the Rwandan justice system. Although concerns over witness intimidation dated back to genocide trials from the 1990s, it was not until the rule 11*bis* process that the NPPA created a dedicated Witness-Victim Services Unit.[55] After the ICTR rejected the first round of transfers, due in part to concerns over the independence of a prosecution-run witness protection scheme, a separate Witness

(eds), *Capacity Development in International Criminal Justice* (DOMAC 2009) 8–12; Horovitz (n 6) 28–30; Oomen (n 25) 898–99.

[50] Richard Karegyesa, 'Empowering Domestic Jurisdictions: Lessons from the ICTR Referral of Cases', International Symposium on the Legacy of the ICTR, Arusha, Tanzania, 6 November 2014 (on file); Horovitz (n 6) 75.

[51] Interviews with Rwandan officials, Kigali, Rwanda, 12 August 2015 and 9 September 2015. Phone interview with former NPPA official, 16 January 2017. See also Martin Ngoga, 'The ICTR Completion Process and Resultant Consequences on Rwanda's Justice System' *New Times Rwanda* (24 October 2008) <newtimes.co.rw/section/read/5493>.

[52] Interviews with Rwandan officials, Kigali, Rwanda, 11 and 12 August 2015.

[53] Phone interview with former ICTR official, 16 January 2017. See also ICTR–OTP, 'Complementarity in Action: Lessons Learned from the ICTR Prosecutor's Referral of International Criminal Cases to National Jurisdictions for Trial' (2015) para 47.

[54] Adama Dieng, 'Capacity-Building Efforts of the ICTR: A Different Kind of Legacy' (2011) 9 Northwestern Journal of International Human Rights 403, 409–10; ICTR–OTP (n 53) para 70. For the ICTY, see Diane Orentlicher, *Some Kind of Justice: The ICTY's Impact in Bosnia and Serbia* (OUP 2018) 365–70.

[55] ICTR–OTP (n 53) para 64; Dieng (n 54) 412–13.

Protection Unit administered by the Supreme Court was created in 2008.[56] Supported by the ICTR, these institutional reforms were expressly cited as one of the reasons why the second round of referrals in 2011–12 succeeded.

In parallel with ICTR capacity building, the Rwandan government developed its own justice sector programmes. Based in Nyanza, the Institute for Legal Practice and Development (ILPD) became the national training academy for judges and prosecutors.[57] Over the years, the ICTR and foreign donors clashed with the ILPD over the content of training for Rwandan justice officials, but the Institute gradually asserted control and became a one-stop shop for training.[58] In 2007, the NPPA established a Genocide Fugitive Tracking Unit with a mandate to locate and initiate the transfer of genocide suspects still at large in Africa, Europe, and beyond.[59] To confront the growing workload, including rule 11*bis* referrals, the NPPA created a specialized International Crimes Unit in 2008 to collect evidence, protect witnesses, and initiate mutual legal assistance requests and communications with the ICTR (later the MICT).[60]

The three ICTR suspects transferred to Rwanda—Jean Uwinkindi, Bernard Munyagishari, and Ladislas Ntaganzwa—were tried by a specialized unit created for this purpose within the High Court. Initially limited to cases transferred from the ICTR, the Chamber of International Crimes (CIC)'s jurisdiction was later expanded to deportation and extradition cases.[61] After ICTR defence teams argued, unsuccessfully, that a 'fair trial' requires Rwanda to integrate foreign judges in cases referred under rule 11*bis,* the CIC's rules were nevertheless amended to allow mixed panels.[62] To date, despite pressure from some extraditing states, Rwanda has

[56] Cited in ICTR-OTP (n 53) para 64. See also ICTR Press Release, 'Tribunal Trains Rwanda Witness Protection Officers' (16 November 2009) <unictr.unmict.org/en/news/tribunal-trains-rwanda-witness-protection-officers>.

[57] Law 22/2006 of 28 April 2006 establishing the Institute of Legal Practice and Development; Law 65/2013 of 27 August 2013 establishing the Institute of Legal Practice and Development and determining its mission, organization and functioning.

[58] Interviews with foreign diplomats, Rwandan attorney and justice officials and foreign experts, Kigali, Rwanda and by phone, 11, 14, and 19 August 2015, 20 July, 2 August and 2 December 2016. See also Horovitz (n 6) 76–79.

[59] Interviews with Rwandan officials, Kigali, Rwanda, 9 September and 19 August 2015. See also AFP, 'Seeking Justice: The Long Hunt for Rwanda's Killers' (2 April 2019) <france24.com/en/20190402-seeking-justice-long-hunt-rwandas-killers>.

[60] Interviews with Rwandan prosecutors, Kigali, Rwanda, 5, 11 August and 8 September 2015.

[61] Interviews with Rwandan prosecutors and judges, Kigali, Rwanda, 11, 12 August and 8 September 2015.

[62] Organic Law 03/2012/OL of 13/06/2012, art 13, para 2, on establishing the functioning and jurisdiction of the Supreme Court, Official Gazette 9 July 2012; 2013 Code of Criminal Procedure, art 210; Sam Rugege and Aimé M. Karimunda, 'Domestic Prosecution of International Crimes: The Case of Rwanda' in Gerhard Werle, Lovell Fernandez and Moritz Vormbaum (eds), *Africa and the International Criminal Court* (TMC Asser Press 2014) 110–11; TC, *Prosecutor v Bernard Munyagishari* (Decision on the Prosecutor's Request for Referral of the Case to Rwanda) ICTR-2005-89-R11*bis* (6 June 2012) paras 193–95; Gahima (n 13) 156.

refused to resort to foreign judges to adjudicate specific cases (the law still allows it, however).[63]

At first sight, the rule 11*bis* referral process constitutes a textbook example of multilevel iteration between international and domestic actors, with each side pushing the other to adjust its expectations and behaviour. But opinions diverge on the merits of the process. While recognizing improvements in domestic capacity flowing from engagement with the ICTR and donors, many Rwandans expressed reservations and frustration about 'external interference', 'imposing foreign standards', and 'double standards'. As one Rwandan official observed, 'who monitored the ICTR?'.[64] A foreign expert confirmed these criticisms, noting that Rwandans often suggested the entire rule 11*bis* process was 'a scam' and that 'the ICTR just wanted these cases back'.[65] Acknowledging challenges in the Tribunal's dealings with Rwandan counterparts, Hassan Jallow noted that most of his work was political and diplomatic in nature.[66] In effect, ICTR leaders served as liaisons between Rwanda, Arusha, and the wider diplomatic community, identifying needs, coordinating donors' often disjointed policies, and making sure support reached where it mattered (e.g. Germans installing videoconferencing facilities, the Dutch reforming prisons, and the British working on witness protection).[67]

Given the complexity of the rule 11*bis* process for both the ICTR and Rwanda, it is important to understand why, despite their differences, including at times overt antagonism, the stakeholders decided to engage in an iterative dialogue. On the ICTR's end, the main incentive for capacity building in Rwanda seems to have been its own cost-cutting needs. Despite the labour-intensive negotiations with Rwandan institutions, this was still cheaper than trials in Arusha. Although the Security Council made the decision for the ICTR in mandating referrals, the reason dialogue was necessary were Goldstone and Arbour's overambitious indictments in the early phases of investigations. In other words, it was an open-ended mandate, primacy and unrealistic planning that made referrals an issue in the first place.

Rwanda's motives for going to such lengths to exercise jurisdiction over a handful of suspects are key. After all, as important as Uwinkindi was to its post-genocide reckoning, he was hardly a genocide mastermind. Negotiations with the ICTR imposed costs on the Rwandan justice sector, and there was always the possibility—admittedly slim as time went by—that the ICTR would invoke primacy and reassert jurisdiction, dealing a blow to Rwanda's legitimacy. As conceded

[63] On foreign judges and extraditions, see UK High Court, *Government of Rwanda v Nteziryayo, Brown, Munyaneza, Mutabaruka, Ugirashebuja*, [28 July 2017] EWHC 1912, paras 236 and 535.

[64] Interviews with Rwandan magistrates, ministry officials, and civil servants, Kigali, Rwanda, August and September 2015. Phone interviews with international experts, 2 August 2016 and 16 January 2017, 9 May 2019. But see Dieng (n 54) 411.

[65] Phone interview with international expert, 2 August 2016.

[66] Interview with Hassan Jallow, Arusha, Tanzania, 10 September 2015.

[67] See also Dieng (n 54) 415–16.

by Martin Ngoga, the decision to push ahead with discussions was not a foregone conclusion: 'there was a strong view that, it was not wise to continue being part of the process that would damage our image, thereby jeopardizing our relations with other national jurisdictions ... [t]he view to pull out was therefore well-founded because further participation would have been a serious gamble'.[68]

Ngoga went on to suggest that Rwanda's decision was motivated by a 'strong desire for justice'.[69] Without discounting this motive (at any rate, it is impossible to discern one rationale behind Rwanda's rule 11*bis* policy), the most likely explanation seems to be a calculation that ICTR approvals of transfers would enhance Rwanda's reputation as a human rights-compliant justice system, which would in turn facilitate hundreds of outstanding extradition (and deportation) requests from around the world. In doing so, the RPF could claim a symbolic victory of sorts in its tussle over genocidaires, twenty years after trials began. Equally important, the government could more credibly argue that its judiciary had handled all allegations of RPF crimes.

Although, in 2016, the Rwandan justice ministry tried but failed to convince the Spanish government to 'cancel' an arrest warrant against RPF officials and send investigation files back for domestic investigation,[70] Rwanda's gamble has worked for the most part. Going back to the 1990s, its extradition and deportation requests had been repeatedly blocked over its justice system's failure to meet international standards. Whereas the ICTR's 2008 rule 11*bis* rejections likely reinforced refusals from France, Germany, and the UK, shortly after the 2011 *Uwinkindi* ruling, the European Court of Human Rights approved Sweden's extradition of a Rwandan suspect, followed by Leon Mugesera's deportation in 2012, after nearly two decades of judicial deadlock in Canada.[71] In 2013, Charles Bandora became the first suspect

[68] Ngoga (n 51).

[69] ibid; see also *Prosecutor v Jean-Bosco Uwinkindi* (*Amicus Curiae* Brief for the Republic of Rwanda in Support of the Prosecutor's Application for Referral pursuant to Rule 11*bis*) ICTR-2001-75-I (18 February 2011) para 1.

[70] Interviews with Rwandan officials and international experts, 2015–20. The Rwandan justice ministry even published a false story claiming that Spain had sent back their case file to Rwanda (Rwandan Ministry of Justice, 'The Ambassador of Spain in Rwanda Paid a Courtesy Visit to Rwandan Minister of Justice and Attorney General' (10 May 2016) (on file with author)). Spain's Prosecutor General office refuted this story. Phone interview with Spanish Prosecutor General's Office, 3 November 2016. In this sense, see also Sara Kendall and Sarah MH Nouwen, 'Speaking of Legacy: Toward an Ethos of Modesty at the International Criminal Tribunal for Rwanda' (2016) 110 American Journal of International Law 212, 224. On the importance of the RPF file, see Lars Waldorf, '"A Mere Pretense of Justice": Complementarity, Sham Trials, and Victor's Justice at the Rwanda Tribunal' (2011) 33 Fordham International Law Journal 1221, 1239–44. See also Chapter 6, section 2.5 in this volume.

[71] ECtHR, *Ahorugeze v Sweden* (Judgment) (App no 37075/09, 27 October 2011). For details of these and other cases, see Yasmine Chubin, 'The Impact of the ICTR 11 Bis Referrals on Rwanda's Legal Reforms, Extradition Requests, and Transfer Case Procedure' (2014) 9–11 <unictr.irmct.org/en/compendium-legacy-ictr-and-development-international-law>. On Mugesera, see William A Schabas, 'Mugesera Case: Yet Another Twist in the Debate about the Rwandan Justice System' (*PhD Studies in Human Rights*, 15 January 2012) <humanrightsdoctorate.blogspot.ch/2012/01/mugesera-case-yet-another-twist-in.html>. On extradition treaties, see further HRW, 'Rwanda: 25 Years on, Solidarity with Victims' (4 April 2019) <hrw.org/news/2019/04/04/rwanda-25-years-solidarity-victims>.

to be physically handed over to Rwanda.[72] In other words, the rule 11*bis* rulings (and subsequent MICT decisions to *not* reassert primacy) provided an important reputational indicator of how extraditing states perceived the Rwandan judiciary.

With the Kagame-led government continuing to negotiate extradition treaties with countries in an effort to prosecute alleged genocidaires, foreign donors made little secret of their reasons for supporting justice reform in Rwanda. Noting that a majority of EU states felt the Rwandan judiciary did 'sufficiently well', an EU ambassador to Rwanda explained that the importance of 'the quality of the Rwandan judiciary ... was more a matter of internal dialogue among [EU] member states for the purpose of their own policies and especially this issue of trials of genocidaires back in Europe'.[73] A Dutch official was more blunt and explained that his government's support was 'important for extradition from the Netherlands ... [we] want to know what the situation is'.[74] Epitomizing the donor community's at times schematic mindset, the Dutch official added 'everything [from] Arusha has to be present here ... it is about [the Rwandans] applying international law as is'.[75]

As will be seen in Chapter 6, disagreement remains as to what exactly 'international law' requires of a national justice system. Concerns have also emerged of a two-tiered system of genocide justice.[76] The High Court's trials of Uwinkindi, Mugesera, and other 'international' genocidaires consist of one set of ICTR-influenced procedures while 'ordinary' local perpetrators do not stand to benefit from the same norms. In turn, this double standard raises further criticisms of the sustainability of ICTR-mandated reforms and the parameters of a fair trial in Rwanda.

2.4. Unfulfilled legacy? Penitentiary reform in Rwanda

Under the ICTR Statute, the Tribunal's sentences 'shall be served in Rwanda' or in other states indicating their 'willingness to accept convicted persons', subject to the ICTR's supervision.[77] Although Rwanda failed to persuade the Security Council to locate the Tribunal in its territory, this norm was expected to provide some consolation by allowing penalties to be enforced in accordance with Rwandan law.

However, this expectation never came to pass. With over 100,000 suspects languishing in pretrial detention in the 1990s, human rights groups denounced the

[72] Chubin (n 71) 10.
[73] Phone interview with former EU ambassador to Rwanda, 5 January 2016.
[74] Interview with Dutch official, Kigali, Rwanda, 14 August 2015.
[75] ibid.
[76] On two-tiered justice, see ICTR–OTP (n 53) paras 74–77; Padraig McAuliffe, 'Bad Analogy: Why the Divergent Institutional Imperatives of the Ad Hoc Tribunals and the ICC Make the Lessons of Rule 11 Bis Inapplicable to the ICC's Complementarity Regime' (2015) 11 International Organizations Law Review 345, 413.
[77] ICTR Statute, art 26.

inhumane conditions in Rwanda's overcrowded prisons.[78] As noted, *gacaca* arose in part from the ordinary justice system's inability to ensure timely trials for so many suspects.[79] Signed in 1999, a memorandum of understanding (MoU) with Rwanda made no mention of hosting convicts on Rwandan soil and when the ICTR finally concluded agreements for the transfers of convicts later that year, Mali and Benin became destinations of choice.[80]

As seen in Chapter 3, rule 11*bis* brought penitentiary standards back into the spotlight, with the ICTR rejecting transfers to Rwanda in 2008 because of, inter alia, the severity of domestic punishments. In anticipation of the ICTR's rulings, the government, supported by foreign donors, developed plans to rehabilitate its prisons. For instance, the EU paid for the construction of a special holding cell in Kigali and later the Dutch government funded the rehabilitation of the prison in Nyanza.[81] In 2008, the ICTR signed an MoU with Rwanda on the enforcement of sentences, allowing inspection of 'the conditions of detention and treatment of the convicted person(s)' and, if necessary, 'the termination of the enforcement of the sentence in Rwanda and transfer the convicted person to another State or to the Tribunal'.[82] A year later, the UN concluded that Rwanda had made such strides in enhancing penitentiary standards that it signed a separate agreement for the detention of people convicted by the SCSL.[83] To date, however, no ICTR convicts have been sent back to Rwanda to serve their prison sentences.[84]

This is no coincidence. Despite advances in penitentiary standards, human rights groups argue that the RPF has complied with the text, but not necessarily the spirit, of these agreements. In 2017, HRW denounced torture and incommunicado detention in military prisons, and a UN body on the prevention of torture suspended its visit to Rwanda due to governmental obstruction.[85] Conditions for 'ordinary' genocidaires (without a link to the ICTR or foreign jurisdictions) and regular criminals are worse, while accusations of serious abuse inside prisons

[78] Amnesty International, 'Rwanda. Gacaca: A Question of Justice' (2002) AFR 47/007/2002 11.

[79] Audrey Boctor, 'The Abolition of the Death Penalty in Rwanda' (2009) 10 Human Rights Review 99, 107–08; Schabas (n 13) 880.

[80] Memorandum of Understanding, 3 June 1999 (on file). For the ICTR's agreements with other states, see <unictr.unmict.org/en/documents/bilateral-agreements>.

[81] UNSC, S/PV.5904 (4 June 2008) 28; Horovitz (n 15) 79–80.

[82] Agreement between the Republic of Rwanda and the United Nations on the Enforcement of Sentences of the International Criminal Tribunal for Rwanda, 4 March 2008, arts 6 and 9(2).

[83] Agreement between the Special Court for Sierra Leone and the Republic of Rwanda on the Enforcement of Sentences of the Special Court for Sierra Leone, 18 March 2009.

[84] On the ICTR's relocation of convicted and acquitted persons to Niger and the ensuing struggle to prevent their deportation to Rwanda, see Balthazar Nduwayezu, 'The Punishment of the Stateless ICTR "Migrants"' (*JusticeInfo*, 9 June 2022) <justiceinfo.net/en/93462-punishment-stateless-ictr-migrants.html>.

[85] HRW, '"We Will Force You to Confess": Torture and Unlawful Military Detention in Rwanda' (2017); OHCHR, 'Prevention of Torture: UN Human Rights Body Suspends Rwanda Visit Citing Obstructions' (20 October 2017) <ohchr.org/en/press-releases/2017/10/prevention-torture-un-human-rights-body-suspends-rwanda-visit-citing>.

persist.[86] After Paul Rusesabagina's controversial rendition to Kigali in 2020, he was held in solitary confinement for several months, and the authorities confiscated confidential documents provided by his attorneys.[87] Government officials counter that any abuses inside Rwandan prisons are not systematic and merely part of the process of penitentiary reform, but the ICTR's legacy in this area is incomplete at best.

2.5. Unpacking primacy's effects on capacity building

In 2015, a few months before the ICTR's closure, the prosecutor published a report entitled 'Complementarity in Action'. In it, Hassan Jallow argued that '[t]ogether with our partners, the ICTR contributed to a host of legal reforms and infrastructure improvements at the national level that were necessary to secure the fair trial rights of the accused'.[88] This assessment is shared by many scholars, including from Rwanda. For instance, Wibabara argues that 'the Tribunal has had an enormous impact on the reform of the judiciary within Rwanda, especially since the adoption of the Tribunal's completion strategy in 2004'.[89] The ICTR's effects on the rule of law are also cited as a core aspect of its legacy.[90]

Despite such laudatory retrospective assessments, the path to institutional revitalization in Rwanda was not linear. Although the Security Council mentioned international capacity building in the ICTR mandate, and donors initially supported projects geared to facilitating domestic genocide trials, stark divergences emerged over time. By the early 2000s, the Rwandan justice sector seemed increasingly isolated, with tensions between, on the one hand, the sovereignty demands of a new political elite looking to consolidate its authority, including through criminal law, and on the other hand, the human rights criticisms of both foreign and domestic actors. Emblematic of the RPF's resolve to provide accountability on its own terms, the specialized chambers comprised only Rwandan magistrates. Similarly, the *gacaca* courts were set up and implemented over the sometimes vocal objections of the human rights community and donors, who nevertheless funded this novel form of traditional justice.

In contrast to the ICTR's absence from domestic rule-of-law reforms in the 1990s, the rule 11*bis* process (like the ICTY's analogous experience in Bosnia and Herzegovina) is often held up as a model for how ICTs should interact with states.[91]

[86] Phone interviews and e-mail exchanges with international advisers and defence counsel, January 2021.

[87] Amnesty International, 'Rwanda: Ensure Remedy after Fair Trial Violations in Paul Rusesabagina Case' (2021).

[88] ICTR–OTP (n 53) ii.

[89] Wibabara (n 46) 73.

[90] Dieng (n 54) 421; see also Chapter 6 in this volume.

[91] See eg William Burke-White, 'The Domestic Influence of International Criminal Tribunals: The International Criminal Tribunal for the Former Yugoslavia and the Creation of the State Court of

However, the conditions that enabled a turn to capacity building are sometimes misunderstood, with some scholars pointing to rule 11*bis* rather than the socio-political environment that opened the door to negotiations in Rwanda specifically. Reforms under the shadow of rule 11*bis* resulted from a confluence of idiosyncratic factors that, combined, produced an iterative process involving the ICTR, Rwandan authorities and foreign states doubling as donors. Despite its resentment of international oversight, the Rwandan government proved susceptible to external pressure because agreement on a handful of cases held the key to a greater prize, namely the extraditions of suspects that Rwandan prosecutors had been trying, unsuccessfully, to gain custody of since the 1990s. It was mainly the RPF's anti-impunity policy (for genocide crimes) that enabled negotiations over the specifics of where and how genocidaires would be held accountable, although a secondary albeit important factor may have been the RPF's desire to shield its own crimes from scrutiny by counteracting claims that its domestic justice system was not impartial. In this regard, the threat of ICTR cases and unenforced French and Spanish indictments against RPF suspects strengthened domestic reforms as well.

The motives of international actors for capacity building in Rwanda deserve scrutiny. The ICTR's early policy of ignoring the domestic realm changed only after the Security Council realigned its mandated goals. Extended negotiations with Rwandan judicial actors over the terms of rule 11*bis* proved important, but the impetus for OTP-, Registry-, and judge-led capacity building came from externally imposed constraints rather than an internal ICTR-centric concern over domestic accountability in Rwanda. Equally important, the iterative process of revitalizing Rwandan judicial institutions was pushed along by the self-interest of foreign states, not coincidentally those with large populations of Rwandan refugees, who expected their courts to eventually allow extraditions or deportations of genocide suspects.

Against this backdrop of complex institutional and sovereignty incentives, it bears emphasizing that, while capacity building under the shadow of rule 11*bis* cannot be explained by institutional design alone, the ICTR's mandate facilitated this iterative process of dialogue and contestation. The Rwanda government's sensitivity to qualitative assessments of its justice system and the reputational effects that flowed therefrom were enabled by two aspects of the ICTR mandate. First, the conditionality scheme of rule 11*bis* based on fair trial rights allowed ICTR officials to engage their Rwandan counterparts over genocide prosecutions, whereas the Rome Statute's anti-impunity ('genuineness') logic would have foreclosed such negotiations (there was no risk that Rwandan courts would shield genocidaires from accountability). Second, the ICTR's residual primacy—the power to revoke cases—and a perception that international judges might enforce this rule, allowed

Bosnia & Herzegovina' (2008) 46 Columbia Journal of Transnational Law 279, 320–24. Critically, see McAuliffe (n 76).

Tribunal officials to push harder negotiations than would have otherwise been possible.

In the end, the ICTR prosecutor and judges extracted greater concessions from Rwandan actors by dangling the carrot of legitimation for the justice sector than by branding the stick of indictments against its leadership. Reforms were made possible by a combination of reputational incentives, namely fair trial rights' conditionalities and the reward of international legitimation. Unexpectedly, rule 11*bis* declinations strengthened, rather than weakened, bilateral interactions, with some reforms, for instance on witness protection, likely not materializing but for external pressure (or taking longer to implement). All in all, the rule 11*bis* process underscores the iterative potential of temporarily antagonistic relations between international and state actors, which must be overcome through negotiation.[92]

At the same time, the Rwandan case study illustrates the limits of external pressure. Although hybrid judicial arrangements have been mooted on at least two separate occasions (early plans to set up a hybrid court with foreign magistrates and recent proposals to integrate foreign judges), they were rejected on sovereignty grounds. Arguably, the Security Council missed an opportunity to promote international participation in Rwandan institutions when the ICTR Completion Strategy, contrary to its ICTY equivalent, failed to mention a hybrid court akin to the War Crimes Chamber in Bosnia and Herzegovina (usually seen as a positive example of hybridity).[93] The Council's less prescriptive approach to ICTR referrals, which reflected ambivalence about the Rwandan justice sector, had the paradoxical effect of decreasing international actors' leverage to shape a justice system that, by its own admission, raised more fair trial concerns than the one in Bosnia and Herzegovina.

Against the backdrop of still ongoing genocide extraditions and deportations, opinions on the Rwandan justice reform remain divided. While analysts recognize the RPF-led government's ambitious policy of post-conflict reconstruction, the shadow effects of a three-tiered accountability response—the ICTR, ordinary courts, and *gacaca*—for Rwandan society's aspirations of emancipatory justice are more debatable. Despite the scale of foreign support for rule-of-law and transitional justice objectives, the RPF's tolerance of a one-sided victors' justice dovetails with its 'deft authoritarianism' that justifies 'restrictions on political parties, civil society, and the media as necessary measures to guard against a recrudescence of ethnic violence' and thereby challenges 'teleological models of political transitions and human rights norm diffusion'.[94] As will be seen in Chapter 6, the Rwandan

[92] Similarly for the ICTY vis-à-vis Serbia, see Orentlicher (n 54) 388–93.

[93] See Chapter 3 in this volume. For appraisals of the Bosnian chamber, see Orentlicher (n 54) 344–82; Padraig McAuliffe, *Transitional Justice and Rule of Law Reconstruction* (Routledge 2013) 197–200 (on the ICTY's impact prior to rule 11*bis*, 190–91).

[94] Scott Straus and Lars Waldorf (eds), *Remaking Rwanda. State Building and Human Rights after Mass Violence* (University of Wisconsin Press 2011) 4 and 16.

judiciary's ability to provide genocidaires with fair trials, in accordance with international human rights standards, remains contested.

3. The Special Court for Sierra Leone

3.1. 'Hybridity', legacy (building), and 'demonstration effects'

Unlike the ICTR, capacity building for the Sierra Leonean justice sector was not mentioned in the SCSL mandate. This omission is surprising. As seen in Chapter 3, not only was the UN aware that domestic institutions required reform; in fact, Sierra Leonean negotiators emphasized the judiciary's lack of capacity as the primary reason for creating a hybrid court (only later would the government emphasize the Lomé amnesty to justify its lack of action on civil war atrocities).[95]

Although domestic rule-of-law reform was formally absent from its mandate, it was widely assumed that, by virtue of its hybridity and *in situ* status, the SCSL would have a 'demonstration effect' on the Sierra Leonean justice system.[96] Equally important, the concept of 'legacy', coined shortly after the SCSL launched operations, emerged as a placeholder for, and driver of, capacity-building initiatives.[97] Originating in civil society consultations, the legacy concept spread rapidly among international and domestic stakeholders. The SCSL's first annual report endorsed the idea of 'leaving a legacy' for the Sierra Leone judiciary, including transfers of equipment, training for lawyers, and a law library.[98]

Over time, the SCSL's 'legacy projects' grew in size and ambition. A legacy working group, created in 2005, and a legacy coordinator, appointed in 2007, were expected to focus on five issues: 'developing the capacity of the national legal profession'; 'promoting the rule of law and accountability in Sierra Leone;' 'promoting human rights and international humanitarian law;' 'promoting the role of civil society in the justice sector;' and 'assisting the government of Sierra Leone in assessing possible uses for the site of the court beyond the lifespan of the trials'.[99]

Coining a concept proved easier than its implementation, however. In 2006, Antonio Cassese argued that '[t]he issue of legacy should be tackled as soon as possible'.[100] Despite his call, legacy remained more a rhetorical slogan than a reality.

[95] Priscilla Hayner, 'Negotiating Peace in Sierra Leone: Confronting the Justice Challenge' (ICTJ and Centre for Humanitarian Dialogue 2007) 25–26.

[96] On demonstration effect, see Chapter 3 in this volume.

[97] HRW, 'Bringing Justice: The Special Court for Sierra Leone. Accomplishments, Shortcomings, and Needed Support' (2004) 36; Report of the Secretary General (n 2) para 46.

[98] President SCSL, 'First Annual Report SCSL' 28.

[99] Open Society Justice Initiative, 'Legacy: Completing the Work of the Special Court for Sierra Leone' (2011) 5. See also President SCSL, 'Third Annual Report SCSL' 28; Viviane E Dittrich, 'Legacies in the Making: Assessing the Institutionalized Legacy Endeavor of the Special Court for Sierra Leone' in Charles C Jalloh (ed), *The Sierra Leone Special Court and Its Legacy* (CUP 2013) 673.

[100] Antonio Cassese, 'Report on the Special Court for Sierra Leone' (2006) para 277.

SCSL judges and prosecutors nominally embraced the idea, but capacity building was not considered part of their core mandate, and early versions of the SCSL Completion Strategy underscored that legacy projects had to be funded by external donors.[101] In other words, even as the Special Court prepared to shut down, legacy projects were ad hoc and secondary to more urgent tasks, such as appeals.

It was only the completion of international trials and appeals in 2008–9 that provided a concrete impetus for the SCSL legacy projects.[102] As Marieke Wierda observes, 'while originally there was resistance to the concept of "legacy" among donors, and an emphasis on pursuing the "core mandate"', the same actors came to criticize the Special Court 'for its inability to have an impact on the domestic legal system'.[103] Ultimately, the SCSL legacy projects crystallized alongside several donor-funded capacity-building initiatives for the justice sector, in particular the UK's Justice Sector Development (2005–11) and Access to Security and Justice (2011–16) programmes.[104] The UN Development Programme, supported initially by the UN's peacekeeping mission, UNAMSIL (until 2005) and later the UN Peacebuilding Commission (starting in 2007) implemented additional rule-of-law projects, with the help of domestic and international civil society groups.[105]

Although the SCSL is now considered a progenitor of the idea that all ICTs should, beyond their international trials, leave a legacy for domestic justice systems, the origins of legacy lie in two seemingly contradictory aspects of the Special Court's mandate.[106] On the one hand, it operated in proximity to Sierra Leonean institutions while its hybrid institutional features aimed to increase Sierra Leoneans' ownership of the Court. On the other hand, the SCSL's restrictive personal jurisdiction and its projected three-year time frame all but ensured that international trials would be an ephemeral experience for Sierra Leoneans.

[101] Thierry Cruvellier, 'From the Taylor Trial to a Lasting Legacy: Putting the Special Court Model to the Test' (ICTJ 2009) 28. Interviews with former SCSL officials, The Hague, Netherlands and London, UK, 19 November 2016 and 9 February 2017. Mohamed A Bangura, 'Delivering International Criminal Justice at the Special Court for Sierra Leone: How Much Is Enough?' in Charles C Jalloh, *The Sierra Leone Special Court and Its Legacy* (CUP 2013) 712.

[102] Interviews with former SCSL officials, Nuremberg, Germany and Washington, DC, 16 and 30 September 2016. Cruvellier (n 101) 38.

[103] Marieke Wierda, 'Transitional Justice in Sierra Leone' in Jeroen de Zeeuw and Krishna Kumar, *Promoting Democracy in Post-Conflict Societies* (Lynne Rienner 2006) 201. For an overview of legacy projects, see Dittrich (n 99) 677–78.

[104] For details, see Mohamed Suma, 'Sierra Leone. Justice Sector and the Rule of Law. A Review by AfriMAP and the Open Society Initiative for West Africa' (Open Society Foundations 2014) 22–23.

[105] UNSC Res 1645 (20 December 2005) S/RES/1645; Ibrahim Bangura, 'Leaving Behind the Worst of the Past: Transitional Justice and Prevention in Sierra Leone' (ICTJ 2021) 20.

[106] Dittrich (n 99) 664; OHCHR, 'Rule-Of-Law Tools for Post-Conflict States. Maximizing the Legacy of Hybrid Courts' (2008) 4–5. On conceptions of legacy, see also Jessica Lincoln, *Transitional Justice, Peace and Accountability: Outreach and the Role of International Courts after Conflict* (Routledge 2011) 122–26. This book dissociates legacy from the SCSL's outreach programme, which disseminated and enhanced knowledge about the court but did not build capacity as such.

3.2. Hybrid staffing: a missed opportunity for iteration?

Required by its mandate to employ Sierra Leonean nationals, one of the SCSL's unique features was its mixed personnel. The Special Court's 'national component' came to be viewed as part of its legacy for the justice sector, with Sierra Leonean legal professionals expected to return to the domestic justice system and increase its capacity by using the skills that they had learned from international colleagues. As Alejandro Chehtman observes, hybrid tribunals are 'at least on paper, in a much better position than internationals in terms of their potential to contribute to developing local capacity through mentoring'.[107]

This assumption ran into various problems. First, the Sierra Leone government proved reluctant to promote national staff, especially to more senior positions at the SCSL. In fact, Kabbah's administration went so far as to secretly amend the SCSL agreement, signed in early 2002 but implemented several months later by Parliament, to ensure that Sierra Leone would *not* be required to appoint one of its nationals as deputy prosecutor.[108] Instead of a Sierra Leonean deputy, the position went to Desmond de Silva, a British barrister (with a history of prior work in Sierra Leone).[109] After De Silva replaced Crane as prosecutor in 2005, freeing up the deputy prosecutor position, the Sierra Leone Bar Association encouraged Kabbah to appoint a national official. The government did not oblige, nominating Christopher Staker, a British national, as deputy prosecutor instead. Other high-ranking appointments, especially among the Special Court's judges, revealed further ambivalence on the government side about the composition of the hybrid tribunal.[110]

It may seem surprising that the government would voluntarily relinquish the opportunity to shape the Special Court's operations, but its position was influenced by several factors. Eke Halloway, then Attorney General, explained '[w]e didn't want someone who had been affected by the atrocities ... We wanted the best person, be he or she a Sierra Leonean or not'.[111] But some argue that Kabbah deliberately declined to appoint experienced Sierra Leone prosecutors and judges

[107] Alejandro Chehtman, 'Developing Local Capacity for War Crimes Trials: Insights from BiH, Sierra Leone, and Colombia' (2013) 49 Stanford Journal of International Law 297, 310; Cassese (n 100) 63.

[108] SCSL Agreement, art 3. See Mohamed Suma, 'The Hybrid Nature of the Special Court Is Fast Dissipating' (*Sierra Leone Court Monitoring Programme (SLCMP)* [date unknown]) <carl-sl.org/pres/the-hybrid-nature-of-the-special-court-is-fast-dissipating-the-sierra-leonean-aspect-should-be-rest/>; McAuliffe (n 93) 229.

[109] On De Silva's ties to Kabbah, see Chris Mahony, 'A Political Tool? The Politics of Case Selection at the Special Court for Sierra Leone' in Kirsten Ainley, Rebekka Friedman and Chris Mahony (eds), *Evaluating Transitional Justice. Accountability and Peacebuilding in Post-Conflict Sierra Leone* (Palgrave Macmillan 2015).

[110] Cruvellier (n 101) 31; International Crisis Group, 'The Special Court for Sierra Leone: Promises and Pitfalls of a "New Model"' (2003) 19–20. But see Alison Smith, 'The Expectations and Role of International and National Civil Society and the SCSL' in Jalloh (n 99) 55–56.

[111] Quoted in International Crisis Group (n 110) 19.

to senior positions for fear that such individuals could inject domestic politics into the SCSL. Binta Mansaray, a former SCSL (and current RSCSL) registrar, has suggested that '[a]t the beginning, there was a deliberate effort to keep away from the national judiciary, for political reasons, in order to remain independent from it'.[112] Others argue that Kabbah may have worried that Sierra Leoneans would influence the prosecutorial strategy in ways not agreeable to the incumbent government. For instance, a former national OTP official noted that 'they were scared of us ... they knew we knew a lot, [and] the government ... fear[ed] that local hires would push the Prosecutor to go after Kabbah'.[113]

Whichever interpretation is more accurate, observers generally agree that Sierra Leonean authorities, especially in the early years, did not take ownership of the SCSL. Former Attorney General, Serry Kamal, is known to have described the SCSL derisively as a 'foreign country'.[114] A number of observers acknowledge that Sierra Leonean judges in particular resented the SCSL's special status, which they viewed with a mix of suspicion and disdain. One former SCSL judge explained that, despite an understandable lack of expertise in matters of international law, their Sierra Leonean counterparts resented being lectured at by international staff.[115] A former Sierra Leonean official noted that the Special Court's 'primacy' over Sierra Leone was a particular bone of contention for national judges who viewed it as an affront to their sovereignty.[116] Despite some improvements over time, such challenges appear to have remained to the end.

Compounding these discrepancies, the Special Court's primarily international principals did not proactively change the balance of power among mid- and low-level staff. On the contrary, a perception existed that there were not enough qualified Sierra Leonean professionals (the Sierra Leonean government made this argument as well).[117] Although many positions in the OTP, the Registry, and the Principal Defender's office could be occupied by either nationals or foreigners, most senior positions remained in the hands of international staff in the first few years, which in turn created resentment among the Sierra Leonean legal profession. In 2004, HRW still pointed out that, although 50 per cent of SCSL staff were Sierra Leonean, they occupied mostly administrative and low-level positions.[118]

[112] Cited in Cruvellier (n 101) 32.

[113] Interview with Sierra Leone attorney, 23 March 2016, Cape Town, South Africa.

[114] Sigall Horovitz, 'Sierra Leone: Interaction between International and National Responses to the Mass Atrocities' (DOMAC 2009) 46; see also Chehtman (n 107) 311; Tom Perriello and Marieke Wierda, 'The Special Court for Sierra Leone under Scrutiny' (ICTJ 2006) 33.

[115] Phone interview with former SCSL judge, 4 August 2016. Similarly, Jane E Stromseth, 'Justice on the Ground? International Criminal Courts and Domestic Rule of Law Building in Conflict-Affected States' (2011) 50 Nomos 169, 174; Open Society Justice Initiative (n 99) 15.

[116] Interview with Sierra Leone attorney, Cape Town, South Africa, 23 March 2016.

[117] Interview with former SCSL officials, Nuremberg, Germany, 29–30 September 2016. Cruvellier (n 101) 31–33; Mohamed Sesay, 'Hijacking the Rule of Law in Postconflict Environments' (2019) 4 European Journal of International Security 41.

[118] HRW (n 97) 36; Chandra L Sriram, 'Wrong-Sizing International Justice? The Hybrid Tribunal in Sierra Leone' (2005) 29 Fordham International Law Journal 472, 500–01; Wierda (n 103) 194.

The ratio of national to international staff gradually shifted in favour of the former, with many international officials leaving and Sierra Leoneans taking their places.[119]

Another problem was that, while the idea of on-the-job learning seemed appealing on paper, practical challenges abounded. For one, translating international criminal law expertise into domestic criminal law practice was not obvious. Horovitz notes that senior government officials, 'highly critical of the [SCSL]', did not 'view it as a role model ... and complained that its proceedings differ from national proceedings, in terms of the use of jurors and rules of evidence'.[120] For another, the number of Sierra Leoneans at the Special Court proved too small to affect practice at the domestic level. When attorneys with experience at the SCSL tried to influence domestic proceedings, they would encounter resentment or a lack of interest in 'foreign' procedures.[121] Also, a perception existed that the SCSL stole the most talented Sierra Leoneans, with many nationals refusing to return to the national judiciary, and opting for more lucrative positions abroad.[122]

Appointments of Sierra Leoneans to senior positions at the SCSL were shaped by domestic politics, but by 2013 hundreds of national attorneys had worked for the prosecution, defence, or in chambers, and many police officers had been seconded to the Special Court, exposing them to complex investigations.[123] Tamba Pujeh Gbekie, a police officer seconded to the Special Court, later became Assistant Inspector General of the Sierra Leonean police.[124] After being promoted deputy prosecutor in 2008, Joseph F. Kamara became Head of the Anti-Corruption Commission (ACC) and later Attorney General. Claire Carlton-Hanciles, who was an SCSL principal defender, went on to chair the Legal Aid Board. Arguably, capacity building remained most limited in the judiciary, with few SCSL judges returning to the Sierra Leonean courts (though, for instance, Nicholas Browne-Marke, an OTP official, was subsequently elevated to the Court of Appeal and Supreme Court).[125]

[119] HRW, 'Justice in Motion. The Trial Phase of the Special Court for Sierra Leone' (2005) 37–38. Critically, see Bangura (n 101) 713–16.

[120] Horovitz (n 114) 46.

[121] Sigall Horovitz, 'How International Courts Shape Domestic Justice: Lessons from Rwanda and Sierra Leone' (2013) 46 Israel Law Review 339, 364; Lincoln (n 106) 128–29.

[122] Bangura (n 101); Michelle Staggs, 'Bringing Justice and Ensuring Lasting Peace. Some Reflections on the Trial Phase at the Special Court for Sierra Leone' (War Crimes Studies Center Berkeley 2006) 25.

[123] Horovitz (n 121) 364.

[124] Cruvellier (n 101) 34–35.

[125] Interview with RSCSL official and Sierra Leonean judge, Freetown, Sierra Leone, 11 and 14 March 2016. Phone interview with international judge, 4 August 2016.

3.3. Legacy in action: witness protection, training, and penitentiary reform

Guaranteeing the safety of victims and witnesses was particularly challenging in Sierra Leone. A relatively small country with tight-knit communities, coupled with the SCSL's *in situ* status—much closer to the affected communities than other ICTs—increased the likelihood that witnesses would be identified and that testifying in court would trigger reprisals. An incident in 2004, where a key witness was almost beaten to death, underscored this risk.[126] Moreover, the SCSL's focus on greatest responsibility—and hence the prosecutor's reliance on 'insider witnesses' who had intimate knowledge of suspects' actions—resulted in nearly 95 per cent of the SCSL's witnesses receiving 'some form of protection' (compared to just 25 per cent and 75 per cent at the ICTY and ICTR respectively).[127]

As foreseen by the SCSL Statute, a Witness and Victim Section (WVS) was created in Freetown to provide 'protective measures and security arrangements, counseling and other appropriate assistance'.[128] Despite various challenges that arose during its years of operation, the Special Court's track record of witness protection is viewed positively by most observers. As Christopher Mahony explains, the WVS 'is often cited as a new international criminal justice model for protecting African witnesses', in particular its 'widening interpretation of witness protection' and 'normative protective modalities to reflect witnesses' psychosocial needs'.[129]

While the WVS fulfilled its mandate during the SCSL's four trials, it was less clear how to provide guarantees to witnesses after the Court shut down. Efforts to create a residual protection mechanism in The Hague collapsed due to budgetary and logistical obstacles, which in turn left the Sierra Leonean judiciary as a natural fallback option.[130] Some aspects of the SCSL's protection mechanisms had over the years seeped into the work of domestic institutions, but the justice system did not have a dedicated witness protection programme that could take over the SCSL's residual functions.[131] Although SCSL officials had recognized a lack of domestic capacity as early as 2004, reforms stalled and it was only as pressure mounted to close the SCSL that a legacy project on witness protection was finally launched.[132]

[126] HRW (n 97) 31; HRW (n 119) 20–24.

[127] On the WVS generally, see Chris Mahony, 'The Justice Sector Afterthought: Witness Protection in Africa' (Institute for Security Studies 2010) 77–78; Elena Naughton, 'Committing to Justice for Serious Human Rights Violations. Lessons from Hybrid Tribunals' (ICTJ 2018) 72.

[128] SCSL Statute, art 16; SCSL RPE, r 34 (originally named Witness and Victim Support Unit, later renamed Witness and Victim Section). See also rscsl.org/WVS.html.

[129] Mahony (n 127) 77.

[130] ibid 92–93.

[131] Sulaiman Bah, 'Legal Reform in Sierra Leone' (Case Matrix Network: Strengthening National Justice for Core International Crimes, The Hague, Netherlands, 28 June 2016) <youtube.com/watch?v=IHPUplQu2N8&index=7&list=PLgMYBJx5GIGqIYQQGzGi1p8IItCY1HF75I>.

[132] Mahony (n 127) 157–59.

Around 2008–9, SCSL officials began providing witness protection and victim management training to Sierra Leonean police officers, some of whom also worked at the WVS on secondment and shared expertise with their national counterparts.[133] As part of its legacy projects, the WVS also helped to develop standard operating procedures for its national counterparts.[134] Building on these initiatives, a National Witness Protection and Assistance Unit, embedded within the Sierra Leonean police, was created and now provides support to witnesses in domestic proceedings on corruption, organized crime, human trafficking, and gender-based violence.[135]

The national witness protection programme is considered one of the SCSL's flagship legacy projects. As one Sierra Leonean police officer explained, we 'were seconded to the Special Court ... and [we] benefit[ed] from ... the Special Court', including through training 'on some of the ways the international system work[ed] ... in investigations and in witness and protection issues'.[136] Highlighting the SCSL's impetus for domestic reforms, another police officer observed that there were 'some high-profile cases that the government came to the Special Court for assistance ... [and] they found out it was very useful to have a witness protection unit in the judicial system in Sierra Leone'.[137] Epitomizing synergies in this area, the RSCSL's sub-office dedicated to witness and victim support collaborates to this day with Sierra Leone's National Witness Protection and Assistance Unit and both are based on the SCSL's former premises in Freetown. Observers agree that capacity building for witness protection succeeded largely due to dynamic interactions between the SCSL and national actors.[138]

In addition to witness protection, the SCSL is recognized to have enhanced police and corrections reform in Sierra Leone. As noted previously, uniquely among Sierra Leonean professionals, national police officers played, from the beginning, an important role in OTP investigations.[139] As part of its legacy projects, the Special Court provided training not only to police officers on criminal investigation and forensic evidence techniques, but also to a variety of legal professionals in a range of areas related to criminal justice.[140] The SCSL's capacity building supplemented

[133] SCSL, 'Special Court Launches Witness Protection Training Programme' (5 November 2009) <rscsl.org/Documents/Press/2009/pressrelease-110609.pdf>; Bangura (n 101) 712.

[134] Open Society Justice Initiative (n 99) 12–13; Fidelma Donlon, 'The Transition of Responsibilities from the Special Court to the Residual Special Court for Sierra Leone: Challenges and Lessons Learned for Other International Tribunals' (2013) 11 Journal of International Criminal Justice 857, 870.

[135] Donlon (n 134) 870. Interviews with Sierra Leonean police officers, Freetown, Sierra Leone, 8 and 14 March 2016.

[136] Interview with Sierra Leonean police officer, Freetown, Sierra Leone, 8 March 2016.

[137] Interview with Sierra Leonean police officer, Freetown, Sierra Leone, 8 March 2016. See also Yandama Kabia and Mamia Sulleh, 'Promoting Justice for Sexual Offenses: Some Persisting Challenges in Sierra Leone' (*Center for the Rule of Law and Accountability*, 4 October 2013) <carl-sl.org/pres/promoting-justice-for-sexual-offences-some-persisting-challenges-in-sierra-leone/>.

[138] But see Cruvellier (n 101) 33–35.

[139] Perriello and Wierda (n 114) 39–40; Horovitz (n 114) 59.

[140] For details, see Bangura (n 101) 711–13.

the efforts of the UK government in police and security sector reform, which led inter alia to the creation of Family Support Units tasked with registering and handling cases of sexual and gender-based violence.[141]

Other areas of reform include Sierra Leone's penitentiary system, which benefited from international donor support, including training by SCSL officials for corrections officers.[142] Given its *in situ* status, the Special Court also implemented capacity-building projects, such as training and material support for Fourah Bay College, the country's premier law school, and the Sierra Leone Bar Association.[143] The Sierra Leone Legal Information Institute, a web-based database on law and practice, started out as a legacy project.[144] It has long been suggested that the Special Court's courthouse, a towering albeit not entirely functional structure in Freetown, should be converted into a training academy or integrated into Fourah Bay law school. However, to the chagrin of Sierra Leonean activists and legal professionals, the judiciary has still not decided what to do with the building, which continues to fall into disrepair.[145]

3.4. Beyond the call of legacy: legal aid and anti-corruption

In his review of the Special Court, Cassese described the Defence Office as 'no doubt a ground-breaking innovation' and 'creative advance that should be considered in all future courts'.[146] While its watershed status in international criminal law is acknowledged,[147] the SCSL's Defense Office also went on to serve as a model for Sierra Leone's criminal justice system. However, unlike its other legacy projects, the Special Court appears to have never actively pushed for reforms; rather, a specialist body modelled on its Defence Office—the Legal Aid Board—emerged organically, through civil society activism, development aid, and government support.[148]

[141] Human Rights Center UC Berkeley School of Law, 'The Long Road Ahead: Accountability for Sexual Violence in Conflict and Post-Conflict Settings. Kenya. Liberia. Sierra Leone. Uganda' (2015) 45.

[142] Interviews with human rights attorneys and RSCSL officials, Freetown, Sierra Leone, 8, 10, and 11 March 2016. See Suma (n 104) 111–16; Cruvellier (n 101) 42.

[143] Horovitz (n 121) 363; Sriram (n 118).

[144] <sierralii.org/content/about-us>.

[145] Interview with Sierra Leone attorney, Freetown, Sierra Leone, 11 March 2016. On the courthouse, see Dittrich (n 99) 676–78.

[146] Cassese (n 100) 1–2; Naughton (n 127) 72.

[147] SCSL RPE, r 45; Vincent O Nmehielle, 'The Defense Office of the Special Court for Sierra Leone: A Watershed in Realizing the Rights of Accused Persons in International Criminal Justice' in Jalloh (n 99). Critically, see Sareta Ashraph, 'The Naked Defense Office: How an Unclear Mandate, Poor Staffing, and Registry Disinterest Stripped the Office of the Principal Defender' in Jalloh (n 99).

[148] Interview with Sierra Leone attorney, 11 March 2016. For early advocacy, see Mohamed Suma, 'Case for an Office of a Public Defender in Sierra Leone' (SLCMP, 2005) <carl-sl.org/pres/a-case-for-an-office-of-a-public-defender-in-system-sierra-leone/>.

The Legal Aid Board's origins can be traced to two pilot legal aid schemes launched in 2009 and 2010, administered by the Sierra Leone Bar Association (with funding from the UNDP) and the Sierra Leonean government (with funding from the UK's JSDP programme) respectively.[149] Building on these experiences, civil society groups lobbied for a permanent legal aid programme, including a national Office of the Public Defender.[150] Although a public defence office was never established, the Legal Aid Act, adopted in 2012, mandated a Legal Aid Board to 'provide, administer, coordinate and monitor the provision of legal aid in civil and criminal matters', including through legal advice, assistance, and representation.[151]

The Board's official launch was delayed until 2015, due in part to the Ebola crisis.[152] Although direct support from the UK and the Sierra Leonean government helped kick-start the Board well after the Special Court had wound up operations in Freetown, many former SCSL staff and Sierra Leonean attorneys suggested that the legal aid programme was rooted conceptually in the Special Court's experiment with a dedicated Defense Office that highlighted defence rights in criminal proceedings.[153] As noted by one activist,[154]

> I can safely say that the protection of accused people in the Sierra Leonean judicial system; the office of principal defender, that is the most important legacy in our judicial system ... the principle of not just the government prosecuting but also giving legal aid so they can defend themselves.

Although the Special Court played mostly a demonstration role, the Legal Aid Board arguably counts among its most durable legacies.

As explained in Chapter 4, the SCSL managed to catalyse neither domestic prosecutions nor a repeal of the Lomé amnesty. Consequently, there was little advocacy—contrary to Rwanda—around specialist institutions for international crimes. A post-2002 initiative to create a War Crimes Office within the justice ministry never got off the ground, and subsequent recommendations to create a dedicated unit for prosecutions of Rome Statute crimes were similarly not heeded.[155] Nevertheless, the SCSL's presence galvanized anti-impunity reforms indirectly, by influencing struggles over Sierra Leone's ACC.

[149] Suma (n 104) 101–03.

[150] ibid 102; Bah (n 131).

[151] Legal Aid Act, 19 July 2012, ss 9 and 20, Supplement to the Sierra Leone Gazette CXLIII, 42, 23 August 2012.

[152] Edna Small, 'President Koroma Launches Sierra Leone Legal Aid Board' (*Sierra Leone News*, 20 November 2015) <awoko.org/2015/11/20/sierra-leone-news-president-koroma-launches-sierra-leone-legal-aid-board/>.

[153] Interviews with government officials and activists, Freetown, Sierra Leone, 10 March 2016.

[154] Interviews with Sierra Leonean activists, Freetown, Sierra Leone, 8 and 15 March 2016. See also Bangura (n 105) 22.

[155] Horovitz (n 114) 59; Sierra Leone Institute of International Law, Communique (14 July 2012) Recommendation 10 (on file with author).

In some ways, the ACC might be seen as a primary accountability response to Sierra Leone's civil war. Established in early 2000, prior to either the SCSL or the TRC, the ACC was expected to tackle the scourge of corruption, which—as the truth commission confirmed in its final report—was considered one of the primary causes of the civil war.[156] As Priscilla Hayner notes, even Foday Sankoh, the RUF leader, argued for accountability for corruption at the Lomé peace talks, though criminal responsibility was not on the table for the RUF.[157]

Like the SCSL's 'greatest responsibility' mandate, the ACC was expected to investigate 'high-profile cases' implicating politicians and government employees suspected of, inter alia, 'corrupt acquisition of wealth' and 'misappropriating public funds, revenue or property'.[158] Although there was no formal overlap in terms of the ACC and SCSL's subject-matter jurisdiction, the close links between organized crime, arms trafficking, and international crimes meant that both institutions could, in theory, deal with similar suspects. The ACC's track record in Sierra Leone also reveals intriguing parallels between the two institutions. Although the ACC, which operated with the UK's financial support, developed procedures to investigate high-profile cases of corruption, only a fraction of its inquiries translated into court cases, and even fewer resulted in prosecutions and convictions. Contrary to expectations, many cases targeted low-level people.[159] Despite Kabbah's nominal support for the fight against corruption, the Attorney General retained the power to approve or decline cases for prosecution submitted by the ACC Head, which undermined the Commission's independence in practice.[160] Amid much controversy, the Kabbah government removed an ACC Commissioner in 2005, prompting the UK to withdraw most of its support and weakening the fight against corruption.[161]

Running on an election promise to reinvigorate anti-corruption efforts, Ernst Koroma announced a revamped 'zero-tolerance for corruption' policy shortly after becoming president in 2007.[162] Abdul Tejan-Cole, a Sierra Leonean national

[156] Witness to Truth, Report of the Sierra Leone TRC, vol 3A (2004) ch 1, paras 105, 111, 146; Suma (n 104) 3.

[157] Hayner (n 95) 12.

[158] Anti-Corruption Act, 26 January 2000, Supplement to the Sierra Leone Gazette CXXXI, 7, 3 February 2000 [2000 ACA], s 7-15. The ACA's mandate extended not only to high-ranking officials, but this was its focus (Derek Poate and others, 'Evaluation of DFID Country Programmes: Sierra Leone. Evaluation Report EV690' 33).

[159] Emmanuel Gaima, 'Sierra Leone', *Effectiveness of Anti-Corruption Agencies in West Africa: Benin, Liberia, Niger, Nigeria, Senegal and Sierra Leone. A Review by Open Society Initiative for West Africa* (2016) 267; Musa Mewa, 'The ACC Act and the Proceeding: An Impediment in the Fight against Impunity' SLCMP [date unknown] <carl-sl.org/pres/the-acc-act-and-the-proceeding-an-impediment-in-the-fight-against-corruption/>.

[160] 2000 ACA, ss 36(1) and 37 [amendments]; Brian Thomson, 'Sierra Leone: Reform or Relapse? Conflict and Governance Reform' (Chatham House 2007) 17–18; International Crisis Group, 'Sierra Leone: A New Era of Reform?' (2008), 18.

[161] Poate and others (n 158) 33, Gaima (n 159) 266.

[162] International Crisis Group (n 160) 1.

who at the time worked in the SCSL prosecutor's office, was chosen to lead the ACC. In 2010, after Tejan-Cole stepped down, another Sierra Leonean official from the SCSL, then deputy prosecutor, Joseph Kamara, took over.[163] The SCSL's influence extended beyond staff appointments. As part of its wide-ranging institutional reforms, which included the Commissioner's power to initiate prosecutions independently from the Attorney General, the ACC adopted some of the Special Court's rules of procedure, including on evidence disclosure.[164] As noted previously, the SCSL also gave training on conducting investigations and using insider witnesses.

Results have been mixed. On the one hand, the ACC has prosecuted a High Court judge and a serving senior minister of government.[165] As Ibrahim Bangura explains, the ACC 'has contributed greatly to curbing the perception of impunity in relation to the misuse of state resources' and 'the arrest of senior government officials sends a strong message that no one is above the law and that culprits will be arrested and investigated'.[166] On the other, a perception lingers that the ACC lacks independence and is used by successive administrations to intimidate the political opposition.[167] Despite an increase in the number of prosecutions, several prominent corruption cases have collapsed amid controversy.[168] As noted by Emmanuel Gaima, '[t]he inability of the ACC to successfully prosecute some high profile cases casts suspicion over the commission and its anti-corruption efforts'.[169] In the end, while its impact on the ACC is indirect, the fight against corruption in Sierra Leone is a continuation of the Special Court's goal of holding accountable those in positions of power, even if the obstacles to overcoming impunity remain entrenched.

3.5. Unpacking a hybrid mandate's effects on capacity building

Great expectations accompanied the establishment of the SCSL. Speaking in 2004, David Crane, then prosecutor, voiced these aspirations in the following terms:[170]

[163] Julia Szybala, 'A Perspective on the Anti-Corruption Commission' (SLCMP 2008) <carl-sl.org/pres/a-prospective-on-the-anti-corruption-commission/>.

[164] Anti-Corruption Act, 1 January 2008, s 7(1)(a) and (d). Interviews with Sierra Leone attorney and judge, 11 and 14 March 2016. Under the 2008 ACA, any party to a dispute before the ACC may apply for an order of non-disclosure of witnesses (s 83).

[165] Gaima (n 159) 260.

[166] Bangura (n 105) 41–42.

[167] ibid 42; George K Kieh, 'State-Building in Post-Civil War Sierra Leone' (2005) 4 African and Asian Studies 163, 180.

[168] Ibrahim Tommy, 'Sierra Leone's Corruption Conundrum: Is the Strategy Working?' (*Centre for Accountability and the Rule of Law*, 10 December 2013) <carl-sl.org/pres/sierra-leones-corruption-conundrum-is-the-strategy-working/>.

[169] Gaima (n 159) 260.

[170] David M Crane, 'Dancing with the Devil. Prosecuting West Africa's Warlords. Current Lessons Learned and Challenges, Colloquium of Prosecutors of International Criminal Tribunals, Arusha, Tanzania, 25–27 November 2004' (on file with author).

> Because the Court is for and about the people of Sierra Leone, the location of the Court must be in Sierra Leone ... It allows the people to see justice begin, work, and end right before their very eyes in a time-frame that causes less trauma to the society at large .... A devastated country needs to rebuild an infrastructure to carry it forward. The cornerstone to that building process is the rule of law. A distant, and seemingly impersonal tribunal has a greater challenge to demonstrate this concept ... We need to leave to [Sierra Leoneans] not just the newly built [courthouse] but a cadre of trained and dedicated Court personnel to carry on the hard work after we depart. The Court works closely with the Sierra Leonean Bar Association, NGOs, and other civil society organizations to develop creative projects ... to rebuild a devastated judiciary. In many ways, the legacy program means that the Court will never leave Sierra Leone.

Although capacity building was not part of its mandate, two aspects of the SCSL's institutional design—its geographical proximity to Sierra Leonean institutions and hybrid composition—were expected to promote local ownership of reforms. Legacy, a concept coined after its creation, became an incubator of reforms in its own right, so much so that by the time the Special Court transitioned to its residual functions some authors had identified a 'legacy turn' in international criminal justice.[171]

Despite these lofty aspirations, the Special Court's different legacies for the Sierra Leonean justice system are contested.[172] To be sure, to a greater extent than other ICTs, international experts on international crimes worked directly with legal professionals from the country over which the Tribunal had jurisdiction. For over a decade, Sierra Leonean attorneys, police officers, and magistrates benefited from exchanges with their international counterparts on a range of legal issues that had never previously been addressed in Sierra Leone. However, many doubt the extent to which this pooling of expertise shaped domestic criminal law practice. Tejan-Cole, one of the most senior Sierra Leonean officials to transition from the SCSL to domestic practice, argued in 2010 that, while '[t]he Court was expected to be an instrument for transforming the local judiciary', its impact '[s]adly ... has been minimal'.[173] Several assessments carried out while the SCSL was still operational reached similarly negative conclusions.[174]

A significant obstacle to capacity building seems to have been the perception that the SCSL's proximity to the affected populations and, by extension, the national judiciary ensured, in and of itself, a transfer of knowledge and skills. Critical of this assumption, Chehtman observes that more creative institutional design

[171] Dittrich (n 99) 665.

[172] ibid 667–69.

[173] Abdul Tejan-Cole, 'Sierra Leone's "Not So" Special Court' in Chandra Lekha Sriram and Suren Pillay (eds), *Peace versus Justice?: The Dilemma of Transitional Justice in Africa* (James Currey 2010).

[174] Perriello and Wierda (n 114) 39; Cruvellier (n 101) 3; Lincoln (n 106) 132–33.

solutions may be needed, enabling international and domestic officials to engage one another on contentious issues, for instance on case distribution or domestic norms.[175] In this sense, relying on a 'demonstration effect' may be insufficient. There also seems to be some evidence that donor investment in justice reform was less generous in Sierra Leone than in other countries. Whether this underfunding can be tied to the SCSL absorbing too much funding requires further research.

It is noteworthy that, although legacy came to be identified with capacity building, it functioned as a rhetorical slogan—similar to complementarity at the ICC—for much of the Special Court's existence. Reforming the Sierra Leone justice sector had intuitive appeal, but capacity building did not take priority over investigations, trials, and appeals—especially given the precarious nature of the Special Court's funding. Tellingly, the catalyst for the SCSL's legacy projects were its own institutional imperatives, especially witness protection that needed to be handled domestically. Aside from such isolated cases of iteration, where international support and domestic capacity were mutually constitutive, legacy projects seemed to be a form of charity, or an afterthought that was desirable but secondary. One senior official referred to the SCSL's capacity building as 'good citizenship' but emphasized it could not distract from prosecutions.[176] The Special Court's convoluted path to embracing legacy points to a key factor—ICT self-interest—underpinning international support for domestic rule-of-law reforms.

By the same token, the capacity-building potential of ICTs depends to a great extent on the receptiveness of national audiences. The Sierra Leonean government has, on occasion, praised the SCSL, for instance when its delegate to the 2010 Kampala Review Conference argued that the SCSL 'made tremendous contributions to accountability ... develop[ing] our national capacity ... [and] contribut[ing] to restoring confidence in the institutions of State and the rule of law'.[177] But, by and large, the Sierra Leonean political establishment avoided entanglement with the SCSL, divorcing its retributive mandate from domestic reconciliation efforts through the truth commission and amnesty. By declining to appoint Sierra Leonean nationals to leadership positions, the government avoided personality-driven contestation over accountability, which in turn facilitated isolation between international and domestic officials who were usually lower in the hierarchy. Unlike in Rwanda, where the rule 11*bis* process enabled a reputational contest between the ICTR and national actors, hybrid staffing may have lost its iterative appeal because of domestic politics.

175 Chehtman (n 107) 316; see also Horovitz (n 114) 66.

176 Interview with former SCSL official, The Hague, Netherlands, 23 November 2015. See also OHCHR (n 106) 7.

177 Statement by the Head of Delegation, Vandi Chidi Minah, Deputy Minister of Foreign Affairs and International Cooperation of the Republic of Sierra Leone to the Review Conference of the Rome Statute for the ICC <asp.icc-cpi.int/iccdocs/asp_docs/RC2010/Statements/ICC-RC-gendeba-Sierra%20Leone-ENG.pdf>.

Although the Special Court's legacy of mixing staff is mixed at best, it seems also that realities and perceptions of legacy are in constant flux.[178] Over time, the SCSL's hybrid staffing seems to have had trickle-down effects for the Sierra Leonean justice sector, for instance by creating a dedicated legal aid institution and influencing the fight against corruption. Whereas during the SCSL's lifespan both international and national officials viewed the colocation of staff as a missed opportunity, interviews in 2016 painted a more nuanced picture, with many former SCSL national staff acknowledging the benefits of international expertise.[179] Although, as will be discussed further in Chapter 6, this may imply that the process of legacy building extends beyond the ICT's lifespan, it should be noted that some scholars continue to challenge how capacity building shaped the justice sector, arguing the Special Court may have even entrenched 'the underlying structures of inequality that precipitated armed violence' while being 'ill-suited for providing affordable, timely, and socially relevant justice for people of low socioeconomic and cultural status'.[180]

4. The International Criminal Court

4.1. Mobilizing the ICC's symbolic shadow: mobile courts and prosecution support cells

After decades of neglect under Mobutu, exacerbated by the First and Second Congo Wars, rebuilding the Congolese justice sector became a priority in the 2000s. Since then, successive administrations have emphasized the fight against impunity (*la lutte contre l'impunité*) as a core objective of rule-of-law reform and transitional justice. Adopted by the justice ministry, a 2007 Action Plan listed the fight against impunity and promotion of human rights as two of four 'strategic priority axes of reform', which were then reincorporated into a 2017–26 National Justice Reform Policy.[181] Partly in response to international pressure, a 'zero tolerance' policy for grave human rights violations was announced in 2009, followed by the appointment, in 2013, of a special representative on sexual violence and child soldier recruitment.[182] In 2015, a countrywide conference on justice reform (*Etats*

[178] Positively, see Bangura (n 101) 716; Smith (n 110) 55–56. David M Crane, 'The Bright Red Thread. The Politics of International Criminal Law—Do We Want Peace or Justice? The West African Experience' in Leila N Sadat (ed), *Forging a Convention for Crimes against Humanity* (CUP 2010) 65–67.

[179] Interviews with Sierra Leonean attorneys, ministers, court staff, and police, Freetown, Sierra Leone, March 2016. See also HRW (n 119); Perriello and Wierda (n 114).

[180] Sesay (n 117) 42; see also Friederike Mieth, 'Bringing Justice and Enforcing Peace? An Ethnographic Perspective on the Impact of the Special Court for Sierra Leone' (2013) 7 International Journal of Conflict and Violence 10.

[181] Ministère de la Justice, 'Plan d'action pour la réforme de la justice' (2007); Ministère de la Justice, 'Politique nationale de réforme de la justice 2017–2026' (2017) Results 14 and 15 (on file).

[182] Trésor Kibangula, 'RDC: Jeanine Mabunda, aux côtés de Kabila contre les violences sexuelles' *Jeune Afrique* (12 January 2015) <jeuneafrique.com/165639/politique/rdc-jeannine-mabunda-aux-c-t-s-de-kabila-contre-les-violences-sexuelles/>.

généraux de la justice) 'pledged to strengthen prosecutions of international crimes as a matter of priority'.[183]

As noted in Chapter 4, donors and NGOs have played a key role in reviving the justice system. Two important initiatives are the mobile courts and prosecution support cells (known by their French acronym, CAPs), which rely on a combination of foreign funding, colocating international and domestic expertise, and civil society engagement on the state's justice priorities.

The UN-backed CAPs programme can be traced to joint international–domestic investigations. Around 2009, MONUSCO began sending joint investigation teams comprising military magistrates and UN human rights officers on human rights fact-finding missions.[184] Building on this collaborative experience, in 2011, MONUSCO deployed magistrates, seconded mainly from African states, to work alongside their Congolese (military) counterparts, to improve accountability for serious crimes.[185] Over the years, CAPs were established across several provinces in eastern DRC, offering technical advice and logistical support for the military justice authorities' investigations and prosecutions.[186] As explained by a senior CAPs official, it is 'technical assistance, for example support in establishing coherent case files that can be used in court proceedings, [establishing] death certificates, medical certificates of rape, and so on'.[187] Although their mandate was limited initially to international crimes, foreign magistrates embedded in the CAPs supported a growing number of prosecutions of serious but 'ordinary' crimes, many administered by another accountability initiative—the mobile courts programme.

In a vast country like the DRC, the revival of *chambres foraines* aims to overcome civilians' main challenge to accessing the justice system: distance and a lack of infrastructure. As Tessa Khan and Jim Wormington explain:[188]

> Everything about the courts is temporary: the court is housed in a community centre or town hall, with magistrates, a registrar, a bailiff, defence attorneys and lawyers brought in from the closest towns and cities. Mobile courts remain in

[183] Daniele Perissi and Karen Naimer, 'Achieving Justice for Child Survivors of Conflict-Related Sexual Violence in the Democratic Republic of the Congo' (2020) 18 Journal of International Criminal Justice 293, 293.

[184] Interview with MONUSCO official, Goma, DRC, 2 September 2015. See also Sofia Candeias and others, 'The Accountability Landscape in Eastern DRC: Analysis of the National Legislative and Judicial Response to International Crimes (2009–2014)' (ICTJ 2015) 25–26.

[185] UNSC Res 1925 (28 May 2010) S/RES/1925, para 12 d. For an overview, see UN Criminal Law and Judicial Advisory Service, 'Combatting Impunity in the Democratic Republic of the Congo. Lessons Learned from the UN Prosecution Support Cell Programme' (2015); UNDP and EU, 'Projet d'appui à La Justice Militaire en République Démocratique du Congo à travers le renforcement du programme des cellules d'appui aux poursuites (February 2015–December 2018)' (2019).

[186] UN Criminal Law and Judicial Advisory Service (n 185) iv.

[187] Interview with senior CAPs official, Kinshasa, DRC, 25 April 2016.

[188] Khan and Wormington, 'Mobile Courts in the DRC: Lessons from Development for International Criminal Justice' [2011] Oxford Transitional Justice Research Working Paper [no pagination].

a given location for a period of between one and two months, hearing as many cases as possible.

Although Congolese domestic law (as in some other African countries) has long allowed temporary deployments of magistrates to rural communities, this method of bringing justice to affected populations spread in the 2000s.[189] Avocats Sans Frontières became one of the first NGOs to launch a programme aimed at deploying more mobile courts for allegations of serious crimes.[190] Focused initially on ordinary crimes, in particular sexual and gender-based violence, mobile courts later turned to more complex cases of international crimes. Operating with technical and logistical support from the UN and NGOs, Congolese magistrates have over the years adjudicated hundreds of cases through temporary deployments, primarily in eastern Congo.[191]

International support for domestic trials in the DRC, in particular through mobile courts, is often associated with the ICC's intervention and complementarity. Viewing the two as part of a mutually reinforcing accountability partnership, NGOs characterize their support for the mobile courts as 'complementarity in action', or—as one activist explained—the 'active complementarity of judicial partners' in national and international anti-impunity programmes.[192] Drawing on the distinction between high- and low-level perpetrators, the Open Society Justice Initiative (OSJI) observes that mobile courts are designed 'to support the concept of "complementarity" ... and hence to complement the work of the [ICC] in The Hague, which is tasked with prosecuting high level suspects otherwise outside the capacity of the domestic court system'.[193]

These and other invocations of complementarity refer to generalist notions of international–national cooperation and implicit divisions of labour rather than the Rome Statute's institutional design, let alone instances of jurisdictional overlap requiring Congolese magistrates to pre-empt ICC jurisdiction. Nevertheless, such claims resonate with donors who see value in connecting their and the ICC's work. One Congolese activist conceded that funding applications made strategic mention of the ICC and complementarity, even though the links between the two were

[189] Loi organique 13/011B du 11 avril 2013 portant organisation, fonctionnement et compétences des juridictions de l'ordre judiciaire, arts 45–48.

[190] Interview with NGO official, Kinshasa, DRC, 25 April 2016.

[191] Adam Day and Jessica Caus, *Rule of Law and Sustaining Peace: Towards More Impactful, Effective Conflict Prevention* (United Nations University, 2021) 163–65.

[192] Interview with NGO official, Kinshasa, DRC, 25 April 2016. Monica Rispo, 'Evaluation of UNDP's Support to Mobile Courts in Sierra Leone, DR Congo, and Somalia' (UNDP 2014) (calling DRC complementarity in action). Daniele Perissi and Elsa Taquet, 'The Kavumu Trial: Complementarity in Action in the Democratic Republic of Congo' (*International Justice Monitor*, 5 February 2018) <ijmonitor.org/2018/02/the-kavumu-trial-complementarity-in-action-in-the-democratic-republic-of-congo/>.

[193] Open Society Justice Initiative, 'Fact Sheet: DRC Mobile Gender Courts' quoted in Christian M De Vos, *Complementarity, Catalysts, Compliance: The International Criminal Court in Uganda, Kenya, and the Democratic Republic of Congo* (CUP 2020) 221.

tenuous, and projects unfolded without any input from The Hague.[194] In a similar vein, Christian De Vos concludes that a 'turn to domestic prosecutions through the use of so-called "mobile" courts ... represents a novel invocation of the complementarity principle', with donors and NGOs 'deliberately ... characteriz[ing] the courts as an extension of and "complementary" to the ICC's work'.[195]

Labels aside, most observers agree that international support for the CAPs and mobile courts has strengthened the capacity of Congolese magistrates to pursue serious crimes. Charles Briefel and Ignacio Tredici, two UN officials, conclude that the CAPs were 'an innovative programme that has had a positive impact on efforts to combat impunity in the DRC, taking the administration of justice to places where it had never been before—closer to victims, witnesses and perpetrators' and that '[a]necdotal feedback received from NGOs indicates that ... without their support most of these investigations and prosecutions would never have taken place'.[196] An observer of the first mobile courts, Kelly Askin went so far as to argue in 2011 that '[w]ith the ICC going after the highest level accused often out of reach of domestic jurisdictions—and the local courts, including mobile courts, going after lower level suspects—accountability can become the norm, and impunity the exception'.[197]

In fact, as explained in Chapter 4, optimistic predictions of a division of labour have not come to pass. In addition to recurring budgetary and personnel constraints, in particular a lack of qualified secondments, one overarching criticism of the CAPs is that they are reactive and focused on technical expertise, while the political dimensions of accountability in the DRC are left unaddressed. Referring to an agreement between MONUSCO and the DRC, which makes UN support dependent on an invitation from Congolese authorities (barring exceptional circumstances), one human rights expert complained that '[CAPs officials] answer requests only—[there is] no initiative ... they have a very passive approach to their mandate, which could be interpreted progressively'.[198] A senior CAPs official confirmed that 'we act on request only ... [we have] authority to intervene unilaterally within 48 hours or 7 days, but this is not used proactively'.[199]

Linked to the CAPs' passivity is the concern that, in practice, MONUSCO and international partners prioritize less serious, ordinary, rather than international, crimes, which indirectly absolves senior suspects. Noting this tendency, a UN official complained: '[they] are doing everything but international crimes—the real

[194] Interview with Congolese attorney, Kinshasa, DRC, 18 August 2016.

[195] De Vos (n 193) 194; on the mobile courts, see further 219–22.

[196] Charles Briefel and Ignacio Tredici, 'The United Nations Prosecution Support Cell Programme in the Democratic Republic of Congo—A Strategy to Combat Impunity for Serious Crimes' (2016) 19 Max Planck Yearbook of United Nations Law 337, 339 and 355.

[197] Quoted in: Baudry Aluma, 'Women's Day: DRC Mobile Court a Sign of Hope' *Inter Press Service* (7 March 2011) <ipsnews.net/2011/03/womens-day-drc-mobile-court-a-sign-of-hope/>.

[198] Interview with NGO official, Goma, DRC, 2 September 2015.

[199] Interview with CAPs official, Kinshasa, DRC, 25 April 2016.

work they should be doing!'.[200] Not only has the UN itself recognized this problem, but CAPs officials acknowledge the sometimes sensitive, political nature of their work. As noted by a senior CAPs adviser, 'there are places we know not to go'.[201]

At the same time, UN officials stress that the international community in the DRC must be careful not to overplay its hand. For instance, attempts to leverage conditionality-type measures, such as the UN human rights due diligence policy that links support for Congolese military operations to international law compliance, can backfire.[202] As will be seen next, the degree to which international partners should support the military, which is aligned with powerful political factions, has been a recurring challenge.

4.2. Military or civilian justice? Unpacking Congo's jurisdictional turf wars

Although the Congolese government has embraced anti-impunity and zero-tolerance policies, international partners struggle to reconcile capacity building with the military's role in Congolese political life, including in the administration of justice. Military justice received little attention prior to the 2000s, but this changed with the UN's growing in-country presence, including the establishment of a human rights office and the deployment of peacekeepers in the late 1990s. Amid the chaos of the two Congo wars, the Cour d'Ordre Militaire, an ad hoc military tribunal operating in Kinshasa from 1998 to 2001, came under sharp criticism for its lack of fair trial standards, politicized decision-making, and extensive use of the death penalty.[203] Compounding the justice system's problems, several rebel groups conducted irregular trials in areas under their control.[204]

As explained in Chapter 4, around the time of the ICC's intervention in 2004, international partners began helping military magistrates to launch prosecutions of serious crimes. Although support for the military—as opposed to the civilian—justice system was based on pragmatic considerations, especially the military's exclusive jurisdiction over international crimes, this was not uncontroversial. Under international law, military justice is considered an exceptional form of justice, which supplements civilian justice on a temporary basis.[205] Concerns grew as

[200] Interview with UN official, Brussels, Belgium, 16 November 2016.

[201] Interview with UN official, Kinshasa, DRC, 16 August 2016. See also Chapter 6, section 4.6 in this volume.

[202] Interview with UN official, Kinshasa, DRC, 16 August 2016.

[203] Mpongo Bokako Bautolinga Edouard, 'La justice militaire et les droits de l'homme: la Cour d'Ordre Militaire' in OHCHR, *Administration de la Justice et droits de l'Homme* (23–25 août 1999) 70–83 (on file with author).

[204] HRW, 'The War within the War: Sexual Violence against Women in Eastern Congo' (2002).

[205] Draft Principles Governing the Administration of Justice through Military Tribunals, E/CN.4/2006/58 (2006), Principle 5.

soon as prosecutions started in the mid-2000s. Criticism focused on the incompatibility of the military's hierarchical command structure with judicial independence, and the norm that civilians should not be prosecuted by military tribunals.[206] Acknowledging concerns that the subservient relationship of military magistrates to their superiors prevents them from investigating, arresting and prosecuting some commanders, one Congolese official observed pithily 'military justice is more military than justice, and that remains a problem'.[207]

Advocated by civil society and donors, legislative reforms dating as far back as 2005 aimed to 'transfer' jurisdiction over international crimes from military to civilian courts. As will be discussed in Chapter 6, these reforms, which were included in Rome Statute legislation, initially collapsed on procedural grounds. However, intense lobbying from some international partners helped an unrelated legislative bill to give civilian courts jurisdiction over international crimes, revolutionizing—so it seemed—the institutional landscape of criminal justice.[208]

Ultimately, the 2013 reforms proved impossible to implement for several reasons. For one, civilian oversight triggered resistance from parts of the political elite, including Kabila-affiliated commanders with potential criminal exposure.[209] Relying on a legalistic argument, namely constitutional guarantees of jurisdictional autonomy, army and police personnel continue to be tried by military tribunals to this day. For another, military judges interpret the existing laws expansively, continuing to arrogate to themselves the power to prosecute civilians in certain circumstances. In short, wresting control over accountability decisions from the military has proved more challenging than legislating to that effect.

Equally important, foreign and domestic actors have, over time, come to appreciate the military's expertise in handling international crimes. Although they now have jurisdictional authority to do so, civilian magistrates are still reluctant to bring cases, due to a lack of training and expertise. Attempts to administer civilian justice, such as a 2016 genocide trial before the Lubumbashi Court of Appeal created serious challenges.[210] According to activists and UN officials, everyone realized, belatedly, that shifting the prosecutorial burden to civilian authorities too

[206] Marcel Wetsh'okonda Koso, 'La République Démocratique du Congo. La Justice Militaire et le respect des droits de l'homme—L'urgence du parachèvement de la réforme' (Open Society Institute for Southern Africa 2009) 9–10; BCUNDH, *Progress and Obstacles in the Fight against Impunity for Sexual Violence in the DRC* (2014) 45.

[207] Interview with UN official, Kinshasa, DRC, 20 April 2016.

[208] Loi organique (n 189) art 91.

[209] Some suggest the law was amended *after* it had been adopted. Interview with Congolese attorney, Kinshasa, DRC, 18 August 2016. See also Candeias and others (n 184) 10–11; HRW, 'Etats Généraux of the Justice System in the Democratic Republic of Congo Recommendations on the Fight Against Impunity for Grave International Crimes' (27 April 2015) <hrw.org/news/2015/04/27/etats-generaux-justice-system-democratic-republic-congo>.

[210] Habibou Bangré, 'RDC: Impasse dans le procès de bantous et pygmées accusés de génocide' (*JusticeInfo*, 3 February 2016) <justiceinfo.net/fr/25796-rdc-impasse-dans-le-proces-de-bantous-et-pygmees-accuses-de-genocide.html>. For an earlier trial of genocide, in 2011, see Eugène Bakama Bope, *La justice congolaise face aux crimes internationaux commis en RDC* (L'Harmattan 2014) 170–89.

quickly could have the effect of decreasing pathways for accountability in the DRC. One activist noted, more damningly, that the civilian justice system may not be the 'solution' at all, as it was 'even more corrupt' than military courts.[211]

In recent years, justice actors seem to be adopting a less dogmatic approach. Even though civilian courts retain primary jurisdiction over international crimes, military tribunals adjudicate crimes committed by army and police agents in practice. Meanwhile, joint military–civilian panels administer trials in several regions, although this is not formally allowed. As noted by a UN official, 'the idea is to allow civilians to learn from [the military's] experience'.[212]

4.3. The struggle for a hybrid court: walking the iteration–isolation tightrope

In the background of the struggle over the military's jurisdictional powers looms the challenge of ensuring accountability for past crimes. Under the Rome Statute, the ICC's temporal jurisdiction extends no further than July 2002, which means that most crimes committed during the two Congo wars are *de jure* excluded from its mandate. Given the unique challenges of prosecutions relating to temporally distant events (and the fact that military tribunals often prioritize new crimes), government and civil society actors have tabled accountability initiatives for pre-2002 crimes, including an ad hoc tribunal, a truth commission, and a hybrid court.

Advocacy for an ad hoc tribunal pre-dates the ICC's investigation, with some NGOs proposing an ICTR-type court as early as the mid-1990s.[213] In 2003, shortly before his ICC self-referral, Kabila also advocated an ad hoc tribunal modelled on the ICTR/Y in a speech before the UN General Assembly.[214] However, given the UN's shift to completion strategies, his proposal received no traction at the time.

Accountability in the DRC is viewed through the prism of the ICC and parallel domestic trials, but both unfolded alongside a truth and reconciliation commission, which operated from 2003 to 2006. Based on the power-sharing ethos of the Inter-Congolese Dialogue that ended the Second Congo War, the commission's

[211] Interview with NGO official, Goma, DRC, 2 September 2015.

[212] Interview with UN official, Kinshasa, DRC, 24 July 2019. See also Chapter 6, section 4.4 in this volume.

[213] Guillaume Ngefa Atondoko, 'Les tribunaux de crimes de guerres et le développement du droit international' *Periodique des droits de l'homme de l'Association zaïroise de défense des droits de l'homme* (November 1994) 11. For post-2000 proposals, see Pascal K Kambale, 'A Story of Missed Opportunities? The Role of the International Criminal Court in the Democratic Republic of Congo' in Christian M De Vos, Sara Kendall and Christian Stahn (eds), *Contested Justice: The Politics and Practice of International Criminal Court Interventions* (CUP 2015) 175; Valérie Arnould, 'Transitional Justice in Peacebuilding: Dynamics of Contestation in the DRC' (2016) 10 Journal of Intervention and Statebuilding 321.

[214] Pascal Kambale and Anna Rotman, 'The International Criminal Court and Congo' (*Global Policy Forum*, October 2004) <globalpolicy.org/component/content/article/164-icc/28474.html>.

leadership was appointed from the main belligerents rather than on the basis of their independence and impartiality.[215] Lacking credibility and buy-in from donors, the commission struggled to obtain funding and, instead of confronting a laundry list of justice-related tasks included in its overambitious mandate stretching back to the 1960s, it ended up conducting only a few election-related activities. The Commission is widely seen as a failure, and one of its recommendations was the establishment of another truth commission.[216]

Although the ICC's and domestic prosecutions took centre stage after 2005, their shortcomings soon became apparent. Advocacy on an additional hybrid court gained traction in the late 2000s, pushed forward by the UN's 2010 Mapping Report. After cataloguing more than 600 serious crimes committed between 1993 and 2003, the UN recommended, among several transitional justice options, the establishment of a treaty-based court modelled on Sierra Leone's Special Court or embedding a mixed court within the Congolese justice system.[217] Shortly thereafter, then justice minister, Luzolo Bambi Lessa, put forward a bill establishing specialized chambers.[218] Luzolo later explained that the idea for a hybrid court had come from consultations with the UN, and that the Mapping Report added momentum.[219]

Comprising both national and international judges and prosecutors, the 'specialized chambers' were initially expected to deal only with international crimes from 1993 and 2002, in deference to the ICC's temporal mandate. Whereas this gave the chambers a distinctly retrospective orientation, subsequent proposals for what became a 'Special Court' expanded its temporal jurisdiction to post-2002 crimes. A hybrid court operating alongside both the DRC's military tribunals and the ICC would give rise to a three-tiered system of justice for serious crimes, which in turn required rules on jurisdictional relations. From the beginning, the Congolese architects of the hybrid tribunal wanted the Special Court to have

[215] ICTJ and Kofi Annan Foundation, 'Challenging the Conventional. Can Truth Commissions Strengthen Peace Processes?' (2014) 46–55; William Burke-White, 'Complementarity in Practice: The International Criminal Court as Part of a System of Multi-Level Global Governance in the Democratic Republic of Congo' (2005) 18 Leiden Journal of International Law 557, 573–74.

[216] Commission vérité et reconciliation, 'Rapport final des activités. De juillet 2003 à février 2007' 76 (on file). See also ICTJ and Kofi Annan Foundation (n 215) 53.

[217] OHCHR, 'Rapport du projet mapping concernant les violations les plus graves des droits de l'homme et du droit international humanitaire commises entre mars 1993 et juin 2003 sur le territoire de la République démocratique du Congo' (2010) 480–86; HRW, 'DR Congo: A "Mixed Chamber" for Congo?' (2009) <hrw.org/news/2009/10/05/dr-congo-mixed-chamber-congo>.

[218] Avant-projet de loi portant création, organisation, fonctionnement, droit applicable, compétence et procédure des chambres spécialisées pour la répression des violations graves du droit international humanitaire, Ministry of Justice and Human Rights, November 2010 and April 2011 (draft laws on file with author); Eric Witte, 'Putting Complementarity into Practice: Domestic Justice for International Crimes in DRC, Uganda and Kenya' (Open Society Foundations 2011) 50.

[219] Interview with Luzolo Bambi Lessa, Kinshasa, DRC, 21 April 2016.

priority, with domestic tribunals enjoying secondary and the ICC merely tertiary jurisdiction.[220]

The proposed hybrid court engendered resistance from various actors, including the Congolese political elite but also some foreign partners. Although its institutional design was compatible with complementarity (and hence domestic primacy, in this case split between the hybrid and domestic courts), the Special Court's expansive temporal jurisdiction and the prospect of jurisdictional conflicts with the ICC created concern. As acknowledged by experts, the ICC initially opposed the hybrid court, though it never formalized a position on the matter.[221] And while ICC opposition dissipated over time, resistance from the EU and some NGOs continued. Objecting, inter alia, on complementarity grounds, the EU feared that a hybrid court would distract from capacity building for the ordinary justice system, creating two-tier justice in the DRC. As explained by an EU official:[222]

> This is complicated … [there are] very clearly different opinions among [EU] member states on [the hybrid chambers]. [The] EU has always been more about domestic justice, [building] Congolese judges' capacity … we are aware of the charge that [hybrid chambers] would be interference and understand this given the history of colonialism, and [we] want domestic justice to take precedence.

As noted by one activist, a 'serious split' emerged between some members of the international community, in particular the US government, who supported the hybrid court, and others who pushed reforms of existing domestic institutions.[223] An NGO official suggested that criticisms of the hybrid tribunal were 'a false problem' but acknowledged that international actors' contradictory positions undermined reform by decreasing their leverage with the government.[224]

Meanwhile, domestic politics loomed large in this debate. Although President Kabila and key government figures endorsed the idea of accountability for past crimes on several occasions, Parliament refused to provide its assent.[225] Two

[220] Patryk I Labuda, 'Applying and "Misapplying" the Rome Statute in the Democratic Republic of Congo' in Christian M De Vos, Sara Kendall and Carsten Stahn (eds), *Contested Justice: The Politics and Practice of International Criminal Court Interventions* (CUP 2015) 416–18.

[221] Interviews with Congolese officials and attorneys, Kinshasa, DRC, 21 and 22 April and 18 August 2016. ICC representatives reacted negatively to the project at an April 2011 seminar in Goma, see also HRW, 'RD Congo: établissement d'une cour spécialisée mixte pour la répression des crimes graves internationaux position commune résultant de l'atelier organisé à Goma le 6–8 avril 2011' <hrw.org/fr/news/2011/04/15/rd-congo-etablissement-dune-cour-specialisee-mixte-pour-la-repression-des-crimes>.

[222] Interview with EU official, Kinshasa, DRC, 16 August 2016. On EU opposition, see 'Women, Peace and Security: Open Debate and Presidential Statement' (*What's in Blue*, 27 October 2014) <whatsinblue.org/2014/10/women-peace-and-security-open-debate-and-presidential-statement.php>.

[223] Interviews with activists, Kinshasa, DRC, 21 and 22 April 2016.

[224] Interview with NGO official, Goma, DRC, 2 September 2015.

[225] 'Cohésion nationale: Discours de Joseph Kabila devant le Congrès' (*Kongo Times*, 23 October 2013) <afrique.kongotimes.info/rdc/politique/6768-cohesion-nationale-discours-joseph-kabila-devant-congres.html>.

different justice ministers spearheaded legislation on a hybrid court, in 2011 and 2014 respectively, but lawmakers voted down the draft bills on both occasions. Among the official reasons evoked during intense parliamentary debates, lawmakers expressed concern that a hybrid court would slow down domestic reforms and infringe on Congolese sovereignty. As one observer explained, 'involving international magistrates was unacceptable ... it would create a two-tier justice system (justice à deux vitesses), [those] well paid and less well paid ... it is an attack on national sovereignty'.[226] Inauspicious timing may have also weakened support for the hybrid court (for instance, calling votes months before the 2011 presidential elections).[227]

However, many observers question such explanations. While acknowledging that turf wars among civil society and donors slowed down reforms, some point to pro-sovereignty factions inside the military with a vested interest in shutting down accountability as a primary cause of the hybrid court's demise. Others go further and question to what extent the executive's commitment to reforms was genuine. As noted by one attorney, 'I asked [the justice minister] why the bill you submitted is chock-full of technical problems that make [the hybrid court] dead on arrival in parliament'.[228] Nick Elebe notes that the 2014 bill in particular, although it was nominally advocated by the justice ministry, 'was marred by procedural errors and ambiguities' and that 'the main problem was the alleged non-alignment of some dispositions of the bill with the Constitution'.[229]

Ultimately, it appears that the prospect of accountability for pre-2002 crimes met with overwhelming resistance from the political and military establishment. As noted succinctly by a top military official, 'the problem with the Special Court is that the political class is afraid it will hold them accountable'.[230] An activist noted that parliamentarians had requested the UN's confidential list of suspects (annexed to the 2010 Mapping report) before voting on whether to establish a hybrid court.[231] According to a top Kabila adviser:

> they wanted to do something along the lines of the Special Court for Sierra Leone, but we didn't like it ... foreign assistance went too far, maybe foreign experts, but

[226] Interview with Nyabirungu Mwene Songa, Kinshasa, DRC, 20 April 2016. On 2011 law, see Patryk I Labuda, 'The Democratic Republic of Congo's Failure to Address Impunity for International Crimes: A View from Inside the Legislative Process' (*International Justice Monitor*, 8 November 2011) <ijmonitor.org/2011/11/the-democratic-republic-of-congos-failure-to-address-impunity-for-international-crimes-a-view-from-inside-the-legislative-process-2010-2011-2/>.

[227] Labuda (n 220) 418–19.

[228] Interview with Congolese attorney, Kinshasa, DRC, 18 August 2016.

[229] Nick Elebe, 'Why DRC Lawmakers Again Rejected Special Chambers to Prosecute International Crimes' (*International Justice Monitor*, 23 May 2014) <ijmonitor.org/2014/05/drc-a-bill-on-special-chambers-rejected-for-the-second-time/>.

[230] Interview with senior military magistrate, Kinshasa, DRC, 23 April 2016.

[231] Interview with NGO official, Goma, DRC, 2 September 2015.

> not foreign staff as such—this is a problem for the sovereignty faction and it implies we don't have the capacity here at the local level, which is not true.[232]

Previously a justice minister and, in that role, government spokesperson for the hybrid court, Luzolo acknowledged in 2016 that government actors were probably only prepared to accept the assistance of international judges, but an independent prosecutor was a step too far: 'in no event would there be international prosecutors, prosecution is a question of "judicial policy" (*politique judiciaire*) ... this is not just a purely judicial matter ... so we can't have internationals interfering'.[233] In short, contrary to countries like CAR, where overwhelming international influence shaped the contours of a nominally hybrid court, Congolese political elites sought to retain control over their domestic accountability process.[234]

In light of the DRC's repeated failure to establish a hybrid court, the UN and NGOs have turned their attention to less controversial proposals, for instance colocating civilian and military magistrates within the ordinary justice system.[235] Civil society groups emphasize, however, that colocation does not address pre-2002 impunity.[236] Following Félix Tshisekedi's ascension to the presidency in 2019, the debate over additional judicial responses has resurfaced. Groups like the Panzi Foundation have argued for both an ad hoc tribunal for 'the big fish' and hybrid mechanisms at the national level.[237] In August 2020, Tshisekedi embraced a transitional justice approach and his human rights minister has reportedly prepared two draft decrees to take matters forward.[238] However, if past experience is anything to go by, it is far from certain that the political elite will approve these measures.

232 Interview with senior Kabila adviser, Kinshasa, DRC, 19 August 2016.

233 Interview with Luzolo Bambi Lessa, Kinshasa, DRC, 18 April 2016.

234 On CAR, see Patryk I Labuda, 'Institutional Design and (Non-)Complementarity: Regulating Relations between Hybrid Tribunals and Other Judicial Institutions' in Kirsten Ainley and Mark Kersten (ed), *Hybrid Justice: Innovation and Impact in the Prosecution of Atrocity Crimes* (OUP forthcoming). For recent challenges, see Amnesty International, 'One Step Forward, Two Steps Backwards: Justice in the Central African Republic' (2021) AFR 19/5038/2021.

235 Interviews with activists and UN officials, 2016–2021. See also Candeias and others (n 184) 13–15.

236 Interviews with activists and UN officials, Kinshasa, DRC and by phone, 22 and 25 April 2016 and 2 August 2016 and 27 September 2021.

237 Isabel Marques da Silva, 'Denis Mukwege's 20-Year Stand against Sexual Violence in DRC' *Euronews* (14 October 2020) <euronews.com/2020/10/14/denis-mukwege-s-20-year-stand-against-sexual-violence-in-drc>.

238 Patrick Maki, 'RDC: Félix Tshisekedi opte pour une "justice transitionnelle" face aux divers crimes et abus commis au pays' (8 August 2020) <actualite.cd/2020/08/08/rdc-felix-tshisekedi-opte-pour-une-justice-transitionnelle-face-aux-divers-crimes-et>; Valérie Arnould, 'Reflections on a Decentralized Approach to Transitional Justice in the DR Congo' (2021) 33 Egmont Institute. Africa Policy Brief; Hans Hoebeke, 'Rumble in the DR Congo: President Tshisekedi Is Taking Control' (Egmont—Royal Institute for International Relations 2021) 112 20. But see Luc Henkinbrant, 'Justice transitionnelle en RDC: Comment l'ONU l'a rangé dans un tiroir' (*JusticeInfo*, 14 January 2022) <justiceinfo.net/fr/86510 justice-transitionnelle-rdc-congo-comment-onu-range-dans-tiroir.html>.

4.4. Positive complementarity (in)action: capacity building with(out) the court?

Despite its fragmented position on the hybrid tribunal, donor support for the justice sector has been a priority since the 2000s. Funded by the EU, Belgium, Netherlands, Sweden, the UK, USA, and Japan, NGOs such as ASF, RCN Justice et Démocratie, the American Bar Association, ICTJ, and Trial International have implemented projects on investigation techniques, sexual, and gender-based violence, forensic skills, case management, information technology, defence rights, and penitentiary reform.[239] MONUSCO has refurbished infrastructure through its quick impact projects, and international criminal law has been incorporated into university curricula.[240]

Despite progress, access to justice and victim and witness protection remain problematic. Victims, who often struggle to pursue court cases due to court and attorney fees, are assisted and represented by NGOs, which—in the absence of state programmes—also provide medical and psychosocial services. Lacking a state-run programme for victim and witness protection, magistrates have also developed stop-gap measures in judicial proceedings, for instance by allowing witnesses and rape victims to testify with masks to shield their identities.[241] However, the lack of a protection framework remains a serious obstacle to pursuing suspects.[242]

Although capacity-building projects are sometimes cast in complementarity language, the term is used by donors and NGOs to convey the general notion of 'international–national cooperation' rather than a specific reference to the ICC or the Rome Statute.[243] For instance, ahead of the 2015 *Etats généraux de la justice*, HRW observed that '[e]ager to promote complementarity between the ICC and national courts, Congolese authorities and international partners have implemented numerous projects to strengthen the capacity of Congo's military justice system to handle grave international crimes', including 'specialized trainings, mobile courts, legal support to victims and assistance with protection'.[244]

[239] Patryk I Labuda, 'Complementarity and Cooperation in the Congo' in Ronald Slye (ed), *The Nuremberg Principles in non-Western Societies: A Reflection on Their Universality, Legitimacy and Application* (International Nuremberg Principles Academy 2016).

[240] Interviews with civil society and foreign experts, Goma and Kinshasa, DRC and by phone, September 2015 and April and August 2016, 27 September 2021.

[241] BCUNDH (n 206) 21–23; Briefel and Tredici (n 196) 344–45; UNDP and EU (n 185) 10. See also Catherine Ramaekers, 'La protection des victimes et témoins de crimes' in RCN Justice et Démocratie (ed), *Les 10 ans de la Cour pénale internationale. Bilans et perspectives. Recueil des actes des journées scientifiques tenues à Kinshasa, RDC du 23 au 25 octobre 2012* (2012).

[242] Interview with human rights activists, Kinshasa, DRC, 18 August 2016 and 6 August 2019. See also HRW, 'DR Congo: Warlord's Conviction Reveals Trial Flaws' (19 April 2019) <hrw.org/news/2019/04/19/dr-congo-warlords-conviction-reveals-trial-flaws>.

[243] Interviews with NGO, UN, and EU officials, Kinshasa, DRC and by phone, 25 April, 16 and 18 August 2016, 12 June 2017.

[244] HRW (n 209).

The ICC itself long avoided capacity building in the DRC, with participation of OTP officials limited to ad hoc initiatives organized by third parties, in their private capacity.[245] Acknowledging this state of affairs, ICC officials noted that it is well known that, notwithstanding positive complementarity, other international actors bear the burden of making the Congolese justice system 'able and willing'.[246]

Yet, as the ICC prepares to potentially exit the DRC, this approach may be evolving. In 2017, amid reports of electoral violence and widespread abuses by the Congolese security services, OTP officials flew to Kinshasa to train the National Human Rights Commission. Aimed at 'sharing best practices, and exchanging views on ways of transferring skills and information sharing in the fight against impunity', the one-off seminar was praised as 'testimony to the vitality of the cooperation between the DRC and the ICC'.[247] Although the Commission deals mainly with fact-finding and cannot launch prosecutions, Michel de Smedt, head of investigations, argued it and the ICC have 'different but complementary mandates'.[248] Another ICC official explained that this form of capacity building was the most the OTP could do to promote accountability in the context of contested elections.[249]

It remains to be seen whether new forms of capacity building—for instance, through a mentoring programme for visiting professionals in The Hague—herald a different approach to how the ICC can support domestic actors.[250] Despite discussions of completion strategies, galvanized by an OTP policy paper in 2021, the ICC has yet to follow in the footsteps of the SCSL or ICTR, which adopted exit strategies, including capacity building for national authorities to enshrine their legacies.[251]

4.5. Deromanticizing domestic justice: how able was/is the Congolese judiciary?

Against the backdrop of the ICC's extended presence in the DRC, a recurring question is the Congolese justice system's capacity to hold perpetrators accountable. After all, the OTP is not expected to open—and should close—investigations if states are able and willing to proceed genuinely on their own. As early as 2005,

[245] Interviews with civil society, UN and ICC officials, 2015–21.

[246] Interview with ICC official, The Hague, Netherlands, 3 December 2019.

[247] ICC, 'The International Criminal Court Takes Part in a Training Seminar for Investigators from the National Human Rights Commission of the Democratic Republic of the Congo' (2017) ICC-CPI-20170418-PR1296 <icc-cpi.int/news/international-criminal-court-takes-part-training-seminar-investigators-national-human-rights>.

[248] ibid.

[249] Interview with ICC official, The Hague, Netherlands, 6 July 2018.

[250] See eg <twitter.com/IntlCrimCourt/status/1242864950273589254?s=20> e-mail exchanges and conversations with ICC–OTP officials, The Hague, Netherlands, March 2020 and January 2021.

[251] ICC–OTP, 'Policy on Situation Completion' (2021). See further Chapter 7 in this volume.

chambers interrogated to what extent Kabila's self-referral, premised on a lack of domestic capacity, reflected facts on the ground.[252]

Given the persistence of impunity in the DRC, the ICC's performance there has come under understandable criticism. More serious critiques, however, allege that OTP-initiated trials may have harmed national responses and undermined local ownership. Notably, Phil Clark argues that the OTP 'has *weakened* the capacity of national institutions to investigate and prosecute international crimes', inter alia by 'usurping' the cases of Lubanga or Katanga from the courts in Ituri, which had more capacity than judicial institutions elsewhere in the DRC.[253] According to Clark, by depriving magistrates of the opportunity to prosecute such cases soon after EU-funded reforms, the ICC undermined the Ituri courts' ability to challenge executive actors 'over the extent of their authority and their ability to hold state actors accountable'.[254] Echoing this critique, others suggest that 'the judiciaries in Uganda and [DRC] appeared fully capable of trying the cases they referred to The Hague'.[255]

These far-reaching critiques require scrutiny. To substantiate his argument, Clark relies primarily on interviews with two Ituri-based prosecutors (both deceased in the meantime), while downplaying documentary evidence of state collapse and other facts about the Congolese justice system.[256] For one, civilian courts in Ituri lacked jurisdiction over international crimes (meaning any cases would necessarily involve ordinary crimes) and it is doubtful that, for instance, Katanga could have ever been prosecuted in an Ituri court—given his high military rank, any military trial would have been transferred to Kisangani or Kinshasa.[257]

For another, many observers reach more nuanced conclusions about Ituri's judiciary. Citing precarious security, witness fears of testifying, insufficient financial and logistical support for judicial personnel, and local prosecutors' limited

[252] See Chapter 3, section 4.4 in this volume.

[253] Phil Clark, *Distant Justice: The Impact of the International Criminal Court on African Politics* (CUP 2018) 186 (emphasis added); Phil Clark, 'The UN Security Council and Transitional Justice: The Democratic Republic of the Congo' in Rebecca Brubaker (ed), *The UN Security Council and Transitional Justice* (United Nations University 2021) 88. Clark's thesis about 'competitive' relations between the ICC and Congolese authorities and Ituri cases being 'usurped' can be traced to a 2008 article (Phil Clark, 'Law, Politics and Pragmatism: The ICC and Case Selection in the Democratic Republic of Congo and Uganda' in Phil Clark and Nicholas Waddell (eds), *Courting Conflict? Justice, Peace and the ICC in Africa* (Royal African Society 2008)).

[254] Clark, *Distant Justice* (n 253) 186.

[255] Padraig McAuliffe, 'From Watchdog to Workhorse: Explaining the Emergence of the ICC's Burden-Sharing Policy as an Example of Creeping Cosmopolitanism' (2014) 13 Chinese Journal of International Law 259, 282; Similarly Oumar Ba, *States of Justice: The Politics of the International Criminal Court* (CUP 2020) 55–58; Kambale (n 213) 186–87; William A Schabas, 'Prosecutorial Discretion v. Judicial Activism at the International Criminal Court' (2008) 6 Journal of International Criminal Justice 731; Karolina Wierczyńska, 'The Rome Statute and the Debate Surrounding the Constitutionalisation, Fragmentation and Pluralisation of International Criminal Law' in Andrzej Jakubowski and Karolina Wierczyńska (eds), *Fragmentation vs the Constitutionalisation of International Law: A Practical Inquiry* (Routledge 2016) 159.

[256] Clark, *Distant Justice* (n 253) 179–83.

[257] Interview with Ituri-based magistrate, Bukavu, DRC, 10 and 13 August 2019.

investigative capabilities, HRW expressed reservations in 2004 as to whether prosecutions of international crimes could move forward in Ituri.[258] Echoing this sentiment, many UN officials and Congolese magistrates question whether the ICC undermined accountability efforts in Ituri or how findings from one province can be extrapolated to the rest of the country. For instance, a senior magistrate with experience in Ituri, after acknowledging the EU's support for justice reform in that province, explained that '[prosecuting] Lubanga would have been very difficult, there was a security threat [undermining] the trust of witnesses to testify before the courts'.[259] The then presiding judge at the Bunia district court explained that the accusation of 'stealing [cases] is a bit harsh; this is foreseen by the Rome Statute; when the state has no capacity, the ICC takes the file', adding that 'Lubanga's case would not have been done locally in reality, victim and witness protection and interference would have made it impossible given the political stakes of this case as opposed to others that took place at this time'.[260] The same judge emphasized the transformative role of international aid for magistrates' work: 'all of this would be impossible without MONUC; to argue that the ICC was not necessary misses the point that domestic justice was completely dependent on external support during this time'.[261] Reacting to the claim that EU support made the Ituri courts 'able' to prosecute Lubanga and others, an African official present in Ituri in 2004 expressed his disagreement succinctly: 'You don't improve the quality of water by exchanging the faucet'.[262]

Divergent perspectives on the capacity of Ituri courts and potential local trials of warlords like Lubanga underscore the challenge of assessing the DRC's 'ability' to prosecute international crimes, especially in light of developments over time. On the one hand, it seems undeniable that international intervention has strengthened the justice system since 2004, with some surveys showing that Congolese have greater trust in the courts.[263] On the other, arguments about the judiciary's ability to handle international crimes and the military's willingness to contest executive power seem to misdiagnose the causes of impunity and risk romanticizing domestic justice in the DRC.[264] To be sure, various aspects of the ICC's cases

[258] HRW, 'Making Justice Work: Restoration of the Legal System in Ituri, DRC' (2004).

[259] Interview with senior military magistrate, Kinshasa, DRC, 26 July 2019.

[260] Interview with senior military magistrate, Goma, DRC, 7 August 2019. References to 'stealing cases' can be found in Clark, *Distant Justice* (n 253) 183 and 185.

[261] Interview with senior military magistrate, Goma, DRC, 7 August 2019.

[262] Interview with UN official, Kinshasa, DRC, 25 July 2019.

[263] Jaïr van der Lijn, Tim Glawion and Nikki de Zwaan, 'Towards Legitimate Stability in CAR and the DRC: External Assumptions and Local Perspectives' (Stockholm International Peace Research Institute 2019).

[264] Henkinbrant (n 238). In this sense, see also Arnould (n 213). On romanticizing the local, see Adam Kochanski, 'The "Local Turn" in Transitional Justice: Curb the Enthusiasm' (2020) 22 International Studies Review 26. But see Clark, *Distant Justice* (n 253) 184 (acknowledging 'we should not romanticise the capacity of the national courts to address serious crimes' but concluding that 'the ICC has not shown that it is capable of prosecuting cases to a higher standard than the Bunia courts').

against mid-level Ituri warlords are controversial—more deserving targets could have been found—but this also downplays the undeniable symbolic value of ICC prosecutions for domestic reform efforts, as seen in Chapter 4.

Rather than weaken reforms or dampen the judiciary's capacity to handle serious crimes, a more tangible problem with the ICC and other partners' support seems to be that, despite extensive capacity building for nearly two decades, the pursuit of accountability remains a fragile work in progress, including in Ituri where mass crimes resumed in 2019. Despite donor aid, concerns persist about victim and witness protection, the independence of military justice, and penitentiary reform (for instance, prisoner escapes still occur too often).[265] As will be seen in Chapter 6, the uncertain genuineness of national proceedings raise further questions about the sustainability of bottom-up accountability initiatives in the DRC.

4.6. Unpacking complementarity's effects on capacity building

Assessments of the ICC's impact on capacity building in the DRC vary. While Clark argues the ICC's 'distant justice' may have undermined the Congolese judiciary's ability to contest executive power, other scholars are generally less critical.[266] For instance, Milli Lake suggests that 'prospects for peace in DR Congo would unlikely be brighter in the absence of any investment in the rule of law ... some aspects of legal capacity building—such as an increased public awareness of human rights violations and the training of lawyers and judges in international criminal law—will contribute positively to an improved human rights climate over time'.[267]

Differences of (scholarly) opinion are likely to persist in this regard. In many ways, the DRC represents a microcosm of the ICC and other international actors' evolving attitudes to capacity building for international crimes. While OTP policy initially envisioned assistance to national judiciaries as a form of positive complementarity—with Ocampo arguing that complementarity 'compels the [OTP] to collaborate with national jurisdictions in order to help them improve

[265] BCUNDH, 'Accountability for Human Rights Violations and Abuses in the DRC: Achievements, Challenges and Way Forward (1 January 2014–31 March 2016)' (2016); BCUNDH, 'Report on Violations of Human Rights and International Humanitarian Law by the Allied Democratic Forces Armed Group and by Members of the Defense and Security Forces in Beni Territory, North Kivu Province and Irumu and Mambasa Territories, Ituri Province, between 1 January 2019 and 31 January 2020' (2020); BCUNDH, 'Rapport public sur les conflits en territoire de Djugu, province de l'Ituri; décembre 2017 à septembre 2019' (2020); BCUNDH, 'Rapport de mission d'enquête spéciale sur les violences intercommunautaires des 16 et 17 décembre 2018 dans le territoire de Yumbi' (2019); BCUNDH (n 206) 19.

[266] Clark, *Distant Justice* (n 253).

[267] Milli Lake, 'Building the Rule of War: Postconflict Institutions and the Micro-Dynamics of Conflict in Eastern DR Congo' (2017) 71 International Organization 281, 308; Elena Baylis, 'Reassessing the Role of International Criminal Law: Rebuilding National Courts through Transnational Networks' (2009) 50 Boston College Law Review 1. More critically than Lake (but with the DRC as a positive case), see De Vos (n 193).

their efficiency'[268]—the ASP subsequently de-emphasized the ICC's involvement but encouraged third parties to spearhead reforms of national institutions. Given the ICC's geographic spread and limited resources, it seemed reasonable to require donors and NGOs to fill the gap. Until recently, the slogan that the ICC was not a 'development agency' symbolized this hands-off approach to capacity building.[269]

But the DRC illustrates both the promise and limitations of multi-stakeholder capacity building in the shadow of ICC investigations. On the one hand, development partners have implemented a variety of projects for the justice sector, ranging from infrastructure rehabilitation to victim support and legal training for practitioners. Although none of these capacity building initiatives aimed to facilitate admissibility challenges against the ICC, a more expansive notion of complementarity qua domestic–international cooperation has proliferated. By providing rhetorical cover for their support to Congolese institutions, the UN and NGOs were able to leverage the ICC's symbolic shadow to market their capacity-building projects as a form of positive complementarity, in particular through the CAPs and mobile courts programme. Similar to the idea of legacy in Sierra Leone, complementarity in the DRC has functioned, arguably with greater success, as a rhetorical slogan to galvanize donor support.

On the other hand, this amalgamation of complementarity with third-party capacity building creates confusion and deflects responsibility for justice reform. In arguing that a hybrid court would distract from reforming ordinary courts and create a two-track system of justice, the EU may have been faithful *à la lettre* to complementarity as enshrined in the Rome Statute, but the emphasis on domestic solutions at all costs may have helped extinguish the prospect of accountability for past crimes altogether. Whereas donors and NGOs in Uganda and Sudan made strategic use of the threat of ICC intervention to help set up specialist institutions for the prosecution of international crimes,[270] a Congolese hybrid tribunal has met with resistance from the political elites, in particular due to disagreement over the extent of the state's authority to pre-empt ICC investigations and the level of international participation in hybrid decision-making. Some government actors have exploited inconsistent messaging from international partners to undermine reforms that could challenge their entrenched interests, with the military maintaining a monopoly on prosecuting international crimes despite legal reforms to the contrary.

Although the ICC has, in line with ASP priorities, allowed third parties to build domestic capacity while avoiding its own involvement in 'positive complementarity'

[268] Statement by Luis Ocampo, 'Statement to the Assembly of States Parties to the Rome Statute of the International Criminal Court' (22 April 2003) New York, ICC–OTP-20030502-10-EN.

[269] ICC–ASP, 'Report of the Bureau on Stocktaking: Complementarity, Taking Stock of the Principle of Complementarity: Bridging the Impunity Gap, ICC–ASP/8/51' (2010) para 16; ICC–OTP, 'Prosecutorial Strategy 2009–2012' (2010) 5.

[270] De Vos (n 193) 23 (critical of these developments).

initiatives, there have been exceptions. Fearing it would need to yield jurisdictional priority to the Congolese judiciary, the OTP initially opposed the hybrid court. Years later, motivated by an opposite set of concerns, the OTP trained the human rights commission, to avoid investigating the crimes of Kabila allies itself. While these two forays into national accountability debates may seem inconsistent at first, on both occasions the OTP intervened when its strategic interests—in maintaining or yielding jurisdictional priority—were at stake. Whereas the hybrid court threatened its privileged position in the institutional landscape, the Commission offered an off-ramp for sensitive investigations.

While its training for the Congolese Human Rights Commission is a rare case of capacity building for state actors in an ongoing investigation, the OTP has reached out to donors and built civil society support more extensively in some preliminary examinations, including in Colombia and Guinea where negotiations with governments on enhancing the state's 'ability' to prosecute, and thereby avoid an ICC investigation, went on for over a decade.[271] Although here again support happened insofar as the OTP's strategic interest in not opening an investigation was served, the shift to completion strategies, especially in long-standing investigations such as the DRC will likely build on the experience of the ad hoc tribunals to explore how ICC organs and development partners can promote a sustainable exit in light of the reputational incentives for, and legitimation side effects, of international support. This seems particularly important in the DRC, a recipient of large amounts of aid through one of the UN's emblematic interventions, where research has shown that support for the executive and military, to the exclusion of other actors and civil society, has strengthened authoritarian dynamics. As Sarah von Billerbeck and Oisín Tansey argue, 'the UN has inadvertently enabled authoritarian practices' in the DRC by 'boost[ing] the material and coercive capacity of the regime' while 'in the wake of flagrant breaches of democratic norms, the UN signalled its tolerance for authoritarianism through muted criticism and continued cooperation with the regime'.[272] Put differently, despite setting out to promote peace, international peacebuilders turn out to be enablers of authoritarianism.[273]

As will be seen in Chapter 6, while positive complementarity initiatives may seem benign, when donors and NGOs focus on building capacity but lose sight of the wider accountability landscape, for instance by enshrining the military's power at the expense of civilian courts, rule-of-law reforms in the ICC's shadow risks romanticizing domestic justice and may enable authoritarian practices as well.

[271] HRW, 'Pressure Point: The ICC's Impact on National Justice. Lessons from Colombia, Georgia, Guinea, and the United Kingdom' (2018). See Chapter 4 and further Chapter 7 in this volume.

[272] Sarah von Billerbeck and Oisín Tansey, 'Enabling Autocracy? Peacebuilding and Post-Conflict Authoritarianism in the Democratic Republic of Congo' (2019) 25 European Journal of International Relations 698, 715.

[273] Adam Day and others, *Peacebuilding and Authoritarianism: The Unintended Consequences of UN Engagement in Post-Conflict Settings* (United Nations University 2021). For the DRC, see also Arnould (n 213) 321–38.

5. Interim Conclusion: Capacity Building in the Court's Shadow

In 2009, Jane Stromseth observed 'we still know surprisingly little' about whether ICTs 'contribut[e] in any enduring way to building domestic capacity for justice'.[274] While there are now numerous mappings of capacity building, including through the ICC–ASP's complementarity platform, international and domestic actors still collaborate mainly on the basis of assumptions about how ICT intervention influences domestic justice systems rather than empirically grounded models.[275]

To different degrees and in different ways, the mandates of the ICTR, SCSL, and ICC foregrounded the importance of state capacity. In this regard, the revival of international criminal law in the 1990s intersected with longer-term rule-of-law promotion efforts, focusing—in the words of the UN Secretary General—on:[276]

> a lack of political will for reform, a lack of institutional independence within the justice sector, a lack of domestic technical capacity, a lack of material and financial resources, a lack of public confidence in [g]overnment, a lack of official respect for human rights, and more generally, a lack of peace and security.

As seen in this chapter, donors and NGOs in Rwanda, Sierra Leone, and the DRC have implemented various projects for national judiciaries, only some of which are linked to accountability for international crimes as such. Against this backdrop, it is not always possible to identify the specific contributions of ICTs or how institutional design choices and national reform policies intersect with one another.[277] While ICTs rarely intervene directly to enhance national institutional capacity, development partners regularly draw on the tribunals' presence—their 'symbolic shadow'—to rationalize capacity building, with concepts like 'positive complementarity' and 'legacy'—born in the interstices of ICT mandates—serving as rhetorical slogans to rationalize transnational cooperation.

[274] Jane E Stromseth, 'Justice on the Ground: Can International Criminal Courts Strengthen Domestic Rule of Law in Post-Conflict Societies?' (2009) 1 Hague Journal on the Rule of Law 81, 88.

[275] International Bar Association War Crimes Committee, 'Analysis of Overcrowded and Under-Examined Areas, Following a Mapping of Organisations' Work on Ameliorating Domestic Capacity to Try Serious International Crimes' (2018).

[276] Report of the Secretary General (n 2) para 3; UNGA, Sustainable Development Goals (2016) Goal 16(3). On longer-term trends, see Randall Peerenboom, Michael Zürn and André Nollkaemper, 'Conclusion: From Rule of Law Promotion to Rule of Law Dynamics' in Michael Zurn, Andre Nollkaemper and Randy Peerenboom (eds), *Rule of Law Dynamics* (CUP 2012); Elena Baylis, 'Transitional Justice and Development Aid to Fragile and Conflict-Affected States: Risks and Reforms' in Roger Duthie and Paul Seils (eds), *Justice Mosaics: How Context Shapes Transitional Justice in Fractured Societies* (ICTJ 2017) 393.

[277] In this sense, Yuval Shany, 'How Can International Criminal Courts Have a Greater Impact on National Criminal Proceedings? Lessons from the First Two Decades of International Criminal Justice in Operation' (2013) 46 Israel Law Review 431, 441–42.

Over time, positive complementarity has become a generic frame of reference for capacity building, due to the appealing semantics of complementarity qua partnership, which is leveraged to secure buy-in from governments in an area of sovereignty as sensitive as international crimes. Accordingly, capacity building for Congolese actors is often rhetorically framed as enhancing complementarity much like the rule 11*bis* process (though it remained grounded on primacy) was marketed as 'complementarity in action'. Even in Sierra Leone, where the government otherwise shunned the ICC, state officials occasionally described the SCSL's legacy as complementarity. By contrast, ICTR and SCSL primacy—associated, rightly or wrongly, with international supremacy—triggered primarily negative reactions from domestic actors, though it eventually translated into the rule 11*bis* process and enabled iterative negotiations with Rwandan authorities.

Beyond their rhetorical resonance, ICT institutional design choices have other, more tangible shadow effects. For instance, the SCSL's emphasis on defence rights trickled down into a state-administered legal aid programme and colocation strengthened domestic expertise on witness protection (similar reforms have proven difficult in the DRC). Similarly, the ICTR's rule 11*bis* triggered negotiations between international civil servants and Rwandan officials over knowledge transfer and institutional reforms. On the other hand, some effects run contrary to expectations. As seen in Sierra Leone, placing a tribunal in-country did not—without further incentives—stimulate iterative practices.[278]

The institutional incentives for ICT involvement in capacity building require further study. Although it is now often assumed that ICTs should support domestic accountability, notably by sharing evidence, this discounts that no tribunal has ever received an *operational* mandate to strengthen national justice systems or domestic prosecutions. Even in its completion phase, the ICTR had no authorization, let alone, budget to build Rwandan capacity. Similarly, the SCSL, seemingly better positioned to influence domestic justice, was only ever expected to cast an indirect shadow—labelled its 'demonstration effect'[279]—over the national justice sector. At both tribunals, where projects materialized, they focused on SCSL (witness protection) or ICTR (referrals) priorities, rather than general domestic needs.

Given the ICC's global remit, a seemingly logical consensus has emerged that it should not even attempt capacity building—as the refrain goes, the ICC is not a 'development agency'—the consequence of which is that Court organs deliberately distance themselves from direct forms of support. This is neither surprising from a division of labour perspective, nor should it be objectionable if the goal is to maximize ICTs' shadow effects. Rather than provide technical or financial assistance for national accountability initiatives as a matter of course, it seems that ICTs are better placed to strengthen domestic justice through targeted interventions or, at a

[278] See Shany (n 277) 444–46; Chehtman (n 107).

[279] On demonstration effect and capacity building, see also Stromseth (n 115) 171–77.

more strategic level, by assessing progress in building state capacity (and norm internalization, as will be discussed in Chapter 6) against agreed-upon standards that can in turn guide reforms. Given that donors and NGOs already have mandates to build capacity—and do so in growing numbers—the question should not be what difference cash-strapped ICTs can make (very little), but rather how other rule-of-law actors, in particular state-based reformers, can harness the shadow of ICTs to promote national reforms.

It is at the intersection of international criminal accountability, development cooperation and states' rule-of-law policies that ICTs arguably have the greatest potential to foster iterative capacity-building dynamics. While ICTs will never be a panacea for national capacity shortfalls, their top-down interventions into complex accountability processes can be beneficial if and when negotiated with states and development partners. For one, ICTs seem to enjoy unique symbolic power to (de)legitimize state efforts to hold perpetrators accountable. As seen in Rwanda, a combination of conditionalities attached to fair trial evaluations and the reward of legitimation spurred domestic reforms, in coordination with development partners (who had their own incentives to build Rwandan capacity). Conversely, in Sierra Leone, where the SCSL and national authorities had few incentives to engage one another, isolationist dynamics prevailed and knowledge transfer took longer to mature.[280]

For another, ICTs seem better placed to activate iterative relationships based on reputational incentives than development partners. Aside from Serbia, where the EU helped the ICTY by deploying hierarchical forms of political conditionality to extract concessions, linking 'material rewards' or 'retribution' to progress on accountability for international crimes has rarely been used in ICC situations.[281] In fact, outside a few preliminary examinations, the OTP has avoided domestic rule-of-law debates, while NGOs rely increasingly on non-hierarchical forms of capacity building, technical assistance, and knowledge diffusion.[282] As such, development partners do not employ conditionalities to tie material rewards to progress on domestic prosecutions of serious crimes in ICC situations. To take one example, while the Cotonou agreement conditions some trade benefits on Rome Statute ratification, the EU has not tried to link trade or other benefits to progress on criminal justice in the DRC or other ICC countries.[283]

[280] Moreover, a lack of donor coordination leads to confusion, overlapping agendas, a waste of resources, and narrow project implementation (Shany (n 277) 448).

[281] On EU conditionality vis-à-vis Serbia, see Orentlicher (n 54) 59–88.

[282] Monika Heupel, 'Rule of Law Promotion through International Organizations and NGOs' in Michael Zurn, Andre Nollkaemper and Randy Peerenboom (eds), *Rule of Law Dynamics* (CUP 2012) 135–36.

[283] Heupel (n 282) 136. On the growing role of China, see Samuli Seppanen, 'Chinese Legal Development Assistance: Which Rule of Law? Whose Pragmatism?' (2018) 51 Vanderbilt Journal of Transnational Law 101; Tanner Larkin, 'China's Normfare and the Threat to Human Rights' (2022) 122 Columbia Law Review 2285. But see Timothy Webster, 'China's Human Rights Footprint in Africa' (2013) 51 Columbia Journal of Transnational Law 626.

In fact, the trend across African situations has been to eschew conditionality, not least to prevent accusations of neocolonialism.[284] Of course, given African states' charges of neocolonialism against the ICC, resorting to benchmarks relating to 'inability' (or 'unwillingness') would have to be done with care, based on a dialogue with government actors, civil society, and development partners, lest it provoke backlash and Rome Statute withdrawals. As noted in Chapter 4, the Kenya precedent serves as a cautionary tale.[285] At the same time, the Kenya experience may have cast too long a shadow and shut down more nuanced debates about the ICC's role in domestic accountability reforms. While the OTP and judges' wariness to set benchmarks based on article 17 criteria may seem like politically neutral interpretation, overly deferential ICC interventions may unnecessarily legitimize governments in Uganda, the DRC, Mali, or Libya.[286] Similarly, Rwanda has long benefited from foreign aid while rejecting external oversight and strategically deflecting human rights criticism.[287]

If nothing else, an uncritical emphasis on capacity building under the banner of positive complementarity carries risks. As donors and NGOs speak the language of partnership to justify their bottom-up rule-of-law initiatives, ICC intervention may—given the flagrant lack of prosecutions of government crimes in most countries—inadvertently romanticize domestic trials and enable authoritarianism 'by providing material support to governments in ways that strengthen centralised regimes' and 'by sending political signals' to political elites about the '[non-]costs of authoritarian behaviour'.[288] As will be seen in Chapter 6, with donors prioritizing narrow project implementation and international civil servants declining to monitor fair trial standards, national elites may be able to redirect ICC intervention for their own ends rather than their populations' expectations of emancipatory justice.

[284] Arguing for a form of conditionality vis-à-vis African countries, see Makau W Mutua, 'Closing the "Impunity Gap" and the Role of State Support of the ICC' in Richard H Steinberg (ed), *Contemporary Issues Facing the International Criminal Court* (Brill Nijhoff 2016) 109. But on conditionality and human rights generally, see Makau W Mutua, 'Savages, Victims, and Saviors: The Metaphor of Human Rights' (2001) 42 Harvard International Law Journal 201.

[285] On reforms and the 'foreign affairs façade' in Kenya, see Lionel Nichols, *The International Criminal Court and the End of Impunity in Kenya* (Springer 2014) 156–75 and 216–25.

[286] Government actors have no qualms leveraging ICC admissibility findings for their own ends. For instance, Libyan actors use the *Al-Senussi* admissibility ruling to argue that their judiciary is 'able', hampering negotiations on reforms of a judiciary that is presented as 'fully compliant' with international standards (author notes, Tripoli, Libya, 2 May 2018).

[287] For a rare analysis of donor aid and its impact on state-led transitional justice in Rwanda, see Stina Petersen, Ingrid Samset and Vibeke Wang, 'Foreign Aid to Transitional Justice: The Cases of Rwanda and Guatemala, 1995–2005' in Kai Ambos, Judith Large and Marieke Wierda (eds), *Building a Future on Peace and Justice* (Springer 2009).

[288] Day and others (n 273) 6.

6
International Intervention and Norm Internalization

1. Introduction

To assess how the shadow of ICTs influences state-driven accountability processes and whether international intervention has generally positive (iteration), neutral (accommodation), or negative (isolation) effects on governments' willingness and ability to pursue accountability for international crimes, this chapter examines to what extent elements of the ICTR, SCSL, and ICC's institutional design encouraged domestic actors in Rwanda, Sierra Leone, and the DRC to enact normative reforms and to what extent international norms are respected in national trials of serious crimes.

Prior to the 1990s, many states' legal systems did not criminalize genocide, crimes against humanity and war crimes, or did so in a fragmentary manner. The revival of ICTs has changed this, so much so that the domestication of international criminal norms is considered an indicator of states' commitment to the fight against impunity. ICT mandates can exert 'normative pull' in different ways. By integrating domestic crimes, the SCSL statute anticipated normative cross-fertilization vis-à-vis the domestic justice sector. Positive complementarity qua 'domestication duty' assumes that states have a legal obligation to implement ICC crimes into domestic law.[1] Primacy created strong incentives to domesticate international norms by conditioning intervention on prosecutions of 'ordinary crimes' (which was equated with bad faith) or, subsequently, by sanctioning rule 11*bis* referrals on adherence to fair trial standards. It bears reiterating that, while rule 11*bis* conditionality revolved around human rights law, the complementarity case law dissociates ICC oversight from human rights standards, with admissibility predicated on 'ungenuine'—but not necessarily unfair—domestic trials.[2]

[1] Jann K Kleffner, 'The Impact of Complementarity on National Implementation of Substantive International Criminal Law' (2003) 1 Journal of International Criminal Justice 86.

[2] On this distinction, see Chapter 3, section 4.5 in this volume. See also Marina Aksenova, 'Human Rights at the International Criminal Court: Testing the Limits of Judicial Discretion' (2017) 86 Nordic Journal of International Law 68; Jessica Almqvist, 'Complementarity and Human Rights: A Litmus Test for the International Criminal Court' (2008) 30 Loyola of Los Angeles International and Comparative Law Review 335.

International Criminal Tribunals and Domestic Accountability. Patryk I. Labuda, Oxford University Press. © Patryk I. Labuda 2023. DOI: 10.1093/oso/9780198868842.003.0006

Focusing on areas of synergy, antagonism, and indifference, this chapter assesses not just how ICTs influence legislative reforms but also to what extent national justice systems internalize international standards in practice. Guided by Harold Koh's definition of norm internalization as 'the complex process' by which 'international legal norms seep into, are internalized, and become entrenched in domestic legal and political processes',[3] this chapter argues that, while the Rome Statute functions as a global code for international crimes, the incentives embedded therein privilege a sovereignty-friendly, outcomes-oriented vision of accountability. Rather than mainstream process-oriented principles grounded on human rights law, states under the shadow of ICC intervention are likely to prioritize the holding of criminal proceedings as such, which is sufficient to repel external scrutiny, but does not necessarily address the underlying conditions of impunity. ICC intervention may even result in 'unintended diversionary complementarity'—trials of lower-level perpetrators for unsystematic ordinary crimes—while eliding questions around the aims of trials in fostering emancipatory justice and transitions towards peace.

2. The International Criminal Tribunal for Rwanda

2.1. Domesticating genocide: keeping internationals at bay

A non-trivial challenge facing the post-genocide Rwandan authorities was that genocide was not a distinct crime under domestic law in 1994. In an ironic twist of history, although Rwanda ratified the Genocide Convention in 1975, its penal code, adopted just two years later, failed to criminalize genocide. As explained by Sam Rugege and Aimé Karimunda, two Rwandan Supreme Court judges, the UN Special Rapporteur for the Prevention and Punishment of the Crime of Genocide in the mid-1970s, who happened to be a Rwandan national, may have convinced the erstwhile Rwandan government that it was unnecessary to domesticate genocide.[4]

This gap in Rwandan law created two problems. First, in line with continental principles, its criminal law prohibited retroactive prosecution and punishment.

[3] Harold Hongju Koh, 'Transnational Legal Process' (1996) 75 Nebraska Law Review 181, 199; Harold Hongju Koh, 'Review: Why Do Nations Obey International Law?' (1997) 106 Yale Law Journal 2599, 2655. Norm internalization is understood here more flexibly than in compliance studies. Borrowing from the literature on legal pluralism, it allows for translation and 'vernacularization' of norms. For this iterative understanding, see Sally Engle Merry, 'Transnational Human Rights and Local Activism: Mapping the Middle' (2006) 108 American Anthropologist 38.

[4] Sam Rugege and Aimé M Karimunda, 'Domestic Prosecution of International Crimes: The Case of Rwanda' in Gerhard Werle, Lovell Fernandez and Moritz Vormbaum, *Africa and the International Criminal Court* (TMC Asser Press 2014) 83–85; Human Rights Commission, 'Study on the Question of the Prevention and Punishment of the Crime of Genocide. Study Prepared by Mr. Nicodème Ruhashyankiko, Special Rapporteur' (1978) E/CN.4/Sub.2/416.

Accordingly, genocidaires could only be prosecuted before Rwandan courts for ordinary crimes, such as murder and rape, which had been criminalized before 1994.[5] Second, in line with primacy, the ICTR Statute gave the prosecutor the power to assert jurisdiction in the event of ongoing and even completed trials if a suspect was prosecuted for an ordinary rather than an international crime.[6] In other words, in late 1994, the domestic legal framework constrained the GNU's policy options in regard to genocide accountability.

Although, in the aftermath of the genocide, Rwandan prosecutors brought charges of ordinary crimes against some suspects, the GNU eventually moved to adopt a more holistic accountability policy. As noted in Chapter 5, with the UN's field operation and NGOs providing capacity building, legislative reform emerged as one core objective.[7] Convened in November 1995, a high-level conference on 'the fight against impunity' developed an early legislative blueprint to enable domestic prosecutions of genocide and crimes against humanity. Among the invitees were European, US, and Canadian experts, although no one from the ICTR appears to have attended. It appears that 'civil' and 'common' lawyers disagreed on the need for new legislation, reflecting the two legal traditions' views on non-retroactivity, but the Rwandan justice ministry built on the conference's recommendations to develop draft legislation that eventually revolutionized the domestic normative landscape.[8]

Adopted by the transitional legislature in August 1996, the organic law on the prosecution of genocide and crimes against humanity was an innovative piece of legislation.[9] To avoid non-retroactivity violations, it established the principle of 'dual incrimination', whereby Rwandan judges had to, first, apply ordinary criminal norms and, second, verify if a criminal act *also* constituted an international crime as defined in one of several international treaties.[10] Equally important, the law devised an original prioritization framework with four degrees of culpability: category 1 planners, which included organizers, instigators of the genocide, those in positions of authority, notorious murderers acting with zeal or excessive

[5] Daniel De Beer, *Loi rwandaise du 30 août 1996 sur l'organisation des poursuites des infractions constitutives du crime de génocide ou de crimes contre l'humanité. Commentaire et jurisprudence* (2nd edn, Alter Egaux 1999) 21.

[6] See Chapter 3, section 2.2 in this volume.

[7] 'Report of the Secretary General on UNAMIR' (4 June 1995) S/1995/457, para 28.

[8] Interview with Rwandan officials and international expert, undisclosed locations, 16 September and 17 November 2016. On this conference, see Olivier Dubois, 'Les juridictions pénales nationales du Rwanda et le Tribunal international' (1997) 79 Revue internationale de la Croix-Rouge 763, 771–72; William A Schabas, 'Genocide, Impunity and Accountability in Rwanda: Is It Reasonable to Expect a Devastated Legal System to Deal Justly with Those Who Destroyed It?' *Inroads: A Journal of Opinion* (1 January 1997).

[9] Organic Law 08/1996 of 1996 on the Organization of Prosecutions for Offenses constituting the Crime of Genocide or Crimes Against Humanity committed since 1 October 1990, Official Gazette, Year 35, 17, 1 September 1996 (1996 organic law).

[10] On dual incrimination and the two step procedure, see De Beer (n 5); Rugege and Karimunda (n 4) 86–88.

malice, and sexual torturers; category 2 perpetrators of intentional homicide or serious bodily assault causing death; category 3 perpetrators of other serious assaults; and category 4 perpetrators of property offenses.[11] Another innovation were plea agreements—a 'common law' concept hitherto alien to Rwandan law—which could be granted in return for an accurate confession, a guilty plea or an apology (though category 1 offenders were excluded from plea bargaining).[12] The organic law also established punishments for each crime and category of perpetrator.[13]

It is impossible to untangle the complex political and legal forces that led to the law's adoption (a difficult task for any legislative process, further compounded by a paucity of contemporary written sources). Behind-the-scenes negotiations on the law included regressive normative proposals, such as a presumption of guilt (instead of the usual presumption of innocence) or reversing the burden of proof for suspects.[14] Both ideas, which would have made it almost impossible for genocide suspects to escape conviction, were rejected. Although the organic law enshrined the right to counsel instead, securing an adequate defence remained contentious, first before the specialized chambers, later in *gacaca* courts and ultimately in the ICTR's rule 11*bis* referrals.[15]

While local and foreign activists agree that the 1996 organic law reflected primarily domestic accountability demands, there is evidence that international advisers embedded within Rwandan ministries contributed to the appropriation of international standards (albeit not always through consistent advice). However, it seems the ICTR played only a minor role in shaping the normative agenda.[16] There is no evidence that concerns over primacy's conditionality scheme (the ordinary crimes and sham trials exceptions) swayed Rwandan officials one way or another to adopt the organic law, although it is likely that Goldstone's assertions of primacy, accelerated the legislative process. One interviewee suggested also that the rush to pass legislation may have caused drafting errors.[17]

A foreign expert involved in the drafting process explained that 'we never discussed the interactions between ICTR and Rwanda during drafting of 1996 law ... the issue was how do we move those thousands of cases here, and to do it with semblance of justice, but no real thought [was] given to how this would interact with ICTR'.[18] According to William Schabas, another expert involved in Rwanda at the time, only the rules on command responsibility were modelled

[11] 1996 organic law, art 2.

[12] Mark A Drumbl, *Atrocity, Punishment, and International Law* (CUP 2007) 73–76.

[13] 1996 organic law, arts 14–18.

[14] De Beer (n 5); Rugege and Karimunda (n 4) 89.

[15] 1996 organic law, art 36.

[16] Interviews with NGO officials and foreign experts, Brussels, Belgium and by phone, 6 September 2016 and 17 November 2016. Interview with former Rwandan government official, undisclosed location, 16 September 2016.

[17] Interview with former ICTR official, Geneva, Switzerland, 25 January 2017.

[18] Phone interview with foreign expert, 6 September 2016.

directly on the ICTR Statute.[19] Significantly, ICTR definitions of international crimes were not domesticated as such—instead, the 1996 organic law criminalized genocide and crimes against humanity through a complex referral scheme to Rwanda's treaty obligations and binding international norms.[20]

While the absence of ICTR definitions in the organic law likely speaks to the complex retroactivity challenges faced by the Rwandan authorities, rather than resistance to the Tribunal per se, the failure to domesticate international crimes decreased the ICTR's normative impact. In his commentary on the 1996 organic law, Daniel de Beer encouraged Rwandan magistrates to use the ICTR Statute's 'much clearer' definition of crimes against humanity, though it appears that few acted on this appeal.[21] In fact, the ICTR Statute's norms and its early case law are mostly absent from early Rwanda jurisprudence. As noted by Schabas:[22]

> [t]he judgments will not be of great interest to international criminal lawyers, because there is little in the way of discussion of the legal issues relating to the prosecution of . . . genocide and crimes against humanity. Instead, they deal principally with the assessment of factual issues, and are of undoubted interest in this respect as an insight into the dynamics of genocide.

Focusing on a relatively high rate of acquittals, Schabas went on to add that 'the judgments provide a reassuring portrait of a judicial system hard at work, contending with the rights of the accused, conflicting evidence and legal questions, and attempting to come to a fair result'.[23]

In fact, the credibility of trials before Rwanda's specialized chambers is contested. The Lawyers Committee for Human Rights condemned group trials with multiple defendants, their lack of access to defence attorneys, lack of translation services, the intimidation of witnesses, and death sentences.[24] Amnesty International excoriated the absence of state-funded legal aid for indigent defendants in capital punishment

[19] 1996 organic law, art 3(2). William A Schabas, 'Justice, Democracy, and Impunity in Post-Genocide Rwanda: Searching for Solutions to Impossible Problems' (1996) 7 Criminal Law Forum 523, 544.

[20] See De Beer (n 5). The organic law references the 1948 Genocide Convention, the 1949 (Fourth) Geneva Convention, 1977 Additional Protocols, and the 1968 Convention on the Non-Applicability of Statutory Limitations to War Crimes and Crimes against Humanity.

[21] De Beer (n 5) 18.

[22] William A Schabas, 'Genocide Trials and Gacaca Courts' (2005) 3 Journal of International Criminal Justice 879, 889.

[23] ibid. Schabas acknowledges NGOs were 'highly critical' (886). See also Drumbl (n 12) 77 ('These judgments are the product of a court system that has grown in sophistication since it began hearing cases, initially somewhat haphazardly, in the aftermath of genocidal devastation').

[24] Lawyers Committee for Human Rights, 'Prosecuting Genocide in Rwanda: A Lawyers Committee Report on the ICTR and National Trials' (1997); Timothy Longman, *Memory and Justice in Post-Genocide Rwanda* (CUP 2017) 110; Mark Drumbl, 'Rule of Law amid Lawlessness: Counselling the Accused in Rwanda's Domestic Genocide Trials' (1998) 29 Columbia Human Rights Law Review 545, 550; Carla J Ferstman, 'Domestic Trials for Genocide and Crimes against Humanity: The Example of Rwanda' (1997) 9 African Journal of International and Comparative Law 857, 869–76.

cases.[25] Many also criticized the proceedings' politicization. Emphasizing the harassment of judicial officials by military and government officials and the lack of fair trial guarantees for Hutu defendants, Alison des Forges and Tim Longman decried the 'weaponization' of genocide trials as an ethnic agenda of the Tutsi-led elite and an intimidation tactic against the political opposition.[26]

Despite sharp criticisms, some observers recognize that fair trial standards improved over time. Reflecting on the different standards in different areas of Rwanda, one NGO official concluded the trials were 'more or less credible ... not the work of great jurists, to be sure'.[27] Another explained that, while the RPF-led authorities were initially 'very sceptical' of claims of innocence and that 'everyone was [initially] found guilty', over time the courts started pronouncing acquittals, especially in cases of blatantly 'false accusations' by private citizens to settle 'personal vendettas'.[28] A former HRFOR official who monitored the trials noted that 'by the time HRFOR was leaving ... we thought suspects could get a fair shake, some [were] convicted, some acquitted, [but] it was not preordained, not a total sham ... [we] couldn't really put our stamp of approval on all this but it was closer to acceptable; some perfunctory, for sure, but not all'.[29]

As noted in Chapter 4, although Goldstone initially foresaw a monitoring role for the ICTR in relation to domestic trials, the OTP abandoned this approach as soon as it acquired custody of its first suspects. As a result, the Tribunal had no direct means of exerting pressure over the quality of domestic proceedings. It bears noting that, while UN officials observed the genocide trials, the UN chose not to issue public reports or to make official recommendations to Rwandan authorities.[30] Internal reporting did feed into the UN's public statements, but HRFOR privileged diplomatic channels of communication, engaging the RPF behind the scenes. However, human rights diplomacy with the RPF had little success. An HRFOR official lamented that the Rwandan government was 'very critical of [our] criticism of the trials' noting how 'Gahima [the deputy justice minister] was willing to engage in private, [and] he recognised shortcomings but the official discourse was always very negative'.[31]

25 Amnesty International, 'Rwanda. Unfair Trials: Justice Denied' (1997) AFR 47/08/97.

26 Alison Des Forges and Timothy Longman, 'Legal Responses to Genocide in Rwanda' in Eric Stover and Harvey Weinstein (eds), *My Neighbor, My Enemy: Justice and Community in the Aftermath of Mass Atrocity* (CUP 2004) 59–62; Longman (n 24) 285–89; Drumbl (n 24) 600–01; Thierry Cruvellier and Ephrem Rugiririza, 'Rwanda: The Most Judged Genocide in History' (*JusticeInfo*, 4 April 2019) <justiceinfo.net/en/40846-rwanda-the-most-judged-genocide-in-history.html>.

27 Interview with former NGO official, Brussels, Belgium, 17 November 2016. In this sense, see also Amnesty International, 'Rwanda: The Troubled Course of Justice' (2000) AFR 47/015/2000.

28 Interview with NGO official, Brussels, Belgium, 17 November 2016.

29 Interview with former HRFOR official, New York, USA, 8 November 2019.

30 Ian Martin, 'After Genocide: The UN Human Rights Field Operation in Rwanda' in Alice H Henkin (ed), *Honoring Human Rights: From Peace to Justice. Recommendations to the International Community* (Aspen Institute 1998) 111.

31 Interview with former HRFOR official, New York, USA, 14 May 2019. Critically on HRFOR, see Todd A Howland, 'Mirage, Magic, or Mixed Bag? The UN High Commissioner for Human Rights' Field Operation in Rwanda' (1999) 21 Human Rights Quarterly 1, 37–55.

Despite the ICTR's isolation from accountability dynamics in Rwanda, its normative standards eventually filtered into domestic criminal law. When, in 2003, the Rwandan parliament revised the criminal code, the definition of crimes against humanity mirrored the ICTR Statute's definition.[32] By opting for the requirement of discriminatory animus, Rwanda rejected other normative standards, including the Rome Statute's definition, and aligned its legislative framework with Arusha.[33]

2.2. Rule 11*bis* and norm dissemination: catalyst or epiphenomenon?

As explained previously, the ICTR and the Rwandan justice system operated largely in isolation from one another until the Completion Strategy when they suddenly found themselves in a mutually dependent arrangement. To enable referrals under rule 11*bis*, Rwanda adopted a series of transfer laws. In March 2007, Parliament enacted a bill regulating referrals from Arusha.[34] When ICTR chambers rejected the first round of transfers in 2008, Arusha and Rwanda worked together to address outstanding fair trial concerns, including sentencing and detention standards, prompting adjustments to the transfer law in 2009, followed by a consolidated transfer law in 2013.[35]

Untangling the normative foundations of criminal law reform in Rwanda is difficult. While many legislative reforms touched upon international crimes *sensu stricto*, and the rule 11*bis* conditionality scheme affected two areas in particular—the death penalty and defence rights—the transfer process was interwoven with a wider normative overhaul of domestic criminal law, driven by general rule-of-law concerns.[36] A new penal code was enacted in 2012, followed by a new code of criminal procedure in 2013.[37] Not surprisingly, therefore, disagreement exists as to

[32] Loi 33*bis*/2003, reprimant le crime de génocide, les crimes contre l'humanité et les crimes de guerre, art 5 (Journal Officiel, 6 September 2003).

[33] On this requirement, see Robert Cryer and others, *An Introduction to International Criminal Law and Procedure* (2nd edn, CUP 2010) 235.

[34] Organic Law 11/2007 of 16 March 2007 Concerning Transfer of Cases to the Republic of Rwanda from the ICTR and from Other States, Official Gazette, 16 March 2017.

[35] Organic Law 03/2009/OL modifying and complementing the Organic Law 11/2007 of 16/03/2007 concerning the Transfer of Cases to the Republic of Rwanda from the International Criminal Tribunal for Rwanda and from Other States, Official Gazette, 26 May 2009 (2007 Transfer Law). Law 47/2013 relating to Transfer of Cases to Republic of Rwanda, Official Gazette, 16 June 2013 (2013 Transfer Law).

[36] See also Nick Huls, 'Constitutionalism à la Rwandaise' in Maurice Adams, Anne Meuwese and Ernst Hirsch Ballin (eds), *Constitutionalism and the Rule of Law* (CUP 2017).

[37] Organic Law 01/2012/OL of 2 May 2012 instituting the Penal Code, Official Gazette, 14 June 2012; Law 30/2013 of 24/5/2013 relating to the Code of Criminal Procedure, Official Gazette, 8 July 2013. On these legislative reforms, see Yasmine Chubin, 'The Impact of the ICTR 11 Bis Referrals on Rwanda's Legal Reforms, Extradition Requests, and Transfer Case Procedure' (2014) <unictr.irmct.org/en/compendium-legacy-ictr-and-development-international-law>.

whether the ICTR catalysed normative reforms, contributed to the consolidation of ongoing reforms, or was epiphenomenal in Rwanda.

At one end of the spectrum, some emphasize the ICTR's contributions. For instance, Rwanda's transfer laws expressly acknowledge the Tribunal, and some ICTR officials tend to emphasize their 'central role' for certain reforms, for instance tweaks to genocide ideology legislation.[38] But most interviewees—Rwandan and international—agree that normative reforms grew out of an extended process of bilateral deliberation, involving senior and mid-level stakeholders from the ICTR's OTP and Registry, the Rwandan NPPA and justice ministry. For instance, Tharcisse Karugarama, justice minister at the time of the rule 11*bis* negotiations, concluded that the ICTR was 'able to influence our attitudes', acknowledging it 'changed the procedures and laws with respect to many issues' and that such changes 'never could have happened without [a] push for international standards of due process'.[39] Nevertheless, even this reading is contested. As explained by one Rwandan judge, changes were made 'not because the ICTR demanded anything ... at most, we [were] inspired by them'.[40]

2.3. Iteration in action: abolition of the death penalty

Abolition is where the ICTR's influence (or lack thereof) is arguably most contested. A thorny issue in pre-genocide Rwanda, the last death sentence was enforced in 1981. In 1992, President Habyarimana commuted the remaining death sentences to life imprisonment, observing a de facto moratorium on the way to abolition.[41]

Unsurprisingly, the scale and cruelty of the genocide put the death penalty at the centre of Rwanda's accountability response. As seen in Chapter 3, the RPF voted against the ICTR in the Security Council, citing the death penalty's exclusion

[38] Interviews with Rwandan officials in August and September 2015 revealed a range of views, but most acknowledged the ICTR's role in catalysing normative change under r 11*bis*. Only two denied that the ICTR had any influence on normative standards. Interviews with ICTR officials, Arusha, Tanzania, 10 September 2015. Interviews with Rwandan magistrates, Kigali, Rwanda, 11 and 12 August 2015, 8 September 2015.

[39] Phone interview with Tharcisse Karugarama, 12 July 2016. But see Statement by Hon Tharcisse Karugarama, Minister of Justice/Attorney General of Rwanda, UNGA Thematic Debate on the Role of International Criminal Justice in Reconciliation, 9 April 2013 (on file) (critical of ICTR and foreign states' role in Rwanda). For official acknowledgement (albeit with criticism) of ICTR role in normative reforms, see also UNSC S/PV.5904, 4 June 2008, 28 (remarks by Martin Ngoga). Martin Ngoga, 'The ICTR Completion Process and Resultant Consequences on Rwanda's Justice System' *New Times Rwanda* (24 October 2008) <newtimes.co.rw/section/read/5493>.

[40] Interview with Rwandan judge, Kigali, Rwanda, 9 September 2015.

[41] William A Schabas, *The Abolition of the Death Penalty in International Law* (3rd edn, CUP 2002) 250–51. On the history of the death penalty in Rwanda, see also Aimé M Karimunda, 'The Death Penalty in Rwanda: Surrounding Politics and the ICTR's Battle for Abolition' in Madoka Futamura and Nadia Bernaz (eds), *The Politics of the Death Penalty in Countries in Transition* (2014) 135.

from its Statute. Rwandans anticipated, correctly, that the absence of capital punishment in Arusha would create a sentencing paradox: lower-level suspects tried in Rwandan courts faced, in some cases mandatory, death sentences, whereas the genocide masterminds risked 'only' life imprisonment.[42] According to some, the RPF's efforts to apprehend 'big fish' fugitives beyond its borders can be explained in part by a desire to deprive the genocide masterminds of 'luxury' conditions in Arusha'.[43]

Although it remained on the books for ordinary crimes such as murder, it was unclear initially how the 1996 organic law would regulate the death penalty. Ultimately, RPF hardliners prevailed, arguing that severe punishments were necessary to prevent similar crimes in the future and the organic law made the death sentence mandatory for category 1 offenders.[44] Yet, while several hundred people were sentenced to death in the first few years, executions took place only once. In April 1998, in different parts of the country, Rwandan authorities publicly executed twenty-two people in football stadiums. Among those executed was Karamira, whom Prosecutor Goldstone 'surrendered' in 1996.[45] An outcry ensued, with the UN, foreign embassies, and human rights groups all condemning the executions. Mary Robinson, then High Commissioner for Human Rights was 'deeply disturbed, and even shocked'.[46]

Following the executions, the entire Rwandan justice sector came under scrutiny from international partners. Although the government publicly dismissed this criticism, it likely had an effect on the political establishment. One activist noted that 'Rwanda's "we don't care what you think" attitude softened considerably after the backlash'.[47] Although no immediate push for abolition ensued, the executions may have amplified splits within the RPF and further executions were put on hold. Analysing the Rwandan authorities' motives, Mark Drumbl concluded that they had 'decided that this particularly retributive sanction no longer promote[d] the goals of genocide prosecutions', although other 'influential' reasons included 'the international community's condemnation of the death penalty, the scepticism of transnational nongovernmental and donor organizations, and the ICTR's position that it will not transfer any cases to the domestic Rwandan authorities where the accused could face the death penalty'.[48]

[42] Audrey Boctor, 'The Abolition of the Death Penalty in Rwanda' (2009) 10 Human Rights Review 99, 102–04. On 'anomalies of inversion', see Madeline Morris, 'The Trials of Concurrent Jurisdiction: The Case of Rwanda' (1997) 7 Duke Journal of Comparative & International Law 349, 371–72.

[43] Interview with NGO official, Brussels, Belgium, 16 November 2016.

[44] Schabas (n 22) 895; Karimunda (n 41) 141–45; Boctor (n 42) 105–06.

[45] Colin M Waugh, *Paul Kagame and Rwanda: Power, Genocide and the Rwandan Patriotic Front* (McFarland 2004) 173–74; Schabas (n 41) 358.

[46] OHCHR, Statement by High Commissioner on executions in Rwanda, 23 April 1998.

[47] Phone interview with activist, 11 May 2017. See also Nicola Palmer, *Courts in Conflict: Interpreting the Layers of Justice in Post-Genocide Rwanda* (OUP 2015) 46. For Rwandan reactions, see also Sigall Horovitz, 'International Criminal Courts in Action: The ICTR's Effect on Death Penalty and Reconciliation in Rwanda' (2016) 48 George Washington International Law Review 505, 515–17.

[48] Drumbl (n 12) 74.

With the death penalty remaining on the books for ordinary crimes and for senior genocide suspects, abolition re-merged as a flashpoint during the rule 11*bis* process. To be eligible to receive cases under rule 11*bis*, all states had to satisfy fair trial conditions. Abolition, however, was particularly onerous for Rwanda. As early as October 2003, the ICTR President, Erik Møse, warned that '[a]t the moment, transfer is made difficult by the fact that Rwandan law prescribes the death penalty as a sentence for certain crimes'.[49] In 2005, the ICTR plenary of judges amended rule 11*bis* to clarify that fair trial included the express condition that a receiving country would not execute defendants.[50] Subsequent Completion Strategy reports, public statements from the ICTR's leadership, and the case law underscored that the death penalty was a non-negotiable impediment to transfers.[51] Given the narrow pool of states willing to entertain rule 11*bis* referrals—in effect, a few European countries and Rwanda—the message was addressed to the RPF.

While Rwanda made no secret of its willingness to receive cases, capital punishment remained a divisive issue among the political elite. Some favoured immediate abolition, others wanted to limit the applicability of the death penalty, while yet others argued the death penalty should be maintained.[52] Against the backdrop of these debates, the first transfer law established life imprisonment as the maximum punishment for ICTR referrals specifically; however, the death penalty remained on the books for other suspects.[53] Yet, just four months later, in July 2007, Parliament abolished the death penalty altogether and, in 2008, Rwanda ratified the Optional Protocol to the ICCPR on abolition of the death penalty.[54]

The decision to abolish the death penalty was contentious inside Rwanda, one of only two countries in the subregion to have taken this step (Burundi being the other).[55] There are divergent views on the extent to which abolition can be traced to rule 11*bis*. Some suggest that abolition grew organically from Rwanda's other rule-of-law reforms. As explained by one Rwandan judge, abolition was 'a homegrown process' in line with Rwanda's broader 'embrace of human rights'.[56]

[49] Report on the ICTR Completion Strategy (6 October 2003) S/2003/946, para 23.

[50] Rule 11*bis*, amendments adopted at the 15th Plenary Session of the Judges, 21 May 2005.

[51] TC, *Prosecutor v Bagaragaza* (Decision on Prosecution's Motion for Referral to the Kingdom of Norway) ICTR-2005-86-R11bis (19 May 2006) para 7; *Report on the ICTR Completion Strategy* (3 May 2004) S/2004/341, para 38; *Report on the ICTR Completion Strategy* (22 November 2004) S/2004/921, para 38.

[52] For an insight into these divisions, see Horovitz (n 47).

[53] Organic Law 11/2007 of 16 March 2007, arts 21 (and 24), Concerning Transfer of Cases to the Republic of Rwanda from the ICTR and from Other States, Official Gazette, 16 March 2017. For details, see Boctor (n 42) 107–09; Horovitz (n 47). As explained in Chapter 3, lingering concerns about solitary confinement blocked the transfer of cases until 2011.

[54] Organic Law 31/2007 of 25 July 2007 Relating to the Abolition of the Death Penalty, Official Gazette Special No of 25 July 2007; Jamil Ddamulira Mujuzi, 'Steps Taken in Rwanda's Efforts to Qualify for the Transfer of Accused from the ICTR' (2010) 8 Journal of International Criminal Justice 237.

[55] HRW, 'Burundi: l'Assemblée nationale abolit la peine de mort et criminalise la torture' (3 December 2008) <hrw.org/fr/news/2008/12/03/burundi-lassemblee-nationale-abolit-la-peine-de-mort-et-criminalise-la-torture>.

[56] Interview with Rwandan judge, Kigali, Rwanda, 8 September 2015.

Similarly, according to Audrey Boctor, 'Rwanda's experience points to the potential that [ICTs] have to force the death penalty debate into the spotlight' but 'that the outcome of the debate ultimately depends on local, not international, forces'.[57]

Others disagree. Karimunda, the Supreme Court judge who also wrote a book on the death penalty, disputes the notion that the death penalty was on its way out and suggests that '[w]ithout the ICTR's insistence, Rwanda would probably still be a retentionist state'.[58] Emphasizing the ICTR's transformative role, Karimunda points to, among other things, active efforts to broaden the applicability of the death penalty prior to 2007. Similarly, drawing on interviews in Rwanda, Sigall Horovitz explains that '[m]ost interviewees felt that Rwanda abolished the death penalty to satisfy the ICTR's referral conditions, even though these conditions merely demanded that the penalty be excluded from transferred cases and not from all cases' and that 'it seems reasonable to conclude that while national dynamics may partly explain the death penalty abolition, the ICTR's referral requirements tipped the scales in favour of abolition'.[59] While this book does not attempt to resolve this question one way or the other, the better view seems to be that abolition would not have occurred when it did without the ICTR.

2.4. Normative mix(-up)? A common law fair trial in the civil law's shadow

As a former German and Belgian colony, Rwanda's legal system at the time of the genocide was based on the continental 'civil law' model, with French serving as its primary working language. However, after 1994, the country's new political elite drawn from the RPF, a rebel group originating in Uganda, gradually imposed English as an official language alongside Kinyarwanda. Over the years, a range of common law imports have influenced the normative landscape, some of which can be traced to the ICTR and its rule 11*bis* process.[60]

As noted in Chapter 5, defence rights were a core concern for human rights organizations involved with the early genocide trials. Under the 1977 procedural code, accused enjoyed few due process safeguards.[61] After the specialized chambers integrated foreign attorneys, the lack of defence rights became a key criticism of the *gacaca* process, which ignored the usual procedural safeguards altogether.

[57] Boctor (n 42) 118.

[58] Karimunda (n 41) 151. See also Aimé Muyoboke Karimunda, *The Death Penalty in Africa: The Path towards Abolition* (Routledge 2014).

[59] Sigall Horovitz, 'How International Courts Shape Domestic Justice: Lessons from Rwanda and Sierra Leone' (2013) 46 Israel Law Review 339, 349–51; see also Horovitz (n 47) 520–30.

[60] Rwanda joined the East African Community and the British Commonwealth in 2007 and 2009 respectively, contributing to the mainstreaming of English-inspired principles. See Huls (n 36) 218–19.

[61] Peter H Sennett and Gregory P Noone, 'Working with Rwanda toward the Domestic Prosecution of Genocide Crimes' (1997) 12 St John's Journal of Legal Commentary 425, 445–46.

Given this chequered history, the fair trial rights of rule 11*bis* defendants—fugitives who had escaped the country in 1994, and whose guilt was largely taken for granted inside Rwanda—were bound to be contentious.

Unlike abolition of the death penalty, where the ICTR's demands were clear, 'ensuring the right to a fair trial', as mandated by rule 11*bis*, was open to interpretation. To meet this standard, Rwanda focused on legislative tweaks to bring its laws in line with international standards, often with the help of external experts who even rewrote drafts of legislative texts.[62] Three main areas underwent reform.

First, the transfer laws guaranteed certain defence rights—for instance, the right to a public hearing; to be informed of the charges; or to appeal—and immunity for defence counsel and witnesses from search, seizure, arrest, and detention.[63] Second, the transfer laws adjusted Rwanda's evidentiary procedures, with suspects enjoying a right to 'examine or have a person to examine on [their] behalf witnesses against [them]' and 'to obtain the attendance and examination of witnesses on [their] behalf under the same conditions as witnesses against [them]'.[64] In practice, this created a presumption that witness testimony was required at trial, whereas under Rwanda's civil law procedure, witness statements could be entered into the trial record without in-court appearances.[65] Third, to address concerns that exculpatory witness testimony during genocide trials might violate genocide denial laws, the transfer law clarified that 'no person shall be criminally liable for anything said or done in the course of a trial'.[66] Although the genocide ideology law was reformed to this effect, the 2012 penal code still criminalizes genocide denial, revisionism and ideology, creating difficulties in practice.[67]

Other areas of Rwandan practice have also been shaped more or less directly by the ICTR. For instance, a Rwandan prosecutor explained that the NPPA's policy was to use ICTR jurisprudence in all genocide cases, not just those transferred from the ICTR, even though this was not legally required.[68] In practice, applying ICTR-inspired norms has not been without its problems, with magistrates and attorneys struggling to adapt Rwanda's (civil law) inquisitorial proceedings to adversarial features of a (common law) fair trial, such as calling witnesses, challenging evidence in court, or cross-examining witnesses. As noted by one Rwandan

[62] Interview with Rwandan judicial official, Kigali, Rwanda, 12 August 2015.

[63] 2013 Transfer Law, arts 14, 15, and 17; 2007 Transfer Law, arts 13–15. Some rights were already guaranteed by the 2003 Constitution and the 1977 Code of Criminal Procedure.

[64] 2013 Transfer Law, art 14(9)–(10); 2007 Transfer Law, art 13(9)–(10).

[65] Chubin (n 37) 7; 2013 Transfer Law, art 8 ('shall not convict a person solely on prior written statements of witnesses who did not give oral evidence during the trial').

[66] 2013 Transfer Law, art 14. See ICTR–OTP, 'Complementarity in Action: Lessons Learned from the ICTR Prosecutor's Referral of International Criminal Cases to National Jurisdictions for Trial' (ICTR OTP 2015) para 62.

[67] Law 84/2013 on the Crime of Genocide Ideology and Other Related Offences, Official Gazette of Rwanda, 11 September 2013. Genocide denial and revisionism is listed as an international crime (2012 Penal Code, art 116).

[68] Interview with Rwandan prosecutor, Kigali, Rwanda, 11 August 2015.

judge, 'calling witnesses as a requirement makes no sense for [the] Rwandan civil law system where [investigative] judges already have a file ... the penal code has been adjusted for the sake of harmonisation ... [but] we are confusing systems'.[69]

Even the ICTR, which has generally emphasized its positive legacy for the Rwandan justice system, acknowledges the challenges of transplanting foreign procedures. In its 2015 Completion report, the OTP notes that 'the referral of international cases to national jurisdictions does not require the wholesale incorporation of international laws and practices into domestic systems'.[70] Asked to assess these challenges, an OTP official was more blunt: 'it's like putting a square peg through a round hole, we have a hybrid system that becomes dysfunctional ... this is a form of neocolonialism ... [there] can't be imposition of common law on a system that operates according to a different logic'.[71]

Opinions vary on how sustainable the infiltration of rule 11*bis* principles will be for the Rwandan justice sector. Most rule 11*bis* reforms were initially restricted to genocide trials before the High Court chambers, but Rwandan attorneys and magistrates have also used these procedures in cases of extradition and deportation from North America and Europe.[72] While some practitioners suggest that 'ICTR-inspired' norms will eventually filter into everyday practice, others underscore the *sui generis* nature of genocide trials and complain about the 'unsustainability' of 'ICTR-imposed' procedures.[73]

To some extent, disagreement over ICTR-induced normative changes mirrors a divide between civil—and common law-trained lawyers, which in turn reflects divisions between French-speaking magistrates and a younger generation of English-speaking and sometimes foreign trained jurists (some of whom also spent time in Arusha). While a French-speaking Rwandan judge noted, with dismay, that 'the civil law lost', others remain more circumspect.[74] It may simply be too early to draw firm conclusions about the possible vernacularization of Rwandan criminal law under the ICTR's shadow.

2.5. In the ICTR's shadow: what counts as a fair domestic trial?

Beginning in 2011, the ICTR approved the transfer of several cases for prosecution in Rwanda. Unlike the rule 11*bis* case law, the ensuing domestic proceedings have elicited limited scholarly analysis. Yet Rwanda's rule 11*bis* trials are a litmus

[69] Interview with Rwandan judge, Kigali, Rwanda, 11 August 2015.
[70] ICTR–OTP (n 66) para 10.
[71] Interview with OTP official, Arusha, Tanzania, 10 September 2015.
[72] Interviews with Rwandan magistrate and justice official, Kigali, Rwanda, 11 and 12 August 2015.
[73] Interviews with Rwandan magistrates and international experts, Kigali, Rwanda and by phone and over e-mail, August 2015, 2 December 2016 and January 2021.
[74] Interview with Rwandan magistrates, Kigali, Rwanda, 8 and 11 and 19 August 2015.

test of domestic accountability transpiring in the shadow of ICTs. Not only do the referrals raise questions about the substantive standards that states ought to apply in domestic proceedings, but the referrals also raises questions about who should evaluate domestic practice—and how should this be done.

Against the backdrop of Rwanda's post-genocide transition, the ICTR had to assess whether, despite the increasingly centralized rule of the RPF Tutsi elite, the justice system was sufficiently independent to provide justice to Hutu defendants. Unlike the ICC, which may assess 'genuineness', the ICTR had the more intrusive task of determining the 'fairness' of Rwandan trials. As reflected in the rule 11*bis* case law, examined in Chapter 3, what counts as 'fair' is open to interpretation. The OTP would later note, 'there [are] no established methods for demonstrating that fair trial rights were available in practice'.[75]

Against the backdrop of common/civil law hybridization, the ICTR monitored compliance with fair trial standards to assess potential challenges from defendants like Uwinkindi who could petition to have their referrals revoked. In line with a two-pronged approach, groups of monitors observed domestic proceedings and then reported their findings, separately, to Arusha. On one hand, the OTP monitors, who had argued for case referrals in collaboration with the Rwandan prosecution service, sought to identify and pre-empt potential problems with case revocations; on the other hand, ICTR judges contracted out their monitoring duties to nominally independent NGOs. In reality, a third group shadowed the ICTR monitors: embassies in Kigali followed the trials to assess whether pending extradition requests from Rwanda could be approved in their home countries.[76]

Interviews with trial observers reveal starkly divergent interpretations of the same sociolegal reality. At one extreme, the ICTR–OTP, a party with a vested interest in ensuring that Rwanda retained jurisdiction over the rule 11*bis* cases, endorsed a hands-off, non-interventionist approach to monitoring, understood as 'observing [but] not interfering', where revocations for fair trial violations were a 'drastic step' and 'a remedy of last resort'.[77] In line with this approach, one ICTR official argued that he had a solid understanding of Rwandan realities, having spoken to various domestic stakeholders, ranging from foreign diplomats to Rwandan judges, prosecutors, and prison wardens. He emphasized that '[our] job was not about passing judgment on the whole legal system but giving facts about the case and leaving interpretation to the judges'.[78]

[75] ICTR–OTP (n 66) 28.

[76] Interviews with diplomats and former ICTR officials, Kigali, Rwanda, Arusha, Tanzania and by phone, 14 August, 10 and 15 September 2015, 16 October and 14 November 2016 and 16 January 2017.

[77] ICTR–OTP (n 66) paras 153, 160, and 167; ICTR President, Guidelines on Monitoring Trials Referred to National Jurisdictions under Rule 11*bis* by ICTR Staff Monitors, 29 June 2012, ICTR-01-75-R11*bis* (based on the principles of non-intervention in the judicial process, objectivity, and harmonization).

[78] Phone interview with former ICTR official, 15 September 2016.

However, most trial monitors expressed a more nuanced vision of their roles and of Rwandan realities. Noting the limited time that monitors spent in Rwanda (usually only several days at a time) and their lack of Kinyarwanda language skills (making it impossible to follow in-court exchanges without the help of translators), one official explained that the ICTR's focus on the trial itself missed the point of observation. They explained:[79]

> you can't get any real impression of meeting the judges, they are all smart and well spoken but none of this means anything in a dictatorship with no culture of independence ... it is hard to expect the judiciary to be somehow independent of [president] Kagame ... the key issue is also that the trial itself is not the real problem, what matters is what leads up to the trial, picking the judges ... and the defence attorneys and [deciding on] their access to funding.

Noting how high-ranking Rwandan officials preselected the magistrates who would participate in ICTR training, an international expert acknowledged that the selection process of judges sitting on rule 11*bis* cases was likely political.[80]

Trial monitoring was beset by other problems. NGO observers sent to Kigali on behalf of ICTR chambers faced logistical and financial problems, including high staff turnover, a lack of adequate language skills, and poor monitoring experience. Some monitors also noted inherent 'conflicts of interest' in the monitoring process. Reiterating critiques raised by defence counsel in Rwanda, two monitors explained that one of their colleagues was removed after writing a critical report (which remains confidential and has never been published) that challenged the prevailing narrative of Rwanda's respect towards fair trial standards. ICTR officials explained that reports became more positive after this 'staff reshuffle'.[81] Others noted that ICTR chambers seemed unwilling to give NGOs too much space, lest the judges be confronted with findings that created too many problems for the Tribunal. One monitor asked rhetorically: 'How much did the ICTR [really] want to know?'[82]

An international expert who spent years in Rwanda emphasized that the 'big concern ... in genocide cases [is] the shared culture of the judges, prosecutors ... there is an official narrative that is enshrined in the law and you can't question it, so it's very difficult to move beyond that'.[83] Yet monitors conceded that ICTR leadership viewed such contextual information as exceeding the scope of their monitoring mandate, which was interpreted as a 'box-ticking exercise' for specific

[79] ibid. In this vein, see also Lars Waldorf, '"A Mere Pretense of Justice": Complementarity, Sham Trials, and Victor's Justice at the Rwanda Tribunal' (2011) 33 Fordham International Law Journal 1221, 1270.

[80] Phone interview with international adviser, 2 December 2016.

[81] Interviews with former ICTR officials, by phone and Arusha, Tanzania 15 September and 16 October 2016.

[82] Phone interview with former ICTR official, 15 September 2016.

[83] Phone interview with international adviser, 2 December 2016.

fair trial rights.[84] Reflecting on these challenges, one monitor concluded, 'this is sensitive . . . the [Rwandan] court pretty skilfully created the illusion of carrying out proceedings in line with basic standards'.[85]

Given these challenges, it is no surprise that ICTR judges struggled to make sense of whether proceedings in Rwanda should be characterized as 'fair'. Although international judges had some reservations about Rwandan proceedings, revocation petitions from defendants alleging fair trial violations have all failed.[86] But interviews with trial monitors reveal ambivalence as well, none of whom suggested that fair trial violations meant that rule 11*bis* defendants should escape conviction. Verbalizing the dilemma of flawed trials occurring against the backdrop of extreme criminality, one expert explained:[87]

> there are some brave judges and lawyers, and the regime is actually motivated to do these trials fairly . . . Bandora . . . did get acquitted on some charges. This is significant . . . the judges said there just wasn't evidence to back up the charges. At the same time, of course some cases are just too hot to take. No one is ever going to be acquitted in Rwanda but this is not the biggest problem for me . . . [the problem is that] rule 11*bis* has not really led to capacity building, and trials are actually less fair, so legacy talk is completely disconnected from reality.

As illustrated by this comment, one concern seems to be the nominal hybridization of Rwandan criminal proceedings. While 'common law' due process principles may increase 'fairness' on paper, Rwandan defence counsel unfamiliar with, for instance, the art of cross-examination may, in fact, find it harder to defend their clients than under procedural rules they apply in domestic proceedings on a regular basis.[88] Ultimately, however, genocide trials in Rwanda point to a greater dilemma: by what standards should 'fairness' be judged and, by the same token, what is the alternative if a state's justice system cannot escape the political and cultural context surrounding certain types of criminality?

As Rwanda continues to request extraditions and deportations around the world, other states struggle with these questions. In 2015, a court in The Hague approved one extradition request, paving the way for further extraditions from the

[84] Phone interview with former ICTR official, 15 September 2016.

[85] Phone interview with former monitor, 14 November 2016.

[86] For instance, after protracted litigation, the chamber that had authorised Uwinkindi's transfer in 2011 declined to revoke his case in 2015. See Oliver Windridge, 'Gone But Not Forgotten—The Ongoing Case of Jean Uwinkindi at the ICTR and MICT' (*Opinio Juris*, 29 July 2015) <opiniojuris.org/2015/07/29/guest-post-gone-but-not-forgotten-the-ongoing-case-of-jean-uwinkindi-at-the-ictr-and-mict/>; Emmanuel Sehene Ruvugiro, 'In Rwanda, the Surprising Confessions of Bernard Munyagishari' (*JusticeInfo*, 20 April 2021) <justiceinfo.net/en/76230-rwanda-surprising-confessions-bernard-munyagishari.html>.

[87] Interview with foreign adviser and e-mail exchanges, undisclosed location, 26 January 2018 and January 2021.

[88] Interview with Rwandan officials, foreign experts, and e-mail exchanges, 2015–21.

Netherlands.[89] Two years later, the UK High Court declined an extradition because trials in Rwanda were deemed unfair.[90] Compounding the paradox, the judges in both cases relied on (conflicting) testimony from the same experts. While partly reflecting the peculiarities of the civil and common law systems, these conflicting rulings illustrate the challenge of establishing what amounts to a fair trial, by what standards fairness should be judged, and the limits of insisting on fair trial rights in the face of serious crimes.[91] Given that the British legal system does not allow prosecutions of genocide pre-dating its own legislation from 2001, the Rwandan suspects residing in the UK effectively benefit from impunity.[92]

2.6. Unpacking primacy's effects on norm internalization

The normative landscape in Rwanda has been overhauled since 1994. Confronted with mass crimes, Rwandan authorities initially implemented legislative reforms to cope with mass prosecutions. Although its influence has varied over time, the ICTR eventually contributed to the hybridization of a traditionally civil law-based criminal justice system with common law principles, especially by mainstreaming fair trial principles towards the end of its mandate.

Yet beyond Rwanda's nominal compliance with international standards, it is less clear to what extent reforms have impacted the fairness of genocide trials. Some scholars are optimistic. For instance, Alhagi Marong and Charles Jalloh argue that '[t]he jurisprudence on referral of cases to Rwanda, illustrates how international institutions' can 'positively influence domestic legal systems'.[93] Drawing on the concept of legacy, Adama Dieng, a former ICTR registrar, goes further and suggests that the Tribunal was 'a role model for the promotion of justice and accountability

[89] Hague Court, *State v claimants*, C/09/494258/KG ZA 15/1217 (27 November 2015).

[90] UK High Court, *Government of Rwanda v. Nteziryayo, Brown, Munyaneza, Mutabaruka, Ugirashebuja* [28 July 2017] EWHC 1912. For more on extraditions to Rwanda, see Nicola Palmer, 'International Criminal Law and Border Control: The Expressive Role of the Deportation and Extradition of Genocide Suspects to Rwanda' (2020) 33 Leiden Journal of International Law 789.

[91] Critically on the UK's original declination, see Mark A Drumbl, 'Prosecution of Genocide v. the Fair Trial Principle: Comments on Brown and Others v. The Government of Rwanda and the UK Secretary of State for the Home Department' (2010) 8 Journal of International Criminal Justice 289. But see Tjitske Lingsma, 'Rwanda Opereert Zoals Oost-Duitsland Met de Stasi' *De Groene Amsterdamer* (6 April 2022) <groene.nl/artikel/rwanda-opereert-zoals-oost-duitsland-met-de-stasi>; Abdil L Dahir, 'Rwandan Court Declines to Extend Sentence for Paul Rusesabagina' *New York Times* (4 April 2022) <nytimes.com/2022/04/04/world/africa/rwanda-paul-rusesabagina-sentence.html>.

[92] On this dilemma, see Drumbl (n 91) 301–04.

[93] Alhagi BM Marong and Charles C Jalloh, 'Transfer of Cases under the Jurisprudence of the ICTR and Lessons Learnt for the ICC' in Alhagi BM Marong and Charles C Jalloh, *Promoting Accountability under International Law for Gross Human Rights Violations in Africa: Essays in Honour of Prosecutor Hassan Bubacar Jallow* (Martinus Nijhoff 2015) 438; see also Padraig McAuliffe, 'Bad Analogy: Why the Divergent Institutional Imperatives of the Ad Hoc Tribunals and the ICC Make the Lessons of Rule 11 Bis Inapplicable to the ICC's Complementarity Regime' (2015) 11 International Organizations Law Review 345, 406–13.

and exporting its knowledge and lessons learned to all sectors of the Rwandan population and across the African continent'.[94]

Despite such laudatory reviews, the ability of Rwanda's justice system to provide fair trials remains contested as are the human rights credentials of the RPF generally. In the 1990s, the RPF's willingness to comply with human rights became a major challenge for NGOs, donors, and the UN. Although early advocacy campaigns yielded some successes, notably the integration of defence counsel in genocide trials, international leverage diminished over time. While Rwandan justice actors implemented reforms with the support—but not at the behest—of international partners, the centralization of the RPF's power dovetailed with an increasingly antagonistic stance to external oversight, culminating in HRFOR's expulsion and the subsequent creation of *gacaca* courts.

Although these dynamics changed when the Completion Strategy created space for dialogue in the mid-2000s, the significance of rule 11*bis* lies in the details of its conditionality scheme, which—contrary to the Rome Statute—had a human rights-based framework to guide negotiations over case distribution, monitoring and revocation. Rule 11*bis* did not force Rwandan authorities to enact progressive legislation, but questions about the fairness of trials did foster contestation within the political elite and empowered some actors to advocate controversial reforms. In this regard, the prospect of referrals likely encouraged or accelerated abolition of the death penalty while helping mainstream some due process norms. While it was not the sole catalyst for abolition or the admixture of fair trial safeguards, the ICTR amplified and solidified these normative trends, with the Registry, OTP, and judges providing training and advice, as seen in Chapter 5. If nothing else, therefore, the ICTR experience suggests that sensitive reforms like the death penalty may benefit from the direct involvement of ICTs.

That being said, while the ICTR's contribution to post-genocide justice is usually equated with the production or domestication of international criminal norms, the rule 11*bis* experiment with human rights conditionality places front and centre the question of how norm dissemination relates to norm internalization and how procedural changes relate to substantive outcomes. Whatever one thinks of the ICTR's rule 11*bis* jurisprudence, its effects on domestic accountability are not just a function of *whether* and *how* international norms were adopted but also *why* and *to what end* Rwanda appropriated these standards. Put differently, did incorporating fair trial principles into the Rwandan legal order produce different substantive—as opposed to procedural—outcomes in its domestic trials?

In this regard, international criminal law exhibits something of a blind spot. Aside from a few transitional justice analyses of Rwanda's post-genocide transition, the ICTR's impact on domestic accountability, including its referrals and

[94] Adama Dieng, 'Capacity-Building Efforts of the ICTR: A Different Kind of Legacy' (2011) 9 Northwestern Journal of International Human Rights 403, 421.

monitoring of fair trial standards, illustrates the limitations of existing scholarship on the aims and justifications of ICTs.[95] The ICTR's (eventually) deferential, 'box-ticking' approach to the realities of domestic trials in Rwanda—similar to Prosecutor Jallow's disregard of *Kabgayi*'s flaws, seen in Chapter 4—underscores that not only are best practices for trial observation in short supply; there is also little agreement on the role of ICTs in monitoring, questioning, and legitimating domestic trials.

With the success of ICTs still measured by 'completed' international (and, to a lesser extent, domestic) trials rather than a critical analysis of their benefits for conflict-affected societies, international civil servants lack incentives to challenge governments or domestic practices. In that sense, a holistic sociolegal inquiry into the legacy of ICTs is usually subordinated to easily measurable outcomes, such as numbers of convictions or types of domesticated norms. As one activist noted perspicaciously in Kigali, 'my conclusion so far of Rwandan domestic reforms is that it has been pretty successful … [but] so what [that] it's effective if this in no way changes the overarching political dynamics in Rwanda which are firmly on the side of the government?'.[96] As this comment underscores, to what extent ICTs are able to act as a counter-hegemonic and emancipatory force in transitional societies is contested.

3. The Special Court for Sierra Leone

3.1. Charging domestic crimes: a missed opportunity for iteration?

Similar to Rwanda, where normative gaps initially foreclosed genocide trials, Sierra Leone's accountability policy was defined, in part, by its legislative landscape. As Kabbah observed in his original request to create the Special Court, 'gaps in Sierra Leonean criminal law', including its failure to criminalize '[crimes] against humanity and some of the gross human rights abuses' prevented national authorities from prosecuting civil war atrocities.[97] Yet, unlike the ICTR, the SCSL took cognizance of domestic realities through its hybrid design. It was hoped that the SCSL, by enabling prosecutions of 'ordinary' Sierra Leonean crimes, might allow national prosecutors to follow its example and bring analogous charges domestically.[98] Moreover, SCSL judges were expected to consider national 'practices

[95] But see Longman (n 24) 120; Palmer (n 47).

[96] Interview with activist, Kigali, Rwanda, 14 August 2015.

[97] Alhaji A Tejan Kabbah, 'Letter Dated 12 June 2000, with an Enclosure, from the President of the Republic of Sierra Leone, to the President of the [UNSC] on the Proposed Special Court for Sierra Leone [Letter Annexed to Letter Dated 9 August 2000 from the Permanent Representative of Sierra Leone]' S/2000/786.

[98] SCSL Statute, art 5.

regarding prison sentences', which could promote cross-fertilization of sentencing standards.[99]

These expectations of normative iteration, or the SCSL's 'demonstration effect', did not come to pass.[100] For all the talk of hybridity, the prosecutor never attempted to charge any domestic crimes due to several reasons. First, there was a lack of familiarity with Sierra Leonean criminal law, as most OTP leadership positions were staffed by foreign experts, especially in the start-up phase when charging decisions were made. Second, domestic crimes were not considered 'grave' enough to merit inclusion. Third, the OTP made a strategic decision to avoid domestic charges, lest defendants be able to litigate their convictions based on national law, including the Lomé amnesty.[101] As David Crane observed later, 'I chose not to get the Sierra Leonean system involved ... I wanted to avoid that'.[102]

Similar isolation transpired in regard to sentencing. While some SCSL judges acknowledged article 19(1) of the Statute, their decisions prioritized international case law and ignored domestic practice, due partly to a lack of 'well-developed and consistent' sentencing standards in Sierra Leone.[103] As noted by Margaret deGuzman, by relying on 'the ICTY and ICTR for guidance on the goals of sentencing', the SCSL 'adopted a strongly international orientation in its sentencing jurisprudence ... [and] missed an opportunity to explore the tensions inherent in its hybrid structure'.[104]

In the end, while it is generally acknowledged that the SCSL contributed to the development of international criminal law, notably for child recruitment and forced marriage, it had less impact on Sierra Leonean law and practice. Noting a 'missed opportunity', a former SCSL official explained that Sierra Leonean officials at the SCSL had unsuccessfully pushed for the prosecution of domestic offences for their 'precedential value', and that national courts could have 'piggy-backed' on the Special Court's potentially broader interpretation of Sierra Leonean law.[105] Similarly, former justice minister, Franklyn Kargbo, explained that, while he

[99] ibid art 19(1).

[100] Thierry Cruvellier, 'From the Taylor Trial to a Lasting Legacy: Putting the Special Court Model to the Test' (ICTJ 2009) 28; Alejandro Chehtman, 'Developing Local Capacity for War Crimes Trials: Insights from BiH, Sierra Leone, and Colombia' (2013) 49 Stanford Journal of International Law 297, 317.

[101] Interviews with former SCSL and RSCSL officials, The Hague, Netherlands, Freetown, Sierra Leone and by phone, 11 March and 19 November 2016 and 7 July 2017. Sara Kendall and Michelle Staggs, 'From Mandate to Legacy: The Special Court for Sierra Leone as a Model for "Hybrid Justice"' (War Crimes Studies Center Berkeley 2005) 7.

[102] Phone interview with David Crane, 25 February 2022.

[103] Mohamed A Bangura, 'Delivering International Criminal Justice at the Special Court for Sierra Leone: How Much Is Enough?' in Charles C Jalloh, *The Sierra Leone Special Court and Its Legacy* (CUP 2013) 719; Yuval Shany, 'How Can International Criminal Courts Have a Greater Impact on National Criminal Proceedings? Lessons from the First Two Decades of International Criminal Justice in Operation' (2013) 46 Israel Law Review 431, 441.

[104] Margaret M deGuzman, 'The Sentencing Legacy of the Special Court for Sierra Leone' in Charles C Jalloh (ed), *The Sierra Leone Special Court and Its Legacy* (CUP 2013) 382 and 384.

[105] Interview with Sierra Leone attorney, Cape Town, South Africa, 23 March 2016.

understood the SCSL's reluctance to charge Sierra Leone's 'archaic' laws, this would have created an incentive to 'update our laws'.[106]

That said, many Sierra Leonean actors actively separated themselves from the SCSL, decreasing the scope for normative cross-fertilization. The Supreme Court's affirmation—in response to a challenge from three SCSL defendants—that that the SCSL was not part of the Sierra Leonean judiciary 'as established by the Constitution', is seen as an overly broad precedent that reduced the prospect of SCSL jurisprudence influencing domestic case law.[107] By emphasizing that SCSL decisions did not bind national courts, the Supreme Court arguably stated more than was necessary and, in doing so, discouraged an exchange of standards. As noted by Horovitz, '[w]hile this decision may have contributed to the Special Court's acceptance in Sierra Leone, it also sent a message to the public that the Court is an external entity to Sierra Leone'.[108] Unlike the ICTR, where rule 11*bis* ensured points of interaction with domestic authorities, both the SCSL (as in its amnesty decision examined in Chapter 4) and the Sierra Leonean judiciary seem to have prevented such linkages from emerging in the first place.[109]

3.2. Domesticating international crimes: international indifference, domestic obstinance, or calculated neglect?

While it is often argued that the Special Court was created because Sierra Leonean courts lacked jurisdiction over war crimes and crimes against humanity to hold perpetrators accountable, the reality is more complex. As a dualist state, where international law is not a direct source of law, Sierra Leone is required to domesticate international norms through implementing legislation.[110] Although the Sierra Leonean Parliament's failure to domesticate treaties has been a recurring problem, one set of war crimes—the 1949 Geneva Conventions' grave breaches—was criminalized by colonial legislation (pre-dating independence in 1961) at the time of the civil war,[111] which means that national courts could have exercised jurisdiction over grave breaches.[112]

[106] Interview with Franklyn Kargbo, Freetown, Sierra Leone, 14 March 2016. See also Horovitz (n 59) 357.

[107] Supreme Court of Sierra Leone, *Issa Sesay & ors v President of the Special Court for Sierra Leone and ors* (Original Application) SC no 1/2003, ILDC 199 (14 October 2005) para 34.

[108] Sigall Horovitz, 'Sierra Leone: Interaction between International and National Responses to the Mass Atrocities' (DOMAC 2009) 47.

[109] For the Appeals Chamber's amnesty decision, see Chapter 4, section 3.3 in this volume.

[110] Mohamed Suma, 'Sierra Leone. Justice Sector and the Rule of Law. A Review by AfriMAP and the Open Society Initiative for West Africa' (Open Society Foundations 2014) 28–31.

[111] ibid 4 and 23.

[112] William A Schabas, 'Amnesty, the Sierra Leone Truth and Reconciliation Commission and the Special Court for Sierra Leone' (2004) 11 University of California Davis Law Review 145, 161.

In practice, Sierra Leone never prosecuted grave breaches domestically and whether this happened deliberately or due to an oversight on the part of national prosecutors will likely never be known (at any rate, only a small subset of civil war atrocities would have qualified as grave breaches).[113] From a normative perspective, President Kabbah's embrace of international criminal law in the late 1990s heralded wider consequences for the national justice sector. In addition to supporting the SCSL's establishment, Kabbah also signed and ratified the Rome Statute, in October 1998 and September 2000, respectively.

Yet, despite this initial enthusiasm for both the SCSL and the ICC, neither Kabbah nor successor governments translated their support into legislative reform. The SCSL proved equally agnostic about legislation. Despite early suggestions that legacy initiatives might include modernizing domestic laws, the SCSL took a hands-off approach.[114] Some court officials participated in the legislative process, including through an NGO created inter alia by SCSL defence attorneys, but these efforts never received the SCSL's endorsement.[115]

In practice, civil society groups spearheaded efforts to domesticate international criminal law, independent of the SCSL's presence in Freetown. For instance, in 2006, the Sierra Leonean Bar Association, in cooperation with domestic and international stakeholders (in particular Manifesto 99 and No Peace Without Justice), convened a workshop in Freetown to debate a draft implementation bill.[116] Attended by Fatou Bensouda, then deputy ICC prosecutor (and, as a Gambian national, an influential voice from the region), the workshop approved and forwarded a draft text to the Attorney General, who was expected to formally table a bill before the Sierra Leonean Parliament for deliberation.[117]

Although this draft bill remains confidential to this day, domestication of the Rome Statute was prioritized over the SCSL Statute for two reasons. The ICC's definitions of crimes were considered more reflective of customary international law and Rome Statute norms more holistic in scope.[118] More importantly, it seems the ICC's definitions of crimes were deemed preferable to SCSL norms due to retroactivity concerns. Whereas it was clear that Rome Statute legislation would operate prospectively, in line with general criminal law principles, transplanting definitions of crimes and other standards from the SCSL Statute could have triggered complex

[113] Bankole Thompson, *Universal Jurisdiction: The Sierra Leone Profile* (TMC Asser Press 2015) 77–78.

[114] ICTJ and UNDP, 'The "Legacy" of the Special Court. Draft for Discussion' (2003) 13 (on file).

[115] Interview with Sierra Leone official, Freetown, Sierra Leone, 15 March 2016. Sulaiman Bah, 'Legal Reform in Sierra Leone' (Case Matrix Network: Strengthening National Justice for Core International Crimes, The Hague, Netherlands, 28 June 2016) <youtube.com/watch?v = IHPUplQu2N8&index = 7&list=PLgMYBjx5GIGqIYQQGzGi1p8HtCY1HF75I>. See also Horovitz (n 108) 50–53.

[116] Interviews with Sierra Leonean and foreign civil society activists, Freetown, Sierra Leone and Nuremberg, Germany, 10 and 15 March 2016 and 20 October 2017.

[117] Bah (n 115).

[118] Interviews with Sierra Leonean activists, 10, 11, and 15 March 2016.

litigation before Sierra Leonean courts. It was feared that, even if the government adhered to the Lomé amnesty, Sierra Leonean attorneys would be able to leverage domesticated international norms in combination with the SCSL's jurisprudence to argue for domestic prosecutions relating to pre-Lomé crimes.[119] As explained by Sierra Leonean activists, it was hoped that forward-looking Rome Statute implementation could be more easily 'sold' to a political elite which still looked askance at the possibility of domestic prosecutions of war-related events.[120]

However, even these more moderate domestication aims proved unpalatable to the Sierra Leonean government. With presidential elections looming in 2007, it appears Kabbah's government had little appetite for a divisive debate over international crimes, and the Rome Statute implementing bill never made it out of the Attorney General's Office. After the 2007 elections and the opposition's rise to power, a separate domestication initiative, led by Parliamentarians for Global Action and the Commonwealth Secretariat, was addressed to the new Attorney General.[121] However, these efforts failed too, notwithstanding assurances from the deputy foreign minister at the 2010 Kampala review conference of his 'commitment to the promotion of international criminal justice', and that Sierra Leone's Parliament was 'on the verge' of domestication.[122]

Rome Statute implementation has resurfaced periodically in the intervening years.[123] For instance, in 2011, draft legislation was submitted to a new Attorney General, but this draft was again never put before Parliament.[124] At yet another 'implementation' workshop, held in Freetown in 2018 on the twentieth anniversary of the Rome Statute's entry into force, the foreign minister offered vague support for the ICC but no concrete commitment to domesticate the Statute. For his part, the chairman of the parliamentary Committee on Human Rights promised to adopt the bill while implying that a draft must first be submitted by the

[119] Interviews with Sierra Leonean activists, 15 March 2016.

[120] On retroactivity, see also Horovitz (n 108) 52.

[121] E-mail exchange with international expert, 18 February 2022. See also Parliamentarians for Global Action, 'PGA Regional Roundtable Discussion on the Implementation of the Rome Statute' <pgaction.org/news/pga-regional-roundtable-discussion-on-the-implementation-of-the-rome-statute.html>.

[122] Emmanuel Turay, 'Kampala: Sierra Leone Commits to Ratify and Implement Rome Statutes' *Patriotic Vanguard* (2 June 2010) <thepatrioticvanguard.com/kampala-sierra-leone-commits-to-ratify-and-implement-rome-statutes>; Statement by the Head of Delegation, Vandi Chidi Minah, Deputy Minister of Foreign Affairs and International Cooperation of the Republic of Sierra Leone to the Review Conference of the Rome Statute for the ICC <asp.icc-cpi.int/iccdocs/asp_docs/RC2010/Statements/ICC-RC-gendeba-Sierra%20Leone-ENG.pdf>.

[123] Interview with Sierra Leonean attorney, Freetown, Sierra Leone, 15 March 2016. Joseph AK Sesay, 'A Case for the Domestication of the Rome Statute in Sierra Leone' <carl-sl.org/pres/a-case-for-the-domestication-of-the-rome-statute-in-sierra-leone/>. See also Bintu A Sesay, 'NMDHR [Network Movement for Democracy and Human Rights] Ends Consultative Meeting for CSOs in Sierra Leone' *Awareness Times* (28 March 2008) <rscsl.org/Clippings/2008/2008-03/pc2008-3-31.pdf>.

[124] 'Hon. Shiaka Musa Sama, Statement Delivered on Behalf of the PGA (Parliamentarians for Global Action) National Group at the Regional Roundtable Conference on [Rome Statute] Implementation' <pgaction.org/pdf/pre/SL%20NG%20Statement%20Liberia.pdf>; SLIIL Communique, 14 July 2012 (on file with author).

Attorney General (which is incorrect, as any lawmaker may introduce a bill of her own volition).[125]

Although the Sierra Leonean executive continued to officially support domestication of the Rome Statute and cites logistical obstacles as the reason for delays, government officials and activists privately acknowledged that Sierra Leone's position on the ICC was being 're-evaluated', due partly to the ICC's difficult relations with the AU. In 2016, the then deputy justice minister explained that the AU's policy on non-cooperation and collective withdrawal may have contributed to Sierra Leone's failure to adopt legislation.[126] For his part, Kargbo denied the decision was 'political' but acknowledged that the AU's position on the ICC likely slowed down the implementation process.[127]

Activists are critical of the political elite's motives. A recurrent argument is that Sierra Leone lacks resources to domesticate the Rome Statute, but interlocutors noted confusion and suspicion of the ICC as likely reasons for stalled reforms.[128] One activist explained, 'they think that domesticating the Rome Statute gives legitimacy to ICC, [and] they don't want to be seen as giving the ICC a win'.[129] Another activist explained that high-ranking politicians fear 'they will be entrapping themselves', with the Al-Bashir warrant serving as a dangerous precedent for politicians.[130]

Despite the executive's ambivalence towards the ICC, the legislature passed legislation on international crimes in 2012. Adopted with little media attention, the Geneva Conventions Act 'giv[es] effect' to the four Geneva Conventions and their two Additional Protocols by establishing that '[a] person of whatever nationality commits an offence if that person, whether within or outside of Sierra Leone commits, aids, abets or procures any other person to commit a grave breach'.[131] Two aspects of the Act are noteworthy. First, the maximum penalty is life imprisonment, abolishing the death penalty for acts that otherwise required this sentence under national law.[132] Second, the Act domesticated the Rome Statute's norms on superior responsibility.[133]

Although the Geneva Conventions Act remains the only legislation on international crimes adopted since 2002, its impact is limited as it recriminalizes a narrow category of crimes that were already part of the national legal order. No

[125] CARL, Press Release, 'On the 20th Anniversary of the Rome Statute, CARL Welcomes the Renewed Commitment of the Government of Sierra Leone to "Domesticate" the Rome Statute, Urges Continued Support to the ICC' (8 August 2018)

[126] Interview with deputy justice minister, Arrow Bockarie, Freetown, Sierra Leone, 15 March 2016.

[127] Interview with former justice minister, Franklyn Kargbo, Freetown, Sierra Leone, 14 March 2016.

[128] Interview with activist and RSCSL official, Freetown, Sierra Leone, 10 and 11 March 2016.

[129] Interview with activist, Freetown, Sierra Leone, 10 March 2016.

[130] Interview with activists and attorneys, Freetown, Sierra Leone, 10, 11 and 15 March 2017. Interview with deputy justice minister, Freetown, Sierra Leone, 15 March 2017.

[131] Geneva Conventions Act, 2012, Supplement to the Sierra Leone Gazette Vol. CXLIII, 74, s 1.

[132] ibid s 2(2)–(4).

[133] ibid s 4 (1)–(3).

grave breaches prosecutions have been initiated to date. Paradoxically, however, the Act may serve as a smokescreen for normative compliance. One activist observed that politicians used the Act to argue that Sierra Leone respected international standards, and that implementing legislation was no longer necessary.[134] Similar to the government's tolerance of the SCSL, which showed the international community that 'enough was being done', the Geneva Conventions Act may have inadvertently displaced more ambitious reforms such as Rome Statute implementation.

3.3. The death penalty: probing the limits of international influence

Aside from domestication, abolitionist campaigns were another battleground for normative reform in Sierra Leone. The death penalty emerged as a flashpoint in the 1990s.[135] In October 1998, at the height of the civil war, a military court sentenced thirty-four AFRC members to death for their role in a coup from the previous year. Twenty-four defendants were executed two weeks later (ten others had their sentences commuted to life imprisonment).[136] Amnesty International and other NGOs condemned both the unfair court-martial, from which no appeal existed under military law, and the executions that followed.[137]

Notwithstanding these controversies, the death penalty remained mandatory for treason, mutiny, murder, and aggravated robbery.[138] At the time of its creation, it was assumed that the Special Court would spur domestic abolitionist efforts (during negotiations on the SCSL, the death penalty was cited among the reasons for a hybrid tribunal).[139] While the SCSL Statute, where life imprisonment was the maximum punishment, created no abolitionist obligation, NGOs hoped that Sierra Leonean courts might adjust their sentencing practices and that ultimately the legislature would eliminate capital punishment altogether.[140]

Initially, the SCSL and Sierra Leone's truth commission seemed to galvanize attention around the death penalty. Among its binding recommendations to the

[134] Interview with activist, Freetown, Sierra Leone, 10 March 2016.

[135] On the politics of treason trials and death sentences in Sierra Leone, see Mohamed Suma, 'Politics of Death Penalty in Post-Conflict Sierra Leone: An Opportunity for Reform or a Missed Opportunity?' in Madoka Futamura and Nadia Bernaz, *The Politics of the Death Penalty in Countries in Transition* (Routledge 2014) 164–67.

[136] Amnesty International, 'Executions of 24 Soldiers after an Unfair Trial: A Blow to Reconciliation in Sierra Leone' (AFR/51/20/98 1998).

[137] ibid; Schabas (n 41) 116. For details, see Abass Bundu, *Democracy by Force? A Study of International Military Intervention in the Civil War in Sierra Leone from 1991–2000* (Universal Publishers 2001) 240–79.

[138] Suma (n 135) 158–60; Abdul Tejan-Cole, 'The Death Penalty in Sierra Leone' (undated manuscript) (on file with author).

[139] Fifth Report on UNAMSIL (31 July 2000) S/2000/751 para 10; ICTJ and UNDP (n 114) 9.

[140] Institute for Security Studies, 'Sierra Leone: A Country Review of Crime and Criminal Justice, 2008' (2009) 66–67.

government, the TRC's final report listed abolition as an immediate and directly enforceable proposal.[141] The TRC reasoned that, unlike expensive infrastructure projects, abolition required mere political will followed by legislative action.[142] In late 2004, after the High Court issued ten death sentences, Amnesty International urged 'an end to the discrepancy between national courts and the [SCSL]', emphasizing that 'a person convicted of the most serious crimes would face a prison sentence, whereas those convicted before national courts of offences which may be less serious could face the death penalty'.[143]

These hopes proved premature. Over the years, the Sierra Leonean political elite's support for abolition waxed and waned. In 2005, the government rejected efforts to abolish the death penalty but promised to continue 'reviewing' the issue.[144] A civil society petition to have the Supreme Court order the government to abolish the death penalty was mooted but failed to materialize.[145] Unlike Rwanda, where mass executions generated condemnation and backlash, Sierra Leonean leaders respected a self-imposed moratorium, which in turn decreased pressure to finalize the process of abolition. Civilian and military courts continued to impose death sentences from time to time, but no executions occurred. In 2006, Kabbah reaffirmed that executions would not take place and his successor, Ernst Bai Koroma, did the same after his election to the presidency in 2007.[146]

Civil society initiatives continued apace—in 2008, the Appeals Court overturned eleven death sentences in a high-profile treason trial, 'opening the possibility of an eventual end to capital punishment'[147]—but it proved impossible to complete abolition through the legislature. Given Parliament's failure to domesticate Rome Statute norms, the absence of the death penalty before the ICC carried little weight.[148] Although the Special Court served as a rhetorical frame for some NGO-led abolitionist campaigns, it appears SCSL officials did not consider advocacy against the death penalty as within their mandate.[149]

As the SCSL wound up operations and international interest in abolition waned, Sierra Leone's official position on the death penalty became increasingly conflicted.

[141] Witness to Truth, Report of the Sierra Leone TRC, vol 2 (2004) ch 3 para 54.

[142] William A Schabas, 'Conjoined Twins of Transitional Justice? The Sierra Leone Truth and Reconciliation Commission and the Special Court' (2004) 2 Journal of International Criminal Justice 1082, 1086–87.

[143] Amnesty International, 'Sierra Leone: Amnesty International Expresses Dismay at Ten Death Sentences for Treason' (21 December 2004) AFR51/009/2004.

[144] Sierra Leone Government White Paper (2005) 6 (on file with author).

[145] Amnesty International, 'Amnesty International Report 2007—Sierra Leone' (23 May 2007) <refworld.org/docid/46558ee12.html>; see also Boctor (n 42) 115.

[146] Jeneba F Kamara, 'The Death Penalty: A Case for Its Abolition' (2006) 19 *The Monitor: Official Newsletter of the Sierra Leone Court Monitoring Programme* 13.

[147] Mohamed Fofanah, 'Death Penalty—Sierra Leone: Successful Appeal Strengthens Case for Abolition' *IPS News Agency* (12 December 2008) <ipsnews.net/2008/12/death-penalty-sierra-leone-successful-appeal-strengthens-case-for-abolition/>; see also Karimunda (n 58) 188–89.

[148] Sesay (n 123).

[149] Horovitz (n 108) 58.

On the one hand, Koroma commuted the sentences of almost everyone on death row to celebrate Sierra Leone's fiftieth anniversary in 2011, followed by a vote in favour—after years of abstaining—of a UNGA resolution calling for a global moratorium in 2012.[150] Then, in 2014, the justice minister assured the UN Human Rights Council that his office was working on legislation abolishing the death penalty that would be ready 'in the space of a few weeks'.[151] On the other hand, capital punishment remained on the books and courts continued to sentence people to death. In 2015, the number of death sentences in domestic proceedings increased for the first time in years.[152] In late 2016, with dozens of individuals on death row, the minister of internal affairs announced that executions would resume, and even supervised the testing of gallows at Pademba Road Prison.[153]

Although these threats did not materialize, there were few indications that Sierra Leone was on the path to abolition. Some government leaders appeared to insist that a new constitution might have to precede abolition, creating an additional hurdle. Yet, in 2021, with the support of a new Attorney General, Parliament finally abolished the death penalty.[154] According to Sabrina Mahtani, although the government of Madaa Bio, which came to power in 2018, made no promises to abolish the death penalty, the tenacity of civil society activism and an innovative legal strategy (piecemeal legislation instead of abolition via constitutional reform followed by a divisive national referendum) allowed reforms to pass.[155]

3.4. The SCSL's incomplete shadow: ordinary criminal justice practice

The SCSL enabled neither the domestication of international crimes nor abolition of the death penalty. Partly for this reason, it is sometimes argued that the Special Court failed to shape the normative landscape and judicial practice in Sierra Leone. To take one example, in 2008, Yada Williams, a prominent Sierra Leonean defence attorney practicing before the SCSL, argued '[i]t's sad ... I don't think [the SCSL]

[150] Sabrina Mahtani, 'How Sierra Leone Abolished the Death Penalty and What Others Could Learn' (*African Arguments*, 2 November 2021) <africanarguments.org/2021/11/how-sierra-leone-abolished-the-death-penalty-and-what-others-could-learn/>.

[151] Amnesty International, 'Sierra Leone to Speed up Death Penalty Abolition (6 May 2014) AFR 51/001/2014.

[152] Elsa Buchanan, 'Could Sierra Leone Revive the Death Penalty to Curb Rising Violence?' *International Business Times* (7 November 2016) <ibtimes.co.uk/could-sierra-leone-revive-death-penalty-curb-rising-violence-1590214>.

[153] Amnesty International, 'Global Report: Death Sentences and Executions 2016' (2017). 38, 36; Cooper Inveen, 'Prepare the Gallows: Sierra Leone and the Death Penalty' (*Al Jazeera*, 31 October 2016) <aljazeera.com/indepth/features/2016/10/prepare-gallows-sierra-leone-death-penalty-161025080542700.html>.

[154] Abolition of the Death Penalty Act 2021, Supplement to the Sierra Leone Extraordinary Gazette CXLXII, 33, 2 July 2021.

[155] Mahtani (n 150).

has impacted the Sierra Leone national system at all'.[156] As noted in Chapter 5, a rift also emerged between the SCSL and the Sierra Leonean legal profession, due partly to divergent work standards in the domestic system compared to the SCSL.[157]

Another problem was that, with just two major trials relating to post-Lomé serious crimes (analysed in Chapter 4), the scope for the cross-pollination of international norms into the daily routine of Sierra Leonean criminal law practice was limited. As noted by one defence attorney, 'the kind of offences they were dealing with were of their own species ... you can have murder and manslaughter being tried locally, but [not] mass murders ... pillage is also unique because it dealt with a war situation'.[158] One exception seems to be sexual crimes, with the Sexual Offences Act internalizing substantive norms and best practices influenced by international criminal law.[159] However, this exception seems to prove the rule. As observed by a (national) RSCSL official, while Sierra Leonean legal professionals are aware of SCSL jurisprudence, 'I am not sure they [can] make a lot of reference to it in their work'.[160]

Yet, over time, the SCSL seems to have influenced criminal justice practice in more discrete ways. Given the different contextual background for ordinary offences, the greatest impact was procedural. In particular, given the high number of Sierra Leonean defence attorneys at the SCSL, defence rights and procedural safeguards filtered into domestic practice. Although 'trial by ambush',[161] whereby Sierra Leonean prosecutors are usually not required to disclose evidence against an accused before trial, is still common, the SCSL's disclosure requirements were gradually domesticated, inter alia at the urging of Sierra Leonean SCSL nationals who returned to the ordinary justice system.[162] In turn, adjustments to practice gave rise to legislative efforts to protect fair trial rights, including revisions to the criminal procedure code. Other procedural changes, such as greater use of written submissions (as opposed to common law oral proceedings) and protective measures for witnesses and victims, manifested primarily in practice, on a case-by-case basis, before efforts were made to amend domestic laws.[163]

[156] Quoted in Cruvellier (n 100) 36.

[157] Open Society Justice Initiative, 'Legacy: Completing the Work of the Special Court for Sierra Leone' (2011) 14–15.

[158] Interview with Sierra Leonean defence attorney, Freetown, Sierra Leone, 15 March 2016.

[159] Interview with Sierra Leonean defence attorney and SCSL official, Freetown, Sierra Leone, 15 March 2016. Sexual Offences Act, Supplement to the Sierra Leone Gazette CXLIII, 60, 1 November 2012; Bah (n 115); Human Rights Center UC Berkeley School of Law, 'The Long Road Ahead. Accountability for Sexual Violence in Conflict and Post-Conflict Settings. Kenya. Liberia. Sierra Leone. Uganda' (2015) 25.

[160] Interview with RSCSL official, Freetown, Sierra Leone, 11 March 2016.

[161] On trial by ambush, see Niobe Thompson, 'Commonwealth Human Rights Initiative. In Pursuit of Justice: A Report on the Judiciary in Sierra Leone' (Commonwealth Human Rights Initiative 2002) 23.

[162] Interviews with Sierra Leone judge, SCSL official and government attorney, Freetown, Sierra Leone, 14 and 15 March 2016.

[163] On efforts to reform domestic criminal law, in particular the 1965 Criminal Procedure Act, see Suma (n 110) 16; University of Nottingham and Human Rights Law Centre, 'Bridging the Gap: Ensuring

Although holistic efforts to overhaul domestic criminal procedure have yet to materialize in Sierra Leone, some practitioners acknowledged the SCSL's impact on everyday practice. One defence attorney described international proceedings as an 'eye-opener'.[164] A Sierra Leonean magistrate noted the Special Court had prompted 'changes in attitude', not just 'in law'.[165] Another attorney noted that, while many reforms were under discussion prior to the SCSL, it remains a fact that 'most innovations of the SCSL have been taken into account'.[166] By contrast, a High Court registrar, who had never previously worked for the SCSL, argued that it had 'no impact for his work'.[167] In sum, while the SCSL's impact on domestic criminal law is partial at best, some domestic practices have changed over time.

3.5. 'No one is above the law': the normative paradox of 'greatest responsibility'?

In 2012, several NGOs published the findings of a broad-based survey to gauge perceptions of the SCSL's performance. Among the core findings, the survey showed that Sierra Leoneans 'overwhelmingly felt that the SCSL had prosecuted those who bear the greatest responsibility for the crimes'.[168] The report then adds 'many people felt a need for additional prosecutions further down the chain of command'.[169] These findings speak to one of the SCSL's less intuitive normative impacts, namely its ability to prosecute and convict a handful of perpetrators and, in doing so, send a message to Sierra Leoneans and the wider region that impunity cannot be tolerated.

As seen in Chapter 4, the SCSL's interpretation of 'greatest responsibility' prompted various criticisms. Among the most serious objections was that the OTP had not actually convicted many high-ranking suspects (it did not help that Sankoh and Norman died prematurely) or that the most brutal perpetrators were deemed 'insufficiently responsible'. As noted by Ibrahim Tommy, '[t]he restrictive nature of the Court's jurisdiction meant that ... many mid-level commanders who actively participated in, and ordered the commission of crimes ... were not tried'.[170]

the Lasting Legacy of the Sierra Leone Special Court and the Truth and Reconciliation Commission' (2012).

[164] Interview with Sierra Leone defence attorney, Freetown, Sierra Leone, 11 March 2016.

[165] Interview with Sierra Leonean magistrate, Freetown, Sierra Leone, 14 March 2016.

[166] Interview with RSCSL official, Freetown, Sierra Leone, 14 March 2016.

[167] Interview with Registrar of High Court, Freetown, Sierra Leone, 11 March 2016.

[168] No Peace Without Justice and others, 'Making Justice Count. Assessing the Impact and Legacy of the Special Court for Sierra Leone in Sierra Leone and Liberia' (2012) 1. On Liberia, see Marlies Glasius, '"It Sends a Message": Liberian Opinion Leaders' Responses to the Trial of Charles Taylor' (2015) 13 Journal of International Criminal Justice 419.

[169] No Peace Without Justice and others (n 168) 1.

[170] Ibrahim Tommy, 'Lessons from the SCSL in the Fight against Impunity' (2012) <asf.be/wp-content/uploads/2012/10/Lessons-from-the-Special-Court-for-Sierra-Leone.pdf>.

Yet, paradoxically, while almost all Sierra Leoneans acknowledge the selective and, therefore, incomplete nature of the SCSL's trials, few deny its contribution to combating impunity. Echoing the findings of the 2012 survey, almost all interviewees acknowledged that the Special Court's 'greatest success' was that it sent a message that 'no one was above the law' or that 'impunity was no longer an option'. As noted by one government official who had previously worked at the SCSL, it 'sent a clear message that having trials was important in and of itself ... [about] sending the big boys to jail'.[171] A civil society leader explained that the Court 'increased national and regional awareness that no one is above the law ... [and] created fear among politicians'.[172] A national prosecutor (with no history at the SCSL) similarly observed that 'the Special Court's strength is that it sends a message, there is no impunity; it will prosecute even despite amnesty'.[173]

There is evidence that such observations about the SCSL's impact in Sierra Leone are more than just anecdotes or self-perpetuating narratives from the UN or the SCSL outreach programme. Even ardent critics of the SCSL, for instance former Attorney General Serry Kamal recognized its deterrent effect, especially in the run-up and aftermath of the 2007 elections—Sierra Leone's first peaceful transfer of power.[174] Others have noted the SCSL's stabilizing role in the 2012 elections as well.[175] Some also emphasize that the Special Court was able to challenge Sierra Leone's 'big man' culture, where power is exercised through paternalistic client–patron relationships, with Charles Taylor's trial 'breaking a glass ceiling' and puncturing the cult of untouchability around West African politicians.[176] Yet others point to Norman's arrest as symbolically important, though his prosecution remains controversial for many Sierra Leoneans.[177] Charles Jalloh concludes that '[t]hough not yet proven empirically', the SCSL likely 'dissuade[d] further violence and in that way helped to restore peace ... [t]hat the SCSL took certain influential military and political leaders out of circulation was thus highly significant'.[178]

[171] Interview with government official, Freetown, Sierra Leone, 11 March 2016.

[172] Interview with activist, Freetown, Sierra Leone, 11 March 2016.

[173] Interview with government official, Freetown, Sierra Leone, 15 March 2016.

[174] Charles C Jalloh, 'Special Court for Sierra Leone: Achieving Justice?' (2011) 32 Michigan Journal of International Law 395, 452–53; Stephen J Rapp, 'The Challenge of Choice in the Investigation and Prosecution of International Crimes in Post-Conflict Sierra Leone' in Charles C Jalloh (ed), *The Sierra Leone Special Court and Its Legacy* (CUP 2013) 29–30.

[175] Ibrahim Bangura, 'Leaving behind the Worst of the Past. Transitional Justice and Prevention in Sierra Leone' (ICTJ 2021) 30–31.

[176] Interview with activists, Geneva, Switzerland and by phone, 7 July 2016 and 6 April 2017. On 'big men', see Tim Kelsall, *Culture under Cross Examination: International Justice and the Special Court for Sierra Leone* (CUP 2009) 75–80. Critically, see Jennifer Easterday, 'The Consequences of Witness Payments at the Special Court for Sierra Leone' in Charles C Jalloh (ed), *The Sierra Leone Special Court and its Legacy* (CUP 2013) 465–68.

[177] Interviews with activists, Freetown, Sierra Leone, 10 and 15 March 2016. But see Chapter 4, section 3.4 in this volume. Critically, see also Kenneth Rodman, 'Justice Is Interventionist: The Political Sources of the Judicial Reach of the Special Court for Sierra Leone' (2013) 13 International Criminal Law Review 63, 63.

[178] Jalloh (n 174) 452–53; Eleanor Thompson, 'Can an International Criminal Tribunal with a Limited Mandate Deter Atrocities? Lessons from the Special Court for Sierra Leone' in Jennifer Schense

All in all, these findings illustrate what can be called the normative paradox of 'greatest responsibility'. While many Sierra Leoneans feel that the SCSL did not prosecute enough or the right perpetrators, its restrictive 'greatest responsibility' jurisdiction—coupled with the government's reconciliation policy—seems to have become something of a self-fulfilling prophecy. A near perfect arrest record and a handful of high-profile trials, carried out in a relatively short time span, may have created a self-perpetuating myth that the most senior people were held to account and sent a message that no one was above the law. In other words, the fact of holding a handful of trials was more important in the long run than the short-term controversies plaguing the SCSL while it operated. As noted by a former (national) SCSL official, the 'greatest success' of the Special Court's 'symbolic justice' was the lesson that 'some is better than no prosecutions'.[179]

3.6. Unpacking a hybrid/restrictive mandate's effects on norm internalization

In 2008, Bankole Thompson, one of the SCSL's national judges, suggested that '[w]e may be assessing [this] too early. I have a feeling that ... 70 percent of the judicial procedure and principles applicable at the SCSL will be transferred to the national system. It will take time.'[180] With the benefit of hindsight, it seems Thompson's hopes have materialized only partially.

A number of factors seem to explain the SCSL's limited contribution to norm internalization. For one, despite its hybridity, it missed opportunities early on to develop an iterative relationship with national justice actors. Prosecutor Crane declined to charge domestic crimes and, by the same token, SCSL judges refused to expand their analysis of the Lomé amnesty's (il)legality to national law. Both decisions augured isolationist dynamics, internalized and reciprocated by Sierra Leoneans. For another, while 'legacy building' and the SCSL's anticipated closure, as seen in Chapter 5, prompted its leadership to reassess a hands-off approach to the national justice sector, this never translated into support for legislative reform. Despite government assurances that the Rome Statute will be domesticated, if Sierra Leone were the site of mass violence today, prosecutions of most international crimes would still not be possible before domestic courts.

Isolationist dynamics in Sierra Leone may have contributed to what Tom Perriello and Marieke Wierda described as the 'spaceship phenomenon ... a

and Linda Carter (eds), *Two Steps Forward, One Step Back: The Deterrent Effect of International Criminal Tribunals* (International Nuremberg Principles Academy 2016).

179 Interview with former SCSL official, Cape Town, South Africa, 23 March 2016.

180 Quoted in Cruvellier (n 100) 37.

Court that is perceived as a curiosity and an anomaly with little impact on citizens' everyday lives.'[181] Yet, while the SCSL's experience suggests that location, the mere presence of a hybrid tribunal *in situ*, is not enough to have a 'demonstration effect' on domestic norms and practice, the SCSL also had downstream effects that its founders may have underestimated. Over time, some aspects of the SCSL's judicial process, especially in terms of defence rights, have taken hold at the national level, not least because former (national) SCSL defence attorneys returned to domestic practice. According to Mohamed Bangura, the SCSL 'contributed very positively in ushering in [a] changing environment of greater respect and compliance with international legal obligations and their domestic application.'[182]

While such laudatory assessments are rare—and it must be recognized that with so few domestic trials of war-related atrocities the scope for cross-pollination of international norms and practices was significantly reduced[183]—the SCSL's greatest normative impact may lie elsewhere. While the Kabbah and Koroma administrations declined to overturn the Lomé amnesty domestically, the Special Court nevertheless placed criminal accountability on the political agenda for over decade. Most striking is Sierra Leoneans' perception that the SCSL challenged a 'big man' culture of impunity (even though the OTP's case selection was contentious during the SCSL's existence and many were unconvinced that the real 'big men' were on trial). However, it may be that the SCSL mandate, which expressly invokes the 'greatest responsibility' of defendants—coupled with the conviction of a head of state—had the paradoxical psychosocial effect of 'elevating' other defendants to the status of high-ranking perpetrators while also consolidating a belief that (some form of) accountability had been achieved.

This research does not attempt to unravel this paradox, nor can it assess the impact of the SCSL's limited prosecutions relative to the contributions of the truth commission or amnesty for most perpetrators. Although it should be acknowledged that the national justice system still faces serious problems,[184] Sierra Leone has not relapsed into conflict and has transitioned to democratic governance, making it an outlier among countries that have experimented with ICTs. As emphasized by Ibrahim Bangura:[185]

[181] Tom Perriello and Marieke Wierda, 'The Special Court for Sierra Leone under Scrutiny' (ICTJ 2006) 2.

[182] Bangura (n 103) 720. However, most observers downplay the SCSL's normative impact. See Sigall Horovitz, 'The Impact of the International Criminal Tribunal for Rwanda and the Special Court for Sierra Leone on Impunity in Rwanda and Sierra Leone' in Vincent O Nmehielle (ed), *Africa and the Future of International Criminal Justice* (Eleven International 2012) 50; Antonio Cassese, 'Report on the Special Court for Sierra Leone' (2006) 61.

[183] Chehtman (n 100) 315–19 and 322–24.

[184] See eg Suma (n 110) 10.

[185] Bangura (n 175) 1.

> Throughout the nearly two decades after the end of the civil war, Sierra Leone has managed to avoid the recurrence of violent conflict. It has held a series of general elections that led to the peaceful transfer of power from one political party to another—democratic changes of government that represent a radical departure from the checkered nature of electioneering processes before 2002. Given the high rate of recidivism among postconflict countries, this is a significant achievement.

While the SCSL's contribution to these developments are open to interpretation, its more restrictive mandate and hybrid features make it worthy of further study.[186]

4. The International Criminal Court

4.1. Joining the ICC club: Congo as a battleground for legislative reform

The DRC was an unlikely candidate for legislative reform. Adopted in 1972, the Code of Military Justice had transplanted genocide, crimes against humanity and war crimes into Congolese law.[187] While, strictly speaking, nothing in the Rome Statute requires states to domesticate ICC crimes, purposive readings of complementarity—lest states be found 'unable or unwilling' to prosecute—are leveraged to promote substantive (definitions of crimes, modes of liability) and procedural (due process guarantees or eliminating amnesties) reforms. With complementarity forming a 'package of norms' necessary to become 'part of the ICC club', the DRC emerged as an early implementation battleground for what was then a new court.[188]

Advocated by prominent NGOs, including Human Rights Watch and Amnesty International, implementation initiatives can be traced to Joseph Kabila's ratification of the Rome Statute in March 2002. In June 2002, the Permanent Commission for the Reform of Congolese Law and the Justice Ministry launched consultations on draft legislation domesticating the Statute, followed by the adoption of a new

[186] In this sense, see Kirsten Ainley, 'Evaluating the Success of Transitional Justice in Sierra Leone and Beyond' in Kirsten Ainley, Rebekka Friedman and Chris Mahony (eds), *Evaluating Transitional Justice. Accountability and Peacebuilding in Post-Conflict Sierra Leone* (Palgrave Macmillan 2015); Padraig McAuliffe, 'Hybrid Tribunals at Ten: How International Criminal Justice's Golden Child Became an Orphan' (2011) 7 Journal of International Law and International Relations 1, 58–59. Critically, see Eka Ikpe, Abiodun Alao and Kamau Nyokabi, 'Beyond Liberal Institution (Re)Building: Conversations on Peacebuilding and Statebuilding in Sierra Leone' (2021) 21 Conflict, Security & Development 431.

[187] Ordonnance-loi 72/060 du 25 septembre 1972, portant institution d'un Code de justice militaire, arts 502, 505, and 530. These post-Second World War norms appear never to have been enforced by the military courts. See Pierre Akele, *Les crimes contre l'humanité en droit congolais* (CEPAS 1999).

[188] Frédéric Mégret, 'Too Much of a Good Thing?: Implementation and the Uses of Complementarity' in Carsten Stahn and Mohamed El Zeidy (eds), *The International Criminal Court and Complementarity* (CUP 2011) 361. See further Chapter 2, section 2 in this volume.

Military Criminal Code (MCC) in November.[189] Surprisingly however, the MCC failed to incorporate ICC norms, with its definitions of crimes diverging from the Rome Statute. For instance, crimes against humanity are defined as 'grave violations of international humanitarian law', and the accompanying list of acts corresponds to many of the ICC's war crimes.[190]

It is not clear why the Congolese legislature passed legislation that, despite civil society pleas, ignored the Rome Statute. As Elena Baylis notes, 'the reasons for this development are mysterious'.[191] According to some Congolese experts, the MCC's outdated norms may have been the by-product of institutional inertia. Efforts to reform military criminal law had begun under Mobutu, and the final version of the MCC may have reproduced draft texts from the pre-ICC era. One Congolese attorney argued that parliamentarians may not have realized they were enacting norms that conflicted with the Rome Statute.[192] However, others suggest that—with the DRC still consumed by civil war in late 2002 and peace negotiations underway in South Africa—lawmakers may have purposely adopted inconsistent legislation in the shadow of the ICC's potential intervention.[193] As explained by one military magistrate, although the legislative impulse behind the MCC's adoption was good ('to break with past abuses'), the Transitional National Assembly subverted the process and did what was 'in the interest' of the Kabila-affiliated authorities.[194]

Against the backdrop of the OTP's growing interest in a DRC investigation in 2003, the MCC's inconsistent definitions re-energized NGO-led 'implementation' campaigns, which shifted to the 2003–6 transitional legislature.[195] Arguing that ICC intervention prompted some Congolese powerbrokers to advocate justice reforms, William Burke-White suggests that Jean-Pierre Bemba and Anastas Ruberwa—both rumoured to be on the ICC's list of suspects—advocated Rome Statute legislation to demonstrate the DRC's ability to do justice domestically and thereby ward off the threat of ICC trials of people like themselves.[196] Ultimately, a

[189] Lawyers Committee for Human Rights and Human Rights Watch, 'Commentaires relatifs à l'avant-projet de loi portant mise en œuvre du Statut de la Cour pénale internationale en RDC' (2003) (on file). For the draft laws, see Godfrey M Musila, 'Between Rhetoric and Action: The Politics, Processes and Practice of the ICC's Work in the DRC' (Institute for Security Studies 2009) annexes 3 and 4.

[190] Loi 024/2002 du 18 novembre 2002 portant code pénal militaire, arts 165–66 (MCC).

[191] Elena Baylis, 'Reassessing the Role of International Criminal Law: Rebuilding National Courts through Transnational Networks' (2009) 50 Boston College Law Review 1, 36.

[192] Interviews with military prosecutor and Congolese attorneys, Kinshasa, DRC, 19, 23 April and 15 August 2016. See also Musila (n 189) 15–17.

[193] Interview with Congolese activist, Kinshasa, DRC, 26 April 2016.

[194] Interview with senior Congolese magistrate, Kinshasa, DRC, 23 April 2016.

[195] On power-sharing, see Laura Davis, 'Power Shared and Justice Shelved: The Democratic Republic of Congo' (2013) 17 International Journal of Human Rights 289.

[196] William Burke-White, 'Complementarity in Practice: The International Criminal Court as Part of a System of Multi-Level Global Governance in the Democratic Republic of Congo' (2005) 18 Leiden Journal of International Law 557, 570–71.

government-backed Rome Statute implementation bill (*loi de mise en œuvre*) died in the Transitional National Assembly without ever coming to a vote.

After Kabila narrowly defeated Bemba in contested presidential elections in 2006, Rome Statute implementing legislation faded from view. Having consolidated power, Kabila increasingly viewed the ICC as a nuisance at best or a threat at worst. Unlike a 2003 draft, supported by the justice ministry, a revised implementation bill failed to gain the executive's endorsement, which significantly decreased its chances of passage. Instead, in 2008, a group of lawmakers submitted a revised bill on their own motion. After clearing the lower chamber (the National Assembly) in late 2010, the bill died in the upper chamber (the Senate) in 2011.[197]

The Senate's decision meant that the 2008 Rome Statute bill failed to gain sufficient support during the 2006–11 legislative term. Although the Congolese legislature usually serves as a rubber stamp for executive policies (and it is likely Kabila allowed the bill to fail), parliamentary debates brought to light four obstacles to implementation.

First, the legislative process was marred by confusion over the aims of implementation, including fears of accountability from some lawmakers. Echoing challenges from the 2003–6 transitional parliament, the 2006–11 legislature still included belligerents from the First and Second Congo Wars, some of whom were accused of committing or facilitating crimes. It is no coincidence that factions implicated in abuses often vocally denounced the need for domestication.[198]

Second, as explained in Chapter 5, efforts to transfer the military's powers to prosecute international crimes to the civilian court system likely amplified turf wars between the legislature and the Kabila-led executive (aligned with the military), which in turn scuttled legislative reforms such as the Rome Statute bill.

Third, the death penalty emerged as a flashpoint in parliamentary debates. Despite a moratorium observed since 2003, capital punishment remained applicable to various offenses, including international crimes. Although the Rome Statute is agnostic about domestic punishments, the fact that the ICC can only impose life sentences was used as an argument by NGOs and foreign embassies to advocate abolition.[199] This generated backlash among some lawmakers and undermined the bill, prompting human rights groups to disentangle abolitionist advocacy from the narrower aims of the implementation bill.[200]

[197] Patryk I Labuda, 'The Democratic Republic of Congo's Failure to Address Impunity for International Crimes: A View from Inside the Legislative Process' (*International Justice Monitor*, 8 November 2011) <ijmonitor.org/2011/11/the-democratic-republic-of-congos-failure-to-address-impunity-for-international-crimes-a-view-from-inside-the-legislative-process-2010-2011-2/>.

[198] Author's notes, Senate debate, Kinshasa, DRC, 11 August 2011.

[199] Rome Statute, art 80. See eg Sofia Candeias and others, 'The Accountability Landscape in Eastern DRC: Analysis of the National Legislative and Judicial Response to International Crimes (2009–2014)' (ICTJ 2015) 13.

[200] Patryk I Labuda, 'Complementarity and Cooperation in the Congo' in Ronald Slye (ed), *The Nuremberg Principles in Non-Western Societies: A Reflection on Their Universality, Legitimacy and Application* (International Nuremberg Principles Academy 2016) 171. Critically on NGO abolition advocacy, see Mégret (n 188) 370.

Fourth, against the backdrop of anti-ICC rhetoric in Africa, accusations of neo-colonialism surfaced in some parliamentary debates. Feeding into pre-existing sovereignty concerns, the AU's denunciations of the ICC seemed to fuel resistance especially from Congolese lawmakers who feared accountability.[201]

In 2003, the ICC prosecutor still argued that 'it should be a high priority ... to actively remind States of their responsibility to adopt and implement effective legislation'.[202] However, the ASP subsequently discouraged the ICC from engaging in outreach to states.[203] With ICC officials avoiding legislative campaigns in the DRC (unlike in Sierra Leone, where Bensouda attended a workshop), civil society accepted the limits of the ICC's shadow for implementation purposes. As Nyabirungu Mwene Songa, a Congolese professor and parliamentarian, explained: 'you must understand the country's history ... there are many warlords among the political class, [and] they feared accountability'.[204]

Unable to overcome the vagaries of legislative politics, some groups shifted their attention to issues that generated consensus across political and belligerent groups, in particular reforms relating to sexual violence and child recruitment. Beginning in the early 2000s, high levels of rape began drawing international attention.[205] In addition to advocacy campaigns directed at the Congolese police and army, the UN and donors provided financial and medical support to victims.[206] Building on this momentum, NGOs and the UN's human rights office advocated legislation to address gaps in Congolese criminal law in regard to sexual violence.[207] Adopted in 2006, two bills criminalized some forms of rape and sexual exploitation for the first time, defined sexual relations with any person under 18 as statutory rape, and provided procedural protections for victims and witnesses.[208] A 2009 child protection law created additional protections for sexual violence against children and imposed a penalty of up to twenty years' imprisonment for the rape of a child.[209]

201 Author's notes, closed parliamentary meeting, Kinshasa, DRC, 15 August 2011.

202 ICC–OTP, 'Informal Expert Paper. The Principle of Complementarity in Practice' (2003) 5.

203 ICC–ASP, 'Report of the Bureau on Stocktaking: Complementarity, Taking Stock of the Principle of Complementarity: Bridging the Impunity Gap, ICC–ASP/8/51' para 42; ICC–OTP, 'Strategic Plan 2016–2018' (2015) para 95.

204 Interview with Nyabirungu Mwene Songa, Kinshasa, DRC, 20 April 2016.

205 Nicola Dahrendorfer, 'Mirror Images in the Congo: Sexual Violence and Conflict' (*Open Democracy*, 27 October 2005) <opendemocracy.net/democracy-resolution_1325/congo_2964.jsp>; HRW, 'Seeking Justice: The Prosecution of Sexual Violence in the Congo War' (2005) 22–45; Office of the UNSG Special Representative on Sexual Violence in Conflict <un.org/sexualviolenceinconflict/countries/democratic-republic-of-the-congo/>.

206 On awareness-raising in the army, see Toussaint Muntazini Mukimapa, *La problématique de la lutte contre les violences sexuelles en droit congolais* (RCN Justice 2009) 5.

207 Global Rights, 'Une loi sur la répression des violences sexuelles. De quoi s'agit-il? Texte d'orientation sur l'avant-projet de loi portant modification du code pénal congolais, du code de procédure pénale et du code de l'organisation et de la compétence judiciaire' (2006) (on file with author).

208 Dunia P Zongwe, 'The New Sexual Violence Legislation in the Congo: Dressing Indelible Scars on Human Dignity' (2012) 55 African Studies Review 37.

209 Loi 001/2009 du 10 janvier 2009, portant protection de l'enfant, art 170. On the two laws, see Muntazini Mukimapa (n 206) 29–60.

In both cases, international and domestic partners succeeded in navigating the DRC's complex legislative politics. A Congolese attorney involved in the passage of the 2006 sexual violence bills explained that they had been submitted for a vote shortly before the expiry of the Transitional National Assembly's term, to avoid potential obstructionism.[210] While the bills do not reference international standards, some analysts suggest that the Rome Statute and the ICTR's case law may have influenced the text.[211] As explained in Chapter 4, the justice sector has built on these reforms to prioritize domestic prosecutions of sexual violence crimes.

Although there have been challenges to implementing these bills—for instance, ten years later, some magistrates still applied the old criminal code—observers note that the increased attention on sexual violence and child recruitment has prompted genuine changes in the behaviour of Congolese actors.[212] Whereas mass rape was previously used as 'a weapon of war', including to punish civilians, UN officials explained that cases of systematic rape no longer occur and that army commanders, responding in part to external pressure, have effected a real 'change in mindset' among rank-and-file troops.[213] Similarly, UN officials and Congolese activists underscore the greater awareness around child recruitment among state actors.[214]

4.2. Complementarity circumvented: direct application of the Rome Statute and fair trial compliance

As explained in Chapter 4, military tribunals—supported by NGOs and the UN—started prosecuting international crimes in the mid-2000s. However, with legislative reform blocked for political reasons, the military justice system faced the practical challenge of applying international norms. Confronted with outdated and sometimes conflicting domestic norms, military magistrates turned to the Rome Statute for guidance.

210 E-mail exchange with Congolese attorney, 6 July 2017.

211 Sigall Horovitz, 'DR Congo: Interaction between International and National Judicial Responses to the Mass Atrocities' (DOMAC 2012) 45; Luke Moffett, *Justice for Victims before the International Criminal Court* (Routledge 2014) 244–45.

212 Interview with officials from Office of the Special Representative, Kinshasa, DRC, 26 April 2016.

213 Interviews cited in Patryk I Labuda, 'With or Against the State? Reconciling the Protection of Civilians and Host State Support in UN Peacekeeping' (International Peace Institute 2020) 8; BCUNDH, *Progress and Obstacles in the Fight against Impunity for Sexual Violence in the DRC* (2014); Ezéchiel Amani Cirimwami and Pacifique Muhindo Magadju, 'Prosecuting Rape as War Crime in the Democratic Republic of the Congo: Lessons and Challenges Learned from Military Tribunals' (2021) 59 Military Law and the Law of War Review 44.

214 Sharanjeet Parmar, 'Dissuasive or Disappointing? Measuring the Deterrent Effect of the International Criminal Court in the Democratic Republic of the Congo' in Jennifer Schense and Linda Carter (eds), *Two Steps Forward, One Step Back: The Deterrent Effect of International Criminal Tribunals* (International Nuremberg Principles Academy 2016) 188–89.

By arguing that in a monist legal system, such as the DRC, it was possible for international law to prevail over domestic norms, military tribunals began applying the Rome Statute to supplement, displace, or even override Congolese criminal law in domestic proceedings.[215] Over the years, magistrates have applied a wide range of international norms to plug gaps and resolve inconsistencies in domestic law, including the Statute's definitions of crimes, its Elements of Crimes and even its RPE. A flexible approach to norm interpretation, often encouraged by international NGOs and partners, has had both positive and negative consequences for judicial practice.

On the one hand, magistrates have replaced incomplete national norms with more comprehensive international norms. In many cases, tribunals applied ICC definitions of crimes to override the MCC's post-Second World War definitions of war crimes and crimes against humanity, or the Rome Statute's rules on victim protection to allow in camera testimony (as domestic law did not provide for such protections). In *Songo Mboyo*, for instance, the judges decided that 'the [ICC] Elements of the Crime ... gives rape a very broad extension including any other inhumane act with a gendered connotation', enabling a conviction for rape against men (which was not criminalized as such under Congolese law).[216] Similarly, applying the Rome Statute's modes of liability has enabled convictions of mid-level perpetrators for crimes of their subordinates.[217]

On the other hand, a selective application of norms creates fair trial concerns. For one, it raises questions about the hierarchy of legal sources and whether all international norms—for instance, procedural norms like the RPE or Elements of Crimes for the internal organization of the ICC's work—have enough legitimacy to displace binding criminal law. For another, it is unclear whether the military's 'pick-and-choose' approach to the applicable law is consistent with the principle of legality. Some question magistrates' seeming willingness to cherry-pick rules that facilitate convictions while ignoring ICC procedural guarantees for defendants. One NGO warns that the 'the existing jurisprudence remains fragmented, inconsistent and, in turn, unpredictable for those brought before Congolese courts'.[218]

[215] Avocats Sans Frontières, 'Etude de jurisprudence. L'application du Statut de Rome de la Cour Pénale internationale par les juridictions de la République démocratique du Congo' (2009).

[216] Tribunal Militaire de Garnison de Mbandaka, *Songo Mboyo*, 12 April 2006, RP 084/05, 27; Jean-Pierre Fofe Djofia Malewa, 'Commentaire du jugement Songo Mboyo: une illustration de l'éclairage de la justice nationale par les textes et la jurisprudence pénaux internationaux' (2006) 2 Revue Horizons 119; Avocats Sans Frontières (n 215) 27 and 37; Jacques B Mbokani, *Jurisprudence congolaise en matière de crimes de droit international* (Open Society Institute 2017) 44.

[217] See Mbokani (n 216) 207–77.

[218] Candeias and others (n 199) 8. For further challenges, see Jacques B Mbokani, 'L'amnistie et la répression des crimes de droit international au regard de l'avènement de la Cour Pénale internationale: le Statut de Rome à l'épreuve des impératifs de la justice transitionnelle' (2015) 75 Annales de droit de Louvain 239, 257.

Similarly, Jacques Mbokani argues 'it is impossible to say that defence rights are respected by Congolese tribunals ... the Congolese state should think to reorganise the justice system, selecting the individuals required to perform judicial functions more diligently'.[219]

Although reactions to the military's admittedly flexible use of the Rome Statute were initially critical, evaluations seem to have become more positive over time. According to the UN, 'court decisions ... are better drafted and reasoned than was hitherto the case'.[220] A military judge observed that applying the Rome Statute was 'not easy' and that it required 'courage' to convince the military hierarchy that this was a worthwhile endeavour.[221] Noting how West African lawyers have turned to the DRC for guidance, one Congolese attorney explained that 'our jurisprudence might be weak, but elsewhere there is no jurisprudence'.[222]

Another dimension to the DRC's use of the Rome Statute is that, unlike the ICTR's rule 11*bis*, complementarity does not condition case (in)admissibility on the observance of fair trial rights but rather the lack of 'genuine' proceedings. As noted in Chapter 3, this means that fair trial violations are not impermissible as long as trials do not end in acquittals. While the Rome Statute's anti-impunity rationale and concomitant agnosticism about fairness has not translated into a lack of interest in defence rights, its effects on domestic judicial practice should not be discounted. Some activists note that the position of the defence has improved, but most also acknowledge that defence rights are not properly regulated by the legal framework, and that, for instance, a system of legal aid for indigent defendants is absent.[223]

More importantly, no systematic trial monitoring exists, including for cases of probable shielding like the *Minova* rape trial (see Chapter 4), which would allow the ICC to exercise jurisdiction under the Rome Statute's 'unwilling genuinely' prong of complementarity. Although it is impossible to draw a direct causal connection, some interviewees pointed to the ICC's passivity in cases like *Minova* or Katanga's secondary domestic trial—as will be seen next—as harmful to the pursuit of principled accountability at the national level.[224]

[219] Mbokani (n 216) 346 (author translation).

[220] Charles Briefel and Ignacio Tredici, 'The United Nations Prosecution Support Cell Programme in the Democratic Republic of Congo—A Strategy to Combat Impunity for Serious Crimes' (2016) 19 Max Planck Yearbook of United Nations Law 337, 355.

[221] Interview with Congolese magistrate, 20 April 2016.

[222] Interview with Congolese attorney, 15 August 2016.

[223] Interviews with Congolese attorneys, Kinshasa, DRC, 25 and 27 April 2016. See Briefel and Tredici (n 220) 358–59.

[224] Interviews with activist and UN officials, Kinshasa, DRC and by phone, 25 April and 2 August 2016.

4.3. Interrogating complementarity's purpose: domestic (re)trials of ICC defendants

Because the ICC's extant complementarity jurisprudence divorces the admissibility of cases from fair trial violations in national proceedings, it is only if a domestic trial (fair or not) produces an acquittal that the ICC will assess the DRC's 'willingness genuinely' to prosecute, with a view to potentially asserting jurisdiction. Although the ICC's jurisprudence, and the perverse incentives it creates for states, are well covered in the literature, its implications in the context of secondary domestic proceedings are rarely analysed. In this regard, the DRC may foreshadow trends in the ICC's complementarity practice in other countries.[225]

In 2016, the ICC had to decide whether to allow Congolese prosecutors to reinitiate domestic proceedings against Katanga, even though the ICC had authorized his Hague trial seven years later based, inter alia, on the DRC prosecution service's assurances that a domestic trial was not possible. In the meantime, the ICC had prosecuted and convicted Katanga, but his relatively short sentence—twelve years' imprisonment—meant he was to be released from prison in early 2016. Displeased with this outcome, Congolese authorities announced that, despite prior assurances to the contrary, Katanga would be prosecuted after he served his ICC sentence.

Katanga's complementarity challenge, his international trial and—as it later turned out—his failed domestic (re)trial illustrate not just the ICC's confusion over the purpose of complementarity but also the contradictions inherent in the OTP's prosecutorial strategy. Exceptionally, on this occasion, the ICC Presidency was required to allow or disallow Congolese authorities to initiate post-ICC proceedings against Katanga. Rather than assess whether the DRC had any genuine intention to prosecute Katanga (ten years after their initial arrest, his co-accused in the original domestic case still languished in *pretrial* detention!), or whether such a trial would meet minimal fair trial guarantees, including the Rome Statute's prohibition of *ne bis in idem*, the presidency gave their permission arguing, with no sense of irony, that a domestic trial was in line with complementarity, which 'is explicitly espoused in ... the [Rome] Statute' and ensures 'effective prosecution ... at the national level'.[226]

That Katanga could be subjected to prosecution before the High Military Court is a logical, albeit perverse, consequence of an ICC prosecutorial strategy that

[225] In late 2015, Katanga was transferred to Kinshasa to serve the remainder of his ICC-mandated sentence. After completing his sentence, a new domestic prosecution was initiated, and Katanga requested the ICC to block his domestic trial. The facts are explained in Patryk I Labuda, 'The Flipside of Complementarity' (2019) 17 Journal of International Criminal Justice 369.

[226] Presidency, *Prosecutor v Germain Katanga* (Decision pursuant to Article 108(1) of the Rome Statute) ICC-01/04-01/07 (7 April 2016) para 23; Presidency, *Prosecutor v Germain Katanga* (Decision on 'Defence Application for Reconsideration of the Presidency "Decision Pursuant to article 108(1) of the Rome Statute"') ICC-01/ 04-01/07-3833 (26 June 2019).

targets suspects who are under domestic investigation, while ICC judges ignore whether the state is unwilling or unable to genuinely prosecute as long as the authorities promise to be inactive. That complementarity could serve to rationalize both Katanga's ICC trial and, seven years later, his secondary domestic trial illustrates the vacuousness of a norm that can be used, depending on the shifting political and institutional interests of the ICC and states, to justify two mutually exclusive outcomes.

Moreover, while avoiding qualitative assessments of domestic proceedings may be convenient to ensure cooperation, it risks making the ICC complicit in fair trial abuses, like Katanga's prolonged and unlawful detention. In 2020, four years after the ICC gave its approval, with no progress in his domestic trial, Katanga was released pursuant to a peace agreement.[227] Given the DRC's patchy adherence to human rights norms, he and his co accused are unlikely to receive compensation for years of unlawful pretrial detention that never translated into a trial.

4.4. Domesticating the Rome Statute: epiphenomenal complementarity

In 2016, the Rome Statute was finally incorporated into the Congolese legal order. Split into four pieces of legislation (to avoid constitutional challenges), *la loi de mise en œuvre* passed nearly unanimously in both chambers of parliament. After the vote, Parliamentarians for Global Action celebrated that '[the bill] will finally allow Congo to give full effect to the principle of complementarity . . . the entirety of the Congolese judicial system will thus be strengthened . . . finally giv[ing] victims access to justice and establish[ing] guarantees of non-repetition'.[228]

The law's most visible aspect was its domestication of the ICC's definitions of genocide, crimes against humanity and war crimes.[229] Yet, while this was initially a core demand for NGOs, the MCC's outdated definitions had, by 2016, become something of a non-issue in practice, with normative cross-pollination occurring through jurisprudence rather than by legislative fiat. With military tribunals applying the Rome Statute on a regular basis, most domestic cases revolved around the ICC's definitions, though the 2016 law expanded on the ICC's protections in

[227] On Katanga's release, see Claude Sengenya, 'DRC: Lubanga and Katanga Freed for Peace in Ituri' (*Justice Info*, 31 March 2020) <justiceinfo.net/en/reconciliation/44065-drc-lubanga-and-katanga-freed-for-peace-in-ituri.html>.

[228] 'PGA Salue l'adoption de la Loi de mise en œuvre du Statut de Rome de la CPI par le Senat de la RDC, 2 November 2015' <pgaction.org/fr/news/drc-adopts-implementing-legislation-rome-statute-icc.html> (author translation).

[229] Article 4 modifiant arts 221–23 du code pénal ordinaire, Loi 15/022 du 31 décembre 2015 modifiant et complétant le Décret du 30 janvier 1940 portant Code pénal, Journal Officiel, 29 February 2016, 2 (hereafter RSLaw1).

two minor ways: the crime against humanity of persecution can now be based on tribal affiliation and the war crime of directing attacks against humanitarian missions extends not only to the UN but also the AU and other international organizations.[230]

Aside from these cosmetic changes, the 2016 law expanded on constitutional fair trial guarantees, in particular the presumption of innocence and the principle of legality.[231] With decade-long efforts to overhaul the 1940 penal code and 1959 criminal procedure code stalled, the 2016 law also updated norms from the colonial period. Equally significant, the law integrated *verbatim* the Rome Statute's complex rules on principal, accessory liability, and superior responsibility, as well as its grounds for excluding criminal liability.[232] Both military and civilian superiors can now be prosecuted as direct perpetrators (military law had previously created obstacles, for example commanders could be tried only as accomplices or co-perpetrators, meaning that accountability depended on whether their subordinates were also prosecuted).

In addition to domesticating the DRC's duty to cooperate with the ICC, the 2016 law clarified which state institutions serve as liaisons to The Hague; provided security guarantees to victims, witnesses, and intermediaries; and resolved lingering jurisdictional issues between civilian and military courts.[233] Contrary to civil society demands, the law expands the death penalty's scope of application in cases of accomplice liability (though a moratorium continues to be observed).[234]

Complementarity played a mainly rhetorical role in the legislative process, but a few provisions address concurrent jurisdiction. Reiterating that 'national jurisdictions have primacy to address [international crimes] and that the ICC 'intervenes only in a subsidiary manner', the law empowers 'the DRC President, further to deliberations in the Council of Ministers, to [self-]refer a situation' and 'request the [ICC] Prosecutor to investigate'.[235] In other words, unlike some states, for instance Spain or CAR, which purport to 'transfer' primacy onto the ICC through domestic

230 ibid art 222(9) CP in conjunction with Rome Statute, art 7(h), which does not recognize tribal groups as a protected category. Rome Statute, art 223(2)(c) and (g) CP in conjunction with art 8(2)(b)(iii) and (vii). There are also two typographic mistakes, see Labuda (n 200) 169–71.

231 ibid art 2 ajoutant art 26*bis* CPC; art 1 ajoutant art 1*bis* CP. The 2006 Congolese Constitution already recognized these rights as a matter of constitutional law.

232 Article 1 modifiant art 1 MCC, Loi 15/023 du 31 décembre 2015 modifiant la loi 024/2002 du 18 novembre 2002 portant code pénal militaire, Journal Officiel, 29 February 2016, p. 17 (RSLaw2); art 2, ajoutant art 21 bis CP and art 2 ajoutant art 22*bis* CP, RSLaw1. The Rome Statute's rules excluding criminal responsibility (arts 31–33) are not incorporated in their entirety (art 2 ajoutant art 23*bis*—quinquies CP, RSLaw1).

233 Article 2 ajoutant art 21 bis—21.31 du CPC, Loi 15/024 du 31 décembre 2015 modifiant et complétant le Décret du 6 août 1959 portant Code de procédure pénal, Journal Officiel, 29 February 2016, 19 (RSLaw3); art 2 ajoutant art 26*ter* CPC; Loi organique 17/003 du 10 mars 2017 modifiant et complétant la loi 023-2002 du 18 novembre portant Code judiciaire militaire, Journal Officiel, 58ème année, 7, 1 April 2017, 7 (RSlaw4).

234 Article 2 modifiant art 21*quater*, last sentence, RSLaw1.

235 Article 2 ajoutant art 21 octies and 10e CPC, RSLaw3.

law, the DRC reasserted its sovereign power and confirmed that the ICC is subsidiary to domestic jurisdiction.[236]

Observers disagree on the reasons for, and the significance of, the Rome Statute bill. For instance, a long-time supporter of implementation emphasized how, despite the government's lukewarm attitude vis-à-vis the ICC, the tenacity of civil society made passage of the law possible.[237] By contrast, some government and military officials downplayed the bill's importance. A high-ranking adviser to Kabila characterized the bill as being 'without much importance', noting the military's application of the Rome Statute.[238] A military commander emphasized that the ICC 'must bend before us, [as] we have priority'.[239] Yet others believe the bill was a missed opportunity. One civil society activist considered the bill 'a failure' due to its insufficient guarantees for victims.[240]

Ultimately, as noted by one of the bill's architects, what secured the bill's passage was that parliamentarians and other Congolese powerbrokers understood that the law itself was not a threat to their positions. In particular, pro-sovereignty factions within the military—placated by the hybrid tribunal's failure, as seen in Chapter 5—seemed to acquiesce to Rome Statute implementation, which did not challenge their authority and implicitly affirmed the ICC's residual jurisdiction over international crimes. 'Fear of the ICC has faded in the meantime', he concluded.[241]

4.5. Rome's anti-impunity shadow: displacing amnesty and immunity

Defined as 'prospectively barring criminal prosecution' or 'retroactively nullifying legal liability', amnesties are a controversial transitional justice tool.[242] On the one hand, they can be used for positive ends, such as, inter alia, 'encouraging combatants to surrender and disarm', 'persuading authoritarian rulers to hand over power', or 'facilitating peace agreements'.[243] On the other, some types of amnesty, especially blanket (unconditional) self-amnesties for international crimes, are considered to be inconsistent with legal obligations to prosecute and, hence, illegitimate (albeit not necessarily illegal).[244]

[236] See Chapter 5, section 4.3 in this volume.
[237] Interview with Nyabirungu Mwene Songa, 20 April 2016.
[238] Interview with senior Kabila adviser, Kinshasa, DRC, 19 August 2016.
[239] Interview with military magistrate, Goma, DRC, 4 September 2015 (commenting on the draft law).
[240] Interview with activist, Kinshasa, DRC, 18 Aug 2016.
[241] Interview with activist, Kinshasa, DRC, 22 April 2016.
[242] OHCHR, *Rule-of-Law Tools for Post-Conflict States. Amnesties* (United Nations 2009) 5.
[243] Transitional Justice Institute, University of Ulster, *The Belfast Guidelines on Amnesty and Accountability: With Explanatory Guidance* (2013) 9.
[244] ibid; OHCHR (n 242).

Strictly speaking, the Rome Statute does not address the (il)legality of amnesties. This was a deliberate choice on the part of its drafters, who realized states would not agree on this issue.[245] However, the consolidation of international criminal law after the 1990s has delegitimized non-retributive forms of accountability. Although there has been some debate as to whether non-retributive mechanisms, such as truth commissions, should make cases inadmissible under article 17, it is likely that cases—otherwise prosecutable but 'immunized' through a national amnesty—would run afoul of the 'inactivity' test and, hence, ICC proceedings would advance without any inquiry as to a state's good or bad faith in adopting said amnesty (however, no direct case law on this point exists so far).

The ICC's presence in the DRC has coincided with four national amnesties, adopted in 2003, 2005, 2009, and 2014 respectively. Although the rationales behind each act varied, the Congolese government has resorted to amnesties primarily to encourage the demobilization of armed groups and their reintegration into the national army.[246] For instance, the 2014 amnesty law, adopted in the aftermath of Ntaganda's M23 rebellion, made Congolese (co-)perpetrators or accomplices eligible for amnesty relating to 'insurrectional acts, acts of war and political offences'.[247] In this case, former rebels needed to submit a letter of commitment that they would abstain from such acts in future, lest their amnesties be revoked.[248]

From a normative perspective, it is noteworthy that all four amnesties have excluded war crimes, crimes against humanity and genocide from their scope of application.[249] Similar to Sierra Leone, where the UN played an important role in circumscribing the Lomé amnesty, it seems international partners at the 2002 Inter-Congolese Dialogue provided the initial impulse for the exclusionary clauses.[250] Going further, the 2014 amnesty—seemingly in response to civil society criticisms of previous laws—excluded rape, sexual violence, the use of child soldiers, and 'other grave and mass violations of human rights'.[251]

Despite the Rome Statute's nominal silence on the (il)legality of amnesties, ICC intervention in the DRC has contributed not only to the delegitimization of amnesties for international crimes but also consolidated a broader anti-impunity

[245] William A Schabas, *Unimaginable Atrocities: Justice, Politics, and Rights at the War Crimes Tribunals* (OUP 2012) 173–76.

[246] Phil Clark, 'The UN Security Council and Transitional Justice: The Democratic Republic of the Congo' in Rebecca Brubaker (ed), *The UN Security Council and Transitional Justice* (United Nations University 2021).

[247] Article 3, Loi 14/006 du 11 février 2014 portant amnistie pour faits insurrectionnels, faits de guerre et infractions politiques, 11 February 2014.

[248] ibid art 5.

[249] Article 1, Décret-Loi 03-001 du 15 avril 2003 portant amnistie pour faits de guerre, infractions politiques et d'opinion, 15 April 2003; Article 3, Loi 05/023 du 2005 portant amnistie pour faits de guerre, infractions politiques et d'opinion, 19 December 2005; Loi 14/006 (n 247).

[250] Pretoria Peace Agreement 16 December 2002, s III, point 8. On the DRC exclusionary clauses' origins, see Laura Davis and Priscilla Hayner, 'Difficult Peace, Limited Justice: Ten Years of Peacemaking in the DRC' (ICTJ 2009) 3.

[251] Loi 14/006 (n 247) art 4.

norm that extends to pardons and immunities.[252] For instance, Mathieu Ngudjolo, reintegrated into the army after being pardoned by Kabila in 2006, was nevertheless surrendered to the ICC three years later. While Ngudjolo's surrender is usually seen as a positive step, it was controversial in other ways. As Phil Clark observes, '[w]hile the Congolese Government was widely hailed for its cooperation in arresting and transferring Ngudjolo to the ICC, its duplicity towards a recipient of a government pardon undermined the broader use of amnesty as an incentive for members of rebel groups to lay down their arms'.[253]

The ICC's anti-impunity shadow has grown over time. Echoing the amnesties' exclusionary clauses, the 2016 Rome Statute implementation law prohibited amnesties for international crimes.[254] Despite some questions as to its constitutionality, the law also abolished domestic immunity for such crimes by domesticating article 27 of the Statute. Accordingly, Congolese law now 'appl[ies] equally to all persons without any distinction based on official capacity', and '[i]n particular, official capacity as a Head of state or government, a member of a government or parliament, an elected representative or a government official shall in no case exempt a person from criminal responsibility'.[255]

Against the backdrop of this law, an electoral crisis unfolded as presidential elections, initially scheduled for 2016, were delayed repeatedly by President Kabila. Although he was barred from running for a third, unconstitutional term, Kabila was reluctant to step down, amid speculation about potential criminal liability.[256] While the elections ultimately took place in late 2018, a contentious issue during the pre-electoral period was legislation on the 'status of former presidents', including the scope of their immunity from prosecution.[257] Promulgated by Kabila just months before the 2018 vote that eventually saw an opposition leader come to power, the law granted 'former elected DRC presidents immunity from criminal prosecution for acts in the exercise of official duties'.[258] Whereas early drafts included an exclusionary clause for genocide, crimes against humanity and war crimes, the final text notes only that 'in regard to crimes against the peace and security of humanity committed by any former elected president national jurisdictions have priority over any international or foreign jurisdiction'.[259] In addition to these legal guarantees, it is rumoured that

[252] On the legal differences between these terms, see OHCHR (n 242).

[253] Clark (n 246) 85–86.

[254] Article 1 modifiant art 34*bis*, RSLaw1.

[255] ibid art 2, ajoutant 20*quater* CP, RSLaw 1 (incorporating Rome Statute, art 27 on the absence of immunities, but it is unclear how this norm is to be reconciled with the Constitution's provision on immunities of heads of state (2006 DRC Constitution, arts 107, 163–64)).

[256] Interview with Congolese attorney. Kinshasa, DRC, 19 April 2016.

[257] 'Sénat: Débat sur la proposition de Loi sur le Statut des anciens présidents de la République' *Radio Okapi* (29 September 2017) <radiookapi.net/2017/09/29/actualite/societe/senat-debat-sur-la-proposition-de-loi-sur-le-statut-des-anciens>.

[258] Loi du 26 juillet 2018 portant status des anciens présidents de la République, art 7 (author translation).

[259] ibid art 9 (author translation).

Kabila struck a pre-electoral deal with the incoming president that immunized him from prosecution.[260]

Government officials' fear of prosecution is not unfounded. As explained in Chapter 4, in addition to trials of armed group members, Congolese courts have prosecuted state actors, including high-ranking political and military officials. In 2014, the High Military Court sentenced Jérôme Kakwavu, an army general, to ten years' imprisonment for the war crimes of rape, murder, and torture.[261] In 2017, a sitting member of the South Kivu parliament was sentenced to life imprisonment for the crime against humanity of raping over forty young girls.[262] On appeal, the judges affirmed that the Rome Statute's principle of irrelevance of official capacity, as domesticated, overrode constitutional immunities. Although the ruling is not a model of clarity—how do international and national laws override constitutional privileges?—practice seems to have consecrated a norm that no one, including sitting government officials, are above the law.[263] This is noteworthy in so far as this stance seems to contradict the AU's position on immunities.[264]

The ICC's anti-impunity shadow is widely acknowledged in the DRC. A prosecutor observed that the political elite, including the prime minister and president, is 'clearly mindful' of the possibility of prosecutions and that 'they are worried'.[265] Echoing this sentiment, an attorney emphasized that the 'political class is scared of the ICC'.[266] By the same token, international actors acknowledge using the ICC to influence the strategic decision-making of Congolese powerbrokers. UN officials explained that the peacekeeping mission has sometimes brandished the threat of ICC prosecutions to influence the behaviour of government and non-state actors with potential criminal exposure. According to a senior UN official, 'the Congolese are terrified of the ICC; they panic when they hear about [the] ICC'.[267] Another UN official noted that 'this relationship between us and ICC is not entirely unhelpful'.[268]

[260] Africa Confidential, 'No Get out of Jail Card' (21 January 2021).

[261] Anneke Van Woudenberg, 'First Congolese General Convicted of Rape' (10 November 2014) <hrw.org/news/2014/11/10/dispatches-first-congolese-general-convicted-rape>. It should be noted, however, that Kakwavu was a former rebel reintegrated into the army.

[262] Daniele Perissi and Karen Naimer, 'Achieving Justice for Child Survivors of Conflict-Related Sexual Violence in the Democratic Republic of the Congo' (2020) 18 Journal of International Criminal Justice 293.

[263] ibid 300–02. Constitutional immunities were also in play in Senator Fidèle Babala's transfer to the ICC in 2013 to face charges of witness tampering (Olivia Bueno, 'Bemba's Colleagues Arrested for Witness Tampering Sparks an Indignant Response in the DRC' (*International Justice Monitor*, 4 December 2013) <ijmonitor.org/2013/12/bembas-colleagues-arrested-for-witness-tampering-sparks-an-indignant-response-in-the-drc/>).

[264] Paola Gaeta and Patryk I Labuda, 'Trying Sitting Heads of State: The African Union versus the ICC in the Al Bashir and Kenyatta Cases' in Ilias Bantekas and Charles C Jalloh (eds), *The International Criminal Court and Africa* (OUP 2018).

[265] Interview with Congolese magistrate, Kinshasa, DRC, 19 April 2016.

[266] Interview with Congolese attorney, Kinshasa, DRC, 19 April 2016.

[267] Interview with senior UN official, Kinshasa, DRC, 27 April 2016. See also Burke-White (n 196) 589.

[268] Phone interview with UN official, 2 August 2016.

Notwithstanding these normative developments, the reach of the ICC's anti-impunity shadow is incomplete. Despite the exclusionary clauses, it is unclear whether Congolese authorities have ever denied amnesty based on an individual's participation in serious crimes. As Patrícia Pinto Soares observes in relation to the 2014 amnesty law, the justice ministry did not seem to have any mechanism in place to assess whether individuals applying for amnesty had committed any of the crimes that required amnesty to be denied.[269] Congolese magistrates struggle, in practice, to distinguish 'legitimate acts of war', which are eligible for amnesty, from international crimes. Military actors also use jurisdictional privileges, whereby military suspects must be tried by someone of equal or higher rank, to prevent some prosecutions from going forward.[270] Moreover, although international partners seem increasingly sceptical about the effectiveness of the DRC's security sector reform, there is still a tacit acceptance of some types of amnesty, especially as the price of demobilization for armed groups.[271]

4.6. The shadow side of article 17: unintended diversionary complementarity

While the DRC is often said to epitomize the potential of international criminal law in Africa, a more complex story lies behind the dozens of trials of international crimes and hundreds of ordinary crimes cases. Drawing on Yahli Shereshevsky's conceptualization of the 'unintended negative effect of positive complementarity', the DRC's accountability landscape is better understood as a case of 'unintended diversionary complementarity', which captures the phenomenon of state authorities trying lower-level, politically unconnected perpetrators for isolated human rights violations while ignoring systematic crimes condoned by senior state officials.[272] By reinforcing rather than challenging power structures in the DRC's political space, unintended diversionary complementarity speaks to the risk of ICTs' 'authoritarian shadow'.

[269] Patrícia Pinto Soares, 'Transitional Justice in the DRC. The 2014 Amnesty Law and the Principle of Complementarity—Quid Juris?' in Triestino Mariniello (ed), *The International Criminal Court in Search of Its Identity and Purpose* (Routledge 2015) 183–88.

[270] Interviews with NGO official and senior UN official, Kinshasa, DRC, 1 September 2015 and 27 April 2016. Military law requires soldiers and police to be tried by judges of equal or higher rank. This rule often shielded high-level commanders from trial since the High Military Court lacked generals among its judges. On the role of constitutional privileges, see BCUNDH (n 213) 18.

[271] On de facto amnesty underpinning DDR processes in the DRC, see Clark (n 246) 85–86.

[272] Yahli Shereshevsky, 'The Unintended Negative Effect of Positive Complementarity' (2020) 18 Journal of International Criminal Justice 1017, 1024–25 (arguing 'the ICC's shadow may induce domestic courts to uphold' policies 'so as not to provide the ICC with "ammunition" in the form of acknowledgement of illegality'). The title of this section refers to Kevin J Heller, 'The Shadow Side of Complementarity: The Effect of Article 17 of the Rome Statute on National Due Process' (2007) 17 Criminal Law Forum 255.

Selectivity is part and parcel of the domestic enforcement of international criminal law in the DRC. Many investigations of serious crimes initially focused on militia groups fighting against government forces, especially in the eastern provinces. More recent data suggest that this trend has been reversed, with courts now prosecuting army troops and police officers at higher rates than armed group members.[273] However, given the government's history of reintegrating rebels into the army, classifying proceedings along a state–non-state binary may obscure the power dynamics behind criminal law enforcement. Acknowledging selectivity in this regard, a senior UN official noted that even when state agents are investigated, it is easier to convince magistrates to bring charges against former rebels reintegrated into the army or low-level suspects with no political connections.[274]

While precise data are lacking, few doubt that trials are used selectively. For instance, the 2011 conviction of Lt. Col. Kibibi for rape as a crime against humanity—characterized as a breakthrough by NGOs—was a politically uncontroversial case against a 'soft target', in this case an officer reintegrated into the army from a Rwandan-backed militia shortly before his arrest.[275] Junior officers are routinely 'scapegoated' to protect their superiors, while informal deals shield some high-ranking military personnel from prosecution altogether.[276] Analysing prosecution trends in South Kivu, Milli Lake argues that cases advance to trial based on factors such as 'political connections', 'intragroup and intergroup rivalries', 'protecting loyalties', 'brokering deals', 'removing challengers and adversaries', or 'deflecting attention from other activities'.[277] She concludes that:[278]

> rather than providing an impartial venue for pursuing legal accountability, human rights trials in eastern DR Congo are inherently political processes ... international stakeholders have proved unable to overcome powerful inter and intragroup alliances that shape who faces trial and who continues to evade justice. As a

[273] E-mail exchanges with UN officials, January 2020. See also Candeias and others (n 199) 22 (in 2014 over half of adjudicated cases still concerned armed groups).

[274] Interview with senior UN official, Kinshasa, DRC 27 April 2016.

[275] 'Congo Army Colonel Guilty of Ordering Mass Rape on New Year's Day' (21 February 2011) AP; Milli Lake, 'After Minova: Can War Crimes Trials Overcome Violence in the DRC?' (*African Arguments*, 8 May 2014) <africanarguments.org/2014/05/08/after-minova-can-war-crimes-trials-overcome-violence-in-the-drc-by-millie-lake/>; Milli Lake, 'Organizing Hypocrisy: Providing Legal Accountability for Human Rights Violations in Areas of Limited Statehood' (2014) 58 International Studies Quarterly 515, 516–17.

[276] Milli Lake, 'Building the Rule of War: Postconflict Institutions and the Micro-Dynamics of Conflict in Eastern DR Congo' (2017) 71 International Organization 281296–300; HRW, 'Justice on Trial: Lessons from the Minova Rape Case in the Democratic Republic of Congo' (2015); BCUNDH (n 213) 13 and 17.

[277] Lake (n 276). For a similar analysis of impunity in Sudan and Uganda, see Sarah MH Nouwen, *Complementarity in the Line of Fire: The Catalysing Effect of the International Criminal Court in Uganda and Sudan* (CUP 2013) 371–78.

[278] Lake, 'After Minova' (n 275).

result, the landscape of violence in eastern DR Congo continues to be characterized by unchecked impunity.

Congolese actors readily acknowledge the political nature of criminal law enforcement. A high-ranking Kabila adviser observed that 'despite the nominal independence of the judiciary', decisions on high-value prosecutions were made by the executive, including the head of state.[279] A senior military magistrate acknowledged political interference in some cases, explaining that, for instance in North Kivu, 'we ask but don't get evidence [from the military]' and that 'military prosecutors [just] don't understand why'.[280] One military prosecutor explained:[281]

> our justice is not so independent, there is strong pressure to not implicate high ranking people, the way this is usually done is that you have mass crimes and yet only one or a few minor people are targeted but we cannot go after more or the main ones. [There is] political pressure to move on to other things, initiate proceedings and that way show that justice is being done, but this is not [real]. We need independence financially [and] logistically and more to be able to do our job.

Acknowledging that support from the UN and NGOs can only overcome some obstacles, international actors calibrate their advocacy to account for prevailing political realities. A senior UN official conceded that 'in sensitive political cases, I told my people to just observe . . . do no harm is a UN guiding principle, [we] don't want to get people killed'.[282] Another UN official conceded that MONUSCO's support for domestic trials was technical and logistical in nature but that the mission would not try to influence prosecutorial policy.[283] Acknowledging a reluctance to advocate trials of Kabila allies, a senior UN official argued 'we wait for opportunities . . . but is the priority to pursue [a perpetrator] if today he is not doing anything, or do I have to focus on pursuing [the perpetrator] who is dangerous today?'.[284]

Given the political nature of criminal justice in the DRC, the UN, and NGOs often redirect support to less sensitive violations. In particular, charges of ordinary

[279] Interviews with senior Kabila adviser, 19 August 2016. This sentiment was confirmed by a number of Congolese state and non-state actors. For similar observations of high-level interference and shielding in the context of the UK–Iraq preliminary examination, see ICC–OTP, 'Situation in Iraq/UK. Final Report' (2020); HRW, 'DR Congo: Sham Trial for Murders of UN Experts' (7 February 2022) <hrw.org/news/2022/02/07/dr-congo-sham-trial-murders-un-experts>; Luc Henkinbrant, 'Justice transitionnelle en RDC: Comment l'ONU l'a rangé dans un tiroir' (*JusticeInfo*, 14 January 2022) <justiceinfo.net/fr/86510-justice-transitionnelle-rdc-congo-comment-onu-range-dans-tiroir.html>.

[280] Interview with senior military magistrate, Kinshasa, DRC, 26 July 2019.

[281] Interview with military magistrate, undisclosed location and date.

[282] Interview with former UN official, Geneva, Switzerland, 12 June 2017.

[283] Labuda (n 213) 20.

[284] Quoted in: ibid.

crimes against isolated perpetrators are prioritized over complex international crimes implicating officers, commanders, and politicians. In other words, isolated charges of rape against insubordinate individuals are pursued rather than coordinated attacks or mass rape by entire units. Another example is advocacy on behalf of consensus topics, such as crimes against children or the environment.[285] Acknowledging this trend, the UN has criticized its own officials for supporting 'serious but "ordinary"' rather than international crimes.[286] At the same time, the UN and NGOs are aware of the limits of their influence. A UN official conceded that 'political pressure' for sensitive prosecutions 'leads nowhere ... [and] we know better than to waste our time'.[287]

Given these and other challenges, opinions on the ICC's impact on domestic accountability in the DRC run the spectrum. Some government actors lament the ICC's insufficient cooperation with domestic proceedings, as noted in Chapter 4. Others criticize its slowness or one-sided prosecutions, while yet others emphasize the Rome Statute's normative impact. Yet, by and large, Congolese stakeholders acknowledge the ICC's emancipatory appeal in the DRC. As one activist observed, 'the ICC allowed Congolese justice to emancipate itself'.[288] Echoing this theme, others argued that 'it served as a catalyst', noting how internal opposition within the army to the transfers of suspects to the ICC 'provoked an internal debate as to why were are not doing it, and as a result now we are [doing it]' or that 'Bosco [Ntaganda] would have never been arrested without the ICC'.[289] At the same time, a senior military magistrate explained that, while the ICC should be careful not to interfere in domestic affairs, greater involvement would be useful for politically sensitive crimes. 'We need the ICC for cases of lack of willingness', he concluded.[290]

How to overcome 'unwillingness'? Herein lies the ICC's greatest challenge. As elsewhere, in the DRC the obstacles to accountability are both structural and personal in nature. To a greater extent than at the ICTR, however, iterative relations

[285] See ICTJ, 'Prosecuting the Plundering of Natural Resources in Eastern DRC to Stem the Violence' (30 January 2017) <ictj.org/news/plundering-natural-resources-drc-violence>; Ephrem Rugiririza and Claude Sengenya, 'In Congo, Mihonya Trial Shows Link Between Environmental and War Crimes' (*JusticeInfo*, 23 September 2021) <justiceinfo.net/en/82441-congo-mihonya-trial-link-environmental-war-crimes.html>; TRIAL International, 'DRC: Former Militiaman Chance Sentenced to Life in South Kivu' (14 September 2021) <trialinternational.org/latest-post/environmental-crimes-brought-before-the-court-in-south-kivu-drc/>.

[286] UN Criminal Law and Judicial Advisory Service, 'Combatting Impunity in the Democratic Republic of the Congo. Lessons Learned from the UN Prosecution Support Cell Programme' (2015) 24. But see Anushka Sehmi, 'Judicializing Economic Violence as Means of Dismantling the Structural Causes of Atrocity in the Democratic Republic of Congo' (2021) 14 International Journal of Transitional Justice 423 (arguing for 'a transformative justice approach' at the ICC and prosecution of 'economic crimes' to 'address the pervasive root causes of conflict' and 'dismantl[e] structural causes of violence').

[287] Phone interview with UN official, 2 August 2016.

[288] Interview with defence attorney, Goma, DRC, 31 August 2015.

[289] Interview with senior military magistrate and activist, Kinshasa, DRC, 23 and 25 April 2016.

[290] Interview with senior military magistrate, Goma, DRC, 7 August 2019.

with state-based actors in countries like the DRC are foreclosed by the Rome Statute's institutional design, compounded by the OTP's risk-averse vision of international intervention and the self-interest (in having triable cases) of judges in The Hague. While the Statute allows the OTP to share information or engage in capacity building, as is advocated by scholars and activists, such support is unlikely to change the accountability landscape. Because the Rome Statute—contrary to the ICTR Statute—lacks an express conditionality mechanism analogous to rule 11*bis* to monitor and revoke ensuing trials, and the prevalent judicial interpretation of article 17 disempowers the OTP (e.g. when it refers evidence) from monitoring fair trial standards, this reading of complementarity creates a dilemma.[291] As the OTP should not facilitate trials absent the power to reassert jurisdiction if state officials renege on promises to respect e.g. witness confidentiality or defence rights, the extant article 17 case law forecloses, rather than stimulates, iteration vis-à-vis state authorities in regard to suspects that both the ICC and states want to prosecute.

Not only does this reading of article 17 foreclose iteration in cases against government rivals; it means that, in practice, the ICC's oversight of domestic proceedings is limited to the hard cases of 'shielding' and 'sham' trials, where states do not want to prosecute suspects at all. Thus, to a greater degree than at the ICTR, the ICC's potential to trigger iteration vis-à-vis domestic authorities is unlikely to follow from strategies of capacity building. And yet, twenty years after it launched operations, the OTP has still failed to devise a strategy that balances its duty to challenge states over sham trials with the operational necessity to maintain cooperation. These dilemmas were exposed most conspicuously in Libya, where the shortcomings of a case law that legitimized flawed proceedings against Gaddafi and Al-Senussi flowed from a deferential and sovereignty-friendly reading of complementarity that glosses over terms like 'genuine' and 'unwilling'.[292]

Echoing the Rwandan experience, another problem in the DRC is that support for domestic prosecutions concentrates on the trial phase while ignoring the pretrial phase. Drawing on her analysis of proceedings in South Kivu, Lake notes that 'looking at due process among only cases that enter the legal system, without examining those that fall out in early stages, obscures the myriad ways in which postconflict institutions ... can be manipulated by elites in pursuit of conflict-related ends'.[293] Yet manipulation of the pretrial phase is ignored entirely by a reading of article 17 that prioritizes binary and facially neutral admissibility tests revolving around the meaning of 'case' rather than the sociolegal parameters of states' willingness, ability, and genuineness to address serious crimes.

[291] Federica Gioia, 'Complementarity and "Reverse Cooperation"' in Stahn and El Zeidy (n 188) 818 (anticipating this problem but downplaying its importance).

[292] See Chapter 3 and further Chapter 7 in this volume.

[293] Lake (n 276) 289.

4.7. Unpacking complementarity's effects on norm internalization

The Congolese normative landscape has changed in the last twenty years. To varying degrees, definitions of international crimes, modes of liability, and defence and victim rights have been incorporated into the domestic legal order. At the same time, amnesties and immunities are viewed with increased scepticism. While complementarity has often served as a rhetorical frame for legislative initiatives, the ICC's contribution to norm internalization in the DRC illuminates certain problems with a Rome Statute-based system of international criminal law enforcement.

Even in countries like the DRC, where the law already criminalized genocide, crimes against humanity and war crimes, NGOs advocated 'implementation' that extended beyond the government's cooperation obligations with the ICC. Although framed as a consequence of complementarity, implementation campaigns proved ineffective, partly because of overambitious priorities that linked ordinary criminal justice and the death penalty to international criminal law enforcement, while potentially slowing down more holistic reforms, such as a new criminal code. The DRC did not implement the Rome Statute to prevent the domestic justice system from being found 'unwilling', nor was advocacy focused on enabling the prosecution of the 'same case' or to otherwise preclude the exercise of ICC jurisdiction.[294] In fact, as long as the political elite viewed the ICC as a threat to its interests, such legislation remained off the table. Thus, rather than enabling, the ICC's shadow may have precluded reforms, while implementation only became possible after the threat of ICC prosecutions had receded.[295] Paradoxically, the implementation law eventually broadened the death penalty's scope of application and, although a moratorium remains in place, magistrates still mete out death sentences.[296]

With legislative reform blocked in Parliament, domestication of international criminal law shifted to the courts. Direct application of the Rome Statute constitutes an innovative albeit a questionable approach to norm internalization, at least from a fair trial perspective. While magistrates, supported by NGOs and donors, override Congolese criminal law to facilitate proceedings, defence rights are sometimes sidelined in a rush to convict. A similar anti-impunity push, at the expense of a more nuanced debate around the fairness of proceedings and non-criminal alternatives, underpins the government's approach to amnesties, which formally

[294] On this expectation, see Burke-White (n 196). But see Baylis (n 191) 51.

[295] Along these lines (with a different focus), see Christian M De Vos, *Complementarity, Catalysts, Compliance: The International Criminal Court in Uganda, Kenya, and the Democratic Republic of Congo* (CUP 2020) 188.

[296] At the time of writing, a moratorium from 2003 remains in place, though tribunals continue to sentence perpetrators of international crimes to mandatory death sentences. See Joseph Mbuyi, 'In Kasai, Justice against All Odds' (*JusticeInfo*, 21 April 2022) <justiceinfo.net/en/91073-kasai-justice-against-all-odds.html>.

exclude international crimes (albeit not necessarily in practice), and the consolidation of a broader anti-impunity norm that extends to domestic immunities.

In light of the government's anti-impunity stance and relatively high numbers of domestic trials, activists generally celebrate the DRC as an example of 'positive complementarity' in action. Yet, while the authorities' motives are complex, including a genuine desire on the part of many Congolese to hold perpetrators to account, in the shadow of the ICC's intervention lies a complex question about the effects of two decades of international support and, in particular, to what extent international norms, as vernacularized in the military courts' jurisprudence, can be said to have been internalized by local actors. Put differently, how genuine (and fair) are proceedings administered by magistrates who are nominally willing and able to prosecute international crimes?

This question is difficult to answer, and statistics about trials, convictions, and acquittals provide scant guidance. Given the national justice system's structural weaknesses, international partners are keen to support domestic prosecutions but rarely interrogate criminal law's role in the DRC's larger scheme of statebuilding. The UN and NGO's agnosticism about criminal law mirrors the ICC's prioritization of '(in-)action over quality' in interpreting complementarity.[297] It is no coincidence that the OTP has still never challenged the DRC's, or any other ICC state party's, exercise of domestic jurisdiction for lack of genuineness.[298] Because, in line with its interpretation of article 17, the ICC may not assert jurisdiction if domestic proceedings 'merely' violate fair trial norms, the OTP is unable to engage—contrary to the ICTR in Rwanda—its national counterparts on cases like *Katanga* that raise questions about the DRC's commitment to basic justice standards. Not only does this reading of article 17, which dissociates complementarity from fair trial norms, reduce the prospects for an iterative dialogue with national authorities; it also increases the likelihood of a binary approach to domestic accountability that ignores questions of process (fairness) at the expense of outcomes (convictions), or conversations about degrees of punishment and non-retributive options—as in Colombia—that may or may not be (in)admissible at the ICC from a transitional justice perspective.[299]

The ICC's reluctance to intervene in domestic accountability debates in the DRC echoes a blind spot in the donor community's statebuilding strategy. Whereas a coalition of actors now advocates rule-of-law reforms and trials in the name of

[297] In this sense, see Milli Lake, *Strong NGOs and Weak States: Pursuing Gender Justice in the Democratic Republic of Congo and South Africa* (CUP 2018) 7–8.

[298] On the nascent Venezuela litigation, see PTC, *Public Redacted Version of 'Decision on the "Request for judicial control submitted to the Pre-Trial Chamber I of the International Criminal Court by the Bolivarian Republic of Venezuela pursuant to Articles 15 and 21.3 of the Statute and Rule 46.2 of the Rules of the regulations of the Court"'*, ICC-02/18-9-Red 02-03-2022 1/12 NM PT (14 June 2021)

[299] On Colombia, see Chapter 4 in this volume.

positive complementarity, there is less analysis of the ends to which states put (international) criminal law. This is not surprising. Even if the UN and NGOs denounce fair trial violations, the ICC has signalled that the Rome Statute supposedly precludes intervention as long as trials end in convictions. Yet equating numbers of trials with positive complementarity ignores whether Congolese magistrates apply the coercive power of prosecution independently and impartially, or conversely whether the military makes strategic use of prosecutions to reinforce its authority and entrench the power of Kinshasa's elites, while doing little to emancipate the justice system from executive and military oversight.

Due to the ICC's deferential approach to trials in the DRC, 'unintended diversionary complementarity' has had at least three under-studied consequences that should be examined in other contexts.[300] First, in the absence of top-down OTP pressure to catalyse or monitor prosecutions of senior government officials, the UN and NGOs redirect their support to individual lower-level suspects whose trials are unlikely to generate political backlash. Second, instead of charges of rape as a crime against humanity against a superior under command responsibility, UN-backed domestic cases implicate less contentious human rights violations and ordinary crimes. Third, although most systematic and high-level cases never become formal proceedings, the UN and NGOs prioritize (including when proceedings implicate state agents) consensus topics such as child recruitment or environmental crimes rather than targeting civilians or election-related crimes.

To be sure, these trends also have positive dimensions, including a focus on violations against children, women, and the environment that are often sidelined. But it must also be recognized that appraisals of positive complementarity that focus on statistical outcomes (numbers of convictions) rather than evaluative sociolegal questions of process and quality (fair trial standards, judicial independence, or civil–military relations) overlook the politics of trials and their impact on statebuilding. As President Tshisekedi considers a new transitional justice strategy, the ICC should reconsider its deferential reading of complementarity and devise an evaluative and relational approach to international criminal law enforcement in the DRC.

5. Interim Conclusion: Norm Internalization in the Court's Shadow

In 2005, Robert Cryer observed that '[t]he ICC may be expected to have a greater promotional role for the incorporation of international crimes into domestic legal

[300] Similarly for Serbia, see Diane Orentlicher, *Some Kind of Justice: The ICTY's Impact in Bosnia and Serbia* (OUP 2018) 406–25.

systems than the *ad hoc* Tribunals'.[301] Ten years later, Padraig McAuliffe concluded that the ICC was 'unlikely to be as fruitful' as the ad hoc tribunals in generating the same 'cycle of interaction, interpretation, and internalization' to make 'penetration of norms a reality'.[302]

To some extent, scholarly disagreement as to how ICTs influence normative standards reflect the different yardsticks by which impact is measured. Whereas the revival of ICTs in the 1990s was expected to reinforce rule-of-law promotion geared to modernizing legislation, some ICT interventions seem to confound conventional diffusion models.[303] Prior to its Completion Strategy, the ICTR influenced domestic law at the margins while Rwandan authorities shunned the ICTR Statute, partly due to its perceived primacy over the national legal order. Despite its hybridity and proximity to Sierra Leone, international standards filtered into domestic law despite—not thanks to—the SCSL, at least in the short term. In the DRC, despite complementarity campaigns, implementation was not facilitated by article 17's admissibility incentives and the threat of ICC intervention may have slowed down criminal justice reform.

Overall, ICTs seem to play more of an 'inspirational' or 'demonstration' role for normative campaigns led by other actors, while ICT institutional design choices—complementarity or hybridity—perform a backdrop function. In Rwanda, Sierra Leone, and the DRC, civil society pressured governments to adjust legal standards, with campaigns geared not only to international crimes but criminal justice generally. At the same time, data suggest that the Rome Statute performs an increasingly centralizing and 'jurisgenerative' role for civil society-led legislative reforms. While the implementation process is not always linear, as seen in the DRC and Sierra Leone, the Statute serves as a 'go-to' legislative source, with 67 out of 120 states parties adopting complementarity legislation.[304] By using the Statute as a checklist of norms and strategically mobilizing the language of complementarity, human rights groups and donors cooperate with governments to enact sovereignty-sensitive reforms, ranging from laws criminalizing sexual violence to changing modes of liability. Significantly, the Rome Statute shapes normative agendas not only in states

[301] Robert Cryer, *Prosecuting International Crimes: Selectivity and the International Criminal Law Regime* (CUP 2005) 171; Leila N Sadat, *The International Criminal Court and the Transformation of International Law: Justice for the New Millennium* (Transnational 2002) 263.

[302] McAuliffe (n 93) 400.

[303] Randall Peerenboom, Michael Zürn and André Nollkaemper, 'Conclusion: From Rule of Law Promotion to Rule of Law Dynamics' in Michael Zurn, Andre Nollkaemper and Randy Peerenboom (eds), *Rule of Law Dynamics* (CUP 2012). On norm diffusion, see Padraig McAuliffe, 'The Roots of Transitional Accountability: Interrogating the "Justice Cascade"' (2013) 9 International Journal of Law in Context 106.

[304] For 'jurisgenerative', see Geoff Dancy and Florencia Montal, 'From Law versus Politics to Law in Politics: A Pragmatist Assessment of the ICC's Impact' (2017) 32 America University International Law Review 645, 685 and 705 (statistics up to date as of 2012; of the 67 ICC state parties, however, 52 had adopted only cooperation legislation).

parties but also non-member states, including in India and Indonesia where authorities are ambivalent about the ICC.[305]

Yet, while bottom-up civil society campaigns have enabled reforms in many countries, the ICTR speaks to the top-down potential of ICT intervention based on a system of conditionalities and multi-stakeholder capacity building. In the shadow of rule 11*bis*, domestic reformers in Rwanda marshalled primacy's coercive power, epitomized by the threat of case revocations, to implement reforms, including on controversial issues such as the death penalty. While the ICC–OTP seemed open to similar involvement, such efforts seem confined to a few preliminary examinations, notably in Colombia where a multi-stakeholder debate has taken place about the permissibility of non-retributive forms of justice. Although debates in the ASP suggest that the ICC is unlikely to be as active as the ICTR, a new Completion policy paper and Prosecutor Khan's turn to 'cooperation agreements' in both Colombia and Venezuela suggest richer conversations about the ICC's involvement in domestic accountability debates may have already begun.[306]

Beyond implementation and formal compliance, ICTs' contributions to norm internalization is contested. Scholars argue that, for instance, primacy was a 'primary [example] of the prioritization of the development of international criminal law over the empowerment of national courts' or that hybrid mandates 'reveal a rather limited level of real impact on the local judicial system'.[307] Meanwhile, complementarity's centralizing and homogenizing tendencies are critiqued for insufficiently accommodating legitimate domestic differences and a plurality of justice perspectives. For instance, Carsten Stahn warns that '[i]f states strengthen domestic systems primarily for the sake of adjudicating specific cases domestically, reform efforts are geared towards ICC priorities rather than long-term domestic interests', which may 'run counter to the objective of … creat[ing] a sustainable "system of justice"'.[308] Critical of the 'mirroring' consequences of the 'same case' standard, Christian De Vos worries that complementarity encourages states to prosecute international rather than ordinary crimes, to establish new exceptional courts rather than reform existing domestic institutions, and to prioritize criminal over alternative justice.[309] In turn, Mark Drumbl argues for 'qualified deference' to

[305] Usha Ramanathan, 'The Surprising Impact of the Rome Statute in India' (*Open Democracy*, 7 November 2014) <opendemocracy.net/en/openglobalrights-openpage/surprising-impact-of-rome-statute-in-india/>.

[306] See further Chapter 7 in this volume.

[307] Padraig McAuliffe, *Transitional Justice and Rule of Law Reconstruction* (Routledge 2013) 188; Shany (n 103) 444.

[308] Carsten Stahn, 'Admissibility Challenges before the ICC: From Quasi-Primacy to Qualified Deference?' in Carsten Stahn (ed), *Law and Practice of the International Criminal Court* (OUP 2015) 239; Karolina Wierczyńska, 'Deference in the ICC Practice Concerning Admissibility Challenges Lodged by States' in Łukasz Gruszczyński and Wouter Werner (eds), *Deference in International Courts and Tribunals: Standard of Review and Margin of Appreciation* (OUP 2014); Mégret (n 188) 363.

[309] De Vos (n 295) 9–10; SMH Nouwen and WG Werner, 'Monopolizing Global Justice: International Criminal Law as Challenge to Human Diversity' (2015) 13 Journal of International Criminal Justice 157.

states that can be rebutted by the ICC under specific conditions that meet the genuineness test.[310]

In line with this, by now, dominant critique of complementarity's 'mirroring' effects, many argue that the ICC gives states insufficient space to craft domestic accountability responses to serious crimes. Yet, while these pluralism-based critiques of the ICC's homogenizing effects have merit, they also seem based on an overly short-term compliance-based reading of what are necessarily longer-term, iterative processes of normative appropriation by states, while also potentially misdiagnosing the obstacles to accountability in situations where only a handful of cases will ever reach The Hague. Contrary to scholarly demands for greater deference to states, the problem with the extant article 17 case law is not that it provides the wrong incentives to states, who—as seen in the DRC's military courts—can adjust international standards to domestic practice, but rather that it facilitates accommodationist practices by giving ICC civil servants the wrong incentives to ignore their role in domestic accountability debates.

While doctrinally sound, the article 17 case law's stark dichotomy between action and inaction and a human rights-averse reading of genuineness, creates a series of pathologies. Notably, the case law allows states to outsource prosecutions to The Hague (legitimating state inaction), prioritizes outcomes (numbers of convictions) rather than processes (how trials materialize, who and why is selected for prosecution, and according to what standards are they tried?), and forecloses richer debates about the relative benefits of domestic and international trials (under what conditions is it justified to take cases away from states?; what benefits do international trials have that domestic trials do not, and vice versa?). Equally important, complementarity, as interpreted by the OTP and judges, provides little guidance on how to establish states' good faith in domesticating and appropriating international criminal law (what is the absence of political will?; under what conditions is non-retributive justice acceptable within a criminal law paradigm?).

It is surprising that, despite Sierra Leone's more appealing trajectory of post-conflict politics, the SCSL's precedent of numerically limited international trials (whether or not we accept the normative paradox of 'greatest responsibility') is rarely considered in ICC situations, where the dogma of 'more domestic trials' seems like the sole reading of (positive) complementarity. As currently framed, case distribution at the ICC avoids questions of why international intervention is necessary in the first place and, by the same token, why states are, more often than not, unwilling to prosecute the most senior state-affiliated perpetrators. By the same token, a statistical focus on domestic trials as evidence of positive

[310] Mark A Drumbl, 'Policy through Complementarity: The Atrocity Trial as Justice' in Stahn and El Zeidy (n 188) 227–31.

complementarity ignores why governments appropriate international criminal norms and whether the coercive power of prosecution serves primarily to entrench the political elite's power. As such, the article 17 case law's legalistic formalism and political agnosticism as to why states do or do not enforce international criminal law stymies conversations about the emancipatory potential—or lack thereof—of domestic prosecutions.

7
In the Court's Shadow
Maximizing Accountability in Unwilling or Unable States

Against the backdrop of the (positive) complementarity turn, defined in this book as a shift towards the domestic enforcement of international criminal law, the preceding chapters examined how the intervention of ICTs influences domestic accountability processes. After Chapter 3 explained how ICT mandates regulate relations with states, Chapters 4–6 assessed how international civil servants and state-based actors influence each other's accountability preferences and to what extent institutional design shaped their interactions in generally positive (iteration), neutral (accommodation), or negative (isolation) ways.

Extrapolating from the book's three case studies, this chapter examines trends in the field of international criminal justice and offers lessons to guide the design of future tribunals. It focuses on the turn from 'coercive' and 'top-down' intervention to 'cooperative' and 'bottom-up' rule-of-law strategies and the phenomenon of 'unintended diversionary complementarity', where states nominally appropriate international norms but systematic crimes committed by incumbent government actors go unpunished. Then, after identifying three intervening factors in ICT–state relations—temporal constraints, intrastate politics, and prosecutorial leadership—the chapter turns to reforms that can be implemented at the ICC to avoid complementarity's 'authoritarian shadow' and enhance the enforcement of international criminal law in an increasingly illiberal political climate. It argues for a more iterative and relational approach based on the relative strengths of ICTs and domestic stakeholders in prosecuting perpetrators of serious crimes.

1. The (Positive) Complementarity Turn: Situating the ICC in a Decentralized and Opportunistic System of Global Justice

International courts and tribunals face criticism and even backlash. However, the question is no longer whether they matter but how they shape the global order. To date, scholars have analysed inter alia how ICTs affect great power politics, peace negotiations, and reconciliation.[1] Less obvious from the burgeoning literature is

[1] David L Bosco, *Rough Justice. The International Criminal Court in a World of Power Politics* (OUP 2014); Janine N Clark, *International Trials and Reconciliation: Assessing the Impact of the International*

International Criminal Tribunals and Domestic Accountability. Patryk I. Labuda,
Oxford University Press. © Patryk I. Labuda 2023. DOI: 10.1093/oso/9780198868842.003.0007

that, during this time, international criminal justice has experienced a paradigm shift. In the 1990s, most observers viewed states as villains who, by their very nature, were ill suited to adjudicating genocide, crimes against humanity, and war crimes. Fast forward to the 2020s, and it is no longer international proceedings in The Hague but rather domestic trials that are the gold standard of the global anti-impunity project. As Devika Hovell observes, the field's 'master narrative' is that 'the future of international criminal justice is domestic'.[2]

Complementarity has emerged as a byword for international criminal law's preoccupation with domestic accountability. At his swearing in, Karim Khan, the third prosecutor, undertook solemnly 'to respect the [Rome] Statute' and 'to comply with complementarity'.[3] But the word complementarity, derived from the Rome Statute, designates not merely the ICC's institutional design vis-à-vis states. More importantly, it has come to embody diverse assumptions, expectations, and beliefs about how international and domestic actors should interact with one another in the anti-impunity project. One especially prominent idea is that international tribunals exist not just to hold trials but also to cast a shadow over states and serve as a 'catalyst' for the domestic rule of law. As noted by Yuval Shany, 'there is an increased tendency to view [ICTs] as mechanisms primarily designed to support and complement the work of national criminal procedures and to pay closer attention to the interaction between the two sets of judicial institutions'.[4]

This process of supporting states is usually called 'positive complementarity', a term that is used in contradistinction to complementarity's 'darker side', whereby the Rome Statute empowers international prosecutors and judges to confront, call out, and shame states for their inability or unwillingness to hold perpetrators to account.[5] While scholars have spilled much doctrinal ink on how the Rome Statute allocates powers between the ICC and states, an equally important development has occurred in the shadow of these interpretive disagreements. Regardless of how one should read articles 17–20 as a matter of legal doctrine, the Statute's emphasis on states' jurisdiction over international crimes has spawned an ideational revolution whereby international intervention is rationalized in terms of its effects on domestic accountability. In this study, the turn to (positive) complementarity refers

Criminal Tribunal for the Former Yugoslavia (Routledge 2014); Mark Kersten, *Justice in Conflict: The Effects of the International Criminal Court's Interventions on Ending War and Building Peace* (OUP 2016).

[2] Devika Hovell, 'The "Mistrial" of Kumar Lama: Problematizing Universal Jurisdiction' (*EJIL: Talk!*, 6 April 2017) <ejiltalk.org/the-mistrial-of-kumar-lama-problematizing-universal-jurisdiction/>.

[3] 'Swearing-in Ceremony: Speech of New ICC Prosecutor Karim A.A. Khan QC' <youtube.com/watch?v=tDldr2ma1S0>.

[4] Yuval Shany, 'How Can International Criminal Courts Have a Greater Impact on National Criminal Proceedings? Lessons from the First Two Decades of International Criminal Justice in Operation' (2013) 46 Israel Law Review 431.

[5] On positive complementarity generally, see HRW, 'Pressure Point: The ICC's Impact on National Justice. Lessons from Colombia, Georgia, Guinea, and the United Kingdom' (2018).

to the phenomenon of why, when, and how international actors work with, despite or against state-based actors to pursue domestic accountability for serious crimes.

Importantly, this turn to (positive) complementarity as a justification-cum-rationale of international intervention is not limited to the ICC or countries where it operates. Over time, the ICTR, ICTY, and SCSL all embraced the ideals and even the vocabulary of positive complementarity, though their institutional design remained grounded on primacy. A similar emphasis on the domestic dimension of international intervention can be observed at newer tribunals, for instance at the CAR hybrid court, where NGOs wield the language of 'complementarity in action' to rationalize its relations with the ICC and maximize its legacy, or at the ACPHR with 'complementary jurisdiction' vis-à-vis African states.[6]

In short, little seems to be left of the idea underpinning primacy in *Tadić* that international trials should be prioritized because states are incapable of enforcing international criminal law. On the contrary, it is states that are now encouraged to provide accountability in the first place.

Yet, while the promise of domestic accountability is rhetorically associated with complementarity, it is less clear how international and state institutions should work together. To inform the practice of international criminal law enforcement, this book extrapolates from its three case studies and analyses ICT–state relations based on iteration, accommodation, and isolation, three types of relationships that reflect whether government actors and international civil servants cooperate with, ignore, or are in conflict with one another. Although the Rome Statute's checks and balances were expected to provide a favourable mix of enforcement incentives to states and the ICC in a global and decentralized system of international justice, this early enthusiasm has abated. Not only is it now contested to what extent the ICC incentivizes states to prosecute serious crimes—this book argues also that the Rome Statute, as currently interpreted, incentivizes mainly accommodation but is unlikely to generate iteration vis-à-vis states. The next section describes three trends that facilitate accommodation before turning to factors that define the conditions of possibility for iterative practices.

2. Three General Trends

2.1. From top-down coercion to bottom-up persuasion: complementarity as cooperation

Despite Louis Henkin's famous observation that 'almost all nations observe almost all principles of international law … almost all of the time', scholars disagree on

[6] See Chapter 2, section 2 in this volume.

why states respect international law.[7] Common hypotheses include self-interest, coercion, reciprocity, reputation, and acculturation.[8] In international criminal law, scholars emphasize how reputation and domestic politics affect states' adherence to international commitments, but less research exists on how ICT institutional design affects tribunal and state choices relating to accountability.[9]

Created in the heyday of liberal internationalism, the two ad hoc tribunals relied initially on coercive power to accomplish their goals. As explained in Chapter 4, prosecutors Goldstone, Arbour, and Del Ponte issued public arrest warrants for high-profile suspects and, if necessary, invoked the ICTY and ICTR's primacy to pre-empt or override national proceedings. Yet, despite the ad hoc tribunals' robust institutional design, underpinned by Chapter VII powers, this top-down vision of international criminal law enforcement quickly ran into challenges. Not only Rwanda and former Yugoslav states but also regional and international actors refused cooperation, which in turn required considerable diplomatic outreach—not always successful—to allow the completion of the ICTY and ICTR mandates.[10] Writing years later, Serge Bammertz, then MICT Prosecutor, observed:[11]

> primacy symbolized and contributed to significant trends perceived to be underway in international law, where international courts applying international law would be able to overcome barriers to justice raised by State sovereignty.

In reality, this vision of international criminal justice, where ICTs and sovereignty were in a tense and even antagonistic relationship, began to fray by the late 1990s. In 2002, the SCSL was created by treaty (consensual by nature) between the UN and Sierra Leonean authorities. A few years later, a similar agreement was struck with the Cambodian government for the ECCC, the consequences of which are being felt to this day.[12] Around the same time, plans to phase out the ICTY and ICTR based on case referrals coalesced.

When Luis Ocampo was sworn in as prosecutor in 2003, the ICC's relationship to states took centre stage. Complementarity, an ill-defined notion inherited from

[7] Louis Henkin, *How Nations Behave* (2nd edn, Columbia UP 1979) 47.

[8] Vera Shikhelman, 'Implementing Decisions of International Human Rights Institutions. Evidence from the UN Human Rights Committee' (2019) 30 European Journal of International Law 753, 755–58.

[9] See eg Courtney Hillebrecht and Scott Straus, 'Who Pursues the Perpetrators? State Cooperation with the ICC' (2017) 39 Human Rights Quarterly 162.

[10] Victor Peskin, 'Croatia's Homeland War, the Battles over Victor's Justice, and the Legacy of the ICTY' in Carsten Stahn and others (eds), *Legacies of the International Criminal Tribunal for the Former Yugoslavia* (OUP 2020) 543–44.

[11] Serge Brammertz, 'Making Complementarity a Reality: The Experiences of the ICTY and IRMCT Office of the Prosecutor' in Carsten Stahn and others (eds), *Legacies of the International Criminal Tribunal for the Former Yugoslavia* (OUP 2020) 34.

[12] Paolo Lobba and Niccolò Pons, 'Rethinking the Legacy of the ECCC' (2020) 18 Journal of International Criminal Justice 599. Heather Ryan, 'And Then, Finally, a Judge Wrote the Shameful End of the Khmer Rouge Tribunal' (*JusticeInfo*, 4 February 2022) <justiceinfo.net/en/87248-finally-judge-wrote-shameful-end-khmer-rouge-tribunal.html>.

negotiations on the Rome Statute, cast a shadow over how the Court and states mediated their respective enforcement roles. Against the backdrop of the OTP's policies and the emerging article 17 case law, the ICC's relations with states took a consensual turn. Showing deference to powerful states, notably the UK (in Iraq), United States (in Afghanistan), and Israel (in Palestine), the first prosecutor concentrated on weaker states on the African continent.[13] Criticized for soliciting self-referrals from Uganda, the DRC, and CAR, which ensured cooperation but required alliances with autocratic leaders, Ocampo tried to balance such investigations with a more confrontational approach in situations referred by the UN Security Council and especially in his outreach to the Kenyan government in the aftermath of the 2007 election violence. In Kenya, its first *proprio motu* investigation, the OTP semi-officially embraced a positive complementarity approach.

As explained in Chapter 4, Kenya remains the only investigation to produce iterative dynamics vis-à-vis incumbent government actors. Yet the OTP's strategy, including its refusal to grant Kenya time to build a domestic response and the failed prosecutions of Kenyan leaders, forced a re-evaluation of prosecutorial strategy. While complementarity remained a rhetorical priority under Fatou Bensouda, who had observed the Kenya inquiry as deputy prosecutor, she shifted the OTP's focus after 2012. Bensouda is remembered for her courageous inquiries into alleged crimes committed by the United States, UK, Russia, and Israel, but it is forgotten that this more confrontational approach vis-à-vis powerful states resulted from the OTP's embrace of preliminary examinations as the main sites for positive complementarity. Meanwhile, relations with states under investigation pivoted to cooperation-based readings of the Rome Statute based on stimulating transnational collaboration. Bensouda would ultimately disavow the ICC qua sword of Damocles imagery in the DRC, though she had previously been comfortable with this type of language.

Against this backdrop, positive complementarity consolidated as a powerful vocabulary for other accountability stakeholders. In particular, civil society and development partners seized on the rhetoric of complementarity-cum-cooperation to rationalize their capacity-building interventions in conflict-affected societies. As Christian De Vos argues, although it 'was initially seen as a mechanism to primarily influence the choices of state actors, [complementarity]'s effects on non-state actors appear to have been far more profound'.[14] Yet, while

[13] Oumar Ba, *States of Justice: The Politics of the International Criminal Court* (CUP 2020).

[14] Christian M De Vos, *Complementarity, Catalysts, Compliance. The International Criminal Court in Uganda, Kenya, and the Democratic Republic of Congo* (CUP 2020) 14. See also Sarah MH Nouwen, *Complementarity in the Line of Fire: The Catalysing Effect of the International Criminal Court in Uganda and Sudan* (CUP 2013) 22–23; Elena Baylis, 'Reassessing the Role of International Criminal Law: Rebuilding National Courts through Transnational Networks' (2009) 50 Boston College Law Review 1.

De Vos and others focus on the ICC and complementarity, it may be that ICTs *tout court* reinvigorate transnational advocacy, irrespective of institutional design choices. Even if primacy was seen as a tool for 'top-down' ICT pressure on states, the ICTR's involvement in Rwanda also served to stimulate 'bottom-up' capacity building. High-profile trials in The Hague, Arusha, or Freetown may have receive(d) the lion's share of international attention, but other state-based actors strategically exploited the 'symbolic shadow' of ICTs to strengthen domestic accountability responses, in line with the UN's broader rule-of-law and transitional justice agendas.

Moreover, while international crimes advocacy provides the initial impetus for reforms, it has knock on effects for the entire criminal justice sector. National contexts explain different priorities—genocide in Rwanda, legal aid in Sierra Leone, or sexual violence in the DRC—but some reforms, including witness protection and abolitionist campaigns, are part and parcel of the broader rule-of-law landscape. In this regard, the Rome Statute has played a centralizing role for legislative reforms, including in non-ICC states parties, facilitated by NGOs who mobilize the language of complementarity to enact reforms as disparate as implementing legislation and infrastructure revitalization. As Mark Kersten observes, such 'downstream, perhaps even unintended, effects do not get nearly as much attention as the dramatic goings-on in The Hague … [but] the Statute has become an indispensable, if sometimes surprising, tool that can be wielded by advocates to achieve accountability and strengthen the rule of law'.[15]

Although some scholars criticize NGO readings of the Rome Statute, in particular doctrinally questionable arguments for domestication and prosecution duties, complementarity has succeeded in reframing international involvement in benign language and, in that sense, has proven a useful rhetorical device to promote reforms in a core area of sovereignty. More problematic may be the ICC's absence from the domestic sphere. At the ICTR, rule 11*bis* conditionalities helped Rwandan reformers to work with international civil servants to enact contentious reforms. However, outside a few preliminary examinations, the ICC has eschewed top-down involvement in domestic accountability debates, while donors and NGOs rely mainly on non-hierarchical forms of capacity building and knowledge diffusion. Although the trend across African investigations has been to avoid conditionalities, notably to prevent accusations of neocolonialism, the current piecemeal approach to capacity building often results in narrow project implementation, with insufficient scrutiny of the ends to which international criminal law is put domestically.

[15] Mark Kersten, 'Making a Distinction: The Rome Statute Is Not the ICC; It Is Much More than That' (*Justice in Conflict*, 17 July 2018) <justiceinconflict.org/2018/07/17/making-a-distinction-the-anniversary-of-the-rome-statute-not-just-the-international-criminal-court/>.

2.2. Unintended diversionary complementarity in the Court's symbolic shadow

Observing that 'states have begun taking steps to amend national law to reflect the jurisdictional scope of the Rome Statute', Bruce Broomhall predicted in 2003 that 'enhancement of the capacity of national law ... could lay the foundations for a significant increase in the number and credibility of national proceedings against international crimes'.[16] Although capacity building for states continues to grow two decades later, it remains unclear to what extent the shadow of ICTs incentivizes governments to prosecute international crimes. Some argue that rule-of-law reform focuses on the wrong problems. For instance, Sarah Nouwen observes that 'steps such as the adoption of domestic laws incorporating ICC crimes or the establishment of special courts ... are politically inexpensive' and 'do not address the real obstacles to domestic proceedings'.[17] Others disagree. After analysing legislative reform in a broader pool of 'newly democratic states', Mark Berlin and Geoff Dancy argue that 'the existence of atrocity laws, on average, correlates with greater numbers of human rights prosecutions' and that '[s]tates with standing atrocity laws are also quicker to initiate trials and reach more verdicts following periods of regime change than states without such laws'.[18]

Disagreements over ICTs' shadow effects on domestic prosecutions reflect varying assumptions about how tribunals should interact with states. In this regard, ambitious claims from early in Ocampo's term—for instance, that the OTP should share evidence to enhance national trials or that the absence of international trials would be an indicator of effectiveness—may have created unrealistic expectations about how international intervention should spur governments into action. Echoing William Burke-White's vision of complementarity qua system of multilevel governance, it is sometimes implicit in scholarly analyses of complementarity that increases in rates of domestic prosecutions should occur not just in the wake of ICC intervention but ideally as a result of admissibility challenges or capacity building.

While it is true that complementarity's mix of incentives was expected to set the ICC apart from other ICTs, practice has confounded such expectations. Like the SCSL, the ICC–OTP has interpreted its mandate to mean jurisdiction over a small group of perpetrators within each situation. Although Ocampo and Bensouda did not always target high-level suspects, their investigations replicated a 'targeted primacy' approach, whereby investigators collected evidence on the assumption that

[16] Bruce Broomhall, *International Justice and the International Criminal Court: Between Sovereignty and the Rule of Law* (OUP 2003) 93.

[17] Nouwen (n 14) 12.

[18] Mark S Berlin and Geoff Dancy, 'The Difference Law Makes: Domestic Atrocity Laws and Human Rights Prosecutions: Domestic Atrocity Laws and Human Rights Prosecutions' (2017) 51 Law & Society Review 533, 534.

ensuing cases would be prosecuted internationally and where complementarity considerations played little role. As early as 2015, Padraig McAuliffe observed that the ICC had 'moved stealthily towards an approximation of the primacy model'.[19]

Another confounding factor seems to be that, by giving judicial imprimatur to policy arguments that admissibility may be uncontested, ICC judges consolidated a Hague-centric interpretation of complementarity that divorced international case selection from state behaviour. In other words, the focus of the article 17 case law is on the OTP (is its case different from the state's case?), not the state (whether, why, and how the state is or is not handling (a) case(s)?). Given that the case law dissociates ICC case selection from state action, the ICC prosecutor may prioritize a handful of uncontroversial—for the state—suspects who happen to be in custody and opposed to the incumbent government, instead of asserting jurisdiction over hard cases that cannot be prosecuted domestically at all. While soft targets do not jeopardize cooperation with governments (accommodation), they also have less potential to shape the prosecutorial preferences of states positively (iteration) or negatively (isolation), for instance by provoking withdrawal.

Scholars have focused on self-referrals and the ICC's targeting of non-state actors therein to expose the ICC's 'limited', 'negative', or 'unintended' effects. Countering such bleak assessments, Geoff Dancy and Florencia Montal defend 'unintended positive complementarity', whereby countries under ICC investigation 'annually try on average four times as many state agents … than do other African nations experiencing violent conflicts'.[20] Identifying a likely catalyst, they suggest that 'latent political struggles between ruling [incumbent government] coalitions and reformer coalitions' exacerbated by ICC intervention, lead to an 'increase in domestic prosecutions … beyond the attention of the ICC'.[21]

Their data are noteworthy in that, while other scholars criticize the OTP's investigative methods or its refusal to share evidence with states, Dancy and Montal focus on the 'hardest' cases involving state agents and emphasize the indirect and prima facie iterative effects of ICC intervention. At first blush, the DRC case study supports this argument, given that—as seen in Chapters 4–6—the national justice system has handled hundreds of international and ordinary but serious crimes in the shadow of the ICC's investigation. Yet, although these figures dwarf domestic prosecutions in other ICC investigations, the Congolese accountability landscape is more complex. While critiques of 'insufficient' deference to states misdiagnose the causes of impunity in the DRC, unintended positive complementarity focuses

[19] Padraig McAuliffe, 'Bad Analogy: Why the Divergent Institutional Imperatives of the Ad Hoc Tribunals and the ICC Make the Lessons of Rule 11 Bis Inapplicable to the ICC's Complementarity Regime' (2015) 11 International Organizations Law Review 345, 373.

[20] Geoff Dancy and Florencia Montal, 'Unintended Positive Complementarity: Why International Criminal Court Investigations May Increase Domestic Human Rights Prosecutions' (2017) 111 American Journal of International Law 689, 691. Dancy and Montal clarify also that their data hold only for investigations, but not preliminary examinations.

[21] ibid 690.

too much on raw numbers but neglects the internal dynamics that allow some—but not other—domestic prosecutions to materialize.

This book uses the term 'unintended diversionary complementarity' to describe the authoritarian 'shadow effect' of international intervention in countries like the DRC and Rwanda. Whereas the existing literature has emphasized how states manipulate the ICC by outsourcing rivals for prosecution in The Hague, an underexplored theme is how domestic elites make strategic use of ICT intervention to implement rule-of-law reforms and then launch less controversial proceedings while blocking high-stakes trials of government-affiliated perpetrators. In the same way that the ICC's investigations and accommodationist case selection have not engendered *vertical* iteration vis-à-vis state authorities over their failure to prosecute government allies, so too the ICC's shadow has failed to galvanize sufficient *horizontal* iteration among state-based actors to disrupt the informal networks that ensure the political elite's survival. Given the OTP and the international community's reluctance to monitor the pretrial phase or denounce sham trials, the domestic enforcement of international criminal law may serve to fight impunity and centralize political authority in equal measure.

Echoing Jelena Subotić's *Hijacked Justice*, unintended diversionary complementarity exposes the disconnect between the utopia of the ICC qua catalyst for cosmopolitan liberal reforms and the reality of national elites using international criminal law to entrench their impunity and centralize power.[22] While Subotić's research anticipated similar dynamics of international intervention and state deflection in other contexts, this book emphasizes the risk of international civil servants 'hijacking' norms to maintain plausible deniability in the face of state non-cooperation and partial enforcement of international law. Whereas ICT mandates can be interpreted to promote iterative practices, ICC prosecutors and judges have embraced sovereignty-friendly readings of complementarity that avoid conflict with governments in exchange for their (limited) cooperation with respect to a handful of Hague-based trials that are mutually acceptable to both sides.

To a greater extent than at the ICTR, the ICC's institutional design, which rewards anti-impunity outcomes (quantity of trials) over human rights-based process (quality of trials), decreases the scope for iterative dynamics vis-à-vis justice actors in countries like the DRC. Put succinctly, the ICC's potential to trigger iteration is unlikely to follow from evidence sharing or capacity building. Yet the OTP has still conspicuously failed to propose a strategy that balances its duty to confront states over shielding and sham trials with the operational necessity to maintain cooperation. As explained in Chapter 6, the OTP's failure to investigate

[22] Jelena Subotić, *Hijacked Justice: Dealing with the Past in the Balkans* (Cornell UP 2009). Similarly in ICC interventions, see De Vos (n 14) 257 and 262–65; Stephen Oola, 'In the Shadow of Kwoyelo's Trial: The ICC and Complementarity in Uganda' in Christian De Vos, Sara Kendall and Carsten Stahn (eds), *Contested Justice* (CUP 2015) Sarah MH Nouwen, 'The ICC's Intervention in Uganda' in Michael Zurn, André Nollkaemper and Randy Peerenboom (eds), *Rule of Law Dynamics* (CUP 2012) 302.

or challenge government allies had several consequences for the DRC's accountability process, which ultimately sanitized the state's record. Similar dynamics of state deflection should be explored in other contexts of high prosecutorial activity, such as Colombia,[23] or where (numerous) domestic investigations fail to translate into (any) prosecutions, such as in the UK and potentially in Israel.[24]

Ultimately, both the DRC and the Rwanda case studies illustrate the perils of associating numbers with qualitative questions of fairness and justice. While there is some evidence of a 'willingness game' between government actors and reformers in both countries, these accountability processes also showcase, albeit for different national reasons, how unequal enforcement of criminal law may consolidate the political elite's power, which in turn suggests that 'positive complementarity' may be less about internalizing norms and more a cautionary tale about the perils of international intervention's (including article 17's) 'authoritarian shadow'.

2.3. From investigation to preliminary examination (and back?)

A permanent, complementarity-based ICC seemed like a departure from how the primacy-based ad hoc tribunals regulated their relations with states. In fact, there are probably more similarities, for instance regarding state non-cooperation, than disjunctures. Yet, among the differences, the selection of situations for investigation is arguably the most impactful.[25]

The ICTR and SCSL never had to decide where they would prosecute crimes, as that decision had been made for them by states, acting through the UN. By contrast, under the Rome Statute, crimes can be referred not only by states parties or the UN Security Council; the prosecutor may also initiate investigations of her own volition. While the OTP's *proprio motu* power was expected to create a more (geographically) varied case docket at the ICC, its most lasting effect to date seems to be the introduction of the preliminary examination phase, as will be seen below.

By contrast, ICC investigations have hewed closely to the SCSL experience. Unlike the ICTR/Y's early open-ended investigations, the ICC prosecutor seems to select a limited pool of cases within each investigation and collects evidence to

[23] Presciently, see Lars Waldorf, '"A Mere Pretense of Justice": Complementarity, Sham Trials, and Victor's Justice at the Rwanda Tribunal' (2011) 33 Fordham International Law Journal 1221, 1223–24. For Colombia, see Avocats Sans Frontières, 'The Principle of Complementarity in the Rome Statute and the Colombian Situation: A Case That Demands More than a "Positive" Approach' (2012); Caroline D Kelly, 'Contextual Complementarity: Assessing Unwillingness and Genuine Prosecutions in Colombia's Special Jurisdiction for Peace' (2017) 48 Georgetown Journal of International Law 807.

[24] Sharon Weill, 'The Situation of Palestine in Wonderland: An Investigation into the ICC's Impact in Israel' in Morten Bergsmo and Carsten Stahn (eds), *Quality Control in Preliminary Examination*, vol 1 (Torkel Opsahl 2018); Thomas O Hansen, 'Complementarity (in)Action in the UK?' (*EJIL:Talk!*, 7 December 2018) <ejiltalk.org/complementarity-inaction-in-the-uk/>.

[25] William A Schabas, 'Victor's Justice: Selecting "Situations" at the International Criminal Court' (2010) 43 John Marshall Law Review 535.

substantiate case hypotheses. Despite an elaborate policy paper on case selection, almost all of the ICC's actual trials appear to be the fruit of opportunistic arrests rather than the maturation of comprehensive case selection processes.[26] As yet, no ICC investigation has produced more than six public arrest warrants, and some have involved a single case. While the number of sealed warrants is unknown, it seems clear the ICC–OTP will remain very selective and not replicate the ICTR/Y's practice of pursuing large numbers of suspects within specific countries.

The SCSL's case selection merits attention in that its restrictive mandate had a chilling effect on domestic prosecutions in Sierra Leone. Mandated to prosecute a small group of suspects bearing greatest responsibility, the SCSL was used by the Sierra Leonean government to deflect attention from its unwillingness to address accountability demands from civil society. Over time, international NGOs also came to see national trials as little more than a sideshow, while SCSL prosecutors (with one exception) concluded that encouraging government officials to launch domestic prosecutions was irreconcilable with their mandate. All in all, the SCSL's restrictive mandate created a contradictory set of isolationist incentives for international actors and civil society, while generating little top-down and bottom-up pressure on national authorities and allowing them to free-ride on international prosecutions.

Yet, while the SCSL's numerically limited trials have been a constant in all ICC investigations to date, the latter's case selection varies qualitatively from the Special Court's 'all-sides' approach. Unlike David Crane's charges against the three main warring factions, no incumbent official has been charged and tried in an ICC self-referral, where relations with state actors are mainly consensual. By contrast, the OTP has pursued suspects from different groups, including from the incumbent government, in *proprio motu* and Security Council-initiated inquiries—with limited effect. No sitting government official has ever appeared involuntarily before the ICC, and—as noted previously—the Kenya investigation against the sitting president and vice-president collapsed amid recriminations of state non-cooperation.

What should one make of these similarities and differences? Relations with over twenty states over a twenty-year period defy a neat categorization,[27] but international–state dynamics at the ICC appear to depend less on complementarity per se and more on jurisdictional triggers and (sometimes evolving) domestic politics. Oscillating between cooperation, indifference and antagonism, the OTP's relations with governments have resembled accommodation in self-referrals (DRC, Uganda, CAR, Côte d'Ivoire, Mali), while isolation has dominated

[26] Independent Expert Review of the ICC and the Rome Statute System (IER), 'Final Report' (2020) paras 658 and 679–83; ICC, 'Overall Response to the "Independent Expert Review". Preliminary Analysis of the Recommendations' (2021) paras 432–36.

[27] But see Ba (n 13) 38–39.

in several *proprio motu* (Burundi and Myanmar) and Security Council-initiated investigations (Sudan before Al-Bashir's ouster). To be sure, these categories do not map neatly onto cases like Libya, where competing state and non-state actors with incomplete control of the country's territory work selectively with the OTP on some issues (migrant crimes) while ignoring ICC arrest warrants. Nevertheless, it remains noteworthy that the ICC has yet to prosecute a case to completion from a non-self-referring state.

To date, iteration between international civil servants and state authorities has featured sporadically at ICTs. The ICTR's conditionality-based rule 11*bis* process stands out as a rare example of a principled dialogue with a government over the merits of a domestic accountability process, yet the catalyst was not Arusha but the UN's cost-cutting imperatives following overambitious investigations by the first prosecutors. By contrast, while ICC investigations sometimes feature iterative practices, the OTP has yet to coordinate prosecutorial strategies, establish divisions of labour, set benchmarks and deadlines, or engage on transitional justice in any investigation,[28] nor is there any evidence of the prosecutor using the threat of prosecution to incentivize a domestic trial along the lines of *Kabgayi*.

In reality, towards the end of Ocampo's term, the iterative ideals of positive complementarity shifted to preliminary examinations. By the late 2000s, with investigations underway in several countries and the first suspects awaiting trial in The Hague, the OTP focused on managing growing demand by deferring to national authorities for a certain amount of time to determine whether genuine proceedings were underway or, absent such proceedings, if the state could be made able and willing to conduct proceedings in the future. With Bensouda placing a 'stronger emphasis' on 'preliminary examination activities',[29] the pre-investigation phase came to assume a central space in the international criminal law imaginary, with the OTP's annual reports on prospective investigations awaited as eagerly as Hague-based trials. Significantly, positive complementarity came to be equated with this pre-investigation phase of international intervention during Bensouda's term.[30]

During this time, several countries served as experimental laboratories for preliminary examinations, with the OTP engaging state authorities over allegations of serious crimes and evaluating the prospects of a purely domestic accountability response that would obviate the need for an ICC investigation. Although the OTP's effectiveness in Colombia has been widely debated, and assessments have varied over time, there is now little doubt that it is a textbook example of iterative,

[28] Even in Kenya, the OTP quickly abandoned efforts to engage after the PTC's authorization of an investigation (Lionel Nichols, *The International Criminal Court and the End of Impunity in Kenya* (Springer 2014) 87).

[29] Fatou Bensouda, 'Foreword' in Carsten Stahn (ed), *The Law and Practice of the International Criminal Court* (OUP 2015).

[30] On this, see IER (n 26) para 734; HRW (n 5) 158–60.

push–pull relations vis-à-vis state authorities.[31] Yet, despite the prominence of OTP involvement in Georgia, Guinea, the UK, Nigeria, and Ukraine, these examinations became more controversial over time. The OTP's refusal to open an investigation in the UK–Iraq situation was heavily criticized, not least because of complementarity—not a single British soldier had been prosecuted—yet the UK's response was deemed 'genuine enough' to forestall an ICC inquiry.[32]

Ultimately, the UK–Iraq declination was an exception that proved the rule: despite the OTP's efforts to boost domestic accountability in over a dozen countries, many preliminary examinations failed to galvanize state action, and most eventually became investigations anyway.[33] By the end of Bensouda's term, there was serious disagreement about their utility. Some viewed them as 'essential for successful trials and to the [ICC]'s external image and perception' and 'a key tool in achieving the broader goals of ending impunity and preventing atrocity crimes'.[34] Others felt that the OTP had 'established its own form of procedure, one not envisaged by the drafters of the Statute', where examinations are used 'for purposes other than the determination of whether to initiate an investigation'.[35]

Preliminary examinations came under sharp attack in the 2020 Independent Expert Review. According to the experts, the fact that preliminary examinations took on average four years to complete was 'untenable, damaging to potential evidence and … frustrating for the victims and civil society, and unsatisfactory to the States Parties'.[36] Significantly, positive complementarity was identified as 'one of the main reasons for … lengthy preliminary examinations', including 'concerns that the annual reporting process is a "naming and shaming" exercise' and that 'public [preliminary examinations] may encourage a state to leave the [ICC]'.[37] The experts emphasized:[38]

> There is a widespread concern among many external stakeholders that by applying the admissibility test prospectively, the OTP is exceeding its mandate. It is

[31] See Chapter 4, section 5 in this volume.

[32] ICC–OTP, 'Situation in Iraq/UK. Final Report' (2020). For a critique, see Clive Baldwin, 'The ICC Prosecutor Office's Cop-out on UK Military Crimes in Iraq' (*Opinio Juris*, 18 December 2020) <opiniojuris.org/2020/12/18/the-icc-prosecutor-offices-cop-out-on-uk-military-crimes-in-iraq/>.

[33] Amnesty International, 'Open Letter to the OTP Requesting Immediate Action on the Situation in Nigeria' (2021) AFR 44/3654/2021; HRW, 'Guinea: Coup Further Complicates Massacre Justice. Efficient, Fair Trial Should Hold 2009 Stadium Abusers Accountable' (26 September 2021) <hrw.org/news/2021/09/26/guinea-coup-further-complicates-massacre-justice>.

[34] Open Society Justice Initiative and Amsterdam Law School, 'Improving Operations of the ICC–OTP: Reappraisal of Structures, Norms, and Practices. Outcome Report and Recommendations' (2020) 2 and 4.

[35] IER (n 26) para 699.

[36] ibid 711; ICC Overall Response (n 26) para 461.

[37] IER (n 26) 720 and 739–40.

[38] ibid 724.

accused of conducting what amounts to 'human rights monitoring', or playing a 'watchdog role'.

Whereas Bensouda began her term hailing preliminary examinations as 'one of the most remarkable efficiency tools we have at our disposal',[39] a decade later the OTP's approach was increasingly criticized, with Human Rights Watch concluding that 'expectations about the OTP's influence need to remain realistic'.[40] In line with the Expert recommendations, Khan launched a reappraisal soon after his swearing in and 'cooperation agreements' with Colombia and Venezuela are widely seen as a new chapter in the ICC's outreach to states.[41] How the OTP and other ICC organs plan to implement positive complementarity is still unknown—a new policy paper on complementarity has yet to be released at the time of writing—but critiques of preliminary examinations seem to foreshadow a rebalancing of priorities at the ICC and potentially a return to investigations as the primary sites of intervention.

3. Three Intervening Factors

Relations between ICTs and states are often examined through the lens of complementarity. In reality, ICT–state relations depend also on other elements of institutional design, such as personal and subject-matter jurisdiction, hybrid institutional features, and considerations flowing, more or less directly, from ICT mandates, for instance resources.[42] While it is beyond the scope of this book to analyse all these factors, it is submitted that the prospect of iterative practices is likely to depend on three issues that deserve more scrutiny going forward.

3.1. Temporal factors: a double-edged sword

Accountability processes are a complex and long-term endeavour, yet temporal factors have played an underappreciated role in ICT mandate design. While ICT

[39] Fatou Bensouda, 'Reflections from the International Criminal Court Prosecutor' (2012) 45 Case Western Reserve Journal of International Law 505, 509.

[40] HRW (n 5) 5; Carsten Stahn, '"The Times They Are a-Changin": Why the ICC Should Revisit Strategies on Preliminary Examination' (*Justice in Conflict*, 10 December 2018) <justiceinconflict.org/2018/12/10/the-times-they-are-a-changin-why-the-icc-should-re-visit-strategies-on-preliminary-examination/>. But see Christian M De Vos, 'Preliminary Examinations and Complementarity' (*International Justice Monitor*, 29 March 2021) <ijmonitor.org/2021/03/ier-blog-series-preliminary-examinations-and-complementarity/>.

[41] Juan Pappier and Liz Evenson, 'ICC Starts Next Chapter in Colombia, But Will It Lead to Justice?' (*EJIL:Talk!*, 15 December 2021) <ejiltalk.org/icc-starts-next-chapter-in-colombia-but-will-it-lead-to-justice/>.

[42] Marieke Wierda and Anthony Triolo, 'Resources' in Luc Reydams, Jan Wouters and Cedric Ryngaert (eds), *International Prosecutors* (OUP 2012).

jurisdiction is always temporally circumscribed in one way or another, operational time frames are not.[43] Neither the ICTR nor the ICTY's lifespans were defined initially, leading to unrealistic, as it turned out, interpretations of their mandates and forcing the UN Security Council to impose completion deadlines. Some tribunals have in the meantime received operational deadlines, for instance the CAR hybrid court or the Bosnia War Crimes Chamber.[44] Yet, because of the ICC's institutional permanence, time frames escaped regulation in its design phase, producing new (and very old) problems in recent years.

A classical dilemma underlying ICT intervention is that justice needs to be swift to matter to states and their populations, yet prosecutions take years to materialize. Deadlines and sunset clauses embedded in ICT mandates may seem like a simple way of addressing temporal quandaries, but their impact on ICT–state relations is complex.[45] One salutary effect of the Security Council requiring the ICTR to shut down by a set date (six years initially, extended later) was that pressure mounted from within the institution to show results as the Tribunal approached the end of its lifespan. At both the SCSL and ICTR, the prospect of closure gave rise to completion strategies, which in turn galvanized attention around their legacy for Sierra Leoneans and Rwandans and their performance came to be assessed not only on the basis of international trials, but also their domestic impacts.

However, aside from legacy's emergence as a *post hoc* rationalization for the ICTR and SCSL's success, temporal factors played a more complex role during their active mandate phase. The SCSL's personal jurisdiction, tight budget, and projected three-year time frame reduced the scope for strategic dialogue with national authorities. In fact, this extremely brief time frame—even though it swelled to seven years in Freetown and longer for the Taylor trial in The Hague—arguably foreclosed *ab initio* any serious consideration of long-term accountability strategies. It is also paradoxical that SCSL civil servants—both foreign and national—ended up ignoring their domestic counterparts and vice versa for much of the Tribunal's existence, though hybridity was expected to galvanize interactions (compared to the ICTR/Y).

One important reason for this isolation was the SCSL's restrictive mandate and the resultant perception that international trials took priority as soon as the 'big fish' were on trial. Crane's successful track record of arrests makes him effective compared to other prosecutors, but the quasi-absence of unenforced warrants against Sierra Leoneans also reduced dependence on the incumbent government, contributing to a comfortable isolationist *modus vivendi* between the international and domestic spheres. By the same token, the shadow of closure reduced the SCSL's

[43] Luc Reydams and Jed Odermatt, 'Mandates' in Reydams, Wouters and Ryngaert (n 42).

[44] Loi organique 15/003 portant création, organisation et fonctionnement de la Cour pénale spéciale, 3 June 2015, art 70.

[45] For an analysis of trade-offs, see Kevin J Heller, 'Completion' in Reydams, Wouters and Ryngaert (n 42) 900–15.

leverage with Sierra Leonean authorities. Knowing that the SCSL had to wind up, national elites could simply wait out their international counterparts and, for instance, Stephen Rapp's pleas for domestic prosecutions were easily ignored. In the end, three issues—a restrictive time frame, restrictive personal jurisdiction, and a robust record of arrests—combined to make the SCSL a transient phenomenon, with little ability or willingness to negotiate hard questions of domestic accountability.

The ICTR shared many elements of institutional design with the SCSL, but temporality played a different role in its relations with Rwanda. Similar to the SCSL, the ICTR began operations with an inward-looking posture. Unlike the SCSL, however, the ICTR managed to use rule 11*bis* to engage Rwandan authorities over domestic reforms and trials, underscoring the iterative potential of international intervention when strategic interests converge. Although ICTR and Rwandan officials disagreed on referrals, an impending deadline had a mobilizing effect and pushed both international and domestic actors to negotiate over solutions. By contrast, where their strategic interests diverged, notably over RPF crimes, the ICTR's closure undermined—like the SCSL's failed attempts to promote national trials—Hassan Jallow's leverage with his domestic counterparts.

The ICTR and SCSL illustrate that deadlines do not per se guarantee iterative relationships: completion strategies are likely to trigger iteration when ICT–state strategic interests converge, but they may have the opposite effect of isolation otherwise. However, it is worth expounding on the conditions under which ICTs and states can productively engage one another on shared objectives. On the one hand, the SCSL's hybrid features and legacy projects had a small effect on Sierra Leone, mainly because international civil servants had no self-interested reason—and, in fact, their budgetary limitations argued against it—to engage state-based actors until the end of their operations. On the other hand, the ICTR's post-Completion about-face and focus on the Rwandan accountability landscape (similar to the ICTY) was underpinned by an element of happenstance, namely too many indictments that needed to be offloaded to comply with cost-cutting measures. Here again, it was the Tribunal's self-interest that enabled iterative relations.

Going forward, more thought needs to be given to the conditions under which tribunals, including the ICC, can benefit from engaging domestic authorities and, conversely, under what conditions state actors, acting in accordance with their interests, will reciprocate entreaties to coordinate accountability strategies. It was long assumed that, as a permanent institution, the ICC's relationship to temporality was different from the ad hoc tribunals.[46] Yet, while the Rome Statute's post-2002 prospective jurisdiction is a strength—most obviously, in terms of deterrence[47]—the ad hoc tribunals' experiences may have lessons for the ICC as well. States

[46] McAuliffe (n 19) 357–58.

[47] Stuart Ford, 'Can the International Criminal Court Succeed? An Analysis of the Empirical Evidence of Violence Prevention' (2020) 43 Loyola of Los Angeles International and Comparative Law

cannot wait the ICC out (the OTP may in theory prosecute indefinitely), but accountability is always retrospective and freedom to keep inquiries open is illusory. As acknowledged by the OTP in 2021, '[w]hile the ICC differs from the ad hoc tribunals because it is a permanent court, exercising jurisdiction over multiple situations rather than only one, it can adopt a similar approach within the context of each of its situations'.[48]

An important commonality with the ad hoc tribunals is that the ICC must show results as quickly as possible. While the ICC's permanency was supposed to shield it from a 'looking for business' mentality, the ICC's track record of apprehending mid-level suspects in countries like the DRC and Mali suggests it may simply suffer from *Tadić* syndrome in each investigation.[49] Swift arrests of perpetrators—more easily available but not necessarily the most senior—may then leave limited capacity for trials of more deserving suspects. For instance, in the CAR 2 situation, ongoing trials of several anti-balaka suspects in The Hague call into question the viability of future cases against more senior commanders from this faction.

A push to score 'quick' wins seems correlated with another operational reality, namely states' greater susceptibility to external influence in the early phases of intervention. Outside the context of *ab initio* isolation, when states simply reject external involvement, as in Burundi, ICTs usually cast a longer shadow when their *modus operandi* is unknown. In the DRC, Sierra Leone, and Rwanda, governments' worries about (additional) cases delimited the influence of each tribunal for many years, but prosecutors' leverage was most pronounced at the beginning when states remained unaware of ICT's strengths and limitations. To date, the ICC has proceeded cautiously, refusing to target incumbent government actors in self-referrals when state cooperation is forthcoming. For instance, in Côte d'Ivoire, the OTP opted for a 'sequencing' strategy, which prioritized cooperation for its Laurent Gbagbo trial but arguably misdiagnosed when the ICC's leverage was greatest.[50] Conversely, Crane's decision to target from the beginning those most responsible within each faction may have avoided sequencing and obstructionism from Sierra Leonean elites.

Similar temporal dilemmas exist in preliminary examinations. In Colombia and Guinea, the ICC's leverage arguably peaked in the early phases of intervention but declined over time.[51] Although preliminary examinations may constitute a paradigmatic convergence of interests, where states and the ICC want to incentivize

Review 101. Benjamin J Appel, 'In the Shadow of the International Criminal Court: Does the ICC Deter Human Rights Violations?' (2018) 62 Journal of Conflict Resolution 3.

[48] ICC–OTP, 'Policy on Situation Completion' (2021) para 10.

[49] See Chapter 4, section 5 in this volume.

[50] Sophie T Rosenberg, 'The International Criminal Court in Côte d'Ivoire' (2017) 15 Journal of International Criminal Justice 471.

[51] Marco Bocchese, '*El Coco* Does Not Frighten Anymore: ICC Scrutiny and State Cooperation in Colombia' (2021) 26 Journal of Conflict and Security Law 157.

domestic accountability to avoid a full investigation, the longer the ICC invests in stimulating domestic trials the more difficult it becomes for the OTP to acknowledge defeat and challenge the state's good faith. This dilemma has surfaced in Guinea and Nigeria, where Bensouda declined repeatedly to open investigations despite civil society demands to that effect.

By the same token, the leverage of prosecutors decreases once a state familiarize itself with their practices and especially when the threat of additional arrests subsides. As noted above, the Rwandan and Sierra Leonean elites ignored international demands, hoping to wait out their international counterparts. While, in theory, government officials cannot ever fully escape the ICC's shadow, this threat is more theoretical than real, as evidence deteriorates, ICC priorities shift, and public attention drifts. In both Uganda and the DRC, the prosecutor should have pushed for a balanced case docket from the beginning, but the longer these situations remained open the more unrealistic the threat of arrest warrants for distant crimes became.

A greater willingness to grapple with the temporal dilemmas of ICC country-specific inquiries is evident. The Independent Experts opted for a standardized two-year time frame for preliminary examinations, with extensions 'only in exceptional and justified circumstances'.[52] Meanwhile, the OTP has put forward a blueprint for 'situation strategies', 'dynamically reviewed and adjusted as the investigation progresses'.[53] Aiming at 'completion of a situation, and identify[ing] the conditions for achieving this, from the outset of its investigation', the OTP emphasizes the role of positive complementarity by 'continu[ing], at all times, to identify opportunities to emphasise and support the primary responsibility of States to exercise their jurisdiction', including by cooperating with states on investigations and 'responding positively as far as possible to requests received under article 93(10)'.[54]

Much remains unknown about 'situation strategies'. For instance, the policy paper mandates 'public notification of the completion of the investigation phase', even though ICTR and SCSL experiences show that too much transparency may decrease leverage with state actors.[55] However, the OTP completion policy paper is a step towards holistic country-specific accountability strategies, from preliminary examination through to investigation and prosecution. A welcome attempt to move beyond a simplistic approach to ICC 'permanency', the paper grapples in a dynamic manner with the temporal aspects of international intervention through tools like prioritization, hibernation, legacy, and closure.[56] It is also a recognition

[52] IER (n 26) paras 717, 720, and R257.

[53] ICC–OTP (n 48) para 23; ICC Forum, *Completion Strategies*, February–May 2020 <iccforum.com/completion>.

[54] ICC–OTP (n 48) paras 23 and 29.

[55] ibid para 51.

[56] Elizabeth M Evenson and Alison Smith, 'Completion, Legacy, and Complementarity at the ICC' in Carsten Stahn (ed), *The Law and Practice of the International Criminal Court* (OUP 2015); Rebecca J Hamilton, 'The ICC's Exit Problem' (2014) 47 New York University Journal of International Law and Policy 1.

that states may require different things at different times. Whereas international support and oversight, including Hague-based trials, may be more necessary at the outset, responsibilities should be shifted back to states over time as their capacity grows.[57]

3.2. Bridging capacity and political will: disaggregating the 'black box' of the 'unable or unwilling' state

The tense relationship between state sovereignty and international criminal law has long been debated. Despite formally accepting cooperation obligations with ICTs, states use various methods to obstruct investigations, prosecutions and, in extreme cases, trials. Notorious examples include Rwanda's effort to strongarm Carla Del Ponte or Kenya's obstruction of the ICC.[58] In addition to overt obstruction, governments regularly execute subtle forms of diversion to prevent international civil servants from discharging their mandates. In many cases, by refraining from acting or delaying, states grind the wheels of international criminal justice to a halt.

Yet, while state non-cooperation is a familiar theme, less understood are the institutional and personal dynamics that contribute to fraught ICT–state relations. The literature speaks generically of a 'lack of political will', without analysing power struggles or the motives of government actors. For instance, the stand-off between Africa and the ICC is often examined on the basis of government statements while minimizing the intrastate contestation spawned by ICC involvement in Sudan and Kenya.[59] In short, the state is often conceptualized as a unitary actor rather than disaggregated and problematized in its own right.[60]

This omission is unfortunate. Although complementarity in the Rome Statute conditions ICC intervention on national authorities failing to exercise jurisdiction, the case law largely ignores the conditions that prevent states from adjudicating serious crimes. It is difficult to miss, however, that post-Cold War ICTs have intervened mainly in situations of mass violence accompanied by the collapse of state institutions (e.g. DRC, Rwanda, or CAR) or state fragility (e.g. Sierra Leone, Côte d'Ivoire, or Libya). While the ICC has more recently initiated inquiries against states that do not meet the 'fragile' state paradigm (UK, USA, Russia, and Israel)

[57] Payam Akhavan, 'Complementarity Conundrums: The ICC Clock in Transitional Times' (2016) 14 Journal of International Criminal Justice 1043.

[58] On Rwanda and Kenya, see Chapter 4 in this volume. For Kenya, see also Laurence R Helfer and Anne E Showalter, 'Opposing International Justice: Kenya's Integrated Backlash Strategy against the ICC' (2017) 17 International Criminal Law Review 1.

[59] But see Kamari Maxine Clarke, *Affective Justice: The International Criminal Court and the Pan-Africanist Pushback* (Duke UP 2019).

[60] On disaggregating the state, see Anne-Marie Slaughter, 'International Law in a World of Liberal States' (1995) 6 European Journal of International Law 503.

and it is too early to tell how these inquiries will unfold, the closure of the UK–Iraq situation and the hibernation of investigations into US crimes in Afghanistan suggest that the ICC will struggle to challenge 'strong' rule-of-law states' accountability shortcomings.[61] In fact, the hitherto divergent trajectories of intervention in 'weak' and 'strong' rule-of-law states seem to reinforce that, as a complementarity-based institution, the ICC is designed primarily to address state inability based on consensual and cooperative engagement, while already 'able' states, such as the UK, will be able to shield their unwillingness from scrutiny by overwhelming the OTP with purportedly genuine domestic inquiries even if they do not translate into any accountability for victims.

While this book's case studies focus on three 'weak' rule-of-law states (each justice system changed to different degrees over time), they speak to the centrality of executive power in international criminal law. Despite there being three branches of government and checks and balances in the DRC, Rwanda, and Sierra Leone, state policy on international crimes was decreed from the presidential office. Efforts to bypass the executive are difficult and, arguably, the ICC's consent-based design makes 'executive backlash' a qualitatively different threat, with national leaders occasionally resorting to withdrawal, for instance in Burundi and the Philippines.[62]

Yet, while interviews revealed a range of opinions on ICT intervention, two strands of thought could be isolated in the DRC, Rwanda, and Sierra Leone: 'pro-sovereignty' actors wary of external interference and more 'international-minded' actors (of course, this binary occludes many shades of grey in between). Despite occasional accusations of neocolonialism from state officials in all three countries, some supported international trials for crimes committed by government-affiliated actors. For instance, some Rwandan officials defended the ICTR's primacy and its ability to 'take away' cases (this was a decidedly minority view), and even Congolese military magistrates critical of the ICC, who defended their ability to handle cases domestically, accepted that prominent suspects benefiting from state protection should be taken to The Hague. Nevertheless, many government actors viewed ICTs with a degree of suspicion and even hostility, as a potential threat to sovereignty.

Given this ambivalence and ICTs' dependence on the executive branch's cooperation, civil society usually plays a mediating role by pressing government officials,

[61] States like Colombia do not map neatly onto this typology. For 'weak' rule-of-law states, see also Thomas Risse, 'Governance in Areas Of Limited Statehood' in David Levi-Faur (ed), *The Oxford Handbook of Governance* (OUP 2012). On US crimes, see Alice Speri, 'How the U.S. Derailed an Effort to Prosecute Its Crimes in Afghanistan' (*The Intercept*, 5 October 2021).

[62] On South Africa's judicial backlash to executive backlash, see Hannah Woolaver, 'Domestic and International Limitations on Treaty Withdrawal: Lessons from South Africa's Attempted Departure from the International Criminal Court' (2017) 111 AJIL Unbound 450.

parliamentarians and judicial actors for action on serious crimes. But dynamics vary depending on the national context. In the DRC, development partners and NGOs enjoy considerable power over domestic proceedings by plugging gaps in the state's capacity.[63] By contrast, while NGOs had some initial success influencing trials in Rwanda, their influence waned once the RPF consolidated its authority. In all three case studies, bottom-up support from NGOs, donors, and international organizations, ran up against the limits of centralized state power.

The three case studies also illuminate an 'activism paradox' in that NGOs and donors, while nominally embracing the ideals of positive complementarity, distrust national institutions and prefer international trials. Scholars have noted similar trends in other countries, including in Kenya, where domestic NGOs challenged the state's legitimacy and argued for Hague-based trials, or more recently in Sudan.[64] While this reluctance to prioritize domestic over international trials reflects well-founded fears about governments' wavering political will, positive complementarity advocacy nevertheless channels a 'managerial' belief in the potential of enhanced state capacity to overcome intrastate power dynamics. In other words, despite a realization that impunity is primarily a political challenge, domestic NGOs together with foreign partners focus on 'enhanced' criminal law enforcement, including new equipment or better training.

A more sophisticated strategy bridging 'capacity building' with 'political will' is still lacking. Drawing on reports from twenty-seven countries, the International Law Association identifies twenty-one obstacles to domestic trials, ranging from legal impediments (immunities) and capacity shortfalls (insufficient evidence) to the hardest subset of 'political impediments' (corruption or lack of judicial independence).[65] Based on an analysis of four preliminary examinations, Human Rights Watch urges the OTP to 'bridge the two pillars of "unwillingness" and "inability"', including by 'focusing public debate through media and within civil society' and 'including accountability in [international actors'] political dialogue with domestic authorities'.[66] Yet, while Khan has signalled openness to engagement and dialogue with both governments and civil society, the ICC's ability to open up the 'black box' of the 'unable' and 'unwilling' state surely remains its greatest challenge going forward.

[63] Milli Lake, *Strong NGOs and Weak States: Pursuing Gender Justice in the Democratic Republic of Congo and South Africa* (CUP 2018).

[64] For Kenya, see Ronald Slye, *The Kenyan TJRC: An Outsider's View from the Inside* (CUP 2018) 231–84. For Sudan, see Elise Keppler, 'Sudan Took Important Step, But Now Should Send the ICC Suspects to The Hague' (19 March 2021) <hrw.org/news/2021/03/19/sudan-took-important-step-now-should-send-icc-suspects-hague>. Labelling this pro-ICC ideology, see Nouwen (n 14) 352.

[65] International Law Association, 'Interim Report on Complementarity in International Criminal Law. Sydney Conference' (2018).

[66] HRW (n 5) 2. Two other strategies are 'equipping human rights activists with information derived from the OTP's analysis', and 'identifying weaknesses in domestic proceedings' to galvanize assistance by international partners.

3.3. Prosecutorial leadership: between arrogance and risk-averseness

Sitting at the intersection of law and politics, the pursuit of international crimes places international prosecutors in a delicate position vis-à-vis states. Lacking enforcement powers, ICTs must reconcile international law's consensual nature in a subfield—criminal law—that relies on coercion for its effectiveness. While engaging, nudging, and even threatening states is a feature, to varying degrees, of multilateral governance, international prosecutors arguably face unique dilemmas in calibrating 'carrots' and 'sticks' to achieve mandated goals.

Prosecutors understand their relationship to politics differently. Crane has emphasized the political nature of his position, arguing inter alia that 'international justice is inherently political' and that '[a] successful Chief Prosecutor has to be a diplomat, a politician, someone who can lead and manage effectively, as well as know the law'.[67] Others separate law from politics, a theme that emerged forcefully during Bensouda's term. 'I don't do politics', she insisted, while acknowledging the political context within which the OTP operated.[68]

Yet, whether one views prosecutorial discretion as primarily political or legally circumscribed decision-making with political consequences, prosecutors' relations with government counterparts reflect a mix of leadership, expertise, management experience, and risk tolerance. While there has been a range of personalities and prosecutorial philosophies among the post-Cold War prosecutors—for instance, Del Ponte acquired a reputation for risk-taking but was accused of political tone-deafness, while Hassan Jallow's diplomatic acumen was contrasted with his overly conciliatory stance towards Rwanda—complementarity has changed prosecutorial practice less than was initially assumed.[69]

Struggling to reconcile their institutional independence with a dependence on state cooperation, prosecutors often err on the side of caution. In doing so, however, they may forsake opportunities for engagement with and the potential to activate civil society coalitions—a problem that has been exacerbated by the OTP's detachment from, and poor grasp of, national realities.[70] At the same time, prosecutors have often experienced the limits of coercive strategies. After Ocampo was criticized for treating the ICC as a 'naming and shaming' organization akin

[67] David M Crane, 'The Chief Prosecutor: Diplomat, Politician, Leader, Manager, and Lawyer' (*Opinio Juris*, 8 April 2020) <opiniojuris.org/2020/04/08/icc-prosecutor-symposium-the-chief-prosecutor-diplomat-politician-leader-manager-and-lawyer/>.

[68] Janet H Anderson, 'ICC Investigations: What Prosecutor Bensouda Leaves Behind' (*JusticeInfo*, 26 January 2021) <justiceinfo.net/en/68812-icc-investigations-what-prosecutor-bensouda-leaves-behind.html>.

[69] Kingsley C Moghalu, *Rwanda's Genocide: The Politics of Global Justice* (Palgrave Macmillan 2005) 133 and 149. Victor Peskin, *International Justice in Rwanda and the Balkans: Virtual Trials and the Struggle for State Cooperation* (CUP 2008) 222–31.

[70] IER (n 26) paras 779–82.

to Amnesty International,[71] Bensouda embraced carrots over sticks as a concession to states willing to cooperate with The Hague while taking on a more interventionist role in preliminary examinations. However, her caution and a perceived reluctance to challenge governments came under criticism from human rights groups towards the end of her term. While conceding that 'the OTP's current approach … appropriately recognize[d] certain inherent limits', Human Rights Watch nevertheless argued that 'the most productive posture of the OTP vis-à-vis national authorities when it comes to encouraging national proceedings is as a "sword of Damocles", that is, as a threat and source of strong pressure'.[72] In similar terms, Amnesty International critiqued the OTP for failing to move the situation in Nigeria to an investigation, despite state authorities' 'willing inability' to address impunity through domestic courts.[73]

Although, upon Khan's swearing in, Amnesty again warned that 'an overly deferential approach to states does not represent complementarity, but rather complicity with major-power impunity',[74] international prosecutors (and judges) seem increasingly reluctant to challenge governments if it jeopardizes otherwise cooperative relations. Where, as in Rwanda, international civil servants engaged government officials on reforms, the impetus came from the UN Security Council, a political body. By contrast, ICC–OTP officials usually argue that negotiations with governments over the terms of their domestic accountability response are not within their mandate. Responding to Human Rights Watch, Emeric Rogier, then head of preliminary examinations, emphasized it was not the OTP's role to 'provide instructions or directions to national prosecutors or to set deadlines for certain investigative steps to be taken—at best, the [OTP] can and does query the plans and timelines of the competent authorities and ensures the requirements of the Rome Statute are made clear'.[75] In interviews, OTP officials delegated to six African situations likewise disclaimed any monitoring role for the ICC, with one OTP official arguing that a 'sword of Damocles' strategy was 'pretentious' and likely 'unhelpful' and emphasized that states understood the 'budgetary limitations' of the ICC.[76] 'The message is conveyed but not in a confrontational manner', noted one OTP official while another explained 'it's the fact of asking questions that pushes them to investigate, we cannot [order] them to do something'.[77]

[71] James Verini, 'The Prosecutor and the President' *New York Times* (26 June 2016) <nytimes.com/2016/06/26/magazine/international-criminal-court-moreno-ocampo-the-prosecutor-and-the-president.html>.

[72] HRW (n 5) 9 and 11.

[73] Amnesty International, 'Willingly Unable. ICC Preliminary Examination and Nigeria's Failure to Address Impunity for International Crimes' (2018) AFR 44/9481/2018.

[74] Amnesty International, 'Open Letter on the Commencement of Your Term of Office as ICC Prosecutor' (2021).

[75] Emeric Rogier, 'The Ethos of Positive Complementarity' (*Justice in Conflict*, 11 December 2018) <justiceinconflict.org/2018/12/11/the-ethos-of-positive-complementarity/>.

[76] Interview with OTP official, The Hague, Netherlands, 3 December 2019. Interviews with OTP officials working on the DRC, Uganda, Mali, Côte d'Ivoire, Libya, and CAR, 2015–21.

[77] Interview with OTP official, The Hague, Netherlands, 24 November 2015.

In response to setbacks, the ICC–OTP has championed bureaucratic reform. After the collapse of the Kenya cases and the acquittals of Laurent Gbagbo and Jean-Pierre Bemba, investigative practices received the lion's share of attention, with reforms focused on better planning, longer periods in-country, and a new policy paper on investigations.[78] However, beyond operational tweaks, philosophical dilemmas await. Not only have ICC prosecutors spent less time in country engaging state actors than their ICTR/Y counterparts; some OTP officials concede that relations with states focus too much on diplomacy.[79] Others explained that OTP leadership refused to accept security risks for investigators, avoiding situations that would be normal for any humanitarian NGO, with the ICC's adherence to UN security protocols cited as an obstacle to effective investigations.[80] Equally important, it remains to be seen if the OTP is willing to use (lawful) covert investigation techniques to overcome state non-cooperation or incorporate evidence from private investigators (not encumbered by ICC security protocols).[81]

At the end of the day, the OTP's posture vis-à-vis governments—striking a balance between risk and caution—will define the ICC's future. To move beyond the institution's track record of trials against mid-level warlords and failed prosecutions of senior government actors, the OTP will need to reconcile cooperative strategies, for instance in CAR, with principled case selection while avoiding backlash in countries like Venezuela. It is early in Khan's term but his decision to hibernate the US prong of the Afghanistan investigation, coupled with assurances that the ICC 'is not in the regime change business' at the 2021 ASP, suggest that the new OTP may be on an increasingly sovereignty-friendly and risk-averse trajectory.[82]

4. Searching for Shadows

Domestic accountability for serious crimes remains a core aspiration. According to the OTP's most recent strategic plan, positive complementarity 'can help to progress the goal of closing the impunity gap' and 'both *maximise* the benefits of [the OTP's] engagement and *minimise* the need for its continuing role'.[83] Along these lines, Nobel Prize laureate Denis Mukwege called for 'investment in positive

[78] IER (n 26) paras 743–47 and R268; ICC (n 26) para 580. Critically, see Douglas Guilfoyle, 'Lacking Conviction: Is the International Criminal Court Broken? An Organisational Failure Analysis' (2019) 20 Melbourne Journal of International Law 401.

[79] IER (n 26) paras 139–41 and 758–60.

[80] Interviews with OTP officials, Bangui, CAR and by phone, 22 June 2019 and 25 May 2019. William Pace in Mark Kersten, 'A Comment in Defence of Luis Moreno Ocampo' (*Justice in Conflict*, 23 June 2016) <justiceinconflict.org/2016/06/23/a-comment-in-defence-of-luis-moreno-ocampo/>.

[81] ICC–OTP, 'Response to OSJI and Amsterdam Law School Report on Improving the Operations of the ICC–OTP: Reappraisal of Structures, Norms and Practices' (2020) 13.

[82] 'ASP 20 First Plenary Meeting: Speech of ICC Prosecutor Karim Asad Ahmad Khan QC', 6 December 2021, <youtube.com/watch?v=RMAMkkPS0ck> (at 47:22, relating to Venezuela).

[83] ICC–OTP, 'Strategic Plan 2019–2021' (2019) para 49 (emphasis in original).

complementarity' soon after Khan's swearing in.[84] Yet, despite complementarity's rhetorical salience, stakeholders are divided on how to accomplish these ambitious aims. Against this backdrop, this section explores how the ICC can work with civil society and government counterparts to cast as long a shadow as possible while avoiding unintended diversionary complementarity and authoritarian statebuilding.

4.1. Reimagining the aims and addressees of international criminal justice

The field of international criminal justice is in semi-permanent crisis and in search of meaning.[85] Although a robust body of case law and practice has consolidated, the ICC's role in the global order is contested. Punishment, prevention, incapacitation, reconciliation, truth-seeking, and expressivism are all cited as justifications for the ICC's existence.[86] Yet, as Florian Jessberger and Julia Geneuss note,

> [i]t is striking that most statements concerning the achievements or shortcomings of the ICC are marked by a lack of clarity regarding the Court's precise task... It is difficult to decide whether a job is done well as long as it is uncertain what exactly that job is.[87]

While the centrality of domestic accountability for serious crimes is now uncontroversial, the role of ICTs in supporting states is not. Some stakeholders argue that other actors are responsible for strengthening domestic justice—'the ICC is not a development agency' has become a rallying cry for this hands-off vision—while others advocate more hands-on involvement. In reality, contestation over the relationship between ICT intervention and state-driven accountability epitomizes divergent understandings not only of international criminal law's goals but also its addressees. At times, it seems to have mutually exclusive audiences—states, the international community, or victims—leading to confusion or missed opportunities.[88]

[84] Denis Mukwege and Kim Thuy Seelinger, 'Lettre ouverte d'un Prix Nobel congolais au procureur de la CPI' (*Le Temps*, 16 July 2021) <letemps.ch/opinions/lettre-ouverte-dun-prix-nobel-congolais-procureur-cpi>.

[85] Elies Van Sliedregt, 'International Criminal Law: Over-Studied and Underachieving?' (2016) 29 Leiden Journal of International Law 1.

[86] Carsten Stahn, *A Critical Introduction to International Criminal Law* (CUP 2019) 428–29; Sarah MH Nouwen, 'International Criminal Law: Theory All Over the Place' in Anne Orford and Florian Hoffmann (eds), *Oxford Handbook of the Theory of International Law* (OUP 2016).

[87] Florian Jessberger and Julia Geneuss, 'The Many Faces of the International Criminal Court' (2012) 10 Journal of International Criminal Justice 1081, 1083.

[88] See generally Shany (n 1) 117–52. For Rwanda, see Nicola Palmer, *Courts in Conflict: Interpreting the Layers of Justice in Post-Genocide Rwanda* (OUP 2015).

Given its potentially global reach, the ICC faces unprecedented challenges in reconciling its international and domestic audiences. In 2003, Aryeh Neier argued '[i]t is generally believed that [the ICC] will be able to bring prosecutions involving no more than about three situations at a time'.[89] By the time Khan took office, he had inherited almost a dozen active (and a few de facto hibernated) investigations, a half dozen preliminary examinations, and more candidates for intervention. Querying the ICC's capacities, some argue for a narrow reading of the Rome Statute, focused on trials and associated functions, such as victim assistance.[90] Two options have received attention: narrowing admissibility by applying a higher gravity threshold and taking feasibility into account during situation selection. But these nominally pragmatic solutions raise many other questions.[91] As the OTP observes, 'if the gravity threshold were to be pitched even higher than it is now, would any of the current situations fail to meet that threshold?'.[92]

For advocates of an expansive vision of the ICC, it must pay more attention to the domestic level. Elizabeth Evenson observes that 'The Hague is not where the ICC matters most. Where the ICC truly needs to matter is in the countries—and indeed in the communities—affected by the crimes.'[93] Valérie Arnould argues similarly:[94]

> ICC success needs to be measured against its local impact, not just by its international effects. The fact that a trial constituted a success for the ICC as an institution does not automatically imply that it was a success in bringing about justice for local communities ... questions of the ICC's success should be approached by exploring the local changes it produces and how this interacts with broader processes of social, political, and institutional change at the local level in which the ICC's operations are necessarily embedded.

Yet, while ICC supporters rhetorically acknowledge victims and affected populations, this impact-based vision of the Court remains controversial.[95] Many fear it invites politics into the ICC's work. As early as 2007, Ocampo argued 'we can't take our impact into consideration. The law must guide us, not our effects on the ground.

[89] Aryeh Neier, 'Accountability for State Crimes: The Past Twenty Years and the Next Twenty Years' (2003) 35 Case Western Reserve Journal of International Law 351, 358.

[90] IER (n 26) paras 643 and 642; Todd Buchwald, 'What Kinds of Situations and Cases Should the ICC Pursue? The Independent Expert Review of the ICC and the Question of Aperture' (*Just Security*, 2 December 2020) <justsecurity.org/73653/part-iii-what-kinds-of-situations-and-cases-should-the-icc-pursue-the-independent-expert-review-of-the-icc-and-the-question-of-aperture/>.

[91] IER (n 26) para 645.

[92] ICC (n 26) para 405.

[93] Elizabeth M Evenson, 'ICC Success Depends on Its Impact Locally' (*Open Democracy*, 26 August 2015) <opendemocracy.net/en/openglobalrights-openpage/icc-success-depends-on-its-impact-locally/>.

[94] Valérie Arnould, 'Rethinking What ICC Success Means at the Bemba Trial' (*Open Democracy*, 14 September 2016) <opendemocracy.net/en/openglobalrights-openpage/rethinking-what-icc-success-means-at-bemba-trial/>.

[95] IER (n 26) para 694.

International justice can't bring change in a country.'[96] Equally important, there is a growing backlash to an impact-driven reading of the ICC's mission among states. Focusing on complementarity, the UK voiced this sentiment in 2018:[97]

> A founding principle of the Court is complementarity. The Court is not there to second guess, still less to review, the decisions of competent, functioning national systems of justice. Justice should in principle be done at the state level. The Court should step in only where States are genuinely unable or unwilling to do so themselves ... the Court has no mandate, and no jurisdiction, nor will it ever have nearly enough capacity, to act as a human rights monitoring organisation for the whole world. It must focus on its core and essential task, set out under the Statute. If it acts otherwise, it risks eroding the confidence States have in the Court and the integrity of the system.

Remarkable for its non-interventionist reading of complementarity, the UK statement dissociates the ICC from reviewing and monitoring state behaviour, lest it illuminate domestic flaws. In fact, backlash against ICC 'interventionism' ties in with wider debates over institutional effectiveness. In 2014, the ASP asked the ICC to 'develop qualitative and quantitative indicators' to assess performance along four axes: expeditiousness, fairness, and transparency of proceedings; effectiveness of leadership and management; security of its own work and of others; and victim access.[98] These indicators promptly came under criticism, because performance was assessed in isolation from national impact. As Carsten Stahn argues, '[p]erformance assessment should not be a one-way street or a self-serving exercise of performance validation ... The ICC matters to states or global audiences, but mostly to countries and societies where the crimes are committed'.[99]

Khan seems open to a wider vision of the ICC's role, arguing inter alia that '[s]uccess does not simply mean the numbers of trials ... in The Hague' but rather 'narrowing accountability, supporting national authorities, looking at imaginative ways in which we work together'.[100] Yet, beyond such rhetorical assurances, ICC

[96] Cited in Phil Clark, *Distant Justice: The Impact of the International Criminal Court on African Politics* (CUP 2018) 43; Paul F Seils, 'Making Complementarity Work: Maximizing the Limited Role of the Prosecutor' in Carsten Stahn and Mohamed M El Zeidy (eds), *The International Criminal Court and Complementarity* (CUP 2011) 1112.

[97] UK Statement to ICC–ASP 17th Session, by Andrew Murdoch, Legal Director <gov.uk/government/speeches/uk-statement-to-icc-assembly-of-states-parties-17th-session>.

[98] ICC–ASP, Strengthening the ICC and the ASP, ICC–ASP/13/Res 5 (2014), Annex I, para 7(b).

[99] Carsten Stahn, 'Is ICC Justice Measurable? Re-Thinking Means and Methods of Assessing the Court's Practice' (*ICC Forum—Performance Debate*, July 2017) <iccforum.com/performance>; Birju Kotecha, 'The ICC's Office of the Prosecutor and the Limits of Performance Indicators' (2017) 15 Journal of International Criminal Justice 543; IER (n 26) para 361.

[100] ICC–OTP, 'Statement of ICC Prosecutor, Karim A.A. Khan QC, to the United Nations Security Council on the Situation in Libya' para 23 <icc-cpi.int/news/statement-icc-prosecutor-karim-aa-khan-qc-united-nations-security-council-situation-libya>.

officials still have few incentives to engage states over domestic accountability. The fact is that too little has changed from an institutional perspective, with the ICC's reputation—as reflected in its budget and performance indicators—dependent on trials in The Hague and especially convictions. Whatever complementarity's rhetorical salience, refocusing on the domestic sphere will require different questions to be asked of the ICC and a more holistic metric of success.[101]

4.2. Rethinking institutional design and (positive) complementarity

ICT–state relations depend on context-specific and contingent circumstances rather than templates such as complementarity, primacy, or hybridity. Opting for complementarity cannot guarantee that states will be incentivized to exercise jurisdiction any more than adoption of a rule 11*bis*-type procedure ensures—as seen in the divergent experiences of Rwanda and Sierra Leone—that domestic authorities will reform laws or prosecute offenders pursuant to referrals. As explained in Chapter 3, these terms can also be understood as dominant ideals or policy preferences for the domestic, international, or mixed enforcement of international criminal law. In practice, however, other institutional (time frames, substantive norms, staffing nationalities), personal (leadership, management experience, risk-averseness), and contextual factors (ongoing conflict or not, a prior rule-of-law history, affiliation of alleged perpetrators with the government in power) condition ICT–state relations.[102]

Yet, while institutional design per se does not predetermine how ICTs and states interact with one another (and international civil servants can and do behave differently, including with the same mandates), the experiences of the ICTR, ICC, and SCSL do not mean that institutional design does not matter. On the contrary, too often ICT–state relations are portrayed simplistically as a by-product of politics (a catch-all term that is then rarely defined). To be sure, politics are central, yet ICT mandates structure and circumscribe how international prosecutors and judges interact with government institutions and civil society actors. While searching for 'optimal arrangements' based on labels such as 'complementarity' or 'hybridity' provide no guarantee of efficacy, policymakers should pay more attention to what incentives institutional design creates for states and ICTs.[103] Future

[101] In this sense, see Alexander Greenawalt, 'Complementarity in Crisis: Uganda, Alternative Justice, and the International Criminal Court' (2009) 50 Virginia Journal of International Law 107, 160; Hillebrecht and Straus (n 9) 173; McAuliffe (n 19). But see Open Society Justice Initiative and Amsterdam Law School (n 34) 15–16.

[102] It is an axiom of transitional justice that no two situations are the same and 'one size fits all' recipes for justice should be avoided (Report of the Secretary General, *The Rule of Law and Transitional Justice in Conflict and Post-Conflict Societies* (2004) S/2004/616).

[103] In this sense, see Alejandro Chehtman, 'Developing Local Capacity for War Crimes Trials: Insights from BiH, Sierra Leone, and Colombia' (2013) 49 Stanford Journal of International Law 297.

research should also probe further how jurisdictional and admissibility norms relate to elements such as personal jurisdiction, triggering mechanisms, or cooperation obligations.[104]

Extrapolating from this book's case studies, it is posited that ICT mandates incentivize three types of relationships between tribunals and states, ranging from iteration through accommodation to isolation, which depend on whether state officials and international civil servants cooperate with, ignore, or are in conflict with one another. However, contrary to the current scholarly emphasis on deference to states, mandates should be designed to *also* ensure a degree of *strategic conflict* in the process of interpreting mandated norms that must then be overcome through creative bargaining tactics. By contrast, where institutional design facilitates *strategic accommodation*, international civil servants will (inevitably) choose non-conflictual means of mandate interpretation that preserve plausible deniability in the face of state opposition. To be sure, a risk-averse posture to norm interpretation can ensure short-term gains, including symbolic cooperation from governments, but it decreases pressure on international and state actors to engage with one another in longer-term dialogue over holistic in-country accountability strategies. Ultimately, ICT mandates provide 'shared ground rules' through which not only to 'find consensus' but also 'to disagree',[105] which is why the fundamental question of when and why states or tribunals should (or not) prosecute serious crimes ought to be mediated through the language of law rather than diplomatic negotiations in the shadow of ICT mandates, recast in the language of (prosecutorial) policy.

Against this backdrop, while the Rome Statute was expected to provide a favourable mix of enforcement incentives to states and the ICC, it is increasingly doubtful whether complementarity actually incentivizes states to prosecute serious crimes. As Stahn notes, while '[t]he idea of complementarity has significant appeal from a systemic perspective . . . it has caused political tensions and unintended side effects in ICC practice'.[106] Going one step further, this book argues that the Rome Statute, as currently interpreted by ICC officials, incentivizes mainly accommodation with states but is unlikely to generate iteration, defined as push–pull relationships between international civil servants and government officials based on evaluative conditionalities for the exercise of jurisdiction. While no ICT mandate can guarantee positive dynamics, some elements of primacy may be more conducive to iterative practices for reasons that can be called legal, ideational, and behavioural.

[104] Two important aspects of the ICC's design are jurisdictional triggers (with self-referrals foreshadowing whether ICT–state relations are generally cooperative) and preliminary examinations (where prosecutorial discretion to the exclusion of judicial oversight has enabled novel practices) (David Bosco, 'Discretion and State Influence at the International Criminal Court: The Prosecutor's Preliminary Examinations' (2017) 111 American Journal of International Law 395, 401 and 414).

[105] Monica Hakimi, 'The Work of International Law' (2017) 58 Harvard International Law Journal 1, 26. For details, see Chapter 2 in this volume.

[106] Stahn (n 86) 226.

First, the conditionalities flowing from the ICTR/Y's primacy provided a principled entry-point and an established process-oriented, human rights-based legal framework for evaluating domestic accountability processes. In applying rule 11*bis*, international judges and prosecutors drew on a rich human rights tradition to ground their conclusions about domestic capacity, political will, and adherence to fair trial standards. Conversely, the Rome Statute's outcome-driven, anti-impunity procedure hampers engagement with states over domestic proceedings and there is no alternative body of norms and practice to draw upon to define the nebulous 'genuineness' standard. It is no coincidence that, with a complementarity case law that has little to say about 'unwilling' and 'genuineness', Prosecutor Bensouda found herself bereft of guidance in evaluating the genuineness of UK's flawed response to allegations of international crimes in Iraq.[107]

Second, although complementarity evokes benign ideas of partnership and cooperation between international and domestic actors, it risks becoming a lowest common denominator that dilutes everyone's responsibility for the enforcement of international criminal norms. Scholars criticize states for outsourcing suspects to The Hague and free-riding on international trials, but it is time to acknowledge that ICTs likewise free-ride on the notion that the impunity gap is ultimately the state's responsibility. While it is usually celebrated for recalibrating accountability incentives away from ICTs and towards states, the Rome Statute's design may ultimately promote a zero-sum form of accommodation where the ICC and states do only as much and as little as is necessary to ward off criticism from the other.

Third, the debate over complementarity's catalytic potential has focused on states' incentives to prosecute international crimes. This framing may inadvertently obscure how institutional design affects the preferences of ICT officials. An anti-impunity reading of article 17 and ideas of complementarity qua cooperation may provide incentives to ICC officials to avoid conflict and seek accommodation with states, rather than confronting them over their failures to provide accountability. In other words, contrary to conventional wisdom, ICT mandates might matter mainly because of the incentives they create for ICTs, rather than states. Although ICTs cannot force states to prosecute under either primacy or complementarity, primacy's strength—especially if personal jurisdiction is 'open-ended', not 'targeted'—may be that it increases the likelihood that international civil servants will eventually be forced to engage governments on impunity gaps. Unlike under article 17, impunity for government crimes remains an international responsibility *as well*.

It must be reiterated that embedding a set of norms labelled primacy, hybridity, or complementarity within an ICT mandate does not predetermine how tribunals interact with states. However, drawing on the experience of the past thirty years,

107 See n 32.

policymakers should be more attentive to the processes of interaction incentivized by ICT mandates, and in particular whether institutional prerogatives can generate iteration rather than mere accommodation. For ICTs to be able to cast a longer shadow, more than cooperation with states is needed. Policymakers must seek institutional checks and balances that oblige international civil servants to challenge states, even when such an approach carries risks for them.

4.3. From accommodation to iteration: enacting relationality at ICTs

Reflecting on primacy's decline and complementarity's rise in international criminal justice, Frédéric Mégret argues that '[f]or better or for worse, complementarity at the ICC is there to stay. Its pedigree is uncontested, its status established, and its utility widely recognized.'[108] Mégret is right about the label, which—like its progeny, positive complementarity—is likely to stay. But his argument also harbours certain assumptions, including that primacy is to be equated with international supremacy, while complementarity is open to interpretation—which is its strength. In fact, the opposite might be closer to the truth. In practice, primacy has lent itself to flexible interpretation, notably through rule 11*bis*, while complementarity—as interpreted by ICC judges—has produced a form of international supremacy.

Labels aside, the current debate over complementarity's strengths and flaws misses an important point. Going forward, the question should not be whether primacy or complementarity is superior in some ideal-type or doctrinal sense, but how ICT institutional design relate to the goals of international criminal justice, and in particular whether mandates are capable of generating iteration between ICTs and states in practice. Ultimately, ICTs should be judged by what difference they make to affected populations and—while they are superficially in opposition to one another—both primacy and complementarity can be interpreted as a rationalization for ICT–state accommodation or as a holistic and relational framework geared to iteration.

Accomplishing iteration requires institutional and ideational shifts at the ICC. Paradoxically, although it was the Rome Statute that was better geared to iterative practices than the ICTR/Y's pre-completion primacy norm, the two came to operate similarly in practice: cases are now prima facie admissible at the ICC just like case selection ended up being the sole prerogative of ICTR/Y prosecutors. Even if the Rome Statute gives different actors a procedural right to challenge admissibility, the ICC case law ignores article 17's conditionality scheme and gives international

[108] Frédéric Mégret, 'The Case against Complementarity' in Carsten Stahn and Mohamed El Zeidy (eds), *The International Criminal Court and Complementarity: From Theory to Practice* (2nd edn, CUP forthcoming).

civil servants unrestrained power to draw lines around cases to 'maintain jurisdiction'.[109] This mirrors the ICTR experience, where rule 9's original conditionality scheme was ignored by prosecutors, making state behaviour largely irrelevant to international case selection, as later reified in judge-made rules of procedure. Thus, while both ICT mandates allowed mutually interdependent concurrent jurisdiction in theory, the challenge remains creating incentives for international civil servants to understand mandates as a system of checks and balances, and their role in international criminal law enforcement vis-à-vis states in iterative terms.

This shift in mentality has yet to happen. In fact, the imbalance between chambers and prosecutors in charting the ICCs' relations with states is growing.[110] By reframing inherently open-ended and contentious questions of case selection and forum allocation in neutral and technical language, judges deflect responsibility for why ICTs should displace domestic jurisdiction and, in so doing, inadvertently delegitimize the exercise of international jurisdiction. Prosecutorial discretion becomes the sole yardstick for the assertion of ICC jurisdiction, with the OTP's case selection—shrouded in secrecy, based on nebulous readings of gravity, and subject to superficial judicial review—becoming the final word on concurrent jurisdiction. In other words, rather than a collective responsibility incumbent upon prosecutors, judges, government officials, and civil society engaged in a relational dialogue about the merits of prosecutions at the national or international levels, the task of guiding relations with states falls to just one (unaccountable) individual: the prosecutor.

Although the shift towards unfettered prosecutorial discretion has received attention, notably in the *Mavi Marmara* litigation and the UK–Iraq declination, the underlying institutional incentives and the chilling effects of complementarity jurisprudence are misconstrued. The ICC's article 17 has been analysed from various perspectives, with legalist–formalist critiques emphasizing an 'objective' or 'neutral' doctrinal reading of the Rome Statute. But many scholars now go further, seeking to counteract the case law's unintended consequences, in particular the circularity of a 'mirroring' obligation for states. Notably, Stahn suggests how the ICC can 'give sufficient space' to states 'while retaining checks and balances', including by imposing a form of conditionality.[111] Proposing to abolish the 'same conduct'

[109] The *Al-Senussi* admissibility decision is not a counterargument, as the prosecutor could have amended the charges to make the international case 'sufficiently' different from Libya's case. It was the OTP's choice to relinquish Al-Senussi to the Libyan authorities, rather than the other way around.

[110] Triestino Mariniello, 'Judicial Control over Prosecutorial Discretion at the International Criminal Court' (2019) 19 International Criminal Law Review 979; Priya Urs, 'Judicial Review of Prosecutorial Discretion in the Initiation of Investigations into Situations of "Sufficient Gravity"' (2021) 18 Journal of International Criminal Justice 851.

[111] Carsten Stahn, 'Admissibility Challenges before the ICC. From Quasi-Primacy to Qualified Deference?' in Carsten Stahn (ed), *Law and Practice of the International Criminal Court* (OUP 2015) 258 (building on Drumbl's 'qualified deference' (see also Chapter 6, section 5 in this volume)).

standard, Kevin Heller advocates 'that as long as a state is making a genuine effort to bring a suspect to justice, the ICC should find his or her case inadmissible'.[112]

A common theme uniting these critiques is that governments should be accorded more leeway, that international judges and prosecutors have gone too far in circumscribing states' freedom to exercise jurisdiction, and that the ICC–OTP must do more to support national institutions by sharing evidence and expertise.[113] While acknowledging and building on this work, it is argued here that a more fundamental rethink of ICT–state relations is required. In particular, concurrent jurisdiction and case selection should not be viewed in binary terms, as a win for either states or the ICC, but rather as a part of a wider accountability puzzle. By uncritically playing up national over international trials, scholars romanticize domestic jurisdiction,[114] place unrealistic demands on international civil servants,[115] and promote awkward partnerships with authoritarian elites in some countries.[116] Importantly, equating the ICC's shortcomings with insufficient flexibility vis-à-vis states misapprehends the obstacles to accountability—how exactly did a handful of trials per country come to be imagined as a threat to sovereignty in the context of mass criminality and mass victimhood?—while arguments for more deference ring hollow to affected populations that get little justice from their courts.

A qualitatively different debate over the merits of forum allocation is needed, bridging (jurisprudential) law and (prosecutorial) policy, on the basis of 'relational complementarity'.[117] To begin with, if the OTP determines that an investigation is warranted, the baseline assumption going forward—albeit rebuttable[118]—must be that the state is unwilling or unable to provide genuine accountability on its own terms (this also applies in self-referrals). Yet international judges have hitherto strenuously avoided any mention of state failure. Stahn, for instance, notes how the article 17 case law has 'detached the method of forum allocation ... from the stigma of "failure" associated with the applicability of the "unwillingness" and "inability" criteria'.[119] Significantly, justifying the exercise of ICC jurisdiction on the basis of technical arguments or conflict-avoidance techniques, while avoiding appraisals

[112] Kevin J Heller, 'Radical Complementarity' (2016) 14 Journal of International Criminal Justice 637, 640.

[113] De Vos (n 14) 103.

[114] Adam Kochanski, 'The "Local Turn" in Transitional Justice: Curb the Enthusiasm' (2020) 22 International Studies Review 26.

[115] Dustin N Sharp, 'What Would Satisfy Us? Taking Stock of Critical Approaches to Transitional Justice' (2019) 13 International Journal of Transitional Justice 570.

[116] Stef Vandeginste, 'Decolonising Human Rights Protection in Africa: Impunity Rhetorically Repackaged?' (Royal Institute for International Relations 2021) 35.

[117] Patryk I Labuda, 'Relational Complementarity (Working Paper)' (2023); Alexander Greenawalt, 'Admissibility as a Theory of International Criminal Law' in Margaret deGuzman and Valerie Oosterveld (eds), *Elgar Companion to the International Criminal Court* (Edward Elgar 2020) 64. For the term 'relational complementarity' (meant differently), see Clark (n 96) 26.

[118] States are, of course, free to challenge admissibility under the Rome Statute, art 18.

[119] Carsten Stahn, 'One Step Forward, Two Steps Back? Second Thoughts on a "Sentence-Based" Theory of Complementarity' (2012) 53 Harvard International Law Journal Online 185, 190.

of domestic alternatives or the goals of case allocation, is considered neutral legal interpretation. As explained by an ICC official:[120]

> all this is done to avoid interfering with state sovereignty. We know what's up, but we don't want to go into it and accuse states of lack of independence or worse; it's enough to just say [the state] is inactive, it's very formalistic ... it's easier [for us], we avoid any controversy over the state's good or bad faith.

Yet this discounts that stigma also creates prospective behavioural incentives for states to avoid shame, while the 'same case' jurisprudence, which elides why states do or do not prosecute, inadvertently incentivizes non-cooperation.[121] Why exactly should Côte d'Ivoire, or anyone else for that matter, care whether a domestic case against Simone Gbagbo is different from the ICC's proposed trial? Although judges will be wary of questioning the 'same case' doctrine in such consequentialist terms, to assume that compliance with orders from The Hague is enough of an incentive to cooperate reveals the limits of an ICC-centric legalist paradigm.[122]

The reality is that, in the absence of pre-existing political will and capacity, a mix of rewards and stigma is the ICC's only tool to incentivize states to cooperate and pursue accountability jointly. At the ICTR, purposive sociolegal readings of rule 11*bis* pushed Rwandan actors to enact reforms—not conflict avoidance that ignored obstacles to fair trials. Put differently, there may be value in the process of negotiating case allocation with states in the language of law rather than diplomacy, which in turn speaks in favour of progressive, conditionality-based interpretations of the Rome Statute's 'unwilling', 'unable', and 'genuineness' criteria.[123] Along these lines, Ezéchiel Amani observes that '[t]here is an urgent need to proceduralize the "unwilling or unable" [formula], which 'is in and of itself a balancing test'.[124]

Relational complementarity also means that the ICC should abandon the doctrinally defensible but self-defeating reading of article 17 whereby national trials'

[120] Interview with ICC official, The Hague, Netherlands, 18 November 2016. Another former ICC official emphasized that labels are 'not innocuous' and that 'refusing to label states as "unwilling" is a big problem because it lets them off the hook' and 'gives political cover to [the state's] lack of cooperation' (interview with former ICC official, Geneva, Switzerland, 28 May 2015).

[121] On naming and shaming, see Emilie M Hafner-Burton, 'Sticks and Stones: Naming and Shaming the Human Rights Enforcement Problem' (2008) 62 International Organization 689.

[122] But see Concurring Separate Opinion of Judge Eboe-Osuji and Judge Bossa, *Judgment on the appeal of Mr Saif Al-Islam Gaddafi against the decision of Pre-Trial Chamber I entitled 'Decision on the "Admissibility Challenge by Dr. Saif Al-Islam Gaddafi pursuant to Articles 17(1)(c), 19 and 20(3) of the Rome Statute"'*, ICC-01/11-01/11-695-Anx (9 March 2020).

[123] For an analogous approach to conditionality—setting benchmarks for states to fulfil, providing time, and holistic monitoring—but within the 'same case' paradigm, see Stahn, 'From Quasi-Primacy to Qualified Deference?' (n 111) 253–58; Mégret (n 108).

[124] Ezéchiel Amani Cirimwami, 'States of Justice Symposium: What If We Took the "Unwilling or Unable" Seriously?' (*Opinio Juris*, 19 August 2020) <opiniojuris.org/2020/08/19/states-of-justice-symposium-what-if-we-took-the-unwilling-or-unable-seriously/> (assimilating U/U with proportionality).

genuineness is divorced from fair trial standards. The shibboleth that 'the ICC is not a human rights court', which has been deployed to deflect responsibility for states' treatment of defendants, lacks a legal basis.[125] The reality is that, when evaluating admissibility under article 17, the ICC is more akin to a human rights court than a criminal court. This may be inconvenient, given the ICC judges' backgrounds and expertise, but the Rome Statute leaves no doubt that the state's justice system—not just the suspect—is on trial in admissibility proceedings.

By the same token, while inward-looking and decontextualized readings of article 17 allow judges and prosecutors to insist that 'unwillingness' should not be read through the lens of fair trial rights, this is a recipe for doctrinally sanctioned arbitrariness. Admissibility is decided on a case-by-case basis, as seen in the contradictory *Al-Senussi* and *Gaddafi* case law or the UK–Iraq declination that relies on human rights law, for lack of a better alternative, but draws arbitrary conclusions about genuineness that ignore inconvenient facts. For better or worse, the human rights system has developed a robust method of assessing when states fail to meet their obligations to victims and defendants, and a temptation to devise a novel 'genuineness' standard rooted in international criminal law should be resisted.[126]

To be clear, relational complementarity is not an argument for more trials in The Hague at the expense of domestic proceedings.[127] On the contrary, it suggests that framing the question of international trials in (binary) opposition to domestic trials may be a red herring. In fact, a relational approach to concurrent jurisdiction is premised on the need for a more nuanced sociolegal debate over the merits of forum allocation.[128] Like Heller, this reading of the Rome Statute emphasizes (lack of) genuine state action as the main criterion for international intervention, but a relational approach means that a handful of ICC trials per country are seen in the context of the entire accountability process—not as a challenge to, but in addition to, state prosecutions. To reframe the narrative around international intervention and normalize limited international trials, the ICC must always justify and, in so

[125] See Chapter 3, section 4.4 (discussion of Libya cases) and Chapter 6, section 4.3 (Katanga's secondary trial) in this volume. On art 21(3) and the centrality of human rights in the Rome Statute, including for complementarity, see Emma Irving, 'The Other Side of the Article 21(3) Coin: Human Rights in the Rome Statute and the Limits of Article 21(3)' (2019) 32 Leiden Journal of International Law 837, 845–47; AC Dissenting Opinion of Judge Ušacka, *Prosecutor v Muthaura, Kenyatta and Ali* (Judgment on the appeal of the Republic of Kenya) ICC-01/09-02/11 OA (20 September 2011) para 16.

[126] In opting for human rights law as its normative frame, the ICC may follow the iterative precedent of human rights courts in Europe and South America (Alexandra Huneeus, 'International Criminal Law By Other Means: The Quasi-Criminal Jurisdiction of the Human Rights Courts' (2013) 107 American Journal of International Law 1). For 'active subsidiarity', see Matthew Saul, 'Shaping Legislative Processes from Strasbourg' (2021) 32 European Journal of International Law 281.

[127] For such a defence of primacy, see Gur-Arye Miriam and Harel Alon, 'Taking Internationalism Seriously: Why International Criminal Law Matters' in Kevin Jon Heller and others (eds), *The Oxford Handbook of International Criminal Law* (OUP 2020).

[128] For a similar argument (with different conclusions), see Frédéric Mégret, 'In Defense of Hybridity: Towards a Representational Theory of International Criminal Justice' (2005) 38 Cornell Journal of International Law 725; Mégret (n 108).

doing, legitimize its assertion of jurisdiction, even when states ask for cases to be tried in The Hague.[129] In other words, any exercise of ICC jurisdiction, even uncontested, must be evaluated, justified, and legitimized in relation to alternatives: a prosecution by the territorial state, the state of the perpetrator's nationality, the victim state, under universal jurisdiction and in relation to non-retributive forms of justice.

While relational complementarity will sometimes be similar in its outcomes, the process is different. Rejecting the assumption of case admissibility, it requires a contextual reinterpretation of articles 17–20, whereby the rationale behind the exercise of ICC jurisdiction is transparently articulated and, by the same token, the ICC's performance can later be judged. While the assertion of jurisdiction by the ICC at the expense of states carries a 'shaming' dimension, it also harbours a prospective, iterative function geared to encouraging 'unwilling' or 'unable' states to improve their performance in accordance with deficiencies publicly identified in the case law. For states 'unwilling' to prosecute genuinely, the ICC identifies obstacles to fair trials. For states 'unable' to adjudicate, the case law provides a baseline for donor-funded capacity building.[130] Significantly, by placing a fair trial at the centre of admissibility proceedings, a relational jurisprudence can also restore human rights to the practice of criminal law, counteracting long-term trends (and critiques) of a criminal turn in human rights.[131]

In so doing, relational complementarity re-establishes a balance between judge-made (admissibility) law and prosecutorial policy, promotes the legitimacy of international trials, and counteracts accusations of neocolonialism by collapsing distinctions between weak and strong states. Rather than a top-down tool for (prosecutorial) case selection that precludes states from showing their bona fide, a conditionality-based process ensures that states have agency to forestall the exercise of international jurisdiction based not on the parameters of international charging but their efforts to provide justice at the national level.[132] An inclusive dialogue, based on *amicus curiae* submissions from civil society, victims groups, expert reports, as contrasted with government statements, should guide evaluations,

[129] For an analysis in the extant case law, see Ben Batros, 'The Evolution of the ICC Jurisprudence on Admissibility' in Stahn and El Zeidy (n 96) 589–602 (noting the ICC's 'conservative understanding' of complementarity).

[130] But see Heller (n 112) 657–58; Jann K Kleffner, *Complementarity in the Rome Statute and National Criminal Jurisdictions* (OUP 2008) 321–22 (noting that unable states are less susceptible to coercive dimension of complementarity).

[131] See Karen Engle, 'Anti-Impunity and the Turn to Criminal Law in Human Rights' (2015) 100 Cornell Journal of International Law 1069; Mattia Pinto, 'Historical Trends of Human Rights Gone Criminal' (2020) 42 Human Rights Quarterly 729.

[132] Stahn, 'From Quasi-Primacy to Qualified Deference?' (n 111) 240. Some may counter that conditionality-based interventions transform the ICC into a hegemonic institution that casts a 'post-colonial' shadow over states, who must justify their bona fide. In fact, this proposal decreases hegemonic tendencies, as *all states* will be subject to the same transparent U/U standard rather than respond to inherently discretionary charging (Labuda (n 117)). For a post-colonial critique, see Nirej Sekhon, 'Complementarity and Post-Coloniality' (2013) 27 Emory International Law Review 799.

lest admissibility become a top-down ICC-centric process.[133] By approximating the extant admissibility case law with prosecutorial practice in preliminary examinations, where the OTP already assesses ability, willingness and genuineness prospectively, relational complementarity will also promote coherence in the ICC's practice in the different prosecutorial phases and reinforce its legitimacy to outside stakeholders. In the end, relational complementarity is a more principled way of enacting (positive) complementarity in both admissibility determinations and in prosecutorial practice. As a form of benchmarking based on analyses of 'unwillingness', 'inability', and 'genuineness' grounded in human rights law, this approach to case distribution brings the Rome Statute closer to rule 11*bis*, whereby states may eventually avoid ICC jurisdiction subject to legal criteria.

Although promoting iterative practices through relational complementarity will require time, especially by revisiting the article 17 case law, many reforms are already underway. This includes the push to formalize the OTP's outreach to states through situation strategies and benchmarking, or ASP complementarity initiatives, such as an ASP Task Force, an OTP Special Adviser on Knowledge Transfer and a Select ASP Committee on e.g. Rome Statute withdrawals.[134] In addition to its support to states, for instance to Libyan authorities or the CAR hybrid court, the OTP's completion policy addresses the monitoring of case admissibility, implicitly for crimes of incumbent state officials and potential sham trials, seemingly accepting a greater supervisory role for the OTP in the investigations phase.[135] In line with the Independent Experts' recommendation to refocus on investigations, Khan concluded the preliminary examination and proceeded with an investigation in Venezuela while signing a 'cooperation agreement', where benchmarking may be enacted for the first time.[136]

The OTP will surely resist proposals to circumscribe its discretion, but positive complementarity and domestic accountability is ultimately a collective responsibility. The ASP, Registry, and the judges, together with the OTP, must find a way to interpret the complementarity norm more creatively, generating dynamic and iterative relationships with states—lest article 17's authoritarian shadow become the norm at the ICC and beyond.

[133] Along these lines, see Mark Ellis, 'International Justice and the Rule of Law' (2009) 1 Hague Journal on the Rule of Law 79, 81–86. Similarly, for 'interests of justice', see Priscilla Hayner, 'Does the ICC Advance the Interests of Justice?' (*Open Democracy*, 31 October 2014) <opendemocracy.net/en/openglobalrights-openpage/does-icc-advance-interests-of-justice/>.

[134] Carsten Stahn, 'Revitalizing Complementarity a Decade after the Stocktaking Exercise', *Policy Brief Series* (Torkel Opsahl 2020).

[135] ICC–OTP (n 48) paras 74–77.

[136] IER (n 26) R264; ICC–OTP, 'Memorandum of Understanding between the Bolivarian Republic of Venezuela and the OTP' (3 November 2021) paras 3–4 (with very few commitments). But see PTC, Public Redacted Version of 'Decision on the "Request for Judicial Control Submitted by the Bolivarian Republic of Venezuela"' (14 June 2021) ICC-02/18-9-Red 02-03-2022, para. 19 ('Venezuela calls upon the [OTP] to provide, in the framework of positive complementarity, roadmaps, directions and a benchmarking framework').

Epilogue

Interrogating the Ideology of (Positive) Complementarity: Should the Future of International Criminal Justice Be Domestic?

The last thirty years have seen a paradigm shift in international criminal justice. States are now the first line of defence in the global anti-impunity project, while international tribunals perform a backup function. As argued by the UN's legal counsel, Miguel Serpa de Soares, '[i]n an ideal future' tribunals such as the ICTY 'will not be necessary and domestic jurisdictions will assume the main responsibility for the prosecution of international crimes'.[1] Put succinctly, the prevailing wisdom is that the future of international criminal justice is domestic.

Yet the normative and empirical foundations of this shift are less clear. For some, internationalism and global governance institutions like the ICC are in crisis. On the heels of a multi-year standoff with the AU, the Bemba and Gbagbo acquittals fuelled further doubts about the viability of international trials, and even triggered an independent review to enhance 'the performance, efficiency, and effectiveness' of the ICC and 'the Rome Statute system'.[2]

Others emphasize the instrumental benefits of domestic trials, especially their greater proximity to local populations and victims. On this view, as argued by Naomi Roht-Arriaza, '[t]he problem is not so much that the international criminal justice project is in decline, as it is that the focus has shifted back to where, arguably, it belongs: to national trials in the courts of the state where the crimes occurred'.[3]

Yet others nuance the crisis discourse altogether, and emphasize resilience in the face of human rights backlash.[4] An emerging disciplinary consensus also stresses the need for modesty. As Fatou Bensouda remarked before leaving office, 'the scale

[1] Miguel de Serpa Soares, 'The Moral Legacy of the ICTY' in Carsten Stahn and others (eds), *Legacies of the International Criminal Tribunal for the Former Yugoslavia: A Multidisciplinary Approach* (OUP 2020) 68.

[2] Independent Expert Review of the ICC and the Rome Statute System, 'Final Report' (2020) para 1.

[3] Naomi Roht-Arriaza, 'Just a "Bubble"? Perspectives on the Enforcement of International Criminal Law by National Courts' (2013) 11 Journal of International Criminal Justice 537, 537.

[4] Joseph Powderly, 'International Criminal Justice in an Age of Perpetual Crisis' (2019) 32 Leiden Journal of International Law 1.

International Criminal Tribunals and Domestic Accountability. Patryk I. Labuda,
Oxford University Press. © Patryk I. Labuda 2023. DOI: 10.1093/oso/9780198868842.003.0008

of criminality we deal with coupled with our severe resource constraints means we have to make tough choices . . . there is a limit to how much we can do'.[5]

While it is now received wisdom that the shadow of ICTs cannot produce 'quick wins' by promoting peace or fostering reconciliation, this book argues that the turn to (positive) complementarity—understood as a shift towards domestic accountability qua *ultima ratio* of the anti-impunity project—has more profound *ideational* consequences for international criminal law than is acknowledged. Grounded in an obscure admissibility norm, complementarity has revolutionized how civil society, scholars, states, and ICTs think, talk, and act in regard to serious crimes. By now, it is secondary whether the ICC promotes domestic accountability. More important is that beliefs originating in the Rome Statute's institutional design have altered the imaginary of international criminal law stakeholders, so much so that complementarity's emphasis on the domestic risks turning into an ideology extending beyond the ICC.[6] In particular, the turn away from international trials towards domestic trials may transform the ontology of international criminal law from a counter-hegemonic project to a consent-based statebuilding enterprise geared to consolidating the authority of governments and directed against non-state actors.

Thus conceived, the (positive) complementarity turn has three ideational dimensions. First, it captures a shift in the balance of power on the global stage. In the past, tribunals such as the ICTR or ICTY had primacy and were expected to override state sovereignty. As noted by Alex Whiting, 'at least initially, [the ad hoc tribunals] were intended as a substitute for the national criminal courts of states deemed unable or unwilling to dispense justice'.[7] By contrast, the Rome Statute legitimizes the opposite premise, namely that a permanent international tribunal with jurisdiction over international crimes functions merely as a 'court of last resort' that must respect domestic trials. The shift could not be starker. Twenty years after the rebirth of international criminal law, the fight against impunity is identified with states while the international community acts in a support role.

Second, a belief has consolidated that not just ICTs but also donors and civil society should work together with states, 'complementing each other', in a collective, collaborative, and consensual struggle to eradicate impunity. Whereas states used to be a primary cause of impunity (and their agents emblematic perpetrators of international crimes), they are now cast and legitimized as a solution to impunity. While ICTs are demonized as selective and incapable of providing impartial justice,

[5] Fatou Bensouda, 'In the Pursuit of International Criminal Justice, without Fear or Favour' *Diplomat* (6 December 2020) <diplomatmagazine.eu/2020/12/06/in-the-pursuit-of-international-criminal-justice-without-fear-or-favour/>. On modesty, see also Mark Kersten, 'Whither the Aspirational ICC, Welcome the "Practical" Court?' *EJIL: Talk!* (22 May 2019) <ejiltalk.org/whither-the-aspirational-icc-welcome-the-practical-court/>.

[6] Tor Krever, 'International Criminal Law: An Ideology Critique' (2013) 26 Leiden Journal of International Law 701.

[7] Antonio Cassese and others, *Cassese's International Criminal Law* (3rd edn, OUP 2013) 292.

the contrary trend to romanticize statebuilding projects geared to the enforcement of (international) criminal law, including in countries with patchy rule-of-law traditions, is rarely interrogated. Against the backdrop of donor-funded capacity building, the state—which is said to bear the primary burden of prosecution regardless of whether it prosecutes anyone at all (e.g. in Mali or Uganda)—is rehabilitated in the eyes of international criminal law.

Third, while positive complementarity implies that cooperative, managerial strategies aimed at 'unable' states can address the root causes of impunity, the ICC and the wider 'international community' seem increasingly incapable of challenging 'unwilling' governments over state-orchestrated crimes. Designed in part as a sword against 'unwilling or unable' states, complementarity risks becoming a shield-cum-justification for international civil servants and governments unwilling to confront state-sanctioned impunity. Until recently, it was well understood that international crimes were largely a state-sponsored phenomenon and hence states were 'enemies' of international criminal justice. Yet a turn to the consensual enforcement of international criminal law legitimizes the opposite premise and recasts states as 'friends' in the fight against impunity. If nothing else, this book is an appeal to rediscover some balance in (positive) complementarity discourse, with states understood as 'frenemies' of the anti-impunity project—at best.

In the end, the turn to domestic accountability as *ultima ratio* of international criminal law has paradoxical effects at both the national and global level. As seen in the ICC's first investigation, which may foreshadow trends elsewhere, accountability in the DRC is equated with bottom-up support for selective national trials, whereas the OTP and donor community long ago stopped interrogating the rationales of criminal law-oriented statebuilding. Rather than a check on state power, complementarity legitimizes capacity building while political elites' failure to account is sanitized through the 'same case' lexicon and readings of article 17 that dissociate justice from human rights considerations. Paradoxically, by refusing to label state institutions 'unwilling or unable', the ICC not only sanitizes state failure to prosecute serious crimes but also inadvertently delegitimizes its own trials.

Moreover, the ICC's divergent trajectories in 'weak' and 'strong' rule-of-law systems suggest that a consent-based ICC will only ever be able to address state inability, while nominally 'able' states shield their unwillingness by appropriating the jurisprudential logic of (in)action to legitimize superficial action for victims. If so, complementarity—reduced to a line-drawing exercise rather than a human rights-based evaluative tool—will reify hierarchies among states. Ultimately, a misguided refusal (lest one offend the state!) to name the real obstacles to domestic justice allows governments—both weak and strong—to hijack intervention for their own purposes, while complementarity stakeholders diffuse a familiar pathology—victor's justice—at the national level.

Twenty years after the Rome Statute's entry into force, the ICC must chart a path forward. While the disciplinary consensus is that the future of international criminal justice is domestic, the effects of international (criminal) intervention at the national level require critical scrutiny. Activists and scholars should consider both the strengths *and weaknesses* of states' increasing use of (international) criminal law, an inherently illiberal tool, in today's increasingly illiberal political climate. It will also be for the ICC and especially its prosecutor to decide if The Hague can function as more than a conduit for consent-based international trials of undesirable domestic rivals and, by the same token, if the ICC's and other ICTs' symbolic shadow can be harnessed by complementarity stakeholders to achieve counter-hegemonic and emancipatory goals domestically.

Bibliography

Adjovi R, 'Regards sur la justice et les droits de l'homme en Afrique. L'affaire Baragaraza' in Paul Tavernier (ed), *Regards sur les droits de l'homme en Afrique* (Harmattan 2008)

Adjovi R, 'L'affaire Gumisiriza devant la justice militaire rwandaise' (2010) 18 African Yearbook of International Law/Annuaire africain de droit international 451

Ainley K, 'Evaluating the Success of Transitional Justice in Sierra Leone and Beyond' in Kirsten Ainley, Rebekka Friedman, and Chris Mahony (eds), *Evaluating Transitional Justice: Accountability and Peacebuilding in Post-Conflict Sierra Leone* (Palgrave Macmillan 2015)

Akele P, *Les crimes contre l'humanité en droit congolais* (CEPAS 1999)

Akhavan P, 'The International Criminal Tribunal for Rwanda: The Politics and Pragmatics of Punishment' (1996) 90 American Journal of International Law 501

Akhavan P, 'International Criminal Justice in the Era of Failed States: The ICC and the Self-Referral Debate' in Carsten Stahn and Mohamed M El Zeidy (eds), *The International Criminal Court and Complementarity* (CUP 2011)

Akhavan P, 'Complementarity Conundrums: The ICC Clock in Transitional Times' (2016) 14 Journal of International Criminal Justice 1043

Aksenova M, 'Human Rights at the International Criminal Court: Testing the Limits of Judicial Discretion' (2017) 86 Nordic Journal of International Law 68

Aksenova M, 'The ICC Involvement in Colombia: Walking the Fine Line between Peace and Justice' in Morten Bergsmo, Carsten Stahn, and Centre for International Law Research and Policy (eds), *Quality Control in Preliminary Examination*, vol 1 (Torkel Opsahl 2018)

Almqvist J, 'Complementarity and Human Rights: A Litmus Test for the International Criminal Court' (2008) 30 Loyola of Los Angeles International and Comparative Law Review 335

Aluma B, 'Women's Day: DRC Mobile Court a Sign of Hope' *Inter Press Service* (7 March 2011) <ipsnews.net/2011/03/womens-day-drc-mobile-court-a-sign-of-hope/>

Alvarez JE, 'Crimes of States/Crimes of Hate: Lessons from Rwanda' (1999) 24 Yale Journal of International Law 365

Amani Cirimwami E, 'States of Justice Symposium: What If We Took the "Unwilling or Unable" Seriously?' (*Opinio Juris*, 19 August 2020) <opiniojuris.org/2020/08/19/states-of-justice-symposium-what-if-we-took-the-unwilling-or-unable-seriously/>

Amani Cirimwami E and Magadju P Muhindo, 'Prosecuting Rape as War Crime in the Democratic Republic of the Congo: Lessons and Challenges Learned from Military Tribunals' (2021) 59 Military Law and the Law of War Review 44

Ambos K, *The Colombian Peace Process and the Principle of Complementarity of the International Criminal Court: An Inductive, Situation-Based Approach* (Springer 2010)

Ambos K, *Treatise on International Criminal Law. Volume III: International Criminal Procedure* (1st edn, OUP 2016)

Ambos K, 'The Return of "Positive Complementarity"' (*EJIL:Talk!*, 3 November 2021) <ejiltalk.org/the-return-of-positive-complementarity/>

Ambos K and I Stegmiller, 'Prosecuting International Crimes at the International Criminal Court: Is There a Coherent and Comprehensive Prosecution Strategy?' (2013) 59 Crime, Law and Social Change 415

Amnesty International, 'Rwanda. Unfair Trials: Justice Denied' (1997) AFR 47/08/97

Amnesty International, 'International Criminal Tribunal for Rwanda. Trials and Tribulations' (1998) IOR 40/003/1998

Amnesty International, 'Executions of 24 Soldiers after an Unfair Trial: A Blow to Reconciliation in Sierra Leone' (1998) AFR/51/20/98

Amnesty International, 'Rwanda. The Troubled Course of Justice' (2000) AFR 47/015/2000

Amnesty International, 'The International Criminal Court: Checklist for Effective Implementation' (2000) IOR 40/011/2000

Amnesty International, 'Rwanda. Gacaca: A Question of Justice' (2002) AFR 47/007/2002

Amnesty International, 'Sierra Leone: Amnesty International Expresses Dismay at Ten Death Sentences for Treason' (21 December 2004) AFR51/009/2004

Amnesty International, 'Amnesty International Report 2007—Sierra Leone' (23 May 2007) <refworld.org/docid/46558ee12.html>

Amnesty International, 'Malabo Protocol: Legal and Institutional Implications of the Merged and Expanded African Court' (2016) AFR 01/3063/2016

Amnesty International, 'Global Report. Death Sentences and Executions 2016' (2017)

Amnesty International, 'Willingly Unable. ICC Preliminary Examination and Nigeria's Failure to Address Impunity for International Crimes' (2018) AFR 44/9481/2018

Amnesty International, '"On Trial, These Warlords Lowered Their Eyes": The Central African Republic's Challenging Pursuit of Justice' (2020) AFR 19/3185/2020

Amnesty International, 'Open Letter to the OTP Requesting Immediate Action on the Situation in Nigeria' (2021) AFR 44/3654/2021

Amnesty International, 'Open Letter on the Commencement of Your Term of Office as ICC Prosecutor' (2021)

Amnesty International, 'Rwanda: Ensure Remedy after Fair Trial Violations in Paul Rusesabagina Case' (2021)

Amnesty International, 'One Step Forward, Two Steps Backwards: Justice in the Central African Republic' (2021) AFR 19/5038/2021

Anderson JH, 'ICC Investigations: What Prosecutor Bensouda Leaves Behind' (*JusticeInfo*, 26 January 2021) <justiceinfo.net/en/68812-icc-investigations-what-prosecutor-bensouda-leaves-behind.html>

Anonymous, 'The Spanish Indictment of High-Ranking Rwandan Officials' (2008) 6 Journal of International Criminal Justice 1003

Appel BJ, 'In the Shadow of the International Criminal Court: Does the ICC Deter Human Rights Violations?' (2018) 62 Journal of Conflict Resolution 3

Aptel C, 'A propos du Tribunal pénal international pour le Rwanda' [1997] International Review of the Red Cross 721

Aravena CC, 'The Admissibility Test before the International Criminal Court under Special Consideration of Amnesties and Truth Commission' in Jann K Kleffner and Gerben Kor (eds), *Complementary Views on Complementarity* (TMC Asser Press 2006)

Arbour L, 'The Crucial Years' (2004) 2 Journal of International Criminal Justice 396

Arbour L and M Bergsmo, 'Conspicuous Absence of Jurisdictional Overreach' (1999) 1 International Law FORUM du droit international 13

Arbour L and A Neier, 'History and Future of the International Criminal Tribunals for the Former Yugoslavia and Rwanda' (1998) 13 American University International Law Review 1495

Arnould V, 'Transitional Justice in Peacebuilding: Dynamics of Contestation in the DRC' (2016) 10 Journal of Intervention and Statebuilding 321

Arnould V, 'Rethinking What ICC Success Means at the Bemba Trial' (*Open Democracy*, 14 September 2016) <opendemocracy.net/openglobalrights/valerie-arnould/rethinking-what-icc-success-means-at-bemba-trial>

Arnould V, 'Reflections on a Decentralized Approach to Transitional Justice in the DR Congo' (2021) 33 Egmont Institute. Africa Policy Brief

Ashraph S, 'The Naked Defense Office: How an Unclear Mandate, Poor Staffing, and Registry Disinterest Stripped the Office of the Principal Defender' in Charles C Jalloh (ed), *The Sierra Leone Special Court and Its Legacy* (CUP 2013)

Avocats Sans Frontières, 'Etude de jurisprudence. L'application du Statut de Rome de la Cour Pénale internationale par les juridictions de la République démocratique du Congo' (2009)

Avocats Sans Frontières, 'The Principle of Complementarity in the Rome Statute and the Colombian Situation: A Case That Demands More than a "Positive" Approach' (2012)

Ba O, *States of Justice: The Politics of the International Criminal Court* (CUP 2020)

Bah S, 'Legal Reform in Sierra Leone' (Case Matrix Network: Strengthening National Justice for Core International Crimes, The Hague, Netherlands, 28 June 2016) <youtube.com/watch?v=IHPUplQu2N8&index=7&list=PLgMYBjx5GIGqIYQQGzGi1p8HtCY1HF75I>

Bakama Bope E, *La justice congolaise face aux crimes internationaux commis en RDC* (Harmattan 2014)

Baldwin C, 'The ICC Prosecutor Office's Cop-out on UK Military Crimes in Iraq' (*Opinio Juris*, 18 December 2020) <opiniojuris.org/2020/12/18/the-icc-prosecutor-offices-cop-out-on-uk-military-crimes-in-iraq/>

Bangré H, 'RDC: Impasse dans le procès de Bantous et Pygmées accusés de génocide' (*JusticeInfo*, 3 February 2016) <justiceinfo.net/fr/25796-rdc-impasse-dans-le-proces-de-bantous-et-pygmees-accuses-de-genocide.html>

Bangura I, *Leaving behind the Worst of the Past: Transitional Justice and Prevention in Sierra Leone* (ICTJ 2021)

Bangura MA, 'Delivering International Criminal Justice at the Special Court for Sierra Leone: How Much Is Enough?' in Charles C Jalloh, *The Sierra Leone Special Court and Its Legacy* (CUP 2013)

Batros B, 'The Evolution of the ICC Jurisprudence on Admissibility' in Carsten Stahn and Mohamed M El Zeidy (eds), *The International Criminal Court and Complementarity* (CUP 2011)

Baylis E, 'Reassessing the Role of International Criminal Law: Rebuilding National Courts through Transnational Networks' (2009) 50 Boston College Law Review 1

Baylis E, 'Transitional Justice and Development Aid to Fragile and Conflict-Affected States: Risks and Reforms' in Roger Duthie and Paul Seils (eds), *Justice Mosaics: How Context Shapes Transitional Justice in Fractured Societies* (ICTJ 2017)

BCUNDH, *Progress and Obstacles in the Fight against Impunity for Sexual Violence in the DRC* (2014)

BCUNDH, 'Preliminary Investigation Report on Human Rights Violations and Violence Perpetrated during Demonstrations in Kinshasa between 19 and 21 September 2016' (2016)

BCUNDH, 'Accountability for Human Rights Violations and Abuses in the DRC: Achievements, Challenges and Way Forward (1 January 2014–31 March 2016)' (2016)

BCUNDH, 'Rapport de Mission d'enquête Spéciale sur les violences intercommunautaires des 16 et 17 décembre 2018 dans le territoire de Yumbi' (2019)

BCUNDH, 'Rapport public sur les conflits en territoire de Djugu, province de l'Ituri; décembre 2017 à septembre 2019' (2020)

BCUNDH, 'Report on Violations of Human Rights and International Humanitarian Law by the Allied Democratic Forces Armed Group and by Members of the Defense and Security Forces in Beni Territory, North Kivu Province and Irumu and Mambasa Territories, Ituri Province, between 1 January 2019 and 31 January 2020' (2020)

Benedetti F, *Negotiating the International Criminal Court: New York to Rome, 1994–1998* (Martinus Nijhoff 2014)

Bennett A, 'Process Tracing: A Bayesian Perspective' in Janet M Box-Steffensmeier, Henry E Brady, and David Collier (eds), *The Oxford Handbook of Political Methodology*, vol 1 (OUP 2009)

Bensouda F, 'Reflections from the International Criminal Court Prosecutor' (2012) 45 Case Western Reserve Journal of International Law 505

Bensouda F, 'Foreword' in Carsten Stahn (ed), *The Law and Practice of the International Criminal Court* (OUP 2015)

Bensouda F, 'In the Pursuit of International Criminal Justice, without Fear or Favour' *Diplomat* (6 December 2020) <diplomatmagazine.eu/2020/12/06/in-the-pursuit-of-international-criminal-justice-without-fear-or-favour/>

Bensouda F, 'Local Prosecution of International Crimes: Challenges and Prospects' (speech delivered at 7th Annual Prosecutors Colloquium, Arusha, Tanzania, November 2014) <icc-cpi.int/iccdocs/otp/otp-statement-141105.pdf>

Benvenuti P, 'The Complementarity of the International Criminal Court to National Criminal Jurisdictions' in Flavia Lattanzi and William Schabas (eds), *Essays on the Rome Statute of the International Criminal Court*, vol 1 (Il Sirente 1999)

Benzing M, 'The Complementarity Regime of the International Criminal Court: International Criminal Justice between State Sovereignty and the Fight against Impunity' (2003) 7 Max Planck Yearbook of United Nations Law 591

Berewa SE, *A New Perspective on Governance, Leadership, Conflict and Nation Building in Sierra Leone* (AuthorHouse 2011)

Bergsmo M, 'The Jurisdictional Régime of the International Criminal Court (Part II, Articles 11–19)' (1998) 6 European Journal of Crime, Criminal Law and Criminal Justice 29

Bergsmo M, 'Institutional History, Behaviour and Development' in Morten Bergsmo, Klaus Rackwitz, and Tianying Song (eds), *Historical Origins of International Criminal Law*, vol 5 (Torkel Opsahl 2017)

Bergsmo M, O Bekou and A Jones, 'Complementarity and the Construction of National Ability' in Carsten Stahn and Mohamed M El Zeidy (eds), *The International Criminal Court and Complementarity* (CUP 2011)

Bergsmo M and T Song, 'The Principle of Complementarity in Practice' in Morten Bergsmo, Klaus Rackwitz and Tianying Song (eds), *Historical Origins of International Criminal Law*, vol 5 (Torkel Opsahl 2017)

Berlin MS, *Criminalizing Atrocity: The Global Spread of Criminal Laws against International Crimes* (OUP 2020)

Berlin MS and G Dancy, 'The Difference Law Makes: Domestic Atrocity Laws and Human Rights Prosecutions: Domestic Atrocity Laws and Human Rights Prosecutions' (2017) 51 Law & Society Review 533

Bernard D, 'Beyond Hierarchy: Standard of Review and the Complementarity of the International Criminal Court' in Lukasz Gruszczynski and Wouter Werner (eds), *Deference in International Courts and Tribunals: Standards of Review and Margin of Appreciation* (OUP 2014)

Boas G, JL Bischoff, NL Reid, and BD Taylor, *International Criminal Procedure* (CUP 2011)

Bocchese M, '*El Coco* Does Not Frighten Anymore: ICC Scrutiny and State Cooperation in Colombia' (2021) 26 Journal of Conflict and Security Law 157

Boctor A, 'The Abolition of the Death Penalty in Rwanda' (2009) 10 Human Rights Review 99

Boehme F, '"We Chose Africa": South Africa and the Regional Politics of Cooperation with the International Criminal Court' (2016) 11 International Journal of Transitional Justice 50

Bohlander M, 'Referring an Indictment from the ICTY and ICTR to Another Court—Rule 11 Bis and the Consequences for the Law of Extradition' (2006) 55 International and Comparative Law Quarterly 219

Bonafé BI, 'Coordinating Concurrent Legal Orders in the Prosecution of International Crimes' (2013) 2 Global Constitutionalism 316

Borello F, 'A First Few Steps. The Long Road to a Just Peace in the Democratic Republic of the Congo' (ICTJ 2004)

Bornkamm PC, *Rwanda's Gacaca Courts: Between Retribution and Reparation* (OUP 2012)

Bosco D, 'Discretion and State Influence at the International Criminal Court: The Prosecutor's Preliminary Examinations' (2017) 111 American Journal of International Law 395

Bosco DL, *Rough Justice: The International Criminal Court in a World of Power Politics* (OUP 2014)

Brammertz S, 'Making Complementarity a Reality: The Experiences of the ICTY and IRMCT Office of the Prosecutor' in Carsten Stahn and others (eds), *Legacies of the International Criminal Tribunal for the Former Yugoslavia* (OUP 2020)

Brammertz S and KC Hughes, 'From Primacy to Complementarity: The International Criminal Tribunal for the Former Yugoslavia, 1993–2015' in Morten Bergsmo and others (eds), *Historical Origins of International Criminal Law. Volume 4* (Torkel Opsahl 2015)

Briefel C and I Tredici, 'The United Nations Prosecution Support Cell Programme in the Democratic Republic of Congo—A Strategy to Combat Impunity for Serious Crimes' (2016) 19 Max Planck Yearbook of United Nations Law 337

Brody R, 'The ICC at 20: Elusive Success, Double Standards and the "Ukraine Moment"' (*JusticeInfo*, 30 June 2022) <justiceinfo.net/en/102866-icc-20-elusive-success-double-standards-ukraine-moment.html>

Broomhall B, *International Justice and the International Criminal Court: Between Sovereignty and the Rule of Law* (OUP 2003)

Brown BS, 'Primacy or Complementarity: Reconciling the Jurisdiction of National Courts and International Criminal Tribunals' (1998) 23 Yale Law Journal 383

Brubacher MR, 'Prosecutorial Discretion within the International Criminal Court' (2004) 2 Journal of International Criminal Justice 71

Buchanan E, 'Could Sierra Leone Revive the Death Penalty to Curb Rising Violence' *International Business Times* (7 November 2016) <ibtimes.co.uk/could-sierra-leone-revive-death-penalty-curb-rising-violence-1590214>

Buchwald T, 'What Kinds of Situations and Cases Should the ICC Pursue? The Independent Expert Review of the ICC and the Question of Aperture' (*Just Security*, 2 December 2020) <justsecurity.org/73653/part-iii-what-kinds-of-situations-and-cases-should-the-icc-pursue-the-independent-expert-review-of-the-icc-and-the-question-of-aperture/>

Bueno O, 'Bemba's Colleagues Arrested for Witness Tampering Sparks an Indignant Response in the DRC' (*International Justice Monitor*, 4 December 2013) <ijmonitor.org/2013/12/bembas-colleagues-arrested-for-witness-tampering-sparks-an-indignant-response-in-the-drc/>

Bundu A, *Democracy by Force? A Study of International Military Intervention in the Civil War in Sierra Leone from 1991–2000* (Universal Publishers 2001)

Burchard C, 'Complementarity as Global Governance' in Carsten Stahn and Mohamed M El Zeidy (eds), *The International Criminal Court and Complementarity: From Theory to Practice* (CUP 2011)

Burke-White W, 'A Community of Courts: Toward a System of International Criminal Law Enforcement' (2002) 24 Michigan Journal of International Law 1

Burke-White W, 'Complementarity in Practice: The International Criminal Court as Part of a System of Multi-Level Global Governance in the Democratic Republic of Congo' (2005) 18 Leiden Journal of International Law 557

Burke-White W, 'Proactive Complementarity: The International Criminal Court and National Courts in the Rome System of Justice' (2008) 49 Harvard International Law Journal 53

Burke-White W, 'The Domestic Influence of International Criminal Tribunals: The International Criminal Tribunal for the Former Yugoslavia and the Creation of the State Court of Bosnia & Herzegovina' (2008) 46 Columbia Journal of Transnational Law 279

Burke-White W, 'Reframing Positive Complementarity' in Carsten Stahn and Mohamed El Zeidy (eds), *The International Criminal Court and Complementarity* (CUP 2011)

Burke-White W and S Kaplan, 'Shaping the Contours of Domestic Justice: The International Criminal Court and an Admissibility Challenge in the Uganda Situation' (2009) 7 Journal of International Criminal Justice 257

Candeias S, L Côté, E Papageorgiou, and M Raymond-Jetté, 'The Accountability Landscape in Eastern DRC: Analysis of the National Legislative and Judicial Response to International Crimes (2009–2014)' (ICTJ 2015)

Canter AS, '"For These Reasons, the Chamber Denies the Prosecutor's Request for Referral": The False Hope of Rule 11 Bis' (2009) 32 Fordham International Law Journal 1614

Carter L, M Ellis and C Jalloh, *The International Criminal Court in an Effective Global Justice System* (Edward Elgar 2016)

Cassese A, 'The Statute of the International Criminal Court. Some Preliminary Reflections' (1999) 10 European Journal of International Law 144

Cassese A, *International Criminal Law* (1st edn, OUP 2003)

Cassese A, 'Role of Internationalized Courts and Tribunals in the Fight against International Criminality' in Cesare Romano, André Nollkaemper, and Jann Kleffner (eds), *Internationalized Criminal Courts. Sierra Leone, East Timor, Kosovo, and Cambodia* (OUP 2004)

Cassese A, 'Report on the Special Court for Sierra Leone' (2006)

Cassese A, *International Criminal Law* (2nd edn, OUP 2008)

Cassese A, P Gaeta, L Baig, M Fan, C Gosnell, and A Whiting, *Cassese's International Criminal Law* (3rd edn, OUP 2013)

Chakravarty A, *Investing in Authoritarian Rule. Punishment and Patronage in Rwanda's Gacaca Courts for Genocide Crimes* (CUP 2016)

Charmaz K, *Constructing Grounded Theory* (Sage 2006)

Chayes A and AH Chayes, *The New Sovereignty: Compliance with International Regulatory Agreements* (Harvard UP 1995)

Chehtman A, 'Developing Local Capacity for War Crimes Trials: Insights from BiH, Sierra Leone, and Colombia' (2013) 49 Stanford Journal of International Law 297

Chehtman A and R Mackenzie, *Capacity Development in International Criminal Justice* (DOMAC 2009)

Chubin Y, 'The Impact of the ICTR 11 Bis Referrals on Rwanda's Legal Reforms, Extradition Requests, and Transfer Case Procedure' (2014) <unictr.irmct.org/en/compendium-legacy-ictr-and-development-international-law>

Clapham A, 'Issues of Complexity, Complicity and Complementarity: From the Nuremberg Trials to the Dawn of the New International Criminal Court' in Philippe Sands (ed), *From Nuremberg to The Hague. The Future of International Criminal Justice* (CUP 2003)

Clark JN, *International Trials and Reconciliation: Assessing the Impact of the International Criminal Tribunal for the Former Yugoslavia* (Routledge 2014)

Clark P, 'Hybridity, Holism, and "Traditional" Justice: The Case of the Gacaca Courts in Post-Genocide Rwanda' (2007) 39 George Washington International Law Review 765

Clark P, 'Law, Politics and Pragmatism: The ICC and Case Selection in the Democratic Republic of Congo and Uganda' in Phil Clark and Nicholas Waddell (eds), *Courting Conflict? Justice, Peace and the ICC in Africa* (Royal African Society 2008)

Clark P, *The Gacaca Courts, Post-Genocide Justice and Reconciliation in Rwanda. Justice without Lawyers* (CUP 2010)

Clark P, 'Chasing Cases: The ICC and the Politics of State Referral in the Democratic Republic of Congo and Uganda' in Carsten Stahn and Mohamed El Zeidy (eds), *The International Criminal Court and Complementarity: From Theory to Practice*, vol 2 (CUP 2011)

Clark P, 'How Rwanda Judged Its Genocide' (Africa Research Institute 2012)

Clark P, *Distant Justice: The Impact of the International Criminal Court on African Politics* (CUP 2018)

Clark P, 'The UN Security Council and Transitional Justice: The Democratic Republic of the Congo' in Rebecca Brubaker (ed), *The UN Security Council and Transitional Justice* (United Nations University 2021)

Clarke KM, *Affective Justice: The International Criminal Court and the Pan-Africanist Pushback* (Duke UP 2019)

Clements R, 'Governing International Criminal Justice: Managerial Practices and the International Criminal Court' (PhD dissertation, Cambridge University, 2019)

Côté L, 'Le Tribunal Pénal International Pour Le Rwanda : Un Tribunal Dans La Tourmente' in Stefaan Marysse and Filip Reyntjens (eds), *L'Afrique des Grands Lacs, Annuaire 2005–2006* (Harmattan 2006)

Côté L, 'Independence and Impartiality' in Luc Reydams, Jan Wouters, and Cedric Ryngaert (eds), *International Prosecutors* (OUP 2012)

Council on Foreign Relations, 'Pursuing International Justice: A Conversation with Luis Moreno Ocampo' (4 February 2010) <cfr.org/event/pursuing-international-justice-conversation-luis-moreno-ocampo-0>

Crane DM, 'Dancing with the Devil. Prosecuting West Africa's Warlords, Current Lessons Learned and Challenges, Colloquium of Prosecutors of International Criminal Tribunals, Arusha, Tanzania, 25–27 November 2004'

Crane DM, 'The Bright Red Thread. The Politics of International Criminal Law—Do We Want Peace or Justice? The West African Experience' in Leila N Sadat (ed), *Forging a Convention for Crimes against Humanity* (CUP 2010)

Crane DM, 'The Take Down: Case Studies Regarding "Lawfare" in International Criminal Justice: The West African Experience' (2010) 43 Case Western Reserve Journal of International Law 201

Crane DM, 'The Chief Prosecutor: Diplomat, Politician, Leader, Manager, and Lawyer' (*Opinio Juris*, 8 April 2020) <opiniojuris.org/2020/04/08/icc-prosecutor-symposium-the-chief-prosecutor-diplomat-politician-leader-manager-and-lawyer/>

Cruvellier T, *Le tribunal des vaincus: Un Nuremberg pour le Rwanda?* (Calmann-Lévy 2006)

Cruvellier T, *From the Taylor Trial to a Lasting Legacy: Putting the Special Court Model to the Test* (ICTJ 2009)

Cruvellier T, 'The Massaquoi Affair: Special Report on the Judas of Sierra Leone' (*JusticeInfo*, 7 April 2020) <justiceinfo.net/en/tribunals/mixed-tribunals/44085-the-massaquoi-affair-special-report-on-the-judas-of-sierra-leone-part-1.html>

Cruvellier T and E Rugiririza, 'Rwanda: The Most Judged Genocide in History' (*JusticeInfo*, 4 April 2019) <justiceinfo.net/en/40846-rwanda-the-most-judged-genocide-in-history.html>

Cryer R, *Prosecuting International Crimes: Selectivity and the International Criminal Law Regime* (CUP 2005)

Cryer R, 'International Criminal Law vs State Sovereignty: Another Round?' (2005) 16 European Journal of International Law 979

Cryer R, H Frman, D Robinson, and E Wilmshurst, *An Introduction to International Criminal Law and Procedure* (2nd edn, CUP 2010)

Dahir AL, 'Rwandan Court Declines to Extend Sentence for Paul Rusesabagina' *New York Times* (4 April 2022) <nytimes.com/2022/04/04/world/africa/rwanda-paul-rusesabagina-sentence.html>

Dahrendorfer N, 'Mirror Images in the Congo: Sexual Violence and Conflict' (*Open Democracy*, 27 October 2005) <opendemocracy.net/democracy-resolution_1325/congo_2964.jsp>

Dancy G and F Montal, 'From Law Versus Politics to Law in Politics: A Pragmatist Assessment of the ICC's Impact' (2017) 32 America University International Law Review 645

Dancy G and F Montal, 'Unintended Positive Complementarity: Why International Criminal Court Investigations May Increase Domestic Human Rights Prosecutions' (2017) 111 American Journal of International Law 689

Da Silva C, 'Will Justice Prevail?' *The Guardian* (4 June 2007) <theguardian.com/commentisfree/2007/jun/04/willjusticeprevail>

Davis L, 'Power Shared and Justice Shelved: The Democratic Republic of Congo' (2013) 17 International Journal of Human Rights 289

Davis L and P Hayner, *Difficult Peace, Limited Justice: Ten Years of Peacemaking in the DRC* (ICTJ 2009)

Day A and J Caus, *Rule of Law and Sustaining Peace: Towards More Impactful, Effective Conflict Prevention* (United Nations University 2021)

Day A, S von Billerbeck, O Tansey, and A Al Maleh, *Peacebuilding and Authoritarianism: The Unintended Consequences of UN Engagement in Post-Conflict Settings* (United Nations University 2021)

De Beer D, *Loi rwandaise du 30 août 1996 sur l'organisation des poursuites des infractions constitutives du crime de génocide ou de crimes contre l'humanité. Commentaire et jurisprudence* (2nd edn, Alter Egaux 1999)

de Búrca G, 'Human Rights Experimentalism' (2017) 111 American Journal of International Law 277

de Búrca G, *Reframing Human Rights in a Turbulent Era* (OUP 2021)

deGuzman MM, 'The Sentencing Legacy of the Special Court for Sierra Leone' in Charles C Jalloh (ed), *The Sierra Leone Special Court and Its Legacy* (CUP 2013)

deGuzman MM, *Shocking the Conscience of Humanity: Gravity and the Legitimacy of International Criminal Law* (OUP 2020)

deGuzman MM, 'SCSL Symposium: Who Bears the Greatest Responsibility for International Crimes?' (*Opinio Juris*, 18 March 2021) <opiniojuris.org/2021/03/18/scsl-symposium-who-bears-the-greatest-responsibility-for-international-crimes/>

Del Ponte C, *Madame Prosecutor: Confrontations with Humanity's Worst Criminals and the Culture of Impunity: A Memoir* (Other Press 2009)

Des Forges A, *'Leave None to Tell the Story': Genocide in Rwanda* (2020 reissue, Human Rights Watch; International Federation of Human Rights 1999)

Des Forges A and T Longman, 'Legal Responses to Genocide in Rwanda' in Eric Stover and Harvey Weinstein (eds), *My Neighbor, My Enemy: Justice and Community in the Aftermath of Mass Atrocity* (CUP 2004)

De Vos CM, 'Investigating from Afar: The ICC's Evidence Problem' (2013) 26 Leiden Journal of International Law 1009

De Vos CM, 'Magical Legalism' and the International Criminal Court: A Case Study of the Kenyan Preliminary Examination' in Morten Bergsmo and Carsten Stahn (eds), *Quality Control in Preliminary Examination*, vol 2 (Torkel Opsahl 2018)

De Vos CM, *Complementarity, Catalysts, Compliance: The International Criminal Court in Uganda, Kenya, and the Democratic Republic of Congo* (CUP 2020)

De Vos CM, 'Preliminary Examinations and Complementarity' (*International Justice Monitor*, 29 March 2021) <ijmonitor.org/2021/03/ier-blog-series-preliminary-examinations-and-complementarity/>

De Waal A, 'Writing Human Rights and Getting It Wrong' [2016] *Boston Review*

Dickinson LA, 'The Promise of Hybrid Courts' (2003) 97 American Journal of International Law 295

Dieng A, 'Capacity-Building Efforts of the ICTR: A Different Kind of Legacy' (2011) 9 Northwestern Journal of International Human Rights 403

Dittrich VE, 'Legacies in the Making: Assessing the Institutionalized Legacy Endeavor of the Special Court for Sierra Leone' in Charles C Jalloh (ed), *The Sierra Leone Special Court and Its Legacy* (CUP 2013)

Donlon F, 'The Transition of Responsibilities from the Special Court to the Residual Special Court for Sierra Leone: Challenges and Lessons Learned for Other International Tribunals' (2013) 11 Journal of International Criminal Justice 857

Drumbl MA, 'Rule of Law Amid Lawlessness: Counseling the Accused in Rwanda's Domestic Genocide Trials' (1998) 29 Columbia Human Rights Law Review 545

Drumbl MA, *Atrocity, Punishment, and International Law* (CUP 2007)

Drumbl MA, 'Prosecution of Genocide v. the Fair Trial Principle: Comments on Brown and Others v. the Government of Rwanda and the UK Secretary of State for the Home Department' (2010) 8 Journal of International Criminal Justice 289

Drumbl MA, 'Policy through Complementarity: The Atrocity Trial as Justice' in Carsten Stahn and Mohamed M El Zeidy (eds), *The International Criminal Court and Complementarity* (CUP 2011)

Drumbl MA, 'Impunities' in Kevin Jon Heller and others (eds), *The Oxford Handbook of International Criminal Law* (OUP 2020)

Dubois O, 'Les juridictions pénales nationales du Rwanda et le Tribunal international' (1997) 79 Revue Internationale de la Croix-Rouge 763

Dunoff JL and MA Pollack (eds), *Interdisciplinary Perspectives on International Law and International Relations: The State of the Art* (CUP 2013)

Du Plessis M, 'The Future of International Criminal Justice Is Domestic' (*iLawyer*, 17 September 2014) <ilawyerblog.com/future-international-criminal-justice-domestic/>

Easterday J, 'The Consequences of Witness Payments at the Special Court for Sierra Leone' in Charles C Jalloh (ed), *The Sierra Leone Special Court and Its Legacy* (CUP 2013)

Ebobrah ST, 'Towards a Positive Application of Complementarity in the African Human Rights System: Issues of Functions and Relations' (2011) 22 European Journal of International Law 663

Elebe N, 'Why DRC Lawmakers Again Rejected Special Chambers to Prosecute International Crimes' (*International Justice Monitor*, 23 May 2014) <ijmonitor.org/2014/05/drc-a-bill-on-special-chambers-rejected-for-the-second-time/>

Ellis M, 'International Justice and the Rule of Law' (2009) 1 Hague Journal on the Rule of Law 79

El Zeidy MM, *The Principle of Complementarity in International Criminal Law: Origin, Development, and Practice* (Martinus Nijhoff 2008)

El Zeidy MM, 'From Primacy to Complementarity and Backwards: (Re)-Visiting Rule11 *Bis* of the Ad Hoc Tribunals' (2008) 57 International and Comparative Law Quarterly 403

Engle K, 'Anti-Impunity and the Turn to Criminal Law in Human Rights' (2015) 100 Cornell Journal of International Law 1069

Engle K, Z Miller and D Davis (eds), *Anti-Impunity and the Human Rights Agenda* (CUP 2016)

Engle Merry S, 'Transnational Human Rights and Local Activism: Mapping the Middle' (2006) 108 American Anthropologist 38

Evenson EM, 'Truth and Justice in Sierra Leone: Coordination between Commission and Court' (2004) 104 Columbia Law Review 730

Evenson EM, 'ICC Success Depends on Its Impact Locally' (*Open Democracy*, 26 August 2015) <opendemocracy.net/en/openglobalrights-openpage/icc-success-depends-on-its-impact-locally/>

Evenson EM and A Smith, 'Completion, Legacy, and Complementarity at the ICC' in Carsten Stahn (ed), *The Law and Practice of the International Criminal Court* (OUP 2015)

Ferdinandusse W and A Whiting, 'Prosecute Little Fish at the ICC' (2022) 19 Journal of International Criminal Justice 759

Ferencz BB, *An International Criminal Court, a Step toward World Peace: A Documentary History and Analysis* (Oceana Publications 1980)

Fernandez de Gurmendi S, 'Foreword' in Carsten Stahn and Mohamed M El Zeidy (eds), *The International Criminal Court and Complementarity* (CUP 2011)

Ferstman CJ, 'Domestic Trials for Genocide and Crimes against Humanity: The Example of Rwanda' (1997) 9 African Journal of International and Comparative Law 857

FIDH, 'Victims in the Balance: Challenges Ahead for the International Criminal Tribunal for Rwanda. Report No. 329/2' (2002)

Fifth Report of the Secretary General on [UNAMSIL], S/2000/751, 31 July 2000

First Annual Report of the ICTY, A/49/342, S/1994/1007, 29 August 1994

Flyvbjerg B, 'Five Misunderstandings about Case-Study Research' (2006) 12 Qualitative Inquiry 219

Fofanah M, 'Death Penalty—Sierra Leone: Successful Appeal Strengthens Case for Abolition' *IPS News Agency* (12 December 2008) <ipsnews.net/2008/12/death-penalty-sierra-leone-successful-appeal-strengthens-case-for-abolition/>

Fofe Djofia Malewa J-P, 'Commentaire du jugement Songo Mboyo: une illustration de l'éclairage de la justice nationale par les textes et la jurisprudence pénaux internationaux' (2006) 2 Revue horizons 119

Ford S, 'Can the International Criminal Court Succeed? An Analysis of the Empirical Evidence of Violence Prevention' (2020) 43 Loyola of Los Angeles International and Comparative Law Review 101

Ford S, 'Senior Leaders and Those Most Responsible at the Extraordinary Chambers in the Courts of Cambodia' (2021) 15 Florida International University Law Review 31

Frulli M, 'The Special Court for Sierra Leone: Some Preliminary Comments' (2000) 11 European Journal of International Law 857

Fry E, 'Between Show Trials and Sham Prosecutions: The Rome Statute's Potential Effect on Domestic Due Process Protections' (2012) 23 Criminal Law Forum 35

Gaeta P, 'Is the Practice of "Self-Referrals" a Sound Start for the ICC?' (2004) 2 Journal of International Criminal Justice 949

Gaeta P and PI Labuda, 'Trying Sitting Heads of State: The African Union versus the ICC in the Al Bashir and Kenyatta Cases' in Ilias Bantekas and Charles C Jalloh (eds), *The International Criminal Court and Africa* (OUP 2018)

Gaeta P and PI Labuda, 'Bilan des quinze premières années de la Cour pénale internationale' in Julian Fernandez and Xavier Pacreau (eds), *Commentaire du Statut de Rome. Commentaire article par article* (Pédone 2019)

Gahima G, *Transitional Justice in Rwanda: Accountability for Atrocity* (Routledge 2013)

Gaima E, 'Sierra Leone' in Gilles Badet, Luc Damiba, Stéphane Enguéléguélé, Emmanuel Gaima, Chijioke Iwuamadi, Semou Ndiaye, and Shine Williams (eds) *Effectiveness of Anti-Corruption Agencies in West Africa: Benin, Liberia, Niger, Nigeria, Senegal and Sierra Leone. A Review by Open Society Initiative for West Africa* (Open Society Foundations 2016)

Gberie L, 'The Civil Defense Forces Trial: Limit to International Justice?' in Charles C Jalloh (ed), *The Sierra Leone Special Court and Its Legacy: The Impact for Africa and International Criminal Law* (CUP 2013)

George AL and A Bennett, *Case Studies and Theory Development in the Social Sciences* (MIT Press 2005)

Gevers C, 'Back to the Future? Civil Society, the "Turn to Complementarity" in Africa and Some Critical Concerns' in Sarah Williams and Hannah Woolaver (eds), *Civil Society and International Criminal Justice in Africa: Challenges and Opportunities* (Juta 2016)

Gibson K, 'Reliance upon and Complications with State Cooperation' (2014) <unictr.irmct.org/sites/unictr.org/files/publications/compendium-documents/ii-reliance-complications-state-cooperation-gibson.pdf>

Ginsburg T and G Shaffer, 'How Does International Law Work?' in Peter Cane and Herbert Kritzer (eds), *The Oxford Handbook of Empirical Research* (OUP 2012)

Ginsburg T and G Shaffer, 'The Empirical Turn in International Legal Scholarship' (2012) 106 American Journal of International Law 1

Gioia F, 'Complementarity and "Reverse Cooperation"' in Carsten Stahn and Mohamed M El Zeidy (eds), *The International Criminal Court and Complementarity* (CUP 2011)

Gissel LE, 'Nomos and Narrative in International Criminal Justice' (2022) 20 Journal of International Criminal Justice 117

Glasius M, *The International Criminal Court: A Global Civil Society Achievement* (Routledge 2006)

Glasius M, '"It Sends a Message": Liberian Opinion Leaders' Responses to the Trial of Charles Taylor' (2015) 13 Journal of International Criminal Justice 419

Global Rights, 'Une loi sur la répression des violences sexuelles. De quoi s'agit-il? Texte d'orientation sur l'avant-projet de loi portant modification du Code pénal congolais, du Code de procédure pénale et du Code de l'organisation et de la compétence judiciaire' (2006)

Goldsmith J and SD Krasner, 'The Limits of Idealism' (2003) 132 Daedalus 47

Goldstone R, P Clark, and D Plesch 'Justice for War Criminals and Human Rights Abusers: Beyond the Nuremberg—ICC Model' (*9BR International*, 31 July 2019) <9bri.com/justice-for-war-criminals-and-human-rights-abusers-beyond-the-nuremberg-icc-model/>

Goldstone RJ, 'Acquittals by the International Criminal Court' (*EJIL:Talk!*, 18 January 2019) <ejiltalk.org/acquittals-by-the-international-criminal-court/>

Goldstone RJ, *For Humanity: Reflections of a War Crimes Investigator* (Yale UP 2000)

Greenawalt A, 'Complementarity in Crisis: Uganda, Alternative Justice, and the International Criminal Court' (2009) 50 Virginia Journal of International Law 107

Greenawalt A, 'Admissibility as a Theory of International Criminal Law' in Margaret deGuzman and Valerie Oosterveld (eds), *Elgar Companion to the International Criminal Court* (2020)

Guichaoua A, *De la guerre au génocide. Les politiques criminelles au Rwanda 1990–1994* (Karthala 2005)

Guilfoyle D, *International Criminal Law* (OUP 2016)

Guilfoyle D, 'Lacking Conviction: Is the International Criminal Court Broken? An Organisational Failure Analysis' (2019) 20 Melbourne Journal of International Law 401

Guilfoyle D, 'This Is Not Fine. The International Criminal Court in Trouble' (*EJIL:Talk!*, 21 March 2019) <ejiltalk.org/part-i-this-is-not-fine-the-international-criminal-court-in-trouble/>

Hafner-Burton EM, 'Sticks and Stones: Naming and Shaming the Human Rights Enforcement Problem' (2008) 62 International Organization 689

Hagan J, *Justice in the Balkans: Prosecuting War Crimes in the Hague Tribunal* (University of Chicago Press 2003)

Hakimi M, 'The Work of International Law' (2017) 58 Harvard International Law Journal 1

Hakimi M, 'Constructing an International Community' (2017) 111 American Journal of International Law 317

Hall CK, 'The First Proposal for a Permanent International Criminal Court' (1998) 322 International Review of the Red Cross 57

Hamilton RJ, 'The ICC's Exit Problem' (2014) 47 New York University Journal of International Law and Policy 1

Hansen TO, 'Complementarity (in)Action in the UK?' (*EJIL:Talk!*, 7 December 2018) <ejiltalk.org/complementarity-inaction-in-the-uk/>

Harhoff F, 'Consonance or Rivalry? Calibrating the Efforts to Prosecute War Crimes in National and International Tribunals' (1997) 7 Duke Journal of Comparative & International Law 571

Haskell L and L Waldorf, 'The Impunity Gap of the International Criminal Tribunal for Rwanda: Causes and Consequences' (2011) 34 Hastings International and Comparative Law Review 49

Hassanein AS, 'Self-Referral of Situations to the International Criminal Court: Complementarity in Practice—Complementarity in Crisis' (2017) 17 International Criminal Law Review 107

Hayner P, 'Negotiating Peace in Sierra Leone: Confronting the Justice Challenge' (ICTJ and Centre for Humanitarian Dialogue 2007)

Hayner P, 'Does the ICC Advance the Interests of Justice?' (*Open Democracy*, 31 October 2014) <opendemocracy.net/en/openglobalrights-openpage/does-icc-advance-interests-of-justice/>

Helfer LR and AE Showalter, 'Opposing International Justice: Kenya's Integrated Backlash Strategy against the ICC' (2017) 17 International Criminal Law Review 1

Heller KJ, 'The Shadow Side of Complementarity: The Effect of Article 17 of the Rome Statute on National Due Process' (2007) 17 Criminal Law Forum 255

Heller KJ, 'A Sentence-Based Theory of Complementarity' (2012) 53 Harvard International Law Journal 202

Heller KJ, 'Completion' in Luc Reydams, Jan Wouters, and Cedric Ryngaert (eds), *International Prosecutors* (OUP 2012)

Heller KJ, 'Radical Complementarity' (2016) 14 Journal of International Criminal Justice 637

Henkin L, *How Nations Behave* (2nd edn, Columbia UP 1979)

Henkinbrant L, 'Justice transitionnelle en RDC: Comment l'ONU l'a rangé dans un tiroir' (*JusticeInfo*, 14 January 2022) <justiceinfo.net/fr/86510-justice-transitionnelle-rdc-congo-comment-onu-range-dans-tiroir.html>

Hentrei S, 'Generalising the Principle of Complementarity: Framing International Judicial Authority' (2013) 4 Transnational Legal Theory 419

Heupel M, 'Rule of Law Promotion through International Organizations and NGOs' in Michael Zurn, Andre Nollkaemper and Randy Peerenboom (eds), *Rule of Law Dynamics* (CUP 2012)

Hillebrecht C, *Domestic Politics and International Human Rights Tribunals: The Problem of Compliance* (CUP 2014)

Hillebrecht C, A Huneeus, and S Borda, 'The Judicialization of Peace' (2018) 59 Harvard International Law Journal 279

Hillebrecht C and S Straus, 'Who Pursues the Perpetrators? State Cooperation with the ICC' (2017) 39 Human Rights Quarterly 162

Hochschild A, 'The Trial of Thomas Lubanga' [2009] The Atlantic <theatlantic.com/magazine/archive/2009/12/the-trial-of-thomas-lubanga/307762/>

Hoebeke H, 'Rumble in the DR Congo: President Tshisekedi Is Taking Control' (Royal Institute for International Relations 2021) 112

Hola B and H Nyseth Brehm, 'Punishing Genocide: A Comparative Empirical Analysis of Sentencing Laws and Practices at the International Criminal Tribunal for Rwanda, Rwandan Domestic Courts, and Gacaca Courts' (2016) 10 Genocide Studies and Prevention 59

Holmes JT, 'The Principle of Complementarity' in Roy S Lee (ed), *The International Criminal Court. The Making of the Rome Statute. Issues, Negotiations, Results* (Kluwer 1999)

Holmes JT, 'Complementarity: National Courts versus the ICC' in Antonio Cassese, Paola Gaeta, and John RWD Jones (eds), *The Rome Statute of the International Criminal Court: A Commentary* (OUP 2002)

Horovitz S, 'Sierra Leone: Interaction between International and National Responses to the Mass Atrocities' (DOMAC 2009)

Horovitz S, 'Rwanda: International and National Responses to the Mass Atrocities and Their Interaction' (DOMAC 2010)

Horovitz S, 'DR Congo: Interaction between International and National Judicial Responses to the Mass Atrocities' (DOMAC 2012)

Horovitz S, 'The Impact of the International Criminal Tribunal for Rwanda and the Special Court for Sierra Leone on Impunity in Rwanda and Sierra Leone' in Vincent O Nmehielle (ed), *Africa and the future of international criminal justice* (Eleven International 2012)

Horovitz S, 'How International Courts Shape Domestic Justice: Lessons from Rwanda and Sierra Leone' (2013) 46 Israel Law Review 339

Horovitz S, 'International Criminal Courts in Action: The ICTR's Effect on Death Penalty and Reconciliation in Rwanda' (2016) 48 George Washington International Law Review 505

Horovitz S, 'Rwanda's Kabgayi Trial between International Justice and National Reconciliation' in Mikkel Jarle Christensen and Ron Levi (eds), *International Practices of Criminal Justice Social and legal perspectives* (Routledge 2017)

Hovell D, 'The "Mistrial" of Kumar Lama: Problematizing Universal Jurisdiction' (*EJIL: Talk!*, 6 April 2017) <ejiltalk.org/the-mistrial-of-kumar-lama-problematizing-universal-jurisdiction/>

Howland TA, 'Mirage, Magic, or Mixed Bag? The UN High Commissioner for Human Rights' Field Operation in Rwanda' (1999) 21 Human Rights Quarterly 1

Howse R and R Teitel, 'Beyond Compliance: Rethinking Why International Law Really Matters' (2010) 1 Global Policy 127

HRW, 'World Report 1996' (1997) <hrw.org/reports/1996/WR96/Africa-08.htm>

HRW, 'The War Within the War. Sexual Violence against Women in Eastern Congo' (2002)

HRW, 'Bringing Justice: The Special Court for Sierra Leone. Accomplishments, Shortcomings, and Needed Support' (2004)

HRW, 'Making Justice Work: Restoration of the Legal System in Ituri, DRC' (2004)

HRW, 'Seeking Justice: The Prosecution of Sexual Violence in the Congo War' (2005)

HRW, 'Justice in Motion. The Trial Phase of the Special Court for Sierra Leone' (2005)

HRW, 'Law and Reality. Progress in Judicial Reform in Rwanda' (2008)

HRW, 'Burundi: l'Assemblée nationale abolit la peine de mort et criminalise la torture' (3 December 2008) <hrw.org/fr/news/2008/12/03/burundi-lassemblee-nationale-abolit-la-peine-de-mort-et-criminalise-la-torture>

HRW, 'Soldiers Who Rape, Commanders Who Condone. Sexual Violence and Military Reform in the Democratic Republic of Congo' (2009)

HRW, 'DR Congo: A "Mixed Chamber" for Congo?' (2009) <hrw.org/news/2009/10/05/dr-congo-mixed-chamber-congo>

HRW, 'Justice Compromised: The Legacy of Rwanda's Community-Based Gacaca Courts' (2011)

HRW, 'RD Congo: établissement d'une cour spécialisée mixte pour la répression des crimes graves internationaux position commune résultant de l'atelier organisé à Goma le 6–8 Avril 2011' (2011) <hrw.org/fr/news/2011/04/15/rd-congo-etablissement-dune-cour-specialisee-mixte-pour-la-repression-des-crimes>

HRW, 'Justice on Trial. Lessons from the Minova Rape Case in the Democratic Republic of Congo' (2015)

HRW, 'Etats Généraux of the Justice System in the Democratic Republic of Congo Recommendations on thc Fight against Impunity for Grave International Crimes' (27 April 2015) <hrw.org/news/2015/04/27/etats-generaux-justice-system-democratic-republic-congo>

HRW, '"We Will Force You to Confess": Torture and Unlawful Military Detention in Rwanda' (2017)

HRW, 'Pressure Point: The ICC's Impact on National Justice. Lessons from Colombia, Georgia, Guinea, and the United Kingdom' (2018)

HRW, 'Rwanda: 25 Years on, Solidarity with Victims' (4 April 2019) <hrw.org/news/2019/04/04/rwanda-25-years-solidarity-victims>

HRW, 'DR Congo: Warlord's Conviction Reveals Trial Flaws' (19 April 2019) <hrw.org/news/2019/04/19/dr-congo-warlords-conviction-reveals-trial-flaws>

HRW, 'Guinea: Coup Further Complicates Massacre Justice. Efficient, Fair Trial Should Hold 2009 Stadium Abusers Accountable' (26 September 2021) <hrw.org/news/2021/09/26/guinea-coup-further-complicates-massacre-justice>

HRW, 'DR Congo: Sham Trial for Murders of UN Experts' (7 February 2022) <hrw.org/news/2022/02/07/dr-congo-sham-trial-murders-un-experts>

Huls N, 'Constitutionalism à La Rwandaise' in Maurice Adams, Anne Meuwese and Ernst Hirsch Ballin (eds), *Constitutionalism and the Rule of Law* (CUP 2017)

Human Rights Center UC Berkeley School of Law, 'The Long Road Ahead. Accountability for Sexual Violence in Conflict and Post-Conflict Settings. Kenya. Liberia. Sierra Leone. Uganda (2015)

Human Rights Commission, 'Study on the Question of the Prevention and Punishment of the Crime of Genocide. Study Prepared by Mr. Nicodème Ruhashyankiko, Special Rapporteur' (1978) E/CN.4/Sub.2/416

Human Security Report Project (ed), *Human Security Report 2009/2010: The Causes of Peace and the Shrinking Costs of War* (OUP 2011)

Huneeus A, 'International Criminal Law by Other Means: The Quasi-Criminal Jurisdiction of the Human Rights Courts' (2013) 107 American Journal of International Law 1

ICC, 'The Office of the Prosecutor Concludes Mission to Colombia' (2 March 2015) ICC-OTP-20150302-PR1090 <icc-cpi.int/Pages/item.aspx?name=pr1090>

ICC, 'Statement by the Prosecutor of the International Criminal Court, Fatou Bensouda, on Her Office's Mission to the Democratic Republic of the Congo from 16 to 20 October 2016' (20 October 2016) <icc-cpi.int/Pages/item.aspx?name=161020-otp-statement-congo>

ICC, 'Statement of the Prosecutor of the International Criminal Court, Fatou Bensouda, Regarding the Situation in the Kasaï Provinces, Democratic Republic of the Congo' (31 March 2017) <icc-cpi.int/Pages/item.aspx?name=170331-otp-stat>

ICC, 'The International Criminal Court Takes Part in a Training Seminar for Investigators from the National Human Rights Commission of the Democratic Republic of the Congo' (18 April 2017) ICC-CPI-20170418-PR1296 <icc-cpi.int/news/international-criminal-court-takes-part-training-seminar-investigators-national-human-rights>

ICC, Press Release, 'ICC Holds High-Level Regional Symposium on Cooperation and Complementarity in Niger' (27 October 2017) ICC-CPI-20171027-PR1340

ICC, 'Response to OSJI and Amsterdam Law School Report on Improving the Operations of the ICC–OTP: Reappraisal of Structures, Norms and Practices' (2020)

ICC, 'Statement by the Prosecutor of the ICC, Fatou Bensouda, Regarding the Situation in Ituri, DRC' (4 June 2020) <icc-cpi.int/Pages/item.aspx?name=200604-icc-prosecutor-statement-ituri-drc>

ICC, 'Statement of the Prosecutor, Fatou Bensouda, on the Conclusion of the Preliminary Examination of the Situation in Nigeria' (11 December 2020) <icc-cpi.int/Pages/item.aspx?name=201211-prosecutor-statement>

ICC, *Overall Response to the 'Independent Expert Review': Preliminary Analysis of the Recommendations* (2021)

ICC, 'ICC Prosecutor, Mr Karim A.A. Khan QC, Concludes the Preliminary Examination of the Situation in Colombia with a Cooperation Agreement with the Government Charting the Next Stage in Support of Domestic Efforts to Advance Transitional Justice' (28 October 2021) <icc-cpi.int/news/icc-prosecutor-mr-karim-khan-qc-concludes-preliminary-examination-situation-colombia>

ICC, 'ICC Prosecutor, Mr Karim A.A. Khan QC, Opens an Investigation into the Situation in Venezuela and Concludes Memorandum of Understanding with the Government' (5 November 2021) <icc-cpi.int/news/icc-prosecutor-mr-karim-aa-khan-qc-opens-investigation-situation-venezuela-and-concludes>

ICC, 'Statement of ICC Prosecutor, Karim A.A. Khan QC, to the United Nations Security Council on the Situation in Libya' (24 November 2021) <icc-cpi.int/news/statement-icc-prosecutor-karim-aa-khan-qc-united-nations-security-council-situation-libya>

ICC, 'ICC Prosecutor, Mr Karim A.A. Khan QC, Concludes First Official Visit to Nigeria' (22 April 2022) <icc-cpi.int/news/icc-prosecutor-mr-karim-aa-khan-qc-concludes-first-official-visit-nigeria>

ICC, Press Release, 'ICC Holds High-Level Regional Symposium on Cooperation and Complementarity in Senegal' (25 May 2022) ICC-CPI-20220525-PR1656 <icc-cpi.int/news/icc-holds-high-level-regional-conference-cooperation-and-complementarity-senegal>

ICC–ASP, 'Report of the Bureau on Stocktaking: Complementarity, Taking Stock of the Principle of Complementarity: Bridging the Impunity Gap' (18 March 2010) ICC-ASP/8/51

ICC–ASP, 'Report of the Court on Complementarity' (16 October 2012) ICC-ASP/11/39

ICC–ASP, 'Report of the Bureau on Complementarity' (6 December 2021) ICC-ASP/20/22'

ICC–OTP, 'Informal Expert Paper. The Principle of Complementarity in Practice' (2003)

ICC–OTP, 'Paper on Some Policy Issues before the Office of the Prosecutor' (2003)

ICC–OTP, 'Report on Prosecutorial Strategy' (14 September 2006)

ICC–OTP, 'Regulations of the Office of the Prosecutor, ICC-BD/05-01-09' (2009)

ICC–OTP, 'Prosecutorial Strategy 2009–2012' (2010)

ICC–OTP, 'Situation in Colombia. Interim Report' (2012)

ICC–OTP, 'Strategic Plan June 2012–2015' (2013)

ICC–OTP, 'Policy Paper on Preliminary Examinations' (2013)

ICC–OTP, 'Strategic Plan 2016–2018' (2015)

ICC–OTP, 'Policy Paper on Case Selection and Prioritisation' (2016)

ICC–OTP, 'Strategic Plan 2019–2021' (2019)

ICC–OTP, 'Situation in Iraq/UK. Final Report' (2020)

ICC–OTP, 'Policy on Situation Completion' (2021)

ICC–OTP, 'Memorandum of Understanding between the Bolivarian Republic of Venezuela and the Office of the Prosecutor of the International Criminal Court' (3 November 2021) <icc-cpi.int/itemsDocuments/otp/acuerdo/acuerdo-eng.pdf>

ICTJ, 'The Special Court for Sierra Leone: The First Eighteen Months' (2004)

ICTJ and Kofi Annan Foundation, 'Challenging the Conventional: Can Truth Commissions Strengthen Peace Processes?' (2014)

ICTJ and UNDP, 'The "Legacy" of the Special Court. Draft for Discussion' (2003) (on file)

ICTR Fourth Annual Report, UN Doc. A/54/315, S/1999/943, 7 September 1999

ICTR Second Annual Report, A/52/582 S/1997/868, 13 November 1997

ICTR–OTP, 'Complementarity in Action: Lessons Learned from the ICTR Prosecutor's Referral of International Criminal Cases to National Jurisdictions for Trial' (2015)

Ikpe E, A Alao and K Nyokabi, 'Beyond Liberal Institution (Re)Building: Conversations on Peacebuilding and Statebuilding in Sierra Leone' (2021) 21 Conflict, Security & Development 431

Independent Expert Review of the ICC and the Rome Statute System, 'Final Report' (2020)

Ingelaere B, 'From Model to Practice: Researching and Representing Rwanda's "Modernized" *Gacaca* Courts' (2012) 32 Critique of Anthropology 388

Ingelaere B, *Inside Rwanda's Gacaca Courts: Seeking Justice after Genocide* (University of Wisconsin Press 2016)

Institute for Security Studies, 'Sierra Leone. A Country Review of Crime and Criminal Justice, 2008' (2009)

International Bar Association War Crimes Committee, 'Analysis of Overcrowded and Under-Examined Areas, Following a Mapping of Organisations' Work on Ameliorating Domestic Capacity to Try Serious International Crimes' (2018)

International Crisis Group, 'Tribunal Pénal international pour le Rwanda: le compte à rebours' (2002)

International Crisis Group, 'The Special Court for Sierra Leone: Promises and Pitfalls of a "New Model"' (2003)

International Crisis Group, 'Tribunal Pénal international pour le Rwanda: pragmatisme de rigueur' (2003)

International Crisis Group, 'Sierra Leone: A New Era of Reform?' (2008)

International Law Association, 'Interim Report on Complementarity in International Criminal Law. Sydney Conference' (2018)

Inveen C, 'Prepare the Gallows: Sierra Leone and the Death Penalty' (*Al Jazeera*, 31 October 2016) <aljazeera.com/indepth/features/2016/10/prepare-gallows-sierra-leone-death-penalty-161025080542700.html>

Irving E, 'The Other Side of the Article 21(3) Coin: Human Rights in the Rome Statute and the Limits of Article 21(3)' (2019) 32 Leiden Journal of International Law 837

Jachtenfuchs M and Krisch N, 'Subsidiarity in Global Governance' (2016) 79 Law and Contemporary Problems 1

Jackson M, 'Regional Complementarity. The Rome Statute and Public International Law' (2016) 14 Journal of International Criminal Justice 1061

Jalloh CC, 'Special Court for Sierra Leone: Achieving Justice?' (2011) 32 Michigan Journal of International Law 395

Jalloh CC, 'Prosecuting Those Bearing "Greatest Responsibility": The Contributions of the Special for Sierra Leone' in Charles C Jalloh (ed), *The Sierra Leone Special Court and Its Legacy: The Impact for Africa and International Criminal Law* (CUP 2013)

Jalloh CC, 'Toward Greater Synergy between Courts and Truth Commissions in Post-Conflict Contexts' in William A Schabas, Margaret M deGuzman, and Diane M Amann (eds), *Arcs of Global Justice: Essays in Honour of William A. Schabas* (OUP 2018)

Jalloh CC, KM Clarke, and VO Nmehielle (eds), *The African Court of Justice and Human and Peoples' Rights in Context: Development and Challenges* (CUP 2019)

Jalloh CC and A Morgan, 'International Criminal Justice Processes in Rwanda and Sierra Leone: Lessons for Liberia' in Charles C Jalloh and Olufemi Elias, *Shielding Humanity: Essays in International Law in Honour of Judge Abdul G. Koroma* (Brill 2015)

Jallow HB, 'Prosecutorial Discretion and International Criminal Justice' (2005) 3 Journal of International Criminal Justice 145

Jensen R, 'Complementarity, "Genuinely" and Article 17: Assessing the Boundaries of an Effective ICC' in Jann K Kleffner and Gerben Kor (eds), *Complementary Views on Complementarity* (TMC Asser Press 2006)

Jessberger F, 'International v. National Prosecutions of International Crimes' in Antonio Cassese (ed), *Oxford Companion to International Criminal Justice* (OUP 2009)

Jessberger F and J Geneuss, 'The Many Faces of the International Criminal Court' (2012) 10 Journal of International Criminal Justice 1081

Johnstone I, *The Power of Deliberation: International Law, Politics and Organizations* (OUP 2011)

Jones NA, *The Courts of Genocide: Politics and the Rule of Law in Rwanda and Arusha* (Routledge 2010)

Jones P and D Smith, 'Notorious Warlord Gives Himself up to International Criminal Court' (*The Guardian*, 19 March 2013) <theguardian.com/world/2013/mar/19/africa-congo>

Kabia Y and M Sulleh, 'Promoting Justice for Sexual Offenses: Some Persisting Challenges in Sierra Leone' (*Center for the Rule of Law and Accountability*, 4 October 2013) <carl-sl.org/pres/promoting-justice-for-sexual-offences-some-persisting-challenges-in-sierra-leone/>

Kagame P, 'Preface' in Phil Clark and Zachary D Kaufman (eds), *After Genocide: Transitional Justice, Post-Conflict Reconstruction and Reconciliation in Rwanda and Beyond* (Hurst 2008)

Kamara JF, 'The Death Penalty: A Case for Its Abolition' (2006) 19 *The Monitor. Official Newsletter of the Sierra Leone Court Monitoring Programme* 13

Kambale P and A Rotman, 'The International Criminal Court and Congo' (*Global Policy Forum*, October 2004) <globalpolicy.org/component/content/article/164/28474.html>

Kambale PK, 'A Story of Missed Opportunities? The Role of the International Criminal Court in the Democratic Republic of Congo' in Christian M De Vos, Sara Kendall, and Christian Stahn (eds), *Contested Justice: The Politics and Practice of International Criminal Court Interventions* (CUP 2015)

Karegyesa R, 'Empowering Domestic Jurisdictions: Lessons from the ICTR Referral of Cases', International Symposium on the Legacy of the ICTR, Arusha, Tanzania, 6 November 2014

Karimunda AM, *The Death Penalty in Africa: The Path towards Abolition* (Routledge 2014)

Karimunda AM, 'The Death Penalty in Rwanda: Surrounding Politics and the ICTR's Battle for Abolition' in Madoka Futamura and Nadia Bernaz (eds), *The Politics of the Death Penalty in Countries in Transition* (2014)

Kaufman ZD, 'The Prospects, Problems and Proliferation of Recent UN Investigations of International Law Violations' (2018) 16 Journal of International Criminal Justice 93

Kelly CD, 'Contextual Complementarity: Assessing Unwillingness and Genuine Prosecutions in Colombia's Special Jurisdiction for Peace' (2017) 48 Georgetown Journal of International Law 807

Kelsall T, *Culture under Cross-Examination: International Justice and the Special Court for Sierra Leone* (CUP 2009)

Kendall S and SMH Nouwen, 'Speaking of Legacy: Toward an Ethos of Modesty at the International Criminal Tribunal for Rwanda' (2016) 110 American Journal of International Law 212

Kendall S and M Staggs, 'From Mandate to Legacy: The Special Court for Sierra Leone as a Model for "Hybrid Justice"' (War Crimes Studies Center Berkeley 2005)

Keppler E, 'Sudan Took Important Step, But Now Should Send the ICC Suspects to The Hague' (19 March 2021) <hrw.org/news/2021/03/19/sudan-took-important-step-now-should-send-icc-suspects-hague>

Kersten M, 'The Complementarity Turn in International Criminal Justice' (*Justice in Conflict*, 30 September 2014) <justiceinconflict.org/2014/09/30/the-complementarity-turn-in-international-criminal-justice/>

Kersten M, *Justice in Conflict: The Effects of the International Criminal Court's Interventions on Ending War and Building Peace* (OUP 2016)

Kersten M, 'A Comment in Defence of Luis Moreno Ocampo' (*Justice in Conflict*, 23 June 2016) <justiceinconflict.org/2016/06/23/a-comment-in-defence-of-luis-moreno-ocampo/>

Kersten M, 'As the Pendulum Swings—The Revival of the Hybrid Tribunal' in Mikkel Jarle Christensen and Levi Ron (eds), *International Practices of Criminal Justice: Social and Legal Perspectives* (Routledge 2017)

Kersten M, 'Making a Distinction: The Rome Statute Is Not the ICC; It Is Much More than That' (*Justice in Conflict*, 17 July 2018) <justiceinconflict.org/2018/07/17/making-a-distinction-the-anniversary-of-the-rome-statute-not-just-the-international-criminal-court/>

Kersten M., 'Whither the Aspirational ICC, Welcome the "Practical" Court?' (*EJIL: Talk!*, 22 May 2019) <ejiltalk.org/whither-the-aspirational-icc-welcome-the-practical-court/>

Khan T and J Wormington, 'Mobile Courts in the DRC: Lessons from Development for International Criminal Justice' [2011] Oxford Transitional Justice Research Working Paper [no pagination]

Kibangula T, 'RDC: Jeanine Mabunda, aux côtés de Kabila contre les violences sexuelles' *Jeune Afrique* (12 January 2015) <jeuneafrique.com/165639/politique/rdc-jeannine-mabunda-aux-c-t-s-de-kabila-contre-les-violences-sexuelles/>

Kieh GK, 'State-Building in Post-Civil War Sierra Leone' (2005) 4 African and Asian Studies 163

Kirabira T, 'Ongwen at the International Criminal Court' (2021) 25(7) ASIL Insights

Kleffner JK, 'The Impact of Complementarity on National Implementation of Substantive International Criminal Law' (2003) 1 Journal of International Criminal Justice 86

Kleffner JK, *Complementarity in the Rome Statute and National Criminal Jurisdictions* (OUP 2008)

Klip A, 'Complementarity and Concurrent Jurisdiction' (2004) 19 Nouvelles Etudes Pénales 173

Kochanski A, 'The "Local Turn" in Transitional Justice: Curb the Enthusiasm' (2020) 22 International Studies Review 26

Koh HH, 'Transnational Legal Process' (1996) 75 Nebraska Law Review 181

Koh HH, 'Review: Why Do Nations Obey International Law?' (1997) 106 Yale Law Journal 2599

Kontic A and D Tolbert, 'The International Criminal Tribunal for the Former Yugoslavia: Transitional Justice, the Transfer of Cases to National Courts, and Lessons for the ICC' in Göran Sluiter and Carsten Stahn (eds), *The Emerging Practice of the International Criminal Court* (Brill 2008)

Koskenniemi M, *From Apology to Utopia the Structure of International Legal Argument* (CUP 2005)

Kotecha B, 'The ICC's Office of the Prosecutor and the Limits of Performance Indicators' (2017) 15 Journal of International Criminal Justice 543

Kress C, '"Self-Referrals" and "Waivers of Complementarity": Some Considerations in Law and Policy' (2004) 2 Journal of International Criminal Justice 944

Krever T, 'International Criminal Law: An Ideology Critique' (2013) 26 Leiden Journal of International Law 701

Krings BL, 'The Principles of "Complementarity" and Universal Jurisdiction in International Criminal Law: Antagonists or Perfect Match?' (2012) 4 Goettingen Journal of International Law 737

Kuhn TS, *The Structure of Scientific Revolutions* (University of Chicago Press 1962)

Labuda PI, 'The Democratic Republic of Congo's Failure to Address Impunity for International Crimes: A View from Inside the Legislative Process' (*International Justice Monitor*, 8 November 2011) <ijmonitor.org/2011/11/the-democratic-republic-of-congos-failure-to-address-impunity-for-international-crimes-a-view-from-inside-the-legislative-process-2010–2011–2/>

Labuda PI, 'Applying and "Misapplying" the Rome Statute in the Democratic Republic of Congo' in Christian M De Vos, Sara Kendall, and Carsten Stahn (eds), *Contested Justice: The Politics and Practice of International Criminal Court Interventions* (CUP 2015)

Labuda PI, 'Complementarity and Cooperation in the Congo' in Ronald Slye (ed), *The Nuremberg Principles in Non-Western Societies: A Reflection on Their Universality, Legitimacy and Application* (International Nuremberg Principles Academy 2016)

Labuda PI, 'The ICC in the DRC: A Decade of Partnership and Antagonism', in Kamari Clarke, Abel Knottnerus, and Eefje de Volder (eds), *Africa and the ICC: Perceptions of Justice* (CUP 2016)

Labuda PI, 'Africa and the ICC: Shattered Taboos, and the Status Quo' (*EJIL: Talk!*, 23 November 2016) <ejiltalk.org/africa-and-the-icc-shattered-taboos-and-the-status-quo/>

Labuda PI, 'The Special Criminal Court in the Central African Republic: Failure or Vindication of Complementarity?' (2017) 15 Journal of International Criminal Justice 175

Labuda PI, 'Taking Complementarity Seriously: Why Is the International Criminal Court Not Investigating Government Crimes in Congo?' (*Opinio Juris*, 28 April 2017) <opiniojuris.org/2017/04/28/33093/>

Labuda PI, 'The Flipside of Complementarity' (2019) 17 Journal of International Criminal Justice 369

Labuda PI, 'Review Essay: The International Criminal Tribunal for Rwanda and Post-Genocide Justice Twenty Five Years on' (2020) 30 European Journal of International Law 1113

Labuda PI, 'With or against the State? Reconciling the Protection of Civilians and Host State Support in UN Peacekeeping' (International Peace Institute 2020)

Labuda PI, 'Institutional Design and (Non-)Complementarity: Regulating Relations between Hybrid Tribunals and Other Judicial Institutions' in Kirsten Ainley and Mark Kersten (eds), *Hybrid Justice: Innovation and Impact in the Prosecution of Atrocity Crimes* (OUP forthcoming)

Labuda PI, 'Relational Complementarity' Working Paper (2023)

Lake M, 'After Minova: Can War Crimes Trials Overcome Violence in the DRC?' (*African Arguments*, 8 May 2014) <africanarguments.org/2014/05/08/after-minova-can-war-crimes-trials-overcome-violence-in-the-drc-by-millie-lake/>

Lake M, 'Organizing Hypocrisy: Providing Legal Accountability for Human Rights Violations in Areas of Limited Statehood' (2014) 58 International Studies Quarterly 515

Lake M, 'Building the Rule of War: Postconflict Institutions and the Micro-Dynamics of Conflict in Eastern DR Congo' (2017) 71 International Organization 281

Lake M, *Strong NGOs and Weak States: Pursuing Gender Justice in the Democratic Republic of Congo and South Africa* (CUP 2018)

Langer M and M Eason, 'The Quiet Expansion of Universal Jurisdiction' (2019) 30 European Journal of International Law 779

Larkin T, 'China's Normfare and the Threat to Human Rights' (2022) 122 Columbia Law Review 2285

Lawyers Committee for Human Rights, 'Establishing an International Criminal Court: Major Unresolved Issues in the Draft Statute' (1996)

Lawyers Committee for Human Rights, 'Prosecuting Genocide in Rwanda: A Lawyers Committee Report on the ICTR and National Trials' (1997)

Lee RS, 'The Rwanda Tribunal' (1996) 9 Leiden Journal of International Law 37

Lewis J and J Ritchie, 'Generalising from Qualitative Research' in Jane Ritchie and Jane Lewis (eds), *Qualitative Research Practice: A Guide for Social Science Students and Researchers* (1st edn, Sage 2013)

Lewis M, *The Birth of the New Justice: The Internationalization of Crime and Punishment, 1919–1950* (OUP 2014)

Lincoln J, *Transitional Justice, Peace and Accountability: Outreach and the Role of International Courts after Conflict* (Routledge 2011)

Lingsma T, 'Rwanda Opereert Zoals Oost-Duitsland Met de Stasi' (*De Groene Amsterdamer*, 6 April 2022) <groene.nl/artikel/rwanda-opereert-zoals-oost-duitsland-met-de-stasi>

LIPRODHOR, 'Rescapés et droits humains. Problèmes actuels des rescapés huit ans après le Génocide' (2002)

Liss R, 'Crimes against the Sovereign Order: Rethinking International Criminal Justice' (2019) 113 American Journal of International Law 727

Liss R, 'The Coherence of Complementarity and the Structure of International Criminal Law' [2023 forthcoming]

Llewellyn J and S Raponi, 'The Protection of Human Rights through International Criminal Law: A Conversation with Madame Justice Louise Arbour, Chief Prosecutor for the International Criminal Tribunals for the Former Yugoslavia and Rwanda' (1999) 57 University of Toronto Faculty Law Review 83

Lobba P and N Pons, 'Rethinking the Legacy of the ECCC' (2020) 18 Journal of International Criminal Justice 599

Lombardi GP, 'Legitimacy and the Expanding Power of the ICTY' (2003) 37 New England Law Review 887

Longman T, *Memory and Justice in Post-Genocide Rwanda* (CUP 2017)

Lorch D, 'As Rwanda Trials Open, A Nation Struggles' *New York Times* (7 April 1995) <nytimes.com/1995/04/07/world/as-rwanda-trials-open-a-nation-struggles.html>

Luban D, 'State Criminality and the Ambition of International Criminal Law' in Tracy Isaacs and Richard Vernon (eds), *Accountability for Collective Wrongdoing* (CUP 2011)

McAuliffe P, 'Hybrid Tribunals at Ten: How International Criminal Justice's Golden Child Became an Orphan' (2011) 7 Journal of International Law and International Relations 1

McAuliffe P, *Transitional Justice and Rule of Law Reconstruction* (Routledge 2013)

McAuliffe P, 'The Roots of Transitional Accountability: Interrogating the "Justice Cascade"' (2013) 9 International Journal of Law in Context 106

McAuliffe P, 'From Watchdog to Workhorse: Explaining the Emergence of the ICC's Burden-Sharing Policy as an Example of Creeping Cosmopolitanism' (2014) 13 Chinese Journal of International Law 259

McAuliffe P, 'Bad Analogy: Why the Divergent Institutional Imperatives of the Ad Hoc Tribunals and the ICC Make the Lessons of Rule 11 Bis Inapplicable to the ICC's Complementarity Regime' (2015) 11 International Organizations Law Review 345

Mahony C, 'The Justice Sector Afterthought: Witness Protection in Africa' (Institute for Security Studies 2010)

Mahony C, 'A Political Tool? The Politics of Case Selection at the Special Court for Sierra Leone' in Kirsten Ainley, Rebekka Friedman, and Chris Mahony (eds), *Evaluating Transitional Justice. Accountability and Peacebuilding in Post-Conflict Sierra Leone* (Palgrave Macmillan 2015)

Mahtani S, 'How Sierra Leone Abolished the Death Penalty and What Others Could Learn' (*African Arguments*, 2 November 2021) <africanarguments.org/2021/11/how-sierra-leone-abolished-the-death-penalty-and-what-others-could-learn/>

Maki P, 'RDC: Félix Tshisekedi opte pour une justice transitionnelle "face" aux divers crimes et abus commis au pays' (8 August 2020) <actualite.cd/2020/08/08/rdc-felix-tshisekedi-opte-pour-une-justice-transitionnelle-face-aux-divers-crimes-et>

Marchand E and L-M Rudi, 'Extraterritorial Cases and National Accountability: The Liberian Quest for Justice' (*Armed Groups and International Law*, 15 June 2020) <armedgroups-internationallaw.org/2020/06/15/extraterritorial-cases-and-national-accountability-the-liberian-quest-for-justice/>

Mariniello T, 'Judicial Control over Prosecutorial Discretion at the International Criminal Court' (2019) 19 International Criminal Law Review 979

Marong A, CC Jalloh, and D Kinnecome, 'Concurrent Jurisdiction at the ICTR: Should The Tribunal Refer Cases to Rwanda?' in Emmanuel Decaux, Adama Dieng, and Malick Sow (eds), *Des droits de l'homme au droit international pénal. Etudes en l'honneur d'un juriste africain, feu le juge Laïty Kama* (Martinus Nijhoff 2007)

Marong ABM and CC Jalloh, 'Transfer of Cases under the Jurisprudence of the ICTR and Lessons Learnt for the ICC' in Alhagi BM Marong and Charles C Jalloh, *Promoting Accountability under International Law for Gross Human Rights Violations in Africa: Essays in Honour of Prosecutor Hassan Bubacar Jallow* (Martinus Nijhoff 2015)

Martin I, 'After Genocide: The UN Human Rights Field Operation in Rwanda' in Alice H Henkin (ed), *Honoring Human Rights: From Peace to Justice. Recommendations to the International Community* (Aspen Institute 1998)

Martin I, 'Hard Choices After Genocide. Human Rights and Political Failures in Rwanda' in Jonathan Moore (ed), *Hard Choices: Moral Dilemmas in Humanitarian Intervention* (Rowman & Littlefield 1998)

Materu SF, *The Post-Election Violence in Kenya: Domestic and International Legal Responses* (Asser 2015)

Mattioli G and A Woudenberg, 'Global Catalyst for National Prosecutions? The ICC in the Democratic Republic of Congo' in Nicholas Waddell and Phil Clark, *Courting Conflict? Justice, Peace and the ICC in Africa* (Royal African Society 2008)

Mbokani JB, 'L'Amnistie et la répression des crimes de droit international au regard de l'avènement de la Cour pénale internationale: le Statut de Rome à l'épreuve des impératifs de la justice transitionnelle' (2015) 75 Annales de droit de Louvain 239

Mbokani JB, *Jurisprudence congolaise en matière de crimes de droit international* (Open Society Institute 2017)

Mbuyi J, 'In Kasai, Justice against All Odds' (*JusticeInfo*, 21 April 2022) <justiceinfo.net/en/91073-kasai-justice-against-all-odds.html>

Mégret F, 'The Politics of International Criminal Justice' (2002) 13 European Journal of International Law 1261

Mégret F, 'In Defense of Hybridity: Towards a Representational Theory of International Criminal Justice' (2005) 38 Cornell Journal of International Law 725

Mégret F, 'Too Much of a Good Thing? Implementation and the Uses of Complementarity' in Carsten Stahn and Mohamed El Zeidy (eds), *The International Criminal Court and Complementarity* (CUP 2011)

Mégret F, 'Is the ICC Focusing Too Much on Non-State Actors?' in Margaret M deGuzman and Diane M Amann (eds), *Arcs of Global Justice: Essays in Honour of William A. Schabas* (OUP 2018)

Mégret F, 'The Case against Complementarity' in Carsten Stahn and Mohamed El Zeidy (eds), *The International Criminal Court and Complementarity: From Theory to Practice* (2nd edn, CUP forthcoming)

Megret F and M Giles Samson, 'Holding the Line on Complementarity in Libya: The Case for Tolerating Flawed Domestic Trials' (2013) 11 Journal of International Criminal Justice 571

Mégret F and I Tallgren (eds), *The Dawn of a Discipline: International Criminal Justice and Its Early Exponents* (CUP 2020)

Meierhenrich J, 'The Practice of International Law: A Theoretical Analysis' (2013) 76 Duke Journal of Comparative & International Law 1

Meierhenrich J, 'How Many Victims Were There in the Rwandan Genocide? A Statistical Debate' (2020) 22 Journal of Genocide Research 72

Melman J, 'The Possibility of Transfer(?): A Comprehensive Approach to the International Criminal Tribunal for Rwanda's Rule 11bis to Permit Transfer to Rwandan Domestic Courts' (2010) 79 Fordham Law Review 1271

Mieth F, 'Bringing Justice and Enforcing Peace? An Ethnographic Perspective on the Impact of the Special Court for Sierra Leone' (2013) 7 International Journal of Conflict and Violence 10

Miller Z, 'Anti-Impunity Politics in Post-Genocide Rwanda' in Karen Engle, Zinaida Miller. and Dennis Davis (eds), *Anti-Impunity and the Human Rights Agenda* (CUP 2016)

Miraglia M, 'Admissibility of Evidence, Standard of Proof, and Nature of the Decision in the ICC Confirmation of Charges in Lubanga' (2008) 6 Journal of International Criminal Justice 489

Miriam G-A and H Alon, 'Taking Internationalism Seriously: Why International Criminal Law Matters' in Kevin Jon Heller and others (eds), *The Oxford Handbook of International Criminal Law* (OUP 2020)

Miskowiak K, *The International Criminal Court. Consent, Complementarity and Cooperation* (DJOF 2000)

Moffett L, *Justice for Victims before the International Criminal Court* (Routledge 2014)

Moghalu KC, *Rwanda's Genocide: The Politics of Global Justice* (Palgrave Macmillan 2005)

Morris JW, 'The Trouble with Transfers: An Analysis of the Referral of Uwinkindi to the Republic of Rwanda for Trial' (2012) 90 Washington University Law Review 505

Morris M, 'The Trials of Concurrent Jurisdiction: The Case of Rwanda' (1997) 7 Duke Journal of Comparative & International Law 349

Morris V and Scharf MP, *The International Criminal Tribunal for Rwanda* (Transnational 1998)

Mphepo T, 'The Residual Special Court for Sierra Leone: Rationale and Challenges' (2014) 14 International Criminal Law Review 177

Mugisha I, 'Rwanda Issues New Indictments for Genocide Suspects' *East African* (12 December 2020) <theeastafrican.co.ke/tea/news/east-africa/rwanda-issues-new-indictments-for-genocide-suspects-3226516>

Mujuzi JD, 'Steps Taken in Rwanda's Efforts to Qualify for the Transfer of Accused from the ICTR' (2010) 8 Journal of International Criminal Justice 237

Mukwege D and KT Seelinger, 'Lettre ouverte d'un Prix Nobel congolais au procureur de la CPI' *Le Temps* (16 July 2021) <letemps.ch/opinions/lettre-ouverte-dun-prix-nobel-congolais-procureur-cpi>

Mundis DA, 'The Judicial Effects of the "Completion Strategies" on the Ad Hoc International Criminal Tribunals' (2005) 99 American Journal of International Law 142

Muntazini Mukimapa T, *La problématique de la lutte contre les violences sexuelles en droit congolais* (RCN Justice 2009)

Muntazini Mukimapa T, 'The Congolese Experience with the Complementary Role of the ICC' (*Justice Info*, 4 August 2016) <justiceinfo.net/en/justice-reconciliation/28669-the-congolese-experience-with-the-complementary-role-of-the-icc.html>

Musila GM, 'Between Rhetoric and Action. The Politics, Processes and Practice of the ICC's Work in the DRC' (Institute for Security Studies 2009)

Mutua M, 'From Nuremberg to the Rwanda Tribunal: Justice or Retribution?' (2000) 6 Buffalo Human Rights Law Review 77

Mutua MW, 'Savages, Victims, and Saviors: The Metaphor of Human Rights' (2001) 42 Harvard International Law Journal 201

Mutua MW, 'Closing the "Impunity Gap" and the Role of State Support of the ICC' in Richard H Steinberg (ed), *Contemporary Issues Facing the International Criminal Court* (Brill Nijhoff 2016)

Naughton E, 'Committing to Justice for Serious Human Rights Violations: Lessons from Hybrid Tribunals' (ICTJ 2018)

Ndahiro A, J Rwagatare and A Nkusi (eds), *Rwanda: Rebuilding of a Nation* (Fountain 2015)

Nduwayezu B, 'The Punishment of the Stateless ICTR "Migrants"' (*JusticeInfo*, 9 June 2022) <justiceinfo.net/en/93462-punishment-stateless-ictr-migrants.html>

Neier A, 'Accountability for State Crimes: The Past Twenty Years and the Next Twenty Years' (2003) 35 Case Western Reserve Journal of International Law 351

Newton MA, 'The Complementarity Conundrum: Are We Watching Evolution or Evisceration?' (2010) 8 Santa Clara Journal of International Law 115

Ngefa Atondoko G, 'Les Tribunaux de crimes de guerres et le développement du droit international' *Periodique des droits de l'homme de l'Association zaïroise de défense des droits de l'homme* (November 1994) 11

Ngoga M, 'The ICTR Completion Process and Resultant Consequences on Rwanda's Justice System' *New Times Rwanda* (24 October 2008) <newtimes.co.rw/section/read/5493>

Nichols L, *The International Criminal Court and the End of Impunity in Kenya* (Springer 2014)

Njikam O, *The Contribution of the Special Court for Sierra Leone to the Development of International Humanitarian Law* (Duncker Humblot 2013)

Nmehielle VO, 'The Defense Office of the Special Court for Sierra Leone: A Watershed in Realizing the Rights of Accused Persons in International Criminal Justice' in Charles C Jalloh (ed), *The Sierra Leone Special Court and Its Legacy* (CUP 2013)

No Peace Without Justice and others, 'Making Justice Count: Assessing the Impact and Legacy of the Special Court for Sierra Leone in Sierra Leone and Liberia' (2012)

Nouwen SMH, '"Hybrid Courts": The Hybrid Category of a New Type of International Crimes Courts' (2006) 2 Utrecht Law Review 190

Nouwen SMH, 'The ICC's Intervention in Uganda' in Michael Zurn, Andre Nollkaemper, and Randy Peerenboom (eds), *Rule of Law Dynamics* (CUP 2012)

Nouwen SMH, *Complementarity in the Line of Fire: The Catalysing Effect of the International Criminal Court in Uganda and Sudan* (CUP 2013)

Nouwen SMH, 'International Criminal Law: Theory All Over the Place' in Anne Orford and Florian Hoffmann (eds), *Oxford Handbook of the Theory of International Law* (OUP 2016)

Nouwen SMH and DM Lewis, 'Jurisdictional Arrangements and International Criminal Procedure' in Göran Sluiter and others (eds), *International Criminal Procedure: Rules and Principles* (OUP 2013)

Nouwen SMH and WG Werner, 'Doing Justice to the Political: The International Criminal Court in Uganda and Sudan' (2010) 21 European Journal of International Law 941

Nouwen SMH and WG Werner , 'Monopolizing Global Justice: International Criminal Law as Challenge to Human Diversity' (2015) 13 Journal of International Criminal Justice 157

Nsanzuwera F-X, *La magistrature rwandaise dans l'étau du pouvoir exécutif* (Collectif des Ligues et Associations des Droits de l'Homme au Rwanda 1993)

Obote-Odora A, 'Transfer of Cases from the International Criminal Tribunal for Rwanda to Domestic Jurisdictions' (2012) 5 African Journal of Legal Studies 147

Ocampo LM, 'Keynote Address' (Council of Foreign Relations, Washington, DC), 4 February 2010 <cfr.org/content/publications/attachments/MorenoOcampo.CFR.2.4.2010.pdf>

Ocampo LM, 'A Positive Approach to Complementarity: The Impact of the Office of the Prosecutor' in Carsten Stahn and Mohamed El Zeidy (eds), *The International Criminal Court and Complementarity* (CUP 2011)

Ocampo LM, 'Prologue. The Prosecutor's Use of Legal Policies' in Martha Minow, Cora C True-Frost, and Alex Whiting, *The First Global Prosecutor* (University of Michigan Press 2015)

Odora-Obote A, 'Investigations and Case Selection' in Anne-Marie de Brouwer and Alette Smeulers (eds), *Elgar Companion to the International Criminal Tribunal for Rwanda* (Edward Elgar 2017)

OHCHR, 'Rule-of-Law Tools for Post-Conflict States: Maximizing the Legacy of Hybrid Courts' (2008)

OHCHR, *Rule-of-Law Tools for Post-Conflict States: Amnesties* (United Nations 2009)

OHCHR, 'Rapport du Projet Mapping concernant les violations les plus graves des droits de l'homme et du droit international humanitaire commises entre mars 1993 et juin 2003 sur le territoire de la République démocratique du Congo' (2010)

OHCHR, 'Prevention of Torture: UN Human Rights Body Suspends Rwanda Visit Citing Obstructions' (20 October 2017) <ohchr.org/en/press-releases/2017/10/prevention-torture-un-human-rights-body-suspends-rwanda-visit-citing>

Ohgushi K, 'A Critical Note on "Hypercritical" Studies of Transitional Justice' (2015) 79 Journal of Social Science 83

O'Keefe R, *International Criminal Law* (OUP 2015)

Oola S, 'In the Shadow of Kwoyelo's Trial: The ICC and Complementarity in Uganda' in Christian De Vos, Sara Kendall, and Carsten Stahn (eds), *Contested Justice* (CUP 2015)

Oomen B, 'Donor-Driven Justice and Its Discontents: The Case of Rwanda' (2005) 36 Development and Change 887

Open Society Foundations, 'Justice in DRC: Mobile Courts Combat Rape and Impunity in Eastern Congo' (2013) <opensocietyfoundations.org/sites/default/files/justice-drc-20130114.pdf>

Open Society Justice Initiative, 'Legacy: Completing the Work of the Special Court for Sierra Leone' (2011)

Open Society Justice Initiative and Amsterdam Law School, 'Improving Operations of the ICC–OTP: Reappraisal of Structures, Norms, and Practices. Outcome Report and Recommendations' (2020)

Orentlicher D, *Some Kind of Justice: The ICTY's Impact in Bosnia and Serbia* (OUP 2018)

Ormston R, L Spencer, M Barnard, and D Snape, 'The Foundations of Qualitative Research' in Jane Ritchie, Jane Lewis, Carol Nicholls, and Rachel Ormston (eds), *Qualitative Research Practice: A Guide for Social Science Students and Researchers* (2nd edn, Sage 2013)

Othman MC, *Accountability for International Humanitarian Law Violations: The Case of Rwanda and East Timor* (Springer 2005)

Palmer N, 'Transfer or Transformation? A Review of the Rule 11 Bis Decisions of the International Criminal Tribunal for Rwanda' (2012) 20 African Journal of International and Comparative Law 1

Palmer N, *Courts in Conflict: Interpreting the Layers of Justice in Post-Genocide Rwanda* (OUP 2015)

Palmer N, 'Who Should Try Félicien Kabuga?' (*Opinio Juris*, 20 May 2020) <opiniojuris.org/2020/05/20/who-should-try-felicien-kabuga/>

Palmer N, 'International Criminal Law and Border Control: The Expressive Role of the Deportation and Extradition of Genocide Suspects to Rwanda' (2020) 33 Leiden Journal of International Law 789

Pappier J and L Evenson, 'ICC Starts Next Chapter in Colombia, But Will It Lead to Justice?' (*EJIL:Talk!*, 15 December 2021) <ejiltalk.org/icc-starts-next-chapter-in-colombia-but-will-it-lead-to-justice/>

Parliamentarians for Global Action, 'PGA Regional Roundtable Discussion on the Implementation of the Rome Statute' (18 January 2008) <pgaction.org/news/pga-regional-roundtable-discussion-on-the-implementation-of-the-rome-statute.html>

Parliamentarians for Global Action, 'PGA salue l'adoption de la loi de mise en œuvre du Statut de Rome de la CPI par le Senat de la RDC' (2 November 2015) <pgaction.org/fr/news/drc-adopts-implementing-legislation-rome-statute-icc.html>

Parmar S, 'Dissuasive or Disappointing? Measuring the Deterrent Effect of the International Criminal Court in the Democratic Republic of the Congo' in Jennifer Schense and Linda Carter (eds), *Two Steps Forward, One Step Back: The Deterrent Effect of International Criminal Tribunals* (International Nuremberg Principles Academy 2016)

Parqué V, 'Le Tribunal pénal international pour le Rwanda' in Stefaan Marysse and Filip Reyntjens (eds), *Annuaire des Grands Lacs 1996–1997* (Harmattan 1997)

Peerenboom R, M Zürn, and A Nollkaemper, 'Conclusion: From Rule of Law Promotion to Rule of Law Dynamics' in Michael Zurn, Andre Nollkaemper, and Randy Peerenboom (eds), *Rule of Law Dynamics* (CUP 2012)

Perissi D and K Naimer, 'Achieving Justice for Child Survivors of Conflict-Related Sexual Violence in the Democratic Republic of the Congo' (2020) 18 Journal of International Criminal Justice 293

Perissi D and E Taquet, 'The Kavumu Trial: Complementarity in Action in the Democratic Republic of Congo' (*International Justice Monitor*, 5 February 2018) <ijmonitor.org/2018/02/the-kavumu-trial-complementarity-in-action-in-the-democratic-republic-of-congo/>

Perriello T and M Wierda, 'The Special Court for Sierra Leone under Scrutiny' (ICTJ 2006)

Peskin V, *International Justice in Rwanda and the Balkans: Virtual Trials and the Struggle for State Cooperation* (CUP 2008)

Peskin V, 'Croatia's Homeland War, the Battles over Victor's Justice, and the Legacy of the ICTY' in Carsten Stahn and others (eds), *Legacies of the International Criminal Tribunal for the Former Yugoslavia* (OUP 2020)

Petersen S, I Samset, and V Wang, 'Foreign Aid to Transitional Justice: The Cases of Rwanda and Guatemala, 1995–2005' in Kai Ambos, Judith Large, and Marieke Wierda (eds), *Building a Future on Peace and Justice* (Springer 2009)

Pinto M, 'Historical Trends of Human Rights Gone Criminal' (2020) 42 Human Rights Quarterly 729

Poate D, P Balogun, I Rothmann, M Knight, and F Sesay, 'Evaluation of DFID Country Programmes: Sierra Leone. Evaluation Report EV690' (2008)

Powderly J, 'International Criminal Justice in an Age of Perpetual Crisis' (2019) 32 Leiden Journal of International Law 1

Prunier G, *The Rwanda Crisis: History of A Genocide* (1st edn, Columbia UP 1995)

Prunier G, *The Rwanda Crisis: History of a Genocide* (2nd edn, Hurst 2002)

Prunier G, *Africa's World War: Congo, the Rwandan Genocide, and the Making of a Continental Catastrophe* (OUP 2010)

Ramaekers C, 'La Protection Des Victimes et Témoins de Crimes' in RCN Justice et Démocratie (ed), *Les 10 ans de la Cour pénale internationale. Bilans et perspectives. Recueil des actes des journées scientifiques tenues à Kinshasa, RDC du 23 au 25 octobre 2012* (2012)

Ramanathan U, 'The Surprising Impact of the Rome Statute in India' (*Open Democracy*, 7 November 2014) <opendemocracy.net/en/openglobalrights-openpage/surprising-impact-of-rome-statute-in-india/>

Rapp SJ, 'The Challenge of Choice in the Investigation and Prosecution of International Crimes in Post-Conflict Sierra Leone' in Charles C Jalloh (ed), *The Sierra Leone Special Court and Its Legacy* (CUP 2013)

Rastan R, 'Complementarity: Contest or Collaboration' in Morten Bergmo (ed), *Complementarity and the Exercise of Universal Jurisdiction for Core International Crimes* (Torkel Opsahl 2010)

Rastan R, 'Situation and Case: Defining the Parameters' in Carsten Stahn and Mohamed M El Zeidy (eds), *The International Criminal Court and Complementarity* (CUP 2011)

Rastan R, 'What Is "Substantially the Same Conduct"?' (2017) 15 Journal of International Criminal Justice 1

Rathbun BC, 'Interviewing and Qualitative Field Methods: Pragmatism and Practicalities' in Janet M Box-Steffensmeier, Henry E Brady, and David Collier (eds), *The Oxford Handbook of Political Methodology*, vol 1 (OUP 2008)

Report of the Secretary General on the establishment of a Special Court for Sierra Leone, S/2000/915, 4 October 2000

Report of the Secretary General on the establishment of the ICTY, S/25704, 3 May 1993

Report of the Secretary General on the United Nations Assistance Mission for Rwanda, S/1995/457

Report of UN High Commissioner for Human Rights on the Human Rights Field Operation in Rwanda, A/53/367, 11 September 1998

Reuters, 'Rwanda Army Opens the Trial of 14 Soldiers' (3 May 1995) <nytimes.com/1995/05/03/world/rwanda-army-opens-the-trial-of-14-soldiers.html>

Reydams L, 'Niyonteze v. Public Prosecutor' (2002) 96 American Journal of International Law 231

Reydams L, 'Belgium's First Application of Universal Jurisdiction: The Butare Four Case' (2003) 1 Journal of International Criminal Justice 428

Reydams L, 'Politics or Pragmatism? The International Criminal Tribunal for Rwanda and the Burying of the Investigation into the Assassination of President Juvénal Habyarimana' (2018) 40 Human Rights Quarterly 989

Reydams L and J Odermatt, 'Mandates' in Luc Reydams, Jan Wouters, and Cedric Ryngaert (eds), *International Prosecutors* (OUP 2012)

Reydams L, J Wouters and C Ryngaert, 'The Politics of Establishing International Criminal Tribunals' in Luc Reydams, Jan Wouters, and Cedric Ryngaert (eds), *International Prosecutors* (OUP 2012)

Reyntjens F, *Political Governance in Post-Genocide Rwanda* (CUP 2013)

Ribaux A, 'Folie meurtrière au pays des mille collines. Carnet de notes d'un enquêteur suisse au Rwanda' [1996] Recueil de jurisprudence neuchâteloise 12

Ricci R, 'Human Rights Challenges in the DRC: A View from MONUC's Human Rights Section' in Mark Malan and Joao Gomes Porto (eds), *Challenges of Peace Implementation: The UN Mission in the DRC* (Institute for Security Studies 2004)

Rispo M, 'Evaluation of UNDP's Support to Mobile Courts in Sierra Leone, DR Congo, and Somalia' (UNDP 2014)

Risse T, 'Governance in Areas of Limited Statehood' in David Levi-Faur (ed), *The Oxford Handbook of Governance* (OUP 2012)

Risse T and TA Börzel, 'Human Rights: The New Agenda' [2012] Working Paper 07. Transatlantic Relationship and the Future Global Governance

Risse-Kappen T, SC Ropp and K Sikkink (eds), *The Persistent Power of Human Rights: From Commitment to Compliance* (CUP 2013)

Robinson D, 'Comments on Chapter 4' in Jann K Kleffner and Gerben Kor (eds), *Complementary Views on Complementarity* (TMC Asser Press 2006)

Robinson D, 'The Mysterious Mysteriousness of Complementarity' (2010) 21 Criminal Law Forum 67

Robinson D, 'The Controversy over Territorial State Referrals and Reflections on ICL Discourse' (2011) 9 Journal of International Criminal Justice 355

Robinson D, 'Three Theories of Complementarity: Charge, Sentence, or Process?' (2012) 53 Harvard International Law Journal Online 65

Robinson P and G Ghahraman, 'Can Rwandan President Kagame Be Held Responsible at the ICTR for the Killing of President Habyarimana?' (2008) 6 Journal of International Criminal Justice 981

Rodman K, 'Justice Is Interventionist: The Political Sources of the Judicial Reach of the Special Court for Sierra Leone' (2013) 13 International Criminal Law Review 63

Rogier E, 'The Ethos of Positive Complementarity' (*Justice in Conflict*, 11 December 2018) <justiceinconflict.org/2018/12/11/the-ethos-of-positive-complementarity/>

Roht-Arriaza N, 'Just a "Bubble"? Perspectives on the Enforcement of International Criminal Law by National Courts' (2013) 11 Journal of International Criminal Justice 537

Rolley S, 'RDC: D'après Michelle Bachelet, "Les crimes contre l'humanité sont confirmés"' *Radio France Internationale* (28 January 2020) <rfi.fr/fr/podcasts/20200128-rdc-apr%C3%A8s-michelle-bachelet-crimes-contre-humanit%C3%A9-sont-confirm%C3%A9s>

Romano C, 'Mixed Criminal Tribunals (Sierra Leone, East Timor, Kosovo, Cambodia)' [2006] *Max Planck Encyclopedia of Public International Law* <opil.ouplaw.com/display/10.1093/law:epil/9780199231690/law-9780199231690-e173>

Rosenberg ST, 'The International Criminal Court in Côte d'Ivoire' (2017) 15 Journal of International Criminal Justice 471

Rugege S and AM Karimunda, 'Domestic Prosecution of International Crimes: The Case of Rwanda' in Gerhard Werle, Lovell Fernandez, and Moritz Vormbaum, *Africa and the International Criminal Court* (TMC Asser Press 2014)

Rugiririza E, 'First Trial in Kasai for Crimes of the Kamuina Nsapu Rebellion' (*JusticeInfo*, 8 November 2021) <justiceinfo.net/en/84096-first-trial-kasai-crimes-kamuina-nsapu-rebellion.html>

Rugiririza E and C Sengenya, 'In Congo, Mihonya Trial Shows Link between Environmental and War Crimes' (*JusticeInfo*, 23 September 2021) <justiceinfo.net/en/82441-congo-mihonya-trial-link-environmental-war-crimes.html>

Ryan H, 'And Then, Finally, a Judge Wrote the Shameful End of the Khmer Rouge Tribunal' (*JusticeInfo*, 4 February 2022) <justiceinfo.net/en/87248-finally-judge-wrote-shameful-end-khmer-rouge-tribunal.html>

Ryngaert C, 'The Principle of Complementarity: A Means of Ensuring Effective International Criminal Justice' in Cedric Ryngaert (ed), *The Effectiveness of International Criminal Justice* (Intersentia; COST Office 2009)

Ryngaert C, 'State Cooperation with the International Criminal Tribunal for Rwanda' in James D Meernik, Thordis Ingadóttir, and Dawn L Rothe (eds), *The Realities of International Criminal Justice* (Brill 2013)

Sabel CF and J Zeitlin, 'Experimentalism in Transnational Governance: Emergent Pathways and Diffusion Mechanisms' [2011] Green Working Paper: Global Re-Ordering: Evolution through European Networks

Sácouto S and K Cleary, 'The *Katanga* Complementarity Decisions: Sound Law But Flawed Policy' (2010) 23 Leiden Journal of International Law 363

Sadat LN, *The International Criminal Court and the Transformation of International Law: Justice for the New Millennium* (Transnational 2002)

Sadat LN, 'Understanding the Complexities of International Criminal Tribunal Jurisdiction' in William A Schabas and Nadia Bernaz (eds), *Routledge Handbook of International Criminal Law* (Routledge 2010)

Sadat LN, 'The Lomé Amnesty Decision of the Special Court for Sierra Leone' in Charles C Jalloh (ed), *The Sierra Leone Special Court and Its Legacy* (CUP 2013)

Sarooshi D, 'Prosecutorial Policy and the ICC: Prosecutor's Proprio Motu Action or Self-Denial?' (2004) 2 Journal of International Criminal Justice 940

Saul M, 'Shaping Legislative Processes from Strasbourg' (2021) 32 European Journal of International Law 281

Schabas WA, 'Justice, Democracy, and Impunity in Post-Genocide Rwanda: Searching for Solutions to Impossible Problems' (1996) 7 Criminal Law Forum 523

Schabas WA, 'Genocide, Impunity and Accountability in Rwanda: Is It Reasonable to Expect a Devastated Legal System to Deal Justly with Those Who Destroyed It?' *Inroads: A Journal of Opinion* (1 January 1997)

Schabas WA, *The Abolition of the Death Penalty in International Law* (3rd edn, CUP 2002)

Schabas WA, 'Amnesty, the Sierra Leone Truth and Reconciliation Commission and the Special Court for Sierra Leone' (2004) 11 University of California Davis Law Review 145

Schabas WA, 'Conjoined Twins of Transitional Justice? The Sierra Leone Truth and Reconciliation Commission and the Special Court' (2004) 2 Journal of International Criminal Justice 1082

Schabas WA, 'Genocide Trials and Gacaca Courts' (2005) 3 Journal of International Criminal Justice 879

Schabas WA, *The UN International Criminal Tribunals: The Former Yugoslavia, Rwanda, and Sierra Leone* (CUP 2006)

Schabas WA, '"Complementarity in Practice": Some Uncomplimentary Thoughts' (2008) 19 Criminal Law Forum 5

Schabas WA, 'Prosecutorial Discretion v. Judicial Activism at the International Criminal Court' (2008) 6 Journal of International Criminal Justice 731

Schabas WA, 'Anti-Complementarity: Referral to National Jurisdictions by the UN International Criminal Tribunal for Rwanda' (2009) 13 Max Planck Yearbook of United Nations Law 29

Schabas WA, 'Victor's Justice: Selecting "Situations" at the International Criminal Court' (2010) 43 John Marshall Law Review 535

Schabas WA, *An Introduction to the International Criminal Court* (4th edn, CUP 2011)

Schabas WA, 'The Rise and Fall of Complementarity' in Carsten Stahn and Mohamed M El Zeidy (eds), *The International Criminal Court and Complementarity* (CUP 2011)

Schabas WA, *Unimaginable Atrocities: Justice, Politics, and Rights at the War Crimes Tribunals* (OUP 2012)

Schabas WA, 'Mugesera Case: Yet Another Twist in the Debate about the Rwandan Justice System' (*PhD Studies in Human Rights*, 15 January 2012) <humanrightsdoctorate.blogspot.ch/2012/01/mugesera-case-yet-another-twist-in.html>

Schabas WA, 'Selecting Cases at the International Criminal Tribunal for Rwanda' in Charles C Jalloh and Alhagi BM Marong (eds), *Promoting Accountability under International Law for Gross Human Rights Violations in Africa. Essays in Honour of Prosecutor Hassan Bubacar Jallow* (Brill 2015)

Schabas WA, *The International Criminal Court: A Commentary on the Rome Statute* (2nd edn, OUP 2016)

Scheffer D, 'Challenges Confronting International Justice Issues' (1998) 4 New England International and Comparative Law Annual 1

Scheffer D, *All the Missing Souls: A Personal History of the War Crimes Tribunals* (Princeton UP 2012)

Schotsmans M, 'La justice transitionnelle pendant la période de la transition en RDC' in Stefaan Marysse, Filip Reyntjens, and Stef Vandeginste (eds), *Annuaire des Grands Lacs 2006–2007* (Harmattan 2007)

Sehene Ruvugiro E, 'In Rwanda, the Surprising Confessions of Bernard Munyagishari' (*JusticeInfo*, 20 April 2021) <justiceinfo.net/en/76230-rwanda-surprising-confessions-bernard-munyagishari.html>

Sehmi A, 'Judicializing Economic Violence as Means of Dismantling the Structural Causes of Atrocity in the Democratic Republic of Congo' (2021) 14 International Journal of Transitional Justice 423

Seils P, 'The Selection and Prioritization of Cases by the Office of the Prosecutor of the International Criminal Court' in Morten Bergsmo (ed), *Criteria for Prioritizing and Selecting Core International Crimes Cases* (2nd edn, Forum for International Criminal and Humanitarian Law 2010)

Seils P, 'Making Complementarity Work: Maximizing the Limited Role of the Prosecutor' in Carsten Stahn and Mohamed M El Zeidy (eds), *The International Criminal Court and Complementarity* (CUP 2011)

Sekhon N, 'Complementarity and Post-Coloniality' (2013) 27 Emory International Law Review 799

Sellars K, 'The First World War, Wilhelm II, and Article 227: The Origin of the Idea of "Aggression" in International Criminal Law' in Claus Kress and Stefan Barriga (eds), *The Crime of Aggression: A Commentary* (CUP 2017)

'Sénat: débat sur la proposition de loi sur le statut des anciens présidents de la République' *Radio Okapi* (29 September 2017) <radiookapi.net/2017/09/29/actualite/societe/senat-debat-sur-la-proposition-de-loi-sur-le-statut-des-anciens>

Sengenya C, 'DRC: Lubanga and Katanga Freed for Peace in Ituri' (*Justice Info*, 31 March 2020) <justiceinfo.net/en/reconciliation/44065-drc-lubanga-and-katanga-freed-for-peace-in-ituri.html>

Sennett PH and GP Noone, 'Working with Rwanda toward the Domestic Prosecution of Genocide Crimes' (1997) 12 St John's Journal of Legal Commentary 425

Seppanen S, 'Chinese Legal Development Assistance: Which Rule of Law? Whose Pragmatism?' (2018) 51 Vanderbilt Journal of Transnational Law 101

Sesay BA, 'NMDHR [Network Movement for Democracy and Human Rights] Ends Consultative Meeting for CSOs in Sierra Leone' *Awareness Times* (28 March 2008) <rscsl.org/Clippings/2008/2008-03/pc2008-3-31.pdf>

Sesay JAK, 'A Case for the Domestication of the Rome Statute in Sierra Leone' <carl-sl.org/pres/a-case-for-the-domestication-of-the-rome-statute-in-sierra-leone/>

Sesay M, 'Hijacking the Rule of Law in Postconflict Environments' (2019) 4 European Journal of International Security 41

Seutcheu M, 'Working Together to Prosecute Human Rights Criminals: An Insider Account of the Relationship between Human Rights Organizations and the International Criminal Tribunal for Rwanda' (unpublished manuscript)

Shany Y, *The Competing Jurisdictions of International Courts and Tribunals* (OUP 2003)

Shany Y, 'The Role of National Courts in Advancing the Goals of International Criminal Tribunals' (2009) 103 Proceedings of the Annual Meeting of the American Society of International Law 210

Shany Y, 'How Can International Criminal Courts Have a Greater Impact on National Criminal Proceedings? Lessons from the First Two Decades of International Criminal Justice in Operation' (2013) 46 Israel Law Review 431

Shany Y, *Assessing the Effectiveness of International Courts* (OUP 2014)

Shany Y, 'Jurisdiction and Admissibility' in Cesare Romano, Karen Alter, and Yuval Shany (eds), *The Oxford Handbook of International Adjudication* (OUP 2014)

Shany Y, *Questions of Jurisdiction and Admissibility before International Courts* (CUP 2016)

Shany Y, *Regulating Jurisdictional Relations between National and International Courts* (OUP 2007)

Sharp DN, 'What Would Satisfy Us? Taking Stock of Critical Approaches to Transitional Justice' (2019) 13 International Journal of Transitional Justice 570

Shereshevsky Y, 'The Unintended Negative Effect of Positive Complementarity' (2020) 18 Journal of International Criminal Justice 1017

Shikhelman V, 'Implementing Decisions of International Human Rights Institutions. Evidence from the UN Human Rights Committee' (2019) 30 European Journal of International Law 753

Shraga D, 'The Second Generation UN-Based Tribunals: A Diversity of Mixed Jurisdictions' in Cesare Romano, André Nollkaemper, and Jann Kleffner (eds), *Internationalized Criminal Courts: Sierra Leone, East Timor, Kosovo, and Cambodia* (OUP 2004)

Shraga D and R Zacklin, 'The International Criminal Tribunal for the Former Yugoslavia' (1994) 5 European Journal of International Law 360

Shraga D and R Zacklin, 'The International Criminal Tribunal for Rwanda' (1996) 7 European Journal of International Law 501

Sikkink K, *The Justice Cascade: How Human Rights Prosecutions Are Changing World Politics* (Norton 2011)

Sikkink K, 'The Age of Accountability: The Global Rise of Individual Criminal Accountability' in Francesca Lessa and Leigh A Payne (eds), *Amnesty in the Age of Human Rights Accountability: Comparative and International Perspectives* (CUP 2012)

Sikkink K, *Evidence for Hope: Making Human Rights Work in the 21st Century* (Princeton UP 2017)

Sikkink K and HJ Kim, 'The Justice Cascade: The Origins and Effectiveness of Prosecutions of Human Rights Violations' (2013) 9 Annual Review of Law and Social Science 269

Simmons BA, *Mobilizing for Human Rights: International Law in Domestic Politics* (CUP 2009)

Slaughter A-M, 'International Law in a World of Liberal States' (1995) 6 European Journal of International Law 503

Slye R, *The Kenyan TJRC: An Outsider's View from the Inside* (CUP 2018)

Smith A, 'The Expectations and Role of International and National Civil Society and the SCSL' in Charles C Jalloh (ed), *The Special Court for Sierra Leone and Its Legacy* (CUP 2013)

Soares M de S, 'The Moral Legacy of the ICTY' in Carsten Stahn and others (eds), *Legacies of the International Criminal Tribunal for the Former Yugoslavia: A Multidisciplinary Approach* (OUP 2020)

Soares PP, 'Transitional Justice in the DRC. The 2014 Amnesty Law and the Principle of Complementarity—Quid Juris?' in Triestino Mariniello (ed), *The International Criminal Court in Search of Its Identity and Purpose* (Routledge 2015)

Speri A, 'How the U.S. Derailed an Effort to Prosecute Its Crimes in Afghanistan' (*The Intercept*, 5 October 2021)

Sriram CL, 'Wrong-Sizing International Justice? The Hybrid Tribunal in Sierra Leone' (2005) 29 Fordham International Law Journal 472

Sriram CL and S Pillay (eds), *Peace versus Justice? The Dilemma of Transitional Justice in Africa* (James Currey 2010)

Staggs M, 'Bringing Justice and Ensuring Lasting Peace. Some Reflections on the Trial Phase at the Special Court for Sierra Leone' (War Crimes Studies Center Berkeley 2006)

Stahn C, 'The Geometry of Transitional Justice: Choices of Institutional Design' (2005) 18 Leiden Journal of International Law 425

Stahn C, 'Complementarity: A Tale of Two Notions' (2008) 19 Criminal Law Forum 87

Stahn C, 'Introduction: Bridge over Troubled Waters?' in Carsten Stahn and Mohamed M El Zeidy (eds), *The International Criminal Court and Complementarity* (CUP 2011)

Stahn C, 'Taking Complementarity Seriously. On the Sense and Sensibility of "Classical", "Positive" and "Negative" Complementarity' in Carsten Stahn and Mohamed M El Zeidy (eds), *The International Criminal Court and Complementarity* (CUP 2011)

Stahn C, 'One Step Forward, Two Steps Back? Second Thoughts on a "Sentence-Based" Theory of Complementarity' (2012) 53 Harvard International Law Journal Online 185

Stahn C, 'Input, Output and "Local" Acceptance: Analyzing Impact and Effects of the International Criminal Court' (*Post-Conflict Justice*, 10 December 2014) <postconflictjustice.com/input-output-and-local-acceptance-analyzing-impact-and-effects-of-the-international-criminal-court/>

Stahn C, 'Admissibility Challenges before the ICC: From Quasi-Primacy to Qualified Deference?' in Carsten Stahn (ed), *The Law and Practice of the International Criminal Court* (OUP 2015)

Stahn C, 'Is ICC Justice Measurable? Re-Thinking Means and Methods of Assessing the Court's Practice' (*ICC Forum—Performance Debate*, July 2017) <iccforum.com/performance>

Stahn C, 'Damned If You Do, Damned If You Don't' (2017) 15 Journal of International Criminal Justice 413

Stahn C, 'The Times They Are a-Changin': Why the ICC Should Revisit Strategies on Preliminary Examination' (*Justice in Conflict*, 10 December 2018) <justiceinconflict.org/2018/12/10/the-times-they-are-a-changin-why-the-icc-should-re-visit-strategies-on-preliminary-examination/>

Stahn C, *A Critical Introduction to International Criminal Law* (CUP 2019)

Stahn C, 'Revitalizing Complementarity a Decade after the Stocktaking Exercise', Policy Brief Series No 115 (Torkel Opsahl 2020)

'State Department Views on the Future for War Crimes Tribunals' (2002) 96 American Journal of International Law 482

Stearns JK, *The War That Doesn't Say Its Name: The Unending Conflict in the Congo* (Princeton UP 2021)

Stigen J, *The Relationship between the International Criminal Court and National Jurisdictions: The Principle of Complementarity* (Martinus Nijhoff 2008)

Straus S, 'The Limits of a Genocide Lens: Violence against Rwandans in the 1990s' (2019) 21 Journal of Genocide Research 504

Straus S and L Waldorf (eds), *Remaking Rwanda: State Building and Human Rights after Mass Violence* (University of Wisconsin Press 2011)

Stromseth JE, 'Justice on the Ground: Can International Criminal Courts Strengthen Domestic Rule of Law in Post-Conflict Societies?' (2009) 1 Hague Journal on the Rule of Law 81

Stromseth JE, 'Justice on the Ground? International Criminal Courts and Domestic Rule of Law Building in Conflict-Affected States' (2011) 50 Nomos 169

Subotic J, *Hijacked Justice: Dealing with the Past in the Balkans* (Cornell UP 2009)

Sullo P, *Beyond Genocide: Transitional Justice and 'Gacaca' Courts in Rwanda: The Search for Truth, Justice and Reconciliation* (TMC Asser Press 2018)

Suma M, 'Case for an Office of a Public Defender in Sierra Leone' (*Sierra Leone Court Monitoring Programme*, September 2005) <carl-sl.org/pres/a-case-for-an-office-of-a-public-defender-in-system-sierra-leone/>

Suma M, 'Politics of Death Penalty in Post-Conflict Sierra Leone: An Opportunity for Reform or a Missed Opportunity?' in Madoka Futamura and Nadia Bernaz (eds), *The Politics of the Death Penalty in Countries in Transition* (Routledge 2014)

Suma M, 'Sierra Leone. Justice Sector and the Rule of Law. A Review by AfriMAP and the Open Society Initiative for West Africa' (Open Society Foundations 2014)

Suma M, 'The Hybrid Nature of the Special Court Is Fast Dissipating' (*Sierra Leone Court Monitoring Programme* [date unknown]) <carl-sl.org/pres/the-hybrid-nature-of-the-special-court-is-fast-dissipating-the-sierra-leonean-aspect-should-be-rest/>

Sung Ho K, 'Max Weber' in Edward N Zalta (ed), *Stanford Encyclopedia of Philosophy* (2021) <plato.stanford.edu/archives/sum2021/entries/weber/>

Swaak-Goldman O, 'Relations between National and International Criminal Courts in the Aftermath of Atrocity Situations', *Proceedings of the Annual Meeting Vol 103* (American Society of International Law 2009)

Tallgren I, 'Completing the "International Criminal Order". The Rhetoric of International Repression and the Notion of Complementarity in the Draft Statute for an International Criminal Court' (1998) 67 Nordic Journal of International Law 107

Tallgren I and T Skouteris (eds), *The New Histories of International Criminal Law: Retrials* (OUP 2019)

Tejan-Cole A, 'The Special Court for Sierra Leone: Conceptual Concerns and Alternatives' (2001) 1 African Human Rights Law Journal 107

Tejan-Cole A 'The Complementary and Conflicting Relationship between the Special Court for Sierra Leone and the Truth and Reconciliation Commission' (2003) 6 Yale Human Rights and Development Journal 139

Thalmann V, 'French Justice's Endeavours to Substitute for the ICTR' (2008) 6 Journal of International Criminal Justice 995

Thompson B, *Universal Jurisdiction: The Sierra Leone Profile* (TMC Asser Press 2015)

Thompson E, 'Can an International Criminal Tribunal with a Limited Mandate Deter Atrocities? Lessons from the Special Court for Sierra Leone' in Jennifer Schense and Linda Carter (eds), *Two Steps Forward, One Step Back: The Deterrent Effect of International Criminal Tribunals* (International Nuremberg Principles Academy 2016)

Thompson N, 'Commonwealth Human Rights Initiative. In Pursuit of Justice: A Report on the Judiciary in Sierra Leone' (Commonwealth Human Rights Initiative 2002)

Thomson B, 'Sierra Leone: Reform or Relapse? Conflict and Governance Reform' (Chatham House 2007)

Thomson SM, *Whispering Truth to Power: Everyday Resistance to Reconciliation in Postgenocide Rwanda* (University of Wisconsin Press 2013)

Tillier J, 'The ICC Prosecutor and Positive Complementarity: Strengthening the Rule of Law?' (2013) 13 International Criminal Law Review 507

Tolbert D and A Kontić, 'The International Criminal Tribunal for the Former Yugoslavia ("ICTY") and the Transfer of Cases and Materials to National Judicial Authorities: Lessons in Complementarity' in Carsten Stahn and Mohamed M El Zeidy (eds), *The International Criminal Court and Complementarity* (CUP 2011)

Tommy I, 'Lessons from the SCSL in the Fight against Impunity' (2012) <asf.be/wp-content/uploads/2012/10/Lessons-from-the-Special-Court-for-Sierra-Leone.pdf>

Tommy I, 'Sierra Leone's Corruption Conundrum: Is the Strategy Working?' (*Centre for Accountability and the Rule of Law*, 10 December 2013) <carl-sl.org/pres/sierra-leones-corruption-conundrum-is-the-strategy-working/>

Townsend G, 'Structure and Management' in Luc Reydams, Jan Wouters, and Cedric Ryngaert (eds), *International Prosecutors* (OUP 2012)

Transitional Justice Institute, University of Ulster, *The Belfast Guidelines on Amnesty and Accountability: With Explanatory Guidance* (2013)

TRIAL International, 'ICC Withdrawal: Kinshasa Issues Alarming Statement' (17 September 2018) <trialinternational.org/latest-post/icc-withdrawal-kinshasa-issues-alarming-statement/>

TRIAL International, 'Universal Jurisdiction Annual Review 2020' (2020)

TRIAL International, 'DRC: Former Militiaman Chance Sentenced to Life in South Kivu' (14 September 2021) <trialinternational.org/latest-post/environmental-crimes-brought-before-the-court-in-south-kivu-drc/>

Turay E, 'Kampala: Sierra Leone Commits to Ratify and Implement Rome Statutes' *Patriotic Vanguard* (2 June 2010) <thepatrioticvanguard.com/kampala-sierra-leone-commits-to-ratify-and-implement-rome-statutes>

UN Criminal Law and Judicial Advisory Service, 'Combatting Impunity in the Democratic Republic of the Congo: Lessons Learned from the UN Prosecution Support Cell Programme' (2015)

UNDP and EU, 'Projet d'appui à la justice militaire en République démocratique du Congo à travers le renforcement du programme des cellules d'appui aux poursuites (février 2015–décembre 2018)' (2019)

University of Nottingham and Human Rights Law Centre, 'Bridging the Gap: Ensuring the Lasting Legacy of the Sierra Leone Special Court and the Truth and Reconciliation Commission' (2012)

UN Joint Human Rights Office, 'Unlawful, Unjustified and Disproportionate Use of Force in the Context of the Management of Public Demonstrations in the DRC from January 2017 to January 2018' (March 2018)

UNGA, Report of the Secretary-General on the Activities of the Office of Internal Oversight Services: Financing of the ICTR, A/51/789 (1997)

Urs P, 'Judicial Review of Prosecutorial Discretion in the Initiation of Investigations into Situations of "Sufficient Gravity" ' (2021) 18 Journal of International Criminal Justice 851

Urueña R, 'Prosecutorial Politics: The ICC's Influence in Colombian Peace Processes, 2003–2017' (2017) 111 American Journal of International Law 104

Vagias M, 'Hybrid Court Resilience and the Selection of Cases' (2020) 33 Leiden Journal of International Law 1029

Vandeginste S, 'Poursuite des présumés responsables du génocide et des massacres politiques devant les juridictions rwandaises' in Stefaan Marysse and Filip Reyntjens (eds), *Annuaire des Grands Lacs 1996–1997*, vol 1 (Harmattan 1997)

Vandeginste S, 'L'approche "vérité et réconciliation" du génocide et des crimes contre l'humanité au Rwanda' in Filip Reyntjens and Stefaan Marysse, *Annuaire des Grands Lacs 1997–1998* (Harmattan 1998)

Vandeginste S, 'Decolonising Human Rights Protection in Africa: Impunity Rhetorically Repackaged?' (Royal Institute for International Relations 2021) 35

Vander Beken T, G Vermeulen and T Ongena, 'Belgium, Concurrent National and International Criminal Jurisdiction and the Principle "ne bis in idem" ' (2002) 73 Revue internationale de droit pénal 811

van der Lijn, Jaïr, Tim Glawion and Nikki de Zwaan, 'Towards Legitimate Stability in CAR and the DRC: External Assumptions and Local Perspectives' (Stockholm International Peace Research Institute 2019)

van der Merwe HJ, 'The Show Must Not Go on: Complementarity, the Due Process Thesis and Overzealous Domestic Prosecutions' (2015) 15 International Criminal Law Review 40

van der Wilt H, A Nollkaemper, MM Dolman and JK Kleffner (eds), *System Criminality in International Law* (CUP 2009)

Van Lierop RF, 'Rwanda Evaluation: Report and Recommendations' (1997) 31 International Lawyer 887 van Schaack B, 'The Building Blocks of Hybrid Justice' (2016) 44 Denver Journal of International Law and Policy 169

Van Sliedregt E, 'International Criminal Law: Over-Studied and Underachieving?' (2016) 29 Leiden Journal of International Law 1

Van Woudenberg A, 'First Congolese General Convicted of Rape' (10 November 2014) <hrw.org/news/2014/11/10/dispatches-first-congolese-general-convicted-rape>

Vasiliev S, 'On Trajectories and Destinations of International Criminal Law Scholarship' (2015) 28 Leiden Journal of International Law 701

Vedantam S and M Penman, 'Fambul Tok: Forgiveness and "Family Talk" in Sierra Leone' *National Public Radio* <npr.org/2016/01/26/463861864/fambul-tok-forgiveness-and-family-talk-in-sierra-leone?t=1655385235966>

Verini J, 'The Prosecutor and the President' *New York Times* (26 June 2016) <nytimes.com/2016/06/26/magazine/international-criminal-court-moreno-ocampo-the-prosecutor-and-the-president.html>

Vlaming F de, 'Selection of Defendants' in Luc Reydams, Jan Wouters, and Cedric Ryngaert (eds), *International Prosecutors* (OUP 2012)

Voeten E, 'Making Sense of the Design of International Institutions' (2019) 22 Annual Review of Political Science 147

von Billerbeck S and O Tansey, 'Enabling Autocracy? Peacebuilding and Post-Conflict Authoritarianism in the Democratic Republic of Congo' (2019) 25 European Journal of International Relations 698

Waldorf L, 'Mass Justice for Mass Atrocity: Rethinking Local Justice as Transitional Justice' (2006) 79 Temple Law Review 1

Waldorf L, '"A Mere Pretense of Justice": Complementarity, Sham Trials, and Victor's Justice at the Rwanda Tribunal' (2011) 33 Fordham International Law Journal 1221

Wallis A, 'International Courts: Justice vs. Politics' *Open Democracy* (27 February 2013) <opendemocracy.net/andrew-wallis/international-courts-justice-vs-politics>

Walpen L, 'La conduite des enquêtes, un défi majeur pour la justice pénale internationale' (2004) 12 Centre international de formation à l'enseignement des droits de l'homme et de la paix: Thématique 35

Waugh CM, *Paul Kagame and Rwanda: Power, Genocide and the Rwandan Patriotic Front* (McFarland 2004)

Webb P and M Bergsmo, 'International Criminal Courts and Tribunals, Complementarity and Jurisdiction' [2010] Max Planck Encyclopedia of Public International Law <opil.ouplaw.com/display/10.1093/law:epil/9780199231690/law-9780199231690-e1381>

Webster T, 'China's Human Rights Footprint in Africa' (2013) 51 Columbia Journal of Transnational Law 626

Weill S, 'The Situation of Palestine in Wonderland: An Investigation into the ICC's Impact in Israel' in Morten Bergsmo and Carsten Stahn (eds), *Quality Control in Preliminary Examination*, vol 1 (Torkel Opsahl 2018)

Wembi S, 'Senior Congo Officials Linked to Kabila Face Sanctions for Rights Abuses' *New York Times* (2 June 2017) <nytimes.com/2017/06/02/world/africa/congo-officials-sanctioned.html>

Werle G and F Jessberger, *Principles of International Criminal Law* (3rd edn, OUP 2014)

Wetsh'okonda Koso M, 'La République démocratique du Congo. La justice militaire et le respect des droits de l'homme—l'urgence du parachèvement de la réforme' (Open Society Institute for Southern Africa 2009)

Wharton S and R Grey, 'The Full Picture: Preliminary Examinations at the International Criminal Court' (2019) 56 Canadian Yearbook of International Law 1

Wibabara C, *Gacaca Courts versus the International Criminal Tribunal for Rwanda and National Courts: Lessons to Learn from the Rwandan Justice Approaches to Genocide* (Nomos 2014)

Wierczyńska K, 'Deference in the ICC Practice Concerning Admissibility Challenges Lodged by States' in Łukasz Gruszczyński and Wouter Werner (eds), *Deference in International Courts and Tribunals: Standard of Review and Margin of Appreciation* (OUP 2014)

Wierczyńska K, *Przesłanki Dopuszczalności Wykonywania Jurysdykcji Przez Międzynarodowy Trybunał Karny* (Wydawnictwo Naukowe Scholar 2016)

Wierczyńska K, 'The Rome Statute and the Debate Surrounding the Constitutionalisation, Fragmentation and Pluralisation of International Criminal Law' in Andrzej Jakubowski and Karolina Wierczyńska (eds), *Fragmentation vs the Constitutionalisation of International Law: A Practical Inquiry* (Routledge 2016)

Wierda M, 'Transitional Justice in Sierra Leone' in Jeroen de Zeeuw and Krishna Kumar (eds), *Promoting Democracy in Post-Conflict Societies* (Lynne Rienner 2006)

Wierda M, 'Comparison of the Legacy of the Special Court for Sierra Leone and the ICC Intervention in Uganda from a Practical Perspective' (2009) 103 Proceedings of the Annual Meeting of the American Society of International Law 218

Wierda M and A Triolo, 'Resources' in Luc Reydams, Jan Wouters, and Cedric Ryngaert (eds), *International Prosecutors* (OUP 2012)

Williams S, *Hybrid and Internationalised Criminal Tribunals: Selected Jurisdictional Issues* (Hart 2012)

Williams SA, 'Article 17: Issues of Admissibility' in Otto Triffterer (ed), *Commentary on the Rome Statute of the International Criminal Court: Observers' Notes, Article by Article* (1st edn, Nomos-Verl-Ges 1999)

Windridge O, 'Gone But Not Forgotten—The Ongoing Case of Jean Uwinkindi at the ICTR and MICT' (*Opinio Juris*, 29 July 2015) <opiniojuris.org/2015/07/29/guest-post-gone-but-not-forgotten-the-ongoing-case-of-jean-uwinkindi-at-the-ictr-and-mict/>

Witte E, 'Putting Complementarity into Practice: Domestic Justice for International Crimes in DRC, Uganda and Kenya' (Open Society Foundations 2011)

Wolfe L, 'What It Takes to Get an Alleged Mass Rapist and 67 Militiamen Arrested in Congo' [2016] *Foreign Policy* <foreignpolicy.com/2016/06/23/how-i-got-an-alleged-mass-rapist-and-67-militiamen-arrested-in-congo/>

Woolaver H, 'Domestic and International Limitations on Treaty Withdrawal: Lessons from South Africa's Attempted Departure from the International Criminal Court' (2017) 111 AJIL Unbound 450

Wrange P, 'The Crime of Aggression: Domestic Prosecutions and Complementarity' in Claus Kress and Stefan Barriga (eds), *The Crime of Aggression: A Commentary* (CUP 2017)

Yang L, 'On the Principle of Complementarity in the Rome Statute of the International Criminal Court' (2005) 4 Chinese Journal of International Law 121

Zahar Alexander and Göran Sluiter, *International Criminal Law: A Critical Introduction* (OUP 2008)

Zongwe DP, 'The New Sexual Violence Legislation in the Congo: Dressing Indelible Scars on Human Dignity' (2012) 55 African Studies Review 37

Index

For the benefit of digital users, indexed terms that span two pages (e.g., 52–53) may, on occasion, appear on only one of those pages.